THE *VILLAGES OF THE FAYYUM*

THE MEDIEVAL COUNTRYSIDE

VOLUME 18

Previously published volumes in this series are listed at the back of the book.

The *Villages of the Fayyum*

A Thirteenth-Century Register of Rural, Islamic Egypt

Edited and Translated by

Yossef Rapoport
and Ido Shahar

BREPOLS

British Library Cataloguing in Publication Data

A catalogue record for this book is available from the British Library.

D/2018/0095/6
ISBN: 978-2-503-54277-5
e-ISBN: 978-2-503-55996-4
DOI: 10.1484/M.TMC-EB.5.106419

Printed in the EU on acid-free paper

Contents

ACKNOWLEDGEMENTS

The initial impetus for this volume came in 1998, upon encountering al-Nābulusī and his text during Avram L. Udovitch's graduate seminar at Princeton University. Professor Udovitch has long been interested in letters of Jewish merchants from the Fayyum preserved in the Cairo Geniza, and this edition and translation is an homage to his life-long commitment to the social and economic history of the medieval Middle East.

The project of editing and translating al-Nābulusī's text was then made possible through a generous research grant from the UK Arts and Humanities Research Council, held from April 2009 to April 2011. The AHRC grant facilitated the bulk of the research for this volume by allowing Ido Shahar to join the project and work full-time on the edition, the translation, and the attached databases and website.

It was at that point that we also received the crucial support of Jim Keenan, whose research on Byzantine Fayyum had already led him to recognize the importance of the text, and to commission a preliminary translation, prepared by Russell Hopley with input from Lennart Sundelin. Jim and his colleagues very generously allowed us to use that translation and offered support throughout the project.

Following Jim Keenan's lead, other archaeologists and papyrologists working on Greek, Roman, Byzantine, and early Islamic Fayyum have guided us through the topography and the habitation patterns. Most of all, we owe a huge debt of gratitude to Dominic Rathbone of King's College London, who has followed this project since its inception and provided a critical eye and invaluable patient support.

We also benefited immensely from the expertise and fresh research of other historians of the Fayyum, and we would like to specifically mention here Brendan Haug, Mohamed Kenawi, Alexei Krol, Daisy Livingstone, Jean-Michel Mouton, Alan Mikhail, Petra Sijpsteijn, and Cornelia Römer. Nicolas Michel's unsurpassable familiarity with the history of the Egyptian countryside in the Mamluk and Ottoman periods influenced our approaches to the text. We would like to particularly thank Wakako Kumakura, whose pioneering research in the Ottoman archives led us to view the Ayasofia manuscript of the work in a new light.

Many scholars working in related fields of the history of medieval Islam have provided us the opportunity to present and discuss preliminary findings. Audiences at the Annemarie Schimmel Kolleg in Bonn have heard us talk about al-Nābulusī more times than we can remember, and we would like to thank our colleagues there: Stephan Conermann, Stuart Borsch, Mohammad Gharaibeh, Anthony Quickel, and, above all, Bethany Walker, for their continuous support. We are also very grateful for the invitations we received from Teresa Bernheimer, Kurt Franz, Micaela Langellotti, Christian Mueller, and David Wengrow, as well as Elisabeth O'Connell at the British Museum.

The final version of the translation owes much to Luke Yarbrough, who has been working concurrently on a beautiful and elegant edition and translation of another treatise by al-Nābulusī, *The Sword of Ambition*. Not only did Luke improve our translation in many ways, but our correspondence also modified our understanding of al-Nābulusī's career.

There were many other friends and colleagues who gave support along the way, more than we could mention here. Amr Saleh, a Fayyumi himself, has been incredibly supportive. At Queen Mary, we would like to particularly acknowledge the support of our medievalist colleagues Jim Bolton, Virginia Davis, and Miri Rubin. The friendship and support of Simon Swain and Emilie

Savage-Smith at Oxford has always been invaluable, and this project could not have materialized without them.

The preparation of the attached database and GIS maps for this project required much professional expertise, and we have been very fortunate to have committed specialists on our side, often giving much more of their time than would normally be expected. Nabih Bashir valiantly oversaw the first draft of the Arabic edition, with good humour. Daniel Burt at the Khalili Research Centre (Oxford) created the initial database, and Adi Keinan guided us through the creation of the set of GIS maps that appear on the website. The map that appears in this volume has been carefully prepared by Max Satchell, who has invested inordinate amount of effort to familiarize himself with the Fayyumi landscape.

The preparation of the map has been made possible through a generous Scouloudi publication grant from the Institute of Historical Research, an equivalent grant from the Isobel Thornley fund at the University of London, and additional support from the School of History, Queen Mary University of London.

Philipp Schofield has been the first to offer us to publish this book as part of Brepols's The Medieval Countryside series and has unwaveringly stuck with us despite lengthy delays. Our editor, Guy Carney, has been delightful to work with, always patient with our whims and efficient with our requests. We are very grateful to Martine Maguire-Weltecke, who spent much time and effort in typesetting the parallel Arabic edition and English translation, and produced such a fantastically elegant book.

We are of course grateful to our families, who suffered Ayyubid tax lists for many years, usually with good spirits. Most of our children don't know a life without the Fayyum at the background. Special thanks go to my daughter Noga Levy-Rapoport for a valiant and crucial round of copy-editing.

Finally, we would like to thank the one person who has made this insight into the villages of medieval Egypt possible, the bureaucrat Abū ʿAmr ʿUthmān ibn al-Nābulusī, whose grandiose literary ambitions and mundane fiscal expertise combined to produce the unique and idiosyncratic *Villages of the Fayyum*.

Part I

Introduction

Editors' Preface

In the spring of 1245, Abū ʿAmr ʿUthman Ibn al-Nābulusī, formerly a high-ranking official in the Ayyubid administration of Egypt, was called out of forced retirement to report on the agricultural conditions in the province of the Fayyum. A roughly triangular depression in Middle Egypt irrigated by a branch of the Nile, the exceptional productivity of the Fayyum was renowned since antiquity, but its fiscal revenues were now perceived to be in decline. Al-Nābulusī surveyed the Fayyum by going from village to village, relying on local tax and irrigation officials and paying careful attention to minute details of agricultural production. He combined the fiscal audit with sections on the irrigation system and the history of the province, and produced a treatise with the rhyming title *Iẓhār Ṣanʿat al-Ḥayy al-Qayyūm fī Tartīb Bilād al-Fayyūm* (Demonstrating the Everlasting Eternal's Design in Ordering the Villages of the Fayyum).

The result is the most detailed cadastral survey to have survived for any region of the medieval Islamic world. Since the archives of medieval Muslim states have been lost, this is as close as we get to the tax registers of any rural province before the Ottoman records of the sixteenth century, a 'Domesday Book' of the medieval Egyptian countryside. Al-Nābulusī provides a first-hand account of the actual conditions in a concrete locality, and his wealth of detail for each of its one hundred villages surpasses, by far, any other source for the rural economy of medieval Islam. It is a unique, comprehensive snap-shot of one rural society at one significant point in its history. Through its descriptions and, especially, through the unparalleled quantitative data, it is possible to draw a picture of the village communities, their internal organization, and their relationship with the state — a unique insight into the way of life of the majority of the population in the medieval Islamic world.

Al-Nābulusī's work has been known to historians for over a century. It first came to the attention of Bernhard Moritz, who found a copy of the work in Cairo. He published an edition of the Arabic text in 1898 under the somewhat misleading title *Taʾrīkh al-Fayyūm wa-bilādihi* (History of the Fayyum and its Villages), a title by which it has been known since.[1] The location of the manuscript used by Moritz, apparently dated to the fifteenth century, is now unknown. A copy of it was made in Cairo in 1897 in connection with Moritz's edition.[2] Moritz knew of the existence of a second copy in the Ayasofia library in Istanbul, but he was unable to use it at the time and had to rely on a single manuscript.

In the following years, the text was primarily studied as a source for the historical geography of the Fayyum. In 1901, Georges M. Salmon published a map of the villages mentioned by al-Nābulusī based on modern place-names, as well as a nutshell paraphrase for each village.[3] His map was then improved by Ali Shafei Bey, a local irrigation engineer with first-hand knowledge of the province. Shafei Bey also provided useful technical explanation of the irrigation system described by al-Nābulusī.[4]

---

[1] Abū ʿUthmān [*sic*] al-Nābulusī, *Taʾrīkh al-Fayyūm wa-bilādihi*, ed. by Bernhard Moritz (Cairo: al-Maṭbaʿa al-Ahliyya, 1898). This edition was reprinted in Beirut in 1974 and reproduced in *Studies of the Faiyūm Together with Taʾrīḫ al-Faiyūm wa-Bilādihī by Abū ʿUthmān an-Nābulusī (d. 1261)*, ed. by Fuat Sezgin and others, Islamic Geography, 54 (Frankfurt: Institute for the History of Arabic-Islamic Science at the Johann Wolfgang Goethe University, 1992).

[2] Abū ʿUthmān al- al-Nābulusī, *Taʾrīkh al-Fayyūm wa-bilādihi*, Cairo, Dār al-Kutub al-Miṣriyya, MS *taʾrīkh* 1594.

[3] Georges M. Salmon, 'Répertoire géographique de la province du fayyoūm d'après le *Kitāb taʾrīkh al-fayyoūm d'an-nāboulsī*', *Bulletin de l'Institut Français d'Archéologie Orientale*, 1 (1901), 29–77.

[4] Ali Shafei Bey, 'Fayoum Irrigation as Described by Nabulsi in 1245 A.D.', *Bulletin de la Société de géographie d'Égypte*, 20. 3 (1940), 283–327; Ingeborg König, 'Die Oase Al-Fayyum nach ʿUtman an-Nabulsi: Ein

Heinz Halm has incorporated the basic details of village names and their fiscal value to his study of Mamluk Egyptian cadastral surveys.[5]

The administrative and fiscal material of the treatise received attention in the pioneering work of Claude Cahen, who in 1956 classified the taxes listed by al-Nābulusī by comparing them to Ayyubid administrative manuals.[6] His work was followed by Hassanein Rabie, who produced an overview of the Ayyubid administration.[7] Tsugitaka Sato incorporated a significant amount of material from the treatise into his 1997 monograph on Egyptian rural society under the *iqṭāʿ* system.[8] Sato's work pays attention to irrigation and the spread of sugarcane cultivation, but his framework of reference remains normative, and anecdotes are taken out of their localized context.

It is striking that in the century since its publication, the *Villages of the Fayyum* was ancillary to the study of taxation or geography but not the focus of attention for its own sake. This is a result of the general weakness of the discipline of rural history in Islamic studies, and the administrative and normative focus of much of the scholarship. The peasant of medieval Islam has been neglected by modern historians: 'a failure of curiosity — and perhaps also a failure (induced by the image of the "timeless East") to suppose that he had any history'.[9] It is also partly a result of the lasting influence of Ibn Khaldūn (d. 1405), who formulated Islamic history as an eternal struggle between the nomads and the townsmen, the *badw* and the *ḥaḍar*, apparently leaving no space or role for the agency of the peasantry.

Recently, this view of the medieval Egyptian peasant as a passive victim has been steadily challenged. In an earlier study, Yossef Rapoport studied the *Villages of the Fayyum* to shed light on the Arab rebellions against the Mamluk sultans, from 1250 and through the fourteenth century.[10] Rapoport points out that in al-Nābulusī's treatise most villagers are described as Arab tribesmen, and that we should therefore view the Arab uprisings as peasant-led revolts. In a recent joint article, we also drew attention to the local management of the complex irrigation system of the Fayyum as described in the treatise, with Arab tribes probably playing a key role in the allocation of water resources.[11] Nicolas Michel's study of the allocation of tax-free privileged lands to village notables and professionals also utilizes al-Nābulusī's work, alongside early Ottoman cadastral surveys, to demonstrate the autonomy of Egyptian peasant communities.[12]

The present edition and translation of the *Villages of the Fayyum* also complements a recent growth in scholarship on earlier periods in the Islamic history of Fayyum. Much of our knowledge of the history of Egypt during its first few centuries under Islamic rule is based on the unique documentary evidence from the province, where abandoned villages were quickly covered by sand. Over the past two decades, historians focused on clusters of Fayyumi archives to reach conclusions regarding the features of early Islamic administration and processes of Arabicization and conversion in the countryside. Petra Sijpesteijn has used documents coming from the archive of an Umayyad local official in south-west Fayyum to describe the early phase of Islamic state formation.[13] Yūsuf Rāġib has brought to light archives of Abbasid and Fatimid merchants and guardsmen.[14] In 2014, Christian Gaubert and Jean-Michel

Beitrage zur Wirtschaftsgeschichte Agyptens um die Mitte des 13. Jahrhunderts n. Chr' (unpublished master's thesis, Albert-Ludwigs-Universitat zu Freiburg im Bresigau, 1966), produces yet a third set of maps of al-Nābulusī's Fayyum, comparing and correcting the earlier maps.

5 Heinz Halm, *Ägypten nach den Mamlukischen Lehensregistern* (Wiesbaden: Reichert, 1982).

6 Claude Cahen, 'Le régime des impôts dans le Fayyûm ayyûbide', *Arabica*, 3. 1 (1956), 8–30.

7 Hassanein Rabie, *The Financial System of Egypt, A.D. 1169–1341* (London: Oxford University Press, 1972).

8 Tsugikata Sato, *State and Rural Society in Medieval Islam* (Leiden: Brill, 1997).

9 R. Stephen Humphreys, *Islamic History: A Framework for Inquiry* (Princeton: Princeton University Press, 1991), p. 284.

10 Yossef Rapoport, 'Invisible Peasants, Marauding Nomads: Taxation, Tribalism and Revolt in Mamluk Egypt', *Mamlūk Studies Review*, 8. 2 (2004), 1–22. See also Alexei A. Krol, 'The "Disappearing" Copts of Fayyām', in *And the Earth is Joyous...: Studies in Honour of Galina A. Belova*, ed. by Sergei Ivanov and Marina Tolmacheva (Москва: ЦЕИ РАН, 2015), pp. 142–62.

11 Yossef Rapoport and Ido Shahar, 'Irrigation in the Medieval Islamic Fayyum: Local Control in a Large-Scale Hydraulic System', *Journal of the Economic and Social History of the Orient*, 55 (2012), 1–31.

12 Nicolas Michel, 'Les services communaux dans les campagnes égyptiennes au début de l'époque ottomane', in *Sociétés rurales ottomanes / Ottoman Rural Societies*, ed. by Mohammad Afifi, Rachida Chih Brigitte Marino, and Nicolas Michel, *Cahier des Annales islamologiques*, 25 (Le Caire: Institut français d'archéologie orientale, 2005), pp. 19–46. See also his 'Devoirs fiscaux et droits fonciers: la condition des fellahs égyptiens (13ᵉ–16ᵉ siècles)', *Journal of the Economic and Social History of the Orient*, 43. 4 (2000), 521–78, where he discusses the impact of the introduction of military *iqṭāʿ* by the Ayyubids on the legal status of the Egyptian peasantry.

13 Petra Sijpesteijn, *Shaping a Muslim State: The World of a Mid-Eighth-Century Egyptian Official* (Oxford: Oxford University Press, 2013).

14 Yūsuf Rāġib, 'Les archives d'un gardien du monastère de

Mouton published a study of rural society in eleventh-century Fayyum based on the exceptional archive of the Banū Bifām, a Coptic family from the village of Dimūh in southern Fayyum. The archive was unearthed in 1998, during excavations in the Naqlūn Monastery.[15]

The exceptionally rich sources for the history of the Fayyum stretch back into the pre-Islamic periods, where a backdrop of rich documentary and material evidence includes thousands of Greek, Latin, and Coptic documents. Together with surviving monuments dotted on the margins of the depression, it is possible to offer an almost uninterrupted history for the province since the Ptolemaic land reclamation of the third century BC. It is against the background of this exceptionally rich documentary evidence that scholars of Roman and Byzantine Egypt have repeatedly called for al-Nābulusī's text to be fully exploited. James Keenan in particular highlighted the importance of the treatise as a point of reference regarding village names and local conditions of agriculture.[16] More recently, Brendan Haug made extensive use of the treatise as part of his research into Fayyum's fluvial landscape during Greek, Roman, and Islamic times.[17] We hope this edition and annotated translation will indeed be of direct benefit for historians and archaeologists of Ptolemaic, Roman, and Byzantine Fayyum, and Egypt more generally.

The present volume offers the first academic edition of the Arabic text of the treatise, based on the edition by Moritz as well as a second copy in the Ayasofia library in Istanbul. It also offers the first translation of the entire text into a European language, with annotations. We preface the edition and the translation with two short chapters. The first chapter introduces al-Nābulusī and his text, discussing the date, structure, and genre of the work. The second chapter offers a guide to the fiscal framework used in the village entries. It sets out to explain the most common agricultural, commercial, and administrative taxes and fees mentioned, remaining faithful to the order in which they are usually listed in the text. It also covers other recurring terms that relate to the allocation of water resources, the tribal system, and the religious landscape.

The map that follows the introductory chapters plots the villages described in the treatise over a modern map of the province. For the production of this map, we have consulted the earlier maps prepared by Shafei Bey and Halm, as well as the K. U. Leuven Fayum Project, an online gazetteer of Graeco-Roman Fayyum.[18] We have adjusted some of the village locations, based on a closer reading of al-Nābulusī's text. Crucially, we set the level of Lake Qarun to be around -30 m below sea level, 15 m higher than its current level. Attestations of village names in other historical records, as well as their presumed locations, are noted at the main entry for each settlement.

The translation has benefited from a draft prepared by James Keenan and Russell Hopley, and reviewed by Lennart Sundelin. The authors have very kindly put this preliminary draft at our disposal. We have also benefited from Luke Yarbrough's 2016 edition and translation of another treatise by al-Nābulusī, his anti-Coptic pamphlet *The Sword of Ambition*.[19] While the topics covered in the *Villages of the Fayyum* are quite different, al-Nābulusī is prone to repeat similar formulae and phrases. Yarbrough prefaces his edition with a very useful biography of al-Nābulusī and the context of anti-Coptic literature in medieval Egypt.

Much of the *Villages of the Fayyum* is taken up by quantitative data, which can be best exploited in a digital format. The numerical sections of the treatise, including the lists of taxes for each village which take up most of the work, have been keyed into Excel spread sheets and made available through a dedicated webpage hosted by the School of History at Queen Mary University of London (<https://projects.history.qmul.ac.uk/ruralsocietyislam>). This is meant as a service to agrarian and economic historians who wish to make further use of

Qalamūn', *Annales Islamologiques*, 29 (1995), 25–57; Rāgib, *Marchands d'étoffes du Fayyoum au IIIe/IXe siècle d'après leurs archives (actes et lettres)* (Le Caire: Institut français d'archéologie orientale, 1982).

[15] Christian Gaubert and Jean-Michel Mouton, *Hommes et villages du Fayyoum dans la documentation papyrologique Arabe (X^e–XIe Siècles)* (Le Caire: Institut français d'archéologie orientale, 2014).

[16] James G. Keenan, 'Fayyum Agriculture at the End of the Ayyubid Era: Nabulsi's Survey', in *Agriculture in Egypt from Pharaonic to Modern Times*, ed. by Alan K. Bowman and Eugene Rogan, Proceedings of the British Academy, 96 (Oxford: Oxford University Press, 1999), pp. 287–99; Keenan, 'Byzantine Egyptian Villages', in *Egypt in the Byzantine World, 300–700*, ed. by Roger S. Bagnall (Cambridge: Cambridge University Press, 2007), pp. 226–43; Keenan, 'Deserted Villages: From the Ancient to the Medieval Fayyum', *Bulletin of the American Society of Papyrologists*, 40 (2003), 119–40; Keenan, 'Landscape and Memory: al-Nabulsi's Ta'rikh al-Fayyum', *Bulletin of the American Society of Papyrologists*, 42 (2005), 203–12.

[17] Brendan J. Haug, 'Watering the Desert: Environment, Irrigation, and Society in the Premodern Fayyūm, Egypt' (unpublished doctoral dissertation, University of California, Berkeley, 2012).

[18] 'Fayum: A Gazetter of the Fayum Area' <http://www.trismegistos.org/fayum/index.php> [accessed 17 December 2017].

[19] Al-Nābulusī, *The Sword of Ambition: Bureaucratic Rivalry in Medieval Egypt*, ed. and trans. by Luke Yarbrough (New York: New York University Press, 2016).

the treatise by following different sets of research questions. It is hoped that sharing the fiscal database with the wider academic community will further the study of the neglected rural history of the Islamic world in general, and of this uniquely rich tax register in particular.

While the present volume is devoted to the edition, translation, and elucidation of the text of the treatise, the fundamental research questions that the treatise allows us to explore are the subject of a companion volume, *Rural Economy and Tribal Society in Islamic Egypt: The Peasants of the Fayyum*. That companion volume, authored by Yossef Rapoport, uses quantitative and qualitative analysis to provide the most detailed microstudy of rural economy for any medieval Islamic context. Following a broader sketch of al-Nābulusī and his time, it explores the history of the province since the Ptolemaic land reclamation to the Fatimid period and proceeds to ultimately address the political and the confessional dimensions of the history of the Egyptian countryside, by assessing the Islamization of rural communities, their tribal identity, and their relations with the state.

Chapter 1

Author and Work

ʿAlāʾ al-Dīn, Abū ʿAmr, ʿUthmān ibn Ibrāhīm ibn Khālid al-Qurashī Ibn al-Nābulusī was born in Cairo on 19 of Dhū al-Ḥijja 588 AH (26 December 1192).[1] Al-Nābulusī's maternal grandfather, a Ḥanbalī preacher from Damascus called Zayn al-Dīn al-Anṣārī, migrated to Egypt during the late Fatimid period, when Ṭalāʾiʿ ibn Ruzzīk was an all-powerful vizier (1154–61). After the overthrow of the Shiʿa dynasty, the staunchly Sunni preacher served under Saladin.[2] Al-Nābulusī himself was initially trained as a religious scholar but then joined the Ayyubid administration, where he advanced rapidly and gained the personal trust of Sultan al-Kāmil (r. 1218–38).[3] By the late 1220s, al-Nābulusī became a chief financial advisor to al-Kāmil, and participated in his daily private council, together with the amir Fakhr al-Dīn ʿUthmān, who was then in charge of all bureaus and taxation.[4] Al-Nābulusī kept his position at the top of Egyptian administration until he was arrested in 1237, on what he claimed were false charges. He spent over a month in jail, during which time his family house was expropriated and sold.

Left outside the corridors of power, and also, according to his own testimony, with limited sources of revenue, al-Nābulusī turned to writing as means of currying favour with al-Kāmil's son and successor, al-Malik al-Ṣāliḥ (r. 1240–49). His first major work was an anti-Coptic treatise, *Tajrīd sayf al-himma li-istikhrāj mā fī dhimmat al-dhimma* (Unsheathing Ambition's Sword to Extract what the Dhimmīs Hoard), where he lashed out at the dishonesty of Copts employed by the Ayyubid administration.[5] The second treatise, *Kitāb lumaʿ al-qawānīn al-muḍiyya fī dawāwīn al-diyār al-miṣriyya* (A Few Luminous Rules for Egypt's Administrative Offices), outlines key problems in the fiscal administration of Ayyubid Egypt and sets out recommendations for increased efficiency and the prevention of fraud. The personal tone of these two works is very marked and allows us to reconstruct al-Nābulusī's career prior to his Fayyum mission. Another work, which survives only in fragments, is *Ḥusn al-sulūk fī faḍl malik Miṣr ʿalā sāʾir al-mulūk* (A Seemly Demonstration of the Superiority of Egypt's King above All Others), apparently extolling the virtues of Egypt and its rulers.[6]

[1] For the biography of al-Nābulusī, see also Luke Yarbrough, 'Introduction'.

[2] Yarbrough, 'Introduction', p. xix; Al-Nābulusī, *Kitāb lumaʿ al-qawānīn al-muḍiyya fī dawāwīn al-diyār al-miṣriyya*, ed. by Carl Becker and Claude Cahen, *Bulletin d'études Orientales*, 16 (1960), 1–78, 119–34 (p. 120 [Introduction], pp. 27, 43 [Arabic]).

[3] On al-Kāmil, see Hans L. Gottschalk, *Al-Malik Al-Kāmil Von Egypten Und Seine Zeit: Eine Studie Zur Geschichte Vorderasiens Und Egyptens in Der Ersten Hälfte Des 7./13. Jahrhunderts* (Wiesbaden: Harrassowitz, 1958).

[4] Al-Nābulusī, *Sword of Ambition*, ed. and trans. by Yarbrough, p. 131.

[5] Here and elsewhere, we follow Yarbrough's elegant translations of the titles of al-Nābulusī's works.

[6] Mentioned at the beginning of the sixth chapter of the treatise. See also *Kitāb lumaʿ*, ed. by Becker and Cahen, pp. 31–34. A related treatise mentioned in medieval sources is *Ḥusn al-sarīra fī ittikhādh al-ḥiṣn biʾl-jazīra* (The Excellent Idea of Establishing the Island Fortress). Al-Maqrīzī cites two short passages from *Ḥusn al-sarīra* that deal with the history of Islamic Egypt, concerning the Tulunid *maydān* and the revolt of the Fatimid commander Shāwar in 557/1162. See Taqī al-Dīn Aḥmad ibn ʿAlī al- Maqrīzī, *Kitāb al-mawāʿiẓ waʾl-iʿtibār fī dhikr al-khiṭaṭ waʾl-āthār*, ed. by Ayman Fu'ad Sayyid, 4 vols (London: Muʾasasat al-Furqān liʾl-Turāth al-Islāmī, 2002), II, 112; I, 231. The treatise celebrated al-Malik al-Ṣāliḥ's construction of a new citadel on the Rawda Island, in the middle of the Nile, opposite Fusṭāṭ. This massive building project began in 1240 or 1241 and lasted at least until 1243, when al-Ṣāliḥ was able to move in with his retinue. On the history of the construction, see Nasser O. Rabbat, *The Citadel of Cairo: A New Interpretation of Royal Mamluk Architecture*, Islamic History and Civilizations: Studies and Texts, 14 (Leiden: Brill, 1995), pp. 86–88 (and the date of 1240); D. S.

In 642/1245, eight years after his forced retirement from government service, al-Nābulusī was called to the Fayyum by orders of al-Malik al-Ṣāliḥ, who was travelling with his entourage through the province. The chronicles for this period in the reign of al-Ṣāliḥ are relatively sparse, and we have no independent testimony of such a royal visit or firm idea of its purpose.[7] According to al-Nābulusī, when al-Malik al-Ṣāliḥ passed through the Fayyum and inspected it, he noticed that the province was less prosperous than it had been, and decided to call al-Nābulusī out of retirement and appoint him to audit the province and its cultivation.

Following his appointment, al-Nābulusī spent more than two months in the Fayyum.[8] This was in the spring of 642/1245, almost certainly from March to May. The exact time of his stay is referred to only once, when he mentions the number of waterwheels in operation in the Fayyum at the time of writing, which is 'the month of Dhū al-Qaʿda of 642', corresponding to 31 March–29 April, 1245. In other instances, he refers to 642 as the current year. He states, with regard to the large village of Minyat Aqnā, that 'in years of lower [Nile] inundations, these lands are exposed and are sown by the villagers. Its revenues then increase, as happened this year, [6]42'.[9] Al-Nābulusī also personally witnessed the garlic harvest of 642, which would have taken place in March or April.[10] He was also told about a cold wind that swept through the province during the winter of 642, prior to his visit.[11] The construction of Muḥraqa Dike (*jisr*) in the district of Giza, discussed as an appendix to the treatise, was ordered at the end of 642, corresponding to May 1245.

The treatise, however, ends with a sentence stating that the work was written in 641, a statement found in both extant manuscripts and in Moritz's edition. This is surely a mistake, but a mistake that is linked to the data al-Nābulusī was compiling. Although al-Nābulusī was in the Fayyum towards the end of 642 AH, he surveyed the tax obligations in the province as they were recorded in the preceding year. Al-Nābulusī explicitly states that:

> I prepared this for the year 641 — this was the year **following** which I received my orders to undertake the survey of the Fayyum (*fa-innahā al-sana allātī umirtu bi'l-naẓar fī al-fayyūm baʿda-ha*). I composed this book thereafter, and the circumstances had not changed in the years [6]42 and [6]43, save for a minor increase in the revenues.[12]

For al-Nābulusī, collecting the data for the preceding fiscal year was simpler than collecting the data for the current year. This was presumably because the tax registers for the current year were still a work in progress and not yet complete. The data for the fiscal year 641 was only occasionally complemented by more up-to-date information. As al-Nābulusī states, after collecting the data for 641, he added some details regarding developments that occurred in 642, and even a sole reference to an event in 643.[13]

The question of dating is complicated by the dual calendar of the fiscal system. Agricultural taxes were collected according to the solar year, known as the *kharājī* year, which followed the Coptic calendar. For all other purposes, the state used the Islamic lunar calendar, which was eleven days shorter. The resultant gap between the *kharājī* solar year of the land tax and the lunar year of other taxes was redressed by occasionally skipping one *kharājī* year, a method known as *taḥwīl*. We know that such an adjustment occurred under Saladin, who ordered to skip the *kharājī* years 565 and 566 so as to make them coincide with the lunar year 567 AH. We do not know of any other adjustment taking place in the Ayyubid period, so we do not know the extent of the gap between the two calendars at the time of al-Nābulusī's visit.[14] It should be noted that al-Nābulusī does not refer

---

Richards, 'al-Ṣāliḥ Nadjm al-Dīn Ayyūb', *The Encyclopedia of Islam*, 2nd edn, VIII, 988–89 (where the date is Shaʿbān 638/ February 1241). *The Sword of Ambition* mentions another work of al-Nābulusī, a scriptural exegesis which attempted to demonstrate the illegality of befriending non-Muslims; Yarbrough, 'Introduction', p. xxii.

[7] Richards, 'al-Ṣāliḥ'. See Muḥammad ibn Sālim Ibn Wāṣil, *Mufarrij al-kurūb fī akhbār banī ayyūb*, ed. by Jamāl al-Dīn al-Shayyāl, Ḥasanayn al-Rabīʿ, and Saʿīd ʿĀshūr (Cairo, 1977), V, 323–47; Shihāb al-Dīn Abū Shāma, *Tarājim rijāl al-qarnayn al-sādis wa'l-sābiʿ al-maʿrūf bi'l-dhayl ʿalā al-rawḍatayn*, ed. by Muḥammad al-Kawtharī (Cairo: Maktab Nashr al-thaqāfa al-Islamiyya, 1947), pp. 168–74.

[8] *Villages of the Fayyum* second chapter, p. 37.

[9] *Villages of the Fayyum*, entry for Minyat Aqnā, p. 211. He also notes that a sugar press in Fānū broke down some years 'prior to this date, which is [6]42'; *Villages of the Fayyum*, p. 191.

[10] *Villages of the Fayyum*, ninth chapter, On the season of harvesting garlic, see Ibn Mammātī, *Kitāb qawānīn al-dawāwīn*, ed. ʿAziz S. ʿAṭiya (Cairo: Al-Jamʿiyya al-zirāʿiyya al-malakiyya, 1943; repr. Cairo: Madbuli, 1996), p. 263.

[11] In the entry for the village of Minyat Aqnā.

[12] *Villages of the Fayyum*, author's introduction, p. 33.

[13] The reference to an event in 643 is in the entry for the village of Fānū (*Villages of the Fayyum*, p. 191).

[14] Rabie, *The Financial System*, p. 133, citing Ibn Mammātī, *Kitāb qawānīn al-dawāwīn*, ed. by ʿAṭiya, p. 358; Shihāb al-Dīn Aḥmad b. ʿAbd al-Wahhāb Al-Nuwayrī, *Nihāyat al-arab fī funūn al-adab*, ed. by Aḥmad Zakī Pāsha and others (Cairo: al-Muʾasasa al-Miṣriyya al-ʿĀmma li'l-Ta'līf wa'l-Tarjama wa'l-Ṭibāʿa wa'l-Nashr, 1923–97), I, 164–65; Shihāb al-Dīn Aḥmad b. ʿAlī Al-Qalqashandī, *Ṣubḥ al-aʿshā fī*

to the term *kharājī* year, and — as seen above — mentions the *hijrī* month of Dhū al-Qaʿda of 642, meaning that his calendar framework was primarily that of lunar years. Nonetheless, it is not certain whether his account of taxes for the year 641 refers to the taxes collected during the *hijrī* year of 641 (June 1243–June 1244), or taxes collected during a fiscal year called 641, based on a solar calendar.

Al-Nābulusī's main effort was to record the tax obligations in each settlement. This involved collecting fiscal documents from local tax-officials, or, when the tax-collectors were not *in situ*, from village headmen. His survey includes records for about 125 different settlements, and his description of the villages' appearance suggests he must have visited them all. At least for part of this time, al-Nābulusī was accompanied by the provincial irrigation official, the *khawlī al-baḥr* (overseer of the canal), who furnished him with information about the complex irrigation system and local history. Al-Nābulusī complemented the information gathered locally by accessing some of the records of the central government in Cairo.

The striking omission from al-Nābulusī's account is any record of actual payments. Al-Nābulusī compiled tax obligations but not the balance of payments at the end of the year. Sporadic information on unpaid or withheld payments is given only in seventeen villages, all of which either belonged to the royal domain of the Sultan at the time of al-Nābulusī's visit, or had been part of the royal domain at some point over the previous decade, which suggests that al-Nābulusī relied on records of the Sultanic fisc for this information. Whatever the explanation, the absence of a record of actual payments gives the treatise a somewhat idealized tone. It is essentially the record of what should have been paid, not of what was actually delivered.

After compiling the records for individual villages, based on local and central registers, al-Nābulusī then aggregated the total tax obligations for the province. His calculations are more or less accurate. For example, al-Nābulusī's aggregate total of taxes in wheat in the province is 72,403 3⁄48 ardabbs, while the taxes and fees in wheat found in the individual village entries amount to just over 71,820. His total of the alms-tax in the province is 1,795 2⁄3 1⁄48 1⁄72 dinars, while the alms-tax in the village entries adds up to over 1,848 dinars. Al-Nābulusī did not aggregate certain categories of local fees, such as seed advances, local allowances for village officials, or the levy of chickens, probably because these payments were not relevant to the assessment of the overall productivity of the province.

Al-Nābulusī's survey was not unusual in itself. It was not uncommon for a bureaucrat from Cairo to be sent to one of the provinces to audit the local accounts.[15] But in al-Nābulusī's own eyes, the mission had taken a much more ambitious turn. After arriving at the Fayyum and examining its administration, al-Nābulusī set himself to write a detailed geographical and historical account of the province. This was to be a book that would truthfully represent every detail of the Fayyum, recreating every aspect of economy and society:

> I aspire that there be no difference between the knowledge of the Fayyum possessed by its inhabitants and that of one who has never seen it but has read this book; and that by means of this book, both those near it and those far away from it may gain equal knowledge of its circumstances. Moreover, I aspire that anyone inquiring about any aspect of the Fayyum, posing questions that are typically asked about similar provinces, would find his query addressed in my account, whether it concerns layout, physical appearance, location, distance from Madīnat al-Fayyūm and the cardinal direction in relation to it, the region's inhabitants, their numbers and to which lineage (*āl*) their section belongs.[16]

The fiscal survey is then presented as an additional layer in the detailed description of the province. The minute fiscal detail — the tax-obligations in total and by category, in cash and in kind, the water quota, local fees, the labour required for the sugar plantations — are all part of a larger, ambitious attempt to capture the Fayyum in its entirety. For al-Nābulusī, the main purpose of the treatise is not to provide information about taxation, even if most of the *Villages of the Fayyum* is eventually taken up by such data. The treatise aims to bring together every bit of information about the Fayyum that may be useful to fellow officials in Cairo, who, hopefully, will never have to bother to visit the province in person.

The structure of the treatise supports this ambitious project of describing the province in its totality. The first chapter sets out the Fayyum's location and topo-

ṣināʿat al-inshāʾ, ed. by Muḥammad ʿAbd al-Rasūl Ibrāhīm (Cairo: Dār al-Kutub al-Khidīwiyya, 1913–22; repr. 1964), XIII, 54. In an example from Fatimid documentary evidence, we find poll-tax receipts for the *kharājī* fiscal year of 412 issued in the *hijrī* year 414; Gaubert and Mouton, *Hommes et villages*, p. 16.

[15] For an example of an official sent to audit Damietta, see al-Nābulusī, *Sword of Ambition*, ed. and trans. by Yarbrough, p. 131.

[16] *Villages of the Fayyum*, author's introduction, p. 32.

graphy, a depression below the level of the Nile. The second and third chapters look at the impact of location and topography on the climate (*mizāj*) and health of the inhabitants, and on the quality of the water and air. The fourth chapter examines the structure of the water system of the Fayyum, explaining the annual cycle of the Nile inundation, and the role of al-Lāhūn Dam in regulating it. Demography is covered in the fifth chapter, which lists the different tribal groups that occupy the Fayyum, each in their own cluster of villages. The sixth chapter picks up the topic of water supply, setting out the causes of its deterioration and previous attempts to revive it. The seventh chapter lists the names of all the settlements in the province by alphabetical order, and the eighth chapter lists all the religious institutions, both Muslim and Christian. The fiscal section begins in the ninth chapter, in which al-Nābulusī provides the aggregate taxes of the province. The tenth and final chapter, which takes up about 80 per cent of the treatise, contains the entries for individual villages and hamlets, roughly by alphabetical order but beginning with Madīnat al-Fayyūm.

The *Villages of the Fayyum* fits no familiar genre in medieval Arabic literature, and there is no obvious model al-Nābulusī was trying to emulate.[17] The desire to bring a region to life through detailed description belongs to the discipline of geography, and several Abbasid authors included fiscal data in their geographical accounts.[18] But the Abbasid geographers were interested in the imperial and the global, and their works are far removed from this micro-study of one individual province. The treatise is a closer match with the genre of historical topography, which later culminates with al-Maqrīzī's famous fifteenth-century account of Egypt and Cairo, the *Khiṭaṭ*. An early representative of this tradition is a younger contemporary of al-Nābulusī, ʿIzz al-Dīn Ibn Shaddād (d. 684/1285). Ibn Shaddād had a career reminiscent of al-Nābulusī, serving under various Ayyubid rulers. He was also sent to conduct a financial audit of an individual province, Ḥarrān, in 640/1242–43.[19] His historical topography of Syria and the Jazīra, known as *al-Aʿlāq al-khaṭīra*, was composed in the 670s/1270s for the Mamluk sultan Baybars. It similarly contains summaries of tax revenues and numbers of troops, but it lacks the fiscal focus of al-Nābulusī's work, not to mention the minute detail at the level of the individual village.[20]

The treatise has traditionally been considered as part of the uniquely rich administrative tradition of the Ayyubid and Mamluk dynasties, and its study was often ancillary to the study of administrative manuals.[21] There is no doubt that the Ayyubid period saw the rise of a rich and novel type of administrative literature, and it is surely not a coincidence that the *Villages of the Fayyum* was composed in that period and in reference to it. The first work in this cluster, the administrative manual of al-Makhzūmī, *Kitāb al-minhāj*, was composed in 565/1169–70 and revised circa 581/1185. The surviving sections of this work deal with military organization and the regulation of international trade.[22] Al-Nābulusī consulted al-Makhzūmī's work, as he notes in his administrative treatise, the *Luminous Rules*.[23] The next administrative work in this group was *Qawānīn al-dawāwīn*, composed by the chief administrator Ibn Mammātī (d. 606/1209). This work, of which a complete manuscript survives, is especially valuable for its expla-

[17] One could note also similarities with the cadastral surveys of Egypt by Ibn Duqmāq and Ibn Jīʿān in the late fourteenth and fifteenth centuries. See summaries in Halm, *Ägypten*; Jo Van Steenbergen, 'Taqwim al-Buldan al-Misriya (CUL Qq 65): Identifying a Late Medieval Cadastral Survey of Egypt', in *Egypt and Syria in the Fatimid, Ayyubid and Mamluk Eras*, IV: *Proceedings of the 9th and 10th International Colloquium Organized at the Katholieke Universiteit Leuven in May 2000 and May 2001*, ed. by U. Vermeulen and Jo Van Steenbergen, Orientalia Lovaniensia Analecta, 140 (Leuven: Peeters, 2005), pp. 477–91; and the thirteenth-century Yemeni almanacs, discussed by Eric Vallet, *L'Arabie marchande: état et commerce sous les sultans rasūlides du Yémen, 626–858/1229–1454* (Paris: Publications de la Sorbonne, 2010). These later sources were obviously not a model for al-Nābulusī.

[18] Paul L. Heck, *The Construction of Knowledge in Islamic Civilization: Qudāma B. Jaʿfar and his Kitāb Al-Kharāj Wa-ṣināʿat Al-kitāba*, Islamic History and Civilizations: Studies and Texts, 42 (Leiden: Brill, 2002), pp. 111–23.

[19] Dominique Sourdel, 'ʿIzz al-Dīn Ibn Shaddād', *The Encyclopedia of Islam*, 2nd edn, III, 933; ʿIzz al-Dīn Ibn Shaddād, *Description de la Syrie du nord*, trans. by Anne-Marie Eddé-Terrasse (Damascus, 1984), p. xii; ʿIzz al-Dīn Ibn Shaddād, *Al-Aʿlāq al-Khaṭīra fī Dhikr Umarāʾ al-Shām wa'l-Jazīra (Taʾrīkh al-Jazīra)*, ed. by Yaḥyā ʿAbbāra, 2 vols (Damascus: Wizārat al-Thaqāfa waʾl-Irshād al-Qawmī, 1977–8), I, 16: 'I was sent to Ḥarrān in 640 to survey it (*li-akshifha-hā*)'

[20] The work was written towards the end of his life between 671/1272–73 and 680/1281–82, so could not have been an inspiration for al-Nābulusī. See Ibn Šaddād, *Description*, trans. by Eddé-Terasse, p. xiv; Humphreys, *Islamic History*, p. 174.

[21] Humphreys, *Islamic History*, 'The Fiscal Administration of the Mamluk Empire', pp. 169–86. Cahen's work on the *Villages of the Fayyum* led to his discovery of al-Makhzūmī's treatise; Cahen, *Makhzūmiyyāt: études sur l'histoire économique et financière de l'Égypte médiévale* (Leiden: Brill, 1977). See also the discussion in Rabie, *The Financial System*, pp. 16–17.

[22] Cahen, *Makhzūmiyyāt*.

[23] Al-Nābulusī, *Kitāb lumaʿ*, ed. by Becker and Cahen, p. 10.

nation of agricultural taxation.[24] Unlike the *Villages of the Fayyum*, however, both al-Makhzūmī and Ibn Mammātī wrote prescriptive works, manuals of the procedures to be followed and not records of actual fiscal obligations.

We do not know whether the *Villages of the Fayyum* made any impression on the sultan al-Malik al-Ṣāliḥ. It is also noticeable that the *Villages of the Fayyum* is not cited by any other medieval author.[25] We have no further information about al-Nābulusī's career, and it therefore seems unlikely that he regained a prominent position in the administration. He died in Cairo about twenty years later, on 25 Jumādā I 660 (17 April 1262), and was buried in the Muqattam Cemetery.[26]

In the *Villages of the Fayyum*, as well as in his other works, al-Nābulusī comes across as an arrogant, self-serving bigot, full of contempt toward both Copts and people of the countryside. His poetry is worse than mediocre. He hated his time outside Cairo. But he is also remarkably observant, with a refreshingly critical approach to his sources. And we must be immensely grateful for al-Nābulusī's literary pretensions. Without them, his mission to the Fayyum would have produced a mundane fiscal report, which would have been lost together with other Ayyubid and Mamluk archives. As it happened, it is precisely because the fiscal material was embedded in a literary work that the *Villages of the Fayyum* has survived so as to give us an unparalleled window onto the taxes, economy, and society of rural Islamic Egypt.

---

[24] Ibn Mammātī, *Kitāb qawānīn al-dawāwīn*, ed. ʿAṭiya; Richard S. Cooper, 'Ibn Mammati's Rules for the Ministries: Translation with Commentary of the Qawānīn al-Dawāwīn' (unpublished doctoral dissertation, University of California, Berkeley, 1973).

[25] Later authors of encyclopaedic works probably did not find it as useful as the works of Ibn Mammātī and al-Makhzūmī. See the comments by Cahen in his introduction to al-Nābulusī, *Kitāb lumaʿ*, ed. by Becker and Cahen, p. 123; and by Sayyid in his edition of al-Maqrīzī, *al-Mawāʿiẓ*, I, 231 n. 3.

[26] ʿAbd al-Muʾmin al-Dimyāṭī, *Le dictionnaire des autorités (Muʿǧam al-Šuyūḫ)*, ed. by Georges Vajda (Paris: CNRS, 1962), p. 164.

Chapter 2

DECODING THE *VILLAGES OF THE FAYYUM*

Al-Nābulusī's survey is written by an experienced administrator, for the benefit of other professional bureaucrats familiar with the Ayyubid tax regime. Not unlike a modern pay-slip or a tax return, it uses terminology intelligible to government officials but which the non-initiate often finds obscure. Given the nature of the source, the aim of this section is to explain the most common categories of taxes, fees, and loans that are listed in the village entries. It also sets out to explain the key terminology used by al-Nābulusī with regard to the allocation of water resources and *iqṭāʿ* grants to military officers, as well as his depiction of village communities and their religious and social identities.

The following discussion builds on, complements, and corrects earlier studies by Cahen, Cooper, Rabie, and Sato.[1] Many of the taxes are explained by Ibn Mammātī in his administrative manual, and further information is supplied by the Mamluk-era manuals of al-Nuwayrī (d. 1333) and al-Qalqashandī (d. 1418). In other cases, the meaning of the terminology has to be inferred from a close reading of al-Nābulusī's text and through reflection on the realities of medieval rural economy.

We aim to explain the terms and categories of the *Villages of the Fayyum* in the order in which they are listed by al-Nābulusī. Each entry starts with an overview of the village, including its status as either *iqṭāʿ*, endowment or part of the royal domain, its nominal fiscal value, tribal affiliation, and water rights. The list of taxes normally begins with the actual revenue (*irtifāʿ*), which consisted of the land tax and taxes on trade. These major categories are followed by a list of fees, including a separate category of pasture fees. In most village entries, the fees are followed by the alms-tax, poll-tax, and payments to the Ministry of Religious Endowments.

Then al-Nābulusī normally lists credit given to the villagers in the form of tax-free privileged land allocated to local officials and dignitaries, seed advances by the government, and advance payments for supplies of barley and beans. The section on credit sometimes ends with a list of arrears from previous years. The last item in village entries is usually the number of chicks to be reared by the local villagers. Information on sugarcane presses and the size of government-owned sugarcane plantations can often be found right at the beginning of the entry, alongside the fiscal revenue, but is sometimes relegated to the concluding sections.

The tax structure of the town of Madīnat al-Fayyūm is quite different, as its lengthy entry contains a number of fiscal terms that are not repeated elsewhere in the treatise. Such terms are explained, as necessary, in the notes to the translated text. Likewise, rare fiscal terms which occur only once or twice in the village entries are also discussed in the notes to the translation and not in this chapter.

For the weights and measurements used in the treatise, see 'Glossary of Measures, Weights, and Monetary Units' that precedes the edition and translation. The nominal exchange rate used throughout the *Villages of the Fayyum* is 1:40 (one gold dinar for 40 silver dirhams). The quantitative data from the treatise is available in digital format through the dedicated webpage.[2]

[1] Cahen, 'Le régime des impôts'; Rabie, *The Financial System*; Cooper, 'Ibn Mammati's Rules'; Sato, *State and Rural Society*.

[2] 'Rural Society in Medieval Islam: *Villages of the Fayyum*' <https://projects.history.qmul.ac.uk/ruralsocietyislam>.

Section I: The Village

I.1. The Village

Throughout the *Villages of the Fayyum*, the village as a unit of agricultural production is called *nāḥiya*. The *nāḥiya* was the administrative building block for the allocation of land and water resources and payment of taxes. When referring to the physical space of the village, al-Nābulusī usually uses the terms *balad* or *balda*.[3]

Hamlets (*kafr*, pl. *kufūr*; also called *munsha'a*, pl. *manāshi'*) were smaller settlements, whose taxes were normally subsumed under the tax-entry of a mother village. A list of the *manāshi'*, organized by their mother villages, is provided towards the end of the treatise. Hamlets were also dependent on a mother village for their water quota. Some hamlets paid alms-tax on livestock separately from their mother village, even if all other taxes, including the land tax, were paid jointly.

I.2. Fiscal Revenue and *Iqṭā*ʿ

Most of the villages in the Fayyum were assigned to holders of *iqṭā*ʿ grants. The holders of the *iqṭā*ʿ grants were officers in the Ayyubid army who had temporary rights to the fiscal revenue (*irtifā*ʿ) in the village in return for providing military service.

The fiscal revenue allocated to *iqṭā*ʿ-holders normally included the land tax, both in cash and in kind, and the commercial taxes. The remaining taxes, including the alms-tax on livestock, the poll-tax on non-Muslims, and fees on the use of pasture, went to the state treasury, the *Dīwān al-Māl*. The *Dīwān al-Māl* also owned most of the sugarcane plantations and all of the sugarcane presses.[4]

A handful of villages were not granted to *iqṭā*ʿ-holders, including three large villages that belonged to the private domain (*khāṣṣ*) of the Sultan. In these three villages the Sultan had a personal right to the fiscal revenue, paralleling rights of *iqṭā*ʿ-holders in other villages.

In addition, three small villages and some individual orchards were endowed as *waqf* for the benefit of religious institutions, both in Cairo and in Madīnat al-Fayyūm. This meant that their fiscal revenues were channelled for the support of the endowed institution.

I.3. Fiscal Value

When a village (or, sometimes, a group of villages) was granted as *iqṭā*ʿ, it was accorded a fiscal value (ʿ*ibra*), designated in a nominal unit of account known as Army Dinar (*dīnār jayshī*). The Army Dinar was supposed to create a standard measure of the income an *iqṭā*ʿ unit was expected to generate, which could then be matched with the rank of the recipient of the *iqṭā*ʿ.

Ibn Mammātī states that the Army Dinar was calculated by multiplying the cash revenue, in gold dinars, by four, then adding to it the expected income in ardabbs of grain. The fifteenth-century author al-Qalqashandī explains that under the Ayyubids each Army Dinar was worth three gold dinars.[5] In the *Villages of the Fayyum*, however, the value of the Army Dinar is not standard.

*Iqṭā*ʿ units usually consisted of a single village, but an *iqṭā*ʿ unit could also consist of a cluster of villages, mostly along the same irrigation canal. The largest clusters of this kind were the Dilya Canal, in south-western Fayyum, which included twelve different villages, and the Tanabṭawayh Canal, also in the south. In villages that formed part of these multi-village *iqṭā*ʿ units, the fiscal value mentioned is of the total *iqṭā*ʿ unit to which the village belonged.

I.4. Bedouin and Non-tribal (*badw* and *ḥaḍar*)

Nearly all villages and hamlets in the Fayyum were inhabited by Arab tribesmen, also called *badw*, or Bedouin. Each village was identified with a tribal section or clan. While the Arabs were the inhabitants in most villages, a handful of villages were inhabited by predominantly non-tribal, or clan-less (*ḥaḍar*) population. In these villages, the Bedouin were the guardsmen or protectors (*khufarā'*).

The segmentary tribal structure is described by al-Nābulusī in his introductory chapters. At the top level were three tribal confederacies (*aṣl* or *āl*), each inhabiting a large number of villages. First in importance were the Banū Kilāb, with as many as fifty villages, followed by the Banū ʿAjlān and the much smaller Lawāta, a Berber tribe. The Banū Kilāb dominated in the centre, south, and west; the ʿAjlān in the east and

[3] Here we differ from Sato, who identifies the *balda* as the administrative unit for the *iqṭā*ʿ: Sato, *State and Rural Society*, p. 179.

[4] Later, in 1315, the collection of the poll-tax was handed over to the *iqṭā*ʿ-holders: see Rabie, *The Financial System*, p. 41; Sato, *State and Rural Society*, pp. 68, 148.

[5] Ibn Mammātī, *Kitāb qawānīn al-dawāwīn*, ed. by ʿAṭiya, p. 369; al-Qalqashandī, *Ṣubḥ*, III, 442–43; Sato, *State and Rural Society*, pp. 153–55; Rabie, *The Financial System*, p. 47; Cooper, 'Ibn Mammati's Rules', pp. 364–67. Stuart Borsch adopts the 1:3 ratio mentioned by al-Qalqashandī: Borsch, *The Black Death in Egypt and England: A Comparative Study* (Austin: University of Texas Press, 2009), pp. 67–90.

the north; while the Lawāta dwelt in villages along the al-Lāhūn gap.

Each tribal confederacy was divided into sections or clans, which al-Nābulusī usually calls *fakhdh* (pl., *afkhādh*) or 'branch' (*far*ʿ). Each tribal section inhabited a varying number of settlements, from one hamlet (the Banū Muṭayr in Sanhūr) to as many as nineteen villages (the Banū Zarʿa of the ʿAjlān). The individual village entries nearly always identify the people of the village (*ahl*) with one particular clan. In the minority of villages where the population is clan-less, the entry identifies the Arab clan that holds the protection rights.

I.5. Water Rights

Most villages were irrigated by gravity-fed canals and were allocated 'water rights', effectively a water quota, determined by the width of the weir at the head of a local feeder canal. Some villages were fed by more than one canal, and then al-Nābulusī lists the water rights for each of these canals separately.

The width of the opening of the weir at the head of the feeder canal was measured in units called *qabḍa*, literally 'fist-length' (approximately 10 cm). A *qabḍa* unit may have also taken into account the slope of the canal or its depth.[6] The water quota of an individual village was taken out of the total water quota of the main branch canal for the surrounding area.

Where a main canal branched off to several feeder canals, each governed by a separate weir, the cluster of weirs was called a divisor (*maqsam*, pl. *maqāsim*). These divisors were found only on the Grand Canal and major branch canals, called the *baḥr*s.

Villages outside of the Fayyum depression itself, mostly north and south of the al-Lāhūn dam, were irrigated in the 'manner of Lower Egypt (*al-rīf*)', that is, by basin irrigation. Villages irrigated by basin irrigation did not have a water quota.[7]

Some villages irrigated by gravity-fed canals also did not have a water quota. This was particularly true for villages lying on higher ground, because the flow in their feeder canal was considered to be too weak and there was no need to regulate it.

[6] A reference to 'small *qabḍas*' (*qubaḍ ṣighār*, in Būr Sīnarū) suggests that the unit was not uniform.

[7] See also the discussion by John Ball, *Contributions to the Geography of Egypt* (Cairo: The Government Press, 1939), p. 220.

I.6. Religious Buildings

Al-Nābulusī relied on a record of churches, monasteries, and mosques in the Fayyum held in Cairo by the Ministry of Endowments of Congregational and Neighbourhood Mosques (*Dīwān Aḥbās al-Jawāmi*ʿ *wa'l-Masājid*), usually abbreviated to the Ministry of Endowments.[8] Al-Nābulusī also notes the existence of some unregistered mosques not on the Ministry's list, usually in smaller villages or hamlets.

Section II: Taxes and Fees

II.1. Land tax in Grains

Taxes in kind were mostly levied through *munājaza* lease contracts. In *munājaza* contracts, a lump sum of ardabbs of grain was assessed based on the estimated area and quality of the village's arable lands, and was levied collectively from the tenants (*muzāri*ʿ*ūn*) of the village.

The taxes in grains consisted mainly of wheat, barley and broad beans. Beyond these staple grains, there was also a range of other summer and winter crops subject to *munājaza* lease contracts, including rice, Jew's mallow, vetch, sesame, rape, cumin, and coriander. There are also rare instances where the *munājaza* is specified in cash, mentioned as a tax on the cultivation of cotton and lentils.[9]

The *munājaza* lease contract was a cheaper alternative to an expensive annual survey of individual plots.[10] The fifteenth-century author al-Qalqashandī explains that a *munājaza* contract is based on average yields: 'the arable land of the village is being tendered (*tunajjaz*) for a specified sum not subject to decrease or increase, and the land tax is being demanded according to that lease'.[11]

Alongside the *munājaza*, a minority of villages paid another category of land tax in grains, called the *mushāṭara*. While *mushāṭara* has the apparent legal meaning of share-cropping, specifically for 50 per cent

[8] This ministry had much discretion over the appointment and reimbursement of religious officials, such as scholars, Qur'an readers and imams. See al-Nābulusī, *Luma*ʿ, ed. by Becker and Cahen, pp. 25–27.

[9] *Munājaza* tax on cotton: Tuṭūn and Buljusūq; on lentils: Miṭr Ṭāris. Unspecified *munājaza* in cash: Ghābat Bāja and Dumūshiyya.

[10] Abū al-Ḥasan Ibn ʿUthmān al-Makhzūmī, *Al-muntaqā min kitāb al-minhāj fī* ʿ*ilm kharāj Miṣr*, ed. by Claude Cahen and Yūsuf Rāghib (al-Qāhirah: Institut français d'archéologie orientale, 1986), p. 59 (fol. 166r). See also Cooper, 'Ibn Mammati's Rules', p. 189.

[11] Al-Qalqashandī, *Ṣubḥ*, III, 458.

of the harvest,[12] in al-Nābulusī's survey the term is practically interchangeable with *munājaza* contracts, and, because it is often specified in round numbers, does not seem to be a fixed share of the produce.[13]

II. 2. Land Tax on Field Cash Crops

Fields of winter and summer cash crops, including the widespread flax, were subject to a 'land tax on feddans' or 'cash land tax on feddans' (*kharāj al-fudun, mufādanāt, kharāj fudun al-ʿayn*). These were taxes on field cultivation, paid in cash according to a scale of tax-rates per feddan. Crops subject to this land tax in cash were flax, cotton, garlic, colocasia, alfalfa, green vegetables, cucurbitaceous fruits, and carrots.

The amount of tax to be paid was calculated according to the area of cultivation (given in feddans) multiplied by the tax-rate (*qaṭīʿa*), which depended on the crop. Al-Nābulusī sometimes provides both the area under cultivation in feddans and the tax assessment in dinars, or sometimes — especially for flax and cotton — just the tax assessment.

The tax-rates mentioned are 1 dinar per feddan on alfalfa;[14] 2 dinars per feddan on garlic,[15] green vegetables (*khuḍar*),[16] henna, indigo,[17] and cucurbitaceous fruits;[18] 3 or 5 dinars per feddan on colocasia;[19] and 3 or 5 dinars per feddan on flax. Cotton was mostly taxed at a rate of 1.5 dinar per feddan, but rates of 1.25 dinar or 2 dinars per feddan are also mentioned.[20]

The cash crop tax category was supplemented by an 'addition' (*iḍāfa*), a 12.5 per cent surcharge over the basic tax.

II. 3. Land tax on Orchards, Palm Enclosures, and Vineyards

The taxes on orchards and vineyards were levied through a category of 'land tax on perennial trees and water-wheels (*kharāj al-rātib wa'l-sawāqī*)'. As the name suggests, this tax was closely associated with year-round irrigation by water-wheels. The tax was levied per feddan and was probably collected in Madīnat al-Fayyūm upon the sale of the produce, a method attested in fourteenth-century Damascus.[21]

Orchards were subject to a standard tax-rate of a 2 dinars, supplemented by a 12.5 per cent surcharge. Land designated for viticulture was subject to a higher rate of 5.33 dinars, plus a surcharge of 12.5 per cent. Young trees were subject to lower rates. Unlike field cultivation, orchards and enclosures were akin to private property, and there are references to named individual owners.

Also included in this category were taxes on lands designated as long-term leases (*aḥkār*). The terms of these long-term leases allowed the lessees freedom of use, but it seems they were mostly planted with trees and vines. Lands subject to long-term leases paid the same rate as orchards, 2 dinars per feddan, made up of a basic tax-rate of one dinar per feddan and an additional tax-rate of another dinar per feddan.

---

[12] For a *mushāṭara* contract from the early Mamluk period in which the produce is divided equally between the landlord and the peasant, see Taqī al-Dīn Ibn Taymiyya, *Majmūʿat al-fatāwā li-Shaykh al-Islām Ibn Taymiyya*, ed. by ʿAbd al-Rahṃān ibn Muḥammad Ibn Qāsim and Muḥammad ibn ʿAbd al-Rahṃān Ibn Qāsim (Riyadh: Maṭābiʿ al-Riyāḍ, 1961), xxx, 119–20.

[13] Ibn Mammātī makes it clear that land subject to *mushāṭara* pays its taxes in kind, but he does not elaborate; Ibn Mammātī, *Kitāb qawānīn al-dawāwīn*, ed. ʿAṭiya, p. 259; Cooper, 'Ibn Mammati's Rules', p. 115 (6.3.14). Al-Makhzūmī distinguishes between land tax on 'feddans of cash and of grains' and feddans of *mushāṭara*; Makhzūmī, *al-minhāj*, p. 60 (fols 166ᵛ–167ʳ). Cahen equates *munājaza* and *mushāṭara* and defines them as the dividing of the total tax of a villages among the individual taxpayers. See his 'Contribution á l'étude des impots dans l'Égypt médiévale', *Journal of the Economic and Social History of the Orient*, 5 (1962), 244–78 (p. 264); Cahen, 'Le régime des impôts', p. 14. See also Rabie, *The Financial System*, p. 75; Cooper, 'Ibn Mammati's Rules', p. 190 ('the process whereby an assessment for an entire district was handed down by the central government and then apportioned among the taxpayers of the district'). See also Cooper, 'The Assessment and Collection of Kharāj Tax in Medieval Egypt', *Journal of the American Oriental Society*, 96. 3 (1976), 365–82.

[14] Compare Cooper, 'Ibn Mammati's Rules', p. 117 (6.3.6), although Ibn Mammātī says there is disagreement on this tax-rate.

[15] Cooper, 'Ibn Mammati's Rules', p. 117 (6.3.7).

[16] Ibn Mammātī reports tax-rate of 2 dinars for lettuce and cabbage; Cooper, 'Ibn Mammati's Rules', p. 121 (6.4.12, 6.4.13).

[17] Ibn Mammātī has 3 dinars for indigo; Cooper, 'Ibn Mammati's Rules', p. 120 (6.3.6, 6.4.09).

[18] Ibn Mammātī has 1–2 dinars; Cooper, 'Ibn Mammati's Rules', p. 118 (6.3.6, 6.4.02).

[19] Ibn Mammātī has the current tax-rate as 4 dinars per feddan, down from 5 under the Fatimids; Cooper, 'Ibn Mammati's Rules', p. 120 (6.4.06).

[20] Ibn Mammātī has cotton taxed at 1 dinar per feddan; Cooper, 'Ibn Mammati's Rules', p. 119 (6.4.04).

[21] Taxes on the fruits and vegetables grown in the Ghūṭa of Damascus were levied after the produce was brought to a central location, called Dār al-Biṭṭīkh wa'l-Fākiha ('Hall of Melons and Fruits'), to be sold and taxed there. See Mathieu Eychenne, 'La production agricole de Damas et de la Ghūṭa au XIVᵉ siècle: diversité, taxation et prix des cultures maraîchères d'après al-Jazarī (m.739/1338)', *Journal of Economic and Social History of the Orient*, 56. 4–5 (2013), 569–630 (p. 597).

II. 4. Lunar-calendar Taxes on Trade (*al-māl al-hilālī*)

Taxes on trade were due from sites of commercial activities, mainly shops, usually in the form of rent or concession. These were known as 'lunar-calendar taxes' (*al-māl al-hilālī*), since they were paid monthly and followed the Islamic, lunar, calendar. This category occasionally also included agricultural activities that did not depend on the solar calendar, such as fishing.

The taxes on trade were levied as rent paid for the usufruct of buildings and structures, such as water-mills, store-houses (*ādur*), weavers' pits, pottery kilns, tanneries, shops, and bath-houses.[22] Often, the taxes on trade are described as 'rent of the Dīwān's shops', 'rent of the shops', or simply revenues 'from the shops', a catch-all category that included small-scale artisanal workshops.

The term surety or concession (*ḍamān*) is also used to designate rent payments on shops, as well as concessions for the operation of ferryboats and the sale of chicken.

II. 5. Fees (*rusūm*)

The process of harvesting, measuring, threshing, and transporting grains was subject to an array of fees, reported in a separate section of the tax record for each village. The fees also included payments to local officials and set payments for armed protection and for religious services. None of these fees is adequately explained in the administrative literature.[23]

II. 5. 1. A threshing-floor fee (*rasm al-ajrān*), in cash and in grains, is mentioned in nearly all villages which were subject to land tax in grains. The threshing floor payments in grains are sub-divided into the different types of crops. For every ardabb of grains paid in threshing-floor fees, cultivators had also to add 0.8–0.9 dirhams in cash.

II. 5. 2. A separate measurement fee (*al-kiyāla*) was paid in kind, again sub-divided into different categories of grains. The aggregate amount of the measurement fees in kind is roughly equivalent to the aggregate threshing-floor fees, but there is no consistent correlation between the two categories.

II. 5. 3. A surcharge payment, called *wafr*, is attested in nine villages with very high grain production. It was calculated as an additional 3 per cent on top of the land tax in kind.[24] A handful of very large villages also had to pay a transport fee, with an inconsistent rate.

II. 5. 4. A uniform harvest fee (*rasm al-ḥiṣād*) of 53 dirhams was levied in nearly all grain-cultivating villages in the province, regardless of the amount of grains they were expected to produce.[25]

II. 5. 5. A uniform and modest protection fee (*rasm al-khafāra*) was collected from most villages, at a fixed value of 15 dirhams. This minimal and uniform tax appears to be a blanket policing fee.[26]

II. 5. 6. A fee for 'supervision of the land survey' (*shadd al-ʿayn*), found in about half the villages in the Fayyum, was linked to the collection of cash land tax on field crops. The largest fees are found in villages which also had substantial cash-crops, especially flax.

II. 5. 7. A 'dredging fee' (*rasm al-jarārīf*) was paid by most villages that lay along gravity-fed canals (a total of sixty-two villages), averaging at around 1 dinar per village. It is not found in villages that relied on basin irrigation.

II. 5. 8. About half the villages along gravity-fed canals made small payments of grains to the official known as *khawlī al-baḥr* (overseer of the canal), who was in charge of the schedule of opening and closing of weirs.

II. 5. 9. A minority of villages paid their taxes on cash field crops in the form of fees, sometimes called 'settlement' (*muṣālaḥa*). This was common with less valuable field crops, such as carrots, where the tax-collectors dispensed with the costly land survey and collected the taxes as fees based on estimates.

---

[22] On this category, see al-Nuwayrī, *Nihāyat al-arab*, VIII, 228. Al-Nuwayrī explains that rent (*ujra*) is levied on covered, or roofed, properties, while surety (*ḍamān*) is levied on uncovered properties.

[23] Al-Nuwayrī states that cash fees (*ḥūqūq*) were paid on every feddan of grain cultivation, at a rate of 2–4 dirhams per feddan; al-Nuwayrī, *Nihāyat al-arab*, VIII, 249. Note that in the *Villages of the Fayyum* the fees are mostly specified in kind and not in cash.

[24] According to al-Nuwayrī, a payment called *wafr* was to be taken by the officials in charge of measuring the grains and buying the crops for cash. In his account the *wafr* seems akin to a fee; al-Nuwayrī, *Nihāyat al-arab*, VIII, 252, 296.

[25] The tiny village of Dimūh al-Dāthir was liable to only 25 dirhams, and was also exempt from the 'protection fee', so must have had its unique arrangements.

[26] This is perhaps the same fee as the one mentioned by al-Nuwayrī in connection with the measurement of crops; al-Nuwayrī, *Nihāyat al-arab*, VIII, 296.

II.6. Pasture Fees

A complex set of fees governed a strict monitoring of grazing. Pasture areas were divided into permanent areas of high quality, known as *rātib*,[27] and seasonal or occasional pasture lands called *ṭāri'*. Each category of pasture area was assigned a tax-rate per head of grazing animal.[28]

The fee for the permanent pasture areas was set at 2.25 dirhams per head of livestock. The fees for seasonal grazing areas were subject to a scale of rates, from 1 dirham per head to 0.25 dirhams per head, apparently depending on the quality of the pasture.

The tax collection and counting of animals was administered by a group of clerks, who received a 'government agents' fee' (*rasm al-mustakhdamīn*), calculated as 6.25 dirham per hundred heads of livestock.[29] The assumption appears to be that the animals remained in the same pasture area throughout the entire season.

Permanent pasture lands (*rātib*) were sometimes subject to a fixed pasture tax (*māl al-marāʿī*), regardless of the number of grazing animals. It was also called the 'permanent pasture tax' (*marāʿī rātib*). A fixed tax on permanent pasture lands was a simpler alternative to the collection of fees per head, and obviated the need to count the numbers of livestock entering the pasture area.[30]

II. 7. Alms-tax (*zakāt*)

Islamic alms-tax, the *zakāt*, was reintroduced to Egypt by Saladin as part of an Islamization project.[31] In Ayyubid Fayyum, it was levied on livestock, categories of dry fruits, capital, and slaves.

II. 7. 1. The principal concern of the alms-tax was livestock. Payment was required from freely pasturing herds or flocks of large and small cattle in full private ownership.[32]

For cows and buffalos, one year-old calf (*tabīʿ*) was levied from a herd of more than thirty cows, and one cow in her second year (*musinna*) for every forty heads.

The alms-tax on sheep and goats was one sheep or goat for a flock of over forty heads, two for 120–200 heads, and then a rate of one animal for every additional hundred. Camels were paid for in heads of goats, one goat for every five camels.[33] The terms used for small livestock are *bayāḍ* (lit., 'white') for sheep and *shaʿriyya* (sing.; pl. *shiʿārā*) for goats. These terms also appear in Ibn Mammātī's section on the alms-tax.[34] Occasionally, a distinction is made between the local small cattle (*qarāriyya*) and transient small cattle (*muntajiʿūn*).

The alms-tax was specified in heads of animals, but actual payment was taken in cash, after the monetary value of the animal was assessed. For example, each head of sheep levied in alms-tax was commuted to around one gold dinar.[35]

II. 7. 2. Alms-tax, probably at a rate of 5 per cent, was levied on the dry fruit of date palms, vineyards, and olives. This alms-tax was levied on privately owned trees and, according to legal literature, was supposed to apply above a minimum threshold of five *awsāq* (about 610 kg). In the *Villages of the Fayyum*, The alms-tax was limited to these three varieties of dry fruit, in line with Shāfiʿī and Mālikī doctrine.[36] Ibn Mammātī reports that alms-tax is levied on the fruits of the date-palm and the grape-vine, but exempts olives.[37]

---

[27] The terminology here is similar to that used for non-Muslims subject to the poll-tax, where *rātib* is a local established resident, *ṭāri'* is a new-comer, and *nāshi'* is one who recently became adult; al-Nuwayrī, *Nihāyat al-arab*, VIII, 242.

[28] Al-Nuwayrī, *Nihāyat al-arab*, VIII, 191, 262. See also Rabie, *The Financial System*, p. 79.

[29] See Rabie, *The Financial System*, pp. 79–80. Rabie argues that the categories of the pasture fee depended on the size and age of the animals.

[30] The two categories of taxes on permanent pasture — fees based on the number of animals and the fixed pasture tax — are mentioned together only in the entry for the village of Shisfa.

[31] Rabie, *The Financial System*, p. 96; Aron Zysow, 'Zakāt', *The Encyclopedia of Islam*, 2nd edn, XI, 406–22.

[32] According to a view ascribed to al-Shāfiʿī, even one day of feeding on fodder would exempt the owner of an animal from paying alms-tax; the Ḥanbalīs view this as a loophole; Ibn Qudāma, *al-Mughnī*, IV, 13. The dominant opinion cited by al-Nawawī is that animals are subject to alms-tax as long as the fodder they receive is not necessary for their survival, which would mean up to three days of fodder. See Yaḥyā bin Sharaf al-Nawawī, *Kitāb al-majmūʿ: Sharḥ al-muhadhdhab*, ed. by Muḥammad Najīb al-Muṭīʿī, 12 vols (Beirut: Dār Iḥyā' al-Turāth al-'Arabī, 2001), V, 231.

[33] Ibn Mammātī, *Kitāb qawānīn al-dawāwīn*, ed. by ʿAṭiya, pp. 311–12; Cooper, 'Ibn Mammati's Rules', pp. 266–67.

[34] Ibn Mammātī, *Kitāb qawānīn al-dawāwīn*, ed. by ʿAṭiya, pp. 351–52.

[35] This is again in line with Ibn Mammātī's recommendations. Al-Makhzūmī is more specific in this regard, stating that the alms-tax on livestock could be levied by the actual sale of the animals or by monetary valuation (*tathmīn*). See Cooper, 'Ibn Mammati's Rules', pp. 291–92.

[36] Al-Nawawī, *Kitāb al-majmūʿ*, V, 310.

[37] The fruits are named as raisins (*zabīb*) and dates (*tamr*). Cooper, 'Ibn Mammati's Rules', p. 267.

The alms-tax on these fruits was calculated as an estimate (*kharṣ*) of the yield. In Islamic law, the alms-tax on grapes, dates, and olives was calculated when the fruits were yet unpicked, leading to an estimate of the projected yield as dried fruit.[38]

II. 7. 3. Alms-tax was also levied on commercial capital and on slaves. According to legal texts, the alms-tax on capital and on slaves was at a rate of 2.5 per cent, above a minimum threshold of 20 dinars. This category was levied almost exclusively in Madīnat al-Fayyūm, suggesting that neither capital nor slaves were widely available beyond the city.

II. 8 Payments for Muslim Religious Endowments (*Dīwān al-Aḥbās*)

The majority of villages, sixty-one settlements, were subject to a tax on religious services paid to the Ministry of Endowments of Congregational and Neighbourhood Mosques. The tax ranged from 0.5 dinar in small villages to a significant 20 dinars in al-Lāhūn.

A small fee, in dirhams, was paid in the same villages for the upkeep of local religious buildings. This fee was closely correlated with the tax due to the Ministry, as a rate of 2–3 dirhams to every dinar of tax (5%–7.5%).

II. 9. Poll-Tax

The poll-tax (*al-jawālī*; the legal term *jizya* does not occur) was levied at a flat rate of 2 dinars per annum on every non-Muslim adult male, in agreement with evidence regarding contemporary practice elsewhere in Egypt. While the majority of the Sunni schools of law exempt the poor, or those incapable of paying, Fatimid and Ayyubid policies were generally to grant no exemptions and to levy a flat rate.[39]

The collection of the poll-tax was undertaken by officials called 'beast-chasers' (*ṭarrādūn al-waḥsh*; also once in singular, *tarrād al-waḥsh*). These officials were given a small annual payment of 0.5 dinar each, deducted from the government's poll-tax revenues.[40]

In the poll-tax register, a quarter of Fayyumi non-Muslims were registered as absentees, either in Upper or in Lower Egypt.

II. 10. Hay Levy

All grain-producing villages were liable to a levy of hay (*muwaẓẓaf al-atbān*), that is, the stalks of grains after the harvest, measured in bales (*shanīf*, pl. *ashnāf*).[41] The hay levy is discussed by Ibn al-Mammātī, who describes a complex tax of which we have only an occasional trace in the treatise. According to Ibn Mammātī, the levy was divided up between the Dīwān, the *iqṭāʿ*-holder and the cultivator. The cultivator could buy the Dīwān's share for cash, at a rate of 4.16 dinar per hundred loads (*ḥiml*).[42]

II. 11. Foodstuff Levy

Iqṭāʿ-holders were entitled to small amounts of cereal dishes of three varieties: *kishk* (dried yogurt with crushed wheat), *sawīq* (parched grain with butter and fat), and *farīk* (green wheat). These taxes were levied in kind, specifically for the benefit of *iqṭāʿ*-holders, and are called in literary sources 'hospitality dues' (*ḍiyāfa*), although the term does not occur in al-Nābulusī's text.

II. 12. Poultry Levy

A levy of chickens is mentioned in eighty-seven villages, amounting to about 55,000 birds. The local tenant cultivators reared chicks, which probably hatched in two major hatcheries (sing. *maʿmal al-farrūj*) in Madīnat al-Fayyūm and Sinnūris. The villagers delivered the mature birds either to the government's kitchens or to the local *iqṭāʿ*-holders. In return they received a 'rearing wage' (*ujrat al-tarbiya*) of one-third of the amount of chickens they were due to deliver.

There are no taxes on chicken, and it seems that poultry production was not permitted beyond this network of hatcheries and village rearing. Monopolies over

[38] This is because the alms-tax on fruits is due when the fruits first appear to be good (*badā ṣalāḥuhā*). See Ibn Qudāma, *al-Mughnī*, IV, 169, 173; al- Nawawī, *Kitāb al-majmūʿ*, V, 325 ff.

[39] This conclusion is based on ample evidence from the Geniza. See Eli Alschech, 'Islamic Law, Practice and Legal Doctrine: Exempting the Poor from the Jizya under the Ayyubids (1171–1250)', *Islamic Law and Society*, 10. 3 (2003), 348–75 (p. 373). Ibn Mammātī, however, still reports rates of 4 1/6 dinars for the rich, 2 dinars as medium rate, and a low rate of 1 7/12 dinar (1.58) for the poor. See Ibn Mammātī, *Kitāb qawānīn al-dawāwīn*, ed. by ʿAṭiya, p. 31.

[40] Ibn Mammātī reports that the poll-tax collectors receive a fee of 2 1/4 dirhams per head; Ibn Mammātī, *Kitāb qawānīn al-dawāwīn*, ed. by ʿAṭiya, p. 319.

[41] Cahen, 'Le régime des impôts', p. 22 n. 3.

[42] Ibn Mammātī, *Kitāb qawānīn al-dawāwīn*, ed. by ʿAṭiya, p. 344; Cooper, 'Ibn Mammati's Rules', p. 288.

the sale of chicken are mentioned in two villages, where small payments for the concession of chicken (*ḍamān al-farrūj*) are mentioned. This may represent a system where a contractor (*ḍāmin*) held a monopoly over the sale of chickens in a given area, as reported for the early Mamluk period.[43]

Section III: Allowances, Advances, and Credit

III. 1. Allowances (*rizaq*)

Large villages allotted tax-free allowances (*rizaq*) of arable land to local officials, including village headmen and guardsmen, supervisors of the sugarcane network, carpenters in charge of maintaining waterwheels, as well as Christian and Muslim clerics.

Allowances were most commonly granted as tax-free plots of arable land, usually measured in feddans but sometimes in ploughshares (*miḥrāth*, pl. *maḥārīth*), a larger unit equal to perhaps a dozen feddans. These plots were exempt from the land tax. Their surplus remained with the local beneficiaries and was not delivered to the *iqṭāʿ*-holder.[44] Since these plots were exempt from the lease contracts affecting other village lands, they were sometimes subject to a canonical land tax on private property, called the tithe (*ʿushr al-rizaq*).[45]

The rationale for the allocation of tax-free allowances was that headmen and other officials provided services to the community which prevented them from attending to the land. The recording of these allowances by al-Nābulusī implies that the *iqṭāʿ*-holders approved these tax-free allowances, deducted from the overall fiscal revenue of the village.

In al-Nābulusī's time there was no distinction between tax-free allowances for civilian and for religious functionaries. This would change a couple of decades later, when al-Ẓāhir Baybars created a separate category of endowed allowances (*rizaq iḥbāsiyya*) in support of Muslim religious institutions. After his reforms, allowances for guardsmen, headmen, and carpenters continued under a separate category, known as *maṣāliḥ al-nāḥiya*.[46]

III. 2. Seed Advances

The Dīwān al-Māl provided annual seed advances (*taqāwī*) for next year's sowing, largely in wheat and barley. The seeds were handed over to *iqṭāʿ*-holders or their agents, who controlled the actual distribution of the seeds to peasants. The *iqṭāʿ*-holder was then expected to reimburse the state with an equivalent amount of seeds at the end of his tenure.[47] The peasants received the seed advances as a loan for the sowing season, which they were supposed to return out of the yield of the spring harvest.

Al-Nābulusī cites from two separate registers of seed advances. One register was of seed advances as recorded (*al-mukhallada*) in the Dīwān. This was a record of the seeds that were to be issued to the *iqṭāʿ*-holders for the cultivation (*ʿimāra*) of the village. The second was a record of the seed advances actually distributed (*al-muṭlaqa*) by the *iqṭāʿ*-holders, according to local practice (*ʿalā mā jarat al-ʿāda*). These seed advances are said to come out of the income of the local *iqṭāʿ*-holders.

For most villages, al-Nābulusī reports either the figure obtained from the records of the Dīwān or the amount of seed advances actually distributed by the *iqṭāʿ*-holders, but not both.

When a village was left without an *iqṭāʿ*-holder, due to death or reassignment, seed advances were recorded under the category of *al-maḥlūl* (seed advances to a village without an *iqṭāʿ*-holder) or *al-murtajaʿ* (the seed advances which should be reclaimed from an *iqṭāʿ*-holder after the end of his tenure).

III. 3. Advance Payments for Barley and Beans

In most large and medium-size villages there is record of contracts to supply the Royal Stables with barley or broad beans as fodder for government-owned animals

---

[43] Rabie, *The Financial System*, p. 103.

[44] Nicolas Michel, 'Les rizaq iḥbāsiyya, terres agricoles en mainmorte dans l'Égypte mamelouke et ottomane: étude sur les dafātir al-aḥbās ottomans', *Annales Islamologiques*, 30 (1996), 105–98 (pp. 109, 114); al-Nuwayrī, *Nihāyat al-arab*, XXXI, 348 (*rizaq al-iḥbāsiyya* for religious buildings and personnel are exempt from being assigned as *iqṭāʿ*).

[45] These tithes, in ardabbs of grains, are listed as an appendix to the land tax of a few villages, after the measurement fees (Sinnūris, Būr Sīnarū). In Babīj Andīr and Ḥaddāda a payment of ardabbs of grain is mentioned as 'land tax on the plough-shares of the allowances' (*kharāj maḥārīth al-rizaq*). In Islamic law, tithe is levied on land which is the private property of Muslims, and varies between a full 10 per cent on naturally irrigated lands and 5 per cent on lands that require artificial irrigation. There is no evidence in the *Villages of the Fayyum* of wider payment of tithes, despite the detailed account by al-Nuwayrī; al-Nuwayrī, *Nihāyat al-arab*, VIII, 252, 259.

[46] See also Michel, 'Les rizaq iḥbāsiyya', pp. 108–11 (Michel corrects the reading to *rizaq*, instead of the classical form *rizq* used by Cahen in his 'Le régime des impôts'); Michel, 'Les services communaux'; Sato, *State and Rural Society*, pp. 185–88.

[47] See Sato, *State and Rural Society*, pp. 200–04.

(*al-ʿawāmil al-dīwāniyya*). In return, the villages received an advance payment.

The contracts are, for the most part, for the supply of barley. The common formula is *wa'l-musallaf ʿalayhi bi-hā min al-shaʿīr bi-rasm al-iṣṭibalāt al-sulṭāniyya* (barley from the village, which had been paid for in advance, assigned to the Royal Stables).[48]

Al-Nābulusī records the amount of barley and beans which the village was contracted to deliver, but not the amount of the advance payments by the government.

III. 4. Arrears

Arrears are mentioned only in seventeen villages. These villages are those which were either under the control of the royal domain (*khāṣṣ*) at the time of al-Nābulusī's visit, or had been under the control of the royal domain at some point over the previous decade. The arrears generally represent the village's debts at the time it was handed over from the royal domain to the *iqṭāʿ*-holders, although the arrears could occasionally also include debts to previous *iqṭāʿ*-holders.

The records identify the creditor — the *Dīwān al-Māl* or a named *iqṭāʿ*-holder — and the type of unpaid fiscal obligation, whether in specie or in kind. This balance of payments carried over from previous years is listed immediately after the seed advances, since both were seen as categories of credit.[49]

The balance of payment is divided into three categories: *al-ḥāṣil* (surplus), *al-mawqūf* (withheld) and *al-bāqī* (outstanding), also called *muta'akhkhar* (delayed). The first category, the surplus (*al-ḥāṣil*), is a record of overpayments from previous years.[50] The second category, the withheld payments (*al-mawqūf*), is of exemptions, mostly in cash, due to flight or death of cultivators, to damage caused by force majeure (e.g., fire or mice), or because of mechanical failures (a malfunctioning mill).[51] The third category, that of 'outstanding payments' (*al-bāqī*), was that of unpaid taxes for which no exemption was granted.

Section IV: Sugarcane

Sugarcane was mostly grown on crown estates, called *ūsīya* (pl. *awāsī*). The crown estates were separate from the main lands of the village and were owned by the Dīwān al-Māl, so were not subject to tax. Instead of taxes, al-Nābulusī records the number of feddans of crown estates in the village and their use.

The sugarcane plantations fed thirteen sugarcane presses, each with one or more pressing-stone, turned by oxen or by water. Each pressing stone was allocated 35–90 feddans of sugarcane. When a sugarcane press was located in a village, al-Nābulusī also lists the feddans of sugarcane and fodder assigned for its supply, which may be located not only in the village itself but also in several nearby villages.

Al-Nābulusī states that the crown estates consisted of 1,654 feddans, of which the vast majority (1,468) were devoted to sugarcane, and the remainder mostly sown with fodder for livestock used for turning the sugar presses. A couple of crown estates were used for crops other than sugar — flowers, fruits, and vegetables in the city, barley and sesame in Ṭalīt in southern Fayyum.

The sugarcane plantations were divided into first and second harvests, with the area of the first harvest always several times larger than the area of the second harvest. A first crop (*ra's*) was planted in March and harvested on January of the following year. After the first harvest, the field was set on fire; the ratoons that emerged after the fire were irrigated until a second harvest (*khilfa*) took place in November–December. Following this two-year cycle, the land had to be left fallow.[52]

Labour for the sugarcane plantations came from villagers, employed either as tenants (*muzāriʿūn*) or as quarter-share wage-labourers (*murābiʿūn*).[53] In Islamic

48 Correctly explained by Cahen ('Le régime des impôts', p. 23). See also al-Nuwayrī, *Nihāyat al-arab*, VIII, 241, for *musallaf* as advance payment.

49 Al-Makhzūmī also lumps together the seed advances and the arrears. He states that when the revenue in kind is collected, the clerks need to distinguish between the land tax of the current year, the arrears (*bāqī*) from the previous year, and the reclaimed seed advances (*murtajaʿ*). See al-Makhzūmī, *al-Muntaqā min kitāb al-minhāj*, p. 62.

50 Al-Nuwayrī, *Nihāyat al-arab*, VIII, 218, 275–76, 284–85. On *ḥāṣil* as the balance in favour of the peasant after the payment of land tax, see VIII, 259.

51 It appears to be equivalent to the term *maḥsūb*, explained by al-Nuwayrī as an exemption due to factors beyond the control of the tax-payer; al-Nuwayrī, *Nihāyat al-arab*, VIII, 289. The term *maḥsūb* is mentioned elsewhere in the treatise with the general meaning of 'deduction'. Al-Nuwayrī mentions the term *mawqūf* as category similar to the arrears (*bāqī*), and lists the *maḥsūb* separately, just after the surplus; al-Nuwayrī, *Nihāyat al-arab*, VIII, 285.

52 Tsugikata Sato, *Sugar in the Social Life of Medieval Islam* (Leiden: Brill, 2014), pp. 34–48; Sato, 'Sugar in the Economic Life of Mamluk Egypt', *Mamlūk Studies Review*, 8. 2 (2004), 87–107 (p. 96).

53 On the *murābiʿūn* in later periods, see Kenneth M. Cuno, *The Pasha's Peasants: Land, Society and Economy in Lower Egypt, 1740–1858* (Cambridge: Cambridge University Press, 1992), p. 181.

law, a *murābaʿa* contract stipulated that a manual labourer only contributed his labour, while seeds and beasts of burden were provided by the land-owner. In return, the *murabiʿ* was to receive a quarter of the yield. In practice *murābaʿa* meant wage-labour. But because it was technically a share-cropping contract, the remuneration the *murābiʿūn* received was classified under the category of seed advances (*taqāwī*).[54]

A handful of villages have references to taxes on canes, which may be either sugarcane or a variety of reeds with no juice, known as Persian cane (*qaṣab fārisī*).[55]

Section V: Ad Hoc Levies

V. 1. Horsemen for Military Campaigns

At the end of the treatise, al-Nābulusī records a levy of four hundred horsemen to be provided by the Arab tribesmen of the villages of the Fayyum as auxiliary forces in the event of a royal campaign. The total of four hundred riders is divided equally between the Banū Kilāb and the Banū ʿAjlān.

V.2. Giza Dike Levy

Al-Nābulusī reproduces a royal decree, dated to the end of 642 (May 1245), ordering the province to raise one hundred dredging units (*jurrāfa*, pl. *jarārīf*) for the construction of the dam of al-Muḥraqa in the nearby province of Giza.[56] Since most villages were ordered to pay a fraction of a *jurrāfa* unit, this levy must have been paid in cash or in labour, not in actual dredging equipment.

According to Ayyubid practice, when a province required a new dam, a levy was divided between the villages of those provinces that would stand to benefit from the dam. Each village was set an amount according to its capabilities at the time and according to the extent of its cultivation.[57] The villages had the option of commuting this levy to cash, at a rate of 10 dinars per unit.[58]

54 This created an artificial parallel with the seed advances handed over to tenant-cultivators of grains, even though the wage-labourers used the cash and grains for sustenance. This point has already been made by Sato, *State and Rural Society*, p. 219.

55 While originally another name for sugarcane, Ibn al-Nafīs refers to *qaṣab fārisī* as a reed with no juice. Ibn Mammātī also mentions a rate of 3 dinars per feddan for the cultivation of Persian canes, separate from sugarcane; Sato, *Sugar*, pp. 30, 98–99.

56 On large irrigation projects by the central government, see Sato, *State and Rural Society*, pp. 227–33.

57 Ibn Mammātī, *Kitāb qawānīn al-dawāwīn*, ed. by ʿAṭiya, pp. 342–44. A later account by al-Qalqashandī describes an annual process of maintenance of royal dikes, led by an amir appointed as the Superintendent of Dikes (*kāshif al-jusūr*) at a given province, and supported by a tax levied in dredging units (*jarārīf*), ploughs and beasts of burden; al-Qalqashandī, *Ṣubḥ*, III, 448–49. See also Rabie, *The Financial System*, p. 115; Nicolas Michel, 'Travaux aux digues dans la vallée du Nil aux époques papyrologique et ottomane: une comparaison', *Cahier de recherches de l'institut de papyrologie et d'égyptologie de Lille*, 25 (2005), 253–76.

58 Al-Maqrīzī, possibly on the basis of Ibn Mammātī, confirms that each village had to pay a certain number of units (*qiṭāʿ*) towards to the royal dikes levy (*muqarrar al-jusūr*). The payment was commuted to cash at a rate of 10 dinars per unit; al- Maqrīzī, *Kitāb al-mawāʿiẓ*, ed. by Sayyid, I, 288, 297. See also Cooper, 'Ibn Mammati's Rules', pp. 313–15, on special taxes for the construction of dams in the provinces of al-Gharbiyya and al-Sharqiyya, called *al-rusūm al-muwaẓẓafa*.

On the Arabic Edition

The treatise survived to the modern era in two known copies. One copy was probably made in the fifteenth century and was used by Bernhard Moritz for his 1898 Būlāq print edition. The location of that manuscript is now unknown. A copy of it was made in Cairo in 1897 in connection with Moritz's edition (Cairo, Dār al-Kutub al-Miṣriyya, MS *ta'rīkh* 1594). Since the original was lost, we know nothing about the circumstances in which it was made, and whether it was the fiscal elements or the historical and literary aspects which attracted the attention of a Mamluk-era copyist.

We know more about the second copy, MS Ayasofia 2960.[1] It was made in the middle of the sixteenth century and presented to Jānim min Qaṣrūh, an amir who served as the inspector of Royal Dikes (*kāshif al-jusūr al-sulṭāniyya*) in the Fayyum and al-Bahnasā under the Ottoman administration. As shown by Wakako Kumakura, the treatise was copied in the context of an Ottoman tax survey of twenty-seven Fayyumi villages conducted in 923/1517–18, the first year of Ottoman rule in Egypt.[2] The copy of this Ottoman survey is found immediately following al-Nābulusī's treatise (fols 172v–175v). The 27 villages included in the Ottoman survey are those which at the time of the Ottoman conquest paid at least some of their taxes to Dīwān al-Dhakhīra, the bureau managing assets under the direct control of the last Mamluk sultans.[3]

The Ayasofia copy of the *Villages of the Fayyum* contains 171 folios, written in multiple types of ink — usually names of villages and categories of taxes appear in red or grey. Names of villages are also written in a more stylized calligraphy than the rest of the text. There are catch words at the bottom left, and a few marginal notes added by later readers, which are noted in our edition.

Our annotated Arabic edition is based on a systematic comparison of Moritz's printed edition (MP, ط. م.) and MS Ayasofia 2960 (AS, أ. س.). Moritz's printed edition is far more reliable, with fewer copyist mistakes and no omissions. This is in part because the Mamluk-era manuscript available to him, now lost, was of superior quality compared to the sixteenth-century Ottoman one. This is attested by the Dār al-Kutub manuscript, copied in 1897 from the Mamluk-era manuscript, which is largely in line with Moritz's edition. But we should also credit Moritz, one of the great Orientalist scholars of the turn of the twentieth century, for a highly accurate transcription of the text.

The Ayasofia manuscript was derived from the same Mamluk-era copy used by Moritz, or from a shared source, as is demonstrated by a pattern of similar copyist mistakes found in both MP and AS. In these cases of mistakes in both source-texts, we provide our amended reading in the body of the text, and indicate in the footnotes the readings found in the manuscripts. In cases of differences between the manuscripts, which are not errors or omissions, we aim to establish the correct version according to the context of the treatise. Variant readings are indicated in the footnotes.

While Moritz's 1898 edition is accurate, it is difficult to get hold of, and even more difficult to use. The edition is printed as a running text, without any paragraphs or tabulation, only highlighting the titles of sections and village entries. That makes the numerical data and fiscal categories practically impossible to follow. In our edition, we not only divided the text into paragraphs but also tried to indicate by indentations the ordering and subordering of lists of taxes. The division to paragraphs and the indentations is paralleled in the English translation.

---

[1] Fakhr al-Dīn ʿUthmān b. al-Nābulusī, *Kitāb Iẓhār Ṣanʿat al-Ḥayy al-Qayyūm fī Tartīb Bilād al-Fayyūm*, Istanbul, Süleymaniye Camii kütüphanesi, MS 2960, Ayasofia 910, fols. 1r – 171r.

[2] Wakako Kumakura, 'Tax Survey Records of the First Year of the Ottoman Rule in Egypt, Contained in the Ayasofia Manuscript with Fakhr al-Dīn ʿUthmān al-Nābulsī's Taʾrīkh al-Fayyūm', *Journal of Asian and African Studies*, 89 (2015), 79–118 (in Japanese, with edited Arabic text).

[3] On Dīwān al-Dhakhīra, see Daisuke Igarashi, *Land Tenure, Fiscal Policy and Imperial Power in Medieval Syro-Egypt* (Chicago: Middle Eastern Documentation Center, 2015). A comparison of the Ottoman tax list with al-Nābulusī's survey three centuries earlier is beyond the scope of this volume, but points to the possibility of writing the history of this exceptional province and its villages well into the early modern period.

Glossary of Measures, Weights, and Monetary Units

Definitions of weights and measures have changed across time and place in Egyptian history. The following is primarily based on the definitions offered by the Mamluk-era author al-Qalqashandī as interpreted by Walther Hinz[4] and Eliyahu Ashtor,[5] and corroborated by the internal evidence in the *Villages of the Fayyum*.

Fractions

Al-Nābulsī uses combinations of the following terms to designate fractions of all types of units, including monetary units, units of volume and units of length and surface:

niṣf = half, 1/2.

thulth = third, ⅓.

rubʿ = quarter, ¼.

suds = sixth, ⅙ (and also half a sixth, 1/12).

thumn = eighth, ⅛ (and also half an eighth, 1/16).

qīrāṭ = carat, 1/24 (and also half a carat 1/48; a quarter of a carat, 1/96).[6]

ḥabba = literally 'grain', 1/72.

dāniq = From Persian, *dāng*, literally 'a sixth', 1/144.[7]

Dry Measures (Volume)

ardabb = about 90 litres, holding approximately 69.6 kg. of wheat and 56 kg. of barley.[8]

wayba = ⅙ ardabb = 15 litres, or 11.6 kg. of wheat.[9]

Length

dhirāʿ (also *dhirāʿ al-ʿamal*) = cubit/ work cubit = 65.6 cm.[10]

qaṣaba (lit. 'cane', or 'reed') = 6 *dhirāʿ* = about 3.9 m.[11]

qabḍa (lit. 'a fist's width') = ⅙ *dhirāʿ* = about 10.9 cm.[12]

[4] Walther Hinz, *Islamische Masse und Gewichte: Umgerechnet ins Metrische System*, Handbuch der Orientalistik, 1 (Leiden: Brill, 1970).

[5] Eliyahu Ashtor, 'Makāyīl and Mawāzīn', *The Encyclopedia of Islam*, 2nd edn, VI, 117–21.

[6] According to Hinz, *qīrāṭ* = 1/32 *qadaḥ* of wheat (Hinz, *Islamische Masse und Gewichte*, p. 50), but in *Villages of the Fayyum* the *qīrāṭ* appears throughout as equal to 1/24. On *qīrāṭ* as a 1/24 share in all contexts, see Cuno, *The Pasha's Peasants*, p. 210; Warren C. Schulz, 'The Mechanisms of Commerce', in *The New Cambridge History of Islam: Volume 4, Islamic Cultures and Societies to the End of the Eighteenth Century*, ed. by Robert Irwin (Cambridge: Cambridge University Press, 2010), pp. 332–54 (p. 347).

[7] On *ḥabbah* and *dāniq* as fractions, rather than units of weight, see Avram L. Udovitch, 'Fals', *The Encyclopedia of Islam*, 2nd edn, II, 768–69; Cuno, *The Pasha's Peasants*, p. 210. For a more literal interpretation, see Hinz, *Islamisch Masse und Gewichte*, pp. 11, 12.

[8] Hinz, *Islamische Masse und Gewichte*, p. 39; Ashtor, 'Makāyīl and Mawāzīn'. According to an anecdote narrated by al-Maqrīzī in the fifteenth century, the ardabb of the Fayyum was 50 per cent larger than that of Cairo; al- Maqrīzī, *Kitāb al-mawāʿiẓ*, ed. by Sayyid, I, 273. This is not mentioned by al-Nābulusī or corroborated by any other source. Note that the ardabb was conceptually defined as the volume of seed of wheat required to sow a standard feddan, in the same way one Roman *artaba* was required to sow a Roman *aroura*.

[9] Hinz, *Islamische Masse und Gewichte*, p. 52.

[10] Hinz, 'dhirāʿ', *The Encyclopedia of Islam*, 2nd edn, II, 232.

[11] Hinz, *Islamische Masse und Gewichte*, p. 63.

[12] Hinz, *Islamische Masse und Gewichte*, p. 63. More precisely, 'from the bottom of the hand to the tip of the extended thumb'; Cuno, *The Pasha's Peasants*, p. 209.

Square Measures (Area)

faddān (pl. *fadādīn*; lit. 'Yoke of oxen') = feddan = 6,368 sq. m.[1]

Weight

qinṭār = 45 kg = 100 *raṭl*.[2]

raṭl = 450 gr = 144 dirham.[3]

qinṭār jarwī = 100 *raṭl jarwī* = 96.7 kg. A weight measure used in Egypt for measuring oil, sugar, and other types of commodities.[4]

maṭar (a measurement unit of liquids) = approximately 16–17 kg.[5]

Monetary Units

dīnār = dinar = gold coin, with canonical weight of 4.233 gr.[6]

dirham = dirham = silver coin, with canonical weight of 3.125 gr. In the *Villages of the Fayyum*, however, the low quality *waraq* or black dirham is always intended.[7]

Exchange Rate

The standard exchange rate used uniformly throughout the treatise is 1 dinar = 40 (*waraq*) dirhams, an exchange rate referred to as the 'exchange rate of Cairo'.[8]

---

[1] Bosworth, s.v. 'Miṣāḥa', *The Encyclopedia of Islam*, 2nd edn, VII, 138. Borsch (*The Black Death*, p. 48) has recently argued that in the Mamluk era, an Egyptian feddan was equal to roughly 1.4 acres (i.e., 5,665 sq. m.). We stick with the traditional interpretation, which is based on the definition of the feddan as 400 square *qaṣaba*, as indicated in literary and documentary sources. In an eleventh-century document from the Fayyum, a surface area of 2 feddans is measured to be 50 *qaṣaba* by 16 *qaṣaba*, i.e., 800 square *qaṣaba*; Gaubert and Mouton, *Hommes et villages*, p. 112 no. 23.

[2] Hinz, *Islamische Masse und Gewichte*, p. 24.

[3] Hinz, *Islamische Masse und Gewichte*, p. 29.

[4] Hinz, *Islamische Masse und Gewichte*, p. 25.

[5] Ashtor, 'Makāyīl and Mawāzīn'; Reinhart Dozy, *Supplément aux dictionnaires arabes*, 2 vols (Leiden: Brill, 1881), II, 600.

[6] Hinz, *Islamische Masse und Gewichte*, p. 11.

[7] Hinz, *Islamische Masse und Gewichte*, p. 29. While mostly the text refers to 'dirhams', without specifying the type of coin, the text contains a few references to *waraq* dirhams and to 'black dirhams', both terms designating the low quality silver coins in circulation in the Ayyubid period; Warren C. Schultz, 'The Monetary History of Egypt, 642–1517', in *The Cambridge History of Egypt*, I: *Islamic Egypt, 640-1517*, ed. by Carl F. Petry (Cambridge: Cambridge University Press, 1998), pp. 318–38 (p. 332). Since the *waraq* dirhams mentioned are said to have the same exchange rate to the dinar of 1:40 observed elsewhere in the treatise, it is likely that all references to dirhams in the treatise are to *waraq*, or black dirhams.

[8] Such an exchange rate also appears in many of the Geniza documents that Goitein analyzed. See Shlomoh D. Goitein, 'The Exchange Rate of Gold and Silver Money in Fatimid and Ayyubid Times: A Preliminary Study of the Relevant Geniza Material', *Journal of the Economic and Social History of the Orient*, 8 (1965), 1–46 (pp. 23, 28, 43).

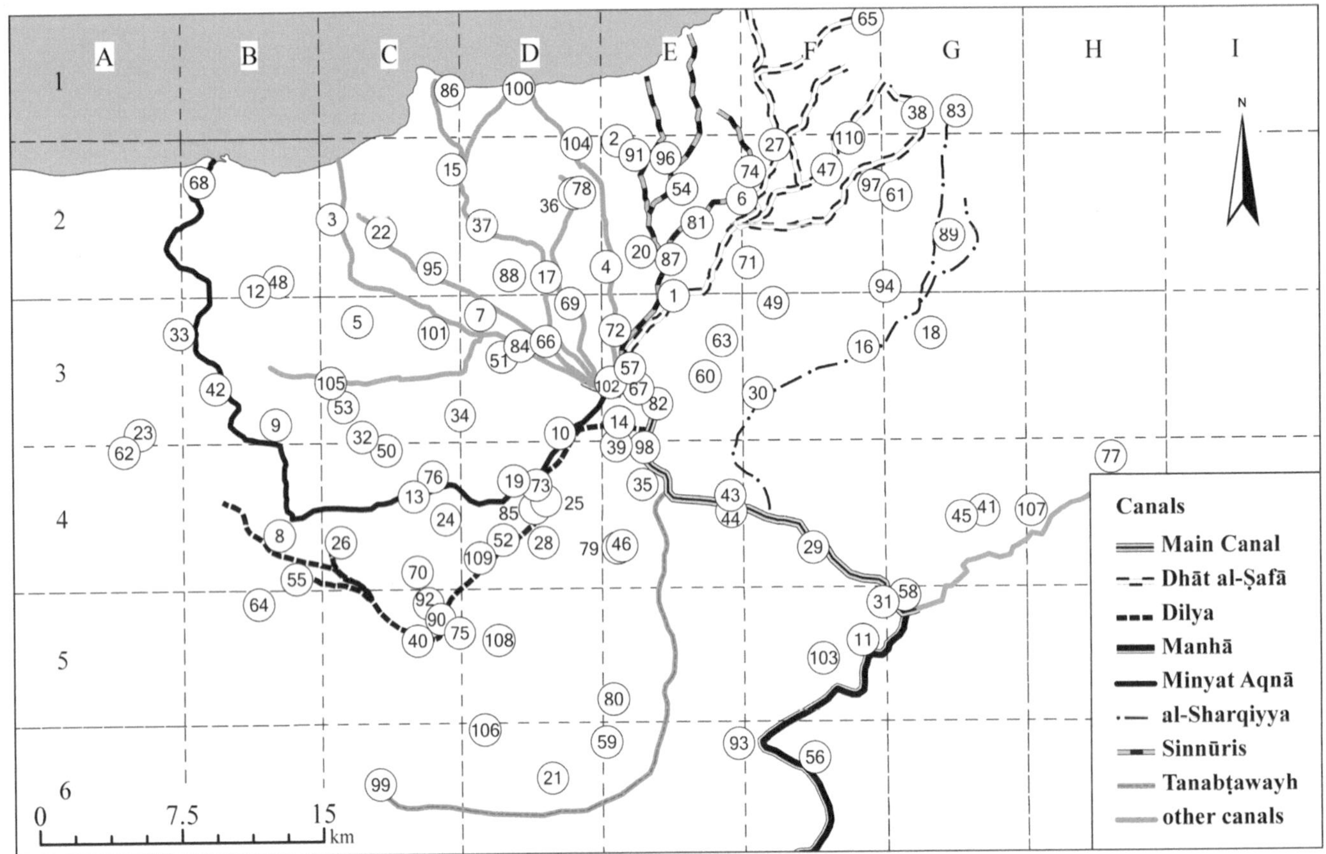

SETTLEMENT	ID	GRID
al-Aʿlām	1	E3
Abhīt	2	E2
Abū Ksā	3	C2
Akhṣāṣ Abū ʿUṣayya	4	E2
Akhṣāṣ al-ʿAjamiyyīn	5	C3
Akhṣāṣ al-Ḥallāq	6	F2
ʿAnz	7	D3
Babīj Andīr	8	B4
Babīj Anqāsh	9	B3
Babīj Faraḥ	10	D3
Babīj Ghaylān	11	F5
Babīj Unshū	12	B2
Baḥr Banī Qurīṭ	13	C4
Bāja	14	E3
Bamawayh	15	C2
Bandīq	16	F3
Banū Majnūn	17	D2
Bayāḍ	18	G3
Bilāla	19	D4
Biyahmū	20	E2
Buljusūq	21	D6
Būr Sīnarū	22	C2
Burjtūt	23	A3
Bushṭā	24	C4
Būṣīr Difidnū	25	D4
Dahmā	26	C4
Dhāt al-Ṣafāʾ	27	F2
Difidnū	28	D4
Dimashqīn al-Baṣal	29	F4
Dimūh al-Dāthir	30	F3
Dimūh al-Lāhūn	31	F5
Dinfāras of Jardū and Ihrīt	32	C3
Diqlawa	33	A3
Disyā	34	C3
Dumūshiyya	35	E4
Fānū	36	D2
Fidimīn	37	D2
Furqus	38	G1
Ghābat Bāja	39	E4
Ḥaddāda	40	C5
al-Ḥammām	41	G4
al-Ḥanbūshiyya	42	B3
Hawwāra al-Baḥriyya	43	E4
Hawwārat Dumūshiyya	44	E4
al-Haysha	45	G4
Hayshat Dumūshiyya	46	E4
Ibrīziyā	47	F2
Ibshāyat al-Rummān	48	B2
al-ʿIdwa	49	F3
Ihrīt	50	C4
al-Istinbāṭ	51	D3
Iṭsā	52	D4
Jardū	53	C3
Jarfis	54	E2
Kanbūt	55	B4
Kawm al-Raml	56	F6
Khawr al-Rammād	57	E3
al-Lāhūn	58	G5
al-Mahīmsī	59	E6
al-Malāliyya	60	E3
Maqtūl	61	G2
Masjid ʿĀʾisha	62	A4
al-Maṣlūb and Kharāb Jundī	63	E3
Mintāra	64	B5
Minyat al-Baṭs	65	F1
Minyat al-Dīk	66	D3
Minyat al-Usquf	67	E3
Minyat Aqnā	68	B2
Minyat Karbīs	69	D3
Minyat Shushhā	70	C4
Miṭr Ṭāris	71	F2
Munshaʾat al-Ṭawāḥīn	72	E3
Munshaʾat Awlād ʿArafa	73	D4
Munshaʾat Ibn Kurdī	74	F2
Muqrān	75	C5
Muṭūl	76	C4
Nāmūsa and Nāmūsa (Nāmūsatayn)	77	H4
Naqalīfa	78	D2
al-Qalhāna	79	E4
Qambashā	80	E5
al-Qubarāʾ	81	E2
Qushūsh	82	E3
al-Rubiyyāt	83	G1
al-Rūbiyyūn	84	D3
al-Ṣafāwina	85	D4
Sanhūr	86	C1
Shallāla	87	E2
Shalmaṣ	88	D2
Shāna	89	G2
Shidmūh	90	C5
Shisfa	91	E2
Shushhā	92	C5
Sidmant	93	E6
Sīla	94	G2
Sīnarū	95	C2
Sinnūris	96	E2
Sirisnā	97	F2
Ṣunūfar	98	E4
Ṭalīt	99	C6
al-Ṭārima	100	D1
Thalāth	101	C3
The City (al-Madina)	102	E3
Ṭimā	103	F5
Tirsā	104	D2
Ṭubhār	105	C3
Tuṭūn	106	D6
Umm al-Nakhārīr	107	H4
Umm al-Sibāʿ	108	D5
Uqlūl	109	D4
al-Zarbī	110	F2

UNLOCATED SETTLEMENTS
al-Aḥkār
al-Bārida
al-Kawm al-Aḥmar
al-Manẓara
Babīj al-Nīla
Birkat ibn Shikla
Iṭfīḥ Shallā
Munshaʾat Abī Sibāʿ
Munshaʾat al-ʿAthāmina
Munshaʾat al-Muṭawwiʿ
Munshaʾat al-Wasaṭ
Munshaʾat Ghaylān
Qumnā Bajūsh

MAP OF THE *VILLAGES OF THE FAYYUM*

The map opposite is intended to represent the landscape of Fayyum as it was in the mid-thirteenth century. It was produced by Dr Max Satchell using ESRI ArcGIS software. The map was created from a variety of sources including geo-rectified scans of 1:100,000 mapping of the US Army Map Service, satellite elevation data, and 100,000 scale maps surveyed under the direction of Pierre Jacotin and published in 1826.[1]

The level of Lake Qārūn (ancient Lake Moeris, modern Birkat Qarun) has fluctuated dramatically throughout history,[2] and since the water level of the lake is the most important factor affecting the size of arable land in the depression, it was crucial to determine the approximate water level of the lake during al-Nābulusī's visit to the region. We followed Ali Shafei Bey's estimate of the lake's water-level at -30 m below sea level at the time of al-Nābulusī's visit.[3] This is about 15 m higher than the current level of -45 m. In recent years, several scientific studies based on pollen records, paleolimnology, and sedimentological analysis have confirmed this as a reasonable estimate for the lake level during the thirteenth century.[4]

Locations of individual villages were reconstructed based on the information provided in the *Villages of the Fayyum*, as well as previous attempts to map the settlements recorded in the survey, especially the map prepared by Shafei Bey in his 'Fayoum Irrigation' essay, and the map of the Fayyum by Heinz Halm in his *Ägypten nach den Mamlukischen Lehensregistern*.[5] Further information on the history of individual settlements was taken from Muḥammad Ramzī, *Al-Qāmūs al-jughrāfī*, and Stefan Timm, *Das Christlich-Koptische Ägypten in Arabischer Zeit*.[6] We have also cross-referenced with modern maps (Google Earth). Explanations and references for villages' locations appear in the footnotes of the English translation.

The routes of the main canals were drawn based on the map produced by Shafei Bey, who was the irrigation engineer of the Fayyum in the 1940s and intimately familiar with local conditions. Some modifications were made, however, in line with the Jacotin maps, and with consideration of the topography of the depression. In particular, the route of the Minyat Aqnā Canal was modified from the route marked by Shafei Bey, so that it follows the route of the Nazla ravine; the location of the large village of Minyat Aqnā, which lay at the end of that canal, near the shores of Lake Qārūn, was changed accordingly. Note that not all settlements have been located. Settlements without any identified location (usually hamlets or smaller villages) are listed separately at the end of the table.

We are thankful to Prof. Dominic Rathbone, Prof. Cornelia Römer, and Dr Brendan Haug for providing us with their sound advice about the topography and geography of the Fayyum. Any faults are entirely ours.

This map was produced with the generous support of the Isobel Thornley Fund.

---

[1] US Army Map Service AMS P671 (GGS 4085) sheets 72/54, 72/60, 68/54, 68/60 (Washington, DC, 1948–49); USGS SRTM 1 Arc-Second Global (6 August 2015); *Carte Topographique de l'Égypte et de plusiers des pays limitrophes...construite par M. Jacotin* (Paris: [n. pub.], 1826), fols 18–19.

[2] See Gertrude Caton-Thompson and Elinor Wight Gardner, *The Desert Fayum: Vol. I* (London: Royal Anthropological Institute of Great Britain and Ireland, 1934), pp. 11–13; Ball, *Contributions*, p. 219; Carl Butzer, *Early Hydraulic Civilization in Egypt: A Study in Cultural Ecology* (Chicago: University of Chicago Press, 1976), p. 37; Peter J. Mehringer, Kenneth L. Peterson, and Fekri Hassan, 'A Pollen Record from Birket Qarun and the Recent History of the Fayum', *Quaternary Research*, 11 (1979), 238–56; Geoff Tassie, 'Modelling Environmental and Settlement Change in the Fayum', *Egyptian Archaeology*, 29 (2006), 37–40; Rebecca Phillipps and others, 'Lake Level Changes, Lake Edge Basins and the Paleoenvironment of the Fayum North Shore, Egypt, during the Early to Mid-Holocene', *Open Quaternary*, 2. 2 (2016), 1–12.

[3] Shafei Bey, 'Fayoum Irrigation', pp. 309, 320. Shafei Bey based this estimation on information provided by al-Nābulusī, as well as on geological and archaeological findings.

[4] See Mehringer, Petersen, and Hassan, 'A Pollen Record', p. 241; Kevin Keatings, and others, 'Ostracods and the Holocene Palaeolimnology of Lake Qarun, with Special Reference to Past Human-Environment Interactions in the Faiyum (Egypt)', *Hydrobiologia*, 654 (2010), 155–76 (p. 159); Hassan M. Baioumy, Hajime Kayanne, and Ryuji Tada, 'Reconstruction of Lake-Level and Climate Changes in Lake Qarun, Egypt, during the Last 7000 Years', *Journal of Great Lakes Research*, 36. 2 (2010), 318–27 (pp. 325–26).

[5] Halm, *Ägypten*.

[6] Ramzī, *Al-Qāmūs al-jughrāfī li'l-bilād al-miṣriyya min 'ahd qudamā' al-Miṣriyyīn ilā sanat 1945* (Cairo: Dār al-Kutub al-Miṣriyya, 1953); Timm, *Das Christlich-Koptische Ägypten*.

Part II

Edition and Translation of the *Villages of the Fayyum*

بسم الله الرحمن الرحيم.

رب زدني علمًا[1] اللهم صل على سيدنا محمد واله وصحبه وسلم تسليما كثيرا.[2] الحمد لله حمدا لا يفنى مدده ولا ينتهي امده واشهد ان لا اله الا الله وحده لا شريك له شهادة لقائلها من عيش الجنة رغده واشهد ان محمدا عبده ورسوله الذي طاب مغيبه ومشهده. صلى الله عليه وعلى اله صلاة تدوم ويفنى يوم الدهر وغده.

اما بعد، فانه لما كان مولانا السلطان الاعظم مالك رقاب الامم سيد ملوك العرب والعجم حامي حوزة الحرمين الشريفين ملك البرين والبحرين سيد ملوك الدنيا سلطان سلاطين الشرق والغرب الملك الصالح نجم الدنيا والدين ايوب، ولد مولانا السلطان السعيد الشهيد الكامل ناصر الدنيا والدين محمد، ولد مولانا السلطان السعيد الشهيد الملك العادل سيف الدنيا والدين ابي بكر، ولد المولى[3] السيد السعيد الشهيد العظيم الشان نجم الدين ايوب الملك[4] الذي تشرفت بذكره المنابر وزهت بوصفه الطروس والمحابر الذي ابتسم به وجه الدهر بعد ان كان عابسا واينع به غصن المجد وقد كان يابسا.

شعر:[5]

ملك ملوك الارض تحت لوائه
كل يروم لِيَاذَهُ بجنابه
لولا مخافتهم سُطاه وسيفَه
كانوا جميعُهُمُ على ابوابه
ورايتَ مس جباههم لترابه
ورايتَ لثم شافههم لركابه

وتواترت[6] مطالعات عبيد دولته وارقاء مملكته باحوال الفيوم وانه ربما فترت الهمة في عمارته واستمر اهمال المباشرين له حتى تغير عن حالته. سلك عظم الله سلطانه سبيل السنة النبوية اليوسفية الصديقية في[7] مرور ركابه العزيز به وتشريفه بالنظر له فراه ذا زروع وضروع وفياف ومروج ومزارع ومسارح ومناهج[8] ومرابح[9] بل ذا بساتين واشجار وجنات تجري من تحتها الانهار وراى خلد الله ملكه مياهه الجارية على الدوام وسلوكها منه تحت الوهاد وفوق الاكام وجرى على جميل شيمه من عمارة البلاد ومصالح العباد.

امر نصره الله تعالى،[10] باستدعائي ببطاقة على جناح طائر من القاهرة المحروسة الى جنب[11] ركابه العزيز فسارعت ممتثلا وامتثلت مسرعا فحين شرفت بالمثول بين يديه شرفني باحسن خطاب واجمل جواب وامرني بالمقام فيه مديدة ريثما يسر خبره ويطيب مخبره. وقال خلد الله ملكه هذه البلاد قد غفل عنها عمالها حتى ظهر اهمالها فاسلك فيها سبيل العدل والسداد وعف[12] منها اثار الظلم والفساد. وجرى عظم الله سلطانه على شيمه من كرم السجية وحسن الوصية.

[1] ساقط من ط. م.: رب زدني علما.

[2] ساقط من أ. س.: اللهم صل على سيدنا محمد وآله وصحبه وسلم تسليما كثيرا.

[3] ط. م.: المؤيد.

[4] ساقط من أ. س.: الملك.

[5] ساقط من ط. م.: شعر.

[6] أ. س.: وتوا ثرت.

[7] ساقط من أ. س.: في.

[8] ط. م.: مناجح.

[9] ولعله مرابع او مرائح.

[10] أ. س. يضيف: تعالى.

[11] ط. م.: حيث.

[12] أ. س.: اعف.

In the name of God, the merciful, the Compassionate.

O God, increase my knowledge![1] Praise be to God, without measure and without end. I testify that there is no god but God, who has no peer, a testimony for which eternal pleasure awaits in Paradise. And I testify that Muhammad is God's servant and messenger, bearing goodness in his absence and in his presence. May God bless him and his family with an everlasting blessing, beyond eternity and its morrow.[2]

Turning to our topic: when our lord the supreme sultan, master of the nations, chief of the Arab and non-Arab kings, protector of the two noble sanctuaries, king of the two continents and the two seas, lord of the kings of the world, sultan of the sultans of east and west, al-Malik al-Ṣāliḥ, Star of this world and of the faith, Najm al-Dīn Ayyūb; who is son of our lord, the blessed, martyred sultan, al-Malik al-Kāmil, Champion of this world and of the faith, Nāṣir al-Dīn Muḥammad; who was son of our lord the blessed, martyred sultan, al-Malik al-ʿĀdil, Sword of this world and of the faith, Sayf al-Dīn Abū Bakr; who was son of the lord, the master, the blessed, martyred and noble Najm al-Dīn Ayyūb (Saladin), the king whose very mention brings honour to the pulpits, and paper and inkwells take pride in describing him; for whom the face of Destiny smiled after it had been frowning, and by whom the branches of glory bloomed after being dry and shrivelled.

Verse:

The kings of the earth rule under his banner
All seek refuge in his might.

Were it not for their fear of his power and his sword
All of them would be at his gates.

You have seen their foreheads touching the ground before him
And you have seen their lips kissing his stirrup.

Reports about the affairs of the Fayyum by the servants of his state and by the slaves of his kingdom have been copious. Indeed, attention to its cultivation has often slackened, and the negligence of its supervisors persisted until its situation had deteriorated. He — may God make his rule mighty! — has proceeded along the path of the righteous prophet Joseph, traveling to the Fayyum with his noble entourage, and honouring it with his inspection. He saw that it is an area of agriculture and animal husbandry, of deserts and meadows, farms and pastures, routes and stopping places. Indeed, it has orchards and trees, as well as 'gardens beneath which rivers flow' (Q 3:15). He — may God preserve his rule! — saw that its waters flow unceasingly, their route going below lowlands and over hills. He proceeded according to his good nature for the cultivation of the land and the benefit of humankind.

He — may God the exalted grant him victory! — ordered that I be summoned, by means of a note attached to the wing of a bird,[3] from the divinely-protected Cairo to the company of his noble entourage. Thus I hastened in obedience and obediently hastened, and when I was honoured by being received in audience, he further honoured me with the finest of discourses and the most appealing of responses, and he ordered that I take up residence in the Fayyum for a while, until the region shall bring good tidings.

[1] The sentence: 'O God, increase my knowledge!' does not appear in Moritz's printed version (herein after: MP); instead MP adds: 'Pray, O God, for our lord Muhammad and his Family and his Companions, and protect [them] mightily'.

[2] Compare the introductory paragraphs in al-Nābulusī, *The Sword of Ambition*, pp. 2–3.

[3] On the use of pigeons in the Ayyubid postal system, see Adam J. Silverstein, *Postal Systems in the Pre-Modern Islamic World* (Cambridge: Cambridge University Press, 2007), p. 168.

ووصلت اليه وباشرته ومررت على بلاده وبحثت عن طارف[13] التدبير فيه وتلاده وعلمت جملا من احواله وجمعت بين تفصيل الامر فيه واجماله عزمت على ان اتحف خزائن مولانا السلطان، عظم الله سلطانه، بكتاب اؤلفه فيه ومصنف ينتفع به في اليوم وما يليه ونزعته عن اكاذيب الاقاويل الماضية وتحريف المؤرخين بوصف الامم الخالية واخبر به وعنه خبرًا يشهد العقل بصحته وتميل النفس الفاضلة الى موافقته.

فان كثيرا من الناس سطروا في كتبهم ان فرعون الذي كان يوسف وزيره لما كبر يوسف قال له حساده على منصبه ان وزيرك قد كبر وانه لا يستحق ان يصرف اليه من خزائنك[14] ما يصرف لوزير صالح التدبير يُخلف بحسن نظره في المملكة اضعاف ما ياخذ منها. فَنَقص مقرره واكشف بالامتحان خبره.

وانه قال ليوسف قد قيل لي كذا وكذا وقص عليه القصة وقال له امض الى هذه الجوبة يعني الفيوم فنصل ماءها وعمرها. وكانت اذ ذاك بركة مملوءة ماء وان يوسف عليه السلام وصل اليها وسال الله عز وجل ان يعينه على تنصيل مائها وعمارتها وان الحق تعالى اعانه على ذلك بملائكته وهداه الى اجراء مائه وعمارته.

والمسافة من عهد يوسف عليه السلام الى الان بعيدة وشروط الموثوق بروايته عزيزة شديدة ولعمري لو كان هذا الامر جرى لضرب في قصصه الواردة في القران بحصة بل بحصص فان الله عز وجل قص في كتابه العزيز جملا من احواله وسماها احسن القصص. ومع هذا فتصديق الكذب وتكذيب الصدق كل عيب والله سبحانه وتعالى اعلم بالغيب.

وحيث ذكرت هذه الجملة من خبره وبينت هذه اللمعة من عينه واثره ناسب ان اشفع ذكر الجملة بالتفصيل واصفه وصف ذي علم به وتحصيل. فحرصت بعد تعب لا يعرف قدره الا من له اهلية التاليف على ان لا يختلف في معرفة الفيوم حال القاطنين به والذي لم يره اذا وقف على هذا الكتاب وان يستوي في العلم باحواله بهذا التاليف القريب منه والبعيد عنه بل على ان لا يسال سائل عن حالة من احواله التي جرت العادة بالسؤال عن مثلها في مثله، الا ويجد الجواب فيه من هيئة وصورة ومحل ونسبة، مسافة من مدينة الفيوم وجهة من الجهات[15] الاربع بالنسبة الى مدينة الفيوم والسكان بها ونفرهم ومن اي ال افخاذهم[16] واسماء بلاده على حروف المعجم ليسهل تناول ذلك على الطالب. وعبرتها الجيشية دون ما ليس له عبرة، وارتفاعها جملة وتفصيلا في مواضعه ومتحصلا، وما على كل بلد من الحقوق والرسوم وعمل في الاقصاب.

[13] أ. س.: الطارق.
[14] أ. س. يضيف: الا.
[15] أ. س.: جهاته.
[16] ط. م.، أ. س.: أي الافخاذ.

He — may God preserve his kingship! — said [to me] that 'the local officials (*ʿummāl*) have been careless with this region until its neglect has become apparent. So proceed in it in a fashion that is both just and firm, and cleanse it of all traces of injustice and iniquity'. He — may God make his rule mighty! — acted according to his nature of noble disposition and good counsel.

Thus I arrived to it [to the Fayyum], observed it and passed through its villages. I also investigated the region's administrative innovations and traditions, and I learned the entirety of its circumstances, combining details with the totality. I was determined to offer to the treasuries of our lord the Sultan — may God make his rule mighty! — a book I would compose about it, a compilation that may be of benefit both in the present day and in days to come. I removed from it the falsehoods of past accounts and the distortions wrought by historians in their descriptions of past nations. I shall present an account of the Fayyum, the soundness of which will be borne out by reason, and with which a lofty mind will be disposed to agree.

Many historians have recorded in their books, concerning the Pharaoh to whom Joseph was vizier, that when Joseph had grown old, those who were envious of his position said to the Pharaoh: 'Your vizier has grown old, and he does not deserve to be paid from your treasuries what is paid to a vizier of competent administration, whose good supervision of the kingdom would raise [income] several times more than what he takes from it. Reduce his salary, and examine his affairs by means of a test'.

And then he [Pharaoh] said to Joseph: 'I was told such and such', and recounted to him what was said against him, and said, 'go to this pit', by which he meant the Fayyum, 'drain its water and bring it under cultivation'. At that time it [the Fayyum] was a lake full of water. And Joseph — peace be upon him — arrived there, and he asked God, the exalted and glorious, to help him to drain its water and bring it under cultivation. And it has been said that the angels of the exalted God helped him in this, and instructed him how to direct the flow of its water and how to bring it under cultivation.

A long time has passed between the times of Joseph — peace be upon him — and the present day, and the requirements for gaining a credible narration are difficult and rigorous. By my life, had that event taken place, it would have been recounted in his [Joseph's] stories that are found in the Qur'an, in more than one place. Yet, God the exalted recounted in His glorious book the whole of his circumstances and designated them 'the most beautiful of stories' (Q 12:3). Indeed, the confirmation of falsehood and the denial of truth are both disgraceful. But God — praise be to Him! — knows best what is hidden from us.

As I recount the affairs of [the Fayyum] in a general way, and briefly explain its nature and history, it is fitting that I pair the general account with some detail and give a knowledgeable and useful description of it. After investing considerable effort — the scope of which may only be realized by those with experience in composition — I aspire that there be no difference between the knowledge of the Fayyum possessed by its inhabitants and that of one who has never seen it but has read this book; and that by means of this book, both those near it and those far away from it may gain equal knowledge of its circumstances. Moreover, I aspire that anyone inquiring about any aspect of the Fayyum, posing questions that are typically asked about similar provinces, would find his query addressed in my account, whether it concerns layout, physical appearance, location, distance from Madīnat al-Fayyūm and the cardinal direction in relation to it, the region's inhabitants, their numbers and to which lineage (*āl*) their sections belong. The names of its villages are arranged by letters of the alphabet for the convenience of anyone consulting this book. Their fiscal value is given in army dinars (*ʿibra jayshiyya*), except for these villages which have no fiscal value. Their fiscal revenue (*irtifāʿu-hā*) is stated both in aggregate and in detail in the appropriate place, along with their taxes collected in kind (*mutaḥaṣṣilu-hā*).[4] The water quota (*ḥuqūq*) and fees (*rusūm*) are listed for every village, as well as the labour required for the sugar plantations.

[4] On *mutaḥaṣṣil* as revenues in kind, distinct from the cash revenues called *mustakhraj*, see al-Nuwayrī, *Nihāyat al-arab*, VIII, 253.

وما بكل بلد من جامع او مسجد بعد حصرها جملة واحدة في موضع واحد ليسهل تناوله على الطالب، وما بها من الديرة والكنائس جملة وما بكل بلد من ذلك. وانما ذكرت الجوامع والمساجد وحصرها[17] لئلا يطول الزمان فيخرب مسجد او جامع وتطول المدد عليه فتبقى ساحته[18] معطلة فيبني بيتا او مبلة او بناء غير المسجد فيكون حصرها مانعا[19] من ذلك. وانما ذكرت الديرة والكنائس لئلا تطول المدد في[20] مستقبل الزمان ويستغفل ولاة الامور لتنائي[21] هذا القطر عن الفسطاط وانزوائه عن مرور السالكين اليه وعنه فيبني احد من النصارى الاقباط الجبابرة الجهال الذين لا ينظرون في العواقب كنيسة او ديرا ويدعى قدمه اذا تنبه اليه[22] احد في مستقبل الزمان فيكون ذكر الجوامع والمساجد[23] مانعا من دعوى النقص فيها. وذكر الديرة والكنائس مانعا من دعوى الزيادة عليها.

وذكرت ما جرت العادة بان يرتفق الديوان من كل بلد من سلف على شعير او فول بالقيمة اليسيرة وما على كل بلد من المراعي والرسوم وجعلت ذلك لسنة ستمائة واحد واربعين فانها السنة التي امرت بالنظر في الفيوم بعدها. والفت هذا الكتاب عقيبها[24] ولم يتغير في سنة اثنتين واربعين وثلاث واربعين[25] شيء من الاوضاع وان حصلت زيادة يسيرة في الارتفاع وما عدا ذلك فقواعد محررة ورسوم مقررة.

وقد جعلت هذا الكتاب عشرة ابواب. والله الموفق للصواب.

الباب الاول، في وصفه من حيث الجملة

الباب الثاني، في ذكر مزاجه

الباب الثالث، في وصف هوائه ومائه

الباب الرابع، في ذكر سبب[26] استمرار جريان مائه مع انقطاع مده من غير ان يجر[27] اليه نهر او يتصل ببحر

الباب الخامس، في ذكر السالكين به وانقسامهم الى البدو والحضر

الباب السادس، في ذكر ما تغير من بحره وسبب ذلك وما دثر من بلاده حتى عسر تداركه الا بالاموال الجزيلة والمدة الطويلة

الباب السابع، في ذكر[28] اسماء بلاده على حروف المعجم

الباب الثامن، في ذكر ما به من الجوامع والمساجد والديرة والكنائس

الباب التاسع، في ذكر ما يشتمل عليه من عين وغلة وغير ذلك من حيث الجملة

الباب العاشر، في وصف بلاده وارتفاعها بلدا بلدا

17 أ. س.: حصرهم.
18 أ. س.: ساحه.
19 أ. س.: نافعا.
20 ساقط من أ. س.: في.
21 أ. س.: لنائي.
22 أ. س.: له.
23 أ. س.: المساجد والجوامع.
24 أ. س.: عقبيا.
25 أ. س. يضيف: فيهما.
26 ساقط من أ. س.: سبب.
27 أ. س.: يجري.
28 ساقط من ط. م.: ذكر.

Congregational mosques (*jāmi*ʿ) and neighbourhood mosques (*masjid*) are mentioned in every village entry, and are also listed together for the convenience of anyone consulting this book. The monasteries and churches in it are also listed both together and by village. I only mentioned and listed congregational mosques and neighbourhood mosques lest, with the passage of time, a neighbourhood mosque or a congregational mosque be deserted and its grounds remain idle for a long time, and then a house be built [there], a flax rettery (*maballa*) or any other building that is not a mosque. This list will prevent that from happening. And I have only mentioned the monasteries and churches, lest, with the passage of time, in the future, if the people of authority be negligent — because of the remoteness of this region from al-Fusṭāṭ, and its seclusion from the path of travellers to and from it — one of the ignorant, conceited Christian Copts, who do not fear the consequences, may build a church or a monastery, claiming its antiquity. Thus, were someone to take note of this book in the future, the list of the congregational mosques and neighbourhood mosques will prevent any claims that there are fewer of them; and the listing of the monasteries and churches will prevent claims that there are more.

I further mentioned the small advance payments which are bestowed by the Dīwān[5] to all villages for [future delivery of] barley or broad beans. I have listed pasture fees and [other] fees imposed on each village.

I prepared this for the year 641 — this was the year following which I received my orders to undertake the survey of the Fayyum. I composed this book thereafter, and the circumstances had not changed in the years [6]42 and [6]43, save for a minor increase in the revenues, and the remaining categories are of established rules (*qawāʿid muḥarrara*) and fixed fees.

I have divided this book into ten chapters — and God grants attainment of what is right:

The first chapter: A general description of the Fayyum

The second chapter: Account of its climate (*mizāj*)

The third chapter: A description of its air and waters

The fourth chapter: Explaining the continuous flow of its water even when it is not inundated [by the Nile], and without any river drawn into it or a canal reaching it.

The fifth chapter: Account of its inhabitants and their division into Bedouins and non-tribal people (*ḥaḍar*).

The sixth chapter: Account of the deterioration of its canal and the reason for that, and of the villages that have so fallen into ruin that their reconstruction could only be achieved by [investing] generous sums of money over a long period of time.

The seventh chapter: List of the names of its villages, arranged by the letters of the alphabet.

The eighth chapter: Account of its congregational mosques, neighbourhood mosques, monasteries and churches.

The ninth chapter: Account of of its aggregate taxes in specie and in grains, and other taxes.

The tenth chapter: A description of its villages and their fiscal revenues, village by village.

5 Here and throughout the treatise, the Dīwān is *Dīwān al-Māl*, the Treasury, unless specifically identified as *Dīwān al-Juyūsh* (Ministry of the Army) or *Dīwān Aḥbās al-Jawāmiʿ wa'l-Masājid* (Ministry of Endowments of Congregational and Neighbourhood Mosques).

الباب الاول

في وصفه من حيث الجملة

اقول وبالله التوفيق ان هذا الفيوم ناحية من قطر الديار المصرية بينه وبين الفسطاط مسافة يوم وليلة للراكب بالجنب الغربي منه. وهي ارض مختلفة التربة ما بين الابليز المحض والطين المختلط بالرمل الذي لا يمنع الزرع ويسمى الدملوف والرمل المشوب بالحصا الذي لا ينبت به شجر ولا زرع.

يكتنف هذه الارض جبل يبتدئ من هرم يعرف بهرم اللاهون وهو اول البلاد الفيومية التي تلي الهرم من هذه[29] الارض ثم يدور هذا الجبل على الفيوم متصلا، ويتصل دائرا الى موضع يقال له كوم درى[30] سوى فوهات هي مسالك اليه من مواضع متعددة. مسافة هذا الجبل للراكب اذا مر عليه من هرم اللاهون المذكور الى كوم دُرى المذكور ثلاثة ايام.

وهذا الفيوم قطر احكمته الصنعة الازلية ودبرته القدرة الالهية وابدعه واهب العقول الصحيحة والافكار الصريحة حتى لحق هذا الموضع السفلي بالعالم العلوي في انه لا يخشى اختلاله ولا تتغير في جريان مائه احواله فهدى الله من اجرى على يديه عمارته وجدد بحسن نظره نضارته بان تامل بالنظر الهندسي والعقل الانسي.

فاذا سمت سطح النيل المبارك عند نهاية انحطاطه يعلو على اعلى ارضه من اول ما يحاذيه الى فسطاطه فاحتفر له بحرا يسمى المنْهَى فوهته المتصلة بالنيل في الطرف القبلي من اعمال الاشمونين فوق قرية تعرف بذروة [دروة] سربام. يمر هذا البحر ما بين بلاد الاشمونين[31] والبهنسا ومدينة البهنسا على حافته ثم يفارق الاشمونين ويبقى سالكا بين بلاد البهنسا والفيوم الى اللاهون المقدم ذكره مسافته اربعة ايام للراكب.

29 ساقط من أ. س.: هذه.

30 أ. س.: درا.

31 ساقط من أ. س.: فوق قرية تعرف بذروة سربام. يمر هذا البحر ما بين بلاد الاشمونين.

The First Chapter

A general description of the Fayyum

And I say — may God grant success! — the Fayyum is a district of the land of Egypt. Between it and al-Fusṭāṭ there is a distance of a day and a night for a horseman riding to its western side. It consists of diverse types of soil, ranging from patches of pure alluvial deposits to clay mixed with sand, which is called *al-damlūf*, and which does not prevent cultivation, to sand spotted with pebbles, in which neither tree nor plant sprouts.

This area is encircled by a mountain range that begins at a pyramid known as the Pyramid of al-Lāhūn,[6] which is the name of the first village of the Fayyum that lies next to the pyramid in this area. These mountains then encircle the Fayyum uninterruptedly and complete a circle at a location known as Kawm Durrī, except for gaps, which allow passageways into it from several places. It takes three days for a horseman to follow this mountain range from the pyramid at al-Lāhūn to Kawm Durrī.

The Fayyum is a region moulded by pre-eternal design, brought about by divine omnipotence, and ingeniously created by the Bestower of right minds and clear thoughts, so that this nether place has come to resemble the heavenly world (*al-ʿulwī*), in that there is no fear of its deterioration, and the flow of its water does not change. God guided the hands of the person who brought about its cultivation, and who restored its prosperity by excellent management through engineering acuity and human reason.

[Even] when the blessed Nile is at its minimum ebb, from where its course starts to run parallel to the Fayyum until [its northern limit in] the direction of Fusṭāṭ, its surface level is above the highest point in the Fayyum. For this reason, a canal (*baḥr*) called al-Manhā was dug, branching off from the Nile at the southern part of the district of al-Ashmūnayn above a village known as Darwat Sarabām.[7] This canal flows between the villages of al-Ashmūnayn and al-Bahnasā, and the city of al-Bahnasā is on its bank. It then leaves al-Ashmūnayn and continues to flow through the villages of al-Bahnasā and the Fayyum toward the previously mentioned al-Lāhūn. Its length is four days of riding.[8]

6 Pyramid of Sesostris II, located south-west of the Fayyum, near the southward turn of al-Manhā Canal.

7 Modern location: Dayrūṭ. Émile Amélineau, *La géographie de l'Égypte à l'époque copte* (Le Caire: Imprimerie nationale, 1893), p. 205, Coptic name: Tarūt Sarābām, in memory of a famous monk called Ṣarābāmūn; Ibn 'Abd Allāh al-Ḥamawī Yāqūt, *Muʿjam al-buldān*, 5 vols (Beirut: Dār Ṣawār li'l-Ṭibāʿah wa'l-Nashr, 1956; this edition will be cited unless otherwise stated), II, 453: Darwat Sarabām ; Asʿad Ibn Mammātī, *Kitāb qawānīn al-dawāwīn*, ed. by ʿAṭiya, p. 112, Darwaṭ Sarābām; al- Maqrīzī, *Kitāb al-Mawāʿiẓ wa'l-iʿtibār fī dhikr al-khiṭaṭ wa'l-āthār*, ed. by Gaston Wiet, 5 vols (Frankfurt am Main: Institute for the History of Arabic-Islamic Science at the Johann Wolfgang Goethe University, 1994), I, 71, 205: Darūṭ Sarabān; al-Qalqashandī, *Ṣubḥ*, I, 413; III, 329–30: Dharwat Sarbām, which is also called Dharwat al-Sharīf, after the Sharīf Ḥiṣn al-Dīn Thaʿlab al-Jaʿrī.

8 Despite medieval Muslim writers' firm belief that the Baḥr Yūsuf/al-Manhā Canal was dug by the biblical Joseph (see Omar Toussoun, *Mémoire sur l'histoire du Nil* [Caire: Imprimerie de l'Institut français d'archéologie orientale, 1925], pp. 174–75), it is actually a natural meandering stream that branches off the Nile (Carl Butzer, *Early Hydraulic Civilization in Egypt: A Study in Cultural Ecology* [Chicago: University of Chicago Press, 1976], p. 16). Throughout the treatise, al-Nābulusī dintinguishes between the Baḥr al-Manhā — the canal that branches off the Nile near Dayrūt (Darwat Sarbām) and flows towards al-Lāhūn — and the Baḥr Yūsuf, the canal that then branches off towards the Fayyūm depression. Indeed, according to Yāqūt (*Muʿjam al-Buldān*, ed. by Muḥammad Amīn Al-Khānḥabī [Cairo: Maṭbaʿat al-Saʿāda, 1906], VIII, 186), al-Manhā is the Coptic name of the region around the mouth of the Baḥr Yūsuf. See also Salmon, 'Répertoire', p. 30, who mentions that the lower parts of Baḥr Yūsuf are called *bahr al-mounha*.

وجعل عند منتهاه بناء محكم[32] على وضع هندسي متقن البناء بتماسيخ الرصاص وزبر الحديد ما بين الاحجار. يعلو هذا البناء على ارض الخليج المحتفر خمسة عشر ذراعا يرد هذا البناء الماء الذي يصل اليه من النيل في البحر المنهى عن ان يخرج في منخفض وراءه الى النيل.

وقد كان راس هذا البحر المنهى فيما سلف يجف كل سنة اربعة اشهر ويمد الفيوم ماؤه الحاصل فيه والنزر بقية السنة وهي ثمانية اشهر فانعكس الحال فيه لاهمال حفره وعدم العناية به فصار يجف الان ثمانية اشهر ويمده النيل اربعة اشهر ومن دليل اهماله انه لم يوجد للاهتمام بحفره ذكر في الديوان ولا حساب يشهد به من مدة تزيد على مائة سنة.

فلما شرف الله تعالى بلاد الفيوم بحلول الركاب المولوي السلطاني الملكي الصالحي النجمي عظم الله سلطانه ومروره عليه امر باحياء هذا الاثر واخراج العوامل لعمارته وندب ولاة الامر القريبين منه لمباشرته وهي سُنة سنها عظم الله سلطانه يرجع بها ماء النيل في امداده البلاد على عادته ويكون سببا لاصلاح الفيوم وعمارته ان شاء الله تعالى.

واحتفر بحرا له فوهة من هذا البحر المنهى بينه وبين هذا البناء المذكور الفان ومائة ذراع يمر هذا البحر المحتفر من شرقي الفيوم الى غربيه في وسط الفيوم بحيث لو قيس من احدى حافتيه الى منتهى ارض الفيوم مما يليه، وقيس من الجانب الاخر الى منتهى ما يليه من الفيوم ومسحا كانا سواءًا.

على هذا البحر وما ينتهي خلجه اليه من بلاد الفيوم جميعها في هذا التاريخ وهو شهر ذي القعدة سنة اثنتين واربعين وستمائة، مائتين اثنان واربعون ساقية، العامر منها مائة وثمانين ساقية والداثر ستة وعشرين ساقية. ومن احجار المعاصر الدائرة بالماء ستة احجار منها اربعة دائرة الى اخر هذه السنة المذكورة[33] وحجران معطلان لسبب اوجب تعطيلهما. ومن الطواحين الدائرة بهذا الماء ثمانية خارجة عن حجر استجد بقرية تعرف بابي كسا في هذه السنة مما يستقبل دورانه اول النيل ان شاء الله تعالى.

وفتح من هذا البحر الداخل من الفيوم ثمانية وخمسين فوهة: في قبليه ثلاثة وعشرين فوهة، وفي بحريه ثلاثين، وفي اخره خمس فوهات، خارجا عن ثمانية مساقي لطاف للاحكار والرواتب لا للبلاد.

تسقى كل فوهة من هذه الفوهات ما تمر عليه من اراضي البلاد سقيا حكميا كفافا لا ينقص عن حاجته ولا يزيد عليها. ومهما فضل من هذا البحر المشار اليه بعد خروج الماء منه في الفوهات المذكورة الى البلاد ينقسم ذيله على خمس فوهات يجري ماؤها الى ما تحته من البلاد لا يضيع من البحر جميعه قطرة واحدة ولا يسلك بجريه منه الا مسلك الفائدة.

At its endpoint, a solid dam (*binā*ʾ) was built, with an orderly layout, reinforced with lead dowels and iron rods between the stones. The dam stands fifteen cubits above the bed of the excavated canal. This dam prevents the water that flows from the Nile, through al-Manhā Canal, from flowing into the low area (*munkhafaḍ*) behind it and back to the Nile.

In the past, the head of this al-Manhā Canal would lie dry for only four months every year. During the rest of the year, that is, for eight months, its water — that which flows into it as well as seepage water — used to reach the Fayyum. This situation has now reversed due to negligence in digging it and to lack of maintenance, and it now lies dry for eight months and the Nile flows into it for only four months. An indication of its neglect is that there is no account in the [records of the] Dīwān [al-Māl, the Treasury] of any attention being given to digging it, and there is no receipt attesting for it, for a period exceeding one hundred years.

When God the exalted honoured the Fayyum with the visit of the entourage of the lord, the sultan al-Malik al-Ṣāliḥ Najm [al-Dunyā wa'l-Dīn] — may God make his rule great! — and with his passing through it, he ordered that this remnant [al-Manhā Canal] be restored and that beasts of burden (*ʿawāmil*) be levied for its restoration. He appointed nearby officials to carry this out. This was an example that he set — may God make his rule great! — in order to bring back the flow of the Nile's water to the villages as it used to be, which would bring about the improvement of the Fayyum and its cultivation, God willing.

[At the time the dam was built], a canal which branched off from al-Manhā canal was dug, at a distance of 2,100 cubits from the aforementioned dam. This excavated canal stretches from the east of the Fayyum to its west, right through the middle. Were one to measure the distance from one of its banks to the edge of the land of the Fayyum in one direction, and then measure from the other bank to the edge of the Fayyum in the other direction, they would be found to be equidistant.

On this canal (*al-baḥr*) and on all its sub-canals (*khuluj*) in the villages of the Fayyum, as of this date, the month of Dhū al-Qaʿda in the year 642 [31 March–29 April, 1245], there are 242 waterwheels, of which 180 were in operation, while 62 have fallen out of use; six stone presses turned by water, of which four are functioning as of the end of this year, while two were inactive due to circumstances that required their going out of use; and eight mills turned by its water, in addition to a new stone mill constructed during that year in a village known as Abū Ksā. The turning of this stone awaits the return of the Nile, God willing.

This canal which flows through the Fayyum has fifty-eight openings: twenty-three openings to the south and thirty to the north, and five openings at its end. In addition, there are eight small irrigation ditches (*masāqī*) which do not go to the villages, but are for lands under long-term lease (*al-aḥkār*) and for perennial plants (*al-rawātib*).

Each of these openings irrigates the lands of the villages through which it passes in a manner that is both wise and sufficient, neither falling short of their need nor exceeding it. Excess water that remains in the canal after the water has been distributed to the villages through these openings is divided into five openings at its end, which take their water to the villages beneath it. Not a single drop of water is lost from the entire canal, and everything which flows through it is put to beneficial use.

32 أ. س.، ط. م.: محكمًا.
33 ساقط من أ. س.: المذكورة.

الباب الثاني
في ذكر مزاجه

اقول وبالله التوفيق ان مزاج الفيوم الغالب عليه الحرارة واليبس لانه غور كما تقدم يكتنفه جبل بعض الجبل من الحجارة الصوان المكسر والرمل والحصا الكبار والصغار وبعضه حجر صفوان يعرض هذا الجبل فيكون مسيرته يوما[34] وليلة للراكب من طريق وهي تعرف بطريق العبيد وبعض هذا الجبل تزيد المسافة منه الى واحات على اليومين والثلاثة[35] يتصل بالبر المقابل له الى اقصى المغرب. وفي بعض المفازات من هذا الجبل يكون عرضه دون اليوم كمفازة سفط[36] ميدوم وزرزا والمحرقة وغير ذلك.

فمتى هبت الريح عليه من جهة من هذه الجهات لا سيما في الصيف وقت الظهيرة واكتسا بها[37] ما تمر عليه حرارة ويبسا ولولا كثرة مائة فانه مع رداءته يرطب في الجملة لكان حال ساكنيها على اشد ما يكون من التغير.

ولقد رايت سكان مدينة الفيوم نفسها[38] كانهم وحش في صورة بني ادم ليس فيهم ولا بهم انس يستوحش الجالس في جمعهم ولا يستانس الوافد في ربعهم حتى انني وجدت الوحشة بدخولي اليها والانفراد بمقامي فيها حتى كتبت لبعض الناس من ابيات:

اشتقت فيها الناس حتى لقد
ناديت واشوقي الى الناس[39]

وانشدني[40] بعض الناس لشاعر دخل الى الفيوم بيتين هما:

يا حبذا بلد الفيوم من بلد
كجنة الخلد انهارا واشجارا
الله يعلم اني مذ حللت بها
وجدت دارا ولكن لم اجد جارا

فاجبته في الحال بديها

ان قال من سكن الفيوم اونة[41]
وجدت دارا ولكن لم اجد جارا
فانني لم اجد مذ جئتها احدا
من الذي قال لا دارا ولا جارا

[34] أ. س.: يوم.
[35] أ. س.: الثلاث.
[36] أ. س.: صفط.
[37] ط. م.: اكسبها.
[38] ساقط من أ. س.: نفسها.
[39] أ. س.: استقت فيها الناس حتى * لقد ناديت واشوقي إلى الناس.
[40] أ. س.: وأنشد.
[41] أ. س.: أوله.

The Second Chapter
Account of the Fayyum's climate (*mizāj*)

I say — may God grant success! — heat and dryness predominate in the Fayyum's climate because it is a basin, as previously explained, encircled by a mountain. Part of the mountain range is made of broken flintstone, and of sand and small and large pebbles, and part of it is made of boulders. The mountain widens, so crossing it requires a day and a night riding along a path known as the 'Slaves' Path'. Part of this mountain range is at a distance of more than two or three days [ride] from [the] Oases (*Wāḥāt*), and it adjoins the open country opposite it towards the Far West [*aqṣā al-maghrib*].[9] The width of some of the desert passages (*mafāza*) of this mountain range requires less than a day to cross, like those of Saft Maydūm,[10] Zirzā,[11] al-Muḥraqa,[12] and others.

When the wind blows upon it from one of these regions, especially during summer afternoons, that which the wind passes over is covered with heat and dryness. And if it were not for the abundance of its water, which helps — despite its putridness — to keep it generally humid, the condition of its inhabitants would take the worst possible turn.

Indeed I have seen the inhabitants of Madīnat al-Fayyūm, and they appeared to be beasts in human form, entirely lacking in sociability. Anyone who joins in their company is repelled by them, and the visitor to their dwellings does not socialize with them. I found loneliness when I entered their company and solitude during my stay among them, so much so that I wrote for someone a few lines of verse:

I longed for people there, so much so /
that I had cried out in desire for company.

Someone recited to me two verses of a poet who had visited the Fayyum; they are as follows:

How wonderful is the land of the Fayyum among countries /
its rivers and trees like the paradise of eternity,

God knows that since I took residence there /
I found a home but have found no neighbour.

I answered him at once, spontaneously:

Whereas the one who had long lived in the Fayyum said /
'I found a home but I have found no neighbour'

I myself have found, since my arrival, not one /
of the things he spoke of, neither home nor neighbour.

[9] The term *al-Maghrib al-Aqṣā* usually denotes in medieval Islamic geographical texts the Western part of North Africa, corresponding to modern Morocco; see Évariste Lévi-Provençal, 'al-Maghrib', *The Encyclopedia of Islam*, 2nd edn, v, 1184–1209 (p. 1184).

[10] Modern day Ṣafṭ al-Sharqiyya (صفت الشرقية), a city located east of the Fayyum, across the mountain range, on the western bank of the Nile. Mentioned also in: Ibn Mammātī, *Kitāb qawānīn al-dawāwīn*, p. 202: Saft Banī Waʿla; Ibn al-Jīʿān, *Kitāb al-tuḥfa as-sanīya bi-asmāʾ al-bilād al-miṣriyya* (Le Caire: Bibliothèque Khédiviale, 1898), p. 158: Saft Banī Waʿlā; Ramzī, *Al-Qāmūs*, ii/iii, 131: Ṣafṭ Al-Sharqiyya.

[11] Modern location: Jirzā. Halm, *Ägypten*, p. 240: Zirzā; Ibn Duqmāq, *Kitāb al-intiṣār li-wāsiṭat ʿiqd al-amṣār*, ed. by Karl Vollers (Le Caire: Imprimerie Nationale, 1893), p. 8 (of al-Bahnasā); Ramzī, *Al-Qāmūs*, ii/iii, 42–43: Jirzā, following Amélineau, *La géographie*: Philadelphie = Kerkei = Zirzā; Trismegistos GEO ID 1760: Philadelphia = Gharabat al-Jirzā.

[12] Unidentified. It is mentioned again at the end of the treatise, in relation to the construction of a new dike in the province of Giza.

ولا يتحركون بحركة الا بمحرك مثل البهائم يقيم الواحد المشهور منهم المدة الطويلة في بيته ولا يخرج من داره[42] ولا يعرف ما الناس فيه ورايت من اقام بها من الغرباء فطالت مدتهم يلحقه ما يلحقهم من حيث لا يشعر والانفراد يوجب الوحشة ويكدر الروح الحيواني ويقتضي تردد العفن في المواضع التي هم بها والرطوبة عليها غالبة فيتراجع العفن اليهم يستنشقونه مع الهواء الذي يمد الحرارة الغريزية والروح الحيواني فيكدره وتقوى السوداء عليهم وتتكاثف الابخرة المتحللة منهم وتبطئ وتقل وتزداد في ابدانهم لعدم الحركة.

لا يعرف احد منهم بمكرمة ولا شجاعة ولا كرم ولا اريحية ولا ترنح ولا[43] منهم ذو صورة جميلة ولا من له صوت حسن البتة ولا بعلم من العلوم ولا بعمل من الاعمال الدقيقة ولا من الصنائع الحسنة والافعال المستحسنة.

قد غلب عليهم الكمد. ولعمري لقد اقمت بالفيوم الى حين تاليف[44] هذا الكتاب[45] مدة تزيد على شهرين في موضع عالي البناء رحب الفناء مكشوف من جهاته الاربع للهواء فما سمعت فيها بعرس ولا اجتماع طائفة لانس ولا مر في طريق من طرقها احد فترنم او غلبه ترنح فغنى او على مذهب الفقراء زمزم.

بَزهم في غاية الغلظ والخشونة قليل البقاء عند استعماله موصوف الغزل بضعفه وانحلاله بخلاف ما حولهم من البلاد واغنامهم لحومها قحلة رخوة كثيرة العروق عديمة الدهن قد غلب عليها العجف مع كثرة العلف لا يوجد فيها سمين البتة كانه في المذاق تبن وكانه في الفم وقت المضغ خرقة يلوكها الانسان او قطعة لبد وضعت فوق اللسان. وطعامهم لعدم الالية بشحم الكلى لا بدهن السلى. والبانهم لا تنعقد ذلك[46] الانعقاد المعروف. وخبزهم رخو الى الغاية لكن اذا بقي يوما وليلة يبس وصار كالبقسماط لا لذة في طعمه. وقصد الاختصار مانع عن الاكثار.

They [the people of the Fayyum] only move when prodded, like beasts. An eminent person among them spends a great deal of time in his home, and is not aware of the affairs of other people. I saw a foreigner who had taken up residence in the Fayyum, and as time went by, he became like them without noticing it. Solitude breeds loneliness and disturbs the vital pneuma (*al-rūḥ al-ḥayawānī*). Decay becomes common in the places where they dwell, as moisture dominates there, and so putrefaction circulates with the air they inhale, which affects the innate heat (*al-ḥarāra al-gharīziya*) and the vital pneuma, and disturbs them. Black bile dominates them, and the dissolving vapours grow thick, linger, decrease (*taqillu*), and accumulate in their bodies because of their lack of movement.

Not one of them is known to be noble or brave, or to be of generous mind or of good spirit, or of merit, and none is attractive in appearance or possessed of a pleasant voice at all; and none have knowledge of any science, or of any refined craft, nor of fine skills or renowned arts.

They are overcome by gloom, and by my life, I have resided in the Fayyum until I composed this book[13] for a period exceeding two months, in a tall building with a spacious courtyard exposed to the four winds — and never did I hear a wedding party or a social gathering. No one passed on its roads singing, nor was anyone overcome by good spirit to the point of chanting, or humming — as is the custom of the mystics (*fuqarāʾ*).

Their cloth is of very low quality and coarse. It doesn't last long when used. The thread is weak and loose, unlike that from surrounding regions. The meat of their sheep is dry, flaccid, laden with sinews, lacking fat, and overly emaciated despite the abundant fodder. There is no fat found on them at all, and they taste like straw; it is as if, when chewing, one masticates a rag or a piece of felt placed on the tongue. As for their food, because of the lack of fatty sheep buttock, [it is cooked] in suet (*shaḥm al-kullā*), rather than with oil made of sheep fat. Their dairy products don't coagulate as they normally do. Their bread is extremely soft, but if left a day and a night it becomes dry, and resembles a hard biscuit entirely devoid of pleasant taste. A desire for brevity keeps me from saying more on this topic.

42 ساقط من أ. س.: ولا يخرج من داره.
43 أ. س. يضيف:فضيلة.
44 أ. س.: تألف.
45 أ. س. يضيف فقرة طويلة تابعة للباب الثالث، تبدأ في عند طلوعها وتنتهي في: مع انه.
46 أ. س.: ذاك.

13 In AS, a long passage which belongs to the third chapter was mistakenly copied here. The passage begins with *ʿinda ṭulūʿi-hā* and ends with *annahu balagha-nī.*

الباب الثالث

في وصف هوائه ومائه

اقول وبالله التوفيق ان الهواء المحيط بالفيوم هواء رديء الى الغاية لانه مخالط الابخرة الرديئة المتراقية من ارضه والعفونة المتفشية منه لان اكثره اجام واقصاب وهيش ومحاطب في طول خلجه. وعلى الخليج[47] نبت كثير واشجار يتحلل منها فضل بخاري وبخار رديء ويمنع البخار المترقي من الارض من الارتقاء ومع هذا بخاره ممازج للعفونات المترقية من مائه.

فان الفيوم يسمى اسفل الارض وصدق مسميه فان اعلى موضع فيه مما يعلوه ماؤه نازل عن سمت سطح ماء النيل في نهاية انحطاطه. ولولا ذلك لما جرى فيه ماؤه فاذا تحركت ريح من الرياح الاربع مزجت تلك العفونات المتفشية من الماء مع البخار الكثيف المتحلل من الارض المخالط للفضلات الناشئة عن الاشجار ومرت على الجهات التي تندفع اليها من الفيوم بعد تكيفها بكيفية ما خالطها مما ذكرت. فاذا لا تبقى[48] الريح من جهة تهب منها على مزاجها ولا مزاج جهتها فهواء الفيوم بهذا الاعتبار هواء[49] رديء الى الغاية. والجبل محيط به يمنعه ان يخرج بقوة فتذهب[50] رداءة الهواء المحيط بها الموصوف كما تقدم وليس في اصلاح هواء الفيوم حيلة الا بالخروج منها الى الفضاء الذي وراء جبله. ولولا قصد الاختصار في هذا الكتاب لبسطت القول فيه وفننته ونوعت الكلام فيه واستوعبته.

واما ماؤه فماء رديء الى الغاية فان الحكماء قالوا ان ماء النيل رديء مع سعته واشتماله على الصفات الحسنة التي وصف الحكماء الماء الحسن بها فانهم قالوا اطيب المياه ما كان صافيا براقا خفيف الوزن عديم الطعم واللون والرائحة مكشوفا للشمس بعيد المجرى يخرج من اودية مقابلة للشمال يسخن سريعا[51] عند طلوعها عليه ويبرد سريعا عند غروبها عنه وينحدر عن المعدة سريعا ويخفف ثقل الطعام الى غير ذلك من اوصافه الحسنة التي تقدم ذكرها.

وقالوا مع هذه الصفات انه رديء الى الغاية لانه يمر على نقائع وبقايا من ارضه ايام زيادته في بطائح ينزل عنها ايام نزوله ويتعفن فيها الحيوان على اختلاف انواعه من الافاعي والاسماك وغيرها. فاذا زاد مر عليها وجرف بها وان ارضه طينية لزجة.[52]

47 أ. س.: الخلج.

48 أ. س.: فلا تبقى اذا.

49 ساقط من أ. س.: هواء.

50 أ. س.: فيذهب.

51 ساقط من أ. س. فقرة طويلة تبدأ في عند طلوعها وتنتهي في: مع انه وهي واردة في ضمن الباب الثاني من أ.س.

52 أ. س.: لزجه.

The Third Chapter

A description of the Fayyum's air and water

I say — may God grant success — the air surrounding the Fayyum is extremely foul because it is mixed with the noxious vapours rising from the soil and the decomposition that spreads from it. The majority of it [of the Fayyum] is covered with thickets, reeds, brush, and scrub wood along the length of its canals. The great number of plants and trees on the canals emit vaporous superfluities and noxious vapours, and these prevent the vapour rising from the soil from lifting. Moreover, these vapours are mixed with the putridity arising from its water.

The Fayyum has been called the lowest place on earth, and rightly so. Indeed, the highest point in it to which its water can rise is lower than the level of the surface of the Nile at its minimum ebb. Were it not so, the Nile's waters would not flow in it. So when one of the four winds blows, it mixes the putridity dissipating from the water with the thick vapour emitted from the land, which is itself mixed with the superfluities produced by the trees. As the wind blows towards any of the regions in the Fayyum, it takes on the qualities of that which it has mixed with, as I have mentioned, since the wind blowing from any area does not retain its original qualities, or the qualities of the area from which it blows. Therefore, the air of the Fayyum is extremely bad. The surrounding mountains prevent it from escaping with any force that would have allowed the foulness of this surrounding air to go away, as described above, and there is no way to improve [one's experience of] the air of the Fayyum except by going out to the open space behind its mountains. Were it not for my intention to make this book brief, I would have elaborated more on this, perfected, expanded and exhausted it.

As for its [the Fayyum's] water, it is vile in the extreme. Learned men have said that the Nile's water is bad despite its great quantity and its possession of those fine features which they say characterize water of good quality. They have said that the best water is that which is pure and sparkling, light in weight, devoid of taste, colour, or smell, exposed to the sun, far-flowing, issuing from valleys facing north, quickly warming with the sun's rise over it and quickly cooling with sunset. The water should also go through the stomach quickly, lightening the heaviness of food, and have the other qualities of fine water noted above.

They also said that despite these qualities, the Nile's water is extremely foul because it passes over swamps, and parts of its river bed become marshes during the period of flooding, and then the river withdraws from them as it recedes. Within these [swamps and standing water] animals of all kinds — snakes and fishes as well as others — decompose. When the Nile floods, the water pass through these swamps and carry them along, since the river bed is clayish and viscous.[14]

[14] Compare Ibn Riḍwān, in Michael W. Dols, *Medieval Islamic Medicine: Ibn Riḍwān's Treatise 'On the Prevention of Bodily Ills in Egypt'*, ed. by Adil S. Gamal, trans. by Michael W. Dols (Berkeley: University of California Press, 1984), p. 84.

فكيف بماء الفيوم وهو كله عن ماء[53] بطيحة ونقعة من النقائع التي نم ماء النيل لمروره على مثلها مع اشتماله على الصفات الحسنة التي تقدم ذكرها ثم ينضاف الى رداءته انه يتصل به نزز من الارض من خروق في ارض بحر المنهى ينز الماء منها ومن ذيول حافاته في بعض الاماكن منه كلما خرج من هذا الماء شيء من فوهات بحر الفيوم الى بلاده اخلفه هذا النزز مع اشتمال النزز على الرداءة المقولة فيه مما يطول بصفته هذا الكتاب وذلك لمخالطته الاجزاء الارضية وانتقاعه فيها حتى وصفه بعض الظرفاء فقال هو اراقة ماء الارض ووصفه اخر فقال كانه ماء خرج من مثانة.

ويكسب هذا الماء الابدان خشونة ويتفق الماء والهواء الموصوف على اهل الفيوم هذا شربا وهذا استنشاقا فيورثان خللا في العقل بالتجفيف ورداءة الكيفية واليبس والسام والضجر وضيق الخلق وفتورا في الاماني والامال وذهولا في الاقوال والافعال وكدورة في الروح الحيواني وخللا في الشهوة الطبيعية وافسادا في الاغراض[54] النفسانية وسوء في الافكار وكمدا في اوقات الليل والنهار.

ولعمري لقد عجبت كيف يسلم اهله القاطنون به من الادواء التي تنشا من مثل هوائه ومائه فلم اجد سببا لذلك سوى احد امرين اما العادة فانه متى تعود شرب السم من الطفولية مع اللبن واستمر لم يؤثر فانهم تعودوا ذلك خلفا عن سلف. واما لان هذا الماء دائم الجريان والحركة مع انقطاع مدده فانه تتقسمه الفوهات ويجري في مضايق من الخليج ينبت في حافاته نبات من الاقصاب وغيرها فيمر عليها ويقرعها فيبقى له مع جريانه وقرع النبات له في مروره حالة يلطف بها واذا طال جريانه ربما فارقته الارضية المخالطة له مع امتحان الشمس له لانه مكشوف كله للشمس فيبقى في صورة ماء مسخن يفارق بذلك ارضيته المخالطة له فاذا عمل في الاواني برد فشربه اهل البلاد قليل الضرر لما ذكرناه.

واما البلاد التي يشرب اهلها من الماء الذي يصل اليهم من ذيل بحر الفيوم بعد مروره على الفيوم ففي البلاء المبرم والذل المحكم فانهم يستعملون الخبائث المحضة والسموم القاتلة فان كنف الفيوم واقذارهم مع كثرتها ورمى جيفهم فيها واستمرارها ودوامها تخالط الماء مع قلته من بَريه مخالطة يظهر[55] اثرها في الطعم على ما بلغني والرائحة واللون على ما شممت ورايت. ولعل ما ذكرته من الاسباب المقللة لضرره خفف ذلك مع تعودهم لاستعماله مع انه[56] بلغني انه كثر فيهم الاستسقاء ووجع الكلى والزمل والحصا واكسبهم[57] استعمال هذا الماء القحول[58] في الجسم والترهل[59] في الابدان.

[53] أ. س.: عماء.
[54] ط. م.: الأعراض.
[55] أ. س.: تظهر.
[56] أ. س.: لأنه.
[57] أ. س.: وأكسبتهم.
[58] أ. س.: النحول.
[59] أ. س.: والتهزل.

All the more so for the Fayyum's water, which consists entirely of stagnant shallow water or swamps. The Nile's water has been condemned, despite having the good qualities previously mentioned, merely for passing through the likes of it. The foul condition of the Fayyum's water is compounded when it comes into contact with ground seepage, either from apertures in the bed of al-Manhā Canal or, in some places, from the lower parts of its banks. Whenever water is channelled towards the villages of the Fayyum through the openings in the Main Canal (*Baḥr al-Fayyūm*),[15] this seepage water replaces it. The seepage contains notorious foulness, which we cannot describe here for the sake of brevity. It is so vile because it is mixed with grains of earth, turning it into a swamp. This has led one witty man to describe it as 'the earth urinating', and another described it as urine dripping from a bladder.

This water makes bodies coarse, and the qualities of the air and the water coincide — the first through drinking and the latter through inhaling — to endow the people of Fayyum with a certain deficiency of reason caused by dryness, as well as base nature, worthlessness, weariness, discontent, impatience, lack of ambition and aspiration, stupor in both word and deed, disturbance of the vital pneuma, deficiency in natural desires, a corruption of mental inclinations, wickedness of thoughts, and sadness during both day and night.

By my life, I was baffled as to how its people, those dwelling in it [in the Fayyum], were unaffected by those illnesses that originate in the likes of its air and water. I have found no reason for this, save for one of the following two explanations. Either it is the power of custom, since when one gets used to drinking poison, having drunk it with one's mother's milk from infancy and having continued to do so, it does not have any effect. So they have become used to it, generation after generation. Or, [they are unaffected] because this water is constantly flowing and moving even when the [Nile's] flooding subsides, since the openings divide the water, and it flows in narrow canals, on the banks of which reeds and other plants grow, and the water knocks against them as it passes. Its flow and its bumping against the vegetation as it passes improve its condition. If its flow is sufficiently prolonged, the earth which had mixed with it may become separated from it. This is so because it is subject to the effects of the sun — since all of it is exposed to the sun — and it acquires the form of warm water, thus separating the earth that got mixed with it. When it is put in vessels and allowed to cool, it causes little harm to the people of the villages who drink it, for the reason I have just mentioned.

But, as for the land whose inhabitants drink the water coming from the lower end of the Main Canal, after it has passed through the Fayyum, they are in a state of undeniable suffering and absolute abasement, as they use sheer filth and deadly poisons. The waste (*kunuf*) of the Fayyum and their abundant foul matters and corpses thrown into it from the two banks, continuously and endlessly, mixes with the scant water of the canal. The effects of this mix, as I have been told, are felt in its taste, and — as I have smelled and seen — in its odour and colour. Perhaps the attenuating reasons that I have mentioned, together with their growing accustomed to it, reduce its harm. However, I have learned that they have frequent cases of dropsy, kidney pain, *zaml* (?) and stones in the kidneys. In addition, the use of this water has resulted in the swelling of their bodies and in bloating.

[15] The main canal that cuts through the Fayyum, from the al-Lāhūn Gap towards the north-west, is called here *Baḥr al-Fayyūm*. Elsewhere in the treatise it is called *al-Baḥr al-Aʿẓam al-Yūsufī* (Joseph's Grand Canal), *al-Baḥr al-Yūsufī* (Joseph's Canal), *al-Baḥr al-Aʿẓam al-Fayyūmī* (the Fayyum's Grand Canal), and *al-Baḥr al-Aʿẓam* (Grand Canal). We do not indicate these variants in the translation, as these terms all appear to refer to the same canal, and not to separate sections of it.

وغلب على سكان الفيوم السوداء حتى انه متى تامل احد من اعيانهم ظهر لمتامله الاختلال في قوله وفعله. واما اختلال العقل فلا فائدة في ذكر اختصاصهم به فان روفس الحكيم ذكر في مقالته في المالينخوليا ما خلا راس ساكن غور قط من مالينخوليا وانشدوا :

من بات في الغوريات الاهل يندبه[60]
فكيف من بات في غور من الغور.

وانما يختلف باختلاف اثاره فتارة يظهر في الصورة وتارة يظهر في السيرة وتارة في القول وتارة في الفعل.

[60] أ. س.: تندبه.

Black bile so predominates among the inhabitants of the Fayyum, that if one of their notables is being observed, the deficiency in his speech and action becomes manifest. As for mental deficiency, there is no benefit in further discussing how much they are characterized by this. Rufus the Physician remarked in his treatise 'On Melancholy'[16] that the head of a person living in a low altitude is never spared from melancholy.

It was recited:

He who sleeps in a pit [that is in a grave], his family mourns for him /
All the more so for someone who spends the night in a pit within a pit.

But the effects may vary, at times manifesting itself in one's appearance, at times in one's demeanour, at times in one's speech and at times in one's actions.

[16] Rufus of Ephesus (lived first century BC) was a renowned Greek physician who wrote numerous influential treatises in various fields of medicine. His treatise 'On Melancholy' was translated to Arabic and quoted extensively by Medieval physicians such as Ibn Sīnā and Isḥāq ibn ʿImrān. See Rufus of Ephesus, *On Melancholy*, ed. by Peter E. Pormann (Tubingen: Mohr Siebeck, 2008).

الباب الرابع

في ذكر سبب[61] استمرار جريان مائه مع انقطاع مده من غير ان يجر اليه نهر او يتصل ببحر

اقول وبالله التوفيق ان بحر المنهى فيه خروق في ارضة متصلة بالنبع ينز منها الماء وكذلك في ذيول حافاته من مواضع فيه متعددة وذلك لنزول سمته عن سمت ماء النيل المبارك[62] ومن الحكمة البالغة انه[63] كلما انجر الماء منه في الفوهات المذكورة الى اراضي[64] البلاد الفيومية ومزارعها وبساتينها واشجارها واقصابها وبالسواقي التي عليه حتى ينقص شيء اخلفه في الحال النزز المتصل به مع الحاصل[65] الذي فيه من ماء النيل. هكذا دائما ابدا.

فاذا تناهى النيل في الاحتراق ظهر نقص هذا الماء لمسامتة سطحه سمت سطح ماء النيل ولولا ما ذكرت من هذه العلة واظهرت من اسرار هذه الحكمة لظهر نقص الماء الذي في المنهى في شهر واحد وازداد نقصه[66] بزيادة استعماله وجريانه ولا سيما وعليه من السواقي بالاشمونين والبهنسا[67] وغيرهما من بَرَيه الجملة الكبيرة التي ليس من غرضنا في هذا الكتاب عدها ولا حصرها.

وهذا المنهى فيه ترع[68] يدخل منها الماء الى اراضي الاشمونين والبهنسا وبلادهما وفوهات يجب لمصلحة الفيوم سد الجميع عند نزول النيل وعمل القطعة عند اللاهون.

فصل: وحيث جرى ذكر القطعة وعملها عند اللاهون ناسب ان اذكرها واصفها[69] حتى لا يبقي في خاطر الواقف على هذا الكتاب فكرة في ما هي ولماذا[70] هي فالقطعة المشار اليها عبارة عن نخلة طويلة يعمل عليها القش والجَب وتربط بحبال حتى يبقى لها بما يعمل عليها غلظ كبير تكون الحبال القوية في طرفها واطراف الحبال في ايدي جمع كثير من الرجال في البر المتصل بالضيعة المسماة باللاهون والبر المقابل لها يرخون الحبال قليلا قليلا مع حمل الماء القطعة المذكورة وجذبه لها الى الفوهة المذكورة وثم في البناء المسمى باللاهون المقدم ذكره بين البنيان المذكور فوهة يخرج منها الماء ايام النيل وتدخل فيها المراكب وتخرج خوفا من ان تمر على الحجر فيكسرها لقوة اضطراب الماء عليه. فاذا نزل النيل وظهر الحجر بقي الماء يخرج من هذه الفوهة وقد جمع جمع كثير من بلاد الفيوم والمهندسون لعمل هذه القطعة الموصوفة وصنعوا بها ما تقدم ذكره يرخونها[71] قليلا قليلا الى ان تصل الى فم الفوهة فتسدها وتمنع الماء من الخروج منها ويعمل الرجال عليها التراب والطين حتى تبقى من جنس البر المتصل بها الى البنيان بحيث يمر الانسان على البناء من اللاهون الى بَر قاي كما يمر على البر المتصل يُقْصَدُ بسد[72] الفوهة توفر الماء الذي يخرج منها على بلاد الفيوم هذا مع مدد النيل له وقبل ان ينقطع جريانه من فوهة المنهى الذي يجف كل سنة كما وصفت.

[61] ساقط من أ. س.: سبب.
[62] أ. س. يضيف: المبارك.
[63] أ. س.: أن.
[64] أ. س.: أرض.
[65] أ. س.: الجاصل.
[66] ساقط من أ. س.: نقصه.
[67] أ. س.: البهنساوية.
[68] أ. س.: تراع.
[69] أ. س.: نذكرها ونصفها.
[70] أ. س.: فيما هي ولا ماذا
[71] أ. س.: أرخوها.
[72] ط. م.: بسند.

The Fourth Chapter

Explaining the continuous flow of its water even when it is not inundated [by the Nile], and without having any river drawn into it or a canal reaching it

I say — may God grant success — there are openings (*khurūq*) in the bed of al-Manhā Canal and in the lower parts of its banks at numerous locations, that are fed by an underground source (*nabaʿ*) from which water seeps. This is because its level is below the level of the blessed Nile. It is part of its ingenious design that whenever water is drawn through these openings towards the lands of the villages of the Fayyum — its cultivated fields, gardens, trees and sugar plantations — or by means of waterwheels, thereby decreasing the water level [in the canal], the seepage immediately substitutes for it, mixing with what was obtained from the Nile's water. This is always and forever the case.

In the period when the Nile reaches its minimum ebb, the lessening of this [seepage] water becomes apparent, as its surface is level with the surface level of the Nile. And were it not for the aforementioned cause that I recounted [that is seepage], and for the secrets of this wise design that I have just explained, the decrease of the water in al-Manhā Canal would occur within one month, and would exacerbate due to the extensive use and flow, in particular because of the waterwheels placed upon al-Manhā Canal at al-Ashmūnayn and al-Bahnasā, and many others at its banks besides these — of which there is a large number, and it is not our aim in this book to enumerate them nor to count them.

On this al-Manhā Canal there are irrigation canals (*turaʿ*), allowing water to reach the lands of al-Ashmūnayn and al-Bahnasā and their villages, as well as openings, which it is in the interests of the Fayyum to close off entirely when the Nile recedes, and the 'bit' (*qiṭʿa*) is installed at al-Lāhūn.

Section: Since the 'bit' at al-Lāhūn and its installation have been mentioned, it is appropriate that I give an account of it and describe it, so that no uncertainty concerning it and its purpose remains in the mind of the reader. The above mentioned 'bit' is a long palm log upon which straw and rags are affixed. These are tied up with ropes, so that it becomes very thick. There are strong ropes at its edges, and the ends of these ropes are in the hands of large groups of men on the bank adjacent to the village (*ḍayʿa*) called al-Lāhūn, and on the opposite bank. They release the ropes little by little, while the water carries the 'bit' and pulls it toward the gap located in the dam of al-Lāhūn, in the midst of the structure. During the days of the [inundation of the] Nile, water escapes through this gap, and boats go in and out through it, as they do not want to risk passing over the stone (*ḥajar*) [i.e., the crest of the dam] for fear of being shipwrecked, due to the power of the water's turbulence. But when the Nile recedes, and the stone is exposed, water continues to escape from this gap. It is then that large groups of men from the villages of the Fayyum, as well as engineers, gather together to install this 'bit' as has been explained. They release it little by little until it comes to the mouth of the gap and blocks it, and thereby prevents the water from escaping. The men pile up soil and clay upon it so that it resembles the bank adjacent to the structure, so much so that a person may cross over the dam from al-Lāhūn to the bank of Qāy,[17] just as he would proceed on the same bank. The purpose of blocking the gap is that the water, which [otherwise would have] escaped through it, will be available for the villages of the Fayyum. This occurs at the time when the Nile still reaches it, before its flow stops at the entrance to al-Manhā Canal, which becomes dry each year as I described.

[17] Qāy, a town located several miles south-west of al-Lāhūn. See Ramzī, *Al-Qāmūs*, II/III, 162: Qāy (قاي).

الباب الخامس

في ذكر الساكنين به وانقسامهم الى البدو والحضر

اقول وبالله التوفيق انه لما رسم لي بالنظر في بلاد الفيوم وعمارتها مررت عليه بلدا بلدا وعرفت ساكنيها ولولا خوفي من استشعارهم لاحصيتهم عددا فوجدت اكثر اهلها العرب وقد تقسموا فيها الى الافخاذ والشعوب[73] وليس فيها من الحضر الا النزر اليسير ولعلها البلدتان او الثلاث مع ان هذا الحضر اليسير تحت خفرهم ياخذون منهم الاجرة على ذلك من رِزْقهم ورِزَقهم ويقتطعون بهذا السبب قطعا من ارضهم ويجعلون اذلالهم من سننهم الجارية عليهم وفرضهم.

وهؤلاء العرب الساكنون كلهم يتفرعون عن ثلاثة اصول: بني كلاب وبني عجلان واللواتيين. وها انا اصف انفارهم في مساكنهم واعينهم فيها باماكنهم خارجا عما يرد اليها ايام جدب[74] البلاد منتجعا وينزل بساحتها اوان حمل الغلال منتفعا.

فاما بنو كلاب فيتفرعون على الانفار التي ياتي ذكرها باماكنهم.

فمنهم بنو جَواب والبلاد التي هم بها: فدمين، الاستنباط، ابو كسا، ثلاث، عنز، نصف سينَرُو، الروبيون.[75]

النفر الاخر، الاضابطة، وبلادهم: منية اقنى[76] وكفورها وهي دِقْلَوه، الفحامة، منشاة حويت، منشاة غيلان، منشاة الوسط، الاثلِة، ابشاية الرمان، نصف سينرو، الحنبوشية فيها ماوى بني زبخ.[77] وبلادهم ايضا: ببيج انشو – كرابسة، بور سينرو، مسجد عائشة.

بنو غصين من بني كلاب، وبلادهم: اهريت بني عطا، دسيا، جردو، دنفارة جردو،[78] دنفارة[79] اهريت، طبهار، اخصاص العجميين،[80] ببيج انقاش، ببيج اندير، ششها،[81] منية ششها، بلالة، منتارة، حدادة، ام السباع، بشطا.

بنو مجنون من بني كلاب، وبلادهم: منية الديك، بنو مجنون، شلمص، وبعض ببيج اندير.

بنو عامر من بني كلاب، وبلادهم: مطول، دفدنو، بوصير، منشاة المطوع من كفور بلالة، الصفاونة، تنفشار، ببيج فرح، اطسا، باجة خفْرًا اهلها حضر نصارى، القلهانة، منشاة اولاد عرفة.

بنو ربيعة من بني كلاب، وبلادهم: قمبشا، دموشية، منية الاسقف خفْرًا، فان سكانها حضر وهم نصارى.

The Fifth Chapter

Account of the [Fayyum's] inhabitants and their division into Bedouin and non-tribal people

I say — may God grant success — when I was appointed to survey the Fayyum and its villages, I passed through it village by village and acquainted myself with their inhabitants; and were it not for my fear of their noticing, I would have made a census of them. I have found that most of the people are Arabs (*al-ʿarab*), and that they are divided up into sections (*afḫādh*) and sub-sections (*shuʿūb*). There are hardly any non-tribal people (*ḥaḍar*) in it, only a few, maybe two or three villages. Moreover, this small non-tribal population is under the protection of the Arabs, who extract from them protection fee, out of their livelihood (*rizqihim*) and their allowances (*rizaqihim*), receiving for this purpose a portion of their [the non-tribal villagers'] land. For the Arabs, humiliation of the non-tribal population is part of their way of life.

These Arabs inhabiting the Fayyum belong to three tribal confederacies (*uṣūl*): the Banū Kilāb, the Banū ʿAjlān, and the Lawātiyyūn. Here I am going to describe their tribal groups according to their places of dwelling and specify them according to their abodes, excluding those who travel to the province in times of drought, or put up their camp sites in its open country in search of livelihood during the transport of the grain harvest.

The Banū Kilāb branch out into subgroups (*anfār*) whose mention will follow, with their abodes. They are:

The Banū Jawwāb. The villages they inhabit are Fidimīn; al-Istinbāṭ; Abū Ksā; Thalāth; ʿAnz; half [the inhabitants] of Sīnarū; al-Rūbiyyūn.

The other group is the Aḍābiṭa. Their villages are Minyat Aqnā and its hamlets — which are Diqlawa, al-Faḥḥāma, Munshaʾat Ḥuwayt, Munshaʾat Ghaylān, Munshaʾat al-Wasaṭ, and al-Athila; Ibshāyat al-Rummān; half [the inhabitants] of Sīnarū; al-Ḥanbūshiyya, which is also the refuge (*maʾwā*) of the Banū Zabakh (?); Babīj Unshū [inhabited by the sub-section of the] Karābisa; Būr Sīnarū; Masjid ʿĀʾisha.

Banū Ghuṣayn of the Banū Kilāb. Their villages are Ihrīt Banī ʿAṭā; Disyā; Jardū; Dinfārat Jardū; Dinfārat Ihrīt; Ṭubhār; Akhṣāṣ al-ʿAjamiyyīn; Babīj Anqāsh; Babīj Andīr; Shushhā; Minyat Shushhā; Bilāla; Mintāra; Ḥaddāda; Umm al-Sibāʿ; Bushṭā.

The Banū Majnūn of the Banū Kilāb. Their villages are Minyat al-Dīk; Banū Majnūn; Shalmaṣ; and some [of the inhabitants] of Babīj Andīr.

The Banū ʿĀmir of the Banū Kilāb. Their villages are Muṭūl; Difidnū; Būṣīr [Difidnū]; Munshaʾat al-Muṭawwiʿ, included in the accounts (*min ḥuqūq*) of Bilāla; al-Ṣafāwina; Tanafshār; Babīj Faraḥ; Iṭsā; Bāja — under their protection (*khafr*[an]), its inhabitants are non-tribal Christians; al-Qalhāna; Munshaʾat Awlād ʿArafa.

The Banū Rabīʿa of the Banū Kilāb. Their villages are Qambashā; Dumūshiyya; Minyat al-Usquf — under their protection, its non-tribal inhabitants are Christians.

The Banū Ḥātim of the Banū Kilāb. Their villages are al-Mahīmsī; Buljusūq; Tuṭūn; Ṭalīt; Kanbūt; Dahmā; Ghābat Bāja; Hayshat Dumūshiyya.

The Banū Qurīṭ and the Banū Shākir. Their villages are Baḥr Banī Qurīṭ, included in the accounts of Muṭūl; Shidmūh; Muqrān.

Banū Jaʿfar of the Banū Kilāb. Their villages are Uqlūl and its hamlet.

---

73 أ. س.: الشعب.
74 أ. س.: جذب.
75 ساقط من أ. س.: الروبيون.
76 ط. م.: افتى.
77 أ. س.: ريح
78 أ. س.: جردو دنفارة .
79 ساقط من أ. س.: دنفارة.
80 ط. م.، أ. س.: الجميين.
81 ساقط من أ. س.: ششها.

بنو حاتم من بني كلاب، وبلادهم: المهيمسي، بلجسوق، تطون، طليت، كنبوت، دهما، غابة[82] باجة، هيشة دموشية.

بنو قُريط وبنو شاكر، وبلادهم: بحر بني قريط من حقوق مطول، شدموه، مقران.

بنو جعفر من بني كلاب، وبلادهم: اقلول وكفرها.

الاصل الثاني، بنو عجلان، وينقسم على الانفار التي ياتي ذكرها:

بنو جابر وقيصر من بني عجلان، وبلادهم: ذات الصفاء منشاة ابن كردى من كفور سنورس، فانو ونقليفة، ونقليفة قياصرة، منية كربيس، اخصاص ابي عصية، سنورس.

للقياصرة كفور[83] وهم من بني عجلان: منشاة الطواحين، بَيَهْمُو، شلالة، شِسْفة، ابهيت، اخصاص الحلاق خَفْرًا، جرفس، القُبَرا – كعبيون.

بنو زرعة من بني عجلان، وبلادهم: شانة، بياض، سيلة، مقطول، الربيات، بنديق، بورها، فرقس، العدوة، سرسنا، مطر طارس، المصلوب، الملالية، الاعلام، قشوش، صنوفر، خور[84] الرماد، دموه الداثر، هوارة البحرية، ابريزيا والزربي – خياثمة.

بنو سمالوس من بني عجلان، وبلادهم: منية البطس، الطارمة، ترسا، بمويه، اهلها حاضرة خفراؤهم بنو سمالوس، وكفورها بنو زُمران وبلادهم: الكوم الاحمر، منشاة نعيم، وغير ذلك.

بنو مُطَير: سنهور خاصة.

الاصل الثالث، اللواتيون.

بنو هاني وهم لواتيون، وبلادهم: سدمنت، ببيج غيلان، كوم الرمل، طما.

بنو سليمان من لواتة، وبلادهم: اللاهون، ام النخارير، هيشة الفردة.

بنو منكنيت، وبلادهم: ناموسة، الحمام.

هوارة، فخذ من لواتة: دمشقين، كوم دري، وهو دموه اللاهون.

82 أ. س.: غار باجة.
83 أ. س.: القياصرة كفورها.
84 أ. س.: غور الرماد.

The second tribal confederacy is the Banū ʿAjlān, and they are divided into sub-groups as follows:

Banū Jābir and the Banū Qayṣar[18] of the Banū ʿAjlān. Their villages are Dhāt al-Ṣafāʾ; Munshaʾat Ibn Kurdī, one of the hamlets of Sinnūris; Fānū and Naqalīfa — in Naqalīfa they are Qayāṣira (Banū Qayṣar); Minyat Karbīs; Akhṣāṣ Abī ʿUṣayya; Sinnūris.

The Qayāṣira of the Banī ʿAjlān live in their own hamlets (*kufūr*).[19] They are: Munshaʾat al-Ṭawāḥīn; Biyahmū; Shallāla; Shisfa; Abhīt; Akhṣāṣ al-Ḥallāq — under their protection; Jarfis.

Al-Qubarāʾ, [inhabited by the] Kaʿbiyyūn [Banū Kaʿb].

Banū Zarʿa of the Banū ʿAjlān. Their villages are Shāna; Bayāḍ; Sīla; Maqṭūl; al-Rubiyyāt; Bandīq; Būr Bandīq; Furqus; al-ʿIdwa; Sirisnā; Miṭr Ṭāris; al-Maṣlūb; al-Malāliyya; al-Aʿlām; Qushūsh; Ṣunūfar; Khawr al-Rammād; Dimūh al-Dāthir; Hawwāra al-Baḥriyya; Ibrīziyā and al-Zarbī of [the sub-section of the] Khayāthima.

Banū Samālūs of the Banū ʿAjlān. Their villages are Minyat al-Baṭs; al-Ṭārima; Tirsā; Bamawayh — its inhabitants are non-tribal, and their protectors are the Banū Samālūs, while its hamlets are of the Banū Zummarān, including al-Kawm al-Aḥmar, Munshaʾat Naʿīm, and others.

Banū Muṭayr: [their] only village is Sanhūr.

The third tribal confederacy is al-Lawātiyyūn [al-Lawāta].

Banū Hāniʾ of the Lawātiyyūn. Their villages are Sidmant; Babīj Ghaylān; Kawm al-Raml; Ṭimā.

Banū Sulaymān of the Lawāta. Their villages are al-Lāhūn; Umm al-Nakhārīr; Hayshat al-Farda.

Banū Munkanīt. Their villages are Nāmūsa; al-Ḥammām.

Hawwāra, a section of the Lawāta. [Their villages are] Dimashqīn [al-Baṣal] and Kawm Durrī, also called Dimūh al-Lāhūn.

[18] The Qayāṣira, i.e., the Banū Qayṣar are sometimes considered by al-Nābulusī to be a sub-section of the Banū Jābir, and sometimes a section of the Banū ʿAjlān.

[19] Only some of the following localities are later identified as hamlets; the rest are villages.

الباب السادس

في ذكر ما تغير من بحره وسبب ذلك وما دثر من بلاده حتى عسر تداركه الا بالاموال الجزيلة والمدة الطويلة

اقول وبالله التوفيق انه قد تقدم في كتابي المسمى بحسن السلوك في فضل ملك مصر على سائر الملوك ان اكثر الحكماء الموصوفين والفضلاء المعروفين من مصر وان سبب[85] اشتغالهم بالحكمة احتياجهم اليها في تدبير ري ارضهم من اقل ما تنتهي[86] اليه في كل سنة زيادة نيلهم انهم دبروه ورتبوه بتوفيق الحق سبحانه وتعالى لهم حتى صارت اراضي الديار المصرية تروى جميعها من اثنى عشر ذراعا ولا يضرها وصول الماء الى عشرين ذراعا.

ولم يعهد انه قصرت زيادته في سنة من السنين عن اثنى عشر ذراعا ولا زاد على عشرين ذراعا وان هذه الاثار والحكم[87] دثرت وعفت من الديار المصرية منذ الفين وستمائة سنة[88] ولم يبق منها شيء الا الفيوم خاصة فانه يروى من اثنى عشر ذراعا ولا يضره العشرون الى سنة ستمائة ثمانية وعشرين فان فيها نظر السلطان السعيد الشهيد الملك الكامل قدس الله روحه ونور ضريحه الى الجيزة[89] ورسم بالاهتمام بجسور عَينها[90] وامر بسد بحر الاهرام فتحامل الماء منه على اراضي الجيزية التي عادتها ان لا تروى الا من ثمانية عشر ذراعها فرويت من اثنى عشر ذراعا فاحيا الله هذا الاثر على يديه.

رجعنا الى ذكر سبب تغير بحر الفيوم وهو ان الذي هداه الله سبحانه وتعالى[91] الى عمل بحر المنهى وعمل البنيان المحكم في نهايته المعروف باللاهون جعله على وضع هندسي بعد ان اخذ بالاصطرلاب[92] ارتفاع مبتدا المنهى ومنتهى البناء المذكور الذي في اخره وجعله على وجه اذا امده النيل مدة[93] محررة وطلع على البنيان وجرى منه جرف بقوة التيار المار عليه ما لعله اجتمع في ارضه من حين انقطاع المدد عنه فاذا علا النيل بزيادته على ذلك الحد الذي يجرف الماء فيه بما رسب فيه وتناهى النيل في زيادته بطل ذلك الى ان ينتهي النيل في زيادته ويعود في نقصانه الى ذلك الحد فيجرف حينئذ ما لعله رسب في طول تلك المدة الى حين سد الفوهة بالقطعة وانقطاع جريان الماء على الحجر لا يزال ذلك كذلك ابدا.

[85] أ. س. يضيف: سبب.
[86] أ. س.: ينتهي.
[87] ساقط من أ. س.: الحكم.
[88] ط. م.:سنة 2600.
[89] ط. م.: الجيزة.
[90] أ. س.: عنيها.
[91] أ. س. يضيف: وتعالى.
[92] ط. م.: الاضطراب.
[93] أ. س.: مددة.

The Sixth Chapter

Account of the deterioration of its canal and the reason for that, and of those villages that have so fallen into ruin that their reconstruction can only be achieved by investing generous sums of money over a long period of time

I say — may God grant success — as already recounted in my book entitled 'A Seemly Demonstration of the Superiority of Egypt's King above All Others', that most celebrated and well-known wise men are from Egypt. The reason the [Egyptians] occupy themselves with science is their need for it in order to irrigate their land, [even] at a minimal level of the Nile flood. And they managed it and organized it, and God almighty granted them success, until all the Egyptian lands were irrigated by [flood level of] 12 cubits, while [flood] water that reached 20 cubits did no harm to the land. At that time, it never happened that the flooding was less than 12 cubits in any year, or that it exceeded 20 cubits.

However, these ancient traditions and sciences have fallen into oblivion and have become obliterated in the Egypt for 2,600 years.[20] And there is nothing left of these sciences with the sole exception of the Fayyum, which is irrigated by 12 cubits, whereas inundation of 20 [cubits] does no harm to it. [This was true] up to the year 628 [1230–31]. In that year the sultan, the blessed martyr al-Malik al-Kāmil — may God sanctify his spirit and illuminate his tomb! — inspected Giza and decreed that attention should be paid to certain dikes which he designated. He ordered the blocking of al-Ahrām Canal, so that the water from it was diverted (*taḥāmala*) onto the lands of Giza that were [until then] only irrigated by [a flood level of] 18 cubits, and since then are irrigated by 12 cubits. So God has thus revived the tradition, by his [the sultan's] hands.

Let us return to the reason for the deterioration of the Main Canal. This is because the one whom God — praise be to Him! — guided to excavate al-Manhā Canal and to build the solid dam (*bunyān*) at its endpoint, known as al-Lāhūn, did this according to principles of engineering, after he had measured with an astrolabe the altitude at the beginning of al-Manhā canal and at the crest of the dam (*bināʾ*) at the other end of the canal. He constructed it in such a fashion, so that when the Nile floods it for a certain period and [the water] rises up over the dam and flows from it, the force of the current, as it flows over the dam, washes away whatever had accumulated on its bed since the end of the [previous] flooding. But when the Nile rises up beyond that level at which the water washes away whatever has silted in it, and the inundation of the Nile reaches its peak (*tanāhā*), this [i.e., the washing away of the silt] ceases. Then, when the inundation of the Nile is over and [its level] decreases, it returns to that level, and washes away what may have accumulated in the course of that period, until the gap is closed with the 'bit' and the flow of water over the stone stops. This is always like that.

[20] Following AS: *mundhu alfaynī wa-sitmiʾa sana* (for 2,600 years). MP: *mundhu sanat alfaynī wa-sitmiʾa* (since the year 2,600). Shafei Bey, 'Fayoum Irrigation', p. 296, following Ball, *Contributions*, p. 221, finds a rationale to this calculation by reference to Herodotus. Since Herodotus writes that King Moeris, the king who supposedly created Lake Moeris (Lake Qārūn), lived nine hundred years before his own time, and since Herodotus himself wrote at 450 BC, the time that had passed since the creation of the lake until al-Nābulusī's day was 900+450+1245 = 2,595 years.

وبلغني من جماعة شتى من العقلاء شيء استفاض بينهم وهو ان ارض هذا البحر المنهى مما يلي اللاهون وهو البناء المحكم المشار اليه كانت مطبقة بالبلاط الثخين بل بالحجارة الملس الكبار المحكوكة الموضوعة حجر الى جنب حجر ليس بينهما خلل على هيئة البلاط وفي منتهى هذا التبليط تحت البناء المحكم بربخان كبيران من الرصاص يخرج منهما على الدوام والاستمرار ماء غليظ بالرمل والطين جعلا لتنظيف قعر البحر يخرج منهما كل ما يصل الى الموضع المبلط من الرسوب. فيؤمن بذلك[94] من ان يعمى هذا البحر ويتربى فيه الربوات ما يعسر عمله لانه لا يزال تحت الماء.

فدثر هذا الاثر وانسدت[95] البرابخ المذكورة من مدة بعيدة لا يعرف مبتداها وعلا على الموضع المبلط المذكور التراب والطين الى ان صار ارتفاع بناء الاهون عن ارض البحر سبعة اذرع فما دونها وصار الذي يرسب من الماء ايام زيادة النيل واتصاله ببحر المنهى اذا وصل الى الحجر وعلا عليه خرج في المنخفض الذي وراءه الى النيل يجرف النيل باكثره.

فلما اقطع الفيوم لامير يقال له فخر الدين عثمان استادار السلطان السعيد الشهيد الملك الكامل قدس الله روحه ونور ضريحه سنة ستمائة وعشرين وكان هذا فخر الدين المشار اليه رحمه الله لعلو همة السلطان السعيد الشهيد الكامل رحمه الله يود ان يظهر له اثر اجتهاده في كل ما يتولاه فبحث عن اسباب عمارة الفيوم فقيل له نظف بحره فقطع ما على حافتيه من سنط وصفصاف وغير ذلك حتى وسعه على ظن ان ذلك يزيد في مائه. فلم يؤثر ذلك شيئا الا عدم الاشجار وذهاب نضارة البحر بما على حافتيه من الشجر لكن لم يضر البحر قطع هذه الاشجار شيئا.

ثم قيل له لو عمل على البناء اليوسفي زيادة في ارتفاعه لكان رد الماء اكثر من رده وهو بهذا الاعتبار فاهتم به وزاد في البنيان المحكم المشار اليه قدر ذراع ونصف بذراع العمل في طول البناء المشار اليه[96] فتربى حينئذ التراب الذي كان يخرج منه وهو بذلك العلو القريب المحكم المقدر بالتقدير الهندسي لهذا الغرض وصار ما كان يخرج منه ويتنظف به ويرمى به النيل[97] لقصر البناء يجد البناء قد علا عن الموضع الحكمي فيترادد[98] التراب والرمل الى ان ربى ربوات في مواضع في[99] البحر المنهى وفي الموضع الذي يخرج منه ماء الفيوم امام فوهته دكة عظيمة من التراب تظهر هذه الدكة كل سنة في بشنش من شهور القبط وينضب[100] عنها الماء فيجتمع لها[101] الرجال من جميع بلاد الفيوم ويقطعونها بالمساحي ويشيلونها بالقفاف هذا والماء حينئذ يدخل من جانبيها في البحر الذي يصل الى الفيوم وبلاده من فوهتين ضيقتين سعة احداهما سبعة اذرع والاخرى خمسة اذرع في عمق لا يبلغ ذراعين.

[94] أ. س.: ذلك.
[95] أ. س.: استددت.
[96] ساقط من أ. س.: قدر ذراع ونصف بذراع العمل في طول البناء المشار إليه.
[97] ساقط من أ. س.: النيل.
[98] ط. م.: فترادد.
[99] ساقط من ط. م.: مواضع في.
[100] أ. س. يضيف الحاشية: الجوهري في صوابه نضب الماء ينضُبُ بالضم نضوبا أي غاد في الأرض وسقاها.
[101] ساقط من أ. س.: لها.

I learned from a group of wise men something that has become well-known among them. The bed of al-Manhā Canal next to al-Lāhūn, that is at the solid dam, was [once] overlaid with compact paving stones — or, more precisely, large smooth scraped stones, placed one next to the other so that there were no gaps between them, like paving stones. At the endpoint of this paving, beneath the solid structure, there were two large lead culverts from which viscid water mixed with sand and clay continuously escaped. The two culverts were made for the purpose of cleaning out the bottom of the canal, and all the silt that had piled up on the paved surface was scoured through them. That ensured that the canal would not be blocked, and prevented the formation of small mounds in it, which are difficult to repair, since they are submerged under water.

But this ancient apparatus has become obsolete, and the culverts have been blocked for a long time, it is not known since when. As a result, soil and clay accumulated on the paved surface until the height of the Lāhūn dam above the bed of the canal has been reduced to no more than seven cubits. Therefore, the sediment that subsides during the days of the Nile's inundation — when the water flows into al-Manhā Canal, reaches the dam and rises up over it to escape into the lower area (*munkhafaḍ*) which is behind it toward the Nile — is now mostly washed away by the Nile.

Then an amir called Fakhr al-Dīn ʿUthmān, the *Ustādār* (majordomo) of the sultan, the blessed martyr al-Malik al-Kāmil — may God sanctify his spirit and illuminate his tomb! — was bestowed the Fayyum as an *iqṭāʿ* in the year 620 [1223–24]. This Fakhr al-Dīn — may God have mercy upon him — because of the lofty concern of the sultan, the blessed martyr al-Malik al-Kāmil — may God have mercy upon him — desired to display to the sultan evidence of his efforts in all that he was in charge of. He looked for ways to bring about prosperity to the Fayyum, and was told: 'clean its canal'. So he cut the acacias and willows and other things on its two banks until he widened it, believing that this would increase its water [volume]. But it had no effect whatsoever, except for having no trees [on the banks], and the greenery of the canal has gone along with the trees on its banks. Yet, cutting these trees did no harm to the canal.

Then he was told that were Joseph's dam [at al-Lāhūn] to be raised, the amount of water it could hold back would be greater than the amount it currently holds. So he occupied himself with this, and he raised the dam by 1 ½ cubits — [measured in] work cubits — across the length of the dam. Thereafter, the soil that had been clearing out from it when it was of a short height, precisely calculated according to [principles of] engineering for this purpose, was forming mounds. Therefore, [the silt that] had been previously cleared out of it, cleaned and discarded by the Nile because of the shortness of the structure, was [now] finding that the structure had risen above its proper place. The soil and the sand were thus held back so that they formed mounds within al-Manhā Canal, and a huge shoal of soil was formed in the place from which the water exits for the Fayyum, in front of the opening.[21] This shoal becomes visible every year in the Coptic month of Bashans [9 May–7 June], and the water gets absorbed[22] in it. Men from all the villages of the Fayyum gather for it and they cut it with shovels, carrying it off with large baskets. Then the water bypasses the shoal from both sides, entering the canal that connects to the Fayyum and its villages through two narrow mouths. The width of one of them is seven cubits, and of the other five cubits, and their depth does not even reach two cubits.

[21] As al-Nābulusī mentions on several occasions, the place from which water enters the Fayyum is located 2,100 cubits west of al-Lāhūn Dam.

[22] AS adds a marginal note (*ḥāshiya*) by a later reader: 'Al-Jawharī [determined] the correct form (*fī ṣawābihi*) as [the verb] *naḍaba al-māʾ* [the water absorbed], *yanḍubu bi'l-ḍamm*; absorption (*nuḍūban*), that is [the water] went into the ground and watered it.' The note refers to the famous lexicographer Abū Naṣr Ismāʿīl al-Jawharī (d. *c.* AD 1005), whose dictionary *Tāj al-lugha wa-ṣiḥāḥ al-ʿArabiyya* (commonly known as *al-Ṣiḥāḥ*), was widely used until the modern era; see L. Kopf, 'al-Djawharī', *The Encyclopedia of Islam*, 2nd edn, II, 495–97.

ثم اراد فخر الدين عثمان المذكور رحمه الله ان يجتهد اجتهادا زائدا فاخذ العوامل الكثيرة ومضى الى راس بحر المنهى واستصحب قوما يعرفون بالمهندسين من اهل القرية المعروفة باللاهون وهي بقرب البناء المشار اليه عادتهم ان يتولوا[102] وضع القطعة المقدم ذكرها في الباب الرابع ولذلك سموا مهندسين لا لعلم بالهندسة ولا عمل فلما مضى بهم الى راس بحر المنهى راوا ان تفتح فوهة تحت فوهته القديمة المتصلة بالنيل بما يناهز مائة قصبة وما حولها ففتحوها بعد تعب وغرامة كثيرة فصار الماء الذي يدخل من فوهة المنهى القديم يخرج بعضه من هذه الفوهة الى النيل. فقصد هؤلاء المسمون بالمهندسين زيادة ماء بحر المنهى فنقص بتدبيرهم لكن تدارك الله عز وجل بحر المنهى بسد الفوهة التي فتحوها تحت الفوهة القديمة فانسدت بالرمل والطين في سنتين واراح الله تعالى الفيوم من ضررها فانها كانت تذهب ببعض مائه الداخل من فوهته الاصلية.

ثم اراد هؤلاء المسمون بالمهندسين ان يغرق جملة من المراكب الكبار في تجاه فوهة المنهى المتصلة بالنيل فغرقها على ظن ان يربي الماء عليها رملا وتبقى جزيرة ترد الماء الى فوهة المنهى فقوي النيل عليها وخرج من ورائها لغلطهم في وضعها غير موضعها وصارت جزيرة كبيرة في راس بحر المنهى يتصوب ماء النيل من ورائها فقل لذلك ماء بحر المنهى وصار راس المنهى يجف كل سنة ثمانية اشهر فهذا سبب اخر من اسباب تغير بحره.

فصل: واما ما دثر من بلاده حتى عسر تداركه الا بالاموال الجزيلة والمدة الطويلة فاقول وبالله التوفيق انه قد شاع وطرق الاسماع ما نقله الخلف عن السلف في امر الفيوم انه كان بركة مملوءة ماء يتنصل اليها ماء الصعيد وانه لما اهتم بها من قدر الله عمارة الفيوم على يديه اما[103] يوسف الصديق كما قيل او غيره من الحكماء واحتفر لها بحر المنهى واحكم البناء المقدم ذكره في اخره واحتفر البحر الذي يدخل الى البحر الذي بينه وبين البناء المحكم الفان ومائة ذراع كما تقدم. ونصل اكثر ماء البركة المحتفرة[104] في هذا البحر الذي يدخل[105] الفيوم بحرين بحرا قبليا يسمى تنبطويه يذهب من القبلة تحت الجبل نحو الغرب يقطع نصف دائرة الفيوم فوق اراض متصلة بسفح الجبل مكشوفة عن الماء. وبحرا بحريا مقابلا للبحر الاول يقال له وردان. يمر هذا البحر الثاني بحريا تحت الجبل نحو الغرب ايضا يقطع نصف دائرة الفيوم الاخرى بحيث يكاد ان يتراءى طرفاه. ينتهي طرف كل واحد[106] منهما الى بركة السمك بحيث لو فضل في[107] احدهما ماء لرمى ماؤه في بركة السمك فبحر وردان ينتهي طرفه الى البركة التي تجاه منية اقنى. وطرف تنبطويه ينتهي الى ماء البركة التي عند قصر قارون.

102 أ. س.: يتولدوا.
103 أ. س.: أيام.
104 أ. س.: المحتفرة; ط. م.: احفر; مخطوطة القاهرة (م. ق.): احتفر.
105 أ. س. يضيف: إلى.
106 ساقط من أ. س.: واحد.
107 أ. س.: من.

Consequently, Fakhr ad-Dīn ʿUthmān — may God have mercy upon him — desired to invest even more efforts, and so he took many beasts of burden and brought them to the head of al-Manhā Canal [i.e., where it branches off from the Nile]. He took along a group of people known as engineers, from among the people of the village called al-Lāhūn. This village lies in the vicinity of the dam, and it is their custom to oversee the operation of installing the 'bit' that was mentioned in the fourth chapter. For that reason they are called engineers, not for their knowledge of engineering or for their experience of it. And when he brought them to the head of al-Manhā Canal, they advised that an opening be cut below the old Nile opening at a distance of about one hundred *qaṣaba* or so. And so they cut it with much toil and cost, but then some of the water that used to enter from the old opening of al-Manhā began to escape from this opening [back] into the Nile. The so-called engineers intended to increase the water of al-Manhā Canal, yet by their scheme it was actually reduced. However, God — the almighty and majestic — replenished al-Manhā Canal by blocking off the opening that they had cut below the old opening with sand and clay over the course of two years. And God the exalted thus relieved the Fayyum from this harm, as it was causing the loss of some of the water entering through the original opening.

Then those so-called engineers wanted to sink several large boats in front of the Nile opening of al-Manhā Canal. So they sank them, believing that the water would pile up sand upon them, forming an island that would divert the water into the opening of al-Manhā Canal. But the force of the Nile's current has overcome it, and because of their mistake in placing the boats in a wrong location, the water was diverted around it. A huge island was formed at the head of al-Manhā Canal, with the water of the Nile flowing behind it. For this reason, the water of al-Manhā Canal has now decreased, and the head of al-Manhā Canal began drying up every year for eight months. This is another reason for the deterioration of its canal.

Section: With regard to those villages that have so fallen into ruin that their redevelopment could only be achieved by investing generous sums of money over a long period of time. I say — may God grant success! — that on the matter of the Fayyum, it has been known for generations, and has spread far and wide, that the Fayyum had been a lake full of water into which the water of Upper Egypt drained. When the one whom God chose to develop the Fayyum — whether it was Joseph the righteous as has been said, or someone else from among the wise men — had become occupied with it, he dug for it al-Manhā Canal, and then ingeniously built the dam at its end. He also dug the canal that flows into the [Main] Canal — at a distance of 2,100 cubits from the reinforced dam, as has been mentioned — and drained off most of the water of the lake.

He then dug two canals issuing from the canal that enters the Fayyum. One is a southern canal called Tanabṭawayh,[23] which flows in a southerly direction, under the mountain towards the west, along the semicircle of the Fayyum, and above lands that are at the foot of the mountain and from which the water had withdrawn. [The second is] a northern canal called Waradān, which is opposite the first canal.[24] This second canal passes in a northern direction, under the mountain and towards the west as well, along the other semicircle of the Fayyum, so that its two ends almost meet each other. Both terminate at the fishery lake, so that any surplus of water in one of them is cast into the fishery lake. Waradān Canal terminates in the lake at a point opposite Minyat Aqnā, and Tanabṭawayh [Canal] terminates in the lake near Qaṣr Qārūn.[25]

23 Al-Maqrīzī, *Kitāb al-mawāʿiẓ*, ed. by Wiet, I, 248: Baḥr Binṭāwh (بحر بنطاوة); Halm, *Ägypten*, p. 243: Baḥr Tanabṭawaih; Salmon, 'Répertoire', p. 70: Baḥr Tanabṭawayh.

24 Halm, *Ägypten*, p. 243: Baḥr Waradān; Salmon, 'Répertoire', p. 31: Baḥr Waradān.

25 Modern location: Qārūn (قارون). Halm, *Ägypten*, p. 268: Qaṣr = Qaṣr Qārūn;

فلما توالت السنون وتعاقبت الدهور واختلفت عليه الاعوام والشهور واستمر اهمال الاهتمام بها وربى الطرح عليها حتى علت بالتراب وصار طرفا كل بحر مسامتا[108] لوسطه في[109] الارض الابليزية وسفا الهواء الرمل فيما مر منه في الاراضي الرملية وانقطع جريان الماء فيها ودثر ما كان من البلاد عليهما.

فاما بحر تنبطويه المذكور اولا، فالذي دثر من بلاده من الجهة القبلية:[110] تنبطويه، وطَبا، وشلاّ، واطفيح، واهريت المنقلبة، وحدادة، وجزازة وقيل زجاجة، وسنهورس، وبَرجتوت،[111] * وسُدُو، وسدرا، وبدريس، وسنهابه، واقنى، وتنهما، وخراب قاسم، وبني برى، وتنهمت السدر، وقصر قارون، وزَرزرة،[112] والريان.

هذه البلاد المذكورة دثرت بحيث ما فيها ساكن ولا بها قاطن.

واما البلاد التي دثرت على هذا البحر المسمى تنبطويه المشار اليه في لحف[113] الجبل، وعوض عنه تحته في الاراضي التي انكشفت من الماء وهي الان عامرة زارعة من الجانب القبلي والغربي. فبُلجسوق في الجبل دثرت وعمر تحتها بلدة عوضها[114] وسميت باسمها بُلجسوق القبلية وهي الان زارعة. وكذلك طِليت دثرت في الجبل وعمر تحتها بلدة تسمى بطليت وهي الان زارعة. وكذلك ام السباع دثرت وعمر تحتها بلدة قريبة من خليج دلية،[115] سميت بام السباع وهي الان زارعة. وكذلك حدادة دثرت وعمر تحتها بلدة وسميت بحدادة وهي الان زارعة.

الجانب البحري دُمَيه عمر عوضها بمويه وهي الان زارعة.

واما البلاد التي دثرت على وردان فهي: اللواسي، وام المعاصر،[116] وام الابراج، ودُمَيديم، وسمسطوس، وشيم، وام الاثل، وسونيس،[117] ودميه، ودار الضرب.

فهذان البحران قد دثرا دثورا لا يمكن عمارتهما الا كما ذكرت في المدة الطويلة بالاموال الجزيلة ولعل اكثر البلاد التي في وسط الفيوم الان محدثة العمارة بعد تنصل ماء الفيوم عنها وربما استغنى بها عما وصفنا من الخراب الداثر وقد رايت في بلاد الفيوم العامرة الان بلادا خرابا داثرة صار اهل البلاد العامرة الان يزرعون اراضي هذه البلاد الداثرة من سنين عديدة حتى لقد استرجعت منها حين تاليف هذا الكتاب ما امكن استرجاعه منها دون ما لم يمكن استرجاعه الا بايلام القلوب وخوف الجاء ساكنيها الى الهروب.

However, as years passed by, and epochs succeeded one another, and years and months came and went, the neglect of the canals continued, and alluvial deposits built up in them so that they were covered with soil, and the elevation at the end of each canal came to be level with the alluvial land in its middle. Moreover, wind scattered sand when it passed through sandy areas. As a result, the flow of water in both was cut off, and the villages on them were deserted.

As for Tanabṭawayh Canal, which was mentioned first, its villages that had been deserted in the southern area are Tanabṭawayh; Ṭabā; Shallā; Iṭfīḥ; Ihrīt al-Munqalaba; Ḥaddāda; Juzāza, or, as some say, Zujāja; Sanhūris; Burjtūt; Sudū; Sidrā; Badrīs; Sanhāba; Aqnā; Tanhamā; Kharāb Qāsim; Banī Barī; Tanhamat al-Sidr; Qaṣr Qārūn; Zarzura; al-Rayyān. These villages were deserted so that there is no dweller or resident in them.

Those deserted villages on this Tanabṭawayh Canal which were located at the foot of the mountain have now been replaced by villages below the canal, on the lands from which water had withdrawn. They are now inhabited and cultivated in the southern and western regions. Buljusūq on the mountain was deserted and a village was built below it in its stead, called by the same name, Buljusūq al-Qibliyya (the Southern). It is now cultivated. Likewise, Ṭalīt on the mountain was deserted, and a village also called Ṭalīt was built below it, now cultivated. Umm al-Sibāʿ was also deserted, and a village called Umm al-Sibāʿ was built below it, near Dilya Canal (*khalīj*),[26] and it is now cultivated. Ḥaddāda was deserted too, and a village called Ḥaddāda was built below it, now cultivated.

In the northern region, Damya was replaced by Bamawayh, which is now cultivated.

The deserted villages on Waradān Canal are al-Lawāsī; Umm al-Maʿāṣir; Umm al-Abrāj; Dumaydīm; Samasṭūs; Shaym; Umm al-Athal; Sūnīs; Damya; Dār al-Ḍarb.

These two canals have fallen into ruin to the extent that it is impossible to refurbish them, except, as I mentioned, over a long period of time and with considerable expense. However, as most of the current villages in the centre of the Fayyum are newly built after the retreat of the Fayyum's water from them, they possibly make up for all the deserted and derelict villages which we have mentioned. [Moreover], I have observed that the people of villages currently inhabited have begun sowing the lands of those villages that had been deserted for many years. So much so, that the land reclaimed at the time of writing this book is all that is possible to reclaim, short of what would be impossible to reclaim without coercion (*īlām al-qulūb*) and risking the flight of the inhabitants.

108 أ. س.: مساقيا.

109 أ. س.: من.

110 ساقط من أ. س.: من الجهة القبلية.

111 أ. س.: بَر شتوت.

112 أ. س.: زَرزوره.

113 أ. س.: لفح.

114 أ. س.: ارضها.

115 ط. م.: دليلة.

116 أ. س.: وام العاص.

117 أ. س.: سرنيس.

Salmon, 'Répertoire', p. 62; Ibn al-Jīʿān, *Kitāb al-tuḥfa*, p. 158: al-Qaṣr min nawāḥī al-jibāl; Ramzī, *Al-Qāmūs*, II/III, 73–74: Qārūn, the Roman Dionysias.

26 Halm, *Ägypten*, p. 243: Khalīj Dīla, as mentioned by al-Maqrīzī (*Kitāb al-mawāʿiẓ*, ed. by Wiet, I, 248–49); Salmon, 'Répertoire', p. 32: Baḥr Dilīa; Shafei Bey, 'Fayoum Irrigation': Baḥr Delahe (on the map).

الباب السابع

في ذكر اسماء بلاده على حروف المعجم ليسهل تناولها على الطالب ويسرع العلم بها على الراغب.

حرف الالف:

المدينة
الملالية
العدوة
الاستنباط
ابريزيا والزربي
ابهيت من كفور سنورس
اخصاص الحلاق من كفور سنورس
القُبَرا من كفور سنورس[118]
اخصاص العجميين
اطسا
ابو كسا
اهريت
ابشاية الرمان
الطارمة
اللاهون وام النحارير
الحمام
ام السباع
الهيشة وهي المفردة[119] باللاهون
المهيمسي من كفور قمبشا[120]
القلهانة من كفور قمبشا[121]
اقلول من حقوق خليج دِلية
الصفاونة وتنفشار من حقوق خليج دلية[122]
الكوم الاحمر من حقوق بمويه
الحنبوشية وقف المدرسة المالكية بمصر المحروسة[123]
الروبيون وقف المدرسة الشافعية التقوية بمدينة الفيوم
الاعلام وقف المدرسة المالكية بمصر

حرف الباء:

بيبج فرح
بوصير دفدنو
باجة
بيبج النيلة من كفور اهريت

118 ساقط من أ. س.: القُبَرا من كفور سنورس.
119 أ. س.: وهو المفرد.
120 أ. س.: قنبشا.
121 أ. س.: قنبشا.
122 ساقط من أ. س.: الصفاونة وتنفشار من حقوق خليج دلية.
123 أ. س. يضيف: المحروسة.

The Seventh Chapter

List of the names of its villages, arranged by the letters of the alphabet for the convenience of anyone consulting it, so as to allow anyone who so wishes to quickly acquaint himself with them

The letter 'alif':

al-Madīna [i.e., Madīnat al-Fayyūm]
al-Malāliyya
al-ʿIdwa
al-Istinbāṭ
Ibrīziyā and al-Zarbī
Abhīt, one of the hamlets of Sinnūris
Akhṣāṣ al-Ḥallāq, one of the hamlets of Sinnūris
al-Qubarāʾ, one of the hamlets of Sinnūris
Akhṣāṣ al-ʿAjamiyyīn
Iṭsā
Abū Ksā
Ihrīt
Ibshāyat al-Rummān
al-Ṭārima
al-Lāhūn and Umm al-Nakhārīr
al-Ḥammām
Umm al-Sibāʿ
al-Haysha, belongs to al-Lāhūn
al-Mahīmsī, one of the hamlets of Qambashā
al-Qalhāna, one of the hamlets of Qambashā
Uqlūl, included in the accounts (*min ḥuqūq*)[27] of Dilya Canal
al-Ṣafāwina and Tanafshār, included in the accounts of Dilya Canal
al-Kawm al-Aḥmar, included in the accounts of Bamawayh
al-Ḥanbūshiyya, an endowment of the Malikite Madrasa in the well-protected city of Miṣr (al-Fusṭāṭ)
al-Rūbiyyūn, an endowment of the Taqawiyya Shafiʿite Madrasa in Madīnat al-Fayyūm[28]
al-Aʿlām, a endowment of the Malikite Madrasa in Miṣr (al-Fusṭāṭ)

The letter 'bāʾ':

Babīj Faraḥ
Būṣīr Difidnū
Bāja
Babīj al-Nīla, one of the hamlets of Ihrīt

[27] The phrase *min ḥuqūq*, literally 'from the rights of', is used throughout the treatise in the sense of a subsidiary village that is reposnsible for its own taxes, yet is also part of a larger *iqṭāʿ* unit, be it an *iqṭāʿ* unit formed of cluster of villages along the same canal, or hamlets attached to a larger mother village.

[28] A madrasa established by the Ayyubid prince Taqī al-Dīn al-Muẓaffar ʿUmar, the nephew of Saladin, who held the Fayyum as *iqṭāʿ* between 579/1183 and 582/1186. It was called the Taqawiyya after his name. See al-Maqrīzī, *Kitāb al-mawāʿiẓ*, ed. by Sayyid, IV, 458; Ibn Khallikān, *Wafayāt al-aʿyān*, ed. by ʿAbbās, III, 456.

بلالة من حقوق خليج دلية	Bilāla, included in the accounts of Dilya Canal
بشطا من حقوق خليج دلية	Bushṭā, included in the accounts of Dilya Canal
بيهمو من حقوق سنورس	Biyahmū, included in the accounts of Sinnūris
بمويه	Bamawayh
ببيج انشو	Babīj Unshū
بور سينرو	Būr Sīnarū
ببيج انقاش	Babīj Anqāsh
ببيج اندير	Babīj Andīr
ببيج غيلان وكوم الرمل	Babīj Ghaylān and Kawm al-Raml
بلجسوق من حقوق خليج تنبطويه	Buljusūq, included in the accounts of Tanabṭawayh Canal
بياض	Bayāḍ
بنديق وبورها	Bandīq and Būr Bandīq
حرف التاء:	**The letter 'tā'':**
ترسا	Tirsā
تطون من حقوق خليج تنبطويه	Tuṭūn, included in the accounts of Tanabṭawayh Canal
حرف الثاء:	**The letter 'thā'':**
ثلاث	Thalāth
حرف الجيم:	**The letter 'jīm':**
جرفس من كفور سنورس	Jarfis, one of the hamlets of Sinnūris
جردو وكفورها	Jardū and its hamlets
حرف الحاء:	**The letter 'ḥā'':**
حدادة	Ḥaddāda
حرف الخاء:	**The letter 'khā'':**
خور الرماد	Khawr al-Rammād
خراب جندي والمصلوب	Kharāb Jundī and al-Maṣlūb
حرف الدال:	**The letter 'dāl':**
دسيا[124]	Disyā
دموشية	Dumūshiyya
دفدنو	Difidnū
دنفارة جردو	Dinfārat Jardū
دنفارة اهريت[125]	Dinfārat Ihrīt
دمشقين البصل	Dimashqīn al-Baṣal
دموه الداثر	Dimūh al-Dāthir
دموه اللاهون	Dimūh al-Lāhūn
دهما من حقوق خليج دلية	Dahmā, included in the accounts of Dilya Canal
حرف الذال:	**The letter 'dhāl':**
ذات الصفاء واخصاص[126] النجار كفرها	Dhāt al-Ṣafā' and Akhṣāṣ al-Najjār, its hamlet
حرف الراء: خال.[127]	**The letter 'rā'':** blank [no village entry for this letter]
حرف الزاى: خال.[128]	**The letter 'zā'':** blank [no village entry for this letter]

---

124 أ. س.: دميا.
125 أ. س.: دنفارة القريب.
126 ط. م.: اجصاص.
127 أ. س. يضيف: خال.
128 أ. س. يضيف: خال.

حرف السين:	The letter 'sīn':
سنهور من حقوق بمويه	Sanhūr, included in the accounts of Bamawayh
سنورس	Sinnūris
سرسنا	Sirisnā
سيلة	Sīla
سينرو	Sīnarū
سدمنت	Sidmant
حرف الشين:	The letter 'shīn':
شسفة من حقوق سنورس	Shisfa, included in the accounts of Sinnūris
شلالة من حقوق سنورس	Shallāla, included in the accounts of Sinnūris
شانة من نواحي الشرقية	Shāna, among the villages of al-Sharqiyya Canal
ششها من حقوق خليج دلية	Shushhā, included in the accounts of Dilya Canal
شدموه من حقوق خليج دلية	Shidmūh, included in the accounts of Dilya Canal
حرف الصاد:	The letter 'ṣād':
صنوفر	Ṣunūfar
حرف الضاد: خال.[129]	The letter 'ḍād':
	blank [no village entry for this letter]
حرف الطاء:	The letter 'ṭā'':
طما	Ṭimā
طليت من حقوق خليج تنبطويه	Ṭalīt, included in the accounts of Tanabṭawayh Canal
طبهار	Ṭubhār
حرف العين:	The letter ''ayn':
عنز	ʿAnz
حرف الغين:	The letter 'ghayn':
غابة باجة	Ghābat Bāja
حرف الفاء:	The letter 'fā'':
فانو	Fānū
فرقس	Furqus
فدمين	Fidimīn
حرف القاف:	The letter 'qāf':
قمبشا	Qambashā
قشوش	Qushūsh
حرف الكاف:	The letter 'kāf':
كنبوت من حقوق خليج دلية	Kanbūt, included in the accounts of Dilya Canal
حرف اللام: خال.[130]	The letter 'lām':
	blank [no village entry for this letter]
حرف الميم:	The letter 'mīm':
منية الاسقف	Minyat al-Usquf
منية كربيس واخصاص بو عصية	Minyat Karbīs and Akhṣāṣ [A]bū ʿUṣayya
منشاة ابن كردى من حقوق سنورس	Munsha'at Ibn Kurdī, included in the accounts of Sinnūris
منشاة الطواحين	Munsha'at al-Ṭawāḥīn
منشاة ابي خزعل من حقوق دنفارة اهريت	Munsha'at Abū Khazʿal, included in the accounts of Dinfārat Ihrīt
منشاة علكان من حقوقها	Munsha'at ʿAlikān (?), [also] included in the accounts of [Dinfārat Ihrīt]
منشاة خلاص من حقوق دنفارة اهريت	Munsha'at Khalāṣ, included in the accounts of Dinfārat Ihrīt

129 أ. س. يضيف: خال.

130 ساقط من ط. م.: حرف اللام: خال.

منية اقنى وكفورها وهي:
دقلوه،
منشاة حويت
منشاة غيلان
منشاة الاثلة[131] تعرف بزيد بن كثير
والفحامة
منشاة شرف وهي للاستنباط
منشاة الوسطى وهي للاستنباط
منشاة الصفصاف وهي للاستنباط
منشاة المقاسم وهي للاستنباط[132]
منشاة سراج وهي للاستنباط
منشاة ابي سالم وهي للاستنباط
منشاة تعرف ببرك البيض للاستنباط
منشاة المعصوبة للاستنباط[133]
منشاة العثمانية لاهريت
منشاة تعرف بابراهيم الجعفري لاقلول
منشاة المطوع وهي لبلالة[134]
منشاة اولاد ابي زكري لبلالة
منشاة عثمان لبلالة
منشاة اولاد زيدان لبلالة المعروفة بالاكراد
منشاة نعيم لبمويه
منشاة المقاسم لبمويه[135]
منشاة شرف لببيج اندير
منشاة ابي حاتم لببيج اندير
منشاة ابريشة لببيج اندير
منشاة الغصيني لببيج اندير
منشاة خامسة
منية ابي سالم لدنفارة جردو
منشاة المرج لدسيا
منشاة موسى لدنفارة جردو[136]
مطر طارس
مسجد عائشة
منشاة اولاد عرفه من حقوق[137] خليج دلية[138] وكفورها
منية البطس القديمة
منية ششها من حقوق دلية
مقران ومنتارة
منية البطس
منية الديك وبني مجنون وشلمص
مجنون
مطول
مقطول والربيات بالشرقية
منشاة الهلالي من كفور جردو

131 أ. س.: الاتله.
132 ساقط من أ. س.: منشأة الصفصاف وهي للاستنباط منشأة المقاسم وهي للاستنباط.
133 ساقط من أ. س.: منشأة تعرف ببرك البيض للاستنباط منشأة المعصوبة للاستنباط.
134 أ. س.: منشأة تعرف بإبراهيم الجعفري لاقلول منشأة المطوع وهي لبلالة منشأة العثمانية لإهريت.
135 أ. س.: مبويه.
136 ساقط من أ. س.: منشأة المرج لدسيا منشأة موسى لدنفارة جردو.
137 ط. م.:كفور.
138 ط. م.: دليلة.

Minyat Aqnā and its hamlets, which are:
Diqlawa
Munshaʾat Ḥuwayt
Munshaʾat Ghaylān
Munshaʾat al-Athila, known as Zayd Ibn Kathīr
al-Faḥḥāma
Munshaʾat Sharaf, [a hamlet] of al-Istinbāṭ
Munshaʾat al-Wusṭā, [a hamlet] of al-Istinbāṭ
Munshaʾat al-Ṣafṣāf, [a hamlet] of al-Istinbāṭ
Munshaʾat al-Maqāsim, [a hamlet] of al-Istinbāṭ
Munshaʾat Sirāj, [a hamlet] of al-Istinbāṭ
Munshaʾat Abū Sālim, [a hamlet] of al-Istinbāṭ
Munshaʾa known as Birak al-Bayḍ, [a hamlet] of al-Istinbāṭ
Munshaʾat al-Maʿṣūba,[29] [a hamlet] of al-Istinbāṭ
Munshaʾat al-ʿUthmāniyya,[30] [a hamlet] of Ihrīt
Munshaʾa known as Ibrāhīm al-Jaʿfarī, [a hamlet] of Uqlūl
Munshaʾat al-Muṭawwiʿ, [a hamlet] of Bilāla
Munshaʾat Awlād Abī Zikrī, [a hamlet] of Bilāla
Munshaʾat ʿUthmān, [a hamlet] of Bilāla
Munshaʾat Awlād Zaydān, [a hamlet] of Bilāla, known as 'al-Akrād' [the Kurds].
Munshaʾat Naʿīm, [a hamlet] of Bamawayh
Munshaʾat al-Maqāsim, [a hamlet] of Bamawayh
Munshaʾat Sharaf, [a hamlet] of Babīj Andīr
Munshaʾat Abī Ḥātim, [a hamlet] of Babīj Andīr
Munshaʾat Ibrīsha,[31] [a hamlet] of Babīj Andīr
Munshaʾat al-Ghuṣaynī, [a hamlet] of Babīj Andīr
A fifth Munshaʾa [of Babīj Andīr]
Minyat Abī Sālim, [a hamlet] of Dinfārat Jardū
Munshaʾat al-Marj, [a hamlet] of Disyā
Munshaʾat Mūsā, [a hamlet] of Dinfārat Jardū
Miṭr Ṭāris
Masjid ʿĀʾisha
Munshaʾat Awlād ʿArafa, a hamlet included in the accounts of Dilya Canal
Minyat al-Baṭs, the old village
Minyat Shushhā, included in the accounts of Dilya [Canal]
Muqrān and Mintāra
Minyat al-Baṭs
Minyat al-Dīk, Banū Majnūn and Shalmaṣ
Muṭūl
Maqṭūl and al-Rubiyyāt on al-Sharqiyya Canal
Munshaʾat al-Hilālī, one of the hamlets of Jardū

29 Elsewhere in the treatise called Munshaʾat al-Makhṣūba.
30 Elsewhere in the treatise called Munshaʾat al-ʿAthāmina.
31 Elsewhere in the treatise called Munshaʾat Awlād Ibrāsha.

حرف النون:	The letter 'nūn':
نقليفة	Naqalīfa
ناموسة وناموسة	Nāmūsa and Nāmūsa
حرف الهاء:	The letter 'hāʾ':
هوارة	Hawwāra
هيشة دموشية المعروفة بمنشاة ربيع	Hayshat Dumūshiyya, known as Munshaʾat Rabīʿ
هوارة البحرية	Hawwāra al-Baḥriyya

الباب الثامن

في ذكر الجوامع والمساجد والديرة والكنائس

اقول وبالله التوفيق لما كانت البلاد يزينها ما بها من الجوامع والمساجد ويحسنها اهل الصلاة ما بين الراكع والساجد اردت ان اصف ما بالفيوم منها واعبر بما شهد به ديوان الاحباس عنها.

والذي يشتمل عليه الفيوم وبلاده[139] من الجوامع والمساجد ثمانين معبدا. تفصيل ذلك:

الجوامع خمسة واربعون جامعا:

الجامع العتيق بالمدينة تقام فيه الجمعة.
الجامع البراني المعروف باليوسفي بحري المدينة.
جامع بسيلة تقام فيه الجمعة، ذكر انه جامع يعقوب عليه السلام.
جامع بابريزيا خرب بحكم خراب الناحية ونقلت الخطبة الى الزربي.
جامع بمطر طارس تقام فيه الجمعة.
جامع بالعدوة تقام فيه الجمعة.
جامع بذات الصفاء، شريف، تقام فيه الجمعة مكتوب فيه ان جماعة من الصحابة مدفونون في البلد حوله.
جامع بسنورس تقام فيه الجمعة.
جامع بابهيت تقام فيه الجمعة.
جامع ببيهمو تقام فيه الجمعة.
جامع بمنيه البطس تقام فيه الجمعة.
جامع بالطارمة تقام فيه الجمعة.
جامع بمويه تقام فيه الجمعة.
جامع بابشاية الرمان تقام فيه الجمعة.
جامع ببيج انقاش تقام فيه الجمعة.
جامع بمنية اقنى تقام فيه الجمعة.
جامع بطبهار تقام فيه الجمعة.
جامع بسينرو تقام فيه الجمعة.
جامع بابي كسا تقام فيه الجمعة.
جامع ببيج انشو تقام فيه الجمعة.
جامع ببيج فرح تقام فيه الجمعة.
جامع جردو تقام فيه الجمعة.
جامع فانو تقام فيه الجمعة.
جامع نقليفة تقام فيه الجمعة.
جامع فدمين تقام فيه الجمعة.
جامع مطول[140] تقام فيه الجمعة.
جامع قشوش تقام فيه الجمعة.
جامع ترسا تقام فيه الجمعة.

[139] ساقط من أ. س.: وبلاده.
[140] أ. س.: نطول.

The Eighth Chapter

Account of its congregational mosques (*jawāmiʿ*), neighbourhood mosques (*masājid*), monasteries, and churches

I say — and may God grant success — as any land is adorned by the congregational mosques and neighbourhood mosques in it, and beautified by the bowing and prostration of the people of prayer, I wanted to describe those which are in the Fayyum, and to relate that which is attested in their regard at the Ministry of Endowments (*Dīwān al-Aḥbās*).

The Fayyum and its villages contain eighty places of worship — congregational mosques and neighbourhood mosques.

This includes 45 congregational mosques, as follows:

The old congregational mosque in Madīnat [al-Fayyūm]. The Friday prayer is held in it.

The extramural congregational mosque, known as 'the Yūsufī', north of the city.

The congregational mosque at Sīla. The Friday prayer is held in it. It is said to be the mosque of Jacob (Yaʿqūb), peace be upon him.

The congregational mosque at Ibrīziyā. It was deserted following the abandonment of the village, and the Friday sermon moved to al-Zarbī.

The congregational mosque at Miṭr Ṭāris. The Friday prayer is held in it.

The congregational mosque at al-ʿIdwa. The Friday prayer is held in it.

A distinguished congregational mosque at Dhāt al-Ṣafāʾ. The Friday prayer is held in it. An inscription inside says that a group of the Companions of the Prophet are buried in the grounds around it.

The congregational mosque at Sinnūris. The Friday prayer is held in it.

The congregational mosque at Abhīt. The Friday prayer is held in it.

The congregational mosque at Biyahmū. The Friday prayer is held in it.

The congregational mosque at Minyat al-Baṭs. The Friday prayer is held in it.

The congregational mosque at al-Ṭārima. The Friday prayer is held in it.

The congregational mosque at Bamawayh. The Friday prayer is held in it.

The congregational mosque at Ibshāyat al-Rummān. The Friday prayer is held in it.

The congregational mosque at Babīj Anqāsh. The Friday prayer is held in it.

The congregational mosque at Minyat Aqnā. The Friday prayer is held in it.

The congregational mosque at Ṭubhār. The Friday prayer is held in it.

The congregational mosque at Sīnarū. The Friday prayer is held in it.

The congregational mosque at Abū Ksā. The Friday prayer is held in it.

The congregational mosque at Babīj Unshū. The Friday prayer is held in it.

The congregational mosque at Babīj Faraḥ. The Friday prayer is held in it.

The congregational mosque at Jardū. The Friday prayer is held in it.

The congregational mosque at Fānū. The Friday prayer is held in it.

The congregational mosque at Naqalīfa. The Friday prayer is held in it.

The congregational mosque at Fidimīn. The Friday prayer is held in it.

The congregational mosque at Muṭūl. The Friday prayer is held in it.

The congregational mosque of Qushūsh. The Friday prayer is held in it.

The congregational mosque of Tirsā. The Friday prayer is held in it.

جامع اللاهون تقام فيه الجمعة، شريف من الايام اليوسفية.
جامع بلجسوق تقام فيه الجمعة.
جامع قمبشا[141] تقام فيه الجمعة.
جامع اقلول تقام فيه الجمعة.
جامع بوصير دفدنو تقام [فيه] الجمعة.
جامع اهريت تقام فيه الجمعة.
جامع اخصاص العجميين تقام فيه الجمعة.
جامع بشطا تقام فيه الجمعة.
جامع فرقس، شريف، تجاب فيه الدعوات، تقام فيه الجمعة.
جامع دموشية تقام فيه الجمعة.
جامع دفدنو تقام فيه الجمعة.
جامع سرسنا تقام فيه الجمعة.
جامع شانة تقام فيه الجمعة.
جامع ششها تقام فيه الجمعة.
جامع منيه ششها تقام فيه الجمعة.
جامع قاي تقام فيه الجمعة.
جامع منشاة قاي تقام فيه الجمعة. وذكرت قاي في الفيوم لانها مضافة اليها[142] في القضاء والاحباس.

واما عدة المساجد بالمدينة[143] وغيرها، فخمسة وثلاثون مسجدا. تفصيله:
مسجد الفرج المطل على السوق.
مسجد بسوق القطانين يعرف بابن الرفعة.
مسجد بسوق القطانين ايضا.
مسجد يعرف باليمنى.
مسجد يعرف بمسجد السلام مجاور الجامع.
مسجد يعرف بالرضى بن الشليل بقناطر[144] الزمام.
مسجد بجوار المدرسة الحسامية.
مسجد يعرف بمسجد الجاولي.
مسجد مطل على سوق البزازين يعرف بابراهيم القوصي.
مسجد يعرف باولاد عبد الوهاب.
مسجد يعرف بانشاء القاضي كمال الدين بن حامد.
مسجد يعرف بمسجد غطاس.
مسجد يعرف بالقاضي ابن جلال الدين.
مسجد يعرف بمسجد القاضي ابن عبد المنعم.
مسجد يعرف بابي الحج.
مسجد يعرف بابي عَبَل.[145]

141 أ. س.: قنبشا.
142 أ. س.: بالمدينة.
143 ساقط من أ. س.: بالمدينة.
144 أ. س.: وقناطر.
145 أ. س.: بأبن عَبَل.

The congregational mosque of al-Lāhūn. The Friday prayer is held in it. It is distinguished, dating back to the days of Joseph.

The congregational mosque of Buljusūq. The Friday prayer is held in it.

The congregational mosque of Qambashā. The Friday prayer is held in it.

The congregational mosque of Uqlūl. The Friday prayer is held in it.

The congregational mosque of Būṣīr Difidnū. The Friday prayer is held in it.

The congregational mosque of Ihrīt. The Friday prayer is held in it.

The congregational mosque of Akhṣāṣ al-ʿAjamiyyīn. The Friday prayer is held in it.

The congregational mosque of Bushṭā. The Friday prayer is held in it.

The congregational mosque of Furqus; a distinguished place, where invocations to God are answered. The Friday prayer is held in it.

The congregational mosque of Dumūshiyya. The Friday prayer is held in it.

The congregational mosque of Difidnū. The Friday prayer is held in it.

The congregational mosque of Sirisnā. The Friday prayer is held in it.

The congregational mosque of Shāna. The Friday prayer is held in it.

The congregational mosque of Shushhā. The Friday prayer is held in it.

The congregational mosque of Minyat Shushhā. The Friday prayer is held in it.

The congregational mosque of Qāy. The Friday prayer is held in it.

The congregational mosque of Munshaʾat Qāy. The Friday prayer is held in it.

And I have mentioned Qāy as part of the Fayyum because it is attached to it[32] in the administration of justice (*al-qaḍāʾ*) and of endowments (*al-aḥbās*).

And as for the number of neighbourhood mosques (*masājid*) in the city and elsewhere, there are 35 mosques:

The mosque of al-Faraj, overlooking the market.

A mosque at the market of the cotton traders, known as Ibn al-Rifʿa.

Another mosque at the market of the cotton traders.

A mosque known as al-Yumnā.

A mosque known as Masjid al-Salām, next to the congregational mosque.

A mosque known as al-Riḍā ibn al-Shalīl, at Qanāṭir al-Zimām.[33]

A mosque near the Ḥusāmiyya Madrasa.

A mosque known as Masjid al-Jāwlī.

A mosque overlooking the market of the cloth merchants, known as Ibrahīm al-Qūṣī.

A mosque known as Awlād ʿAbd al-Wahhāb.

A mosque known to be founded by the *Qāḍī* Kamāl al-Dīn ibn Ḥāmid.

A mosque known as Masjid Ghiṭās.

A mosque known as Qāḍī Ibn Jalāl al-Dīn.

A mosque known as Masjid Qāḍī Ibn ʿAbd al-Munʿim.

A mosque known as Abū al-Ḥajj.

A mosque known as Abū ʿAbal.[34]

32 AS variant: *bi'l-madīna* (in the city) instead of *ilayhā* (to it).

33 Not mentioned elsewhere in the treatise.

34 AS: Ibn ʿAbal.

مسجد يعرف بغرس الدين بجوار دار الولاية.
مسجد يعرف بمسجد القبة قبالة المدرسة.
مسجد يعرف بحسام الدين الموسكي بحارة الارمن.
مسجد يعرف بالباجي بسوق الابزاريين.
مسجد يعرف بمسجد اقبال بجوار المعمل.
مسجد يعرف بمسجد القبو.
مسجد يعرف بفخر الدولة بجوار قناطر الزمام.
مسجد مطل على البركة في القبور يعرف بجلال الدين.
مسجد يعرف بالمسجد المظفري على خليج سنورس.
مسجد يعرف بابن فحل على خليج ذات الصفاء.
مسجد يعرف بمسجد الدكة قريب من خليج منية اقنى قبالته.
مسجد يعرف بسويقة الارمن.
مسجد يعرف بانشاء الامير بدر الدين المرندزي[146] على الخليج الاعظم.
مسجد بسيلة على كوم ابيض عال.[147]
مسجد بالعدوة يعرف بالقبة.
مسجد بمويه ظاهرها بجوار طاحون الماء.
مسجد بابي كسا يعرف بابي رباح.
مسجد برجتوت.
مسجد بسنهور غير مدون.

واما عدة الديرة، فثلاثة عشر ديرا. تفصيله:
دير ابي اسحاق[148] بجوار اللاهون وهو بحريه.
دير سيلة قبليها.
دير العامل قبلي العدوة.
دير سدمنت على بحر الفيوم وهو بحري سدمنت في الجبل.
دير النقلون في الجبل قريب من القمبشا[149] وهو بالشرق منها.

A mosque known as Ghars al-Dīn, near the Governor's House (*Dār al-Wilāya*).

A mosque known as Masjid al-Qubba (lit., the Dome), in front of the Madrasa.

A mosque known as Ḥusām al-Dīn al-Mawsikī, in the Armenian quarter (*ḥārat al-Arman*).

A mosque known as al-Bājī at the spice market.

A mosque known as Masjid Iqbāl, near the hatchery.

A mosque known as Masjid al-Qabw (lit., the Vault).

A mosque known as Fakhr al-Dawla, near Qanāṭir al-Zimām.

A mosque overlooking the pond at the cemetery, known as Jalāl al-Dīn.

A mosque known as the Muẓaffarī Mosque, on Sinnūris Canal.

A mosque known as Ibn Fiḥl, on Dhāt al-Ṣafāʾ Canal.

A mosque known as Masjid al-Dikka, near Minyat Aqnā Canal, in front of it.

A mosque known as the Little Market of the Armenians (*Suwayqat al-Arman*).

A mosque known to be founded by the amir Badr al-Dīn al-Marandizī,[35] on the Main Canal.

A white mosque at Sīla, on a high mound.

A mosque at al-ʿIdwa known as al-Qubba [the Dome].

The mosque of Bamawayh, outside of it, near the watermill.

A mosque at Abū Ksā, known as Abū Rabbāḥ.

The mosque of Burjtūt.

An unregistered mosque at Sanhūr.

And as for the number of monasteries, there are 13 monasteries:

The Monastery of Abū Isḥāq in the vicinity of al-Lāhūn, north of it.[36]

The Monastery of Sīla, to its south.[37]

The Monastery of al-ʿĀmil, south of al-ʿIdwa.

The Monastery of Sidmant on the Fayyum Canal (i.e., al-Manhā Canal), north of Sidmant, on the mountain.

The Monastery of Naqlūn, on the mountain near Qambashā, to its east.[38]

---

[35] Badr al-Dīn al-Marandizī (vocalization uncertain) is later mentioned as a former governor of the Fayyum. He has not been identified in other sources. The name is likely to be of Kurdish origin.

[36] Abū Sāliḥ the Armenian, *Churches and Monasteries of Egypt*, ed. and trans. by Basil T. A. Evetts, Anecdota Oxoniensia, Semitic Series, 7 (Oxford: Clarendon Press, 1895), p. 210: Monastery of Isaac.

[37] Abū Sāliḥ, *Churches and Monasteries*, pp. 209–10, known as the Monastery of the Brothers.

[38] Modern Monastery of Naqlūn. Abū Sāliḥ, *Churches and Monasteries*, p. 205, it was known as the 'Monastery of the Log/Wood?' (*Dayr al-Khashab*). See also Amélineau, *La géographie*, pp. 133, 273.

---

146 أ. س.: المريدزي.
147 أ. س.: عالي.
148 ط. م.: اسحق.
149 أ. س.: القنبشا.

دير دموشية وهو قبليها.
دير ابي شنودة قبلي منشاة اولاد عرفة.
دير بمويه وهو شرقيها.
دير فانو وهو غربيها.
دير سنورس وهو غربيها.[150]
دير دسيا وهو بحريها.
دير ذات الصفاء وهو قبليها.
دير القلمون وهو اخر الاعمال قريب من البهنسا.

واما عدة الكنائس، فخمسة وعشرون كنيسة:
بالمدينة[151] اربعة كنائس عامرة.[152]
باجة ثلاث كنائس، منها واحدة متهدمة.
منية الاسقف كنيسة واحدة.
دمشقين كنيستان.
سيلة كنيسة عامرة.
سنورس كنيستان، واحدة عامرة وكنيسة متهدمة في حدود شونة الغلات[153] السلطانية.
نقليفة كنيسة واحدة.
فانو ثلاث كنائس متهدمة.
ذات الصفاء كنيستان.
ابو كسا كنيسة واحدة.
سينرو كنيسة واحدة.
بمويه كنيستان.
دفدنو كنيسة واحدة.

150 ساقط من أ. س.: دير سنورس وهو غربيها.
151 أ. س.: المدينة.
152 أ. س.: عامة.
153 أ. س.: الغلال.

The Monastery of Dumūshiyya, to its south.

The Monastery of Abū Shinūda (Shenute), south of Munshaʾat Awlād ʿArafa.

The Monastery of Bamawayh, to its east.

The Monastery of Fānū, to its west.[39]

The Monastery of Sinnūris, to its west.

The Monastery of Disyā, to its north.

The Monastery of Dhāt al-Ṣafāʾ, to its south.

The Monastery of al-Qalamūn, [at] the edge of the province, near al-Bahnasā.[40]

And as for the number of churches, there are 25 churches:[41]

In Madīnat [al-Fayyūm] there are four functioning (*ʿāmira*) churches.[42]

Bāja: three churches, one of them in ruins.

Minyat al-Usquf: one church.

Dimashqīn [al-Baṣal]: two churches.

Sīla: a functioning church.

Sinnūris: two churches, one functioning and another one in ruins on the boundaries of the Sultan's granaries.

Naqalīfa: one church.

Fānū: three churches in ruin.

Dhāt al-Ṣafāʾ: two churches.

Abū Ksā: one church.

Sīnarū: one church.

Bamawayh: two churches.

Difidnū: one church.

[39] Abū Sāliḥ, *Churches and Monasteries*, p. 209, known as the Monastery of the Cross, in which the liturgy is celebrated once a year, on the feast of the cross.

[40] Modern Monastery of Qalamūn. Abū Sāliḥ, *Churches and Monasteries*, pp. 206–08: In 1178 there were 130 monks in this monastery.

[41] The list below has twenty-four churches.

[42] Abū Sāliḥ, *Churches and Monasteries*, pp. 204–05, mentions that there are four churches in the city: the Church of Angel Michael, a large church that stands near the gate of the city called Sūrus; the Church of Virgin Mary, outside of the city; the Church of Martyr Mercurius; and a Church of the Melkites in the quarter of the Armenians.

الباب التاسع

في ذكر ما اشتمل عليه من عين وغلة وغير ذلك من حيث الجملة

اقول وبالله التوفيق انه لما خرجت الاوامر العالية المطاعة المولوية السلطانية الصالحية النجمية عظم الله شانها ونصر سلطانها لي بالنظر في مصالح الفيوم وعمارته رسم بعمل اوراق بارتفاعه[154] من عين وغلة وصنف فاسترفعت بذلك اوراقا اما من البلاد الجارية في الخاص فمن مستخدمي البلاد[155] يومئذ اما من الوقف فمن النواب فيه واما من البلاد المقطعة فمن وجد من كتاب المقطعين[156] ومن مشايخ البلاد التي لا كتاب للمقطعين بها اخذت عليهم الايمان الشرعية والقسامات الوضعية بانهم صادقون فيما اخبروا عن ارتفاع البلاد وانهم لم ينقصوا منها شيئا. واحببت ان افرد هذه الجملة المفردة في باب ليسهل الاطلاع على جملته واعقبه في الباب الذي يتلوه وهو العاشر بوصف البلاد وارتفاعها بلدا بلدا.

فجملة ارتفاع الفيوم في سنة ستمائة واحد واربعين من العين، عشرون الفا وسبعمائة وسبعة واربعون دينارا وقيراط ونصف[157] حبة؛ ومن الغلات مائة الف واربعون الفا وسبعمائة واحد وثلاثون اردبا وقيراط. تفصيله:

قمح، اثنان وسبعون الفا واربعمائة وثلاثة ارادب وقيراط ونصف.
شعير وفول، ثلاثة وستون الفا وثلاثمائة واثنان وستون اردبا وثلث ونصف قيراط.[158]
سمسم، ثلاثمائة وخمسة وثلاثون اردبا وربع ونصف ثمن.
ارز بقشره، الفان وتسعمائة[159] وستون اردبا وقيراطان.
كمون، سبعمائة واثنان وثلاثون اردبا وربع وسدس وثمن.
كراويا، سبعة ارادب ونصف وربع.
سلجم، ثلاثة وتسعون[160] اردبا ونصف وثلث وثمن.
جلبان، ثلاثمائة واردبان وربع.
كزبرة، تسعة عشر اردبا وسدس ونصف ثمن.
فريك، ثمانية ارادب ونصف.
ملوخية، ستة ارادب.

ومن القطن، اربعة واربعون قنطارا.

ومن الثوم اليابس، ثلاثة وعشرون قنطارا وسدس.

ومن عسل النحل، ثلاثة وعشرون قنطارا.

154 أ. س.: بارتفاع.
155 أ. س.، ط. م.: مستجد في البلاد.
156 ط. م.: من الكتاب المقطعين; أ. س.: في كتاب المقطعين.
157 ساقط من أ. س.: نصف.
158 ساقط من أ. س.: قيراط.
159 أ. س.: سبعمائة.
160 أ. س.: سبعون.

The Ninth Chapter

Account of its aggregate taxes in specie and in grains, and other taxes

I say — may God grant success — that when I was issued the exalted orders, which must be obeyed, of our lord the sultan al-Ṣāliḥ Najm al-Dīn — may God make them mighty and their rule victorious — to inspect the administration of the Fayyum and its cultivation, it was decreed that its fiscal revenue in cash, in grains and in foodstuff varieties (*aṣnāf*) were to be recorded. I compiled documents in accordance with that: For the villages belonging to the private domain of the sultan (*al-khāṣṣ*), from the agents of the villages (*mustakhdamī al-bilād*); for the endowed properties, from their administrators (*al-nuwwāb fihi*); and as for the villages held in *iqṭāʿ*, from the clerks of the *iqṭāʿ*-holders (*min kuttāb al-muqṭaʿīn*) where found, and from the headmen (*mashāyikh*) of the villages in which the *iqṭāʿ*-holders keep no clerks. [From these headmen] I exacted legal oaths and prescriptive vows (*al-qasāmāt al-waḍʿiyya*), [attesting] that they were truthful in what they reported about the revenues of the villages, and that they had not underreported anything.[43] I have decided to dedicate a separate chapter to this aggregate total, so as to make it easy to consult, and then to follow it up in the subsequent chapter — the tenth chapter — with a description of the villages and their fiscal revenues, village by village.

The entire fiscal revenues of the Fayyum in the year 641 are, in specie, 20,747 1/24 1/144 dinars; and in grains, 140,731 1/24 ardabbs:

- wheat (*qamḥ*), 72,403 3/48 ardabbs;
- barley (*shaʿīr*) and broad beans (*fūl*), 63,362 1/3 1/48 ardabbs;
- sesame (*simsim*), 335 1/4 1/16 ardabbs;
- rice in hull (*aruzz bi-qishrihi*), 2,960 2/24 ardabbs;
- cumin (*kammūn*), 732 1/4 1/6 1/8 ardabbs;
- caraway (*karawyā*), 7 1/2 1/4 ardabbs;
- turnip rape (*saljam*), 93 1/2 1/3 1/8 ardabbs;
- chickling vetch (or green pea, *jullubān*), 302 1/4 ardabbs;
- coriander (*kuzbara*), 19 1/6 1/16 ardabbs;
- *farīk*, 8 1/2 ardabbs;
- Jew's mallow (*mulūkhiyya*), 6 ardabbs.

In cotton, 44 qinṭārs.

In dry garlic, 23 1/6 qinṭārs.

In honey, 23 qinṭārs.

[43] On the use of *qasāmāt* in Mamlūk society, see D. S. Richards, 'The Qasāma in Mamlūk Society: Some Documents from the Ḥaram Collection in Jerusalem', *Annales Islamologues*, 25 (1990), 245–84. According to Richards, *qasāmāt or qasāʾim* were written documents attesting that the parties had duly sworn before witnesses that they would do, or not do, certain things (p. 248). In one of the documents discussed by Richards, the *qasāma* contains an oath taken by several village headmen, who swore before the court in Jerusalem that their fields had not produced revenue during the last four years (case VI, pp. 267–70).

ومن الفدن، الف وستمائة واربعة وخمسون فدانا وربع وسدس ودانق. تفصيله:

قصب السكر، راس وخلفة، الف واربعمائة وثمانية وستون فدانا وثمن ودانق.

قلقاس، اربعة فدادين وربع وثمن.

قرط وفول برسم عوامل بلاد الخاص، مائة واحد وثمانون فدانا وثلثان وربع.

والذي اشتمل عليه ارتفاع الزكوات المبرورة بالاعمال الفيومية الف وسبعمائة وخمسة وتسعون[161] دينارا وثلثان ونصف قيراط وحبة. تفصيل ذلك:

الدولبة، مائتان وثمانية وستون دينارا ونصف وثلث وحبة.

عن الرقيق، سبعة وعشرون دينارا وقيراط وحبة.

عن العقار، دينار واحد ونصف وثمن.

عن الصادر، ديناران ونصف.

خرص العنب والنخل والزيتون، ستمائة وتسعة عشر دينارا وثلثان ونصف قيراط وحبة. تفصيل ذلك:

خرص العنب اربعمائة وتسعة عشر دينارا وثلث وربع وثمن ودانق.[162]

خرص النخل، مائة واربعة وستون دينارا وثلث وربع وحبتان.

خرص الزيتون، خمسة وثلاثون دينارا وربع وثمن.

ثمن الماشية، عن الف ومائة واثنين وعشرين راسا، ثمانمائة وخمسة وسبعون دينارا وثلثان وربع وحبة. تفصيله:

ابقار، عن خمسين راسا، ثلاثة وتسعون[163] دينارا وقيراط وحبة.

جاموس، عن ثمانية ارؤس، ستة عشر دينارا وربع وثمن. تفصيله:

مسنات، عن خمسة ارؤس، اثنا عشر دينارا ونصف وربع وثمن.

تبعان، عن ثلاثة ارؤس، ثلاثة دنانير ونصف.

بقر احمر، عن اثنين واربعين راسا، سبعة وسبعون دينارا وثلثان وحبة. تفصيله:

مسنات، عن احد عشر راسا، اثنان وثلاثون دينارا ونصف وثلث.

تبعان، عن احد وثلاثين راسا، ثلاثة واربعون دينارا ونصف وثلث وحبة.

اغنام، عن الف واثنين وسبعين راسا، سبعمائة واثنان وثمانون دينارا ونصف وربع وثمن. تفصيله:

بياض، عن خمسمائة واربعة واربعين راسا، خمسمائة واثنان وثمانون دينارا وثلثان وربع وحبة.

شعارى، عن خمسمائة وثمانية وعشرين راسا، مائة وتسعة وتسعون دينارا وثلثان وربع وحبتان.

[161] أ. س.: سبعون.

[162] ط. م.: دانق.

[163] أ. س.: سبعون.

Feddans of [crown estates], 1,654 ¼ ⅙ 1/144 feddans:

sugarcane, first and second harvest (*ra'ˀs wa-khilfa*), 1,468 ⅛ 1/144 feddans;

colocasia, 4 ½ ⅛ feddans;

alfalfa and broad beans, assigned for the beasts of burden in the lands that belong to the Sultan's private domain (*al-khāṣṣ*), 181 ⅔ ¼ feddans.

The entire revenue from the blessed alms-tax (*zakawāt*) in the lands of the Fayyum is 1795 ⅔ 1/48 1/72 dinars:

merchandise (*al-dawlaba*), 268 ½ ⅓ 1/72 dinars;

slaves (*al-raqīq*), 27 1/24 1/72 dinars;

real estate (*al-ʿaqār*), 1 ½ ⅛ dinar;

al-ṣādir,[44] 2 ½ dinars.

Estimate (*kharṣ*) for grapes, dates and olives, 619 ⅔ 1/48 1/72 dinars:

estimate of grapes, 419 ⅓ ¼ ⅛ 1/144 dinars;

estimate of dates, 164 ⅓ ¼ 2/72 dinars;

estimate of olives, 35 ¼ ⅛ dinars.

Monetary value of livestock, for 1,122 heads, 875 ⅔ ¼ 1/72 dinars:

cattle, for 50 heads, 93 1/24 1/72 dinars.

water buffalo, for eight heads, 16 ¼ ⅛ dinars:

two-year old cows (*musinnāt*), for 5 heads, 12 ½ ¼ ⅛ dinars;

yearling calves (*tubʿān*), for three heads, 3 ½ dinars.

Cows, for 42 heads, 77 ⅔ 1/72 dinars:

two-year old cows, for 11 heads, 32 ½ ⅓ dinars;

yearling calves, for 31 heads, 43 ½ ⅓ 1/72 dinars.

Small cattle (*aghnām*), for 1,072 heads, 782 ½ ¼ ⅛ dinars:

sheep (*bayāḍ*), for 544 heads, 582 ⅔ ¼ 1/72 dinars;

goats (*shiʿārā*), for 528 heads, 199 ⅔ ¼ 2/72 dinars.

[44] Possibly alms-tax on merchandise taken out from the province. In the administrative literature, the term *ṣādir* has the meaning of exports. See Claud Cahen, 'Douanes et commerce dans les ports méditerranéens de l'Égypte médiévale d'après le Minhādj d'al-Makhzūmī', *Journal of the Economic and Social History of the Orient*, 7. 3 (1964), 217–314 (p. 244).

وجملة ارتفاع الجوالي، بما فيه من المحسوب عن طرادين الوحش، وهو عن احد واربعين نفرا، عشرون دينارا ونصف، الفان وثلاثمائة واربعة وخمسون دينارا. تفصيله:

ما تضمنه عمل الذمة عن الف ومائة واثنين واربعين نفرا، الفان ومائتان واربعة وثمانون دينارا. تفصيله:

المقيمون بالاعمال، عن ثمانمائة وتسعة واربعين نفرا، الف وستمائة وثمانية وتسعون دينارا.

الناؤون[164] عن الاعمال، عن مائتين وثلاثة وتسعين نفرا، خمسمائة وستة وثمانون دينارا. تفصيله:

الوجه البحري، عن مائة[165] واربعة وخمسين نفرا، ثلاثمائة وثمانية دنانير.

الوجه القبلي، عن مائة وتسعة وثلاثين نفرا[166]، مائتان وثمانية وسبعون دينارا.

تتمة الجملة عن عجز العدة، سبعون دينارا.

والموظف على البلاد من الاتبان، مائة الف وتسعة واربعون الفا وتسعمائة وستة عشر شنيفًا. تفصيله:

ما تضمنه العمل المخلد بالديوان لسنة ثلاث وثلاثين وستمائة، الذي لم يوجد بعده حساب للاتبان، احد وتسعون الفا وستمائة وخمسون شنيفا.

ما لم يرد العمل المذكور على بقية نواحي الاعمال الفيومية المهمل حالها ولم يوجد ما يدل عليها، مما تعين تحصيل ذلك نظير المقرر على النواحي المتضمنة العمل، ثمانية وخمسون الفا ومائتان وستون شنيفا.

واما ارتفاع المواريث، فان جملته لسنة احد واربعين وستمائة عينا، اربعمائة واربعة وثلاثون دينارا ونصف وربع وحبة. تفصيله:

اجرة الاملاك الديوانية خارجا عن الادر الخراب والمستهدمة بالنيل المبارك والادر المبيعة نظير سنة اربعين وستمائة، عن الف وثمانمائة وثلاثين[167] درهما، خمسة واربعون دينارا ونصف وربع وثمن وحبتان.

الاحكار، ثلاثة عشر[168] دينارا وقيراط وحبتان.

ثمرة الانشاب، اربعون دينارا.

العقود، دينار واحد وربع وثمن.

الترك، مائة وعشرون دينارا وثمن.

البذل[169]، مائتان واربعة عشر دينارا وسدس وثمن.

164 أ. س.: النائبون.

165 أ. س.: مائتين.

166 أ. س. يضيف: نفرا.

167 أ. س.: ألف وثلاثمائة وستة وثلاثين.

168 أ. س.: ثمانيه عشر.

169 أ. س.; ط. م.: البذل

The entire revenue of the poll-tax (*al-jawālī*), after deducting [the wages of] the 'beast-chasers' (*ṭarrādūn al-waḥsh*)[45] — which are for 41 individuals, 20 ½ dinars — is 2,354 dinars:

That which is included in the register of the non-Muslims (*ʿamal al-dhimma*), for 1,142 individuals, 2,284 dinars:

those who reside in the district [of the Fayyum], for 849 individuals, 1,698 dinars;

absentees, for 293 individuals, 586 dinars:

the northern regions [of Egypt] (*al-wajh al-baḥrī*): for 154 individuals, 308 dinars;

the southern regions [of Egypt] (*al-wajh al-qiblī*): for 139 individuals: 278 dinars.

Adjustment (*tatimma*) to the aggregate, as the total is too low, 70 dinars.[46]

The hay levy (*al-muwaẓẓaf*) in the villages: 149,916 bales (*shanīfan*):

That which is recorded in the register of the Dīwān (*al-ʿamal al-mukhallad bi'l-dīwān*)[47] for the year 633, after which date no calculation for hay was found, 91,650 bales.

The remaining villages in the Fayyum are not found in the register, and their circumstances have been neglected, so there is nothing to indicate [their hay levy]. This required calculation (*taḥṣīl*) on the basis of what was determined for the localities which are recorded in the register, 58,260 bales.

The total revenues from [intestate] inheritances (*mawārīth*)[48] for the year 641 are, in specie, 434 ½ ¼ 1/72 dinars:

Rent for the properties belonging to the Dīwān (*al-amlāk al-dīwāniyya*) excluding the disused or demolished buildings near the blessed Nile, and the buildings that were sold — on the basis of the accounts for 640 [AD 1242–3], 1,836 dirhams, equal to 45 ½ ¼ ⅛ 2/72 dinars.

Lands subject to long-term lease (*al-aḥkār*), 13 1/24 2/72 dinars.

Fruits of plantations (*thamarat al-anshāb*), 40 dinars.

Contracts (*al-ʿuqūd*), 1 ¼ ⅛ dinar.

Bequests (*al-tirak*), 120 ⅛ dinars.

Badhl,[49] 214 ⅙ ⅛ dinars.

45 The context here and elsewhere points to officials in charge of collecting the poll-tax. The term appears to be used pejoratively towards the non-Muslims who are to be 'chased' by the poll-tax collectors.

46 The *tatimma* is an adjustment to the balance. For example, if the cadastral survey shows that the tenant has less land than he was registered for, then the land tax that is taken is in proportion to the difference. See Cooper, 'Ibn Mammati's Rules', p. 317.

47 On *khallada* as the act of making a record in an official register, see al-Nuwayrī, *Nihāyat al-arab*, VIII, 208, 229, and passim.

48 The account of inheritances passed on to the state, in part or in full, when there were no other legal heirs, or when the legal heirs were entitled to only part of the inheritance; see Rabie, *The Financial System*, p. 47. This category is mentioned only in Madīnat al-Fayyūm.

49 The *badhl* appears to be an accounting term for some form of cash revenues, probably an additional payment for the tax-collectors. The later common meaning of *badhl* as bribe, attested in Mamluk sources, is doubtlessly derivative. Elsewhere it is also mentioned as 'the *badhl* of the government agents' in the entry for Fānū, in the category of cash revenues, and as an item of cash revenue in Miṭr Ṭāris. Al-Nuwayrī states that a record of the *budhūl* should come at the end of the document recording an allocation of *iqṭāʿ* revenue. See al-Nuwayrī, *Nihāyat al-arab*, VIII, 202.

والذي اشتمل عليه ارتفاع احباس الجوامع والمساجد المعمورة بذكر الله عز وجل، الف وثلاثمائة وستة وثمانون دينارا وسدس وحبتان. تفصيله:

مال الهلالي، ستمائة وستة وتسعون دينارا.

المعجل من اجر[170] الحوانيت، ثلاثون دينارا وربع وسدس ونصف ثمن.

الاحكار، سبعة وستون دينارا وثلث وثمن وحبتان.

مواقف الصيادين، ثمانية دنانير.

العقود، نظير سنة اربعين وستمائة، مما يوردونه اصلا ومحسوبا حفظا لذكره بحكم ان الاحكار بالاعمال استوعبت، خمسة وثمانون دينارا ونصف.

الخراجي، ثلاثمائة وثلاثة واربعون دينارا ونصف وربع. من ذلك على قاي ومنشاة قاي، تسعة عشر دينارا، على جاري العادة.

وتتمة الجملة على نواحي الاعمال الفيومية:

ثمن ثمرة الانشاب الواردة اصلا ومحسوبا[171] في كلف المساجد، عشرة دنانير ونصف وقيراط وحبة.

زائد صرف الخراجي، سبعة وعشرون دينارا وقيراط وحبة.

تتمة الجملة من جملة ما استظهر به عما[172] ورد مضاف الختمات المخلدة بالديوان[173] المعمور في الاحكار واجرة الحوانيت، مائة وسبعة عشر دينارا ونصف وربع وثمن وحبة.

ويتلو ذلك في البلاد بما بكل منهم من الرزق وما عليهم من الرسم لخولي البحر والمربى من الفروج وما يزرعه[174] اهل البلاد من اقصاب السكر وما تسلف[175] عليه من الشعير برسم الاصطبلات السلطانية والفول برسم العوامل الديوانية والتقاوي وغير ذلك على ما ياتي بيانه.

The revenue of the [Ministry of] Endowments of Congregational and Neighbourhood Mosques, built in remembrance of God the almighty and exalted, is 1,386 1/6 2/72 dinars:

Lunar calendar taxes (*māl al-hilālī*), 696 dinars.

Advance payments (*al-muʿajjal*) of the rents of the shops, 30 dinars 1/4 1/6 1/16.

Lands subject to long terms lease (*al-aḥkār*), 67 1/3 1/8 2/72 dinars.

Berths of the fishermen (*mawāqif al-ṣayyāḍīn*), 8 dinars.

Contracts, on the basis of the accounts for 640 [AD 1242–3], of what was conveyed as basic assessment and following deductions (*aṣl*[an] *wa-maḥsūb*[an]): 85 1/2 dinars. This is mentioned only for the record, since the long-term leases in the provinces were subsumed (?, *istawʿabat*).

The land tax, 343 1/2 1/4 dinars. Of that, the share of Qāy and Munshaʾat Qāy is 19 dinars, as is customary.

Adjustment to the aggregate [of the revenues of the Ministry of Endowments] for the villages of the Fayyum:

The monetary value of the fruits of plantations, as basic assessment and following deductions on the expenses of the mosques, 10 1/2 1/24 1/72 dinars.

The land-tax overpayments (*zāʾid ṣarf al-kharājī*),[50] 27 1/24 1/72 dinars.

Another adjustment to the aggregate: The total of recently added[51] sealed records (*al-khatamāt*)[52] of revenues registered in the prosperous Dīwān, from lands subject to long-term lease and from rent of shops: 117 1/2 1/4 1/8 1/72 dinars.

I will follow with the allowances (*al-rizaq*) in each of the villages; the fee for the overseer of the canal (*khawlī al-baḥr*); the chickens reared; the sugarcane sown by the people of the villages; the advance payments for barley assigned for the sultan's stables and for broad beans assigned for the beasts of burden of the Dīwān; the seed advances (*al-taqāwī*), and other things, as will be seen.

170 أ. س.: أجرة.
171 أ. س. يكرر: ومحسوبا.
172 أ. س.: عن ما.
173 ط. م.: للديوان.
174 أ. س.: يزرعونه.
175 أ. س.: يسلف.

50 Al-Nuwayrī refers to *zāʾid al-mustakhraj* as an over-payment of taxes that should be deducted from the tax obligations of the following year; al-Nuwayrī, *Nihāyat al-arab*, VIII, 232.

51 On *al-mustaẓhar bi-hi* (or *bi-hā*) as 'recently introduced', see al-Nuwayrī, *Nihāyat al-arab*, VIII, 201, 209.

52 For discussion of *khatma* as an annual record of cash revenues, see al-Nuwayrī, *Nihāyat al-arab*, VIII, 275. According to Cahen, the term designated sealed records of monthly poll-tax revenues and of alms-tax; Cahen, 'Le régime des impôts', pp. 251, 257; Cahen, 'Douanes et commerce', p. 246.

فصل: لا يظن من وقف على هذا الكتاب فراى ما ذكر في ارتفاعه من الاصناف من السمسم والارز والكمون والكراويا والسلجم والجلبان والكزبرة والفريك والملوخية والقطن والثوم اليابس والعسل النحل وقصب السكر والقلقاس والقرط والفول عن مقادير هذه الاصناف هي كل ما في الفيوم. بل هذا ما يخص الديوان السلطاني عن زراعة الاواسي الديوانية والرسوم المقررة خارجا عما يحصل للمزارعين ويزرع في البلاد بالخراج.

Section: Anyone consulting this book should not think – having seen the account of revenues in the categories of sesame, rice, cumin, caraway, rape, chickling vetch, coriander, green wheat, Jew's mallow, cotton, dry garlic, honey, sugarcane, colocasia, alfalfa and broad beans – that the above mentioned amounts are all that is found in the Fayyum. Rather, this is what belongs to the sultan's Dīwān from the cultivation of the crown estates (*al-awāsī al-dīwāniyya*) and from the fixed fees (*al-rusūm al-muqarrara*). It excludes what the tenants (*muzāriʿūn*) sow in the villages, which is subject to the land tax.[53]

وها انا اذكر صنفا من الاصناف يستدل به على ما ذكر، وهو ان الذي ذكر من الارتفاع من الثوم ثلاثة وعشرون قنطارا واني احتطت على ثوم زرع بمطر طارس، وهي بلد من بلاد الفيوم، بالخراج لسنة اثنتين واربعين وستمائة فاحصيتها وزنا. فاذا هي الفا قنطار واثنان وستون قنطارا ونصف وربع وثمن قنطار، مما قطيعته دينار ان الفدان وذلك عن دون الثلاثين فدانا. فهذا حاصل هذه القطيعة من هذا البلد فما ظننا بباقي البلاد وعلى هذا القياس.

Here I will mention one of these categories to demonstrate this. The garlic revenue mentioned above is 23 qinṭārs; yet I have taken note of the amount of garlic subject to land tax on cash crops for the year 642 [AD 1244–5] sown in Miṭr Ṭāris, one of the villages of the Fayyum. I have measured it by weight, and it is 2,062 ½ ¼ ⅛ qinṭārs of garlic subject to a tax rate of 2 dinars per feddan. [This amount of garlic was cultivated] on less than 30 feddans. This is the yield for this plot of land in this village, and one can infer from this for the rest of the villages.

[53] Al-Nābulusī is making the point that the list of revenues in kind mentioned in the preceding pages does not represent the full fiscal revenue of the province but only includes revenues in kind from the crown estates. There appears to a confusion here, as the totals mentioned above for minor grains (rice, sesame, cumin, caraway, rape, vetch, coriander, and Jews' mallow) are actually accurate aggregations of the revenues in kind collected in the different villages. His remark is therefore only correct for cotton and garlic: The crown estates produced revenues of cotton and garlic in kind, but in the villages garlic and cotton were subject to a land tax in cash, so the full extent of garlic and cotton cultivation is not revealed by the aggregates in kind.

الباب العاشر
في وصف بلاده وارتفاعها بلدا بلدا

المدينة: اقول[176] وبالله التوفيق هذه اللفظة تطلق في الفيوم على المدينة التي بلاد الفيوم قراها وهي عبارة عن نقطة في الدائرة التي يكتنفها الجبل المحيط بالفيوم. وهي ذات شقين يمر بينهما بحر الفيوم فاذا انتهى البحر الى قريب ثلثي العمارة منها لقى في[177] وجهه جامعها المعقود على قناطر اربع يخرج الماء[178] منها الى بقية العمارة التي على حافتيه ثم الى البلاد. وكل شق من هذين الشقين فيه اسواق وعمائر ودور ومساكن والاسواق متصلة على التسقيف الذى على البحر المشار اليه وعلى غيره.

فيها[179] الحاكم والعدول والمدرسون ووكيل بيت المال والطبيب والجوامع والمساجد والمدارس والحمامات ودار الوكالة والبزازون والعطارون وكثير مما في المدن.

والفواكه[180] ايام الفواكه والخضر واكثر الفواكه التي بها التين والكمثرى والتفاح الاخضر والمخضب والمشمش الا انه يسير والرطب والعنب وفي بساتينها شجر الخروب والتوت وفيها من الزهر الورد الكثير والياسمين العطر والنوفر البري واما النسرين فكثير حتى ان ماءه يستخرج لكثرته.

وفيها التناة[181] وارباب البساتين والمواشي والزروع وفيها الركاضون يجلبون اليها ويجلبون منها ويكسبون في ذهابهم وايابهم. واهلها اهل خير سذج في غفلة كانهم بها وهي اوطانهم غرباء ذو البستان[182] في بستانه وذو الزرع[183] في زرعه نافرون عن الغرباء متباعدون من القرباء غفلة لا قصدا.

176 أ. س.: فاقول.
177 ساقط من أ. س.: في.
178 ساقط من أ. س.: الماء.
179 أ. س.: من.
180 ساقط من أ. س.: والفواكه.
181 أ. س.: التنات; ط. م.: التناة.
182 أ. س.: بساتين.
183 أ. س.: الزروع.

The Tenth Chapter
A description of its villages and their fiscal revenues, village by village

The City (*al-madīna*):[54] I say — may God grant success — this term applies in the Fayyum to the city, for which the villages of the Fayyum are the rural hinterland (*qurā*). It is like a point within the circle formed by the mountains that enclose the Fayyum. It is divided into two parts by the Main Canal. After the [Main] Canal passes through two thirds of its inhabited area, it encounters the congregational mosque of the city, which is vaulted (*maʿqūd*) over four arches, and the water runs through them to the remaining urban area located on its two banks, and then to the villages. Each of the two parts of the city has its own marketplaces, buildings, halls (*dūr*) and residences. The marketplaces are connected by a roof, which runs over the [Main] Canal; other canals are also covered in such a way.

In the city there is a judge, notaries, teachers, the agent of the treasury, and a physician; congregational mosques, neighbourhood mosques, madrasas, public baths, and the merchandise warehouse (*dār al-wakāla*); the cloth merchants and the perfumers; and much else which is found in cities.

Fruits are found during the seasons of fruits and vegetables. Most of the fruits in it are figs, pears, green and pigmented (*mukhaḍḍab*)[55] apples, apricots — albeit in small quantity — as well as ripe dates and grapes. In its orchards there are carob-bean and mulberry trees. Its flowers include many roses, fragrant jasmine and wild water lily. As for the eglantine roses (*nisrīn*), they are so numerous that their abundant sap is being extracted.

In the city there are townsmen (*tunnāʾ*), as well as farmers who own orchards, livestock and fields. Travelling merchants are also to be found, bringing goods in and out of the city, and making their livelihood by their goings and comings. The people of the city are good and simple, but are in a state of apathy, as if they were strangers in their own land. The owner of an orchard stays in his orchard, and the owner of a field stays in his field, eschewing strangers and keeping their distance from those who live nearby. This is done out of apathy rather than by intention.

[54] Modern location: Madīnat al-Fayyūm (مدينة الفيوم). Timm, *Das Christlich-Koptische Ägypten*, pp. 1506–25: Krokodilopolis/ Arsinoē; Trismagistos GEO ID 327; Salmon, 'Répertoire', pp. 42–44; Ibn al-Jīʿān, *Kitāb al-tuḥfa*, p. 150; Antoine Isaac Silvestre De Sacy, *État des provinces et des villages de l'Égypte* (Strassburg: Treuttel et Würtz, 1810), p. 680; Yāqūt, *Muʿjam al-Buldān*, IV, 287; Marie Jules-César Savigny, *Description de l'Égypte, ou recueil des observations et des recherches qui ont été faites en Égypte pendant l'expédition de l'armée française, publié par les ordres de sa majesté l'empereur Napoléon le Grand: planches*, Histoire naturelle, 18 (Paris: Panckoucke, 1827), p. 129; Étienne M. Quatremére, *Mémoires géographiques et historiques sur l'Égypte, et sur quelques contrées voisines: recueillis et extraits des manuscrits coptes, arabes, etc., de la Bibliothèque Impériale*, 2 vols (Paris: Schoell, 1811), I, 391; Aḥmad Bey Zéki, 'Une description arabe du fayyoūm au VIIe siècle de l'hégire', *Bulletin de la société Khédiviale de Géographie*, 5 (1899), 253–95 (p. 30); Abū Ṣāliḥ, *Churches and Monastries*, p. 202; Amélineau, *La géographie*, p. 331; Ramzī, *Al-Qāmūs*, II/III, 96: Madīnat al-Fayyūm.

[55] On *tufāḥ mukhaḍḍab* as a variety of apple, probably red and green, see Mathieu Eychenne, 'La production agricole de Damas et de la Ghūṭa au XIVe siècle: diversité, taxation et prix des cultures maraîchères d'après al-Jazarī (m.739/1338)', *Journal of Economic and Social History of the Orient*, 56. 4–5 (2013), 569–630.

يحف بهذه المدينة كثير من البساتين لها صورة الغوطة الحسنة للمقبل عليها من جميع جهاتها حسنة المرائي كثيرة المراعي تصلح ماوى للصعلوك لا مقرا للملوك. يرتفق الفقراء الساكنون بها ارتفاق الساكنين بالارياف لوجود الماء والكلا والصيد في البر والبحر والاسترزاق في[184] الديس والحطب والخب والبردى وما في معناه من المباح.

وهذه البلدة باردة الاسحار بارزة الاشجار كثيرة الثمار قليلة الامطار يشرب اكثر اهل[185] هذه البلدة من ماء البحر المار في وسطها مع ان كنفهم عليه واغنياؤهم يشربون من الابار الا ان كل بئر له كنيف يرشح اليه.

يسقى اكثر بساتينها بالسواقي. ولبعض البساتين من البر البحري ثلاث مساقى: مسقاة لبركة مؤنسة وما معها، ومسقاة لورثة محيي الدين بن الاشقر، ومسقاة لحكر القاضي الاسعد بن جلال الدين وحكر راجح.

فاما ارتفاعها، فالعين — الفان واربعمائة دينار واربعة دنانير وثمن وحبة؛ الغلة اربعة وعشرون اردبا وثلث وثمن.
تفصيله:
سمسم ستة عشر اردبا وثلث وربع وثمن.
كراويا سبعة ارادب ونصف وربع.

ثوم يابس، ثلاثة وعشرون قنطارا وثلث.

عسل نحل، ثلاثة وعشرون قنطارا.

فدن مائة واثنان وستون فدانا وثلثان[186] وربع ونصف ثمن.
تفصيله:
قصب سكر، مائة وتسعة فدادين ونصف وربع ونصف ثمن.
تفصيله:
راس، اثنان وتسعون فدانا وقيراط ونصف؛
خلفة، سبعة عشر فدانا ونصف.
من ذلك ما يزرع بالمرابعين ويسقى، احد وثمانون فدانا وربع ونصف قيراط. تفصيله:
راس، باراضي منية كربيس، احد وسبعون فدانا وربع ونصف قيراط؛
خلفة، باراضي خور الرماد، عشرة فدادين.
ومنه ما هو زراعة المزارعين بالنواحي، ثمانية وعشرون فدانا وسدس وثمن. تفصيله:
راس، عشرون فدانا وثلثان وثمن؛
وخلفة، سبعة فدادين ونصف.
تفصيل ذلك:
خور الرماد، خمسة فدادين ونصف. تفصيله:
راس، ثلاثة ونصف:
خلفة، فدانين.
ببيج فرح، ستة فدادين وربع:
راس، اربعة فدادين؛
خلفة، فدانين وربع.

[184] أ. س.: من.
[185] ساقط من ط. م.: اهل.
[186] أ. س.: ثلث.

Many orchards surround this city, and, in the eyes of a person approaching it from any direction, it resembles a beautiful fertile valley. It is a beautiful sight, with plenty of pasture. But it is a refuge suitable for the destitute, not an abode for kings. The poor who reside in it subsist in the same way as those living in rural areas, owing to the availability of water and grass, hunting and fishing, and the use of thickets, firewood, bark of trees, papyrus and similar things free for public use.

This town is of chilly dawns, lofty trees, abundant fruits, and little rain. Most of the town's people drink water from the [Main] Canal that passes through it, even though their latrines flow into it. The wealthy people among them drink from wells, but each of these wells has a latrine that oozes water into it.

Most of its orchards are irrigated by means of waterwheels. Some orchards on the northern bank [of the Main Canal] are fed by three irrigation ditches (*masāqī*): an irrigation ditch for Birkat Muʾnisa and its adjacent area; an irrigation ditch for the heirs of Muḥyī al-Dīn Ibn al-Ashqar; and an irrigation ditch for the leased land (*ḥikr*) of the judge al-Asʿad Ibn Jalāl al-Dīn, and the leased land of Rājiḥ.

The revenue in specie is 2,404 ⅛ 1/72 dinars; and in grains, 24 ⅓ ⅛ ardabbs:
- Sesame, 16 ⅓ ¼ ⅛ ardabbs.
- Caraway, 7 ½ ¼ ardabbs.

Dry garlic, 23 ⅓ qinṭārs.

Honey, 23 qinṭārs.

Feddans [of crown estate], 162 ⅔ ¼ 1/16 feddans:[56]
- Sugarcane, 109 ½ ¼ 1/16 feddans:
  - First harvest, 92 3/48 feddans.
  - Second harvest, 17 ½ feddans.
  - Of these, 81 ¼ 1/48 feddans are sown and irrigated by quarter-share laborers (*murābiʿīn*):
    - First harvest in the lands of Minyat Karbīs, 71 ¼ 1/48 feddans.
    - Second harvest in the lands of Khawr al-Rammād, 10 feddans.
- The other 28 ⅙ ⅛ feddans are sown by tenants (*al-muzāriʿīn*) in the villages:
  - First harvest, 20 ⅔ ⅛ feddans
  - Second harvest, 7 ½ feddans.
- [The feddans sown by tenants, in detail]:
  - Khawr al-Rammād, 5 ½ feddans:
    - First harvest, 3 ½ [feddans].
    - Second harvest, 2 feddans.
  - Babīj Faraḥ, 6 ¼ feddans:
    - First harvest, 4 feddans.
    - Second harvest, 2 ¼ feddans.

[56] The number cited here reflects the amount of feddans of sugarcane plantations assigned for the supply of the local sugar press. The plantations could be located in nearby villages, as is the case here.

قشوش، فدانين:
راس،[187] فدان؛
خلفة، فدان وربع.[188]
منية كربيس، اربعة عشر فدانا وربع وسدس وثمن:
راس، اثنا عشر فدانا وسدس وثمن؛
خلفة، فدانان وربع.
قرط، ثلاثة وعشرون فدانا وثلثان وربع.
فول اخضر، سبعة وعشرون فدانا ونصف.
قلقاس، فدانان.

تفصيل ذلك جميعه:

مال الهلالي بما فيه من المقطع للامراء وهو الف ومائة دينار، الف وسبعمائة وثلاثة وعشرون دينارا وثلث وثمن ودانق. تفصيله:
الوكالة، خمسمائة واربعة وسبعون دينارا وثلث ونصف قيراط.
الحمام الديوانية، مائة وسبعون دينارا.[189]
عقر الماء عما استعمله الحمام الجارية في الوقف الفخري من بئر الحمام الديوانية، خمسون دينارا.
معمل الفروج، ثلاثمائة وسبعة واربعون دينارا ونصف.
المدبغة والغرابيل، مائتان وخمسة دنانير.
عود القصارة، مائة واربعة وسبعون دينارا وربع.
حانوتي الشمع والحرير، ثلاثة وثلاثون دينارا ونصف وثلث.
اجرة الحوانيت الديوانية وقباب الفاخورة، خارجا عن الحوانيت الديوانية الداخلة في عقد ايجار[190] مستاجري الابواب، وهو في الشهر ثلاثة وعشرون درهما ونصف. تفصيله:
حانوت القصار، خمسة دراهم.
حانوتي الشمع والحرير، اربعة عشر درهما.
حانوت الغرابيل، اربعة دراهم ونصف.
وبما في ذلك من اجرة الحوانيت المرتبة لائمة المساجد، وهو في السنة ثلاثون دينارا، مائة وثمانية وستون دينارا ونصف وحبتان. تفصيله:[191]
اجرة الحوانيت، خاصة مائة واربعة واربعون دينارا ونصف وحبتان.
اجرة قباب الفاخورة، اربعة وعشرون دينارا.

مال الخراجي، خارجا عن خراج الفدن ببركة ابن شكلة المنتقلة بالاقطاع لمغل سنة اربعين وستمائة بمقتضى ما تضمنته المناشير السلطانية، خارجا عن ثمن الكرات وهو خمسة دنانير، ستمائة وثمانون دينارا وثلثان[192] ودانق، والسمسم، والكراويا، والثوم، والفدن على ما تقدم شرحه زراعة المزارعين، مائة وثمانية وسبعون دينارا وربع وثمن. تفصيله:

187 رأس يكرر في أ. س.
188 ساقط من ط. م.: وربع.
189 ساقط من أ. س.: وثلث ونصف قيراط الحمام الديوانية مائة وسبعون دينارا.
190 أ. س.: اجاير.
191 ساقط من أ. س.: تفصيله.
192 أ. س.: ثلثي.

Qushūsh, 2 feddans:
First harvest, 1 feddan.
Second harvest, 1 feddan.
Minyat Karbīs, 14 ¼ ⅙ ⅛ feddans:
First harvest, 12 ⅙ ⅛ feddans.
Second harvest, 2 ¼ feddans.
Alfalfa, 23 ⅔ ¼ feddans.
Green broad beans, 27 ½ feddans.
Colocasia, 2 feddans.

The revenues in detail:

Lunar-calendar tax (*māl al-hilālī*) is 1,723 ⅓ ⅛ 1/144 dinars. It incorporates the taxes handed over as *iqṭāʿ* for the amirs, 1,100 dinars. [The lunar-calendar tax in detail]:

The merchandise warehouse, 574 ⅓ 1/48 dinars.
The baths of the Dīwān, 170 dinars.
Indemnity (*ʿuqr*) for the water drawn from the well of the Dīwān's bath-houses and used by the baths of the endowment of al-Fakhrī, 50 dinars.
The chick hatchery (*maʿmal al-farrūj*), 347 ½ dinars.
The tannery and the sieves, 205 dinars.
The fulling and bleaching boards (*ʿūd al-qiṣāra*), 174 ¼ dinars.
The two wax and silk shops, 33 ½ ⅓ dinars.
Rent of the Dīwān's shops and the pottery kilns [*qubāb al-fākhūra*], 168 ½ 2/72 dinars. This sum excludes the Dīwān's shops subject to the tenancy contract of those who rent the [shops at the?] gates, amounting to 23 ½ dirhams per month:
the fuller's shop, 5 dirhams;
the two wax and silk shops, 14 dirhams;
the sieve shop, 4 ½ dirhams.[57]
The [rent from the Dīwān's shops] incorporates the rent of the shops allocated to the imams of the mosques, 30 dinars annually.
The [total rent for the Dīwān's shops] is 168 ½ 2/72 dinars:
the rent of the shops, 144 ½ 2/72 dinars;
the rent of the arched pottery kilns, 24 dinars.

Land tax, in specie, 680 ⅔ 1/144 dinars. This sum excludes the land tax assessed by feddans for [the lands of] Birkat Ibn Shikla, which were transferred to *iqṭāʿ*-holders as of the yield (*mughall*) of the year 640 [AD 1242–3], in conformity with royal decrees (*al-manāshīr al-sulṭāniyya*). It [also] excludes the value of the leek, at 5 dinars. As for the sesame, the caraway, the garlic, and the [crown estate] feddans cultivated by tenants, see above.

Of the land tax, 178 ¼ ⅛ dinars, in detail:

57 The rent from the fuller's, wax and silk, and sieve shops is listed separately, perhaps because they were located outside the city walls.

خراج الراتب والاحكار، مائة[193] وخمسة وستون دينارا وثمن ونصف قيراط وحبة. تفصيله:[194]

المستقر، مائة واثنا عشر دينارا ونصف وثلث وثمن وحبتان. تفصيل:

الاصل عن مائة واثنى عشر فدانا وثلثين[195] ونصف قيراط وحبة، مائة وديناران ونصف وثمن وحبتان. تفصيل:

راتب، قطيعة دينارين، عن تسعة فدادين ونصف تسعة عشر دينارا.

حكر، عن مائة وثلاثة فدادين وسدس ونصف قيراط وحبة، ثلاثة وثمانون دينارا ونصف وثمن وحبتان. تفصيله:

قطيعة اربعة دنانير وثلث وثمن ودانق الفدان، عن احكار[196] الادر، عن اربعة فدادين وسدس وحبتين، عشرون دينارا وثمن ودانق.

قطيعة دينار واحد الفدان، عن ثمانية وعشرين فدانا وقيراط، ثمانية وعشرون دينارا وقيراط.

قطيعة نصف دينار الفدان، عن سبعين فدانا ونصف وثلث وثمن ودانق، خمسة وثلاثون دينارا وربع وسدس ونصف ثمن.

الاضافة، عشرة دنانير وثلث.

زائد القطيعة، اثنان وخمسون دينارا وسدس ودانق.

المقرر عن خراج الزراعة ببركة ابن شكلة عن المزدرع عما يجب للديوان عن الماء المحمول على اعناق الابقار بالسواقي الديوانية وحرث الاراضي بالابقار والمحاريث الديوانية، ثلاثة عشر دينارا وخمسة قراريط ودانق.

زراعة الاواسي الديوانية بالسواقي وغيرها، خارجا عما تاخر بيعه من الكرات، وهو خمسة دنانير، خمسمائة وديناران وسدس وثمن ودانق. والسمسم والكراويا والثوم والفدن على ما تقدم في الجملة. وذلك المبلغ عن ثمن الزهر، وثمرة النخل، والباذنجان، والعجور، والفول الاخضر، واللوبيا، واليقطين، وجميع اصناف الخضر.

رسم خلايا النحل بالاعمال الفيومية ثلاثة وعشرون قنطارا.

بها معصرة قصب سكر بظاهرها ذات حجرين دائرين بالابقار.

بها من الجوامع والمساجد، احد وثلاثون معبدا. تفصيله:

جوامع، اثنان: جامع الصلاة بالمدينة، والجامع اليوسفي بظاهرها من الجهة البحرية.

مساجد، تسعة وعشرون مسجدا.

مدارس، خمس: ثلاث شافعية واثنتان مالكية.

كنائس، اربع.

والذي يشتمل عليه ارتفاع زكاتها، ثلاثمائة واحد وخمسون دينارا وربع وسدس وحبتان. تفصيله:

الدولبة، مائتان واربعة واربعون دينارا وقيراط وحبة.

عن الرقيق، ستة وعشرون دينارا وخمسة قراريط وحبة.

العقار، نصف وثمن دينار.

الصادر، ديناران ونصف.

الخرص، اثنان واربعون دينارا وخمسة قراريط. تفصيله:

193 ساقط من أ. س.: مائة.

194 أ. س. تفصيل ذلك.

195 أ. س.: ثلث.

196 أ. س.: حكر.

Land tax on perennial plants and on lands subject to long-term lease (*kharāj al-rātib wa'l-aḥkār*), 165 ⅛ 1/48 1/72 dinars:

Established tax (*al-mustaqarr*), 112 ½ ⅓ ⅛ 2/72 dinars:

Basic assessment (*aṣl*), for 112 ⅔ 1/48 1/72 feddans, 102 ½ dinars, ⅛ 2/72:

Land tax on perennial plants at the rate of 2 dinars [per feddan], for 9 ½ feddans, 19 dinars;

Land tax on land under long-term lease, for 103 ⅙ 1/48 1/72 feddans, 83 ½ ⅛ 2/72 dinars:

At the rate of 4 ⅓ 1/144 dinars per feddan for long term lease of buildings, for 4 ⅙ 2/72 feddans, 20 ⅛ 1/144 dinars;

at the rate of 1 dinar per feddan, for 28 1/24 feddans, 28 1/24 dinars;

at the rate of ½ dinar per feddan, for 70 ½ ⅓ ⅛ 1/144 feddans, 35 ½ ⅙ 1/16 dinars;

The addition (*iḍāfa*), 10 ⅓ dinars.

Added tax-rate [on long-term lease] (*zā'id al-qaṭīʿa*), 52 ⅙ 1/144 dinars.

This also includes the established (*al-muqarrar*) land tax on what has been sown at Birkat Ibn Shikla, which is owed to the Dīwān in return for water delivered upon the necks of cattle in the Dīwān's waterwheels, and for ploughing the land by means of the Dīwān's cattle and ploughs, 13 5/24 1/144 dinars.

The cultivation of the crown estates by means of waterwheels and other means: 502 ⅙ ⅛ 1/144 dinars. This excludes the leek, whose sale has been delayed, and its value is 5 dinars. The totals of the sesame, the caraway, the garlic and the [crown estate] feddans are mentioned above. This sum represents the monetary value of flowers, the fruit of date palms, eggplants, green melons (*ʿajūr*), green beans (*lūbiyā*), pumpkins (*yaqṭīn*), and all kinds of green vegetables.

The fee on beehives in the district of the Fayyum, 23 qinṭārs.

In the city, at its outskirts, there is a sugarcane press with two stones turned by cattle.

In it there are thirty-one places of worship, congregational mosques and neighbourhood mosques, including:

Two congregational mosques: the congregational mosque in the city, and the Yūsufī congregational mosque in its outskirts in the northern direction;

Twenty-nine neighbourhood mosques.

Five madrasas: three Shafiʿite and two Malikite.

Four Churches.

The revenues of the alms-tax in it are 351 ¼ ⅙ 2/72 dinars:

merchandise (*al-dawlaba*), 244 1/24 1/72 dinars;

slaves (*raqīq*), 26 5/24 1/72 dinars;

real estate (*al-ʿaqār*) ½ ⅛ dinar;

al-ṣādir, 2 ½ dinars;

خرص العنب دينار.
خرص النخل احد واربعون دينارا وخمسة قراريط.
ثمن الماشية، عن سبعة وعشرين راسا، خمسة وثلاثون دينارا ونصف وثلث. تفصيله:
ابقار، عن تسعة ارؤس، سبعة عشر دينارا وربع وثمن.
جاموس، عن ثمانية ارؤس، ستة عشر دينارا وربع وثمن. تفصيله:
مسنات، عن خمسة ارؤس،[197] اثنا عشر دينارا ونصف وربع وثمن.
تبعان، عن ثلاثة ارؤس، ثلاثة دنانير ونصف.
بقر احمر، تبيع واحد، دينار واحد.
اغنام، عن ثمانية عشر راسا، ثمانية عشر دينارا وثلث وثمن. تفصيله:
بياض، عن ستة عشر راسا، سبعة عشر دينارا وربع وثمن.
شعارى، عن راسين، دينار واحد وقيراطان.

الجوالي، عن ثلاثمائة وثلاثة واربعين نفرا، ستمائة وستة وثمانون دينارا. تفصيله:
المقيمون بها، عن مائتين وتسعة وستين نفرا، خمسمائة وثمانية وثلاثون دينارا.
الناعون عنها، بالوجه البحري والقبلي، عن اربعة وسبعين نفرا، مائة وثمانية واربعون دينارا. تفصيله:
الوجه البحري، عن تسعة وعشرين نفرا، ثمانية وخمسون دينارا.
الوجه القبلي، عن خمسة واربعين نفرا، تسعون دينارا.

والذي اشتمل عليه ارتفاع المواريث الحشرية لسنة احدى واربعين وستمائة، اربعمائة واربعة وثلاثون دينارا وربع وثمن وحبتان على ما تقدم تفصيله.

ارتفاع الاحباس بها، الف واثنان واربعون دينارا وربع وسدس وحبتان. تفصيله:
الهلالي، ستمائة وستة وتسعون دينارا.
المعجل من اجرة الحوانيت ثلاثون دينارا وربع وسدس ونصف ثمن.
الاحكار، سبعة وستون دينارا وثلث وثمن وحبتان.
مواقف للصيادين، ثمانية دنانير.
العقود، نظير سنة اربعين، خمسة وثمانون دينارا ونصف.[198]
زائد صرف الخراجي، سبعة وعشرون دينارا وقيراط وحبة.
ثمن ثمرة الانشاب بالمدينة والنواحي، عشرة دنانير ونصف قيراط وحبة.

estimate [of dates, grapes and olives], 42 5/24 dinars:
estimate of grapes, 1 dinar;
estimate of dates, 41 5/24 dinars.
Monetary value of livestock, for 27 heads, 35 1/2 1/3 dinars:
cattle, for nine heads: 17 1/4 1/8 dinars:
water buffalo, for eight heads: 16 1/4 1/8 dinars:
two-year old cows, for five heads, 12 1/2 1/4 1/8 dinars;
monetary value of yearling calves, for three heads, 3 1/2 dinars;
cows, one yearling calf, 1 dinar.
small cattle, for 18 heads, 18 1/3 1/8 dinars:
sheep, for 16 heads, 17 1/4 1/8 dinars;
goats, for two heads, 1 2/24 dinar.

The poll-tax, for 343 individuals, 686 dinars:
those who reside in it, for 269 individuals, 538 dinars;
absentees, in the northern and southern regions, for 74 individuals, 148 dinars:
the northern region, for 29 individuals, 58 dinars;
the southern region, for 45 individuals, 90 dinars.

The revenue from intestate inheritances (*al-mawārīth al-ḥashriyya*) for 641 [AD 1243–4], 434 1/4 1/8 2/72 dinars, as previously mentioned and listed.

The entire revenue of the [Ministry of] Endowments in it, 1,042 1/4 1/6 2/72 dinars:
lunar calendar [taxes], 696 dinars.
the advance payments of the rents of the shops, 30 1/4 1/6 1/16 dinars;
land tax on lands under long term lease, 67 1/3 1/8 2/72;
berths of the fishermen, 8 dinars;
contracts, on the basis of the year [6]40 [AD 1242–3], 85 1/2 dinars;
the land-tax overpayment (?, *zāʾid ṣarf al-kharājī*), 27 1/24 1/72 dinars;
monetary value of the fruit of plantations in the city and its localities, 10 1/48 1/72 dinars.

197 أ. س.: ارس.
198 ساقط من أ. س.: ونصف.

تتمة الجملة من جملة ما استظهر به عما ورد مضاف الختمات[199] في الاحكار[200] واجرة الحوانيت وغير ذلك، مائة وسبعة عشر دينارا ونصف وربع وثمن[201] وحبة.

المراعي بها، عن خمسمائة وستين راسا، ثلاثمائة وستون درهما ونصف، تسعة دنانير وحبة. تفصيله:

راتب، عن خمسين راسا، مائة واثنا عشر درهما ونصف.

طارئ، عن خمسمائة وعشرة اروس، مائتان وثلاثة عشر درهما. تفصيله:

قطيعة خمسين درهما المائة، عن ثلاثمائة، مائة[202] وخمسون درهما.

قطيعة ثلاثين درهما المائة، عن مائتين وعشرة اروس، ثلاثة وستون درهما.

رسم المستخدمين، خمسة وثلاثون درهما.[203]

الكيالة، الف ومائتا دينار.

حفر[204] القزازين، اربعمائة واربعة وثمانون دينارا.

سوق الدواب، مائة وخمسة وخمسون دينارا. ذكر انه قرر لاستقبال سنة احدى واربعين وستمائة بما مبلغه مائة وعشرون دينارا.[205]

الصبغ، مائتان واربعون دينارا.

والمرتب لائمة المساجد على اجر الحوانيت الديوانية بمدينة الفيوم ما مبلغه ثلاثون دينارا. تفصيله:

القاضي الاجل مجد الدين عبد الله بن نصر بن علي بن[206] المجاور، امام مسجد ابن فحل المعلق على بحر ذات الصفاء، ثمانية عشر دينارا.

الفقيه عبد العزيز بن معافى، امام مسجد القبة، ستة دنانير.

الفقيه القطب ثعلب بن طاهر، مما هو الان بيد ولده، امام المسجد المعروف بابن فخر الدولة، ستة دنانير.

والذي بها من التقاوي الديوانية المستقرة الى اخر سنة احدى واربعين وستمائة والمطلقة لسنة اثنتين واربعين وستمائة الى حين عمله، عينا، مائة وعشرون دينارا[207] وثلث ودانق؛ غلة مائة واربعة ارادب وربع وسدس ونصف قيراط وربع قيراط. تفصيله:

قمح، ستة وستون اردبا ونصف وثلث.

شعير، اردب واحد وربع.

فول، تسعة عشر اردبا.

برسيم، ستة عشر اردبا وثلث.

كراويا، ثلثا اردب.

زريعة نيلة، نصف وربع قيراط.

بزق بصل، ثلث اردبا.

---

199 ط. م.: الحتمات.

200 ساقط من أ. س.: في الاحكار (لكنه يضيفها على هامش الصفحة).

201 وثمن ساقط من أ. س.

202 ط. م. يكرر الكلمة مائة.

203 ساقط من أ. س.: رسم المستخدمين خمسة وثلاثون درهما.

204 أ. س.: جفر.

205 أ. س.: مائة دينار وعشرون.

206 ساقط من أ. س.: بن.

207 أ. س. يضيف وسدس.

The adjustment to the aggregate, which is the total of recently added sealed records of revenues registered in the prosperous Dīwān, from lands subject to long-term lease, from rent of shops, and other sources: 117 ½ ¼ ⅛ 1/72 dinars.

The pasture fee in it, for 560 heads, 360 ½ dirhams, which are 9 1/72 dinars:

Permanent pasture lands (*rātib*), for 50 heads, 112 ½ dirhams;

Seasonal pasture lands (*ṭāriʾ*), for 510 heads, 213 dirhams:

at the rate of 50 dirhams per 100 [heads], for 300 [heads], 150 dirhams;

at the rate of 30 dirhams per 100 [heads], for 210 heads, 63 dirhams;

The government agents' fee (*rasm al-mustakhdamīn*), 35 dirhams.

The measurement fee (*al-kiyāla*), 1,200 dinars.

The pit looms of the weavers (*ḥufar al-qazzāzīn*[58]), 484 dinars.

The riding animals market (*sūq al-dawābb*), 155 dinars. It has been mentioned that it was fixed, from the beginning of 641 [AD 1243–4], at 120 dinars.

The dye, 240 dinars.

The payment allocated to the imams of the mosques from the rent of the Dīwān's shops in Madīnat al-Fayyūm is 30 dinars:

The eminent judge, Majd al-Dīn ʿAbdallāh ibn Naṣr ibn ʿAlī ibn al-Mujāwir, imam of the mosque of Ibn Fiḥl, which is arched over Dhāt al-Ṣafāʾ Canal, 18 dinars;

the jurist ʿAbd al-ʿAzīz ibn Muʿāfā, imam of the mosque of al-Qubba, 6 dinars;

the eminent jurist Thaʿlab ibn Ṭāhir, imam of the mosque known as Ibn Fakhr al-Dawla — although it is now held by his son — 6 dinars.

The Dīwān's seed advances (*al-taqāwī al-dīwāniyya*) in it, as established by the end of the year 641, and distributed (*al-muṭlaqa*) for the year 642, up to the preparation of this account, are, in specie, 120 ⅓ 1/144 dinars; [and in] grains, 104 ¼ ⅙ 1/48 1/96 ardabbs:

wheat, 66 ½ ⅓ ardabbs;

barley, 1 ¼ ardabb;

broad beans, 19 ardabbs;

clover (*birsīm*), 16 ⅓ ardabbs;

caraway, ⅓ ardabb;

seeds (*zarīʿa*) of indigo (*nīla*), 1/48 1/96 ardabb;

onion seeds (?, *bazq baṣal*),[59] ⅓ ardabb.

---

[58] On *qizāza* as weaving in general, and not just weaving of silk, see Ibn al-Ḥajj, *al-Madkhal*, 4 vols (Beirut: Dār al-Fikr, 1990), IV, 233 (*al-ḥiyāka wa-hiya al-qizāza*). His section on *ṣināʿat al-qizāza* is clearly about weaving in general, not silk-weaving specifically, even if silk is mentioned (IV, 239–43). In a recent contribution, Mahmood Ibrahim identifies the *qazzāzūn* as silk-weavers, but there is no explicit reference to silk in any of the passages which he discusses. See Mahmood Ibrahim, 'The 727/1327 Silk Weavers' Rebellion in Alexandria: Religious Xenophobia, Homophobia, or Economic Grievances', *Mamlūk Studies Review*, 16 (2012), 123–42.

[59] The term *bazq* appears three more times in the treatise in connection with onions. The meaning may be derived from *bazaqa al-arḍ*, to sow. It may also be a mistake for *bizr* (seeds) and indeed in one instance both AS and MP have *bizr*.

والموقوف والمتاخر الباقي[208] الى اخر سنة احدى واربعين وستمائة، عينا، مائة وتسعة عشر دينارا ونصف قيراط وحبة. وعسل نحل، اربعة قناطير وخمسة وثلاثون رطلا ونصف وثلث.

والموقوف خاصة، باسم القصار المنفصل، سبعة دنانير وربع ونصف قيراط.

الباقي، مائة واحد عشر دينارا ونصف وربع وحبة والعسل النحل.

الملالية: عبارة عن بليدة صغيرة من ضواحي المدينة وزنارها بجوار اراضي دار الرماد والاعلام والمصلوب وقشوش. جدارها في ارض المصلوب ولها اريضة ليس فيها نخل ولا شجر قد غرس فيها ودي صغير فيها برج حمام وبيوت يسيرة قريبة الى المدينة جدا من شرقي الفيوم على سكة الطريق المسلوك على يسار السائر الى مصر. مقطعة حينئذ لعلاء[209] الدين الساقي وجمال الدين بن يغمور. عبرتها الجيشية الف ومائة دينار. اهلها بنو زرعة، فخذ من بني كلاب. تشرب من البحر[210] الاعظم ولها خليج خاص من الجهة البحرية؛ عبرته خمس قبض.

ارتفاعها، عينا، عن خراج ثلاث سواقي احداها على خليج ذات الصفاء لوصول اراضيها اليه وساقيتان على دار الرماد قصب وخضراوات وقطاني ستون دينارا؛ وغلة مائتان وستة عشر اردبا. تفصيله:

قمح مائة وستة وستون اردبا.

شعير خمسون اردبا.

وعليها كيالة ورسوم ومراعي، مائة وسبعون درهما وربع وثمن، نقد مصر اربعة دنانير وربع وحبة. وغلة اربعة عشر اردبا وربع وسدس.[211] تفصيله:

قمح اثنا عشر اردبا ونصف وثمن.

شعير اردب واحد وثلثان[212] وثمن.

The withheld payments (*al-mawqūf*) and the outstanding payments until the end of 641 [AD 1243–4]: in specie, 119 1/48 1/72 dinars; and in honey, 4 qinṭārs, 35 ½ ⅓ raṭls:

Withheld payments, which relate to the dismissed fuller (*al-qaṣṣār al-munfaṣil*): 7 ¼ 1/48 dinars.

Outstanding payments: 111 ½ ¼ 1/72 dinars; and the honey.

Al-Malāliyya:[60] This is a small village, at the outskirts of the city. It is adjacent to the lands of Dār[61] al-Rammād, al-Aʿlām, al-Maṣlūb and Qushūsh. Its fences (*jidārihā*) are in the lands of al-Maṣlūb. It has small plot of land (*urayḍa*), in which there are no date palms or trees, although it had been planted with small palm shoots. It has a dovecote and a few houses. It is very close to the city, on the eastern side of the Fayyum, to the left of one traveling towards Cairo on the main road. At that time it was allocated as an *iqṭāʿ* to ʿAlāʾ al-Dīn al-Sāqī and Jamāl al-Dīn ibn Yaghmūr.[62] Its fiscal value is 1,100 army dinars. Its people are the Banū Zarʿa, a section of the Banū ʿAjlān.[63] It gets its water from the Main Canal, through its own dedicated canal that issues from the north bank [of the Main Canal], with a water quota of five *qabḍas*.

Its revenue:

In specie, from land tax on sugar plantation, vegetables and legumes (*qaṭānī*), irrigated by three waterwheels, one of which is on Dhāt al-Ṣafāʾ Canal, since its lands reach it, and two others on Dār al-Rammād [Canal]: 60 dinars.

In grains, 216 ardabbs:

wheat, 166 ardabbs;

barley, 50 ardabbs.

The measurement fee, other fees and the pasture tax are 170 ¼ ⅛ dirhams, which in the currency of Cairo is 4 ¼ 1/72 dinars;[64] and in grains, 14 ¼ ⅙ ardabbs:

wheat, 12 ½ ⅛ ardabbs;

barley, 1 ⅔ ⅛ ardabb.

---

208 أ. س.: والباقي.

209 أ. س.: لعلاي.

210 أ. س.: البحر.

211 أ. س.، ط. م. يضيفا الفقرة: وعليها زكاة عن ثمن ماشية، عن عشرة أرؤس، ثمانية دنانير وثلث. تفصيله:
بياض، ستة أرؤس، ستة دنانير وسدس. شعارى، أربعة أرؤس، ديناران وسدس. ونوردها في محلها.

212 أ. س.: ثلثاي.

---

60 Modern location (uncertain): Kufūr al-Nīl (كفور النيل). Halm, *Ägypten*, p. 262, identifies al-Malāliyya with Shallāla, but this identification is questionable, as al-Nābulusī has the two villages quite distant from each other. Ramzī, *Al-Qāmūs*, I, 114, identifies al-Malāliyya with ʿIzbat Ḥusayn Bek Ramzī, near Dār al-Rammād, but we could not locate that ʿIzba. In line with Nābulusī's description, which places al-Malāliyya near the lands of Dār al-Rammād, al-Aʿlām, al-Maṣlūb and Qushūsh, we locate it in modern Kufūr al-Nīl.

61 Elsewhere: Khawr al-Rammād.

62 Jamāl al-Dīn Mūsā ibn Yaghmur al-Yārūqī was an amir of Turcomen origin, mentioned as governor of Cairo under al-Ṣāliḥ in 1248 and later, by 1250, as governor of Damascus. See R. Stephen Humphreys, *From Saladin to the Mongols* (Albany: State University of New York Press, 1977), p. 294; Humphreys, 'The Emergence of the Mamluk Army', *Studia Islamica*, 45 (1977), 67–99 (p. 73); Humphreys, 'The Emergence of the Mamluk Army (Conclusion)', *Studia Islamica*, 46 (1977), 147–82 (p. 157); Reuven Amitai-Preiss, 'The Mamluk Officer Class during the Reign of Sultan Baybars', in *War and Society in the Eastern Mediterranean, 7th 15th Centuries*, ed. by Yaacov Lev (Leiden: Brill, 1997), pp. 267–300 (p. 299); Anne-Marie Eddé, 'Kurdes et Turcs dans l'armée ayyoubide de Syrie du Nord', in *War and Society in the Eastern Mediterranean, 7th–15th Centuries*, ed. by Yaacov Lev (Leiden: Brill, 1997), pp. 225–36 (pp. 229, 234).

63 AS and MP: Banū Kilāb.

64 In both MP and AS, the section on alms-tax of the village is inserted here, apparently out of place. We have placed it after the discussion of fees.

تفصيل ذلك:

الرسوم والكيالة مائة واثنان واربعون درهما ونصف وربع وثمن، واربعة عشر اردبا وربع وسدس على ما فصل. تفصيل ذلك:

شد العين، احد وعشرون درهما ونصف وربع.
رسم الجراريف، خمسة واربعون درهما.
رسم الحصاد، ثلاثة وخمسون درهما.[213]
رسم الخفارة، خمسة عشر درهما.
رسم[214] الاجران، ثمانية دراهم وثمن وتسعة ارادب وربع وثمن، غلة:
قمح، سبعة ارادب ونصف وثلث.
شعير، اردب واحد وربع وسدس وثمن.
الكيالة، خمسة ارادب وقيراط:
قمح، اربعة ارادب وثلثان[215] وثمن.
وشعير ربع اردب.
المراعي، عن ثمانية وخمسين راسا طارئ، سبعة وعشرون درهما ونصف. تفصيله:
قطيعة درهم، عن اثنى عشر راسا، اثنا عشر درهما.
قطيعة خمسة وعشرين المائة، عن ستة واربعين راسا، احد عشر درهما ونصف.
رسم المستخدمين، اربعة دراهم.[216]

وعليها زكاة عن ثمن ماشية، عن عشرة اروس، ثمانية دنانير وثلث. تفصيله:
بياض، ستة اروس، ستة دنانير وسدس.
شعارى، اربعة اروس، ديناران وسدس.

ليس فيها للاحباس شيء.

فيذكر[217] لخولي البحر[218] عليها، قمح، نصف اردب.

عليها من الاتبان خمسمائة وستون شنيفا.

المربى فيها من الفروج ثلاثمائة وعشرة. تفصيله:
للديوان، مائتان وعشرة.
وللمقطعين مائة.

ومن حرف[219] الالف، العدوة: هذه البلدة بلدة حسنة تحفها البساتين من جهاتها الاربع. ذات نخيل وثمار وبساتين[220] واشجار وكروم وخراج معلوم. محلها من شرقي بلد الفيوم. وبها معصرة ذات حجر واحد يدور بالابقار. ولها من الماء سبع قبض من البحر الاعظم من الجهة البحرية، يزرع عليه الصيفي والشتوي. وبها جامع، تقام فيه الجمعة، ومسجد يعرف بالقبة. اهلها بنو زرعة، فخذ من بنى عجلان.

In detail:

The fees and the measurement fee, 142 ½ ¼ ⅛ dirhams, and 14 ¼ ⅙ ardabbs, as specified above. [The fees] include:

supervision of the land survey, 21 ½ ¼ dirhams;
dredging fee, 45 dirhams;
harvest fee, 53 dirhams;
protection fee, 15 dirhams;
threshing-floor fee, 8 ⅛ dirhams; and in grains, 9 ¼ ardabbs:
wheat, 7 ½ ⅓ ardabbs;
barley, 1 ¼ ⅙ ardabb.
The measurement fee, 5 1/24 ardabbs:
wheat, 4 ⅔ ⅛ ardabbs;
barley, ¼ ardabb.
The pasture tax, for 58 heads, on seasonal pasture lands, 27 ½ dirhams:
at the rate of one dirham per head, for 12 heads, 12 dirhams;
at the rate of 25 [dirham] per hundred [heads], for 46 heads, 11 ½ dirhams;
the government agents' fee, 4 dirhams.

The alms-tax imposed on it, for the monetary value of 10 heads of livestock, 8 ⅓ dinars:
sheep, for six heads, 6 ⅙ dinars;
goats, for four heads, 2 ⅙ dinars;

For the [Ministry of] Endowments, nothing to be mentioned.

For the overseer of the canal, wheat, ½ ardabb.

Hay, 560 bales.

The chicken reared in it, 310:
210 for the Dīwān;
100 for the *iqṭāʿ*-holders.

Also from the letter 'alif': al-ʿIdwa.[65] This is a pleasant village, surrounded by orchards on four sides, with date palms, fruits, trees and vineyards, and some [crops subject to] land tax. It is towards the east of the Fayyum. It has a press of one stone, turned by cattle. Its water quota is seven *qabḍas*, from the northern bank of the Main Canal. It sows summer and winter crops. It has a congregational mosque, in which the Friday prayer is held, and a neighbourhood mosque known as al-Qubba [lit., the Dome]. Its people are of the Banū Zarʿa, a branch of the Banū ʿAjlān.

213 ساقط من أ. س.: رسم الحصاد ثلاثة وخمسون درهما.
214 ساقط من أ. س.: رسم.
215 أ. س.: ثلثاي.
216 وفي كلا المخطوطين فقرة الزكاة واردة في غير مكانها، ضمن رسم الكيالة.
217 أ. س.: فنذكره.
218 أ. س.: الحسد.
219 أ. س.: حروف.
220 ساقط من أ. س.: وبساتين.

65 Modern location: al-ʿEdwa (العدوة). Halm, *Ägypten*, p. 276: ʿUdwat Saila; Salmon, 'Répertoire', p. 46; Ibn al-Jīʿān, *Kitāb al-tuḥfa*, p. 152; de Sacy, *État des provinces*, p. 681 (also ʿUdwat Sayla); Savigny, *Description de l'Égypte*, p. 129; Amédée Boinet Bey, *Dictionnaire géographique de l'Égypte* (Le Caire: Imprimerie nationale, 1899), p. 177: Al-Adawa or al-Edwa; Ramzī, *Al-Qāmūs*, II/III, 94: Al-ʿIdwa.

ارتفاعها، عينا، مائتان وتسعة وثمانون دينارا وثلث وثمن وحبتان؛ وغلة الف وتسعمائة وسبعة ارادب وسدس. تفصيله:

قمح، ثمانمائة واثنان وسبعون اردبا ونصف وربع ونصف قيراط.

شعير، اربعمائة وتسعة وثلاثون اردبا وثلث وربع ونصف ثمن.[221]

فول، اربعمائة واربعون اردبا وربع اردب.

ارز احمر بقشره، مائة واربعة وخمسون اردبا ونصف.

ومن القصب السكر، زراعة المرابعين، ثمانون فدانا. تفصيله:

راس، خمسة وستون فدانا.

خلفة، خمسة عشر فدانا.

تفصيل ذلك:

مال الهلالي، ثمانية وعشرون دينارا:

الحانوت، ستة عشر دينارا ونصف وربع.

الكتاني، سبعة دنانير ونصف.

القزازين، ديناران وربع.

الفروج، دينار ونصف.

خراج الراتب[222] والحكر، مائتان وخمسة عشر دينارا وسدس وثمن وحبتان. تفصيله:

الاصل، عن ثمانية وثمانين فدانا وقيراط ودانق، مائة واحد وثمانون دينارا وربع ودانق. تفصيله:

كرم، قطيعة خمسة دنانير وثلث الفدان، عن اربعة فدادين ونصف وثلث وثمن، ستة وعشرون دينارا وثلث وثمن.

راتب، عن احد وسبعين فدانا وثلث وربع وثمن، مائة وثلاثة واربعون دينارا وربع وسدس.

حكر، عن احد عشر فدانا وربع وثمن ودانق.

الاضافة، اثنان وعشرون دينارا وثلثان[223] وحبة.

زائد القطيعة، احد عشر دينارا وربع وثمن ودانق.

خراج فدن[224] الزراعة، اربعة دنانير وخمسة قراريط ودانق. تفصيل:

الاصل، ثلاثة دنانير ونصف وربع:

ثوم، عن فدان واحد وثلث وربع ونصف ثمن، ثلاثة دنانير وسدس وثمن.

قلقاس، عن ثمن وحبتين، ثلث وثمن دينار.

الاضافة، ثلث وثمن ودانق.

خراج حكر الديوان بالعدوة، ديناران وربع.

خراج المناجزة، الف وثمانمائة واربعون اردبا. تفصيله:

قمح، ثمانمائة وخمسة واربعون اردبا.

شعير، اربعمائة واثنان وعشرون اردبا ونصف.

ارز بقشره، مائة وخمسون اردبا.

فول، اربعمائة واثنان وعشرون اردبا ونصف.

مشاطرة المقاث، سبعة وثلاثون دينارا ونصف ثمن.

221 ط. م.: وثمن.

222 أ. س.: التراب.

223 أ. س.: ثلث.

224 ساقط من أ. س.: فدن.

Its revenues in specie are 289 1/3 1/8 2/72 dinars; and in grains, 1,907 1/6 ardabbs:

wheat, 872 1/2 1/4 1/48 ardabbs;

barley, 439 1/3 1/4 1/16 ardabbs;

broad beans, 440 1/4 ardabbs;

red rice in hull, 154 1/2 ardabbs.

The sugarcane sown by quarter-share labourers, 80 feddans:

first harvest, 65 feddans;

second harvest, 15 feddans.

[The revenue in detail]:

lunar calendar tax, 28 dinars:

the shop, 16 1/2 1/4 dinars;

the flax merchants, 7 1/2 dinars;

the weavers, 2 1/4 dinars;

chicken [concession],[66] 1 1/2 dinar;

Land tax on perennial plants and on lands subject to long-term lease, 215 1/6 1/8 2/72 dinars:

Basic assessment, for 88 1/24 1/144 feddans, 181 1/4 1/144 dinars:

vineyards, at the rate of 5 1/3 dinars per feddan, for 4 1/2 1/3 1/8 feddans, 26 1/3 1/8 dinars;

perennial plants, for 71 1/3 1/4 1/8 feddans, 143 1/4 1/6 dinars;

land subject to long-term lease, for 11 1/4 1/8 1/144 feddans [at a rate of 1 dinar per feddan].

the addition, 22 2/3 1/72 dinars;

the added tax-rate [on long-term lease], 11 1/4 1/8 1/144 dinars.

Land tax on cash crops assessed by feddans, 4 5/24 1/144 dinars:

the basic assessment, 3 1/2 1/4 dinars:

garlic, for 1 1/3 1/4 1/16 feddan, 3 1/6 1/8 dinars;

colocasia, for 1/8 2/72 feddan, 1/3 1/8 dinar.

the addition, 1/3 1/8 1/144 [dinar].

Land tax on the Dīwān's land in al-ʿIdwa which is subject to long-term lease (*kharāj ḥikr al-dīwān*), 2 1/4 dinars.

Munājaza land tax, 1,840 ardabbs:

wheat, 845 ardabbs;

barley, 422 1/2 ardabbs;

rice in hull, 150 ardabbs;

broad beans, 422 1/2 ardabbs.

66 Elsewhere a concession for the sale of chicken, *ḍamān al-farrūj*.

قرط بالعدوة من زراعة الاوسية، ديناران وسدس ونصف قيراط وحبة.

زراعة الاوسية، فدن[225] قصب سكر، زراعة المرابعين، ثمانون فدانا:
راس، خمسة وستون فدانا.
خلفة، خمسة عشر فدانا.

الوفر، خمسة وخمسون اردبا وسدس:
قمح، خمسة وعشرون اردبا وثلث.
شعير، اثنا عشر اردبا وثلثان.
فول، اثنا عشر اردبا وثلثان.
ارز بقشره، اربعة ارادب ونصف.

الحمولة، اثنا عشر اردبا:
قمح، اردبان وربع وسدس ونصف قيراط.
شعير، اربعة ارادب[226] وربع وسدس ونصف ثمن.
فول، خمسة ارادب وقيراطان.

والمربى من الفروج بها، ستمائة. تفصيله:
المستقر تربيته للديوان المعمور، مائة وخمسون فروجا.
المرتب تربيته، بما فيه من اجرة التربية عما يخص المزارعين بحق الثلث، اربعمائة وخمسون.

وعليها من الزكاة، اثنان وعشرون دينارا وقيراط ونصف وحبة. تفصيله:
الخرص، ستة عشر دينارا ونصف وربع ونصف ثمن وحبة.
ثمن الاغنام، عن ستة اروس، خمسة دنانير وربع.

وعليها لديوان الاحباس، ديناران.

والمطلق بها من الرزق،[227] ثمانية وستون فدانا:
اولاد نجم بن رحيم خفراء الطريق، خمسون فدانا.
خفراء الناحية، ثمان فدادين.
النجارون،[228] اربعة فدادين.
خولي الاقصاب، ستة فدادين.

وعلى مزارعيها لخولي البحر، قمح، اردب واحد.

وعليها من الرسوم والمراعي والكيالة، عن الف وخمسة وخمسين درهما وربع وثمن، ستة وعشرون دينارا وربع وثمن وحبة؛ وغلة، مائة واربعة وثلاثون اردبا وثلثان وثمن. تفصيله:
قمح، خمسة وستون اردبا.
شعير، احد واربعون اردبا وربع وثمن.
فول، ثلاثة وعشرون اردبا وربع.
ارز بقشره، خمسة ارادب وسدس.

The *mushāṭara* land tax on cucurbitaceous fruits, 37 1/16 dinars.

Alfalfa in al-ʿIdwa, cultivated in the crown estate, 2 1/6 1/48 1/72 dinars.

The cultivation of the crown estate by quarter-share labourers, 80 feddans:
first harvest, 65 feddans;
second harvest, 15 feddans.

The surcharge (*wafr*), 55 1/6 ardabbs:
wheat, 25 1/3 ardabbs;
barley, 12 2/3 ardabbs;
broad beans, 12 2/3 ardabbs;
rice in hull, 4 1/2 ardabbs.

Transport fee (*al-ḥamūla*), 12 ardabbs:
wheat, 2 1/4 1/6 1/48 ardabbs;
barley, 4 1/4 1/6 1/16 ardabbs;
broad beans, 5 2/24 ardabbs.

The chicken reared in it, 600:
the established (*al-mustaqarr*) rearing for the prosperous Dīwān, 150 chicks.
the set rearing (*al-murattab tarbiyata-hu*), including the rearing wage for the tenants by their right to a third, 450.

The alms-tax, 22 1/24 1/48 1/72 dinars:
the estimate, 16 1/2 1/4 1/16 1/72 dinars;
monetary value of small cattle, for six heads, 5 1/4 dinars.

For the Ministry of Endowments, 2 dinars.

That which is distributed (*al-muṭlaqa*) as allowances (*rizaq*), 68 feddans:
[for] the sons of Najm ibn Raḥīm, watchmen of the road, 50 feddans;
[for] the watchmen of the village, 8 feddans;
[for] the carpenters, 4 feddans;
[for] the overseer of the sugarcane, 6 feddans;

For the overseer of the canal, wheat, 1 ardabb.

The fees, the pasture tax and the measurement fee, 1,055 1/4 1/8 dirhams, which are 26 1/4 1/8 1/72 dinars; and in grains, 134 2/3 1/8 ardabbs:
wheat, 65 ardabbs;
barley, 41 1/4 1/8 ardabbs;
broad beans, 23 1/4 ardabbs;
rice in hull, 5 1/6 ardabbs.

225 ساقط من أ. س.: فدن.
226 أ. س.: أردب بدل من اربع أرادب.
227 أ. س.: الزرق.
228 أ. س.: النجارة.

تفصيله:
الرسوم والكيالة، ثلاثمائة واثنان وسبعون درهما، ومائة واربعة وثلاثون اردبا وثلثان وثمن. تفصيله:
قمح، خمسة وستون اردبا.
شعير، احد واربعون اردبا وربع وثمن.
فول، ثلاثة وعشرون اردبا وربع.
ارز بقشره، خمسة ارادب وسدس.
تفصيله:
شد الاحباس، اربعة دراهم ونصف.
رسم جراريف، تسعون درهما.
رسم حصاد، ثلاثة وخمسون درهما.
رسم خفارة، خمسة عشر درهما.
رسم قلقاس، سبعة عشر درهما.
رسم جزر، سبعة وسبعون درهما ونصف.
رسم ثوم، خمسة وسبعون درهما.
رسم الاجران، سبعون درهما وثمانون اردبا وسدس:
قمح، اربعون اردبا وربع وسدس وثمن.
شعير، ستة عشر اردبا وربع وثمن.
فول، ثلاثة وعشرون اردبا وربع.
الكيالة، اربعة وخمسون اردبا ونصف وثمن:
قمح، اربعة وعشرون اردبا وثلث وثمن.
شعير، خمسة وعشرون اردبا.
ارز بقشره، خمسة ارادب وسدس.
المراعي، عن خمسمائة وستة وستين راسا، ستمائة وثلاثة وستون درهما وربع وثمن. تفصيله:
راتب، عن مائة واربعة وثمانين راسا، اربعمائة واربعة عشر درهما.
طارئ، عن ثلاثمائة واثنين وثمانين راسا، مائتان[229] واربعة عشر درهما:
قطيعة مائة درهم المائة راس، تسعة عشر راسا، تسعة عشر درهما.
قطيعة سبعين المائة راس، عن مائتين وخمسة عشر راسا، مائة وخمسون درهما ونصف.
قطيعة ثلاثين درهما المائة، عن مائة وثمانية واربعين راسا، اربعة واربعون درهما ونصف.
رسم المستخدمين، خمسة وثلاثون درهما وربع وثمن.[230]

والمطلق لها من التقاوي للمعاملين، ستمائة وستة وسبعون اردبا وسدس وثمن. تفصيله:
قمح، ثلاثمائة واربعون اردبا ونصف وثلث وثمن.
شعير، مائة واحد واربعون اردبا وقيراطان.
فول، مائة وستة وخمسون اردبا وسدس.
سلجم، نصف اردب وثلث.
ارز بقشره، سبعة وثلاثون اردبا وربع.

تقاوي المرابعين، عينا، ثلاثة وستون دينارا ونصف وربع؛ قمح، اربعة واربعون اردبا ونصف.

عليها من الاتبان، الف وسبعمائة شنيف.

[229] أ. س.: مائة.
[230] أ. س.: وسدس.

The [fees, the pasture tax and the measurement fee] include:
the fees and the measurement fee, 372 dirhams, and 134 ⅔ ⅛ ardabbs:
wheat, 65 ardabbs;
barley, 41 ½ ⅛ ardabbs;
broad beans, 23 ¼ ardabbs;
rice in hull, 5 ⅙ ardabbs.
In detail:
supervision of endowments, 4 ½ dirhams;
dredging fee, 90 dirhams;
harvest fee, 53 dirhams;
protection fee, 15 dirhams;
colocasia fee, 17 dirhams;
carrot fee, 77 ½ dirhams;
garlic fee, 75 dirhams;
threshing-floor fee, 70 dirhams; and 80 ⅙ ardabbs:
wheat, 40 ¼ ⅙ ⅛ ardabbs;
barley, 16 ¼ ⅛ ardabbs;
broad beans, 23 ¼ ardabbs;
measurement fee, 54 ½ ⅛ ardabbs:
wheat, 24 ⅓ ⅛ ardabbs;
barley, 25 ardabbs,
rice in hull, 5 ⅙ ardabbs.
The pasture tax, for 566 heads, 663 ¼ ⅛ dirhams:
permanent pasture lands, for 184 heads, 414 dirhams;
seasonal pasture lands, for 382 head, 214 dirhams:
at the rate of 100 dirhams per 100 head, for 19 head, 19 dirhams;
at the rate of 70 [dirhams] per 100 head, for 215 head, 150 ½ dirhams;
at the rate of 30 dirhams per 100 head, for 148 head, 44 ½ dirhams;
The government agents' fee, 35 ¼ ⅛ dirhams.

The seed advances distributed for the cultivators (*al-muʿāmilīn*), 676 ⅙ ⅛ ardabbs:
wheat, 340 ½ ⅓ ⅛ ardabbs;
barley, 141 ²⁄₂₄ ardabbs;
broad beans, 156 ⅙ ardabbs;
rape, ½ ⅓ ardabb;
rice in hull, 37 ¼ ardabbs.

Seed advances for the quarter-share labourers: in specie, 63 ½ ¼ dinars; [and in grains,] wheat, 44 ½ ardabbs.

Hay, 1700 bales.

ومن حرف[231] الالف، الاستنباط ومناشئها، مما ذكر في حرف الميم في باب ذكر البلاد على حروف[232] المعجم، وهي[233] ثمان مناشئ. هذه البلدة عبارة عن بلد قديمة قريبة[234] من المدينة من غربي الفيوم، مسافة نصف ساعة. ذات نخيل يسيرة جميز وسنط.[235] ليس بها بساتين ولا كروم. يحف بها شيء من الطرفاء. جارية في اقطاع جماعة من المقطعين. اهلها بنو جواب، فخذ من بنى كلاب. عبرتها جيشية، سبعة الاف وتسعمائة دينار وستة وسبعون دينارا. تسقى من خليج مبنى مجصص من الجانب القبلي، بحري خليج دسيا، عبرته ست قبض.

ارتفاعها، عينا، ستة وخمسون دينارا وسدس؛ وغلة الف وثمانمائة واثنان وعشرون اردبا:

قمح، تسعمائة.
شعير، تسعمائة.
سمسم، عشرون.
كشك وفريك، اردبان.

تفصيله:

المراعي، خمسة عشر دينارا وثلث ودانق.
خراج الراتب، ستة دنانير ونصف وثلث وحبة.
ثمن المقاث، خمسة عشر دينارا وربع وثمن.
خراج النخل، احد عشر دينارا.
ثمن ثلث التبن، سبعة دنانير وثلث وربع ونصف قيراط.

المناجزة، غلة، الف وثمانمائة واثنان وعشرون اردبا.

وعليها لديوان الاحباس، ديناران.

والرسوم والمراعي والكيالة، سبعة دنانير وربع وثمن؛ وغلة اثنان وثمانون اردبا وثلثان ونصف قيراط:

قمح، خمسة وخمسون اردبا وقيراطان.
شعير خمسة وعشرون اردبا ونصف وثلث.
فول، نصف وربع اردب ونصف قيراط.
سمسم، اردب واحد.

تفصيله:

الرسوم والكيالة، مائتان وخمسة عشر درهما وربع؛ وغلة اثنان وثمانون اردبا وثلثان ونصف قيراط على ما فصل.
تفصيله:

شد العين، ثلاثة عشر درهما وربع.
رسم الجراريف، تسعون درهما.
شد الاحباس، اربعة دراهم.
رسم الحصاد، ثلاثة وخمسون درهما.
رسم الخفارة، خمسة عشر درهما.
رسم الاجران، اربعون درهما؛ وغلة خمسة واربعون اردبا ونصف وربع. تفصيله:

قمح، اربعة وثلاثون اردبا ونصف وربع وثمن.
شعير، تسعة ارادب وثلث ونصف قيراط.
فول، نصف وربع اردب ونصف قيراط.
سمسم، نصف وربع اردب.

الكيالة، ستة وثلاثون اردبا وثلثان وربع ونصف قيراط:

231 أ. س.: حروف.
232 أ. س.: الحروف.
233 أ. س.: وهم.
234 ساقط من أ. س.: قريبة.
235 ط. م.: صنط.

Also beginning with the letter 'alif': al-Istinbāṭ[67] and its eight hamlets, as mentioned in the letter 'mīm' in the chapter describing the villages according to the letters of the alphabet. It is an ancient village, located close to the city, half an hour's [ride] to the west. It has a few date palms, sycamores and acacias, but no orchards or vineyards. It is surrounded by tamarisks. It is allocated as *iqṭā*ʿ to a group of *iqṭā*ʿ-holders. Its people are the Banū Jawwāb, a section of the Banū Kilāb. Its fiscal value is 7,976 army dinars. It is irrigated by a plastered canal with a weir (*mubnā mujaṣṣas*),[68] [issuing from] the southern side [of the Main Canal], north of Disyā Canal. Its [water] quota is six *qabḍas*.

Its revenue in specie, 56 ⅙ dinars; and in grains, 1,822 ardabbs:

wheat, 900;
barley, 900;
sesame, 20;
kishk and *farīk*, 2 ardabbs.

[The revenue in specie]:

the pasture tax, 15 ⅓ 1/144 dinars;
land tax on perennial plants, 6 ½ ⅓ 1/72 dinars;
monetary value of cucurbitaceous fruits, 15 ¼ ⅛ dinars;
land tax on date palms (*kharāj al-nakhl*), 11 dinars;
monetary value of a third of the hay [levy], 7 ⅓ ¼ 1/48 dinars.

Munājaza land tax, in grains, 1,822 ardabbs.

For the Ministry of Endowments, 2 dinars.

The fees, the pasture tax and the measurement fee, 7 ¼ ⅛ dinars; and in grains, 82 ⅔ 1/48 ardabbs:

wheat, 55 2/24 ardabbs;
barley, 25 ½ ⅓ ardabbs;
broad beans ¾ 1/48 ardabb;
sesame, 1 ardabb.
[Of that], the fees and the measurement fee: 215 ¼ dirhams; and in grains, 82 ⅔ 1/48 ardabbs, as listed above. In detail:

supervision of the land survey, 13 ¼ dirhams;
dredging fee, 90 dirhams;
supervision of endowments, 4 dirhams;
harvest fee, 53 dirhams;
protection fee, 15 dirhams;
threshing-floor fee, 40 dirhams; and in grains, 45 ½ ¼ ardabbs:

wheat, 34 ½ ¼ ⅛ ardabbs;
barley, 9 ⅓ 1/48 ardabbs;
broad beans, ½ ¼ 1/48 ardabb;
sesame, ¾ ardabb.

67 Modern location: al-Sumbāṭ (السمباط). Salmon, 'Répertoire', p. 60; Zéki, 'Une description', p. 38; Savigny, *Description de l'Égypte*, p. 128; Boinet Bey, *Dictionnaire géographique*, p. 510; Ramzī, *Al-Qāmūs*, II/III, 94, following Amélineau, *La géographie*, Jebnouti = Sebnouti = Al-Sunbāṭ.

68 Several sub-canals are described in the text as having or lacking a *bunyān*, literally 'structure'. In the variant here, the canal is described as *mubnā*, i.e., having a *bunyān* structure on it. As the terms *bunyān* and *mabnā* are used earlier in the treatise to describe the spill-way dam at al-Lāhūn, we suggest that the structure referred to here is a weir that regulated the flow of the water to the canal.

قمح، عشرون اردبا وخمسة قراريط.
شعير، ستة عشر اردبا وربع وسدس ونصف ثمن.
سمسم، ربع اردب.
المراعي، طارئ، عن مائتين واثنين واربعين راسا، تسعة وسبعون درهما ونصف وثمن:
قطيعة ثلاثين درهما المائة راس، عن خمسة وثمانين راسا، خمسة وعشرون درهما وربع.[236]
قطيعة خمسة وعشرين درهما المائة، عن سبعة وخمسين راسا، تسعة وثلاثون درهما وربع.
رسم المستخدمين، خمسة عشر درهما وثمن.

عليها من الزكاة، عن ثمن ماشية، عن ثمانية ارؤس،[237] تسعة دنانير وثلث. تفصيله:
بقر احمر، مسنة واحدة، ثلاثة دنانير.
اغنام، عن سبعة ارؤس، ستة دنانير وثلث.

والذى جرت العادة لها من التقاوي، اربعمائة وثمانون اردبا. تفصيله:
قمح، مائتان[238] وستة وعشرون اردبا.
شعير، مائتان واحد عشر اردبا.
فول، ثلاثة واربعون اردبا.

وعليها من الاتبان، الفان وستمائة وخمسون شنيفا.

والمربى بها من الفروج للديوان والمقطعين، بما فيه من اجرة التربية، الف ومائتان وخمسون طائرا. تفصيله:
للديوان السلطاني، اربعمائة وخمسون طائرا.
للمقطعين، ثمانمائة طائر.

لخولي البحر، هبة على المقطعين، قمح، اردبان.

اهلها يزرعون من الاقصاب ويسقون من الخلف برسم حجر سنهور، عشرين فدانا ونصف وربع.

والمسلف عليها بها من الشعير، برسم الاصطبلات السلطانية، مائتا اردب.

ومن حرف[239] الالف، ابريزيا والزربي. من شرقي الفيوم الى بحريه. هاتان البلدتان احداهما قديمة وهي ابريزيا والثانية مستجدة وهي الزربي. وهما يذكران معا في الحساب ويقطعان كذلك. بينهما وبين مدينة الفيوم ثلاث ساعات للراكب. ليس عليهما ولا على واحدة منهما بساتين ولا كروم ولا غروس سوى قريب من عشرين نخلة ودي في هذا التاريخ. اهلهما[240] بنو زرعة من بنى عجلان، خياتمة. عبرتهما[241] جيشية سبعة الاف واربعمائة دينار. لهما من الماء من جملة بحر ذات الصفاء، عما يخصهما من الماء المساق[242] الى الفسقية اليوسفية تحت القبرا من خليج مجصص للصيفي والشتوي، عشر قبض. وبالزربي جامع تقام فيه الجمعة.

ارتفاعهما مما جميعه مستخرجا ومتحصلا، عينا، خمسة عشر دينارا؛ غلة الف ومائة وخمسة وثمانون اردبا:

236 ساقط من أ. س.: وربع.
237 أ. س.: عن مائتي راس.
238 أ. س.: مائة.
239 أ. س.: حروف.
240 أ. س.: أهلها.
241 أ. س.: عبرتها.
242 أ. س.: المسوق.

measurement fee, 36 ⅔ ¼ 1/48 ardabbs:
wheat, 20 5/24 ardabbs;
barley, 16 ¼ ⅙ 1/16 ardabbs;
sesame, ¼ ardabb.
The pasture tax for seasonal pasture lands, for 249 heads, 79 ½ ⅛ dirhams:
at the rate of 30 dirhams per 100 heads, for 85 head, 25 ¼ dirhams;
at the rate of 25 dirhams per 100 [heads], for [1]57 head, 39 ¼ dirhams.
The government agents' fee: 15 ⅛ dirhams.

The alms-tax, for the monetary value of eight heads of livestock, 9 ⅓ dinars:
cows, for a two-year old cow, 3 dinars;
small cattle, for seven heads, 6 ⅓ dinars.

The seed advances customarily distributed, 480 ardabbs:
wheat, 226 ardabbs;
barley, 211 ardabbs;
broad beans, 43 ardabbs.

Hay, 2,650 bales.

The chicken reared in it, for the Dīwān and the *iqṭāʿ*-holders, including the rearing wage, 1,250 birds:
for the royal Dīwān, 450 birds;
for the *iqṭāʿ*-holders, 800 birds.

For the overseer of the canal, as a gift from the *iqṭāʿ*-holders, wheat, 2 ardabbs.

Its people sow 10 ½ ¼ feddans of sugarcane and they irrigate them for the second harvest. These are assigned to the stone at Sanhūr.

The barley assigned for the royal stables, which was paid for in advance, 200 ardabbs.

Also beginning with the letter 'alif': Ibrīziyā[69] and al-Zarbī,[70] in the north-east of the Fayyum. These two villages — one of them, Ibrīziyā, is ancient, and the second, al-Zarbī, is new — are registered together in the accounts, and are allocated jointly as *iqṭāʿ*. They are three hours' ride from Madīnat al-Fayyūm. In neither of them are there any orchards, vineyards or plantations, except for — at that time — nearly twenty shoots of date palms. Their people are Banū Zarʿa, of the Banū ʿAjlān, and they belong to the [sub-section of the] Khayāthima. Their joint fiscal value is 7,400 army dinars. They get water from the overall [water quota] of Dhāt al-Ṣafāʾ Canal. They take a share of the water channelled towards the [divisor known as] al-Fasqiyya al-Yūsufiyya, below al-Qubarāʾ, by a plastered canal. This water is used for summer and winter cultivation. [Their share is] 10 *qabḍas* [of water]. In al-Zarbī there is a congregational mosque, in which the Friday prayers are held.

69 Ibrīzyā's modern location: Kafr ʿUmayra (كفر عميرة). Halm, *Ägypten*, p. 259: Ibrīzyā/al-Zarbī; Salmon, 'Répertoire', p. 48; Ibn al-Jīʿān, *Kitāb al-tuḥfa*, p. 150; Ibn Mammātī, *Kitāb qawānīn al-dawāwīn*, p. 103; de Sacy, *État des provinces*, p. 680: Ibrīryā wa'l-Zarbī; Ramzī, *Al-Qāmūs*, I, 110: Ibrīzyā = Kafr ʿUmayra.

70 Modern location: al-Zirbī (عزبة الشرايع/ الزربي). Halm, *Ägypten*, p. 259: al-Zarbī; Savigny, *Description de l'Égypte*, p. 130: Al-Zarābī; Ramzī, *Al-Qāmūs*, II/III, 110: al-Zirbī.

قمح، ستمائة واحد وخمسون اردبا.
شعير، اثنان وستون اردبا.
فول، خمسة وثلاثون اردبا.
ارز بقشره، ثلاثمائة واثنان وثمانون اردبا.
جلبان، خمسة وخمسون اردبا.

تفصيله:
الهلالي، عشرة دنانير.
المراعي، خمسة دنانير.

مشاطرة الغلات، الف ومائة وخمسة وثمانون اردبا على ما فصل.

وعليها من الزكاة عن ثمن اغنام، عن اربعة ارؤس، ثلاثة دنانير وثلث وربع وثمن. تفصيله:
بياض، عن ثلاثة ارؤس، ثلاثة دنانير وسدس.
شعرية واحدة، ربع وسدس وثمن دينار.

وعليها من الرسوم والمراعي والكيالة، عن مائتين وثلاثة وثمانين درهما وربع وثمن، سبعة دنانير وقيراطان؛ قمح، اربعة وستون اردبا وسدس. تفصيله:
الرسوم، مائتان واربعة وخمسون درهما وقمح اربعة وستون اردبا وسدس. تفصيله:
شد العين، ثلاثة وثلاثون درهما ونصف.
شد الاحباس، ستة وعشرون درهما ونصف.
رسم الجراريف، تسعون درهما.
رسم الحصاد، ثلاثة وخمسون درهما.
رسم الخفارة، خمسة عشر درهما.
رسم الجزر، ستة دراهم.
رسم الاجران، ثلاثون درهما، وقمح، اربعة وثلاثون اردبا وسدس.
الكيالة، قمح ثلاثون اردبا.
المراعي، تسعة وعشرون درهما وربع وثمن.
قطيعة خمسة وعشرين درهما المائة، عن اثنين وتسعين راسا، ثلاثة وعشرون درهما.
رسم المستخدمين، ستة دراهم وربع وثمن.

وعليهما من خراج الاستنباط لسنورس، غلة، ستون اردبا وثلث وثمن. تفصيله:
قمح، ثمانية وعشرون اردبا وربع وثمن.
شعير، احد عشر اردبا وربع وسدس وثمن.
سمسم، اثنا عشر اردبا.
فول، ثمانية ارادب وربع وسدس وثمن.

وعليها لديوان الاحباس، عينا، ثمانية دنانير.

وعليهما لخولي البحر، قمح، اردب واحد.

وعليها من الشعير المسلف عليه برسم الاصطبلات السلطانية، مائة واربعون اردبا.

وعليها من الاتبان، ثمانمائة شنيف.

Their entire revenue in cash and in kind, in specie, 15 dinars; and in grains, 1,185 ardabbs:

wheat, 651 ardabbs;
barley, 62 ardabbs;
broad beans, 35 ardabbs;
rice in hull, 382 ardabbs;
chickling vetch, 55 ardabbs.

In detail:

Lunar calendar tax, 10 dinars;
pasture tax, 5 dinars.

Mushāṭara land tax, in grains, 1,185 ardabbs, as specified.

The alms-tax, for the monetary value of four heads of small cattle, 3 ⅓ ¼ ⅛ dinars:

sheep, for three heads, 3 ⅙ dinars;
one goat, ¼ ⅙ ⅛ dinar.

The fees, the pasture tax and the measurement fee are 283 ¼ ⅛ dirhams, which are 7 ²⁄₂₄ dinars and 64 ⅙ ardabb:

The fees: 254 dirhams; and wheat, 64 ⅙ ardabbs:
supervision of the land survey, 33 ½ dirhams;
supervision of endowments, 27 ½ dirhams;
dredging fee, 90 dirhams;
harvest fee, 53 dirhams;
protection fee, 15 dirhams;
carrot fee, 6 dirhams;
threshing-floor fee, 30 dirhams; wheat, 34 ⅙ ardabbs.
The measurement fee, wheat, 30 ardabbs.
The pasture tax, 29 ¼ ⅛ dirhams:
at the rate of 25 dirhams per hundred [heads], for 92 heads, 23 dirhams.
Government agents' fee, 6 ¼ ⅛ dirhams.

Land tax on al-Istinbāṭ, part of [the land-tax revenues of] Sinnūris, in grains, 60 ⅓ ⅛ ardabbs:[71]

wheat, 28 ¼ ⅛ ardabbs;
barley, 11 ¼ ⅙ ⅛ ardabbs;
sesame, 12 ardabbs;
broad beans, 8 ¼ ⅙ ⅛ ardabbs.

For the Ministry of Endowments, in specie, 8 dinars.

For the overseer of the canal, wheat, 1 ardabb.

The barley assigned for the royal stables, which was paid for in advance, 140 ardabbs.

Hay, 800 bales.

---

[71] This minor tax is mentioned in four villages in the north-east of the province — Ibrīziyā, Sirisnā, Minyat al-Baṭs, and Furqus. It appears that peasants from these villages cultivated plots in an area called al-Istinbāṭ (not the village of the same name, located in the western part of the province). The revenues, in small amounts of grain, were included within the accounts of the larger village of Sinnūris. The land tax was divided among the peasants of the four villages, with the larger village of Sirisnā paying three times more than the smaller villages of Ibrīziyā and Furqus. The auxiliary costs of the measurement of the grains were not picked up by any of the villages, and al-Nābulusī lists them in one of the appendices, together with other dues which were not tagged to any individual village.

والذي جرت العادة باطلاقه لها من التقاوي، ثلاثمائة واحد وسبعون اردبا وربع وسدس. تفصيله:

قمح، مائتان واحد وعشرون اردبا.

شعير وفول، ستة وسبعون اردبا.

ارز بقشره، اربعة وسبعون اردبا[243] وربع وسدس.

والمربى بها من الفروج ثمانمائة وخمسون فروجا. تفصيله:[244]

للمقطعين، ستمائة فروج.

وللديوان المعمور من الفروج السلطاني، بما فيه من اجرة التربية، مائتان وخمسون.

والمقرر عليها من الفريك والكشك، اردبان ونصف:

فريك، اردب واحد.

كشك اردب واحد ونصف.

ومن حرف[245] الالف، ابهيت. هذه البلدة من كفور سنورس، بحري مدينة الفيوم، غربي سنورس. مسافتها من المدينة ساعتان للراكب. تشمل على بساتين وكروم نخل وتين وزيتون. اهلها قياصرة من بنى جابر، فرع من فروع بنى عجلان. وعبرتها جيشية اربعة الاف دينار. تشرب من خليج سنورس من الشاذروان المتفرع لسنورس وما معها للشتوي[246] والصيفي بما عدته ست قبض. وبها جامع تقام فيه خطبة[247] الجمعة. ارتفاعها عينا، على ما قرره المقطعون، ستة وثلاثون دينارا وستمائة اردب:

قمح، اربعمائة اردب.

شعير، مائتا اردب.

خراج الراتب، ستة وثلاثون دينارا.

خراج المناجزة، ستمائة اردب على ما فصل.

وعليها من الزكاة، ثلاثة دنانير وثلث وربع ونصف قيراط. تفصيله:[248]

خرص العنب، ديناران.

ثمن الاغنام، عن راسين، دينار وثلث وربع ونصف قيراط. تفصيله:

بياض، راس واحد، دينار واحد وقيراط ونصف.

شعريه واحدة، ربع وسدس وثمن دينار.

وعليها من المراعي والرسوم والكيالة، عن ثلاثمائة واثنين وخمسين درهما ونصف، ثمانية دنانير ونصف وثلث واربعون اردبا وربع وسدس. تفصيله:

قمح، ثلاثة وعشرون اردبا وثلثان.

شعير، احد عشر اردبا وقيراطان.

فول، خمسة ارادب وثلثان.

The seed advances customarily distributed in it are 371 ¼ ⅙ ardabbs:

wheat, 221 ardabbs;

barley and broad beans, 76 ardabbs;

rice in hull, 74 ¼ ⅙ ardabbs.

The chickens reared in it, 850 chickens:

for the *iqṭāʿ*-holders, 600 chickens;

for the prosperous Dīwān, including the rearing wage, 250 chickens assigned to the royal [kitchens].

The established levy of *farīk* and *kishk*, 2 ½ ardabbs:

farīk, 1 ardabb;

kishk, 1 ½ ardabb.

Also beginning with the letter 'alif': Abhīt.[72] This is one of the hamlets of Sinnūris, two hours' ride north of Madīnat al-Fayyūm, and west of Sinnūris. It has orchards, vineyards, date palms, fig trees and olives. Its people belong to the Qayāṣira of the Banū Jābir, one of the branches of the Banū ʿAjlān. Its fiscal value is 4,000 army dinars. It gets its water from Sinnūris Canal, through [the divisor called] al-Shādhrawān, which supplies water to Sinnūris and its hamlets. It uses the water for winter and summer cultivation, six *qabḍas*. It has a congregational mosque, in which the Friday prayer is held.

Its revenue, in specie [and in kind], according to what was confirmed by the *iqṭāʿ*-holders, is 36 dinars and 600 ardabbs:

wheat, 400 ardabbs;

barley, 200 ardabbs.

Land tax on perennial plants, 36 dinars.

Munājaza land tax, 600 ardabbs, as specified.

The alms-tax is 3 ⅓ ¼ 1/48 dinars:

estimate of grapes, 2 dinars;

monetary value of small cattle, for two heads, 1 ⅓ ¼ 1/48 dinar:

sheep, one head, 1 1/24 1/48 dinar;

one goat, ¼ ⅙ ⅛ dinar.

The pasture tax, the fees and the measurement fee, 352 ½ dirhams, which are 8 ½ ⅓ dinars; and 40 ¼ ⅙ ardabbs:

wheat, 23 ⅔ ardabbs;

barley, 11 2/24 ardabbs;

broad beans, 5 ⅔ ardabbs.

243 ساقط من أ. س.: أرز بقشره أربعة وسبعون أردبا.

244 ساقط من أ. س.: تفصيله.

245 أ. س.: حروف.

246 أ. س.: من الشتوي.

247 ساقط من ط. م.: خطبة.

248 ساقط من أ. س.: تفصيله.

72 Modern location: Abhīt al-Ḥajar (ابهيت الحجر). Halm, *Ägypten*, p. 244: Abhit = al-Ḥajar al-Lāhūni; Salmon, 'Répertoire', p. 52; Ibn al-Jīʿān, *Kitāb al-tuḥfa*, p. 151: Ibhayt; de Sacy, *État des provinces*, p. 680: Abhayt; Savigny, *Description de l'Égypte*, p. 130: Bahbīt al-Ḥajar; Ramzī, *Al-Qāmūs*, II/III, 108: Abhīt al-Ḥajar; notes, following Amélineau, *La géographie*, that the Roman name of this village was Peīthīsis.

تفصيله:

الرسوم، مائة وتسعة واربعون درهما ونصف وربع واثنان وعشرون اردبا وربع وسدس. تفصيله:

شد الاحباس، ستة دراهم.

رسم الجراريف، اربعون درهما.

رسم الحصاد، ثلاثة وخمسون درهما.

الخفارة، خمسة عشر درهما.

رسم قلقاس، سبعة عشر درهما.

رسم الاجران، ثمانية عشر درهما ونصف وربع، وغلة اثنان وعشرون اردبا وربع وسدس. تفصيله:

قمح، احد عشر اردبا وثلثان.

شعير، خمسة ارادب وقيراطان.

فول، خمسة ارادب وثلثان.

الكيالة، ثمانية عشر اردبا:

قمح، اثنا عشر اردبا.

شعير ستة ارادب.

المراعي، عن مائتين واحد عشر راسا، مائتان وثلاثة دراهم ونصف وربع. تفصيله:

راتب، قطيعة درهمين وربع الراس، عن احد وثلاثين راسا، تسعة وستون درهما ونصف وربع.

طارئ، عن مائة وثمانين راسا، مائة وعشرون درهما ونصف وربع وثمن. تفصيله:

قطيعة درهم الراس، عن اربعة واربعين راسا، اربعة واربعون درهما.

قطيعة سبعين درهما المائة، عن تسعين راسا، ثلاثة وستون درهما.

قطيعة ثلاثين درهما المائة، عن ستة واربعين راسا، ثلاثة عشر درهما ونصف وربع وثمن.

رسم المستخدمين، ثلاثة عشر درهما وثمن.

وعليها لديوان الاحباس، عينا، ديناران ونصف.

وعليها من الاتبان، الف ومائة وعشرون شنيفا.

والمربى بها من الفروج، للديوان، بما فيه من اجرة التربية، ثلاثمائة وعشرون فروجا. تفصيله:

للديوان، مائتان.

وللمقطعين مائة وعشرون.

والذى جرت به العادة من التسليف على الناحية من الشعير برسم الاصطبلات السلطانية، خمسة وثلاثون اردبا.

والذي بالناحية من التقاوي السلطانية، غلة، مائة وستة وتسعون اردبا ونصف وثلث:

قمح، اربعة وثلاثون وثلثان.

شعير، اربعة وعشرون اردبا.

فول، سبعة وثلاثون اردبا.

سمسم، اردب وسدس.

والذي على الناحية من الباقي في الايام الكاملية لسنة اربع وثلاثين وستمائة وما قبلها، قبل انتقالهما من الخاص الى المقطعين، داخل في الباقي المذكور في سنورس وكفورها.

[In detail:] the fees, 149 ½ ¼ dirhams and 22 ¼ ⅙ ardabbs:

supervision of endowments, 6 dirhams;

dredging fee, 40 dirhams;

harvest fee, 53 dirhams;

protection [fee], 15 dirhams;

colocasia fee, 17 dirhams;

threshing-floor fee, 18 ½ ¼ dirhams; and in grains, 22 ¼ ⅙ ardabbs:

wheat, 11 ⅔ ardabbs;

barley, 5 ²⁄₂₄ ardabbs;

broad beans, 5 ⅔ ardabbs.

The measurement fee, 18 ardabbs:

wheat, 12 ardabbs;

barley, 6 ardabbs.

The pasture tax, for 211 heads, 203 ½ ¼ dirhams:

Permanent pasture lands, at a rate of 2 ¼ dirhams per head, for 31 heads, 69 ½ ¼ dirhams;

Seasonal pasture lands, for 180 heads, 120 ½ ¼ ⅛ dirhams:

at the rate of one dirham per head, for 44 heads, 44 dirhams;

at the rate of 70 dirhams per hundred [heads], for 90 heads, 63 dirhams;

at the rate of 30 dirhams per hundred [heads], for 46 heads, 13 ½ ¼ ⅛ dirhams;

The government agents' fee, 13 ⅛ dirhams.

For the Ministry of Endowments, in specie, 2 ½ dinars.

Hay, 1,120 bales.

The chickens reared in it for the Dīwān, including the the rearing wage, 320 chickens:

for the Dīwān, 200;

for the *iqṭā*ʿ-holders, 120.

The barley customarily assigned for the royal stables, which was paid for in advance, 35 ardabbs.

The royal seed advances [distributed] in the village, in grains, 196 ½ ⅓ ardabbs:

wheat, 134 ⅔ [ardabbs];

barley, 24 ardabbs;

broad beans, 37 ardabbs;

sesame, 1 ⅙ ardabb.

The arrears of the village, dating back to the days of [al-Malik] al-Kāmil, for the year 634 and prior to that — before it was transferred from the private domain of the sultan to the *iqṭā*ʿ-holders — are subsumed in the arrears listed in the entry of Sinnūris and its hamlets.

والذي جرت به العادة مما يزرعه[249] اهل الناحية ويسقونه من الاقصاب برسم المعاصر لسنورس[250] بابقارهم ورجالهم، ويتسلمون عنه الاجرة، عشرون فدانا ونصف وربع وثمن وحبتان. تفصيله:

راس، مما يتسلمون اجرته عن كل فدان ديناران، اربعة عشر فدانا وثلثان وثمن.[251]

خلفه، مما يتسلمون اجرته عن كل فدان نصف وربع دينار، ستة فدادين وقيراطان وحبتان.

ومن حرف[252] الالف، اخصاص الحلاق. من كفور سنورس بحري مدينة الفيوم، مما يلي الشرق قبلي سنورس، مسافتها من المدينة ساعة للراكب. هذه البلدة عبارة عن بساتين وانهار وغروس وثمار تكتنفها البساتين من جميع جهاتها، عروس من عرائس الفيوم، ذات النخيل والكروم والفواكه المتنوعة والازهار الكثيرة والثمار الغزيرة تمير مدينة الفيوم وما حولها من البلاد حتى تتعدى الى كورة بوش والبهنسا والارياف والى المدن كالقاهرة ومصر واسكندرية ودمياط. وهي قليوب قاهرة الفيوم. فيها البساتين مما يباع بالقيمة الحسنة والجملة المستحسنة حتى انه ذكر عن بستان فيها، مساحته تسعة فدادين ونصف وثلث ونصف ثمن وحبة، ان من جملة ثمره اربعمائة قنطار بالفيومي كمثرى، ومائة اردب تفاح مخضب وغيره سوى ما فيه من الورد والعنب وغير ذلك. يحسب السالك في هذه البلاد والجالس في بساتينها انه سالك بدمشق وبساتينها من كثرة ظلها وجريان[253] المياه فيها من جميع جهاتها بالخلج والانهار في الليل والنهار.

ومع هذا[254] خراجها بمائها السيح ديناران وثمن الفدان محتملة الزيادة لمن اراده الا انها كما قيل للشهيد صلاح الدين، قدس الله روحه ونور ضريحه، وقد سال عن ثغر الاسكندرية جدي للام زين الدين[255] الواعظ رحمه الله تعالى، فقال له: الاسكندرية صحن صيني فيه صير. اهل هذه الاخصاص غليظو المزاج كثيرو اللجاج. في هذه البلدة رباط فيه فقراء وشيخ لهم وبسبب الشيخ والفقراء والرباط تطيلس فلاحو هذه البلدة وصاروا يدعون بالفقهاء والقضاة من غير فقه ولا قضاء.

وهذه البلدة تسقى من الماء المطلق في خليج ذات الصفاء بما ينساق منه الى الفسقية اليوسفية تحت القبرا في خليجين مجصصين لسقى البساتين، ست قبض:

خليج شرقي، اربع قبض.

خليج غربي، قبضتان.

249 أ. س.: يزرعونه.

250 أ. س.: بسنورس.

251 أ. س.: ثلثاي.

252 أ. س.: حروف.

253 أ. س.: وبساتين.

254 أ. س.: ذلك.

255 ساقط من ط. م.: الدين.

The sugar plantations, assigned to the presses in Sinnūris, which are customarily sown and irrigated by the people of the village, by their cattle and their men, and for which they obtain a wage: 20 ½ ¼ ⅛ ²⁄₇₂ feddans:

first harvest, for which they obtain a wage of 2 dinars per feddan: 14 ⅔ ⅛ feddans;

second harvest, for which they obtain a wage of ¾ dinar per feddan: 6 ²⁄₂₄ ²⁄₇₂ feddans.

Also beginning with the letter 'alif': Akhṣāṣ al-Ḥallāq.[73] It is one of the hamlets of Sinnūris, one hour's ride north-east of Madīnat al-Fayyūm, and south of Sinnūris. This village has orchards, streams, plantations and fruits. Orchards surround it on all its sides; It is one of the beautiful brides of the Fayyum. It has date palms, vineyards, various fruits, many flowers and abundant yield. Its produce provides for Madīnat al-Fayyūm and its environs, and even reaches the rural districts of Būsh, al-Bahnasā, the villages (*al-aryāf*), and the cities, such as Cairo, Miṣr,[74] Alexandria and Damietta. It is to the capital of the Fayyum what Qalyūb[75] is to Cairo. The produce of its orchards is sold at a fine price and in considerable quantity. It has been said that one orchard in it, with an area of 9 ½ ⅓ ¹⁄₁₆ ¹⁄₇₂ feddans, has a yield of 400 Fayyūmī qinṭārs of pears, and 100 ardabbs of pigmented apples (*mukhaḍḍab*) and other fruits, not including the roses, the grapes and other produce in it. Anyone who passes through this village and sits in its orchards feels as if he is passing through Damascus and its orchards, due to the ample shade they offer, and to the constant flow of water in its canals and streams from all directions, night and day.

Yet, the land tax of the village, despite its flowing water, is [at a rate of] 2 ⅛ dinars per feddan. An increase is possible if one so desired. However, it is like what was said to the martyr Salāḥ al-Dīn [Saladin], may God sanctify his soul and illuminate his tomb. When he [i.e., Saladin] asked my maternal grandfather, Zayn al-Dīn the preacher, may God have mercy on him, about the port of Alexandria, the latter told him: 'Alexandria is a porcelain dish with a crack (?, *ṣīr*) in it'. The people of these Akhṣāṣ [lit., 'shacks'] are hot tempered and quarrelsome. In this village there is a Sufi lodge (*ribāṭ*), in which there are Sufis and their sheikh. On account of the sheikh, the Sufis and the lodge, the peasants of this village have began wearing the cowls (*ṭaylasān*),[76] and are being called jurists and judges, while possessing neither jurisprudence nor judgment.

This village is irrigated by the water of Dhāt as-Ṣafā' Canal, from which it is channelled for the irrigation of the orchards through the [divisor called] al-Fasqiyya al-Yūsufiyya, below al-Qubarā', by two plastered canals. [It gets] six *qabḍas*:

from an eastern canal, four *qabḍas*;

from a western canal, two *qabḍas*.

[73] Modern location: al-Ikhṣāṣ (الإخصاص). Halm, *Ägypten*, p. 245; Salmon, 'Répertoire', pp. 48–49; Zéki, 'Une description', p. 36; Yāqūt, *Muʿjam al-Buldān*, I, 123; Ibn al-Jīʿān, *Kitāb al-tuḥfa*, p. 151: Akhṣāṣ al-Ḥallāf; de Sacy, *État des provinces*, p. 680; Savigny, *Description de l'Égypte*, p. 129: al-Iḥsās; Ramzī, *Al-Qāmūs*, II/III, 108: al-Ikhṣāṣ.

[74] In al-Nābulusī's time, Fatimid Cairo was still distinct from the older city of Miṣr-Fusṭāṭ. See Carl Becker, 'Miṣr, c. 2. The Historical Development of the Capital of Egypt', *The Encyclopedia of Islam*, 2nd edn, VII, 147–52.

[75] Qalyūb, a town 20 kilometres north of Cairo, was well known during the Fatimid and Ayyubid times for its gardens and trees. See A. Richter, 'al-Ḳalyūb', *The Encyclopedia of Islam*, 2nd edn, IV, 514–15; Ramzī, *Al-Qāmūs*, II/I, 11, 57–8.

[76] A shawl-like garment, worn over head and shoulders as a mark of Islamic piety and scholarship. See also al-Nābulusī's mocking of the *ṭaylasān* worn by converted Copts and rustics in his *Sword of Ambition*, ed. and trans. by Yarbrough, pp. 165–67.

وبها جامع تقام فيه[256] الجمعة، مستجد غير مدون. وهي جارية في اقطاع الامير فخر الدين امير شكار الاشرفي، وهي خفر[257] الجابريين وبنى كعب المفرعين من بني عجلان.

ارتفاعها خارجا عن ثمن ثمرة البستان المنتقل الى ملك الشريف العلوي، ومبلغه ستون دينارا، ستمائة واحد عشر دينارا عينا وثلثان وحبتان. تفصيله:

خراج الاحكار، خمسمائة وسبعون دينارا وربع وسدس وحبتان. تفصيله:

الاصل، عن مائتين وثمانية وستين فدانا وربع وسدس وحبتين، مائتان وثمانية وستون دينارا وربع وسدس وحبتان.

الاضافة، ثلاثة وثلاثون دينارا وربع وسدس وثمن وحبة.

زائد القطيعة، مائتان وثمانية وستون دينارا وربع وسدس وحبتان.

خراج فدن العين، احد واربعون دينارا وربع. تفصيله:

الاصل ستة وثلاثون دينارا وثلثان. تفصيله:[258]

قلقاس، عن تسعة فدادين وثلث ونصف قيراط وحبة، ثمانية وعشرون دينارا وقيراطان.

قرط، عن اربعة فدادين، اربعة دنانير.

خضر، عن فدانين وربع ونصف قيراط وحبة، اربعة دنانير وثلث وربع.

الاضافة، اربعة دنانير وثلث وربع.

والمرتب بها عن حكر الطاحون الدائرة بالماء، سبعة دنانير وثلثان ونصف قيراط.

وعليها من الزكاة، ثلاثون دينارا وثلث وربع وثمن ودانق. تفصيله:

الدولبة، ستة دنانير وثمن.

الخرص، سبعة عشر دينارا وربع وسدس وثمن ودانق. تفصيله:

عن العنب، ثلاثة دنانير وثلث وحبة.

عن النخل، اربعة عشر دينارا وسدس ونصف قيراط وحبة.

ثمن الماشية، عن سبعة اروس، سبعة دنانير وقيراط. تفصيله:

بقر احمر، عن مسنة واحدة، ديناران ونصف وثلث.

ثمن اغنام، عن ستة اروس اربعة دنانير وخمسة[259] قراريط. تفصيله:

بياض، عن راسين، ديناران وثمن.

شعارى، عن اربعة، ديناران وقيراطان.

وعليها الديوان الاحباس مما هو منسوب في[260] الضرائب الديوانية عن القبراء، دينار واحد وثمن.

[256] أ. س. يضيف: الخطبة.

[257] ط. م.: الجفر.

[258] ساقط من أ. س.: تفصيله.

[259] أ. س.: وخمس.

[260] أ. س.: من.

It has a new unregistered congregational mosque, in which the Friday prayer is held. It is allocated as *iqṭāʿ* to the amir Fakhr al-Dīn *amīr shikār* al-Ashrafī.[77] It is under the protection (*khafr*) of the Banū Jābir and the Banū Kaʿb, branches of the Banū ʿAjlān.

Its revenue is 611 ⅔ ²⁄₇₂ dinars. This excludes the sale-price of the fruits of the orchard conveyed to the ownership (*mulk*) of al-Sharīf al-ʿIlwī, for the sum of 60 dinars. [The cash revenues] in detail:

- Land tax on lands subject to long lease, 570 ¼ ⅙ ²⁄₇₂ dinars:
  - the basic assessment, for 268 ¼ ⅙ ²⁄₇₂ feddans, 268 ¼ ⅙ ²⁄₇₂ dinars;
  - the addition: 33 ¼ ⅙ ⅛ ¹⁄₇₂ dinars.
  - the added tax-rate [on long-term leases]: 268 ¼ ⅙ ²⁄₇₂ dinars.
- Land tax on cash-crops, assessed by feddans, 41 ¼ dinars:
  - basic assessment, 36 ⅔ dinars:
    - colocasia, for 9 ⅓ ¹⁄₄₈ ¹⁄₇₂ feddans, 28 ²⁄₂₄ dinars;
    - alfalfa, for 4 feddans, 4 dinars;
    - green vegetables, for 2 ¼ ¹⁄₄₈ ¹⁄₇₂ feddans, 4 ⅓ ¼ dinars.
  - the addition: 4 ⅓ ¼ dinars.

The set payment for the long-term lease of the water-mill, 7 ⅔ ¹⁄₄₈ dinars.

The alms-tax is 30 ⅓ ¼ ⅛ ¹⁄₁₄₄ dinars:

- merchandise, 7 ⅛ dinars;
- the estimate, 17 ¼ ⅙ ⅛ ¹⁄₁₄₄ dinars:
  - grapes, 3 ⅓ ¹⁄₇₂ dinars;
  - date palms, 14 ⅙ ¹⁄₄₈ ¹⁄₇₂ dinars.
- The monetary value of livestock, for seven heads, 7 ¹⁄₂₄ dinars:
  - on cows, a two-year old cow, 2 ½ ⅓ dinars;
  - the monetary value of small cattle, for six heads, 4 ⁵⁄₂₄ dinars:
    - sheep, for two heads, 2 ⅛ dinars;
    - goats, for four [heads], 2 ²⁄₂₄ dinars.

For the Ministry of Endowments, listed in the Dīwān's register (*ḍarāʾib*) of the village of al-Qubarāʾ, 1 ⅛ dinar.

[77] The Ashrafī *nisba* may designate this amir as a former slave of al-Ashraf Mūsā, Ayyubid prince of Damascus (d. 1237). The title of *amīr shikār* designated the officer as Master of the Hunt, although the actual responsibilities of an amir carrying this rank are unclear.

والذي يزرعه[261] اهل هذه الناحية من الاقصاب الراس بابقارهم ورجالهم ويسوقونه من الخلف ويعزقونه[262] ويخدمونه بالاجر لمعاصر سنورس، ثمانية وعشرون فدانا وثلث. تفصيله:

راس، مما يتسلمون اجرته حسابا عن كل فدان ديناران، تسعة عشر فدانا ونصف وثلث وثمن.

خلفة، مما يتسلمون عنه الاجرة حسابا عن كل فدان نصف وربع دينار، ثمانية فدادين وربع وثمن.

والمربى بها من الفروج، ثلاثمائة وتسعون. تفصيله:

للديوان السلطاني، بما فيه من اجرة التربية وهو الثلث، ثلاثمائة وعشرة فراريج.

المقطع، ثمانون طائرا.

ومن حرف[263] الالف، القبرا. هذه البلدة صغيرة الحجم، قبلي اخصاص الحلاق الى الغرب، ارضها متاخمة لارضها بحيث يسمع اهل البلدة نداء الاخرى. تشتمل على بساتين تين ونخل وكروم وتفاح وخوخ، وبساتينها منها ما هو مجتمع كالغوطة ومنها ما هو متفرق. اهلها من عرب بني كعب من بني عجلان. ارضها مسجلة على اهل الاخصاص يزرعونها، واهل هذه البلدة يزرعون في شلالة فهم في ترك[264] ما يزرع بارضهم وزرعهم في ارض الغير، كالنعامة تترك بيضها وتسرح فتجد في طريقها بيض غيرها فتقعد عليه وتحضنه. وفيها يقول الشاعر:

كتاركة بيضها بالعراء
ومكسية[265] بيض اخرى جناحا

وهؤلاء القوم، نفر عصاة جهال من اجلاف العرب ومن عادتهم التسحب والهرب. خرب والي الفيوم الامير[266] بدر الدين المرندزي مرة ديارهم وقطع لفسادهم اثارهم ونزحهم عن هذه[267] البلدة. فلما راح بدر الدين المذكور عادوا اليها.

وهى بغير عبرة وبها معصرة[268] ذات حجر واحد. اقصابه تزرع في اراضي مطر طارس وهو داخل في[269] ارتفاعها. تسقى[270] من الشاذروان المتفرع[271] من بحر سنورس بخليج مفرد. عبرته لسقى الشتوي والصيفي اربع قبض.

ارتفاعها مائة وتسعة عشر[272] دينارا وسدس؛ غلة، مقررة على اهل اخصاص الحلاق،[273] ستمائة وستة وسبعون اردبا وقيراط ونصف. تفصيله:

قمح، ثلاثمائة وسبعة وثمانون اردبا ونصف وثمن.

شعير، مائتان وسبعة ارادب وثلث وربع وثمن.

261 أ. س.: يزرعونه.
262 ساقط من أ. س.: ويعزقونه.
263 أ. س.: حروف.
264 ساقط من أ. س.: ترك.
265 أ. س.: مكسية; ط. م.: مكسبة.
266 ساقط من أ. س.: الأمير.
267 ساقط من أ. س.: هذه.
268 أ. س. : وهي بمعصرة.
269 ساقط من أ. س.: في.
270 أ. س. : يسقي.
271 أ. س. : المتفرغ.
272 أ. س. : وعشرون.
273 ساقط من أ. س.: الحلاق.

The first harvest of sugarcane, sown by the people of the village, by means of their cattle and their men, and the second harvest which they irrigate, hoe[78] and maintain for wages, assigned to the presses of Sinnūris, 28 ⅓ feddans:

first harvest for which they obtain a wage, calculated as 2 dinars per feddan, 19 ½ ⅓ ⅛ feddans;

second harvest, for which they obtain a wage, calculated as ¾ dinar for feddan, 8 ¼ ⅛ feddans.

The chickens reared in it, 390:

for the Royal Dīwān, including the rearing wage of a third, 310 chickens;

for the *iqṭāʿ*-holder, 80 birds.

Also beginning with the letter 'alif': al-Qubarāʾ.[79] This is a small village, south-west of Akhṣāṣ al-Ḥallāq. Its land is adjacent to the land of Akhṣāṣ al-Ḥallāq, so much so that the people of one village hear someone calling in the other village. It contains orchards of figs, date palms, vine, apples and peaches. Some of its orchards are clustered together like a fertile valley, and some are dispersed. Its people are Arab, the Banū Kaʿb of the Banū ʿAjlān. Its land is registered (*musajjala)* in the name of the people of al-Akhṣāṣ [al-Ḥallāq], who sow it, whereas the people of this village sow in Shallāla. By not sowing their own land and sowing the land of another instead, they are like an ostrich that leaves its eggs and goes to graze, then finds in its path the eggs of another ostrich, sits on these and broods upon them. On this topic the poet says:

Like the one who leaves her eggs in the open
And covers[80] the eggs of another by her wing[81]

These people are a disobedient and ignorant lot, from among the boorish Arabs, and it is their custom to withdraw (*al-tasaḥḥub*) and flee. At one point, the governor of the Fayyum, the amir Badr al-Dīn al-Marandizī, destroyed their homes (*diyāra-hum*) and suppressed the traces of their cultivation (*qaṭaʿa āthāra-hum*)[82] due to their transgression, and he removed them from this village. But when Badr al-Dīn left, they returned.

It has no fiscal value. It has a press with one stone. Its sugarcane is sown in the lands of Miṭr Ṭāris, and subsumed in the revenue register of that village. It is irrigated from a separate canal, which branches out from the [divisor known as] al-Shādhrawān on Sinnūris Canal. Its quota, for irrigating winter and summer crops, is four *qabḍas*.

Its entire revenue [in specie] is 119 ⅙ dinars; and in grains, levied on the people of Akhṣāṣ al-Ḥallāq, 676 1/24 1/48 ardabbs:

wheat, 387 ½ ⅛ ardabbs;

barley, 207 ⅓ ¼ ⅛ ardabbs;

78 Arabic *ʿazq*: to hoe up the soil and clean it from the weeds that grow with the sugarcane; al-Nuwayrī, *Nihāyat al-arab*, VIII, 265.

79 Modern location: Al-Kaʿābī al-Qadīma/Munshàat ʿUṭayfa (منشاة عطيفة/الكعابي القديمة). Salmon, 'Répertoire', p. 50; Ramzī, *Al-Qāmūs*, II/III, 11: al-Kaʿābī al-Qadīma; I, 299 (under the entry of Shallāla): Ḥūḍ al-Turba, number 9, in the lands of Munshàat ʿUṭayfa. Shafei Bey, 'Fayoum Irrigation', p. 309, confirms this identification and states that the local peasants still remembered the weir, or flow divisor, that used to be there (al-Fasqiyya al-Yūsufiyya).

80 AS: *mukassiyya*. MP: *mukassiba*. The canonical version of the verse has *mulbisat*^{an} (covers).

81 The verses are taken from a poem by Ibn Harma (b. 709 in Medina). See Abū Manṣūr al-Thaʿālibī, *Thimār al-Qulūb fī al-Muḍāf wa'l-Mansūb* (Cairo: Dār al-Maʿārif, 1982), p. 445; On Ibn Harma, see Charles Pellat, 'Ibn Harma', *The Encyclopedia of Islam*, 2nd edn, III, 786.

82 The phrase may have the specific meaning of 'discontinued their right to cultivate'. The term *athar* is used in the Ottoman period to designate rights of usufruct by tenants. See Cuno, *The Pasha's Peasants*, pp. 64 ff.

فول، سبعة وسبعون اردبا وثلثان[274] وربع ونصف ثمن.
سمسم، اثنا عشر اردبا ونصف وربع.

تفصيله:
خراج الرواتب باسم المزارعين وارباب الاملاك بالقبرا، اربعة وتسعون دينارا وقيراط ودانق. تفصيله:
الاصل، عن ثلاثة واربعين فدانا ونصف ونصف قيراط وحبة، ثمانون دينارا وربع وسدس وثمن ودانق. تفصيله:
كرم، قطيعة خمسة دنانير وثلث، عن ربع وسدس ونصف ثمن فدان، ديناران وربع وسدس وثمن وحبة.
راتب، عن ثلاثين فدانا وثمن ونصف قيراط وحبة، ثمانية وخمسون دينارا وسدس وثمن ودانق. تفصيله:
كامل، عن ثمانية وعشرين فدانا وثمن وحبة، ستة وخمسون دينارا وربع وحبتان.
غرس عامين، عن فدانين ونصف قيراط، ديناران ونصف قيراط.
حكر، عن سبعة فدادين وثلث ونصف ثمن، احد عشر دينارا وربع وسدس وحبتان. تفصيله:
قطيعة دينارين، عن اربعة فدادين وقيراط ودانق، ثمانية دنانير وقيراطين وحبة.
قطيعة دينار، عن ثلاثة فدادين وثلث وحبة، ثلاثة دنانير وثلث وحبة.
قطن، عن خمسة فدادين ونصف، ثمانية دنانير وربع.
الاضافة، ثلاثة عشر دينارا ونصف.

خراج المناجزة، غلة، ستمائة وستة وسبعون اردبا وقيراط ونصف على ما فصل باضافته في الجملة.

وعليها من الزكاة، دينار واحد وربع وسدس وثمن. تفصيله:
خرص النخل، دينار واحد.
زكاة الغنم، عن شعرية واحدة، ربع وسدس وثمن دينار.

وعليها من الرسوم والمراعي والكيالة شركة اخصاص الحلاق، عن تسعمائة وثمانية وثلاثين درهما[275] وربع وثمن، ثلاثة وعشرون دينارا وخمسة قراريط، واثنان وعشرون اردبا ونصف قيراط:
قمح، اربعة عشر اردبا ونصف قيراط.
شعير، اربعة ارادب.
فول، اربعة ارادب.

تفصيله:
الرسوم، ثلاثمائة واحد وستون درهما وثمن، وقمح تسعة ارادب ونصف ونصف قيراط. تفصيله:
رسم الجراريف، ستة وعشرون درهما.
رسم الحصاد، ثلاثة وخمسون درهما.
شد الاحباس، اربعة دراهم.
رسم الخفارة، خمسة عشر درهما.
رسم القلقاس، مائة وثمانون درهما.
رسم الثوم، خمسة وسبعون درهما.
رسم الاجران، ثمانية دراهم وثمن، وقمح تسعة ارادب ونصف ونصف قيراط.

---

broad beans, 77 ⅔ ¼ 1/16 ardabbs;
sesame, 12 ½ ¼ ardabbs.

[The revenue in specie]:
Land tax on perennial plants, in the name of the tenants and the owners of the properties at al-Qubarāʾ, 94 1/24 1/144 dinars:
basic assessment, for 43 ½ 1/48 1/72 feddans, 80 ¼ ⅙ ⅛ 1/144 dinars:
vineyards, at the rate of 5 ⅓ dinars, for ¼ ⅙ 1/16 feddan, 2 ¼ ⅙ ⅛ 1/72 dinars.
perennial plants, for 30 ⅛ 1/48 1/72 feddans, 58 ⅙ ⅛ 1/144 dinars:
fully-grown plants (*kāmil*), for 28 ⅛ 1/72 feddans, 56 ¼ 2/72 dinars;
two-year old plants (*ghars ʿāmayn*), for 2 1/48 feddans, 2 1/48 dinars;
land subject to long-term lease, for 7 ⅓ 1/16 feddans, 11 ¼ ⅙ 2/72 dinars:
at the rate of 2 dinars [per feddan], for 4 1/24 1/144 feddans, 8 2/24 1/72 dinars;
at the rate of 1 dinar [per feddan], for 3 ⅓ 1/72 feddans, 3 ⅓ 1/72 dinars.
cotton, for 5 ½ feddans, 8 ¼ dinars.
the addition, 13 ½ dinars.

Munājaza land tax, in grains, 676 1/24 1/48 ardabbs, as specified above in the aggregates.

The alms-tax is 1 ¼ ⅙ ⅛ dinar:
estimate of date palms, 1 dinar;
alms-tax on small cattle, for one goat, ¼ ⅙ ⅛ dinar.

The fees, the pasture tax and the measurement fee, jointly with Akhṣāṣ al-Ḥallāq — 938 ¼ ⅛ dirhams, which are 23 5/24 dinars; [and in grains,] 22 1/48 ardabbs:
wheat, 14 1/48 ardabbs;
barley, 4 ardabbs;
broad beans, 4 ardabbs.

[The fees, the pasture tax and the measurement fee] in detail:
the fees, 361 ⅛ dirhams; wheat, 9 ½ 1/48 ardabbs:
dredging fee, 26 dirhams;
harvest fee, 53 dirhams;
supervision of endowments, 4 dirhams;
protection fee, 15 dirhams;
colocasia fee, 180 dirhams;
garlic fee, 75 dirhams;
threshing-floor fee, 8 ⅛ dirhams; and wheat, 9 ½ 1/48 ardabbs.

---

274 ط.م.: وثللثان.
275 أ.س.: دينار.

الكيالة، اثنا عشر اردبا ونصف:

قمح، اربعة ارادب ونصف.

شعير، اربعة ارادب.

فول، اربعة ارادب.

المراعي، عن اربعمائة وسبعة وخمسين راسا، خمسمائة وسبعة وسبعون درهما وربع. تفصيله:

راتب، قطيعة درهمين وربع الراس، عن مائة وثمانية وعشرين راسا، مائتان وثمانية وثمانون درهما.

طارئ، عن ثلاثمائة وتسعة وعشرين راسا، مائتان وستون درهما ونصف وثمن. تفصيله:

قطيعة درهم الراس، عن مائة وخمسة وعشرين راسا، مائة وخمسة وعشرين درهما.

قطيعة سبعين درهما المائة، عن مائة وستة وثمانين راسا، مائة وثلاثون درهما وربع.

قطيعة ثلاثين درهما المائة، عن ثمانية عشر راسا،[276] خمسة دراهم وربع وثمن.

رسم المستخدمين، ثمانية وعشرون درهما ونصف وثمن.[277]

وعليها من الاتبان، ستمائة واربعة واربعون شنيفا.

والذي يسلف عليه من الشعير باسم اهل الاخصاص الذى عليهم مغل الناحية، خمسون اردبا.

ومن حرف[278] الالف، اخصاص العجميين. هذه البلدة غربي مدينة الفيوم، مسافة ساعتين للراكب منه. عليها جملة مستكثرة من الكروم والتفاح اليسير والنخل، ويسير من التين والخوخ. اهلها عرب وهم بنو غصين من بني كلاب. متاخمة لاراضي ببيج انشو، حتى انه ثبت في الديوان بالمشاريح[279] المشهود فيها، ان[280] اهلها استولوا على قطعة من اراضي ببيج انشو. وصدق على[281] ذلك نقص[282] ارتفاع ببيج انشو بانقطاع هذه الارض منها وما زاد من ارتفاع هذه البلدة التي هي اخصاص العجميين عن ارتفاعها قبل استيلائهم على هذه الارض.

عبرتها جيشية، ثلاثة الاف ومائة[283] وخمسون دينارا. جارية في اقطاع جماعة من المقطعين: شمس الدين بن شرره[284] ومن معه. شربها من الجهة القبلية من البحر الاعظم الفيومي من خليج بغير بنيان يعرف بدفد لاله، عبرته ثمان قبض. وبها جامع تقام فيه الجمعة.

ارتفاعها مما جميعه مستخرجا ومتحصلا، عينا، مائتان وثمانية وعشرون دينارا وقيراط وحبة، غلة الفان وستة ارادب:

قمح، تسعمائة واربعة وعشرون اردبا.

شعير، تسعمائة وثلاثون اردبا.

The measurement fee, 12 ½ ardabbs:

wheat, 4 ½ ardabbs;

barley, 4 ardabbs;

broad beans, 4 ardabbs.

The pasture tax, for 457 heads, 577 ¼ dirhams:

Permanent pasture lands, at the rate of 2 ¼ dirhams per head, for 128 heads, 288 dirhams;

seasonal pasture lands, for 327 heads, 260 ½ ⅛ dirhams:

at the rate of a dirham per head, for 125 heads, 125 dirhams;

at the rate of 70 dirhams per 100 [heads], for 186 heads, 130 ¼ dirhams;

at the rate of 30 dirhams per 100 [heads], for 18 heads, 5 ¼ ⅛ dirhams.

Government agents' fee, 28 ½ ⅛ dirhams.

Hay, 644 bales.

The barley paid for in advance, for the people of al-Akhṣāṣ who are the ones liable for the annual grain yield of the village, 50 ardabbs.

Also beginning with the letter 'alif': Akhṣāṣ al-ʿAjamiyyīn.[83] This village is two hours' ride west of Madīnat al-Fayyūm. It has very extensive vineyards, a few apple trees and date palms, as well as some figs and peaches. Its people are Arabs, the Banū Ghuṣayn of the Banū Kilāb. It is adjacent to the lands of Babīj Unshū. It was confirmed by attested submissions (*al-mashārīḥ al-mashhūd fīhā*)[84] in the Dīwān that its people took over a portion of the lands of Babīj Unshū. This is corroborated by the decrease in the revenues of Babīj Unshū, as this land was taken from it, and the increase in the revenues of this village, namely Akhṣāṣ al-ʿAjamiyyīn, compared to what it was before they took over this land.

Its fiscal value is 3,150 army dinars. It is allocated as *iqṭāʿ* for a group of *iqṭāʿ*-holders, who are Shams al-Dīn ibn Shirwa/Sharara and those with him. Its water comes from the southern side of the Main Canal, from a canal without a weir (?, *bunyān*), known as Dafd Lāla. Its water quota is eight *qabḍas*. It has a congregational mosque, in which the Friday prayers are held.

Its revenues in cash and kind are, in specie, 228 1/24 1/72 dinars; and in grains, 2,006 ardabbs:

Wheat, 924 ardabbs;

barley, 930 ardabbs;

---

276 ساقط من أ. س.: مائة وثلاثون درهما وربع قطيعة ثلاثين درهما المائة عن ثمانية عشر رأسا.

277 ساقط من أ. س.: رسم المستخدمين ثمانية وعشرون درهما ونصف وثمن.

278 أ. س.: حروف.

279 أ. س.: بالمشائيخ.

280 أ. س.: انها.

281 أ. س. يضيف: على.

282 ط. م.: بعض.

283 أ. س.: دينار.

284 أ. س.: شروة.

[83] Modern location: ʿAjamiyyīn (العجميّين). Halm, *Ägypten*, p. 245: ʿAjamiyyīn; Salmon, 'Répertoire', pp. 59–60; Zéki, 'Une description', p. 35; de Sacy, *État des provinces*, p. 680: Aḥṣāṣ; Savigny, *Description de l'Égypte*, p. 128: El-ʿAgmyyn (in the map: ʿAgmīineh); Ibn Mammātī, *Kitāb qawānīn al-dawāwīn*, p. 103; Ibn al-Jīʿān, *Kitāb al-tuḥfa*, p. 151; Ramzī, *Al-Qāmūs*, II/III, 72: ʿAjamiyyīn.

[84] On *mashārīḥ* as documents attesting to a decrease in revenues, see al-Nuwayrī, *Nihāyat al-arab*, VIII, 243 ff. One example is that of documents submitted by owners of orchards that their trees had been submerged by the Nile's flood. Another example is of a document submitted to the officials in charge of the poll-tax, which lists the names of those who converted to Islam, died, or left the province.

كمون، مائة واربعون اردبا.
سلجم، اثنا عشر اردبا.

تفصيله:
الهلالي، عن اجرة الحانوت، سبعة دنانير.
المراعي، دينار واحد.
خراج الراتب، عن ستة واربعين فدانا وثلثين[285] وحبة، مائتان وعشرون دينارا وقيراط وحبة. تفصيله:
كرم، اربعة وثلاثون فدانا وثلث وربع، بما فيه من غرس عامين وغرس عام وهو فدانان وثلثان[286] وثمن وحبتان، مائة واحد وتسعون دينارا وثلث.
شجر مثمر،[287] عن اثني عشر فدانا وقيراطين وحبة ثمانية وعشرون دينارا وثلث وربع وثمن[288] وحبة.

المناجزة،[289] الفان وستة ارادب على ما فصل.

وعليها من الزكاة، مائة وعشرون دينارا ونصف وثمن وحبتان. تفصيله:
الخرص، مائة وخمسة عشر دينارا ونصف. تفصيله:
خرص العنب، مائة وخمسة عشر دينارا.
خرص النخل، نصف دينار.
ثمن الماشية، عن خمسة عشر راسا، خمسة دنانير وثمن وحبتان. تفصيله:[290]
بقر احمر، عن تبيع واحد، دينار وربع وثمن.
ثمن اغنام، عن اربعة عشر راسا، ثلاثة دنانير ونصف وربع وحبتان:
شعارى، عن ثلاثة عشر راسا، ديناران وثلث وربع وثمن وحبتان. تفصيله:
عن راسين، دينار وقيراطان.
الابل للمنتجعين للناحية، عن احد عشر راسا، دينار ونصف وثمن وحبتان.

وعليها من الرسوم[291] والكيالة، عن مائتين واثنين وخمسين درهما ونصف وربع، ستة دنانير وربع وسدس وثمن وحبتان؛ وغلة، اربعة وثمانون اردبا وثلث ونصف ثمن. تفصيله:
قمح، تسعة واربعون اردبا وثلث.
شعير، احد وعشرون اردبا وربع وسدس وثمن.
فول، تسعة ارادب ونصف ونصف قيراط.
كمون، اربعة ارادب.

تفصيله:
شد العين، خمسة وستون درهما.
شد الاحباس، اربعة دراهم.
رسم الجراريف، خمسة واربعون درهما.
رسم الحصاد، ثلاثة وخمسون درهما.
رسم الخفارة، خمسة عشر درهما.
مصالحة السلجم، خمسة وثلاثون درهما.

cumin, 140 ardabbs;
rape, 12 ardabbs.

[The revenue in detail]:
lunar-calendar tax, for the rent of the shop, 7 dinars;
pasture tax, 1 dinar;
land tax on perennial plants, for 46 2/3 1/72 feddans, 220 1/24 1/72 dinars:
vineyards, [for] 34 1/3 1/4 feddans — inclusive of two-year and one-year old plants, which account for 2 2/3 1/8 2/72 feddans — 191 1/3 dinars.
fruit-bearing trees,[85] for 12 2/24 1/72 feddans, 28 1/3 1/4 1/8 1/72 dinars.

Munājaza land tax, 2,006 ardabbs, as specified.

The alms-tax is 120 1/2 1/8 2/72 dinars:
the estimate, 115 1/2 dinars:
estimate of grapes, 115 dinars;
estimate of date palms, 1/2 dinar;
monetary value of livestock, for 15 heads, 5 1/8 2/72 dinars:
cows, for one yearling calf, 1 1/8 dinar;
monetary value of small cattle, for 14 heads, 3 1/2 1/4 2/72 dinars:
goats, for 13 heads — 2 1/3 1/4 1/8 2/72 dinars:
for two heads [of goats], 1 2/24 dinar;
for camels of those seeking pasture in the village, 11 heads, 1 1/2 1/4 1/8 2/72 dinar.

The fees and the measurement fee, 252 1/2 1/4 dirhams, which are 6 1/4 1/6 1/8 2/72 dinars; and in grains, 84 1/3 1/16 ardabbs:
wheat, 49 1/3 ardabbs;
barley, 21 1/4 1/6 1/8 ardabbs;
broad beans, 9 1/2 1/48 ardabbs;
cumin, 4 ardabbs.

[The fees] include:
Supervision of the land survey, 65 dirhams;
supervision of endowments, 4 dirhams;
dredging fee, 45 dirhams;
harvest fee, 53 dirhams;
protection fee, 15 dirhams;
settlement (*muṣālaḥa*) for rape, 55 dirhams;

285 أ. س.: ثلثي.
286 أ. س.: وثلثاي.
287 ساقط من ط. م.: وغير مثمر.
288 ساقط من أ. س.: وثمن.
289 أ. س. يضيف: ثمانية وعشرون دينارا.
290 ساقط من أ. س.: تفصيله.
291 أ. س.: الرسم.

85 AS adds: 'and those not bearing fruit'.

رسم الاجران، خمسة وثلاثون درهما ونصف وربع،
وغلة،[292] ثلاثة واربعون اردبا وثلث ونصف ثمن:
قمح، تسعة وعشرون اردبا وثلث.
شعير،[293] اردب وربع وسدس وثمن.
فول، تسعة ارادب ونصف ونصف قيراط.
كمون، ثلاثة ارادب.[294]
الكيالة، احد واربعون اردبا:
قمح، عشرون اردبا.
شعير، عشرون اردبا.
كمون، اردب واحد.[295]

وعليها من الاتبان، الفا شنيف.

وعليها لديوان الاحباس، ديناران.

رسم خولي البحر، قمح، اردب واحد.[296]

وما يسلف بها من الشعير برسم الاصطبلات السلطانية ما جملته مائتان وخمسون اردبا.

والذي جرت به العادة للناحية[297] من التقاوي، مائتان وستة ارادب. تفصيله:
قمح، مائة وعشرون اردبا.
شعير، اربعة وثمانون اردبا.
كمون، اردبان.

والمستقر اطلاقه لارباب الرزق، ثلاثة فدادين. تفصيله:
المشايخ، فدانان.
النجار،[298] فدان.

والمقرر على المزارعين، كشك وفريك، خمسة ارادب. تفصيله:
كشك، ثلاثة ارادب.
فريك، اردبان.

والمربى بها من الدجاج تسعمائة طائر. تفصيله:
للديوان، بما فيه من اجرة التربية وهو الثلث، ستمائة.
للمقطعين، ثلاثمائة.

اهلها يزرعون الاقصاب برسم معصرة ببيج انشو بابقارهم ورجالهم. والذي استقر عليه زراعة الراس[299] منها، خارجا عن الخلف الذى لم يتحرر،[300] ثلاثون فدانا.

threshing-floor fee, 35 ½ ¼ dirhams; and in grains, 43 ⅓ 1/16 ardabbs:
wheat, 29 ⅓ ardabbs,
barley, 1 ¼ ⅙ ⅛ ardabb;
broad beans, 9 ½ 1/48 ardabbs;
cumin, 3 ardabbs.
measurement fee, 41 ardabbs:
wheat, 20 ardabbs;
barley, 20 ardabbs;
cumin, 1 ardabb.

Hay, 2,000 bales.

For the Ministry of Endowments, 2 dinars.

Fee for the overseer of the canal, wheat, 1 ardabb.

The barley assigned for the royal stables, which was paid for in advance, 250 ardabbs.

The seed advances customarily distributed to the locality, 206 ardabbs:
wheat, 120 ardabbs;
barley, 84 ardabbs;
cumin, 2 ardabbs.

The confirmed allocation for those entitled to allowances (*arbāb al-rizaq*), 3 feddans:
the headmen, 2 feddans;
the carpenter, 1 feddan.

The confirmed levy of *kishk* and *farīk* dishes from the tenants, 5 ardabbs:
kishk, 3 ardabbs;
farīk, 2 ardabbs.

The chickens reared in it, 900 birds:
for the Dīwān, including the rearing wage of a third, 600 birds;
for the *iqṭāʿ*-holders, 300.

Its people sow sugarcane, which is assigned to the press in Babīj Unshū, by their own cattle and their men. It has been confirmed that the sowing of first harvest is 30 feddans. This excludes the second harvest, which has not yet been ascertained (*lam yataḥarrar*).

292 ساقط من أ. س.: خمسة وثلاثون درهما ونصف وربع وغلة.
293 أ. س. يضيف: اربع أرادب.
294 ساقط من أ. س.: ونصف قيراط كمون ثلاثة أرادب.
295 أ. س. يضيف:رسم خولي البحر قمح أردب واحد.
296 ساقط من أ. س.: رسم خولي البحر قمح أردب واحد.
297 ساقط من أ. س.: للناحية.
298 ط. م.: النحار.
299 أ. س.: الرواتب.
300 أ. س.: عن الخلفة التي لم تتحرر.

ومن حرف[301] الالف، اطسا. هذه البلدة بلدة صغيرة قبلي الفيوم، مجاورة لدفدنو. فيها[302] نخل متفرق ودويرات يسيرة؛ فيها كرم[303] وخوخ. مسافتها من مدينة الفيوم ساعة ونصف للراكب. اهلها عرب من بني عامر، وهم فخذ من بني كلاب. عبرتها جيشية، الف دينار. شربها من خليج مجصص من البر القبلي ينقسم من قبلي بوصير، يخص الناحية اربع قبض.

ارتفاعها مما جميعه مستخرجا ومتحصلا، عينا، اثنا عشر دينارا؛ غلة، اربعمائة واثنان وثلاثون اردبا. تفصيله:
قمح، مائتان وستة عشر اردبا.
شعير وفول، مائتان وستة عشر اردبا.

تفصيله:
مراعي، ديناران.
خراج الراتب، عشرة دنانير.

مناجزة الغلة، اربعمائة واثنان وثلاثون اردبا، على ما فصل.

عليها من الزكاة، خمسة دنانير ونصف وربع وثمن. تفصيله:
خرص النخل، ثلاثة دنانير وربع.
ثمن الماشية، عن ثلاثة ارؤس، ديناران ونصف وثمن.
تفصيله:
بقر احمر، تبيع واحد، دينار.
اغنام، راسان[304]، دينار واحد ونصف وثمن.
تفصيله:
بياض، عن راس واحدة،[305] دينار واحد وقيراطان.
شعارى، عن راس، ربع وسدس وثمن دينار.

وعليها من الرسوم والكيالة والمراعي، عن مائة وعشرة دراهم ونصف وثمن، ديناران ونصف وربع وحبة، غلة تسعة عشر اردبا وقيراطان. تفصيله:
قمح، خمسة عشر اردبا وثلث وربع.
شعير، اردبان ونصف وربع.
فول، نصف وربع اردب.

تفصيله:
الرسوم، مائة ودرهم واحد وربع؛ غلة ثمانية ارادب وثلث.
تفصيله:
قمح، خمسة ارادب وثلث وربع.
شعير، اردبان ونصف وربع.
تفصيله:
شد العين، ثمانية عشر درهما.
شد الاحباس، اربعة دراهم.
رسم الحصاد، ثلاثة وخمسون درهما.
رسم الخفارة، خمسة عشر درهما.
رسم الاجران، احد عشر درهما وربع؛ غلة ثمانية ارادب وثلث:
قمح، خمسة ارادب وثلث وربع.
شعير[306]، اردبان ونصف وربع.

Also beginning with the letter 'alif': Iṭsā.[86] This is a small village, in the south of the Fayyum, close to Difidnū. It has scattered date palms and a few small enclosures, in which there are vineyards and peach trees. Its distance from Madīnat al-Fayyūm is an hour and a half's ride. Its people are Arabs from the Banū ʿĀmir, a branch of the Banū Kilāb. Its fiscal value is 1,000 army dinars. It gets its water from a plastered canal, which issues from the south bank [of the Main Canal], south of Būṣīr [Difidnū]. The village is allotted four *qabḍas* [of water].

Its revenues in cash and in kind are, in specie, 12 dinars; in grains, 432 ardabbs:
- wheat, 216 ardabbs;
- barley and broad beans, 216 ardabbs.

[The revenue in detail]:
- pasture tax, 2 dinars;
- land tax on perennial plants, 10 dinars;

Munājaza [land tax] on grains, 432 ardabbs, as specified.

The alms-tax is 5 ½ ¼ ⅛ dinars:
- estimate of date palms, 3 ¼ dinars;
- monetary value of livestock, for three heads, 2 ½ ⅛ dinars:
  - cows, for one yearling calf, 1 dinar;
  - small cattle, for two heads, 1 ½ ⅛ dinar:
    - sheep, for one head, 1 2/24 dinar;
    - goats, for one head, ¼ ⅙ ⅛ dinar.

The fees, the measurement fee and the pasture tax, 110 ½ ⅛ dirhams, which are 2 ½ ¼ 1/72 dinars; and in grains, 19 2/24 ardabbs:
- wheat, 15 ⅓ ¼ ardabbs;
- barley, 2 ½ ¼ ardabbs;
- broad beans ½ ¼ ardabb.

[The fees] include:
- the fees, 101 ¼ dirhams; in grains, 8 ⅓ ardabbs:
  - wheat, 5 ⅓ ¼ ardabbs;
  - barley, 2 ½ ¼ ardabbs.
- [The fees in detail]:
  - supervision of the land survey, 18 dirhams;
  - supervision of endowments, 4 dirhams;
  - harvest fee, 53 dirhams;
  - protection fee, 15 dirhams;
  - threshing-floor fee, 11 ¼ dirhams; in grains, 8 ⅓ ardabbs:
    - wheat, 5 ⅓ ¼ ardabbs;
    - barley, 2 ½ ¼ ardabbs.

301 أ. س.: حروف.
302 أ. س.: منها.
303 ساقط من أ. س.: كرم.
304 أ. س.: راسين.
305 أ. س.: واحد.
306 ساقط من ط. م.: شعير.

86 Modern location: Iṭsā (اطسا). Timm, *Das Christlich-Koptische Ägypten*, pp. 1205–06: Tsē; Halm, *Ägypten*, p. 260; Salmon, 'Répertoire', p. 65; Zéki, 'Une description', p. 38; de Sacy, *État des provinces*, p. 680; Description de l'Égypte, p. 126; Yāqūt, *Muʿjam al-Buldān*, I, 218: Aṭsā; Ibn al-Jīʿān, *Kitāb al-tuḥfa*, p. 151; Ramzī, *Al-Qāmūs*, II/III, 81: Iṭsā.

الكيالة، عشرة ارادب ونصف وربع. تفصيله:
قمح، عشرة ارادب.
فول، نصف وربع اردب.
المراعي، تسعة دراهم وربع وثمن. تفصيله:
قطيعة خمسة وعشرين درهما المائة، عن ثلاثين راسا، سبعة دراهم ونصف.
رسم المستخدمين، عن ثلاثين راسا، درهم ونصف وربع وثمن.

وعليها لديوان الاحباس، ديناران.

وعليها من الاتبان، اربعمائة وعشرون شنيفا.

ورسم[307] خولي البحر، ثلاث ويبات.

والذي جرت به العادة للناحية من التقاوي، ستون اردبا. تفصيله:
قمح، اثنان وثلاثون اردبا.
شعير، اربعة عشر اردبا.
فول، اربعة عشر اردبا.

والمربى بها من الفروج، اربعمائة وعشرة. تفصيله:
للديوان السلطاني، بما فيه من اجرة التربية وهو الثلث، مائتان وعشرة.
للمقطعين مائتان.

والذي يسلف عليه بها من الشعير للاصطبلات السلطانية، ثلاثون اردبا.

ومن حرف الالف، اهريت. هذه البلدة بلدة متوسطة، بين البلد الكبير والصغير. فيها نخل وجميز وسدر وكروم. بينها وبين مدينة[308] الفيوم مسافة ساعتين للراكب. اهلها عرب، وهم من بني غصين وهو فخذ من بني كلاب. وهى تعرف ببببيج النيلة. عبرتها جيشية، خمسة الاف ومائتا دينار. تشرب من خليج بالبر القبلي بغير بنيان، عبرته ثمان قبض. وبها جامع تقام فيه الجمعة.

ارتفاعها مما جميعه مستخرجا ومتحصلا، عينا، سبعة عشر دينارا وسدس وثمن ودانق؛ وغلة، الف وثلاثمائة اردب:
قمح، ستمائة وخمسون اردبا.
شعير، ستمائة وخمسون اردبا.

تفصيله:
حفر[309] القزازين، اربعة دنانير وثلثان[310] وثمن ودانق.
المراعي، خمسة دنانير.
خراج الراتب، سبعة دنانير ونصف.

خراج المناجزة والحمولة، الف وثلاثمائة اردب على ما فصل.

وعليها من الزكاة، اربعة عشر دينارا. تفصيله:
اهريت، عن ثمن الماشية، عن اربعة ارؤس، اربعة دنانير وثمن. تفصيله:
بقر احمر، تبيع واحد، ديناران.
اغنام، عن ثلاثة ارؤس، ديناران وثمن. تفصيله:
بياض، عن راس واحد، دينار واحد وقيراط.
شعارى، عن راسين، دينار واحد وقيراطان.

307 أ. س.: وبرسم.
308 ساقط من أ. س.: مدينة.
309 أ. س.: جفر.
310 أ. س.: وثلثاي.

The measurement fee, 10 ½ ¼ ardabbs:
- wheat, 10 ardabbs;
- broad beans, ½ ¼ ardabb.

The pasture tax, 9 ¼ ⅛ dirhams:
- at the rate of 25 dirhams per hundred [heads], for 30 heads, 7 ½ dirhams.
- the government agents' fee, for 30 heads, 1 ½ ¼ ⅛ dirham.

For the Ministry of Endowments, 2 dinars.

Hay, 420 bales.

The fee of the overseer of the canal, 3 *wayba*.

The seed advances which are customarily assigned to the locality, 60 ardabbs:
- wheat, 32 ardabbs;
- barley, 14 ardabbs;
- broad beans, 14 ardabbs.

The chickens reared in it, 410 [birds]:
- for the Dīwān, including the rearing wage of a third, 210;
- for the *iqṭāʿ*-holders, 200.

The barley assigned for the royal stables, which was paid for in advance, 30 ardabbs.

Also beginning with the letter 'alif': Ihrīt.[87] This is a medium-sized village, two hours' ride from Madīnat al-Fayyūm. It has date palms, sycamores, sidr trees (Ziziphus, Christ's thorn) and vineyards. Its people are Arabs from the Banū Ghuṣayn, a branch of the Banū Kilāb. It is [also] known as Babīj al-Nīla.[88] Its fiscal value is 5,200 army dinars. It gets its water from a canal without a weir, which issues from the south bank [of the Main Canal]. Its [water] quota is eight *qabḍas*. It has a congregational mosque in which the Friday prayer is held.

Its revenues in cash and in kind are, in specie, 17 ⅙ ⅛ 1/144 dinars; and in grains, 1,300 ardabbs:
- wheat, 650 ardabbs;
- barley, 650 ardabbs.

[The revenue in detail]:
- pit looms of the weavers, 4 ⅔, ⅛ 1/144 dinars;
- the pasture tax, 5 dinars;
- land tax on perennial plants, 7 ½ dinars;

Munājaza land tax and the transport fee, 1,300 ardabbs, as specified.

The alms-tax, 14 dinars:
- Ihrīt, monetary value of livestock, for four heads, 4 ⅛ dinars:
  - cows, a yearling calf, 2 dinars;
  - small cattle, for three heads, 2 ⅛ dinars:
    - sheep, for one head, 1 1/24 dinar;
    - goats, for two heads, 1 2/24 dinar.

87 Modern location: Ihrit al-Gharbiyya (اهريت الغربية). Timm, *Das Christlich-Koptische Ägypten*, p. 1175: Hrit; Halm, *Ägypten*, p. 260: Ihrit/Disyā; Salmon, 'Répertoire', p. 62; de Sacy, *État des provinces*, p. 681; Savigny, *Description de l'Égypte*, p. 127: Aheryt; Ibn Mammātī, *Kitāb qawānīn al-dawāwīn*, p. 103; Yāqūt, *Muʿjam al-Buldān*, I, 284: Ihrīt; Ibn al-Jīʿān, *Kitāb al-tuḥfa*, p. 152; Ramzī, *Al-Qāmūs*, II/III, 83: Ihrit al-Gharbiyya.

88 Mentioned above in Chapter 7 as 'Babīj al-Nīla, one of the hamlets of Ihrīt'.

ببيج النيلة، سبعة دنانير وربع. تفصيله:
خرص العنب، خمسة دنانير وربع.
ثمن اغنام، بياض، عن راسين، ديناران.
منشاة العثامنة،[311] ثمن خمس شعارى، ديناران ونصف وثمن.

وعليها من الرسوم والكيالة والمراعي، عن مائتين واربعة وثمانين درهما، سبعة دنانير وقيراطان وحبة؛ وغلة، ثمانية وسبعون اردبا وثلثان وثمن. تفصيله:
قمح، اربعة وثلاثون اردبا وسدس وثمن.
شعير، ستة وثلاثون اردبا وربع وثمن.
فول، ثمانية ارادب وثمن.

تفصيله:
الرسوم، مائتان وستة وخمسون درهما، وتسعة وثلاثون اردبا ونصف وثلث وثمن. تفصيله:
قمح، تسعة عشر اردبا وثلثان[312] وربع.
شعير، سبعة عشر اردبا وثلثان[313] وثمن.
فول، اردبان وربع.

تفصيله:
شد العين، اربعة وخمسون درهما.
شد الاحباس، تسعة دراهم.
رسم الجراريف، تسعون درهما.
رسم الحصاد، ثلاثة وخمسون درهما.
رسم الخفارة، خمسة عشر درهما.
رسم الاجران، خمسة وثلاثون درهما، وتسعة وثلاثون اردبا ونصف وثلث وثمن، على ما فصل.
الكيالة، ثمانية وثلاثون اردبا ونصف وثلث. تفصيله:
قمح، اربعة عشر اردبا وربع وثمن.
شعير، ثمانية عشر اردبا وثلث وربع.
فول، خمسة ارادب ونصف وربع وثمن.
المراعي، ثمانية وعشرون درهما، طارى، عن ستة وسبعين راسا، ثمانية وعشرون درهما. تفصيله:
قطيعة ثلاثين درهما المائة، عن احد وثلاثين راسا، تسعة دراهم ونصف.
قطيعة خمسة وعشرين درهما المائة، عن خمسة واربعين راسا، ثلاثة عشر درهما ونصف وربع.
رسم المستخدمين، اربعة دراهم وربع.

وعليها لديوان الاحباس، اربعة[314] دنانير عينا.

وعليها من الاتبان، الف وخمسمائة شنيف.

رسم خولي البحر، اردب واحد.

والذي جرت العادة باطلاقه لها من التقاوي، مائة وثلاثة وثمانون اردبا. تفصيله:
قمح، ثمانية وثمانون اردبا.
شعير، خمسة وتسعون اردبا.

311 أ. س.: العتامنة.
312 أ. س.: وثلثاي.
313 أ. س.: وثلثاي.
314 ط. م.: ربعة.

Babīj al-Nīla, 7 ¼ dinars:
the estimate of grapes, 5 ¼ dinars;
monetary value of small cattle, sheep, for two heads, 2 dinars.
Munsha'at al-ʿAthāmina,[89] the monetary value of five goats, 2 ½ ⅛ dinars.

The fees, the measurement fee and the pasture tax, 284 dirhams, which are 7 ²⁄₂₄ ¹⁄₇₂ dinars; and in grains, 78 ⅔ ⅛ ardabbs:
wheat, 34 ⅙ ⅛ ardabbs;
barley, 36 ¼ ⅛ ardabbs;
broad beans, 8 ⅛ ardabbs.

The fees are 256 dirhams and 39 ½ ⅓ ⅛ ardabbs:
wheat, 19 ⅔ ¼ ardabbs;
barley, 17 ⅔ ⅛ ardabbs;
broad beans, 2 ¼ ardabbs.

[The fees] include:
supervision of the land survey, 54 dirhams;
supervision of endowments, 9 dirhams;
dredging fee, 90 dirhams;
harvest fee, 53 dirhams;
protection fee, 15 dirhams;
threshing-floor fee, 35 dirhams and 39 ½ ⅓ ⅛ ardabbs, as specified.
measurement fee, 38 ½ ⅓ ardabbs:
wheat, 14 ¼ ⅛ ardabbs;
barley, 18 ⅓ ¼ ardabbs;
broad beans, 5 ½ ¼ ⅛ ardabbs.
The pasture tax, on seasonal pasture lands, for 76 heads, 28 dirhams:
at the rate of 30 dirhams per hundred [heads], for 31 heads, 9 ½ dirhams;
at the rate of 25 dirhams per hundred [heads], for 45 heads, 13 ½ ¼ dirhams.
The government agents' fee, 4 ¼ dirhams.

For the Ministry of Endowments, 4 dinars in specie.

Hay, 1,500 bales.

The fee of the overseer of the canal, 1 ardabb.

The seed advances customarily distributed in it, 183 ardabbs:
wheat, 88 ardabbs;
barley, 95 ardabbs.

89 Mentioned above in Chapter 7 as 'Munsha'at al-ʿUthmāniyya'.

والمقرر على المزارعين من الاصناف، خمسة ارادب. تفصيله:
كشك، اردبان.
فريك، اردبان.
سويق، اردب واحد.

The confirmed levy of foodstuffs from the tenants, 5 ardabbs:
kishk, 2 ardabbs;
farīk, 2 ardabbs;
sawīq, 1 ardabb.

والذي جرت العادة بتربيته من الفروج، ثمانمائة وخمسون طائرا:
للديوان، بما فيه من اجرة التربية وهو الثلث، اربعمائة وخمسون.
وللمقطعين، اربعمائة طائر.

The chickens that are customarily reared, 850 birds:
for the Dīwān, including the rearing wage of a third, 450;
for the *iqṭāʿ*-holders, 400 birds.

والذي جرت العادة ببرشه وزراعته وسقيه بابقارهم ورجالهم، راس وخلفة، برسم معاصر الاقصاب بسنورس، احد وعشرون فدانا ونصف وربع ونصف ثمن. تفصيله:
راس، اربعة عشر فدانا وخمسة قراريط.
خلفة، سبعة فدادين وثلث وربع ونصف قيراط.

The land which is customarily ploughed (*bi-barshihi*),[90] sown and irrigated by their cattle and their men, first harvest and second harvest, assigned to the sugarcane presses at Sinnūris, 21 $\frac{1}{2}$ $\frac{1}{4}$ $\frac{1}{16}$ feddans:
first harvest, 14 $\frac{5}{24}$ feddans;
second harvest, 7 $\frac{1}{3}$ $\frac{1}{4}$ $\frac{1}{48}$ feddans.

وعليها من الجوالي، عن احد وثلاثين نفرا، اثنان وستون دينارا. تفصيله:
المقيمون بها، عن خمسة وعشرين نفرا، خمسون دينارا.
الناعون عنها، عن ستة اشخاص، اثنا عشر دينارا. تفصيله:
الوجه البحري، نفر، ديناران.
الوجه القبلي، خمسة انفار، عشرة دنانير.

The poll-tax, for 31 individuals, 62 dinars:
those residing in it, for 25 individuals, 50 dinars;
those absent from it, for six individuals, 12 dinars:
the northern region, one individual, 2 dinars;
the southern region, five individuals, 10 dinars.

والذي يسلف بها من الشعير للاصطبلات السلطانية، مائتا اردب.

The barley assigned for the royal stables, which was paid for in advance, 200 ardabbs.

ومن حرف[315] الالف، ابو كسا. هذه البلدة بلدة كبيرة، عليها نخل كثير في[316] واد مستطيل يليها وكروم حسنة على هيئة الحجاز في واديها ونخلها، على ما اخبرني من راى الحجاز. بينها وبين مدينة الفيوم ثلاث ساعات للراكب. اكثر اهلها حاضرة وفيها قليل من العرب وهم بنو جواب، فخذ من بني كلاب. خفر هذه البلدة لهم وسكنى بعضهم فيها. جارية في اقطاع المقطعين. بها معصرة ذات حجرين، حجر دائر بالابقار،[317] وحجر دائر بالماء.

Also beginning with the letter 'alif': Abū Ksā.[91] This is a large village, with many date palms in a long ravine that lies nearby, where there are also fine vineyards. Its ravine with its date palms resembles the Hejaz, as I was told by someone who visited the Hejaz. It is three hours' ride from Madīnat al-Fayyūm. Most of its people are non-tribal (*ḥāḍira*), with a few Arabs of the Banū Jawwāb, a branch of the Banū Kilāb. The protection of this village is in their hands, and some of them reside in it. It is allocated as *iqṭāʿ* to *iqṭāʿ*-holders.

It has a press with two stones: one turned by cattle and one turned by water.

اقصابها تزدرع باراضيها واراضي[318] ابشاية الرمان وهي لسنة احدى واربعين وستمائة، خارجا عن الزيادة لسنة اثنتين واربعين وستمائة، مائة واربعة وستون فدانا وقيراط. تفصيله:
راس، مائة وثلاثة عشر فدانا.
خلفة، احد وخمسون فدانا وقيراط للديوان السلطاني.

Its sugarcane is sown in its lands and in the lands of Ibshāyat al-Rummān. They amounted to 164 feddans $\frac{1}{24}$ in 641 [AD 1243–4], without the addition in the year 642 [AD 1244–5]:
first harvest, 113 feddans;
second harvest, 51 $\frac{1}{24}$ feddans.

That is for the royal Dīwān.

والمزدرع بها من القرط والفول للعوامل الديوانية، سبعة عشر فدانا.

The alfalfa and broad beans sown in it for the cattle of the Dīwān, 17 feddans.

عبرتها جيشية، خمسة عشر الفا وخمسة وثمانون دينارا ونصف. شربها من خليج اخر البحر اليوسفي من الجهة البحرية، شركة ببيج انشو وابشاية[319] الرمان وطبهار وجردو، تتقسم[320] بخشبة واحدة؛ يخص الناحية ثلاثة عشر قبضة. بها جامع تقام فيه الجمعة ومسجد شريف يعرف برباح.

Its fiscal value is 15,085 $\frac{1}{2}$ army dinars. It gets its water from a canal at the end of the Main Canal, from the northern side, which is shared with Babīj Unshū, Ibshāyat al-Rummān, Ṭubhār and Jardū. [The water to these villages] is divided by a single wooden [divisor]. The village is allotted 13 *qabḍas*. It has a congregational mosque, in which Friday prayers are held, and a distinguished neighbourhood mosque, known as Rabāḥ.

ارتفاعها مما جميعه مستخرجا ومتحصلا، خارجا عن اجرة الحمولة وهي ثلاثمائة وتسعة وثلاثون اردبا ونصف وربع. تفصيله:
قمح، مائة واثنان وسبعون اردبا وثلث.
شعير، مائة وسبعة وستون اردبا وقيراطان.

That excludes the transport fee, which is 339 $\frac{1}{2}$ $\frac{1}{4}$ ardabbs:
wheat, 172 $\frac{1}{3}$ ardabbs;
barley, 167 $\frac{2}{24}$ ardabbs.

315 أ. س.: حروف.
316 ساقط من أ. س.: في.
317 ط. م.: بالنفار.
318 أ. س.: وأراضيها.
319 أ. س.: ابتوطية.
320 أ. س.: ينقسم.

90 On *barsh* as preparing land for sugarcane plantations with heavy ploughs called *muqalqilāt*, see al-Nuwayrī, *Nihāyat al-arab*, VIII, 264.

91 Modern location: Abū Ksāh (ابو كساة). Timm, *Das Christlich-Koptische Ägypten*, pp. 48–9: Philoxenou; Trismegistos GEO ID 4825: Philoxenou; Halm, *Ägypten*, p. 244: Abūksā; Salmon, 'Répertoire', p. 57; Zéki, 'Une description', p. 35; de Sacy, *État des provinces*, p. 680: Abū Kisā; Savigny, *Description de l'Égypte*, p. 129: Abou Ksé; Ibn Mammātī, *Kitāb qawānīn al-dawāwīn*, p. 118; Ibn al-Jīʿān, *Kitāb al-tuḥfa*, p. 151; Ramzī, *Al-Qāmūs*, II/III, 72: Abū Ksāh.

عينا، مائة واحد وثلاثون دينارا ونصف؛ غلة اربعة الاف ومائة وعشرون اردبا ونصف وربع. تفصيله:
قمح، الفان وخمسة وسبعون اردبا.
شعير وفول، الفان وخمسة ارادب وقيراطان.
كمون، اربعون اردبا وثلثان.

تفصيل ذلك:
الحانوت، اربعون دينارا.
بيع الكتان، اربعة عشر دينارا.
المراعي، اثنا عشر دينارا ونصف.
خراج الراتب، خمسة وستون دينارا.

خراج المناجزة، غلة، اربعة الاف ومائة وعشرون اردبا ونصف وربع، على ما فصل.

وعليها من الزكاة، عينا، سبعون دينارا وقيراطان. تفصيله:[321]
دولبة، نصف دينار.
الخرص، اربعة واربعون دينارا. تفصيله:
خرص العنب، اربعون دينارا.
خرص النخل، اربعة دنانير.
ثمن الماشية، عن سبعة وثلاثين راسا خمسة وعشرون دينارا وثلث وربع. تفصيله:
بقر احمر، عن تبيع واحد، دينار واحد وثلث وربع وثمن.
ثمن الاغنام، عن ستة وثلاثين راسا، ثلاثة وعشرون دينارا ونصف وربع وثمن. تفصيله:
بياض، عن ثمانية عشر راسا، تسعة عشر دينارا وربع.
شعارى، عن ثمانية عشر راسا، اربعة دنانير ونصف وثمن. تفصيله:
عن الاغنام، عن خمسة ارؤس، ديناران وثلثان.
عن الابل، عن ثلاثة عشر راسا، دينار واحد ونصف وثلث وثمن.

وعليها من الجوالي، عن ثمانية عشر نفرا مقيمين بها، ستة وثلاثون دينارا.

وعليها من الرسوم والمراعي والكيالة، عن سبعمائة واحد وسبعين[322] درهما، تسعة عشر دينارا وربع وحبتان، ومائة واحد وسبعون[323] اردبا وربع غلة. تفصيله:
قمح، اثنان وسبعون اردبا ونصف وثلث وثمن.
شعير، اثنان وثمانون اردبا وثلثان[324] وربع.
فول، ثلاثة عشر اردبا وربع وثمن.
سلجم، اردبان.

الرسوم، اربعمائة وعشرة دراهم ونصف، وغلة خمسة وتسعون اردبا وربع. تفصيله:
قمح، ثمانية وثلاثون اردبا وقيراطان.
شعير، ثلاثة واربعون اردبا ونصف وربع.
فول، احد عشر اردبا ونصف وربع وثمن.
سلجم، اردب واحد وربع وسدس وثمن.

321 ساقط من أ. س.: تفصيله.
322 أ. س.: عشرين.
323 أ. س.: تسعون.
324 أ. س.: ثلثاي.

Its revenues in cash and in kind are, in specie, 131 ½ dinars; and in grains, 4,120 ½ ¼ ardabbs:
- wheat, 2,075 ardabbs;
- barley and broad beans, 2,005 2/24 ardabbs;
- cumin, 40 ⅔ ardabbs.

[The revenues in specie] include:
- the shop, 40 dinars;
- the sale of flax, 14 dinars;
- pasture tax, 12 ½ dinars;
- land tax on perennial plants, 65 dinars;

Munājaza land tax, in grains, 4,120 ½ ¼ ardabbs, as specified.

The alms-tax, in specie, 70 2/24 dinars:
- merchandise (*dawlaba*), ½ dinar;
- estimate, 44 dinars:
  - estimate of grapes, 40 dinars;
  - estimate of date palms, 4 dinars.
- monetary value of livestock, for 37 heads, 25 ⅓ ¼ dinars:
  - cows, for a yearling calf, 1 ⅓ ¼ ⅛ dinar.
  - small cattle, for 36 heads, 23 ½ ¼ ⅛ dinars:
    - sheep, for 18 heads, 17 ¼ dinars;
    - goats, for 18 heads, 4 ½ ⅛ dinars:
      - [levied on] small cattle, for five heads, 2 ⅔ dinars;
      - [levied on] camels, for 13 heads, 1 ½ ⅓ ⅛ dinar.

The poll-tax, for 18 individuals dwelling in it, 36 dinars.

The fees, the pasture tax and the measurement fee, 771 dirhams, which are 19 ¼ 2/72 dinars; and in grains, 171 ¼ ardabbs:
- wheat, 72 ½ ⅓ ⅛ ardabbs;
- barley, 82 ⅔ ¼ ardabbs;
- broad beans, 13 ¼ ⅛ ardabbs;
- rape, 2 ardabbs.

The fees are 410 ½ dirhams; and, in grains, 95 ¼ ardabbs:
- wheat, 38 2/24 ardabbs;
- barley, 43 ½ ¼ ardabbs;
- broad beans, 11 ½ ¼ ⅛ ardabbs;
- rape, 1 ¼ ⅙ ⅛ ardabb.

تفصيله:

الاجران، اثنان وثمانون درهما ونصف، وغلة خمسة وتسعون اردبا وربع، على ما فصل.

شد العين، سبعون درهما.[325]

شد الاحباس، عشرة دراهم.

رسم الجراريف، تسعون درهما.

رسم الحصاد، ثلاثة وخمسون درهما.[326]

رسم الخفارة، خمسة عشر درهما.

مصالحة السلجم، تسعون درهما.

الكيالة، ستة وسبعون اردبا:

قمح، اربعة وثلاثون اردبا ونصف وربع وثمن.

شعير، تسعة وثلاثون اردبا وسدس.

فول اردب واحد ونصف.

سلجم، ثلث وثمن اردب.

المراعي، طارئ، عن سبعمائة وخمسين راسا، ثلاثمائة وستون درهما ونصف. تفصيله:

قطيعة درهم واحد، عن اربعة وتسعين راسا، اربعة وتسعون درهما.

قطيعة ستين درهما المائة، عن مائة وعشرين راسا، اثنان وسبعون درهما.

قطيعة ثلاثين درهما المائة، عن مائتين واثنين وسبعين راسا، احد وثمانون درهما ونصف وثمن.

قطيعة خمسة وعشرين درهما المائة، عن مائتين واربعة وستين راسا، ستة وستون درهما.

رسم المستخدمين، ستة واربعون درهما ونصف وربع وثمن.

وعليها لديوان الاحباس، ثلاثة عشر دينارا عينا.

وعليها من الاتبان، اربعة الاف شنيف.

رسم خولي البحر، قمح اردبان.

اهلها يزرعون الاقصاب باراضيها برسم معصرتها، خارجا عن الزائد لسنة اثنتين واربعين وستمائة[327]، ستة وستون فدانا ونصف. تفصيله:

راس، خمسة واربعون فدانا ونصف.

خلفة، احد وعشرون فدانا.

المسلف بها من الشعير برسم الاصطبلات السلطانية، سبعمائة اردب.

والذي جرت العادة به لعمارة الناحية من التقاوي[328]، خمسمائة واربعة[329] وستون اردبا:

قمح، مائتان واثنان وثمانون اردبا.

شعير، مائتان واثنان وثمانون اردبا.

المربى بها من الفروج، الف وسبعمائة وسبعون فروجا:

للديوان المعمور، بما فيه من اجرة التربية وهو الثلث، تسعمائة وسبعون فروجا.

للمقطعين، ثمانمائة طائر.

325 ساقط من أ. س.: شد العين سبعون درهما.

326 ساقط من أ. س.: رسم الحصاد ثلاثة وخمسون درهما.

327 ساقط من ط. م.: وأربعين وستمائة.

328 أ. س. يضيف: السلطانية.

329 أ. س.: أردب.

[The fees] include:

threshing-floor fee, 82 ½ dirhams, and in grains, 95 ¼ ardabbs, as specified.

Supervision of the land survey, 70 dirhams;

supervision of endowments, 10 dirhams;

dredging fee, 90 dirhams;

harvest fee, 53 dirhams;

protection fee, 15 dirhams;

settlement for rape, 90 dirhams;

measurement fee, 76 ardabbs:

wheat, 34 ½ ¼ ⅛ ardabbs;

barley, 39 ⅙ ardabbs;

broad beans, 1 ½ ardabb;

rape, ⅓ ⅛ ardabb.

The pasture tax, for 750 heads of seasonal pasture lands, 360 ½ dirhams:

at the rate of 1 dirham [per head], for 94 heads, 94 dirhams;

at the rate of 60 dirhams per 100 [heads], for 120 heads, 72 dirhams;

at the rate of 30 dirhams per 100 [heads], for 272 heads, 81 ½ ⅛ dirhams;

at the rate of 25 dirhams per 100 [heads], for 264 heads, 66 dirhams.

the government agents' fee, 46 ½ ¼ ⅛ dirhams.

For the Ministry of Endowments, 13 dinars, in specie.

Hay, 4,000 bales.

The fee for the overseer of the canal, 2 ardabbs of wheat.

Its people sow in its lands sugarcane, assigned to its press, 66 ½ feddans:

first harvest, 45 ½ feddans;

second harvest, 21 feddans.

This excludes the increment of the year 642.

The barley assigned for the royal stables, which was paid for in advance, 700 ardabbs.

The seed advances[92] customarily assigned for the village's cultivation (*li-ʿimārat al-nāḥiya*), 564 ardabbs:

wheat, 282 ardabbs;

barley, 282 ardabbs.

The chickens reared in it, 1,770 chickens:

for the prosperous Dīwān, including the rearing wage of a third, 970 chickens;

for the *iqṭāʿ*-holders, 800 birds.

92 AS adds: *al-sulṭāniyya*, 'the royal seed advances'.

والمرتب لارباب الرزق:
المشايخ والخفراء، اثنا عشر فدانا؛
القصاص عشرون اردبا، قمح وشعير نصفان.

ومن حرف[330] الالف، ابشاية الرمان. هذه البلدة بلدة[331] كبيرة، بينها وبين مدينة[332] الفيوم مسافة اربع ساعات للراكب، من غربي الفيوم ليس بعدها الى الجبل من الجانب الغربي الا منية اقنى، ارضها متلخمة لارضها. فيها شجر يسير من النخل والزيتون وشجيرات معدودة كمثرى. وبها ساقية على بئر معين يشرب منها اهل البلدة في الصيف، اذا تاخر عنهم ماء البحر لقلته. قبليها حديقة نخل بموضع يسمى تمدورة. عبرتها جيشية اربعة عشر الفا وسبعمائة وتسعة[333] وخمسون دينارا. تشرب من خليج في اخر البحر الاعظم اليوسفي شركة ابي كسا وببيج انشو وطبهار وجردو، تقسم[334] لهذه النواحي بخشبة واحدة. يخص هذه الناحية في خليجها من المقسم المذكور ستة عشر قبضة. بها جامع تقام فيه الجمعة.

ارتفاعها مما جميعه مستخرجا ومتحصلا، عينا، اثنان وتسعون دينارا و غلة ستة الاف وسبعمائة وستة عشر اردبا ونصف وثلث ونصف قيراط. تفصيله:
قمح، ثلاثة الاف ومائة وسبعة وثلاثون اردبا وثلثان ونصف قيراط.
شعير، ثلاثة الاف وسبعة وعشرون اردبا وثلثان وربع ونصف قيراط.
كمون، ثلاثمائة وتسعة ارادب ونصف وربع وثمن.[335]
سلجم، ثلاثة واربعون اردبا وثلثان وثمن.
كزبرة، ستة عشر اردبا وقيراط[336] ونصف.[337]
فول، مائة واحد وثمانون اردبا ونصف.

تفصيله:
المراعي، خمسة عشر دينارا.[338]
الهلالي، ستون دينارا.
خراج الراتب، سبعة عشر دينارا. تفصيله:
كرم، عن قيراطي فدان، نصف دينار.
شجر، عن سبعة فدادين وثلث، ستة عشر دينارا ونصف.

خراج[339] الغلة، ستة الاف وسبعمائة وستة عشر اردبا ونصف وثلث[340] ونصف قيراط على ما فصل. تفصيله:
المناجزة، خمسة الاف وثمانمائة وسبعة وثمانون اردبا ونصف وربع ونصف قيراط:
قمح، الفان وسبعمائة وثلاثة وستون اردبا وثلث وربع ونصف قيراط.
شعير، الفان وستمائة وثلاثة وخمسون اردبا وثلث وربع ونصف قيراط.
فول، مائة وعشرة ارادب.
كمون، ثلاثمائة واردبان وربع وسدس[341] وثمن.
سلجم، اثنان واربعون اردبا ونصف وثمن.
كزبرة، خمسة عشر اردبا ونصف ونصف ثمن.

The established allowances:
the headmen and guardsmen, 12 feddans;
the 'fable-tellers' (*quṣṣāṣ*),[93] 20 ardabbs, half wheat and half barley.

Also beginning with the letter 'alif': Ibshāyat[94] al-Rummān. This is a large village, four hours' ride from Madīnat al-Fayyūm, in the west of the province. There is nothing beyond it in the direction of the mountain on the western side except Minyat Aqnā, whose lands border those of this village. It has a few date palms and olive trees, and some small pear trees. It has a waterwheel standing upon a well that flows to the surface (*maʿīn*), from which the people of the village drink in the summer, when the canal water fails to reach them due to its scantiness. South of it there is a garden of date palms in a place called Tmdwrh (?). Its fiscal value is 14,759 army dinars. The village gets its water from a canal [that branches off] from the end of the Main Canal. The same canal also supplies water to Abū Ksā, Babīj Unshū, Ṭubhār and Jardū. The water is divided to these villages by a single wooden [divisor]. The amount of water allotted to the village by that divisor is 16 *qabḍas*. It has a congregational mosque, in which the Friday prayers are held.

Its revenues in cash and in kind are, in specie, 92 dinars; and in grains, 6,716 ½ ⅓ 1/48 ardabbs:
wheat, 3,137 ⅔ 1/48 ardabbs;
barley, 3,027 ⅔ ¼ 1/48 ardabbs;
cumin, 309 ½ ¼ ⅛ ardabbs;
rape, 43 ⅔ ⅛ ardabbs;
coriander, 16 1/24 1/48 ardabbs;
broad beans, 181 ½ ardabbs.

[The revenue in detail]:
fixed pasture tax, 15 dinars;
lunar-calendar tax, 60 dinars;
land tax on perennial plants, 17 dinars:
vineyards, for 2/24 of a feddan, ½ dinar;
trees, for 7 ⅓ feddans, 16 ½ dinars.

Land tax in grains (*kharāj al-ghilla*), 6,716 ½ ⅓ 1/48 ardabbs, as specified:
Munājaza land tax, 5,887 ½ ¼ 1/48 ardabbs:
wheat, 2,763 ⅓ ¼ 1/48 ardabbs;
barley, 2,653 ⅓ ¼ 1/48 ardabbs;
broad beans, 110 ardabbs;
cumin, 302 ¼ ⅙ ⅛ ardabbs;
rape, 42 ½ ⅛ ardabbs;
coriander, 15 ½ 1/16 ardabbs.

330 أ. س.: حروف.
331 ساقط من أ. س.: بلدة.
332 ساقط من أ. س.: مدينة.
333 ساقط من أ. س.: وتسعة.
334 أ. س.: ينقسم.
335 أ. س. يضيف: كزبرة ستة عشر أردبا وقيراط.
336 ساقط من أ. س.: كزبرة ستة عشر أردبا وقيراط.
337 ساقط من أ. س.: ونصف، لكنه يضيفها على الحاشية.
338 أ. س.: أردبا.
339 أ. س. يضيف: الراتب.
340 أ. س. يضيف: وثمن.
341 ساقط من ط. م.: وسدس.

93 The *quṣṣāṣ* are probably Christian officials, perhaps priests (*qusūs*). Elsewhere in the treatise the *quṣṣāṣ are* twice mentioned alongside monks. The literal meaning is 'story-tellers' or 'fable-tellers', and parallels the derogatory use of 'beast-chasers' to refer to poll-tax officials.

94 Modern location: Ibshawāy (ابشواي). Timm, *Das Christlich-Koptische Ägypten*, pp. 44–45: Pisais; Trismegistos GEO ID 1836: Pisais; Halm, *Ägypten*, p. 260; Salmon, 'Répertoire', pp. 57–58; Zéki, 'Une description', p. 44; Ibn Mammātī, *Kitāb qawānīn al-dawāwīn*, p. 103; Yāqūt, *Muʿjam al-Buldān*, I, 73: Abshiyah, known as Abshiyat al-Rummān; Ibn al-Jīʿān, *Kitāb al-tuḥfa*, pp. 150–51; de Sacy, *État des provinces*, p. 680; Savigny, *Description de l'Égypte*, p. 129: Ibshāy al-Rummān; Ramzī, *Al-Qāmūs*, III/III, 71: Ibshawāy.

المشاطرة، ثمانمائة وتسعة وعشرون اردبا وقيراطان:
قمح، ثلاثمائة واربعة وسبعون اردبا وقيراطان.
شعير، ثلاثمائة واربعة وسبعون اردبا وثلث.
فول، احد وسبعون اردبا ونصف.
كمون، سبعة ارادب ونصف.
سلجم، اردب وسدس.
كزبرة، ثلث اردب.

وعليها من الزكاة، ثمانية وعشرون دينارا وثمن وحبتان. تفصيله:
دولبة، دينار واحد.
خرص النخل، دينار واحد ونصف.
ثمن المواشي، ثلاثون راسا، خمسة وعشرون دينارا ونصف وثمن وحبتان. تفصيله:
بقر احمر، عن مسنة واحدة، ثلاثة دنانير وثمن وحبتان.
اغنام، عن تسعة وعشرين راسا، اثنان وعشرون دينارا ونصف:
بياض، عن سبعة عشر راسا، ثمانية عشر دينارا.
شعاري، عن اثنى عشر راسا، اربعة دنانير ونصف:
عن الاغنام، عن سبعة ارؤس، ثلاثة دنانير ونصف وربع.
عن الابل، عن خمسة ارؤس، نصف وربع دينار.

وعليها من الرسوم والكيالة والمراعي، عن ثمانمائة ودرهمين وربع، عشرون دينارا وقيراط وحبة؛ غلة مائتان وسبعة وثلاثون اردبا وثلثان وربع. تفصيله:
قمح، مائة واربعة وثلاثون اردبا وربع وسدس.
شعير، خمسة وسبعون اردبا وثلثان وربع.
فول، احد وعشرون اردبا وثلث وربع.
كمون، ستة ارادب.

تفصيله:
الرسوم، خمسمائة واحد واربعون درهما ورقا، وغلة مائة وثلاثة وثلاثون اردبا وثلث:
قمح، ستون اردبا وربع وثمن.
شعير، ستة واربعون اردبا ونصف وربع.
فول، احد وعشرون اردبا وثلث وربع.
كمون، اربعة ارادب ونصف وثمن.
تفصيله:
شد العين، ثمانية وعشرون درهما.
شد الاحباس، عشرون درهما.
الجراريف، مائة واثنان وثمانون درهما ونصف.
رسم الحصاد، ثلاثة وخمسون درهما.
الخفارة، خمسة عشر درهما.
مصالحة السلجم، مائة وعشرون درهما.
رسم الاجران، مائة واثنان وعشرون درهما ونصف، وغلة مائة وثلاثة وثلاثون[342] اردبا وثلث، على ما فصل.

mushāṭara land tax, 829 2/24 ardabbs:
wheat, 374 2/24 ardabbs;
barley, 374 ⅓ ardabbs;
broad beans, 71 ½ ardabbs;
cumin, 7 ½ ardabbs;
rape, 1 ⅙ ardabb;
coriander, ⅓ ardabb.

The alms-tax, 28 ⅛ 2/72 dinars:
merchandise, 1 dinar;
estimate of date palms, 1 ½ dinar;
monetary value of livestock, [for] 30 heads, 25 ½ ⅛ 2/72 dinars:
cows, for a two-year old cow, 3 ⅛ 2/72 dinars;
small cattle, for 29 heads, 22 ½ dinars:
sheep, for 17 heads, 18 dinars;
goats, for 12 heads, 4 ½ dinars:
[levied on] small cattle, for seven heads, 3 ½ ¼ dinars;
[levied on] camels, for five heads, ½ ¼ dinar.

The fees, the measurement fee and the pasture fee, are 802 ¼ dirhams, which are 20 1/24 1/72 dinars; and in grains, 237 ⅔ ¼ ardabbs:
wheat, 134 ¼ ⅙ ardabbs;
barley, 75 ⅔ ¼ ardabbs;
broad beans, 21 ⅓ ¼ ardabbs;
cumin, 6 ardabbs.

[The fees] include:
the fees are 541 *waraq* dirhams,[95] and in grains, 133 ⅓ ardabbs:
wheat, 60 ¼ ⅛ ardabbs;
barley, 46 ½ ¼ ardabbs;
broad beans, 21 ⅓ ¼ ardabbs;
cumin, 4 ½ ⅛ ardabbs.
[The fees] in detail:
supervision of the land survey, 28 dirhams;
supervision of endowments, 20 dirhams;
dredging fee, 182 ½ dirhams;
harvest fee, 53 dirhams;
protection fee, 15 dirhams;
settlement for rape, 120 dirhams;
threshing-floor fee, 122 ½ dirhams; and in grains, 133 ⅓ ardabbs, as specified.

342 أ. س. يضيف: درهما ونصف.

95 The *waraq* dirhams, or black dirhams, were minted during the late Fatimid period. They were of poor silver quality, and were therefore very dark, almost black. In the Geniza, the term *waraq* dirham was used as a generic term for low-quality dirhams during the Ayyubid period. See Goitein, 'The Exchange Rate', p. 38; Cécile Bresc, 'Quseir al-Qadim: A Hoard of Islamic Coins from the Ayyubid Period', *Revue numismatique*, 6. 164 (2008), 407–36 (p. 410). Al-Nābulusī always refers to *waraq* dirhams, even when the type of dirham is not specified. Another reference to the *waraq* dirhams (in the accounts of the Malikite Madrasa, at the end of the treatise) shows the same exchange rate of 40 dirhams to the dinar as applied elsewhere in the treatise.

الكيالة، ثمانية وتسعون اردبا وثلث وربع:
قمح، احد وسبعون اردبا وقيراط.
شعير، ستة وعشرون اردبا وسدس.
كمون، اردب واحد وربع وثمن.

عشر الرزق، ستة ارادب:
قمح، ثلاثة ارادب.
شعير، ثلاثة ارادب.

المراعي الطارئ، عن سبعمائة واثنين وخمسين راسا، مائتان واحد وستون درهما وربع. تفصيله:
قطيعة درهم واحد الراس، عن عشرة اروس، عشرة دراهم.
قطيعة ثلاثين درهما المائة، عن ثلاثمائة وسبعة وسبعين راسا، مائة وثلاثة عشر درهما.
قطيعة عشرين درهما المائة، عن ثلاثمائة وخمسة وستين راسا، احد وتسعون[343] درهما وربع.
رسم المستخدمين، سبعة واربعون درهما.

وعليها لديوان الاحباس، عشرة دنانير.

وعليها من الاتبان، سبعة الاف شنيف.

رسم خولي البحر، قمح، اردبان.

اهلها يزرعون الاقصاب باراضيها برسم معصرة ابي كسا، سبعة وتسعون فدانا وربع وسدس وثمن. تفصيله:
راس، سبعة وستون فدانا ونصف.
خلفة، ثلاثون فدانا وقيراط.

والمقرر بها من التقاوي برسم عمارة الناحية، تسعمائة وستة وستون اردبا وسدس. تفصيله:
قمح، اربعمائة وتسعة وسبعون اردبا.
شعير، اربعمائة وخمسة وثمانون اردبا ونصف وثلث.
كمون، اردب واحد وثلث.

والمربى بها من الفروج، الفان وتسعمائة وثلاثون فروجا. تفصيله:
للديوان المعمور، بما فيه من اجرة التربية وهو الثلث، الف وسبعمائة وثلاثون فروجا.
للمقطعين، الف ومائتان.

والمقرر على المزارعين بها من الكشك والفريك، احد عشر اردبا وثلث، نصفان.

والذي يسلف بها من الشعير برسم الاصطبلات السلطانية، سبعمائة اردب.

ومن حرف الالف، الطارمة. هذه البلدة بحري الفيوم، بينها وبين مدينة الفيوم اربع ساعات للراكب. متاخمة لمنية البطس وبمويه، بينهما. فيها نخل يسير مستجد اطعم بعضه. عبرتها جيشية تسعة الاف دينار. اهلها بنو سمالوس فخذ من بني لواتة [= عجلان].[344] تشرب من خليج شركة بين ترسا والناحية، من باب مجصص، اخر الجهة الشرقية من المدينة، تتقسم[345] من اسفل في خليجين على الناحيتين. يخص هذه الناحية للشتوي خاصة ثلاث عشرة قبضة ونصف. وبها جامع تقام فيه الجمعة.

343 أ. س.: ستون.
344 أ. س.، ط. م.: لواته.
345 أ. س.: ينقسم.

The measurement fee, 98 ⅓ ¼ ardabbs:
wheat, 71 1/24 ardabbs;
barley, 26 ⅙ ardabbs;
cumin, 1 ¼ ⅛ ardabb;

The tithe on allowances (*ʿushr al-rizaq*), 6 ardabbs:
wheat, 3 ardabbs;
barley, 3 ardabbs.

The pasture tax, for 752 heads of seasonal pasture lands, 261 ¼ dirhams:
at the rate of one dirham per head, for 10 heads, 10 dirhams;
at the rate of 30 dirhams per 100 [heads], for 377 heads, 113 dirhams;
at the rate of 25 dirhams per 100 [heads], for 365 head, 91 ¼ dirhams;
the government agents' fee, 47 dirhams.

For the Ministry of Endowments, 10 dinars.

Hay, 7,000 bales.

The fee of the overseer of the canal, wheat, 2 ardabbs.

Its people sow sugarcane, assigned to the press in Abū Ksā, in the lands of the village, 97 ¼ ⅙ ⅛ feddans:
first harvest, 67 ½ feddans;
second harvest, 30 1/24 feddans.

The established seed advances, assigned for the village's cultivation, 966 ⅙ ardabbs:
wheat, 479 ardabbs;
barley, 485 ½ ⅓ ardabbs;
cumin, 1 ⅓ ardabb.

The chickens reared in it, 2,930 chickens:
for the prosperous Dīwān, including the rearing wage of a third, 1,730 chickens;
for the *iqṭāʿ*-holders, 1,200.

The confirmed levy of *kishk* and *farīk* on the tenants, 11 ⅓ ardabbs, half in each.

The barley assigned for the royal stables, which was paid for in advance, 700 ardabbs.

Also beginning with the letter 'alif': al-Ṭārima.[96] This is a village at the north of the province, four hours' ride from Madīnat al-Fayyūm. It is adjacent to Minyat al-Baṭs and Bamawayh, and is located between the two of them. It has a few recently planted date palms, some of which have borne fruit. Its fiscal value is 9,000 army dinars. Its people are the Banū Samālūs, a branch of the Banū Lawāta [= ʿAjlān].[97] It gets its water from a canal shared between Tirsā and this village, issued from a plastered sluice gate (*bāb mujaṣṣaṣ*) at the eastern edge of the city. The canal splits lower down to two sub-canals for the two villages. The [water quota] allotted to this village, specifically for winter cultivation, is 13 ½ *qabḍas*. It has a congregational mosque, in which the Friday prayers are held.

96 Modern location: Al-Saʿīdiyya (السعيدية). Halm, *Ägypten*, p. 274; Salmon, 'Répertoire', p. 53; Ibn al-Jīʿān, *Kitāb al-tuḥfa*, p. 152; Ramzī, *Al-Qāmūs*, I, 79; II/III, 117: al-Saʿīdiyya.

97 AS and MP: al-Lawāta.

ارتفاعها مما جميعه مستخرجا ومتحصلا، على ما قرره المقطعون، عينا، تسعون دينارا؛ غلة، الفا اردب:

قمح، الف[346] ومائتان وستة وستون اردبا وثلثان.

شعير، سبعمائة وثلاثة وثلاثون اردبا وثلث.

تفصيله:

مال الهلالي، سبعون دينارا.

مال المراعي، عشرون دينارا.

مناجزة الغلات[347]، الفا اردب على ما فصل.

وعليها لمقطعي العشر المعروف بابن المهراني، غلة ثمانون اردبا، قمح وشعير نصفان.

وعليها من الزكاة، عن ثمن اغنام، عن احد وثلاثين راسا، خمسة وعشرون دينارا وقيراط وحبتان:

بياض، عن عشرين راسا، احد وعشرون دينارا ونصف.

شعارى، عن احد عشر راسا، ثلاثة دنانير وربع وسدس وثمن وحبتان. تفصيله:

عن الاغنام، عن[348] خمسة اروس، ديناران وثلثان.

عن الابل، ستة اروس، نصف وربع وثمن وحبتان.

وعليها من الرسوم والمراعي الطارئ والكيالة،[349] عن اربعمائة واثنين واربعين درهما ونصف وربع، احد عشر دينارا وقيراط وحبتان؛ وغلة، مائة واثنان واربعون اردبا وسدس وثمن:

قمح، ستة وستون اردبا وثلث وربع وثمن.

فول، خمسة وسبعون اردبا وثلث وربع.

تفصيله:

الرسوم، مائتان وخمسة وخمسون درهما ونصف وربع، وغلة سبعة وتسعون اردبا وسدس وثمن:

قمح، احد واربعون وثلث وربع وثمن.

فول، خمسة وخمسون اردبا وثلث وربع.

تفصيل ذلك:

شد الاحباس، اربعة عشر درهما.

رسم الجراريف، تسعون درهما.

رسم الحصاد، ثلاثة وخمسون درهما.

رسم الخفارة، خمسة عشر درهما.

رسم الاجران، ثلاثة وثمانون درهما ونصف وربع، وغلة سبعة وتسعون اردبا وسدس وثمن، على ما فصل.

الكيالة، خمسة واربعون اردبا:[350]

قمح، خمسة وعشرون اردبا.

فول، عشرون اردبا.

المراعي الطارئ، عن خمسمائة وثمانية وثمانين راسا، مائة وسبعة وثمانون درهما. تفصيله:

قطيعة ثلاثين درهما المائة، عن خمسة وستين راسا، تسعة عشر درهما ونصف.

قطيعة خمسة وعشرين درهما المائة، عن خمسمائة وثلاثة وعشرين راسا، مائة وثلاثون درهما ونصف وربع.

رسم المستخدمين، ستة وثلاثون درهما ونصف وربع.

346 أ. س. يضيف: أردب.

347 أ. س.: الغلال.

348 ساقط من ط. م.: عن.

349 أ. س.: الكيالة والطارئ.

350 أ. س، ط. م.: درهما.

Its revenues in cash and in kind are, according to what was confirmed by the *iqṭāʿ*-holders, in specie, 90 dinars; in grains, 2,000 ardabbs:

wheat, 1,266 ⅔ ardabbs;

barley, 733 ⅓ ardabbs.

[The revenue in detail]:

lunar-calendar taxes, 70 dinars;

pasture tax, 20 dinars;

Munājaza land tax in grains, 2,000 ardabbs, as specified.

For the *iqṭāʿ*-holders of the tithe (*al-ʿushr*) known as Ibn al-Mihrānī, in grains, 80 ardabbs [of] wheat and barley, half in each.[98]

The alms-tax, from the monetary value of small cattle, for 31 heads, 25 $\frac{2}{24}$ $\frac{2}{72}$ dinars:

sheep, for twenty heads, 21 ½ dinars;

goats, for eleven heads, 3 ¼ ⅙ ⅛ $\frac{2}{72}$ dinars:

[levied on] small cattle, for five heads, 2 ⅔ dinars;

[levied on] camels, for six heads, ½ ¼ ⅛ $\frac{2}{72}$ dinar.

The fees, the pasture fee on seasonal pasture lands and the measurement fee, 442½¼ dirhams, which are 11 $\frac{1}{24}$ $\frac{2}{72}$ dinars; and in grains, 142 ⅙ ⅛ ardabbs:

wheat, 66 ⅓ ¼ ⅛ ardabbs;

broad beans, 75 ⅓ ¼ ardabbs.

[The fees, the seasonal pasture lands pasture tax and the measurement fee] in detail:

The fees, 255 ½ ¼ dirhams; and in grains, 97 ⅙ ⅛ ardabbs:

wheat, 41 ⅓ ¼ ⅛ ardabbs;

broad beans, 55 ⅓ ¼ ardabbs.

[the fees] in detail:

supervision of endowments, 14 dirhams;

dredging fee, 90 dirhams;

harvest fee, 53 dirhams;

protection fee, 15 dirhams;

threshing-floor fee, 83 ½ ¼ dirhams, and in grains, 97 ⅙ ⅛ ardabbs, as specified.

The measurement fee, 45 ardabbs:[99]

wheat, 25 ardabbs;

broad beans, 20 ardabbs.

The pasture tax on seasonal pasture lands, for 588 heads, 187 dirhams:

at the rate of 30 dirhams per 100 [heads], for 65 heads, 19 ½ dirhams;

at the rate of 25 dirhams per 100 [heads], for 523 heads, 130 ½ ¼ dirhams.

The government agents' fee, 36 ½ ¼ dirhams.

98 A levy 'for the *iqṭāʿ*-holders of the *ʿushr* known as Ibn al-Mihrānī' is reported for six villages across the Fayyum: Minyat al-Dīk, Babīj Unshū, Babīj Anqāsh, al-Ṭārima, Bushṭā, and Dimashqīn al-Baṣal. While the first three were located close to each other in the west of the province, the remaining three were spread across the province. The payments consisted of small amounts of grains, 5 to 80 ardabbs, with the exception of Dimashqīn al-Baṣal, where the payment was levied in gold dinars (probably because the village paid its taxes almost entirely in specie). It appears to be a payment due to *iqṭāʿ*-holders who held a concession on a particular kind of tithe.

99 MP and AS: dirham.

وعليها لديوان الاحباس، عينا، ستة دنانير.

وعليها من الاتبان، الفا شنيف.

والمقرر على المزارعين بالناحية كشك وفريك، اربعة ارادب، نصفان.

والذي بها من التقاوي للمحلول والمرتجع، مائة وسبعة وسبعون اردبا وثلثان ونصف ثمن:
قمح، ثلاثة وثمانون اردبا ونصف وربع.
شعير، ستة وعشرون اردبا وثلث ونصف ثمن.
فول، سبعة وستون اردبا ونصف وثلث.[351]

والذي جرت العادة باطلاقه لها من التقاوي[352]، خمسمائة وستة ارادب:
قمح، مائتان وثلاثة وخمسون اردبا.
شعير وفول، مائتان وثلاثة وخمسون اردبا، نصفان.

والمقرر تربيته من الفروج بها، ثمانمائة وخمسون:
للديوان المعمور، بما فيه من اجرة التربية وهو الثلث، اربعمائة وخمسون طائرا.
للمقطعين، اربعمائة.

والذي يسلف بها من الشعير برسم الاصطبلات السلطانية، مائة وعشر ارادب.

وبها من الرزق:
للخطيب، نصف محراث؛
النجار، ثمانية فدادين؛
طرادون الوحش، اربعة فدادين.

ومن حرف الالف، اللاهون وام النخارير. هذه البلدة بلدة متوسطة بين الكبيرة والصغيرة، عند البناء المحكم المعروف باليوسفي وباللكند وبالفردة. وبها جميز على ساحلها ونخل حولها، وهي منتهى شرقي الفيوم مما يلى البحر المنهى. عليها سواقي من جملة السواقي المقدم ذكرها. يزرعها اهلها من ماء النيل ايام النيل اسوة بلاد الكورة من غير سقي على عادة الفيوم. وفيها حبوب يسيرة تزرع. واما النخارير فهي موضع عبارة عن غيط منسوب الى اللاهون داخلة[353] في اقطاع مقطع اللاهون. عبرتها اربعة الاف دينار جيشية تروى اراضيها اسوة بلاد الريف. وباللاهون جامع شريف من الايام اليوسفية تقام فيه الجمعة. خفارتها[354] لبني سليمان، فخذ من لواتة.

351 أ. س.: وثمن.
352 أ. س.: من التقاوي لها.
353 أ. س.: دائر.
354 أ. س.: خفرها.

For the Ministry of Endowments, in specie, 6 dinars.

Hay, 1,000 bales.

The confirmed levy of *kishk* and *farīk* dishes on the tenants in the village, 4 ardabbs, half in each.

The seed advances for [*iqṭāʿ* units] which are vacant or reclaimed from *iqṭāʿ*-holders (*li'l-maḥlūl wa'l-murtajaʿ*),[100] 177 ⅔ 1/16 ardabbs:
wheat, 83 ½ ¼ ardabbs;
barley, 26 ⅓ 1/16 ardabbs;
broad beans, 67 ½ ⅓ ardabbs.[101]

The seed advances customarily distributed in it, 506 ardabbs:
wheat, 253 ardabbs;
barley and broad beans, 253 ardabbs, half of each.

The confirmed rearing of chickens, 850:
for the prosperous Dīwān, including the rearing wage of one-third, 450 birds;
for the *iqṭāʿ*-holders, 400.

The barley assigned for the royal stables, which was paid for in advance, 110 ardabbs.

The allowances (*rizaq*):
for the Friday preacher, half of a ploughshare (*miḥrāth*);[102]
[for] the carpenter, 8 feddans;
[for] the 'beast-chasers' (*ṭarrādūn al-waḥsh*), 4 feddans.

Also beginning with the letter 'alif', al-Lāhūn[103] and Umm al-Nakhārīr.[104] This is a medium-size village, located near the reinforced dam known as Joseph's Dam, as well as 'al-Lakand' and 'al-Farda'. It has sycamores upon its bank, and date palms around it. It is at the eastern edge of the Fayyum, next to al-Manhā Canal. It has waterwheels, included in the total number of waterwheels mentioned earlier. At the season of the Nile's flooding, its people cultivate its lands with the water of the Nile, like the other rural districts of Egypt, without irrigating the land in the manner of the Fayyum. Small amounts of grains are sown in it. Umm al-Nakhārīr is a field (*ghayṭ*) attached to al-Lāhūn, and included in the *iqṭāʿ* of the *iqṭāʿ*-holder of al-Lāhūn. [Al-Lāhūn's] fiscal value is 4,000 army dinars. Its lands are watered like the villages of Lower Egypt (*al-rīf*). In al-Lāhūn there is a distinguished congregational mosque dating to the days of Joseph, in which the Friday prayers are held. Its protection is at the hands of the Banū Sulaymān, a branch of the Lawāta.

100 For *iqṭāʿ maḥlūl* as an *iqṭāʿ* without an *iqṭāʿ*-holder, see al-Nuwayrī, *Nihāyat al-arab*, VIII, 202, 211.

101 AS variant: *thumn* (an eighth) instead of: *thulth* (third).

102 The plough-shares were shares in the village arable lands, probably indicating the amount of land that could be cultivated by one plough. The list here, and other references to the plough-share in other villages, suggests that a plough-share was equivalent to a dozen feddans. They are mentioned in the survey only in connection with the *rizaq*, the tax-free allowances of land allocated to local officials.

103 Modern location: Al-Lāhūn (اللاهون). Timm, *Das Christlich-Koptische Ägypten*, pp. 1485–86: Ptolmais Hormou; Halm, *Ägypten*, p. 261: Lahūn; Salmon, 'Répertoire', p. 38; Zéki, 'Une description', p. 38; Savigny, *Description de l'Égypte*, p. 126: Alāhūn; Ibn Mammātī, *Kitāb qawānīn al-dawāwīn*, p. 103; Ibn al-Jīʿān, *Kitāb al-tuḥfa*, p. 150; Ramzī, *Al-Qāmūs*, II/III, 97: Al-Lāhūn, notes, following Amélineau, *La géographie*, that its ancient Egyptian name was Rohount ('the culvert'), and its Coptic name Lahoun.

104 Modern location: Banī Khalīfa (بني خليفة). Ibn al-Jīʿān, *Kitāb al-tuḥfa*, p. 151: Umm al-Bakhārīr; de Sacy, *État des provinces*, p. 680: Umm al-Bakārīr; Halm, *Ägypten*, p. 258: Umm an-Nakhārīr; Salmon, 'Répertoire', p. 38; Ramzī, *Al-Qāmūs*, II/III, 130: Banī Khalīfa.

ارتفاعها مما جميعه مستخرجا ومتحصلا من جملة عينا، الف دينار ومائة واربعة وثمانون دينارا وربع، وغلة مائتان واربعة وتسعون اردبا ونصف وثمن. تفصيله:

قمح، خمسة وخمسون اردبا وسدس وثمن.

شعير، عشرة ارادب وثلث.

فول، خمسة واربعون اردبا.

جلبان، مائة واربعة وثمانون اردبا.

تفصيل ذلك:

الهلالي، خمسون دينارا. تفصيله:

الحانوت، اربعون دينارا.

القزازون، ديناران ونصف.

المعدية، دينار واحد ونصف.

ضمان الفروج، اربعة دنانير.

الفوال، ديناران.

المراعي، عشرة دنانير.

المصايد، ستة وعشرون دينارا.

الخراجي، الف وثمانية وتسعون دينارا وربع:

كتان، تسعمائة وتسعة وخمسون دينارا وربع.

قرط ثمانية وستون دينارا.

خراج السواقي، احد وسبعون دينارا.

والغلة، مشاطرة، على ما تقدم.

بعد ما منه عن ثلث الهيشة، وهو مائة وخمسة وخمسون دينارا وخمسة قراريط البارز عما يخص اللاهون وام النخارير، عينا، الف وتسعة وعشرون دينارا وقيراط غلة مائتان واربعة وتسعون اردبا ونصف وثمن. تفصيله:

قمح، خمسة وخمسون اردبا وسدس وثمن.

شعير، عشرة ارادب وثلث.[355]

فول، خمسة واربعون اردبا.

جلبان، مائة واربعة وثمانون اردبا.

وعليها من الزكاة، عينا، ستة عشر دينارا وربع. تفصيله:

دولبة، ثمانية دنانير.

ثمن المواشي، عن ثمانية ارؤس، ثمانية دنانير وربع. تفصيله:

بقر احمر، تبيع واحد، ديناران.

ثمن اغنام، عن سبعة[356] ارؤس، ستة دنانير وربع:

بياض، عن خمسة ارؤس، خمسة دنانير وسدس.

شعارى، راسان، دينار وقيراطان.

وعليها من الجوالي، عن نفر واحد مقيم بها، ديناران.

وعليها لديوان احباس الجوامع والمساجد، عينا، عشرون دينارا.

وعليها من الرسوم والكيالة والمراعي، عن اربعمائة وستة دراهم ونصف وثمن، عشرة دنانير[357] وسدس. وغلة، اثنا عشر اردبا. تفصيله:

قمح، اربعة ارادب.

فول، اربعة ارادب.

جلبان، اربعة ارادب.

355 ساقط من أ. س.: وثلث.
356 أ. س.: ستة.
357 أ. س.: دراهم.

Its revenue in cash and in kind is, in specie, 1,184 ¼ dinars; and in grains, 294 ½ ⅛ ardabbs:

wheat, 55 ⅙ ⅛ ardabbs;
barley, 10 ⅓ ardabbs;
broad beans, 45 ardabbs;
chickling vetch, 184 ardabbs.

[The revenue in detail]:

Lunar-calendar tax, 50 dinars:
the shop, 40 dinars;
the weavers, 2 ½ dinars;
the ferry-boat (*al-ma*ʿ*diyya*), 1 ½ dinar;
concession [on the sale of] chicken, 4 dinars;
the bean-seller, 2 dinars.

The pasture tax, 10 dinars.

The fishing (*al-maṣāʾid*), 26 dinars.

Land tax [on cash crops], 1,098 ¼ dinars:
flax, 959 ¼ dinars;
alfalfa, 68 dinars;
land tax on [lands irrigated by] waterwheels, 71 dinars.

In grains, *mushāṭara* land tax, as above.

After deducting the third of the revenue [of the hamlet] of al-Haysha,[105] amounting to 155 ⁵⁄₂₄ dinars, the balance (*bāriz*)[106] [of the revenues] of al-Lāhūn and Umm al-Nakhārīr is, in specie, 1,029 ¹⁄₂₄ dinars; in grains, 294 ½ ⅛ ardabbs:

wheat, 55 ⅙ ⅛ ardabbs;
barley, 10 ⅓ ardabbs;
broad beans, 45 ardabbs;
chickling vetch, 184 ardabbs.

The alms-tax, in specie, 16 ¼ dinars:
merchandise, 8 dinars;
monetary value of livestock, for eight heads, 8 ¼ dinars:
cows, one yearling calf, 2 dinars;
monetary value of small cattle, for seven heads, 6 ¼ dinars:
sheep, for five heads, 5 ⅙ dinars;
goats, two heads, 1 ²⁄₂₄ dinar.

The poll-tax, for one individual residing in it, 2 dinars.

For the Ministry of the Endowments of Congregational and Neighbourhood Mosques, in specie, 20 dinars.

The fees, the measurement fee and the pasture tax, 406 ½ ⅛ dirhams, which are 10 ⅙ dinars; and in grains, 12 ardabbs:

wheat, 4 ardabbs;
broad beans, 4 ardabbs;
chickling vetch, 4 ardabbs.

105 A hamlet of al-Lāhūn, whose lands only partially fell within the boundaries of the *iqṭā*ʿ of al-Lāhūn; see the separate entry for al-Haysha.

106 The *bāriz* is the remainder after a sum was deducted from the total. See also al-Nuwayrī, *Nihāyat al-arab*, VIII, 201.

تفصيله:
الرسوم، مائتان وتسعة وثلاثون درهما وربع، وسبعة ارادب وثلث وربع وثمن. تفصيله:
قمح، اردب وربع وسدس وثمن.
فول، ثلاثة ارادب وقيراطان.
جلبان، ثلاثة ارادب وقيراطان.
تفصيله:
شد العين، مائة وعشرون درهما.
شد الاحباس، خمسة واربعون درهما.
رسم الحصاد، ثلاثة وخمسون درهما.
رسم الخفارة، خمسة عشر درهما.
رسم الاجران، ستة دراهم وربع، وسبعة ارادب وثلث وربع وثمن، على ما فصل.
الكيالة، اربعة ارادب وسدس وثمن:
قمح، اردبان وثلث وثمن.
فول، ثلثان[358] وربع اردب.
جلبان، ثلثان[359] وربع اردب.
المراعي الطارئ، عن اربعمائة واحد واربعين راسا، مائة وسبعة وستون درهما وربع وثمن. تفصيله:
قطيعة درهم واحد الراس، عن اربعة وثلاثين راسا، اربعة وثلاثون درهما.
قطيعة ثلاثين درهما المائة، عن احد وثمانين راسا، اربعة وعشرون درهما وربع وثمن.
قطيعة خمسة وعشرين المائة، عن ثلاثمائة وستة وعشرين راسا، احد وثمانون درهما ونصف.
رسم المستخدمين سبعة وعشرون درهما ونصف.

وعليها من الاتبان، ثلاثمائة شنيف.[360]

والذي جرت العادة بتربيته[361] من الفروج،[362] بما فيه من اجرة التربية بحق الثلث، ثلاثمائة وستون.

ومن حرف الالف، الحمام. هذه البلدة بلدة حسنة مجاورة البحر اللطيف الذي ينزل منه[363] الماء من البناء المحكم عند اللاهون، شرقيه[364]، ايام النيل الى البحر الكبير. وتدخل المراكب منه الى الفيوم وتخرج قبالة بوصير من الكورة. عليها ساقيتان، وفيها كتان مزدرع في الارض المستجدة بها،[365] التي هي للديوان غير داخلة في الاقطاع، تعرف بارض بلجسوق. مما يجب على مقطعيها حق ثلاث سنين خراج هذه الارض التي تغلبوا عليها وسال مقطعوها يومئذ[366] ان يصالح الديوان على اربعمائة دينار ولم يقنع منهم بذلك. عبرتها جيشية، ثلاثة الاف دينار. تروى ري ريف، اهلها بنو منكنيت، فخذ من بني لواتة.

ارتفاعها مما جميعه مستخرجا ومتحصلا، عينا، ستمائة وسبعة وتسعون دينارا، وغلة ثلاثمائة وخمسون اردبا. تفصيله:
قمح، مائتا اردب.
فول، مائة وخمسون اردبا.

358 أ. س.: ثلثاي.
359 أ. س.: ثلثاي.
360 أ. س.: شنيفا.
361 أ. س.: جرت به العادة تربيته.
362 أ. س.: الفراريج.
363 ساقط من أ. س.: منه.
364 أ. س. يضيف: منه.
365 ساقط من أ. س.: بها.
366 ساقط من أ. س.: يومئذ.

In detail:
the fees: 239 ¼ dirhams; and 7 ⅓ ¼ ⅛ ardabbs:
wheat, 1 ¼ ⅙ ⅛ ardabb;
broad beans, 3 ²⁄₂₄ ardabbs;
chickling vetch, 3 ²⁄₂₄ ardabbs.
[The fees] include:
supervision of the land survey, 120 dirhams;
supervision of endowments, 45 dirhams;
harvest fee, 53 dirhams;
protection fee, 15 dirhams;
threshing-floor fee, 6 ¼ dirhams; and 7 ⅓ ¼ ⅛ ardabbs, as specified.
The measurement fee, 4 ⅙ ⅛ ardabbs:
wheat, 2 ⅓ ⅛ ardabbs;
broad beans, ⅔ ¼ ardabb;
chickling vetch, ⅔ ¼ ardabb.
Pasture tax, for 441 heads of seasonal pasture lands, 167 ¼ ⅛ dirhams:
at the rate of one dirham per head, for 34 heads, 34 dirhams;
at the rate of 30 dirhams per hundred [heads], for 81 heads, 24 ¼ ⅛ dirhams;
at the rate of 25 [dirhams] per hundred [heads], for 326 heads, 81 ½ dirhams.
The government agents' fee, 27 ½ dirhams.

Hay, 300 bales.

The chicken customarily reared, including the wage of the breeders, which is a third, 360.

Also beginning with the letter 'alif': al-Ḥammām.[107] This is a pleasant village, neighbouring the small canal through which the water descends — [during] the days of the Nile's flood — from the reinforced dam at al-Lāhūn, towards the east, into the the main branch of the Nile (*al-baḥr al-kabīr*). Boats use this canal to enter into the Fayyum. The exit is in front of Buṣīr[108] in the rural area (*al-kūra*) [outside the Fayyum]. The village has two waterwheels. It has flax, sown in recently reclaimed land, known as Buljusūq's land, which belongs to the Dīwān and is not included in the *iqṭāʿ*. Its *iqṭāʿ*-holders are required to pay three years of the land tax on this land, over which they have seized control (*taghallabū ʿalayhā*). The *iqṭāʿ*-holders requested at that time that the Dīwān would settle for a payment of 400 dinars, but the Dīwān was not persuaded. Its fiscal value is 3,000 army dinars. It is watered like Lower Egypt. Its people are the Banū Munkanīt, a branch of the Banū Lawāta.

Its revenue in cash and in kind is, in specie, 697 dinars; and in grains, 350 ardabbs:
wheat, 200 ardabbs;
broad beans, 150 ardabbs.

107 Modern location: al-Ḥammām (الحمّام). Halm, *Ägypten*, p. 258: Ḥammām/Umm an-Nakhārīr; Salmon, 'Répertoire', p. 38; Ibn al-Jīʿān, *Kitāb al-tuḥfa*, p. 151; de Sacy, *État des provinces*, p. 680; Savigny, *Description de l'Égypte*, p. 127; Ramzī, *Al-Qāmūs*, II/III, 151: al-Ḥammām.

108 Modern Maasarat Abu Sir, in the Bani Sweif Governorate; see Ramzī, *Al-Qāmūs*, II/III, 135.

تفصيله:
الهلالي، خمسة عشر دينارا.
المراعي، ستة عشر دينارا وربع.
الخراجي، ستمائة وخمسة وستون دينارا ونصف وربع،[367]
والغلة على ما تقدم تفصيله.

وعليها من الزكاة، عن ثمن اغنام، عن سبعة عشر راسا، سبعة عشر دينارا ونصف وثمن:
بقر احمر، تبيع واحد، دينار واحد.
ثمن الاغنام، عن ستة عشر راسا، ستة عشر دينارا ونصف وثمن. تفصيله:
بياض، خمسة عشر راسا، ستة عشر دينارا وقيراطان.
شعارى، عن راس واحد، ربع وسدس وثمن دينار.

وعليها من الرسوم والكيالة والمراعي، عن خمسمائة وثلاثة وثلاثين درهما وثمن، ثلاثة عشر دينارا وثلث، وغلة تسعة وثلاثون اردبا وربع ونصف قيراط:
قمح، ستة وعشرون ونصف وثلث.
شعير، نصف وربع ونصف قيراط.[368]
فول، احد عشر[369] اردبا وثلثان.

تفصيله:
الرسوم، مائة وثلاثة وثمانون درهما وتسعة وعشرون اردبا:
قمح، ستة عشر اردبا ونصف ونصف ثمن.
شعير، نصف وربع ونصف قيراط.
فول، احد عشر اردبا وثلثان.
تفصيله:
شد العين، تسعون درهما.
رسم الحصاد، ثلاثة وخمسون درهما.
رسم الخفارة، خمسة عشر درهما.
رسم الاجران، خمسة وعشرون درهما، والغلة على ما تقدم.
الكيالة، قمح، عشرة ارادب وربع ونصف قيراط.
المراعي، عن اربعمائة وسبعة[370] وستين راسا طارئ، ثلاثمائة وخمسون درهما وثمن.

والذي يسلف بها من الفول برسم العوامل الديوانية، خمسون اردبا. ومن الشعير، برسم الاصطبلات السلطانية، خمسون اردبا.

وعليها من الاتبان، ثمانمائة شنيف.

وبها من الرزق، اربعة فدادين. تفصيله:
الخطابة، فدانان.
رهبان دير ابي اسحق[371]، فدانان.

والمربى بها من الفروج للديوان والمقطعين، ستمائة فروج نصفان.

ومن حرف الالف، ام السباع. هذه البلدة بلدة صغيرة، في[372] قبلي الفيوم. فيها جميزة واحدة وسنطات. عبرتها جيشية، اربعة الاف دينار. اهلها بنو غصين، فخذ من بني كلاب. والمطلق لها[373] من الماء من بحر دلية من المقسم المعروف بالقلنبو، عشرون قبضة وثلثان.

367 ساقط من أ. س.: الخراجي ستمائة وخمسة وستون دينارا ونصف وربع.
368 ساقط من أ. س.: قمح ستة وعشرون ونصف وثلث شعير نصف وربع ونصف قيراط.
369 أ. س.: وعشرون.
370 أ. س.: ستة.
371 أ. س.: إسحاق.
372 أ. س.: من.
373 أ. س.: بها.

[The revenues in specie] include:
lunar-calendar tax, 15 dinars;
pasture tax, 16 ¼ dinars;
land tax [on cash crops], 665 ½ ¼ dinars;

In grains, as specified above.

The alms-tax, for the monetary value of 17 heads of livestock, 17 ½ ⅛ dinars:
cows, a yearling calf, 1 dinar;
monetary value of small cattle, for 16 heads, 16 ½ ⅛ dinars:
sheep, 15 heads, 16 2/24 dinars;
goats, for one head, ¼ ⅙ ⅛ dinar.

The fees, the measurement fee and the pasture tax, 533 ⅛ dirhams, which are 13 ⅓ dinars; and in grains, 39 ¼ 1/48 ardabbs:
wheat, 26 ½ ⅓ [ardabbs];
barley ½ ¼ 1/48 [ardabb];
broad beans, 11 ⅔ ardabbs.

[This includes]:
the fees, 183 dirhams and 29 ardabbs:
wheat, 16 ½ 1/16 ardabbs;
barley ½ ¼ 1/48 [ardabb];
broad beans, 11 ⅔ ardabbs.
[The fees] in detail:
supervision of the land survey, 90 dirhams;
harvest fee, 53 dinars;
protection fee, 15 dirhams;
threshing-floor fee, 25 dirhams; and in grains, as specified.
The measurement fee, wheat, 10 ¼ 1/48 ardabbs.
The pasture tax on seasonal pasture lands, for 467 heads, 350 ⅛ dirhams.

The broad beans assigned for the cattle of the Dīwān, which was paid for in advance, 50 ardabbs. The barley assigned for the royal stables, [paid for in advance], 50 ardabbs.

Hay, 800 bales.

The allowances, 4 feddans:
for the Friday preachers, 2 feddans;
for the monks of the monastery of Abū Isḥāq, 2 feddans.

The chickens reared for the Dīwān and the *iqṭāʿ*-holders, 600 chickens — half for each.

Also beginning with the letter 'alif': Umm al-Sibāʿ.[109] This is a small village in the south of the Fayyum. It has one sycamore tree and some acacia trees. Its fiscal value is 4,000 army dinars. Its people are the Banū Ghuṣayn, a branch of the Banū Kilāb. The water allocated to it from Dilya Canal, by means of the divisor known as al-Qalanbū, is 20 ⅔ *qabḍas*.

109 Modern location (uncertain): ʿIzbat Muḥammad ʿĀmir (عزبة محمد عامر). Halm, *Ägypten*, p. 276: Umm as-Sibāʿ/Bushṭā; Salmon, 'Répertoire', p. 67; de Sacy, *État des provinces*, p. 681; Ramzī, *Al-Qāmūs*, I, 126: ʿIzbat Wāsif Ghalī Bāsha near al-Ghāba. We could not identify this ʿIzba. In line with the geographical information provided by al-Nābulusī on this village, we located it near the village of ʿIzbat Muḥammad ʿĀmir.

ارتفاعها، مما جميعه مستخرجا ومتحصلا، شعير، ستمائة اردب وثمانون اردب.

عليها من الزكاة، عن القرارية والمنتجعين عن ثمن[374] اغنام، عن سبعة عشر راسا، اربعة عشر دينارا.

تفصيله:

بياض، عن تسعة ارؤس، تسعة دنانير ونصف.

شعارى، عن ثمانية ارؤس، اربعة دنانير ونصف.

وعليها من الرسوم والكيالة، عن خمسة وثمانين درهما ونصف، ديناران وثمن وحبة، وغلة تسعة وثلاثون اردبا وثلثان ونصف ثمن. تفصيله:

قمح، سبعة ارادب ونصف وثمن.

شعير، تسعة وعشرون اردبا ونصف قيراط.

وفول، ثلاثة ارادب وقيراطان.

الرسوم، خمسة وثمانون درهما ونصف. تفصيله:

رسم الحصاد، ثلاثة وخمسون درهما.

رسم الخفارة، خمسة عشر درهما.

رسم الاجران، سبعة عشر درهما ونصف، وغلة تسعة عشر اردبا وثلثان ونصف ثمن.

الكيالة، شعير، عشرون اردبا.

وعليها من الاتبان، ستمائة شنيف.

مزارعوها يربون من الفروج مائتين وعشرين فروجا. تفصيله:

للديوان المعمور، بما فيه من اجرة التربية، وهو الثلث، مائة وعشرون طائرا.

للمقطعين بها، مائة طائر.

والذي يسلف عليه بها من الشعير، برسم الاصطبلات السلطانية، خمسة وخمسون اردبا.

وبالناحية من تقاوي المحلول، ثمانية عشر اردبا قمحًا.

ومن حرف الالف، الهيشة المفردة باللاهون. هذه الهيشة عبارة عن غيط في اللاهون، مثل ام النخارير، بعضها داخل في اقطاع اللاهون وبعضها خارج عنه. عبرتها الف وخمسمائة ودينار واحد جيشية. تروى من ماء النيل. مزارعوها من اهل اللاهون وغيرها.

ارتفاعها، مما جميعه مستخرجا، عينا، اربعمائة وخمسة وستون دينارا ونصف وثمن. تفصيله:

خراج الثلثين منها، ثلاثمائة وعشرة دنانير وربع وثمن. تفصيله:[375]

كتان، عن سبعة وخمسين فدانا وثلث، مائتان وستة وثمانون دينارا وثلثان.

قرط ثلاثة وعشرون دينارا ونصف وربع.

خراج المستثنى به باللاهون، على ما تقدم شرحه فيها، مائة وخمسة وخمسون دينارا وخمسة قراريط.

374 أ. س.: ثمانية.

375 ساقط من أ. س.: خراج الثلثين منها ثلاثمائة وعشرة دنانير وربع وثمن تفصيله.

Its revenues in cash and in kind are, in barley, 680 ardabbs.

The alms-tax, on local animals as well as animals seeking pasture (*al-qarāriyya wa'l-muntajiʿīn*),[110] for the monetary value of 17 heads of small cattle, 14 dinars:

sheep, for nine heads, 9 ½ dinars;

goats, for eight heads, 4 ½ dinars.

The fees and the measurement fee are 85 ½ dirhams, which is 2 ⅛ 1/72 dinars; and in grains, 39 ⅔ 1/16 ardabbs:

wheat, 7 ½ ⅛ ardabbs;

barley, 29 1/48 ardabbs;

broad beans, 3 2/24 ardabbs.

The fees, 85 ½ dirhams:

harvest fee, 53 dirhams;

protection fee, 15 dirhams;

threshing-floor fee, 17 ½ dirhams; and in grains, 19 ⅔ 1/16 ardabbs.

The measurement fee, barley, 20 ardabbs.

Hay, 600 bales.

Its tenants rear 220 chickens:

for the prosperous Dīwān, including the rearing wage, at a third, 120 birds;

for the *iqṭāʿ*-holders, 100 birds.

The barley assigned for the royal stables, which was paid for in advance, 55 ardabbs.

The seed advances, for a vacant [*iqṭāʿ*-holding] (*taqāwī al-maḥlūl*), 18 ardabbs in wheat.

Also beginning with the letter 'alif': al-Haysha,[111] attached to al-Lāhūn. This al-Haysha is a field in al-Lāhūn, like Umm al-Nakhārīr. Some of it is included in the *iqṭāʿ* of al-Lāhūn, and some of it is outside of it. Its fiscal value is 1,501 army dinars. It is irrigated from the water of the Nile. Its tenants are from the people of al-Lāhūn and elsewhere.

Its revenue, entirely collected in cash, is, in specie, 465 ½ ⅛ dinars:

land tax on ⅔ [of its land], 310 ¼ ⅛ dinars:

flax, for 57 ⅓ feddans, 286 ⅔ dinars;

alfalfa, 23 ½ ¼ dinars;

land tax on land excluded (*al-mustathnā bi-hi*) for the revenue of al-Lāhūn, as previously explained, 155 5/24 dinars.

110 On *al-qarāriyya* as a term designating local tenants, see al-Nuwayrī, *Nihāyat al-arab*, VIII, 248.

111 Modern location (uncertain): between al-Lāhūn and Umm al-Nakhārīr. Halm, *Ägypten*, p. 258; Salmon, 'Répertoire', p. 38; Ramzī, *Al-Qāmūs*, II/III, 162: Ghīṭ al-Baḥḥārī, but we could not identify this place-name. In line with al-Nābulusī's description, we located it on the tail of the mountain, in between al-Lāhūn and Umm al-Nakhārīr.

ومن حرف الالف، المَهيمسِي، من كفور قمبشا.[376] هذه البلدة بلدة[377] صغيرة وبها اثر نخيلات. مسافتها للراكب اربع ساعات. وهي[378] اخر الفيوم، من القبلة، وهي مفازة البهنسا. وهي كفر من كفور خليج تنبطويه،[379] داخل في عبرة اقطاعها من جملة مبلغها، ستة وعشرون الفا جيشية ومائتان وخمسون دينارا. اهلها بنو حاتم، فخذ من بني كلاب، يعرفون بالمياحيه (ط.م.)/المياجبة (ا.س.). تشرب من بحر تنبطويه[380] من جملة عبرة[381] الماء المطلق في البحر المذكور، بما عدته سبع قبض ونصف ماء.

ارتفاعها ستة عشر دينارا ونصف وثلث وحبة، وغلة اربعمائة وخمسة وخمسون اردبا وسدس. تفصيله:

قمح، ثلاثمائة وثلاثة ارادب وثلث.

شعير وفول، مائة واحد وخمسون اردبا ونصف وثلث.

تفصيله:

خراج القطن، عن ستمائة واربعة وسبعين درهما، سبعة عشر دينارا ونصف وثلث وحبة.

خراج الغلة، اربعمائة وخمسة وخمسون اردبا وسدس، على ما فصل.

وعليها من الزكاة،[382] عن ثمن اغنام القرارية والمنتجعين، عن خمسة عشر راسا،[383] عشرة دنانير ونصف وربع وحبة. تفصيله:

بياض، عن سبعة ارؤس، تسعة دنانير وقيراطان.

شعارى، عن ستة ارؤس، دينار وثلثان وحبة.

وعليها من المراعي والرسوم والكيالة، عن مائتين وسبعة وعشرين درهما ونصف وثمن، خمسة دنانير وثلثان ونصف قيراط، وغلة ثلاثة وثلاثون اردبا وثلثان ونصف قيراط:

قمح، عشرون اردبا وثلثان.

شعير، تسعة ارادب وسدس.

فول، ثلاثة ارادب ونصف وثلث ونصف قيراط.

تفصيله:

شد الاحباس، ستة دراهم ونصف.

رسم جراريف، احد واربعون درهما ونصف.

رسم الحصاد، ثلاثة وخمسون درهما.

رسم خفارة، خمسة عشر درهما.

رسم الاجران، اثنان وعشرون درهما، وغلة عشرون اردبا وربع ونصف ثمن، على ما فصل.

الكيالة، ثلاثة عشر اردبا وربع وثمن:

قمح، عشرة ارادب وربع وثمن.

شعير، ثلاثة ارادب.

المراعي، عن مائة وثلاثة واربعين راسا طارئ، تسعة وثمانون درهما ونصف وثمن. تفصيله:

قطيعة درهم واحد الراس، عن ستين راسا، ستون درهما.[384]

قطيعة خمسة وعشرين درهما المائة، عن ثلاثة وثمانين راسا عشرون درهما ونصف وربع.

رسم المستخدمين، ثمانية دراهم ونصف وربع وثمن.

Also beginning with the letter 'alif': Al-Mahīmsī,[112] one of the hamlets of Qambashā. This is a small village, with traces of small date palms. It is four hours' ride [from the city], at the southern edge of the Fayyum, on the passage (*mafāza*) to al-Bahnasā. It is one of the hamlets of Tanabṭawayh Canal, and included in its *iqṭā*ʿ, which has a total fiscal value of 26,250 army dinars. Its people are the Banū Ḥātim, a branch of the Banū Kilāb; they are known as al-Myajbh (?).[113] It gets its water from Tanabṭawayh Canal, out of the total water quota allocated to that canal, 7 ½ *qabḍas* of water.

Its revenues are 16 ½ ⅓ 1/72 dinars; and in grains, 455 ⅙ ardabbs:

wheat, 303 ⅓ ardabbs;

barley and broad beans, 151 ½ ⅓ ardabbs.

[The revenues in specie] consist of land tax on cotton, 674 dirhams, which are 17 ½ ⅓ 1/72 dinars.

Land tax on grains, 455 ⅙ ardabbs, as specified.

The alms-tax, for the monetary value of 15[114] heads of small cattle, both local and those seeking pasture, 10 ½ ¼ 1/72 dinars:

sheep, for seven heads, 9 2/24 dinars;

goats, for six heads, 1 ⅔ 1/72 dinar.

The pasture tax, the fees and the measurement fee, 227 ½ ⅛ dirhams, which are 5 ⅔ 1/48 dinars; and in grains, 33 ⅔ 1/48 ardabbs:

wheat, 20 ⅔ ardabbs;

barley, 9 ⅙ ardabbs;

broad beans, 3 ½ ⅓ 1/48 ardabbs.

[The fees] in detail:

supervision of endowments, 6 ½ dirhams;

dredging fee, 41 ½ dirhams;

harvest fee, 53 dirhams;

protection fee, 15 dirhams;

threshing-floor fee, 22 dirhams, and in grains, 20 ¼ 1/16 ardabbs, as specified.

The measurement fee, 13 ¼ ⅛ ardabbs:

wheat, 10 ¼ ⅛ ardabbs;

barley, 3 ardabbs.

The pasture tax, for 143 heads on seasonal pasture lands, 89 ½ ⅛ dirhams:

at the rate of one dirham per head, for 60 heads, 60 dirhams;

at the rate of 25 dirhams per 100, for 83 heads, 20 ½ ¼ dirhams;

the government agents' fee, 8 ½ ¼ ⅛ dirhams.

---

376 أ. س.: قنبشا.

377 ساقط من ط. م.: بلدة.

378 أ. س. يضيف: في.

379 ط. م.: تنبطوه.

380 أ. س. يضيف ويشطب: داخل في عبرة إقطاعها.

381 ساقط من أ. س.: عبرة.

382 أ. س. يضيف ويشطب: أربعمائة وخمسة وخمسون أردبا.

383 ساقط من أ. س.:رأسا.

384 ساقط من أ. س.: درهم واحد الرأس عن ستين رأسا ستون درهما.

---

112 Modern location (uncertain): Al-Ḥamdiyya (الحمدية). Halm, *Ägypten*, p. 261: Mahmasī = Bahmasī; Salmon, 'Répertoire', pp. 71–72; Zéki, 'Une description', p. 44: al-Mahīmsī; Ibn al-Jīʿān, *Kitāb al-tuḥfa*, p. 151; de Sacy, *État des provinces*, p. 680; Ramzī, *Al-Qāmūs*, I, 118: al-Mahmasī. In line with al-Nābulusī's description, we located it near the modern village of al-Ḥamdiyya — a location which is also in line with Shafei Bey's map.

113 AS: myajbh; MP: myaḥyh.

114 According to the numbers specificed below, the total should be 13.

عليها من الاتبان، ثمانمائة شنيف.

Hay, 800 bales.

وبها من التقاوي الديوانية، ستة وثلاثون اردبا وربع:
قمح، اثنان وثلاثون اردبا.
شعير، اربعة ارادب.
سمسم، ربع اردب.

The seed advances from the Dīwān, 36 ¼ ardabbs:
wheat, 32 ardabbs;
barley, 4 ardabbs;
sesame, ¼ ardabb.

وعليها من الباقي عند ما كانت جارية في الخاص ما يذكر في قمبشا[385] من جملة ما يخصها من المقاسمة لسنة اربع وثلاثين وستمائة وما قبلها.

The arrears owed from the time it belonged to the Sultan's private domain will be mentioned in the entry for Qambashā, included in its total apportionment (*muqāsama*) for the year 634 and earlier.

والمربى بها من الفروج، خمسمائة وسبعون. تفصيله:
للديوان السلطاني بما فيه من اجرة التربية بحق الثلث، ثلاثمائة.
للمقطعين، مائتان وسبعون.

The chickens reared in it, 570:
for the royal Dīwān, including the rearing wage of a third, 300;
for the *iqṭā*ʿ-holders, 270.

اهلها يزرعون من القصب السكر بدموشية لسنة احدى واربعين وستمائة، راس، فدانان.

Its people sow some sugarcane at Dumūshiyya. For the year 641, [it amounted to] 2 feddans of first harvest.

والمسلف عليه[386] بها من الشعير برسم الاصطبلات السلطانية، سبعة وعشرون اردبا ونصف.

The barley assigned for the royal stables, which was paid for in advance, 27 ½ ardabbs.

ومن حرف الالف، القلهانة. هذه البلدة قبلي دموشية من كفور خليج تنبطويه داخلة في عبرة اقطاعه الجيشي وجملته، ستة وعشرون الفا ومائتان وخمسون دينارا. اهلها بنو عامر معروفون[387] بالشبيتيين، فخذ من بني كلاب. تشرب من بحر تنبطويه بعبرة عدتها خمس قبض برسم الشتوي بها واقصاب دموشية.

Also beginning with the letter 'alif': Al-Qalhāna.[115] This village, south of Dumūshiyya, is one of the hamlets of Tanabṭawayh Canal. It is included in its total fiscal value, which is 26,250 army dinars. Its people are the Banū ʿĀmir, known as al-Shubaytiyyīn (?), a branch of the Banū Kilāb. It gets its water from Tanabṭawayh Canal, a quota of five *qabḍas*, assigned for winter cultivation and for the sugarcane of Dumūshiyya.

ارتفاعها، غلة، خمسمائة وخمسة وثلاثون اردبا. تفصيله:
قمح، ثلاثمائة وستة وخمسون اردبا وثلثان.
شعير وفول، مائة وثمانية وسبعون اردبا وثلث.

Its revenues in kind, 535 ardabbs:
wheat, 356 ⅔ ardabbs;
barley and broad beans, 178 ⅓ ardabbs.

وعليها من الزكاة، عن اغنام، عن ستة ارؤس، اربعة دنانير وخمسة قراريط. تفصيله:
بياض، عن راسين، ديناران وثمن.
شعارى، عن اربعة ارؤس، ديناران وقيراطان.

The alms-tax, for six heads of small cattle, 4 ⁵⁄₂₄ dinars:
sheep, for two heads, 2 ⅛ dinars;
goats, for four heads, 2 ²⁄₂₄ dinars.

وعليها من الرسوم والكيالة، عن ثلاثة عشر درهما وثمن، ثلث دينار، وغلة احد وعشرون اردبا ونصف وثمن. تفصيله:
قمح، خمسة عشر اردبا وربع.
شعير، ستة[388] ارادب وربع وثمن.
الكيالة، تسعة ارادب ونصف وربع وثمن. تفصيله:
قمح، اربعة ارادب ونصف وربع وثمن.
شعير، خمسة ارادب.[389]
الرسوم، ثلاثة عشر درهما وثمن، وغلة احد عشر اردبا ونصف وربع:
قمح، عشرة ارادب وربع وثمن.
شعير، اردب واحد وربع وثمن.

The fees and measurement fee are 13 ⅛ dirhams, which is ⅓ dinar; and in grains, 21 ½ ⅛ ardabbs:
wheat, 15 ½ ardabbs;
barley, 6 ¼ ⅛ ardabbs.
The measurement fee is 9 ½ ¼ ⅛ ardabbs:
wheat, 4 ½ ¼ ⅛ ardabbs;
barley, 5 ardabbs;
The fees are 13 ⅛ dirhams; and in grains, 11 ½ ¼ ardabbs:
wheat, 10 ¼ ⅛ ardabbs;
barley, 1 ¼ ⅛ ardabb.

وعليها من الاتبان، خمسمائة شنيف.

Hay, 500 bales.

اهلها يزرعون الاقصاب بدموشية وهو فدان واحد وثلثان وربع.

Its people sow sugarcane in Dumūshiyya, 1 ⅔ ¼ feddan.

385 أ. س.: قنبشا.
386 ساقط من أ. س.: عليه.
387 أ. س.: يعروفون.
388 أ. س.: خمسة.
389 ساقط من أ. س.: وربع وثمن. الكيالة تسعة أرادب ونصف وربع وثمن. تفصيله قمح أربعة أرادب ونصف وربع وثمن. شعير خمسة أرادب.

115 Modern location: Qalhāna (قلهانة). Halm, *Ägypten*, p. 267; Salmon, 'Répertoire', p. 72; Ibn al-Jīʿān, *Kitāb al-tuḥfa*, p. 152; de Sacy, *État des provinces*, p. 681: al-Qilhānah; Ramzī, *Al-Qāmūs*, II/III, 86: Qalahāna, ancient Tkalahitis/Lalahitis (following Amélineau, *La géographie*).

وبها من التقاوي الديوانية، سبعة واربعون اردبا وثمن. تفصيله:

قمح، ثمانية وثلاثون اردبا.

شعير، ستة ارادب.

فول، اردبان وثلث.

سمسم، ثلثان[390] وثمن اردب.

والمربى بها من الفروج، مائتان وثمانون فروجا. تفصيله:

للديوان المعمور، بما فيه من اجرة التربية وهو الثلث، مائة وثمانون طائرا.

[للمقطعين، مائة طائرا].

ومن حرف الالف، اقلول. من نواحي خليج دلية. هذه البلدة بلدة صغيرة، قبلي الفيوم، دائرها نخل وبها ايضا شجر ونخل. مسافتها للراكب ساعتان. داخلة في عبرة اقطاع الخليج المذكور، وهى سبعة وعشرون الفا وستمائة وخمسة وعشرون دينارا. تشرب من بحر دلية من الخليج المقسم المعروف بالقلنبو، بما عبرته عشر قبض وثلثان ماء. بها جامع تقام فيه الجمعة. اهلها بنو جعفر، فخذ من بني كلاب.

ارتفاعها مما جميعه مستخرجا ومتحصلا،[391] عن احد وعشرين درهما وربع وثمن، نصف دينار وحبتان[392]، عن خراج احكار; غلة، الف وستة وستون اردبا وثلثان.

قمح، ستمائة واربعون اردبا.

شعير، مائتان وثلاثة[393] عشر اردبا وثلث.

فول، مائتان وثلاثة عشر اردبا وثلث.[394]

وعليها من الزكاة، عن اغنام، عن راسين، دينار واحد ونصف. تفصيله:

بياض، عن راس واحد، دينار واحد.

شعرية، نصف دينار.

وعليها من الرسوم والكيالة والمراعي، عن مائة واحد وثمانين درهما ونصف وربع وثمن، اربعة دنانير وربع وسدس وثمن وحبة; وغلة، احد وسبعون اردبا ونصف وثمن:

قمح، تسعة وعشرون اردبا ونصف وثلث.

شعير، سبعة وثلاثون اردبا وثلثان.

فول، اربعة ارادب وثمن.

تفصيله:

الرسوم، مائة وستة وخمسون درهما ونصف، وستة وثلاثون اردبا وثلث وربع ونصف قيراط:

قمح، ثمانية عشر اردبا وثلثان.

شعير، ثلاثة عشر اردبا ونصف وربع ونصف ثمن.

فول، اربعة ارادب وثمن.

شد العين، خمسة دراهم.

رسم الجراريف، احد واربعون درهما.

رسم الحصاد، ثلاثة وخمسون درهما.

رسم الخفارة، خمسة عشر درهما.

رسم الاجران، اثنان وثلاثون درهما ونصف، وغلة ستة وثلاثون اردبا وثلث وربع ونصف قيراط على ما فصل.

390 أ. س.: ثلثا.

391 ساقط من ط. م.: مما جميعه مستخرجا ومتحصلا.

392 ساقط من أ. س.: وحبتان.

393 أ. س.:ثلثة.

394 ساقط من أ. س.:فول مائتان وثلاثة عشر أردبا وثلث.

The seed advances from the Dīwān, 47 ⅛ ardabbs:

wheat, 38 ardabbs;

barley, 6 ardabbs;

broad beans, 2 ⅓ ardabbs;

sesame, ⅔ ⅛ ardabb.

The chicken reared in it, 280 chickens:

for the prosperous Dīwān, including the rearing wage of a third, 180 birds.

[for the *iqṭāʿ*-holders, 100 birds].[116]

Also beginning with the letter 'alif': Uqlūl,[117] one of the villages of Dilya Canal. This is a small village in southern Fayyum, two hours' ride [from the city]. It is surrounded by date palms, and trees and date palms are also found inside the village. It is included in the fiscal value of the *iqṭāʿ* of the above mentioned canal, which is 27,625 [army] dinars. It gets its water from Dilya Canal, through the divisor known as al-Qalanbū. Its water quota is 10 ⅔ *qabḍas*. It has a mosque, in which the Friday prayers are held. Its people are the Banū Jaʿfar, a branch of the Banū Kilāb.

Its revenues in cash and in kind are, from land tax on lands subject to long-term lease, 21 ¼ ⅛ dirhams, which is ½ 2/72 dinar; and in grains, 1,066 ⅔ ardabbs:

wheat 640 ardabbs;

barley, 213 ⅓ ardabbs;

broad beans, 213 ⅓ ardabbs.

The alms-tax imposed on it, for [the monetary value] of two heads of small cattle, 1 ½ dinar:

sheep, for one head, 1 dinar;

goats, for one head, ½ dinar.

The fees, the measurement fee and the pasture tax are 181 ½ ¼ ⅛ dirhams, which are 4 ½ ⅙ ⅛ 1/72 dinars; and in grains, 71 ½ ⅛ ardabbs:

wheat, 29 ½ ⅓ ardabbs;

barley, 37 ⅔ ardabbs;

broad beans, 4 ⅛ ardabbs.

[The fees, the measurement fee and the pasture tax] in detail:

the fees, 156 ½ dirhams, and 36 ⅓ ¼ 1/48 ardabbs:

wheat, 18 ⅔ ardabbs;

barley, 13 ½ ¼ 1/16 ardabbs;

broad beans, 4 ⅛ ardabbs.

[the fees include]:

supervision of the land survey, 5 dirhams;

dredging fee, 41 dirhams;

harvest fee, 53 dirhams;

protection fee, 15 dirhams;

threshing-floor fee, 32 ½ dirhams; and in grains, 36 ⅓ ¼ 1/48 ardabbs, as specified.

116 Missing in both manuscripts.

117 Modern location: al-Jaʿāfra (الجعافرة). Halm, *Ägypten*, p. 276; Salmon, 'Répertoire', p. 67; de Sacy, *État des provinces*, p. 680; Ibn al-Jīʿān, *Kitāb al-tuḥfa*, p. 151; Ramzī, *Al-Qāmūs*, II/III, 81: al-Jaʿāfra. Uqlūl is well represented in documents from the Fatimid period; see most recently Yūsuf Rāgib, *Transmission de biens, mariage et répudiation a Uqlul, village du Fayyoum, au Ve-XIe siècle* (Le Caire: Institut français d'archéologie orientale, 2016).

الكيالة، خمسة وثلاثون اردبا ونصف قيراط. تفصيله:
قمح، احد عشر اردبا وسدس.
شعير، ثلاثة وعشرون اردبا ونصف وثلث ونصف قيراط.
المراعي طارئ، عن سبعة وسبعين راسا، خمسة وعشرين درهما وربع وثمن. تفصيله:
قطيعة ثلاثين المائة، عن احد وعشرين راسا، ستة دراهم ونصف.
قطيعة خمسة وعشرين درهما المائة، عن ستة وخمسين راسا، اربعة عشر درهما.
رسم المستخدمين، اربعة دراهم ونصف وربع وثمن.

وعليها لديوان الاحباس اربعة دنانير.

وعليها من الاتبان، تسعمائة شنيف.

تزرع من[395] الاقصاب بدموشية فدانين.

والمربى بها من الفروج، خمسمائة وستون طائرا. تفصيله:
للديوان، مائتان وعشرة، بما فيه من اجرة التربية.
للمقطعين، ثلاثمائة وخمسون طائرا.

ومن حرف الالف، الصفاونة وتنفشار. عبارة[396] عن غيط من حقوق دلية. هذه البلدة بلدة صغيرة وهي قبلي الفيوم. دائرها نخل على بحر دلية وشجر يسير. مسافتها ساعتان للراكب. من جملة اقطاع الخليج المذكور، على ما يشهد به ديوان الجيوش. لها من الماء من بحر دلية بما فيه من الخفارة [397] اربع قبض. اهلها بنو عامر، فخذ من بني كلاب.

ارتفاعها عن خراج الراتب، مقرر على المعاملين، عن مائتين وثمانية دراهم ونصف وثمن، خمسة دنانير وخمسة قراريط ونصف.[398] وغلة، اربعمائة واحد وستون اردبا ونصف وثلث. تفصيله:
قمح، مائتان واثنان وثمانون اردبا وسدس وثمن.
شعير، مائة واربعة ارادب ونصف قيراط.
فول، اربعة وسبعون اردبا ونصف وربع ونصف قيراط.

قصب سكر، عشرون فدانا.

وعليها من الزكاة، عن اغنام، عن اربعة ارؤس، ثلاثة دنانير وثمن. تفصيله:
بياض، عن راسين، ديناران وثمن.
شعارى، عن راسين، دينار واحد.

وعليها من الرسوم والكيالة والمراعي، عن مائة واربعة عشر درهما ونصف، ديناران ونصف وثلث وحبتان؛ وغلة، ثلاثة وثلاثون اردبا ونصف:
قمح، ثمانية وعشرون اردبا وربع.
شعير، خمسة ارادب وربع.

تفصيله:
الرسوم مائة واحد عشر درهما وثمن، قمح عشرون اردبا وربع وسدس. تفصيله:
شد العين، ثمانية دراهم.
شد الاحباس، ثلاثة دراهم.
رسم الجراريف، اربعة عشر درهما ونصف وثمن.
رسم الحصاد، ثلاثة وخمسون درهما.
رسم الخفارة، خمسة عشر درهما.

395 ساقط من أ. س.: من.
396 ساقط من أ. س.:عبارة.
397 ولعله الصفاونة.
398 أ. س.: ودانق.

the measurement fee, 35 1/48 ardabbs:
wheat, 11 1/6 ardabbs;
barley, 23 1/2 1/3 1/48 ardabbs.
The pasture tax on seasonal pasture lands, for 77 heads, 25 1/4 1/8 dirhams:
at the rate of 30 [dirhams] per 100 [heads], for 21 heads, 6 1/2 dirhams;
at the rate of 25 dirhams per 100 [heads], for 56 heads, 14 dirhams;
the government agents' fee, 4 1/2 1/4 1/8 dirhams.

For the Ministry of Endowments, 4 dinars.

Hay, 900 bales.

Sugarcane sown at Dumūshiyya, 2 feddans.[118]

Chickens reared in it, 560 birds:
for the Dīwān, 210, including the rearing wage;
for the *iqṭāʿ*-holders, 350 birds.

Also beginning with the letter 'alif': al-Ṣafāwina and Tanafshār,[119] included in the accounts of Dilya [Canal]. This is a small village in southern Fayyum, two hours' ride [from the city]. It is surrounded by date palms and a few trees near Dilya Canal. It is included in the *iqṭāʿ* of the above mentioned canal, as attested by Dīwān al-Juyūsh (Ministry of the Army). Its water quota from Dilya Canal, including the allowance for protection (*al-khafāra*), is four *qabḍas*. Its people are the Banū ʿĀmir, a branch of the Banū Kilāb.

Its revenue from land tax on perennial plants, as established on the cultivators, is 280 1/2 1/8 dirhams, which are 5 5/24 1/48 dinars; and in grains, 461 1/2 1/3 ardabbs:
wheat, 282 1/6 1/8 ardabbs;
barley, 104 1/2 1/4 1/48 ardabbs;
broad beans, 74 1/2 1/4 1/48 ardabbs.

Sugarcane, 20 feddans.

The alms-tax, for four heads of small cattle, 3 1/8 dinars:
sheep, for two heads, 2 1/8 dinars;
goats, for two heads, 1 dinar.

The fees, the measurement fee and the pasture tax are 114 1/2 dirhams, which are 2 1/2 1/3 2/72 dinars; and in grains, 33 1/2 ardabbs:
wheat, 28 1/4 ardabbs;
barley, 5 1/4 ardabbs.

[The fees, the measurement fee and the pasture tax] in detail:
The fees are 111 1/8 dirhams, [and in grains] wheat, 20 1/4 1/6 ardabbs:
supervision of the land survey, 8 dirhams;
supervision of endowments, 3 dirhams;
dredging fee, 14 1/2 1/8 dirhams;
harvest fee, 53 dirhams;

118 The sugarcane plantations in the village of Dumūshiyya were cultivated by peasants coming from nine different villages in southern Fayyum.

119 Modern location: Al-Ṣawāfna (الصوافنة). Halm, *Ägypten*, p. 268; Salmon, 'Répertoire', p. 67; de Sacy, *État des provinces*, p. 680: al-Ṣafāwiyya; Ibn al-Jīʿān, *Kitāb al-tuḥfa*, p. 152: al-Ṣafāwiyya; Savigny, *Description de l'Égypte*, p. 126: al-Ṣufāwiya; Ramzī, *Al-Qāmūs*, II/III, 101: al-Ṣawāfna.

رسم الاجران، سبعة عشر درهما ونصف، وقمح عشرون اردبا وربع وسدس.
كيالة، ثلاثة[399] عشر اردبا وقيراطان. تفصيله:
قمح، سبعة ارادب ونصف وثلث.
شعير، خمسة ارادب وربع.
المراعي، ثلاثة دراهم وربع وثمن:
قطيعة خمسين درهما المائة، عن[400] ستة اروس، ثلاثة دراهم.
رسم المستخدمين، عن الصفاونة(?)[401]، ربع وثمن درهم.

وعليها لديوان الاحباس، نصف وثلث دينار. تفصيل ذلك:
الصفاونة، نصف دينار.
تنفشار، ثلث دينار.

وعليها من الاتبان، اربعمائة وخمسون شنيفا.

والذي يسلف بها من الشعير للاصطبلات السلطانية، ثلاثون اردبا.

اهلها يزرعون من القصب السكر بدموشية، راس، فدان واحد وثلث.

والمربى بها من الفروج، ثلاثمائة وسبعة وعشرون طائرا:
للديوان المعمور بما فيه من اجرة التربية، مائتان وعشرة.
للمقطعين، مائة وسبعة عشر طائرا.

ومن حرف الالف، الحنبوشية. وقف الملك الناصر للمالكية بمصر المحروسة.[402] هذه البلدة عبارة عن بلدة كبيرة، وهي اخر عمل الفيوم غربيه ما وراءها الا الجبل، بحريها منية اقنى، مفازة واح. عليها نخل وشجر كثير، تين وتفاح وكمثرى. مسافتها للراكب اربع ساعات. وبها جامع تقام فيه الجمعة، غير مدون. لها من الماء من بحر منية اقنى، شركة ببيج انقاش مما يقسم ذلك[403] بخشبة. يخص الناحية من المقسم المعروف بالعرين، اربع عشرة قبضة.

ارتفاعها، عينا، عشرة دنانير، غلة، الف وستمائة وخمسون اردبا:
قمح، ثمانمائة اردب.
شعير، ثمانمائة اردب.
كمون، خمسون اردبا.

وعليها من الزكاة، ثمن اغنام، عن خمسة عشر راسا، عشرة دنانير وحبة. تفصيله:
بياض، عن سبعة اروس، سبعة دنانير وربع.
شعارى، ثمانية اروس، ديناران ونصف وربع وحبة.

protection fee, 15 dirhams;
threshing-floor fee, 17 ½ dirhams; and wheat, 20 ¼ ⅙ ardabbs.
The measurement fee, 13 ²⁄₂₄ ardabbs:
wheat, 7 ½ ⅓ ardabbs;
barley, 5 ¼ ardabbs.
The pasture tax, 3 ¼ ⅛ dirhams:
at the rate of 50 dirhams per 100 [heads], for six heads, 3 dirhams;
the government agents' fee, for al-Ṣafāwina (?),[120] ¼ ⅛ dirham.

For the Ministry of Endowments, ½ ⅓ dinar:
al-Ṣafāwina, ½ dinar;
Tanafshār, ⅓ dinar.

Hay, 450 bales.

The barley assigned for the royal stables, which was paid for in advance, 30 ardabbs.

Its people sow sugarcane in Dumūshiyya, 1 ⅓ feddan of first harvest.

The chickens reared in it, 327 birds:
for the prosperous Dīwān, including the rearing wage, 210 birds;
for the *iqṭāʿ*-holders, 117 birds.

Also beginning with the letter 'alif': al-Ḥanbūshiyya.[121] It is an endowment of al-Malik al-Nāṣir for the Malikite [jurists] in Miṣr (al-Fusṭāṭ). This is a large village, at the western edge of the Fayyum. There is nothing beyond it [in the Western direction] except the mountain. North of it is Minyat Aqnā, and the passage to the oases (*wāḥ*). It has date palms and many trees: figs, apples and pears. It is four hours' ride [from the city]. It has an unregistered congregational mosque, in which the Friday prayers are held. It gets its water from Minyat Aqnā Canal, shared with Babīj Anqāsh, by means of a single wooden [divisor]. The water quota allocated to this village through the divisor known as al-ʿArīn is 14 *qabḍas*.

Its revenues are, in specie, 10 dinars; and in grains, 1,650 ardabbs:
wheat 800 ardabbs;
barley, 800 ardabbs;
cumin, 50 ardabbs.

The alms-tax, for monetary value of 15 heads of small cattle, 10 ¹⁄₇₂ dinars:
sheep, for seven heads, 7 ¼ dinars;
goats, for eight heads, 2 ½ ¼ ¹⁄₇₂ dinars.

399 أ. س.:ثلثة.
400 ساقط من أ. س.:عن.
401 أ. س.: الحزوبه; ط. م.: الحزونه.
402 ساقط من ط. م.: المحروسة.
403 ساقط من ط. م.: ذلك.

120 MP: al-ḥzwnh: AS: al-ḥrwnh.

121 Modern location: Al-Nazla (النزلة). Halm, *Ägypten*, p. 258; Salmon, 'Répertoire', p. 61; de Sacy, *État des provinces*, p. 680; Ibn Mammātī, *Kitāb qawānīn al-dawāwīn*, p. 103; Ibn al-Jīʿān, *Kitāb al-tuḥfa*, p. 151: al-Khanbūshiyya; Ramzī, *Al-Qāmūs*, II/III, 72–73: al-Nazla. Al-Maqrīzī reports that the village of al-Ḥanbūsiyya was endowed by Saladin in 1170–71 in favour of the Malikite al-Nāṣiriyya Madrasa in Cairo. Because the teaching staff and the students in the al-Nāṣiriyya Madrasa received their salaries in the form of wheat (*qamḥ*) transported directly from the Fayyumi village, the Madrasa came to be known as al-Qamḥiyya; *Kitāb al-mawāʿiẓ*, ed. by Sayyid, IV, 455.

الارض المعروفة بالاحكار بخليج دلية، معروفة برزقة حصن ابن مترف. جارية في اقطاع المقطعين. لها من الماء من بحر دلية، من المقسم المعروف بالتبرون، قبضتان. ارتفاعها، قمح وشعير، مائتان وخمسون اردبا نصفان.

ومن حرف الالف، الروبيون. وهي الارض المعروفة بالغابة، وقف مدرسة الشافعية التقوية بمدينة الفيوم. هذه البلدة بلدة صغيرة، غربي الفيوم، مسافتها من مدينة الفيوم نصف ساعة للراكب. وبها نخل يسير وسنط[404] ولها من الماء[405] بخليج من البر القبلي، مبنى مجصص. عبرته اربع قبض.

ارتفاعها، عينا، تسعة وستون دينارا وربع وسدس وثمن وحبتان، وغلة، سبعمائة اردب: قمح وشعير نصفان. تفصيله:

خراج الزراعة، عن الشتوي والصيفي، عينا، خمسون دينارا، وغلة على ما فصل.

خراج الاحكار، تسعة عشر دينارا وربع وسدس وثمن[406] وحبتان.

وعليها من الزكاة، عن ثمن ماشية، عن ثلاثة ارؤس، ثلاثة دنانير ونصف وثمن:

بقر احمر، تبيع واحد، دينار واحد ونصف.

اغنام بياض، عن راسين، ديناران وثمن.

وعليها كيالة، احد وعشرون اردبا: قمح وشعير نصفان.

ومن حرف الالف، الاعلام. هذه البلدة عبارة عن بلدة صغيرة وهي وقف على الفقهاء المالكية بالمدرسة الناصرية بمصر المحروسة. بينها وبين مدينة الفيوم نصف ساعة، وهي بحري الفيوم الى الشرق. تشتمل على بيوت قليلة على جبل رمل. هذا الجبل الرمل متصل الى العدوة. فيها دويرات مستجدة تين وجميزة واحدة صغيرة. تشرب من خليج مبني مجصص من البر البحري. عبرته خمس قبض. اهلها بنو زرعة.

ارتفاعها، عينا، ثلاثون دينارا؛ غلة، ستمائة وستة وخمسون اردبا وربع:

قمح، ثلاثمائة وثمانية وعشرون اردبا وثمن.

شعير، ثلاثمائة وثمانية وعشرون اردبا وثمن.

[404] ط. م.: صنط.

[405] ساقط من أ. س.: الماء.

[406] ساقط من أ. س.: وثمن.

[Also beginning with the letter 'alif']: The area known as al-Aḥkār,[122] on Dilya Canal, also known as the allowance of Ḥiṣn ibn Mutrif (?).[123] It is allocated as *iqṭāʿ* to *iqṭāʿ*-holders. It has a quota of two *qabḍas* of water of Dilya Canal, from the divisor known as al-Tabrūn. Its entire revenue is 250 ardabbs of wheat and barley, half in each.

Also beginning with the letter 'alif': Al-Rūbiyyūn.[124] It is the area known as al-Ghāba, which is an endowment of the Shafiʿite al-Taqawiyya Madrasa in Madīnat al-Fayyūm. This is a small village in western Fayyum, half an hour's ride from Madīnat al-Fayyūm. It has a few date palms and acacias. It gets its water from the southern bank [of the Main Canal], by a plastered canal with a weir. Its [water] quota is four *qabḍas*.

Its revenue is, in specie, 69 ¼ ⅙ ⅛ 2/72 dinars; and in grains, 700 ardabbs of wheat and barley, half in each.

[The revenue in detail]:

land tax on winter and summer crops, in specie, 50 dinars; and in grains, as specified;

land tax on lands subject to long-term lease, 19 ¼ ⅙ ⅛ 2/72 dinars.

The alms-tax, for the monetary value of three heads of livestock, 3 ½ ⅛ dinars:

cows, for a yearling calf, 1 ½ dinar;

small cattle, for two heads of sheep, 2 ⅛ dinars.

The measurement fee, 21 ardabbs, wheat and barley, half in each.

Also beginning with the letter 'alif': al-Aʿlām.[125] This is a small village, endowed as a waqf for the Malikite jurists of the al-Nāṣiriyya Madrasa in the protected city of Miṣr. It is half an hour's [ride] from Madīnat al-Fayyūm, towards the north-east. It contains a few houses on a sandy hill, which stretches until al-ʿIdwa. It has recently planted enclosures of fig trees, as well as a one small sycamore tree. It gets its water from the northern bank of [the Main Canal] by a plastered canal with a weir. Its [water] quota is five *qabḍas*. Its people are the Banū Zarʿa.

Its revenues are, in specie, 30 dinars; and in grains, 656¼ ardabbs:

Wheat, 328 ⅛ ardabbs;

Barley, 328 ⅛ ardabbs.

[122] Modern location (uncertain): ʿIzbat al-ʿĪsāwī (عزبة العيساوي). There are no references in other sources to this village. In line with al-Nābulusī's description, we placed it near the modern village of ʿIzbat al-ʿĪsāwī, which is located in an area that was served by al-Tabrūn, near modern Minyat al-Ḥayṭ (Minyat Shushhā).

[123] This is possibly the same as the allowance of ʿIzz al-Dīn ibn Ḥiṣn, mentioned in the entry for Minyat Shushhā as receiving ½ *qabḍa* of water from the Tabrūn divisor on Dilya Canal.

[124] Modern location (uncertain): ʿIzbat al-Awqāf, which lies on the Disyā Canal, near al-Sunbāṭ/ Nazlat Bashīr (نزلة بشير). Halm, *Ägypten*, p. 268: Rūbīyīn; Salmon, 'Répertoire', p. 61; de Sacy, *État des provinces*, p. 680: al-Rūbīyīn; Ibn al-Jīʿān, *Kitāb al-tuḥfa*, p. 152: al-Rūbīyīn; Ramzī, *Al-Qāmūs*, I, 63: ʿIzbat al-Awqāf near al-Sunbāṭ. We could not locate the modern ʿIzbat al-Awqāf. In line with al-Nābulusī's description we located it near the modern village of Nazlat Bashīr. This location is also in line with Shafei Bey's map.

[125] Modern location: al-Aʿlām (الأعلام). Halm, *Ägypten*, p. 245; Salmon, 'Répertoire', p. 47; Ibn Mammātī, *Kitāb qawānīn al-dawāwīn*, p. 104: al-Iʿlām = al-Aʿlām; Ibn al-Jīʿān, *Kitāb al-tuḥfa*, p. 152: notes that it belongs to the endowment of al-Madrasa al-Ṣāliḥiyya in Cairo; de Sacy, *État des provinces*, p. 681; Savigny, *Description de l'Égypte*, p. 129; Ramzī, *Al-Qāmūs*, II/III, 94: al-Aʿlām.

ومن حرف الباء، ببيج فرح. هذه البلدة عبارة عن بلدة متوسطة، بين الكبير والصغير[407]. تشمل على دويرات تين وحدائق نخل واصول سنط[408]. بينها وبين مدينة الفيوم اقل من نصف ساعة. غربي خليج منية اقنى. عبرتها جيشية خمسة عشر الف دينار. وبها جامع تقام فيه الجمعة. لها من الماء بخليج من الجهة القبلية، مبنى مجصص، في ارض وقف الخانقاه. عبرته اربع قبض. اهلها بنو عامر، فخذ من افخاذ بني كلاب.

ارتفاعها مما جميعه مستخرجا ومتحصلا، عينا، ثمانية عشر دينارا، مما جميعه مراعي راتب؛ غلة، عن خراج الزراعة، بما فيه من الاضافة، الف وستمائة ثمانية واربعون اردبا. تفصيله:[409]

قمح، ثمانمائة واربعة وعشرون اردبا.

شعير وفول، ثمانمائة واربعة وعشرون اردبا.

عليها من الزكاة، خمسة وعشرون دينارا ونصف وثلث. تفصيله:

دولبة، نصف دينار.

ثمن ماشية، عن اربعة وعشرين راسا، خمسة وعشرون دينارا وثلث. تفصيله:

بقر احمر، تبيع واحد، ديناران.

اغنام، عن ثلاثة وعشرين راسا، ثلاثة وعشرون دينارا وثلث:

بياض، عن احد وعشرين راسا، اثنان وعشرون دينارا وربع.

شعارى، عن راسين، دينار وقيراطان.

وعليها من الرسوم والكيالة والمراعي، عن اربعمائة وستة عشر درهما، عشرة دنانير وربع وثمن وحبتان؛ وغلة، اثنان وتسعون اردبا وثلثان ونصف قيراط:

قمح، سبعة وخمسون اردبا وثمن ونصف قيراط.

شعير، ثلاثة وعشرون اردبا وربع وسدس وثمن.

فول، اثنا عشر اردبا.

تفصيله:

الرسوم، مائتان وستة دراهم، وغلة، تسعة واربعون اردبا وثلثان. تفصيله:

قمح، ستة وعشرون اردبا وثمن.

شعير، احد عشر اردبا وربع وسدس وثمن.

فول، اثنا عشر اردبا.

تفصيله:

شد الاحباس، خمسة دراهم.

رسم الجراريف، تسعون درهما.

رسم الحصاد، ثلاثة وخمسون درهما.

رسم الخفارة، خمسة عشر درهما.

رسم الاجران، ثلاثة واربعون درهما، وغلة تسعة واربعون اردبا وثلثان، على ما فصل.

الكيالة، اربعون اردبا ونصف قيراط:

قمح، ثمانية وعشرون اردبا ونصف قيراط.

شعير، اثنا عشر اردبا.

عشر الرزق: قمح، ثلاثة ارادب.

Beginning with the letter 'bā'': Babīj Faraḥ.[126] This is a medium-sized village, with small enclosures of fig trees and gardens of date palms and acacia trunks (*uṣūl*). It is less than half an hour's [ride] from Madīnat al-Fayyūm, to the west of Minyat Aqnā Canal. Its fiscal value is 15,000 army dinars. It has a congregational mosque in which the Friday prayers are held. It gets its water from a plastered canal with a weir on the southern side [of the Main Canal], in the land of the endowment of the Khānaqāh [al-Ṣalāḥiya, in Madīnat al-Fayyūm]. Its [water] quota is four *qabḍas*. Its people are the Banū ʿĀmir, a branch of the Banū Kilāb.

Its revenues in cash and in kind are, in specie, 18 dinars, all of which is permanent pasture tax; and in grains, for land tax on crops, including the addition, 1,648 ardabbs:

- wheat, 824 ardabbs;
- barley and broad beans, 824 ardabbs.

The alms-tax is 25 ½ ⅓ dinars:

- merchandise, ½ dinar;
- monetary value of livestock, for 24 heads, 25 ⅓ dinars:
  - cows, for a yearling calf, 2 dinars;
  - small cattle, for 23 heads, 23 ⅓ dinars:
    - sheep, for 21 heads, 22 ¼ dinars;
    - goats, for two heads, 1 2/24 dinar.

The fees, the measurement fee and the pasture tax are 416 dirhams, which are 10 ¼ ⅛ 2/72 dinars; and in grains, 92 ⅔ 1/48 ardabbs:

- wheat, 57 ⅛ 1/48 ardabbs;
- barley, 23 ¼ ⅙ ⅛ ardabbs;
- broad beans, 12 ardabbs.
- The fees are 206 dirhams, and in grains, 49 ⅔ ardabbs:
  - wheat, 26 ⅛ ardabbs;
  - barley, 11 ¼ ⅙ ⅛ ardabbs;
  - broad beans, 12 ardabbs.
- [The fees] in detail:
  - supervision of endowments, 5 dirhams;
  - dredging fee, 90 dirhams;
  - harvest fee, 53 dirhams;
  - protection fee, 15 dirhams;
  - threshing-floor fee, 43 dirhams; and in grains, 49 ⅔ ardabbs, as specified.
- The measurement fee, 40 1/48 ardabbs:
  - wheat, 28 1/48 ardabbs;
  - barley, 12 ardabbs.
- The tithe on the allowances (*ʿushr al-rizaq*), wheat, 3 ardabbs.

407 أ. س.: الكبيرة والصغيرة.

408 ط. م.: صنط.

409 ساقط من أ. س.: تفصيله.

126 Modern location: Abjīj (ابجيج). Halm, *Ägypten*, p. 248; Salmon, 'Répertoire', p. 64; Zéki, 'Une description', p. 44; Yāqūt, *Muʿjam al-Buldān*, I, 64: Ibjīj; de Sacy, *État des provinces*, p. 681: Babīj Faraj; Savigny, *Description de l'Égypte*, p. 129: Babjīj; Ibn Mammātī, *Kitāb qawānīn al-dawāwīn*, p. 119; Ibn al-Jīʿān, *Kitāb al-tuḥfa*, p. 153: Babīj Faraj; Ramzī, *Al-Qāmūs*, II/III, 94: Abjīj.

المراعي طارئ، عن خمسمائة وستة عشر راسا، مائتان وعشرة دراهم.[410] تفصيله:
قطيعة مئة درهم المئة راس، عن خمسة ارؤس، خمسة دراهم.
قطيعة سبعين درهما المائة، عن[411] ستة عشر راسا، احد عشر درهما وربع.
قطيعة خمسين درهما المائة، عن مائة واحد وخمسين راسا، خمسة وسبعون درهما ونصف.
قطيعة خمسة وعشرين درهما المائة راس، عن ثلاثمائة اربعة واربعين راسا، ستة وثمانون درهما.[412]
رسم المستخدمين، اثنان وثلاثون درهما وربع.

رسم خولي البحر بها، قمح، اردب واحد.

وعليها من الاتبان، الف وتسعمائة وخمسون شنيفا.

وعليها لديوان الاحباس، ديناران.

اهلها يزرعون من الاقصاب برسم معصرة المدينة باراضي منية كربيس وغيرها، خارجا عن الزائد لسنة اثنتين، ستة فدادين وربع:
راس، اربعة فدادين.
خلفة، فدانين وربع.

والذي يربى بها من الفروج، خمسمائة طائر. تفصيله:
للديوان المعمور بما فيه من اجرة التربية، وهو الثلث، ثلاثمائة فروج.
للمقطعين، مائتا طائر.

والمطلق بها من التقاوي برسم عمارتها، مائتان وثلاثة وسبعون اردبا وثلث. تفصيله:
قمح، مائة وخمسة عشر اردبا وسدس.
شعير، احد وثمانون اردبا وسدس.
فول، سبعة وسبعون اردبا.

والذي يسلف عليه بها من الشعير برسم الاصطبلات السلطانية، مائة اردب.

ومن حرف الباء، بوصير دفنو. هذه البلدة عبارة عن بلدة كبيرة، عامرة، تشتمل على حدائق نخل وجميزة واحدة صغيرة مجاورة لخليج دلية. بينها وبين مدينة الفيوم ساعة للراكب، قبلي مدينة الفيوم. عبرتها شركة مع دفنو في الاقطاع بما مبلغه عشرة الاف دينار. جارية في اقطاع علم الدين الجولاني. والمطلق لها من الماء عما خصها[413] بحق الثلث من شركة دفنو ودموشية، سبع قبض وربع وثمن قبضة وربع قيراط. وبها جامع تقام فيه الجمعة. اهلها بنو عامر، فخذ من بني كلاب.

ارتفاعها، عينا، عن اربعمائة وسبعة وسبعين درهما وثمن، احد عشر دينارا وثلثان وربع ودانق. تفصيله:
الحانوت، عشرة دراهم.
حفر[414] القزازين، تسعة عشر درهما.
خراج الاحكار، مائة وتسعة وتسعون درهما وربع.
المراعي، مائة وثمانية وتسعون درهما ونصف.
رسم الاجران، خمسون درهما وربع وثمن.

410 أ. س.: دنانير.
411 أ. س. يضيف: مائة احد وخمسين.
412 ساقط من أ. س.: درهما.
413 ساقط من أ. س.: عما خصها.
414 أ. س.: جفر.

Pasture tax on seasonal pasture lands, for 516 heads, 210 dirhams:
- at the rate of 100 dirhams per 100 heads, for five heads, 5 dirhams;
- at the rate of 70 dirhams per 100 [heads], for 16 heads, 11 ¼ dirhams;
- at the rate of 50 dirhams per 100 [heads], for 151 heads, 75 ½ dirhams;
- at the rate of 25 dirhams per 100 heads, for 344 heads, 86 dirhams;
- the government agents' fee, 32 ¼ dirhams.

The fee for the overseer of the canal, wheat, 1 ardabb.

Hay, 1,950 bales.

For the Ministry of Endowments, 2 dinars.

Its people sow sugarcane, assigned for the press in the city, in the lands of Minyat Karbīs and in other places. It amounts to 6 ¼ feddans, excluding the increment for the year [64]2:
- first harvest, 4 feddans;
- second harvest, 2 ¼ feddans.

The chickens reared in it, 500 birds:
- for the prosperous Dīwān, including the rearing wage of a third, 300 chickens;
- for the *iqṭāʿ*-holders, 200 birds.

The seed advances distributed in it, assigned for its cultivation, 273 ⅓ ardabbs:
- wheat, 115 ⅙ ardabbs;
- barley, 81 ⅙ ardabbs;
- broad beans, 77 ardabbs.

The barley assigned for the royal stables, which was paid for in advance, 100 ardabbs.

Also beginning with the letter 'bāʾ': Būṣīr Difidnū.[127] This is a large, populous village, with gardens of date palms, and a small single sycamore tree near Dilya Canal. It is one hour's ride south of Madīnat al-Fayyūm. The fiscal value of its *iqṭāʿ*, which is joint with Difidnū, is 10,000 [army] dinars. It is assigned as *iqṭāʿ* to ʿAlam al-Dīn al-Jawlānī.[128] The water allocated to it, which is a third of what it gets jointly with Difidnū and Dumūshiyya, is 7 ¼ ⅛ 1/96 *qabḍas*. It has a congregational mosque, in which the Friday prayers are held. Its people are the Banū ʿĀmir, a branch of the Banū Kilāb.

Its revenues in cash are 477 ⅛ dirhams, which are 11 ⅔ ¼ 1/144 dinars:
- the shop, 10 dirhams;
- pit looms of the weavers, 19 dirhams;
- land tax on land subject to long-term lease, 199 ¼ dirhams;
- pasture [tax], 198 ½ dirhams;
- threshing-floor fee, 50 ¼ ⅛ dirhams.

127 Modern location: Abū Šīr Difinnū (ابوصير دفنو). Halm, *Ägypten*, p. 244; Salmon, 'Répertoire', p. 65; Ibn al-Jīʿān, *Kitāb al-tuḥfa*, p. 151: Abūṣīr Difidnū; Savigny, *Description de l'Égypte*, p. 127: Abūṣīr Difidnūr; Ramzī, *Al-Qāmūs*, II/III, 81: Abū Ṣīr Difinnū.

128 An amir by the name of al-Jawlānī is mentioned as a commander of troops sent to Damietta by al-Ṣāliḥ in 647; al-Dhahabī, *Taʾrīkh*, ed. by Tadmurī, Ḥawādith wa-wafayāt 641–50 H, p. 45.

غلة، الف وثلاثمائة واحد وسبعون اردبا وثلث وربع. تفصيله:
قمح، تسعمائة واردب واحد وربع وثمن.
شعير وفول، اربعمائة وسبعون اردبا وخمسة[415] قراريط.

تفصيله:
الخراج والوفر والكيالة، الف وثلاثمائة وخمسة وثلاثون اردبا ونصف وثمن:
قمح، ثمانمائة وتسعون اردبا وربع وثمن.
شعير وفول، اربعمائة وخمسة واربعون اردبا وربع.
رسم الاجران، خمسة وثلاثون اردبا ونصف وثلث وثمن. تفصيله:[416]
قمح، احد عشر اردبا.
شعير، اربعة وعشرون اردبا ونصف وثلث وثمن.

وعليها من الرسوم والكيالة، خارجا عما هو جار في اقطاع المقطعين، عن مائة واربعة وثمانين درهما ونصف، اربعة دنانير وثلث وربع وحبتان؛ وغلة،[417] مائة وثمانية ارادب وقيراط. تفصيله:
قمح، تسعة وخمسون اردبا وثلثان وثمن.
شعير، عشرون اردبا وثلثان.
فول، ستة وعشرون اردبا وثلث وربع.
سمسم، اردب واحد.

تفصيله:
شد العين، ثلاثة دراهم.
شد الاحباس، ثمانية دراهم.
رسم الجراريف، خمسة واربعون درهما.
رسم الحصاد، ثلاثة وخمسون درهما.
رسم الخفارة، خمسة عشر درهما.
رسم المدقات، درهم واحد.
رسم الاجران، تسعة وخمسون درهما ونصف، وثمانية وستون اردبا وثلثان وربع ونصف ثمن:
قمح، ثلاثة وثلاثون اردبا.
شعير، اربعة عشر اردبا وثلثان.
وفول، عشرون اردبا وثلث وربع.
سمسم، ثلثان ونصف ثمن.
الكيالة، تسعة وثلاثون اردبا وقيراط ونصف:
قمح، ستة وعشرون اردبا وثلثان وثمن.
شعير، ستة ارادب.
فول، ستة ارادب.
سمسم، ربع ونصف[418] قيراط.

وعليها من الزكاة، عن ثمن الماشية، عن اربعة عشر راسا، اثنا عشر دينارا وثلثان:
بقر احمر، تبيع واحد، دينار واحد.
اغنام، ثلاثة عشر راسا، احد عشر دينارا وثلثان:
بياض، عن تسعة اروس، تسعة دنانير ونصف.
شعارى، عن اربعة اروس، ديناران وسدس.

And in grains, 1,371 ⅓ ¼ ardabbs:
wheat, 901 ¼ ⅛ ardabbs;
barley and broad beans, 470 5⁄24 ardabbs.

[The revenue in grains] in detail:
the land tax, the surcharge and the measurement fee: 1,335 ½ ⅛ ardabbs:
wheat, 890 ¼ ⅛ ardabbs;
barley and broad beans, 445 ¼ ardabbs;
The threshing-floor fee, 35 ½ ⅓ ⅛ ardabbs:
wheat, 11 ardabbs;
barley, 24 ½ ⅓ ⅛ ardabbs.[129]

The fees and the measurement fee — excluding that which [was mentioned above] as part of the *iqṭāʿ* of the *iqṭāʿ*-holders — 184 ½ dirhams, which are 4 ⅓ ¼ 2⁄72 dinars; and in grains, 108 1⁄24 ardabbs:
wheat, 59 ⅔ ⅛ ardabbs;
barley, 20 ⅔ ardabbs;
broad beans, 26 ⅓ ¼ ardabbs;
sesame, 1 ardabb.

[The fees] include:
supervision of the land survey, 3 dirhams;
supervision of endowments, 8 dirhams;
dredging fee, 45 dirhams;
harvest fee, 53 dirhams;
protection fee, 15 dirhams;
grinding fee (*midaqqāt*), 1 dirham;
threshing-floor fee, 59 ½ dirhams, and 68 ⅔ ¼ 1⁄16 ardabbs:
wheat, 33 ardabbs;
barley, 14 ⅔ ardabbs;
broad beans, 20 ⅓ ¼ ardabbs;
sesame ⅔ 1⁄16 [ardabb].
The measurement fee, 39 1⁄24 1⁄48 ardabbs:
wheat, 26 ⅔ ⅛ ardabbs;
barley, 6 ardabbs;
broad beans, 6 ardabbs;
sesame, ¼ 1⁄48 [ardabb].

The alms-tax, for the monetary value of 14 heads of livestock, 12 ⅔ dinars:
cows, a yearling calf, 1 dinar;
small cattle, thirteen heads, 11 ⅔ dinars:
sheep, for nine heads, 9 ½ dinars;
goats, for four heads, 2 ⅙ dinars.

415 أ. س.: وخمس.
416 ساقط من أ. س.: تفصيله.
417 ساقط من أ. س.: مائة وأربعة وثمانين درهما ونصف أربعة دنانير وثلث وربع وحبتان وغلة.
418 ساقط من أ. س.: نصف (لكنه يضيفه في الحاشية).

129 In this village, unusually, part of the fees are included in the fiscal revenue allocated to the *iqṭāʿ*-holders, while the rest are listed under the standard category of fees, below.

وعليها من الجوالي، عن عشرين نفرا، اربعون دينارا. تفصيله:
المقيمون بها، اربعة عشر نفرا، ثمانية وعشرون دينارا.
الناعون عنها، ستة نفر، اثنا عشر دينارا:
بالوجه البحري، اربعة نفر، ثمانية دنانير.
الوجه القبلي، نفران، اربعة دنانير.

وعليها من الاتبان الف واربعمائة شنيف.

وعليها لديوان الاحباس، من العين، اربعة دنانير.

رسم خولي البحر، قمح، اردب واحد.

والذي يربى بها من الفروج، ثلاثمائة وتسعون. تفصيله:
للديوان المعمور، بما فيه من اجرة التربية وهو الثلث، مائتان واربعون.
المقطعون، مائة وخمسون.

يزرع[419] من الاقصاب بدموشية، اربعة فدادين ونصف وربع وحبتان، خارجا عن الزيادة في سنة اثنتين.

والذي[420] يسلف بها من الشعير برسم الاصطبلات السلطانية، مائة واحد واربعون اردبا.

وعليها من الكشك والفريك، اردب واحد.

ومن حرف الباء، باجة. هذه البلدة عبارة عن بلدة صغيرة ذات بساتين واشجار وسواقي تدور الليل والنهار. تشرب ايام النيل بالسيح. ولها مسقاة نيلي، تعرف باقنى، بينها وبين منية الاسقف. وبعد نزول النيل على اعناق الابقار. وليس لها زرع فيذكر الا يسير قصب وخضر على السواقي. اكثر اهلها نصارى. عبرتها جيشية مجموعة مع غابتها المعروفة بمنشاة الحاتميين بما مبلغه ستة الاف دينار.

ارتفاعها، عينا، مائتان واثنان وتسعون دينارا وربع وسدس ونصف ثمن وحبة. تفصيل ذلك:
حفر[421] القزازين، تسعة دنانير.
خراج المفادنات، عن مائتين واحد وعشرين فدانا وربع وسدس وثمن وحبتين، مائتان واحد وخمسون دينارا وثلثان وربع ونصف ثمن وحبة. تفصيله:
خراج الراتب، احد وثلاثون دينارا وخمسة قراريط وحبة. تفصيله:
الاصل، عن ثلاثة عشر فدانا وثلثين وثمن وحبتين، سبعة وعشرون دينارا ونصف وثمن وحبة.
الاضافة، ثلاثة دنانير وثلث وربع.
خراج الاحكار، مائتان وعشرون دينارا ونصف وربع ونصف قيراط. تفصيله:
الاصل، عن مائتين وسبعة فدادين ونصف وربع، مائتان وسبعة[422] دنانير ونصف وربع.
الاضافة، ثلاثة عشر دينارا ونصف قيراط.
نفط النخل، سبعة دنانير ونصف.
مساقاة البستان المعروف بمعز الدين، اربعة دنانير.
خراج القصب، قطيعة دينارين الفدان، عن عشرة فدادين، عشرون دينارا.

خفرها لبنى عامر، فخذ من بني كلاب.

بها ثلاث كنائس، احدها[423] متهدمة.

419 أ. س.: تزرع.
420 ساقط من ط. م.: والذي.
421 أ. س.: جفر.
422 أ. س.: عشرين.
423 أ. س.: أحدهم.

The poll-tax, for twenty individuals, 40 dinars:
those residing in it, fourteen individuals, 28 dinars;
those absent from it, six individuals, 12 dinars:
the northern region, four individuals, 8 dinars;
the southern region, two individuals, 4 dinars.

Hay, 1,400 bales.

For the Ministry of Endowments, in specie, 4 dinars.

The fee of the overseer of the canal, wheat, 1 ardabb.

The chickens reared in it, 390:
for the prosperous Dīwān, including the rearing wage of a third, 240;
for the *iqṭāʿ*-holders, 150.

Sugarcane sown in Dumūshiyya: 4½ ¼ 2/72 feddans. This excludes the increment for the year [64]2.

The barley assigned for the royal stables, which was paid for in advance, 141 ardabbs.

In addition, *kishk* and *farīk* dishes, one ardabb.

Also beginning with the letter 'bā'': Bāja.[130] This is a small village with orchards, trees and waterwheels that turn day and night. During the days of the Nile's inundation, it is watered by its flow. It has an irrigation ditch of Nile water (*misqāh nīlī*), known as Aqnā, between it and Minyat al-Usquf. After the Nile recedes, [it gets its water] on cattle's necks. It has no field crops worthy of note, except for some sugarcane and green vegetables [irrigated] by waterwheels. The majority of its people are Christians. Its fiscal value, combined with that of its hamlet known as Ghāba (Ghābat Bāja), also known as the hamlet of al-Ḥātimiyyīn, is 6,000 army dinars.

Its revenues in specie are 292 ¼ ⅙ 1/16 1/72 dinars:
pit looms of the weavers, 9 dinars;
land tax assessed by feddans, for 221 ¼ ⅙ ⅛ 2/72 feddans, 251 ⅓ ¼ 1/16 1/72 dinars:
land tax on perennial plants, 31 5/24 1/72 dinars:
the basic assessment, for 13 ⅔ ⅛ 2/72 feddans, 27 ½ ⅛ 1/72 dinars;
the addition, 3 ⅓ ¼ dinars.
land tax on lands subject to long-term lease, 220 ½ ¼ 1/48 dinars:
the basic assessment, for 207 ½ ¼ feddans, 207 ½ ¼ dinars;
the addition, 13 1/48 dinars.
Date palm oil (*nafṭ*), 7 ½ dinars.
The share-cropping (*musāqāh*) of the orchard known as Muʿizz al-Dīn, 4 dinars.
Land tax on sugarcane at the rate of 2 dinars per feddan, for 10 feddans, 20 dinars.

Its protection is in the hands of the Banū ʿĀmir, a branch of the Banū Kilāb. It has three churches, one of them is deserted.

130 Modern location (uncertain): Munshảat Abū Khalaf (منشاة ابو خلف). Halm, *Ägypten*, p. 249; Salmon, 'Répertoire', p. 41; de Sacy, *État des provinces*, p. 681; Ramzī, *Al-Qāmūs*, I, 139: Jabāna/Maqām al-Sheikh Khalaf, near Madīnat al-Fayyūm. We identified it with Munshảat Abū Khalaf.

عليها من المراعي الطارئ، عن اربعة ارؤس اربعة دراهم.

عليها من الزكاة، عن خرص النخل، ثمانية دنانير ونصف.

وعليها من الجوالي، عن مائة ونفرين، مائتان واربعة دنانير. تفصيله:
المقيمون بها، عن تسعين نفرا، مائة وثمانون دينارا.
الناءون عنها بالوجه البحري، عن اثنى عشر نفرا، اربعة وعشرون دينارا.

والمربى بها من الفروج للديوان المعمور، بما فيه من اجرة التربية وهو الثلث، ثلاثمائة وعشرون طائرا.

بركة ابن[424] شكلة. بها نخل كثير وسدر وياسمين ونرجس واشجار متنوعة. جارية في اقطاع المقطعين. شربها من خليج ترسا وخليج سنورس بالسواقي والراحة بظاهر المدينة، شرقيها. ارتفاعها عينا اثنان وسبعون دينارا.

ومن حرف الباء،[425] بلالة. هذه البلدة عبارة عن بلدة صغيرة. بينها وبين مدينة الفيوم مسافة ساعة للراكب. تشتمل على بيوت يسيرة ونخل ويزرع[426] بها الاقصاب. ولها مناشئ عدة تذكر في حرف الميم. ولها زرع شتوي. كفورها ومناشئها اربعة مناشئ:
منشاة المطوع، معروفة بابي علاق.
منشاة اولاد ابي زكري.
منشاة عثمان.
منشاة اولاد[427] زيدان المعروفة بالاكراد.

داخلة في اقطاع خليج دلية. لها من الماء من جملة بحر دلية، عشر قبض وربع وسدس وثمن. اهلها بنو غصين فخذ من بني كلاب.

بها معصرة قصب ذات حجر واحد. والمزدرع لها[428] من القصب السكر اربعون فدانا. تفصيله:
بمنشاة الصفاونة، عشرون فدانا.
باراضي الناحية المقدم ذكرها، عشرون فدانا.

ارتفاعها، عينا، سبعة عشر دينارا وسدس وثمن وحبة، وغلة الف ومائتان وثلاثون اردبا. تفصيله:
قمح، سبعمائة وثمانية وثلاثون اردبا.
شعير وفول، اربعمائة[429] واثنان وتسعون اردبا.

وعليها من الرسوم والكيالة والمراعي، عن مائتين واربعة[430] وتسعين درهما وربع، سبعة دنانير وثلث وحبتان؛ وغلة، سبعون اردبا. تفصيله:
قمح، ستة وثلاثون اردبا.
شعير، ثلاثة وعشرون اردبا وربع وسدس وثمن.
فول، عشرة ارادب وثلث وثمن.

تفصيله:
الرسوم، مائة وخمسة وسبعون درهما ونصف، وغلة، ستة واربعون اردبا. تفصيله:
قمح، اثنان وعشرون اردبا.
شعير، ثلاثة عشر اردبا وربع وسدس وثمن.
فول، عشرة ارادب وثلث وثمن.

The pasture tax for four heads, on seasonal pasture lands, 4 dirhams.

The alms-tax, for the estimate of dates, 8 ½ dinars.

The poll-tax, for 102 individuals, 204 dinars:
for those residing in it, for 90 individuals, 180 dinars;
for those absent from it in the northern region, for 12 individuals, 24 dinars.

The chickens reared in it for the prosperous Dīwān, including the rearing wage of a third, 320 birds.

[Also beginning with the letter 'bā'']: Birkat ibn[131] Shikla.[132] It has many date palms and sidr trees, jasmine, narcissus and various trees. It is assigned as an *iqṭāʿ* to *iqṭāʿ*-holders. It gets its water from the canals of Tirsā and Sinnūris by waterwheels and basin irrigation (*wa'l-rāḥa*). It is at the outskirts of the city, to its east. Its revenues, in specie, are 72 dinars.

Also beginning with the letter 'bā'': Bilāla.[133] This is a small village, one hour's ride from Madīnat al-Fayyūm. It has a few houses and date palms, and sugarcane is sown in it. It also has several hamlets, which will be mentioned under the letter 'mīm'. It has winter cultivation. Its hamlets are four: Munshaʾat al-Muṭawwiʿ, known as Abū ʿAllāq; Munshaʾat Awlād Abī Zikrī; Munshaʾat ʿUthmān; Munshaʾat Awlād Zaydān, known as al-Akrad [lit, the Kurds].

It is included in the *iqṭāʿ* of Dilya Canal, and gets its water — 10 ¼ ⅙ ⅛ *qabḍas* — from the total of Dilya Canal. Its people are the Banū Ghuṣayn, a branch of the Banū Kilāb.

It has a sugar press with one stone. There are 40 feddans of sugarcane assigned for it:
in Munshaʾat al-Ṣafāwina, 20 feddans;
in the lands of the village [i.e., Bilāla], 20 feddans.

Its revenue in specie, 17 ⅙ ⅛ 1/72 dinars; and in grains, 1,230 ardabbs:
wheat, 738 ardabbs;
barley and broad beans, 492 ardabbs.

The fees, the measurement fee and the pasture tax, 294 ¼ dirhams, which are 7 ⅓ 2/72 dinars; and in grains, 70 ardabbs:
wheat, 36 ardabbs;
barley, 23 ¼ ⅙ ⅛ ardabbs;
broad beans, 10 ⅓ ⅛ ardabbs.

[The fees, the measurement fee and the pasture tax] in detail:
the fees, 175 ½ dirhams; and in grains, 46 ardabbs:
wheat, 22 ardabbs;
barley, 13 ¼ ⅙ ⅛ ardabbs.
broad beans, 10 ⅓ ⅛ ardabbs.

424 ساقط من أ. س.: ابن.
425 أ. س.: الألف.
426 أ. س.: تزرع.
427 أ. س. يضيف: أبي زكري منشاة عثمان منشاة أولاد.
428 أ. س.: بها.
429 أ. س. يضيف: أردب.
430 أ. س.: مائة واثنان.

131 AS: 'Birkat Shikla'.

132 Modern location (uncertain): at the north-eastern outskirts of the city, following Salmon, 'Répertoire', p. 50, but no references in other sources.

133 Modern location: Kafr al-Zaʿfrānī (كفر الزعفراني). Halm, *Ägypten*, p. 251; Salmon, 'Répertoire', p. 66; Ibn al-Jīʿān, *Kitāb al-tuḥfa*, p. 153; de Sacy, *État des provinces*, p. 68; Ramzī, *Al-Qāmūs*, II/III, 86: Kafr al-Zaʿfrānī.

تفصيله:

شد الاحباس، ثمانية دراهم.

شد العين، ثمانية عشر درهما.

رسم الجراريف، احد واربعون درهما ونصف.

رسم الحصاد، ثلاثة وخمسون درهما.

رسم الخفارة خمسة عشر درهما.

رسم الاجران، اربعون درهما، وغلة، ستة واربعون اردبا، على ما تقدم ذكره وتفصيله باصنافه في جملة[431] الرسوم.

الكيالة، اربعة وعشرون اردبا:

قمح، اربعة عشر اردبا.

شعير، عشرة ارادب.

المراعي، عن مائتين واربعة وثمانين راسا طارئ ورسومها[432] مائة وثمانية عشر درهما ونصف وربع. تفصيله:

قطيعة مائة درهم المائة راس، عن احد واربعون راسا، احد واربعون درهما.

قطيعة خمسة وعشرين درهما، عن مائتين وثلاثة واربعين راسا، ستون درهما.

رسم المستخدمين، حسابا عن كل مائة راس ستة دراهم وربع، سبعة عشر درهما ونصف وربع.

وعليها من الزكاة سبعة دنانير وثلث وربع. تفصيله:

بلالة، عن ثمن الاغنام، عن خمسة اروس، ثلاثة دنانير وثلث وربع. تفصيله:

بياض، عن راسين، ديناران.

شعارى، عن ثلاثة اروس، دينار وثلث وربع.

منشاة المطوع، اربعة دنانير:

خرص النخل، دينار واحد ونصف.[433]

اغنام، ديناران ونصف. تفصيله:

بياض، عن راسين ديناران.

شعارى، عن راسين، نصف دينار.

عليها من الاتبان، الف ومائتا شنيف.

رسم خولي البحر، اردب واحد وثلثان، قمح وشعير نصفان، وعسل مطران.

وعليها لديوان الاحباس، ثلاثة دنانير ونصف.

اهلها يربون من الفروج ثمانمائة. تفصيله:

للديوان المعمور[434] السلطاني، بما فيه من اجرة التربية، وهو الثلث، خمسمائة فروج.

للمقطعين، ثلاثمائة.

والمسلف بها من الشعير برسم الاصطبلات السلطانية، ستون اردبا.

والذي بها من التقاوي، على ما تضمنه حساب مستخدمي الامير جمال الدين بن الهمام عن ثلثي الناحية، ثمانية وتسعون اردبا ونصف وربع:

قمح، ثلاثة وخمسون اردبا ونصف.

شعير، سبعة وعشرون اردبا ونصف.

فول، سبعة عشر اردبا ونصف.

431 أ. س.: جملته.

432 أ. س.: ورسومهم.

433 أ. س.: وثمن.

434 ساقط من ط. م.: المعمور.

[The fees] include:

supervision of endowments, 8 dirhams;

supervision of the land survey 18 dirhams;

dredging fee, 41 ½ dirhams;

harvest fee, 53 dirhams;

protection fee, 15 dirhams;

threshing-floor fee, 40 dirhams; and in grains, 46 ardabbs, as mentioned and specified above, according to its various categories, in the aggregate of the fees.

The measurement fee, 24 ardabbs:

wheat, 14 ardabbs;

barley, 10 ardabbs.

The pasture tax, for 284 heads of seasonal pasture lands, 118 ½ ¼ dirhams:

at the rate of 100 dirhams per 100 heads, for 41 heads, 41 dirhams;

at the rate of 25 dirhams [per 100 heads], for 243 heads, 60 dirhams.

the government agents' fee, calculated as 6¼ dirhams for every 100 heads, 17 ½ ¼ dirhams.

The alms-tax, 7 ⅓ ¼ dinars:

Bilāla, for the monetary value of small cattle, for five heads, 3 ⅓ ¼ dinars:

sheep, for two heads, 2 dinars;

goats, for three heads, 1 ⅓ ¼ dinar;

Munshaʾat al-Muṭawwiʿ, 4 dinars:

estimate of dates, 1 ½ dinar;

monetary value of small cattle, 2 ½ dinars:

sheep, for two heads, 2 dinars;

goats, for two heads, ½ dinar.

Hay, 1,200 bales.

The fee of the overseer of the canal, 1 ⅔ ardabb of wheat and barley, half in each category; and two maṭars of molasses.

For the Ministry of Endowments, 3 ½ dinars.

Its people rear 800 chickens:

for the prosperous Dīwān, including the rearing wage of a third, 500 chickens;

for the *iqṭāʿ*-holders, 300.

The barley assigned for the royal stables, which was paid for in advance, 60 ardabbs.

The seed advances [distributed] in it, according to the accounts of the agents of the amir Jamāl al-Dīn ibn al-Humām, for the two-thirds of the village [that belong to his *iqṭāʿ*], 98 ½ ¼ ardabbs:

wheat, 53 ½ ardabbs;

barley, 27 ½ ¼ ardabbs;

broad beans, 17½ ardabbs.

ومن حرف الباء، بشطا. هذه البلدة عبارة عن بلدة كانت كبيرة عامرة، فلما تعدى اهلها وقووا بجمعهم على المقطع، نقصهم حقها من الماء وصرفه الى غيرها من البلاد المطيع اهلها. فبقيت الان صغيرة فيها يسير من المزارعين وارضها متسعة تبور كل سنة لتحريك[435] الماء عنها الى غيرها. بينها وبين مدينة الفيوم مسافة ساعتين للراكب. ليس بها نخل ولا شجر ولا بساتين سوى اصل جميز.

وهي من نواحي خليج دلية مجموعا في عبرة الاقطاع بنواحي الخليج المذكور وهو[436] بما فيه من الزائد وهو[437] خمسة وثمانون دينارا وربع وسدس وثمن، سبعة وعشرون الفا وستمائة وخمسة وعشرون دينارا[438] جيشية. لها من الماء من بحر خليج دلية من المقسم المعروف بالقلنبو، اربع قبض وثلث ماء. وبها جامع تقام فيه الجمعة. اهلها من بنو غصين، فخذ من بنى كلاب.

ارتفاعها، شعير، مائة وستون[439] اردبا، خارجا عما يخص الامير جمال الدين بن الهمام[440] بها من الارتفاع[441] الذي نقله الى اقلول.

عليها لمقطعي العشر المعروف بابن المهراني، شعير خمسة ارادب.

عليها من الرسوم والكيالة والمراعي، عن[442] مائة وتسعة وخمسين درهما ونصف وربع، ثلاثة دنانير ونصف وثلث وثمن وحبتان؛ وشعير، تسعة ارادب وثمن. تفصيله:

الرسوم، مائة وثلاثة وثلاثون درهما وربع، وشعير تسعة ارادب وثمن. تفصيله:

شد العين، عشرة دراهم.

رسم الجراريف، احد وخمسون درهما ونصف.

رسم الحصاد، ثلاثة وخمسون درهما.

رسم الخفارة، خمسة عشر درهما.

رسم الاجران، ثلاثة دراهم ونصف وربع، وشعير اربعة ارادب وثمن.

الكيالة، خمسة ارادب.

المراعي، عن خمسة وثمانين راسا، ستة وعشرون درهما ونصف. تفصيله:

قطيعة خمسة وعشرين درهما المائة، عن خمسة وثمانين راسا، احد وعشرون درهما وربع.

رسم المستخدمين، خمسة دراهم وربع.

وعليها من[443] الزكاة، عن ثمن اغنام، عن ثلاثة اروس، ديناران وقيراط. تفصيله:

بياض، عن راس واحد، دينار واحد.

شعارى، عن راسين، دينار وقيراط.

عليها من الاتبان، خمسمائة شنيف.

وعليها لديوان الاحباس، خمسة دنانير.

اهلها يربون من الفروج مائة وستين فروجا:

للديوان المعمور، بما فيه من اجرة التربية، ستون طائرا.

وللمقطعين مائة طائر.

Also beginning with the letter 'bā'': Bushṭā.[134] This village was formerly large and populous. However, when its people became impudent (*taʿaddā*), and in their numbers prevailed over the *iqṭāʿ*-holder, he reduced their water quota and transferred it to other villages, whose people are obedient. So now it has become a small village, with few tenants, and spacious land that lies fallow every year, because of the reallocation of the water to other villages. It is two hours' ride from Madīnat al-Fayyūm. It has no date palms, trees and orchards, except for acacia tree trunks.

It is one of the villages of Dilya Canal, and it is included in the fiscal value of the *iqṭāʿ* of the villages of the canal, which is — including the increment (*al-zāʾid*) of 85 ¼ ⅙ ⅛ dinars — 27,625 army dinars. It gets water from Dilya Canal, from the divisor known as al-Qalanbū, 4 ⅓ *qabḍas* of water. It has a mosque in which the Friday prayers are held. Its people are the Banū Ghuṣayn, a branch of the Banū Kilāb.

Its revenue in barley is 160 ardabbs. This excludes the revenue assigned to the amir Jamāl al-Dīn ibn al-Humām, which he transferred to Uqlūl.

For the *iqṭāʿ*-holders of the tithe known as Ibn al-Mihrānī, 5 ardabbs of barley.

The fees, the measurement fee and the pasture tax are 159 ½ ¼ dirhams, which are 3 ½ ⅓ ⅛ 2/72 dinars; and barley, 9 ⅛ ardabbs.

[The fees, the measurement fee and the pasture tax] in detail:

The fees, 133 ¼ dirhams; and barley, 9 ⅛ ardabbs. In detail:

supervision of the land survey, 10 dirhams;

dredging fee, 51 ½ dirhams;

harvest fee, 53 dirhams;

protection fee, 15 dirhams;

threshing-floor fee, 3 ½ ¼ dirhams; and barley, 4 ⅛ ardabbs.

The measurement fee, 5 ardabbs.

The pasture tax, for 85 heads, 26 ½ dirhams:

at the rate of 25 dirhams per 100 [heads], for 85 heads, 21 ¼ dirhams;

the government agents' fee, 5 ¼ dirhams.

The alms-tax, for the monetary value of three heads of small cattle, 2 1/24 dinars:

sheep, for one head, 1 dinar;

goats, for two heads, 1 1/24 dinar.

Hay, 500 bales.

For the Ministry of Endowments, 5 dinars.

Its people rear 160 chickens:

for the prosperous Dīwān, including the rearing wage, 60 birds;

and for the *iqṭāʿ*-holders, 100 birds.

435 أ. س.: لتحويل.

436 أ. س.: وهي.

437 أ. س.: وهي.

438 ساقط من ط. م.: دينارا.

439 أ. س.: وستة.

440 ساقط من أ. س.: بن الهمام.

441 أ. س.: الإقطاع.

442 ساقط من أ. س.: عن.

443 ساقط من أ. س.: من.

134 Modern location (uncertain): near al-Ghāba (الغابة). Halm, *Ägypten*, p. 252; Ibn al-Jīʿān, *Kitāb al-tuḥfa*, p. 153: Busṭā; Salmon, 'Répertoire', p. 67: Bouchtā; Zéki, 'Une description', p. 37; de Sacy, *État des provinces*, p. 681: Busṭā wa-Umm al-Sibāʿ; Ramzī, *Al-Qāmūs*, I, 159: ʿIzbat Muḥammad Efendī Ṣabrī near al-Ghāba. We could not locate this ʿIzba, and we therefore have no positive identification of this village. We located it north of the modern village of al-Ghāba, a location which is also in accord with Shafei Bey's map.

ومن حرف الباء، بيهمو. هذه البلدة عبارة عن بلدة متوسطة، بين الكبر والصغر.[444] تشتمل على بساتين وكروم ودويرات تين وحدائق نخل وزيتون. بينها وبين مدينة الفيوم مسافة ساعة للراكب. يزرع فيها[445] الاقصاب المنسوبة الى سنورس.

بها صنمان من احجار كبار قديمة رومية، وجه احدهما الى ناحية الغرب ووجه الثاني مما يلي القبلة الى جهة الرمل. وهما في الارض الابليز عليها خطوط قدماء من[446] جنس الاهرام والبرابي. انهى بعض الناس اشتمالهما[447] على كنوز فهدم من اعاليهما[448] احجار ولم يظهر فيهما[449] شيء. ونكر ان تحتهما[450] حفر متسع ينكر من دخل هذا الحفر انه[451] راه متسعا وهذا الحفر بازائهما من القبلة. ياتيها اهل البلاد اذا اصابهم مرض ويستعملون ماءها استشفاء به كما يستعملون مياه طبرية. ويلقى فيها العوام الخروب والمرسين والدراهم وربما اوقدوها[452] على الدوام بالزيت والشمع.

وهي جارية في اقطاع الاجل نور الدين ابن صاحب حمص، والامير صمصام الدين محمد بن داود[453] والامير ناصر الدين وبدر الدين اخوة الشجاع بيرم، والامير فتح الدين بن ناصر الدين، ومماليك ابى شعرة وغيرهم. عبرتها جيشية ثلاثة الاف دينار. تشرب من بحر سنورس بخليج ينقسم ويتفرع من الشذروان عبرته عشر قبض ماء تسقى[454] الشتوي والصيفي والبساتين. اهلها قياصرة، يرجعون لبني جابر فخذ من بني عجلان. بها جامع تقام فيه الجمعة.

ارتفاعها، عينا، ثلاثمائة واحد وستون دينارا وثلثان؛ وغلة، تسعمائة اردب:

قمح، ستمائة اردب.[455]

شعير وفول، ثلاثمائة اردب.

تفصيله:

خراج الراتب واجرة الحانوت بما فيه من الموقوف عن الداثر، وهو ثلاثة وثلاثون دينارا، ثلاثمائة واثنان وعشرون دينارا.

خراج الخضراوات، تسعة وثلاثون دينارا وثلثان.

خراج المناجزة، تسعمائة اردب، على ما فصل.

عليها من الرسوم والكيالة والمراعي، عن خمسمائة وستة عشر درهما ونصف وربع، اثنا عشر دينارا وثلثان وربع؛ وغلة، تسعون اردبا وثلث ونصف ثمن. تفصيله:

قمح، تسعة وعشرون اردبا وقيراطان.

شعير، اردب واحد وربع وسدس وثمن.

فول، تسعة ارادب ونصف وربع قيراط.

Also beginning with the letter 'bā'': Biyahmū.[135] This is medium-sized village, one hour's ride from Madīnat al-Fayyūm. It has orchards and vineyards, enclosures of fig trees and gardens of date palms and olives. Sugarcane is sown in it, and it is assigned to [the press in] Sinnūris.

In this village there are two idols, made of large ancient, Byzantine (*rūmiyya*) stones. One of them faces the western direction, and the other the southern direction, towards the sandy area. They stand on alluvial land, and are covered with ancient writings, of the kind found on the pyramids and ancient temple ruins. It has been reported by some people that they contain treasures. Stones were removed from their tops, but nothing was found in them. It has also been said that an expansive crevice lies beneath both, and those who entered this crevice confirm it to be so. This crevice lies across from the two idols, to the south. The people of the region come to it if they fall sick, and they use its water for healing, in the same way the water of (Lake) Tiberias is used. The commoners throw carob, myrtle and dirhams in it. Sometimes they light it up continuously with oil lanterns and candles.

It is assigned as *iqṭā*ʿ to the honoured Nūr al-Dīn, son of the ruler of Homs;[136] and to the amir Ṣamṣām al-Dīn Muḥammed ibn Dāwūd;[137] and to the amirs Nāṣir al-Dīn and Badr al-Dīn, brothers of Shujāʿ [al-Dīn] Bayram; and to the amir Fatḥ al-Dīn ibn Nāṣir al-Dīn; and to the *mamlūk*s of Abū Shaʿra, and others. Its fiscal value is 3,000 army dinars. It gets its water from Sinnūris Canal by a channel that branches off from the [divisor called] al-Shādhrawān. Its quota, ten *qabḍa*s of water, is used for irrigating winter and summer cultivation, as well as orchards. Its people are Qayāṣira, a sub-section of the Banū Jābir, a branch of the Banū ʿAjlān. It has a mosque in which the Friday prayers are held.

Its revenue in specie is 361 ⅔ dinars; and in grains, 900 ardabbs:

wheat, 600 ardabbs;

barley and broad beans, 300 ardabbs.

[the revenue] in detail:

land tax on perennial plants and rent of the shop — including the withheld payments relating to derelict property, which amount to 33 dinars — 322 dinars;

land tax on green vegetables, 39 ⅔ dinars;

Munājaza land tax, 900 ardabbs, as specified.

The fees, the measurement fee and the pasture tax are 516 ½ ¼ dirhams, which are 12 ⅔ ¼ dinars; and in grains, 90 ⅓ 1/16 ardabbs:

wheat, 29 2/24 ardabbs;

barley, 1 ¼ ⅙ ⅛ ardabb;

broad beans, 9 ½ ¼ 1/96 ardabbs.

444 أ. س.: الكبيرة والصغيرة.
445 أ. س.: بها من.
446 أ. س.: في.
447 أ. س.: اشتمالها.
448 أ. س.: أعاليها.
449 أ. س.: فيها.
450 أ. س.: تحتها.
451 أ. س.: من.
452 أ. س.: وقدوها.
453 أ. س.: داوود.
454 أ. س.: يسقى.
455 ساقط من ط. م.: أردب.

135 Modern location: Biyahmū (بيهمو). Timm, *Das Christlich-Koptische Ägypten*, pp. 415–16: Biyahmū; Trismegistos GEO ID 3442: Bihamu; Halm, *Ägypten*, p. 250; Salmon, 'Répertoire', pp. 49–50; Ibn al-Jīʿān, *Kitāb al-tuḥfa*, p. 153; Zéki, 'Une description', pp. 37, 42; de Sacy, *État des provinces*, p. 682; Savigny, *Description de l'Égypte*, p. 129: Byhmou; Richard A. Pococke, *A Description of the East, and Some Other Countries*, 2 vols (London: Bowyer, 1745), I, 57: Baiamout; Ramzī, *Al-Qāmūs*, II/III, 111: Biyahmū.

136 The ruler of Homs at the time was the the Ayyubid prince al-Manṣūr Ibrāhīm, who had succeeded his father al-Mujāhid ibn Shirkūh in 637/1240; Humphreys, *From Saladin to the Mongols*, p. 263. The authority of the Egyptian Sultan al-Ṣāliḥ over Homs was recognized only in 641/1243 (p. 272).

137 Possibly al-Khāzindār al-ʿĀdilī, who was governor of Mecca in 1223. See Abū al-Maḥāsin Yūsuf Ibn Taghrībirdī, *Al-Nujūm al-zāhira fi mulūk Miṣr wa'al-Qāhira* (Cairo: al-Muʾasasa al-Miṣriyya al-ʿĀmma li'l-Taʾlīf wa'l-Ṭibāʿa wa'l-Nashr, 1963–71), VII, 252; Halm, *Ägypten*, p. 250.

تفصيله:

الرسوم، مائتان وستة وعشرون درهما وربع، وغلة، خمسة وعشرون اردبا وثمن ونصف قيراط. تفصيله:

قمح، اربعة عشر اردبا وقيراطان.

شعير، اردب واحد وربع وسدس وثمن.

فول، تسعة ارادب ونصف ونصف قيراط.

تفصيله:

شد الاحباس، خمسة دراهم.

رسم الجراريف، احد وخمسون درهما ونصف.

رسم الحصاد ثلاثة وخمسون درهما.

رسم الخفارة، خمسة عشر درهما.

رسم القلقاس، ثمانون درهما.

رسم الاجران، احد وعشرون درهما ونصف وربع، وغلة، خمسة وعشرون اردبا وثمن ونصف قيراط على ما فصل.

الكيالة، خمسة عشر اردبا وربع. تفصيله:

قمح، خمسة عشر اردبا.

فول، ربع اردب.

المراعي، عن ثلاثمائة وثلاثة وعشرون راسا ورسومها، مائتان وتسعون درهما ونصف. تفصيله:

راتب، قطيعة درهمين وربع الراس، عن ثمانية وخمسين راسا، مائة وثلاثون درهما ونصف.

طارئ، عن مائتين وخمسة وستين راسا، مائة وتسعة وثلاثون درهما ونصف وربع وثمن. تفصيله:

قطيعة درهم الراس، عن ثمانية وعشرين راسا، ثمانية وعشرون درهما.

قطيعة سبعين درهما المائة راس، عن مائة[456] وراسين، احد وسبعون درهما وربع وثمن.

قطيعة ثلاثين درهما المائة، عن مائة وخمسة وثلاثين راسا، اربعون درهما ونصف.

رسم المستخدمين، عشرون درهما وثمن.

وعليها من الزكاة، تسعة وعشرون دينارا وثلث وربع وثمن ودانق. تفصيله:

الخرص، اربعة وعشرون دينارا وثلثان وربع ونصف قيراط. تفصيله:

خرص العنب، ثمانية دنانير وثلثان ونصف قيراط.

خرص النخل، دينار ونصف.

خرص الزيتون، ثلاثة عشر دينارا ونصف وربع.

ثمن الماشية، عن خمسة اروس، اربعة دنانير ونصف وربع وحبتان. تفصيله:

بقر احمر، تبيع واحد، دينار ونصف وثمن وحبتان.[457]

ثمن الاغنام، عن اربعة اروس، ثلاثة دنانير وثمن. تفصيله:

بياض، عن راسين، ديناران وقيراطان.

شعارى، عن راسين، دينار واحد وقيراط.

وعليها من الجوالي، عن عشرة نفر، عشرون دينارا. من ذلك ما هو محسوب عن طرادين الوحش، عن اربعة نفر ديناران. تفصيله:

المقيمون بها، عن سبعة نفر، اربعة عشر دينارا.

الناءون عنها بالوجه البحري، ثلاثة نفر، ستة دنانير.

وعليها من الاتبان، الف وستمائة شنيف.

456 أ. س.: مائتين.

457 ساقط من أ. س.: بقر أحمر تبيع واحد دينار ونصف وثمن وحبتان.

[The fees, the measurement fee and the pasture tax] in detail:

The fees are 226 ¼ dirhams; and in grains, 25 ⅛ 1/48 ardabbs:

wheat, 14 2/24 ardabbs;

barley, 1 ¼ ⅙ ⅛ ardabb;

broad beans, 9½ 1/48 ardabbs.

[The fees] include:

supervision of endowments, 5 dirhams;

dredging fee, 51 ½ dirhams;

harvest fee, 53 dirhams;

protection fee, 15 dirhams,

colocasia fee, 80 dirhams,

threshing-floor fee, 21½¼ dirhams, and in grains, 25 ⅛ 1/48 ardabbs, as specified.

The measurement fee is 15 ¼ ardabbs:

wheat, 15 ardabbs;

broad beans, ¼ ardabb.

The pasture tax, for 323 heads, fees of 290 ½ dirhams:

permanent pasture lands, at the rate of 2 ¼ dirhams per head, for 58 heads, 130 ½ dirhams;

seasonal pasture lands, for 265 heads, 139 ½ ¼ ⅛ dirhams:

at the rate of one dirham per head, for 28 heads, 28 dirhams;

at the rate of 70 dirhams per 100 heads, for 102 heads, 71 ¼ ⅛ dirhams;

at the rate of 30 dirhams per 100 [heads], for 135 heads, 40 ½ dirhams;

the government agents' fee, 20 ⅛ dirhams.

The alms-tax, 29 ⅓ ¼ ⅛ 1/144 dinars:

the estimate, 24 ⅔ ¼ 1/48 dinars:

estimate of grapes, 8 ⅔ 1/48 dinars;

estimate of dates, 1 ½ dinar;

estimate of olives, 13 ¼ dinar.

Monetary value of livestock, for five heads, 4 dinars ½ ¼ 2/72:

cows, a two-year-old cow: 1 dinar ½ ⅛ 2/72;

monetary value of small cattle, for four heads, 3 ⅛ dinars:

sheep, for two heads, 2 dinars 2/24;

goats, for two heads, 1 dinar 1/24.

The poll-tax, for 10 individuals, 20 dinars. From this sum, one should deduct payments for 'beast-chasers' (*ṭarrādūn al-waḥsh*), which are 2 dinars for four individuals.

[The poll-tax] in detail:

those residing in it, for seven individuals, 14 dinars;

those absent from it, in the northern region, for three individuals, 6 dinars.

Hay, 1,600 bales.

عليها لديوان الاحباس، ديناران ونصف.

اهلها يزرعون من[458] اقصاب السكر برسم[459] المعاصر بسنورس، خارجا عن الزيادة في سنة اثنتين واربعين وستمائة، ثلاثون فدانا وثلث وثمن:

راس، خمسة عشر فدانا وربع وسدس.

خلفة، خمسة عشر فدانا وقيراط.

اهلها يربون من الفروج خمسمائة وعشرين طائرا. تفصيله:

للديوان المعمور، بما فيه من اجرة التربية بما يخص المزارعين وهو الثلث، ثلاثمائة.

للمقطعين، مائتا طائر وعشرون طائرا.

والذي بها من التقاوي السلطانية، غلة، مائتان واحد وتسعون اردبا وسدس:

قمح، مائتان وثلاثة ارادب.

شعير، خمسة وثلاثون اردبا وسدس.[460]

فول، ثلاثة وخمسون اردبا.[461]

والتقاوي المرتجعة عن النكر [= النكز ؟] العمادي، اربعة ارادب وسدس:

قمح، اردبان وربع وسدس

فول، اردب ونصف وربع.[462]

والذي جرت العادة بانفاقه [=بايقافه][463] في جهة من بعد وتسحب او سقط بالوفاة ولم يكن له موجود ولا زراعة عن الداثر لاستقبال سنة ثلاثين والى اخر سنة اربع وثلاثين، ستة وثمانون دينارا وسدس وحبة.

والذي بها من الباقي في الايام السلطانية الكاملية من جملة الباقي المساق في معاملة سنورس، بحكم ان هذه الناحية من حقوقها وهي داخلة في حسابها عند ما كانت جارية في الخاص.

ومن حقوقها حجر معصرة كان دائرا بالماء، معروف بتندود، معطل.

ومن حرف الباء، بمويه. هذه البلدة عبارة عن بلدة كبيرة. بينها وبين مدينة[464] الفيوم مسافة ساعتين للراكب. تشتمل هذه البلدة على بساتين وكروم وحدائق نخل وزيتون. وهي من غربي الفيوم. وبها سوق وهو يقوم يوم الخميس. وبها العطارون ودكاكين بزازين. يسكنها اعيان من قضاة مدينة[465] الفيوم، اولاد حامد، وهي جارية في اقطاع اصحاب الطواشي جمال الدين محسن والطواشي عزيز الدولة الصالحي والاجناد الصالحية. عبرتها اربعة وثلاثون الفا ومائة وعشرة دنانير جيشية، على حكم الاقطاع. تشرب من بحر يعرف بالناحية منهدم المعالم بغير بنيان، ليس له عبرة قبض.

458 ساقط من ط. م.: من.

459 أ. س. يضيف: برسم.

460 ساقط من أ. س.: قمح مائتان وثلاثة أرادب شعير خمسة وثلاثون أردبا وسدس.

461 ساقط من أ. س.: وخمسون أردبا.

462 ط. م.: وثمن.

463 أ. س.، ط. م.: بإنفاقه.

464 ساقط من أ. س.: مدينة.

465 ساقط من ط. م.: مدينة.

For the Ministry of Endowments: 2½ dinars.

Its people sow 30 ⅓ ⅛ feddans of sugarcane assigned for the presses at Sinnūris, excluding the increment of the year 642:

first harvest, 15 ¼ ⅙ feddans;

second harvest, 15 feddans 1/24.

Its people rear chickens, 520 birds:

for the prosperous Dīwān, including the one-third rearing wage that belongs to the tenants, 300;

for the *iqṭāʿ*-holders, 220 birds.

The royal seed advances in it, in grains, 291 ardabbs ⅙:

wheat, 203 ardabbs;

barley, 35 ⅙ ardabbs;

broad beans, 53 ardabbs.

The reclaimed seed advances (*al-taqāwī al-murtajaʿa*) from al-Dhikr [Ildekiz ?] al-ʿImādī,[138] 4 ardabbs ⅙:

wheat, 2 ¼ ⅙ ardabbs;

broad beans, 1 ½ ¼ ardabb.

The revenue customarily withheld[139] on account of those those who kept away, withdrew, or perished without leaving an heir, and those whose disused lands were not cultivated, from the outset of the year [6]30 to the end of [6]34, 86 dinars ⅙ 1/72.

The outstanding payments owed since the days of sultan al-Kāmil [r. 615/1218–635/1238] are recorded in the total arrears in the accounts of Sinnūris (*muʿāmalat Sinnūris*),[140] since this village was included in the accounts [of Sinnūris] when it belonged to the private domain of the sultan.

A press made of stone turned by water, known as Tandūd, is included in the *iqṭāʿ*. It is currently out of order.

Also beginning with the letter 'bā'': Bamawayh.[141] This is a large village, two hours' ride from Madīnat al-Fayyūm. It has orchards, vineyards and gardens of date palms and olives. It lies toward the west of the province. It has a market held on Thursdays, perfume vendors and shops of cloth merchants. The Awlād Ḥāmid, among the notable judges of Madīnat al-Fayyūm, live here. It is assigned as an *iqṭāʿ* to the followers of the *ṭawāshī* Jamāl al-Dīn Muḥsin and the *ṭawāshī* ʿAzīz al-Dawla al-Ṣāliḥī, and to the soldiers of the Ṣāliḥiyya regiment.[142]

138 AS and MP: *al-dhikr*. In the context of reclaimed seed advances, which are elsewhere associated with the balance of *iqṭāʿ*-holders at the end of their tenure, we expect to find here a name of a military officer. An amir by the name of Ildekiz (again, reading uncertain) is named as *iqṭāʿ*-holder in Qushūsh.

139 MP and AS: '*bi-infāqihi*', corrected to '*bi-īqāfihi*'.

140 Al-Nuwayrī refers to *muʿāmala* as a fiscal account (*Nihāyat al-arab*, VIII, 289). In Ibn Mammātī, *Kitāb qawānīn al-dawāwīn*, p. 307ff, the term appears to refer to all types of revenues that go to the Dīwān. In al-Nābulusī's text, it is mostly used in relation to registers of arrears of unpaid taxes, both to the Dīwān and to *iqṭāʿ*-holders. See also Sato, *State*, p. 128 n.

141 Modern location: Sanhūr (سنهور). Timm, *Das Christlich-Koptische Ägypten*, p. 315: Anbā Kāw (Bamawēh, in Arabic); Halm, *Ägypten*, p. 249; Salmon, 'Répertoire', pp. 55–56: Bamūya; de Sacy, *État des provinces*, p. 681: Bamawaīh; Amélineau, *La géographie*, p. 101: بموىro بماى; Ibn Mammātī, *Kitāb qawānīn al-dawāwīn*, p. 118; Ibn al-Jīʿān, *Kitāb al-tuḥfa*, p. 153: Bamawayh; Ramzī, *Al-Qāmūs*, II/III, 112: Sanhūr.

142 The *ṭawāshī* Jamāl al-Dīn Muḥsin was in charge of al-Ṣāliḥ's mamluks, which came to form the Ṣāliḥiyya regiment. He was instrumental in the rise of Shajar al-Durr to the throne at the end of the decade. See Amalia Levanoni, 'The Mam-

بها جامع تقام فيه الجمعة. وبها مسجد بظاهرها، بجوار طاحون الماء. وبها كنيستان وبظاهرها من شرقيها دير. اهلها حضر. خفر بمويه خاصة لبنى سمالوس، والكوم الاحمر والباردة لبنى زمران، فخذ من بني عجلان، وسنهور لبني مطير. وبها معصرة ذات حجر واحد، وبسنهور معصرة ذات حجرين: حجر دائر وحجر مستجد.

ارتفاعها مما جميعه مستخرجا ومتحصلا، عينا، ثلاثمائة واثنان وثلاثون دينارا ودانق; وغلة، ستة الاف وثلاثمائة وسبعة عشر اردبا وربع وسدس. تفصيله:

قمح، اربعة الاف ومائتان وتسعة ارادب ونصف وثلث وثمن.

شعير وفول، الفان ومائة وسبعة ارادب وثلث وثمن.

تفصيل ذلك:

الهلالي، عن اجرة طواحين الماء والحوانيت الديوانية والعطر وغير ذلك، مائتان وتسعة دنانير وثلثان وحبتان.

ضمان الفروج، ثمانية دنانير.

خراج الراتب، بما فيه من الداثر، ثلاثة وتسعون دينارا وربع ونصف ثمن.

خراج القرط ومؤنة النواب، احد وعشرون دينارا.

خراج المناجزة، ستة الاف وثلاثمائة وسبعة عشر اردبا وربع وسدس، على ما فصل.

وعليها من الرسوم والكيالة والمراعي، عن الفين وستمائة واحد عشر درهما وربع وثمن، خمسة وستون دينارا وربع ونصف قيراط وحبة. وغلة، مائتان واردبان وربع وسدس ونصف قيراط. تفصيله:

قمح، تسعة وتسعون اردبا وسدس ونصف ثمن.

شعير، ستة وثمانون اردبا ونصف.

فول، اربعة عشر اردبا وثلث وربع وثمن.

سلجم، اردبان.

تفصيله:

الرسوم، خمسمائة وستة دراهم ونصف; وغلة، مائة وعشرون اردبا وثلث وربع ونصف قيراط:

قمح، تسعة واربعون اردبا وسدس ونصف ثمن.

شعير، ستة وخمسون اردبا وثلثان.

فول، اربعة عشر اردبا وثلث وربع وثمن.

تفصيله:

شد الاحباس، ثمانية وثلاثون درهما ونصف.

رسم الجراريف، مائتان اثنان[466] وتسعون درهما ونصف.

رسم الحصاد، ثلاثة وخمسون درهما.

رسم الخفارة، خمسة عشر درهما.[467]

رسم الاجران، مائة وسبعة دراهم ونصف، وغلة مائة وعشرون اردبا وثلث وربع ونصف قيراط. تفصيله:

قمح، تسعة واربعون اردبا وسدس ونصف ثمن.

شعير، ستة وخمسون اردبا وثلثان.

فول، اربعة عشر اردبا وثلث وربع وثمن.

[466] ساقط من ط. م.: اثنان.

[467] ساقط من أ. س.: الخفارة خمسة عشر درهما.

Its fiscal value is 34,210 army dinars, based on the rules of *iqṭāʿ* [assessment]. It gets its water from a canal which takes its name from the village. The canal's structures (*al-maʿālim*) are destroyed, and it is without a weir or a water quota.

It has a congregational mosque, in which the Friday prayers are held, and a neighbourhood mosque in its outskirts, near the watermill. It has two churches, and in its outskirts, to the east, there is a monastery. Its people are non-tribal. The protection of Bamawayh proper is in the hands of the Banū Samālūs. Al-Kawm al-Aḥmar and al-Bārida[143] are of the Banū Zummarān, a branch of the Banū ʿAjlān; and Sanhūr belongs to the Banū Muṭayr. It has a press with one stone, and in Sanhūr there is a press with two stones, one in service and the second a new one.

Its revenues in cash and in kind are in specie, 332 1/144 dinars; and in grains, 6,317 ¼ ⅙ ardabbs:

wheat, 4,209 ½ ⅓ ⅛ ardabbs;

barley and broad beans, 2,107 ⅓ ⅛ ardabbs.

[The revenue in detail]:

Lunar-calendar taxes, for the rent of the watermills, the Dīwān's shops, the perfume shops and other things, 209 ⅔ 2/72 dinars;

Concession for [sale of] chicken, 8 dinars;

Land tax on perennial plants, including what fell into disuse, 93 ¼ 1/16 dinars;

Land tax on alfalfa and the provisions for the agents (*al-nuwwāb*), 21 dinars;

Munājaza land tax, 6,317 ¼ ⅙ ardabbs, as specified.

The fees, the measurement fee and the pasture tax are 2,611 ¼ ⅛ dirhams, which are 65 dinars ¼ 1/48 1/72; and in grains, 202 ¼ ⅙ 1/48 ardabbs:

wheat, 99 ⅙ 1/16 ardabbs;

barley, 86 ½ ardabbs;

broad beans, 14 ⅓ ¼ ⅛ ardabbs;

rape, 2 ardabbs.

[The fees, the measurement fee and the pasture tax] in detail:

the fees, 506 ½ dirhams; and in grains, 120 ⅓ ¼ 1/48 ardabbs:

wheat, 49 ⅙ 1/16 ardabbs;

barley, 56 ⅔ ardabbs:

broad beans, 19 ⅓ ¼ ⅛ ardabbs.

[The fees] include:

supervision of endowments, 38 ½ dirhams;

dredging fee, 292 ½ dirhams;

harvest fee, 53 dirhams;

protection fee, 15 dirhams;

threshing-floor fee, 107 ½ dirhams; and in grains, 120 ⅓ ¼ 1/48 ardabbs:

wheat, 49 ⅙ 1/16 ardabbs;

barley, 56 ⅔ ardabbs:

broad beans, 14 ⅓ ¼ ⅛ ardabbs.

luks' Ascent to Power in Egypt', *Studia islamica*, 72 (1990), 121–44 (p. 130); Halm, *Ägypten*, p. 249 (al-Muḥassin). The honorific title *ṭawāshī* has in Ayyubid sources the meaning of a horseman or a knight, and, unlike later usage, is not reserved exclusively for eunuchs.

[143] This village is not otherwise mentioned among the hamlets of Bamawayh; it may be a copyist's mistake for the hamlet of al-Qilāwa (القلاوة).

الكيالة، احد وثمانون اردبا ونصف وثلث. تفصيله:
قمح، خمسون اردبا.
شعير، تسعة وعشرون اردبا ونصف وثلث.
سلجم، اردبان.
المراعي، عن الفين وستمائة واربعة عشر راسا، الفان ومائة واربعة دراهم ونصف وربع وثمن. تفصيله:
راتب، عن ثلاثمائة وستة وثمانين راسا، قطيعة درهمين وربع الراس، ثمانمائة وسبعون درهما.
طارئ، عن الفين ومائتين وثمانية وعشرين راسا، الف واحد وسبعون درهما ونصف. تفصيله:
قطيعة درهم الراس، عن مائتين وستة وعشرين راسا، مائتان وستة وعشرون درهما.
قطيعة سبعين درهما المائة، عن خمسمائة وسبعة عشر راسا، ثلاثمائة واثنان وستون درهما ونصف.
قطيعة خمسين درهما المائة، عن مائة وثلاثة وتسعين راسا، ستة وتسعون درهما ونصف.
قطيعة ثلاثين درهما المائة، عن الف ومائتين اثنين وسبعين راسا، ثلاثمائة واحد وثمانون درهما ونصف وربع وثمن.
قطيعة خمسة وعشرين درهما المائة، عن عشرين راسا، خمسة دراهم.
رسم المستخدمين مائة وثلاثة وستون درهما وربع وثمن.

وعليها من الزكاة، خمسة واربعون دينارا وسدس وحبتان. تفصيله:[468]
الزكاة ببمويه خاصة، اربعون دينارا وثلث وربع وحبتان:
دولبة، ديناران وثلثان.
عن رقيق، نصف وربع وثمن دينار.
الخرص، تسعة دنانير ونصف وربع وثمن. تفصيله:
خرص العنب، ديناران.
خرص النخل، ديناران ونصف.
خرص الزيتون، خمسة دنانير وربع وثمن.
ثمن الماشية، عن احد واربعين راسا، سبعة وعشرون دينارا وسدس وحبتان. تفصيله:
بقر احمر، مسنة واحدة، ثلاثة دنانير.
اغنام، عن اربعين راسا، اربعة وعشرون دينارا وسدس وحبتان. تفصيله:
بياض، عن ثمانية عشر راسا، تسعة عشر دينارا وثلث.
شعارى، عن اثنين وعشرين راسا، اربعة دنانير ونصف وثلث وحبتان. تفصيله:
عن الاغنام، عن اربعة ارؤس، ديناران وسدس.
عن الابل، عن ثمانية عشر راسا، ديناران وثلثان وحبتان.
الكوم الاحمر، ثمن اغنام، عن راسين، دينار واحد وثلث وربع. تفصيله:
بياض، عن راس واحد، دينار واحد وقيراط.
شعارى، عن راس واحد ربع وسدس وثمن دينار.
سنهور، اغنام، عن اربعة ارؤس، ثلاثة دنانير:
بياض، عن راسين، ديناران.
شعارى، عن راسين، دينار واحد.

وعليها من الجوالي، عن مائة وستين نفرا، ثلاثمائة وعشرون دينارا. تفصيله:
المقيمون بها، عن مائة وتسعة نفر، مائتان وثمانية عشر دينارا.
الناءون عنها بالوجه البحري والقبلي، عن احد وخمسين نفرا، مائة وديناران. تفصيله:
الوجه البحري، تسعة واربعون نفرا، ثمانية وتسعون دينارا.
الوجه القبلي، نفران، اربعة دنانير.

The measurement fee, 81 ½ ⅓ ardabbs:
wheat, 50 ardabbs;
barley, 29 ½ ⅓ ardabbs;
rape, 2 ardabbs.
The pasture tax, for 2,614 heads, 2,104 ½ ¼ ⅛ dirhams:
permanent pasture lands, for 386 heads at the rate of 2 ¼ dirhams per head, 870 dirhams;
seasonal pasture lands, 2,228 heads, 1,071 ½ dirhams:
at the rate of one dirham per head, for 226 heads, 226 dirhams;
at the rate of 70 dirhams per 100 [heads], for 517 heads, 362 ½ dirhams;
at the rate of 50 dirhams per 100 [heads], for 193 heads, 96 ½ dirhams;
at the rate of 30 dirhams per 100 [heads], for 1,072 heads, 381 ½ ¼ ⅛ dirhams;
at the rate of 25 dirhams per 100 [heads], for 20 heads, 5 dirhams;
the government agents' fee, 163 ¼ ⅛ dirhams.

The alms-tax, 45 ⅙ 2/72 dinars:
The alms-tax for Bamawayh proper, 40 ⅓ ¼ 2/72 dinars:
merchandise, 2 ⅔ dinars;
slaves ½ ¼ ⅛ dinar;
the estimate, 9 ½ ¼ ⅛ dinars:
estimate of grapes, 2 dinars;
estimate of date palms, 2 ½ dinars;
estimate of the olives, 5 ¼ ⅛ dinars.
monetary value of livestock, for 41 heads, 27 ⅙ 2/72 dinars:
cows, for a two-year old cow, 3 dinars;
small cattle, for 40 heads, 24 ⅙ 2/72 dinars:
sheep, for 18 heads, 19 ⅓ dinars;
goats, for 22 heads, 4 ½ ⅓ 2/72 dinars:
[levied on] goats, for four heads, 2 ⅙ dinars;
[levied on] camels, for 18 heads, 2 ⅔ 2/72 dinars.
[The alms-tax for] al-Kawm al-Aḥmar:
monetary value of small cattle, for two heads, 1 ⅓ ¼ dinar:
sheep, for one head, 1 1/24 dinar;
goats, for one head, ¼ ⅙ ⅛ dinar.
[The alms-tax for] Sanhūr:
[monetary value of] small cattle, for four heads, 3 dinars:
sheep, for two heads, 2 dinars;
goats, for two heads, 1 dinar.

The poll-tax, for 160 individuals, 320 dinars:
those residing in it, for 109 individuals, 218 dinars;
those absent from it in the northern and southern regions, for 51 individuals, 102 dinars:
the northern region, 49 individuals, 98 dinars;
the southern region, two individuals, 4 dinars.

---

468 ساقط من أ. س.: تفصيله.

وعليها لديوان الاحباس، ثمانية عشر دينارا.

وعليها من الاتبان، ستة الاف وثلاثمائة شنيف.

رسم خولي البحر، قمح، اردبان.

والمستقر بها من الرزق، احد وستون فدانا. تفصيله:

المشيخة، ستة فدادين.

طرادون الوحش، اربعة فدادين.

الجامع والمساجد، اربعة فدادين. تفصيله:[469]

الجامع، فدان واحد.

ابن المعلم، فدان واحد.

مسجد ابن عبد السميع، فدانان.

الخفارة، ستة عشر فدانا.

خولي القصب، ستة فدادين.

الخطابة، اربعة وعشرون فدانا.

المسجد بسنهور فدان واحد.

اهلها يزرعون من الاقصاب السكر برسم[470] معصرة الناحية الدائرة بالابقار، خارجا عن الزائد[471] في سنة اثنتين واربعين وستمائة، ثمانين فدانا وربع. تفصيله:

راس، تسعة وخمسون فدانا ونصف.

خلفة، عشرون فدانا ونصف وربع.

المزدرع بها من القرط والفول، خمسة عشر فدانا.

والمزدرع برسم معصرة سنهور باراضي فدمين، مائة وعشرة فدادين[472] وثلثان. تفصيله:

قصب سكر، مائة فدان:

راس، تسعة وستون[473] فدانا.

خلفة، احد وثلاثون[474] فدانا وسدس.

فول اخضر، عشرة فدادين وذلك[475] لسنة اثنتين واربعين وستمائة.

والمربى بها من الفروج، الفان واربعمائة فروج. تفصيله:

للديوان المعمور، بما فيه مما يسقط عن المزارعين عن اجرة التربية بحق الثلث، الف فروج.

للمقطعين، الف واربعمائة فروج.

والذي يسلف بها من الشعير برسم الاصطبلات السلطانية، خارجا عما نقل الى غيرها بحكم قلة الصنف المذكور بها وهو مائتا اردب، ستمائة اردب.

والذي بها من التقاوي السلطانية برسم عمارة الناحية، الفان وثلاثمائة واثنا عشر اردبا وثمن. تفصيله:

قمح، الف واثنان وتسعون اردبا وثلث وربع ونصف قيراط.

شعير، خمسمائة وثمانون اردبا وسدس.

فول، اربعمائة وتسعة وتسعون اردبا ونصف وثمن.

سلجم، اربعة اردب وثلثان وثمن.

سمسم، احد وعشرون اردبا وثلث.

كمون، احد عشر اردبا ونصف وثلث.

كزبرة، اردب واحد وثلث ونصف ثمن.

زريعة نيلة، ربع وثمن اردب.

469 ساقط من أ. س.: تفصيله.
470 ساقط من أ. س.: رسم.
471 ط. م.: البلد.
472 أ. س.: مائة وعشرة فدان.
473 أ. س.: وتسعون.
474 ط. م.: جلبان ثلاثون.
475 ط. م. يضيف: خالصا.

For the Ministry of Endowments, 18 dinars.

Hay, 6,300 bales.

The fee for the overseer of the canal, wheat, 2 ardabbs.

The established allowances in it, 61 feddans:

the headmen, 6 feddans;

'beast-chasers' (*ṭarrādūn al-waḥsh*), 4 feddans;

the congregational mosque and the neighbourhood mosques, 4 feddans:

the congregational mosque, 1 feddan;

[the mosque of] Ibn al-Muʿallim, 1 feddan;

the mosque of Ibn ʿAbd al-Samīʿ,[144] 2 feddans.

the guardsmen, 16 feddans;

the overseer of the sugarcane, 6 feddans;

the Friday preachers, 24 feddans;

the mosque at [the hamlet of] Sanhūr, 1 feddan.

Its people sow sugarcane assigned for the press of the village, which is turned by cattle. Excluding the increment for the year 642, this amounts to 80 ¼ feddans:

first harvest, 59 ½ feddans;

second harvest, 20 ½ ¼ feddans.

Alfalfa and broad beans sown in it, 15 feddans.

They sow, in the land of Fidimīn, 110 ⅔ feddans assigned for the press at Sanhūr:

sugarcane, 100 feddans:

first harvest, 69 feddans;

second harvest, 31 ⅙ feddans.

green beans, 10 feddans. This is for 642 [AD 1244–5].

The chickens reared in it, 2,400 chickens:

for the prosperous Dīwān, including what is deducted for the tenants as their rearing wage of a third, 1,000 chickens;

for the *iqṭāʿ*-holders, 1,400 chickens.

The barley assigned for the royal stables, which was paid for in advance, 600 ardabbs. This excludes what was transferred elsewhere, due to the shortage of this category [i.e., barley] in the village, 200 ardabbs.

The seed advances from the royal Dīwān, assigned for the village's cultivation, 2,312 ⅛ ardabbs:

wheat, 1,192 ⅓ ¼ 1/48 ardabbs;

barley, 580 ⅙ ardabbs;

broad beans, 499 ½ ⅛ ardabbs;

rape, 4 ⅔ ⅛ ardabbs;

sesame, 21 ⅓ ardabbs;

cumin, 11 ½ ⅓ ardabbs;

coriander, 1 ⅓ 1/16 ardabb;

seeds of indigo, ¼ ⅛ [ardabb].

144 In Chapter 8 above, al-Nābulusī mentions the existence of only one unnamed neighbourhood mosque in Bamawayh, which lies outside of the village, near the watermill.

والذي ينساق بها من الحواصل[476] والموقوف والباقي في الايام الكاملية لاستقبال سنة احدى وثلاثين والى اخر سنة اربع وثلاثين عن الحاصل والموقوف والباقي، قبل انتقالها للمقطعين[477]، عينا، مائتان وسبعة دنانير وقيراط وحبتان؛ وغلة، سبعة عشر الفا وثلاثمائة وخمسة وثمانون اردبا وثلث وربع وثمن. تفصيله:

قمح، ثلاثة عشر الفا ومائة وستة وخمسون اردبا وثلثان وثمن.
وشعير، ثلاثة الاف واحد وعشرون اردبا وثلث ونصف قيراط.
وفول، الف ومائة وستة عشر اردبا وثلثان وربع ونصف ثمن.
وسمسم، اثنان وعشرون اردبا وثمن.
وسلجم، خمسة واربعون اردبا ونصف وثلث ونصف قيراط.
كمون، عشرون اردبا وقيراط.
كزبرة، اردبان ونصف ونصف[478] ثمن.
ثوم يابس، مائة وثلاثة واربعون قنطارا وربع ونصف ثمن.
الحاصل خاصة، ثلاثة ارادب وثمن:
سمسم، ثلثا اردب.
سلجم، اردب واحد وقيراطان.
كمون، ثلث وثمن.
كزبرة، ثلثان وربع اردب.
الموقوف عن الخراب الداثر في مدة خمس سنين، مائة واحد وثمانون دينارا ونصف ودانق.
الباقي، خمسة وعشرون دينارا ونصف ونصف ثمن، وغلة سبعة عشر الفا وثلاثمائة واثنان وثمانون اردبا وثلث وربع[479]، على ما فصل.

ومن حرف الباء، ببيج انشو. هذه البلدة عبارة عن بلدة جيدة متوسطة بين الكبر والصغر من غربي الفيوم. بينها وبين مدينة الفيوم مسافة دون الساعتين واكثر من الساعة للراكب. وبها النخيل والاعناب والبساتين والاقصاب قريب من خليج منية اقنى. وهي جارية في اقطاع الامير شهاب الدين ابن الامير سعد الدين بن كمشبغا[480]. شربها من خليج الجهة البحرية، اخر البحر الاعظم اليوسفي، ينقسم بخشبة، شركة ابي كسا وابشاية الرمان وطبهار وجردو. ويخص الناحية، من جملة اربعة وخمسين قبضة في الخليج المذكور للنواحي المذكورة، تسع قبض. بها معصرة قصب ذات حجرين بالابقار. وبها جامع تقام فيه الجمعة. اهلها الاضابطة كرابسة، فخذ من بني كلاب.

ارتفاعها، عينا، مائتان واربعة وعشرون دينارا وقيراط وحبتان؛ وغلة، الف وسبعمائة واحد وخمسون اردبا. تفصيله:
قمح، ثمانمائة وخمسة وستون اردبا وثمن.
شعير، ثمانمائة[481] وستة وثلاثون اردبا وربع وثمن.
وكمون، خمسة وثلاثون اردبا.
سلجم، اربعة عشر اردبا ونصف.

فدن، خارجا عن السمسم المستهلك بالفار، مائة واربعة عشر فدانا:
قصب سكر، راس،[482] مائة فدان.
قرط برسم العوامل، اربعة عشر فدانا وربع.

الهلالي، ثمانية عشر دينارا وربع وثمن. تفصيله:
الحانوت، اربعة عشر دينارا وربع وثمن.
الفاخورة، اربعة دنانير.

476 أ. س.: الحاصل.
477 ط. م، أ. س.: للمقطعين قبل انتقالها .
478 ساقط من ط. م.: ونصف.
479 ساقط من أ. س.: وثلث وربع.
480 ط. م.: كمشبا.
481 أ. س.: مائة.
482 ساقط من ط. م.: رأس.

The surplus, withheld and outstanding payments carried forward since the days of al-Kāmil, from the beginning of the year [6]31 to the end of the year [6]34, before the village was transferred [from the private domain of the sultan] to the *iqṭāʿ*-holders, are, in specie, 207 1/24 2/72 dinars; and in grains, 17,385 ⅓ ¼ ⅛ ardabbs:

wheat, 13,156 ⅔ ⅛ ardabbs;
barley, 3,021 ⅓ 1/48 ardabbs;
broad beans, 1,116 ⅔ ¼ 1/16 ardabbs;
sesame, 22 ⅛ ardabbs;
rape, 45 ½ ⅓ 1/48 ardabbs;
cumin, 20 1/24 ardabbs;
coriander, 2 ½ 1/16 ardabbs;
dry garlic, 143 ¼ 1/16 qinṭārs.
The surplus (*ḥāṣil*)[145] proper, 3 ⅛ ardabbs:
sesame, ⅔ ardabb;
rape, 1 2/24 ardabb;
cumin ⅓ ⅛ [ardabb];
coriander ⅔ ¼ ardabb.
Withheld payments relating to derelict and deserted property for a period of five years, 181 ½ 1/144 dinars.
The outstanding payments are 25 ½ 1/16 dinars; and in grains, 17,382 ⅓ ¼ ardabbs, as specified above.

Also beginning with the letter 'bāʾ': Babīj Unshū.[146] This is a fine village, medium-sized, in the west of the Fayyum, between one and two hours' ride from Madīnat al-Fayyūm, close to Minyat Aqnā Canal. It has date palms, grapes, orchards and sugarcane. It is assigned as an *iqṭāʿ* to the amir Shihāb al-Dīn, son of the amir Saʿd al-Dīn ibn Kumushbughā. It gets its water from a canal that issues from the northern side of the Main Canal, at its end, by a wooden [divisor]. The canal is shared with Abū Ksā, Ibshāyat al-Rummān, Ṭubhār and Jardū. The village is allotted 9 *qabḍas* from the total of 54 *qabḍas* [of water] in the aforementioned canal. It has a sugar press with two stones, turned by cattle. It has a congregational mosque, in which the Friday prayers are held. Its people are Karābisa, of the Aḍābiṭa, a branch of the Banū Kilāb.

Its revenues in specie are 224 1/24 2/72 dinars; and in grains, 1,751 ardabbs:
wheat, 665 [= 865][147] ⅛ ardabbs;
barley, 836 ¼ ⅛ ardabbs;
cumin, 35 ardabbs;
rape, 14 ½ ardabbs;

[crown estate] feddans, excluding the sesame consumed by mice, 114 feddans:
sugarcane, first harvest, 100 feddans;
alfalfa, assigned for the cattle [of the Dīwān], 14 ¼ feddans.

Lunar-calendar taxes, 18 ¼ ⅛ dinars:
the shop, 14 ¼ ⅛ dinars;
the pottery kilns, 4 dinars;

145 On *ḥāṣil* as the surplus carried over from previous years, see al-Nuwayrī, *Nihāyat al-arab*, VIII, 218.

146 Modern location: Abū Junshū (ابو جنشو). Halm, *Ägypten*, p. 248: Babīj Anshū; Salmon, 'Répertoire', p. 57: Babīj Anshū; Ibn Mammātī, *Kitāb qawānīn al-dawāwīn*, p. 118: Babīj Inshū; Yāqūt, *Muʿjam al-Buldān*, I, 334; de Sacy, *État des provinces*, p. 681; Savigny, *Description de l'Égypte*, p. 129: Abū Jinshū; Ibn al-Jīʿān, *Kitāb al-tuḥfa*, p. 153; Ramzī, *Al-Qāmūs*, II/III, 71: Abū Junshū.

147 The correct number should be 865 in order for the sums to add up. See also below, where the land tax in wheat, excluding fees, is said to be 840 ardabbs.

مال الخراجي، ماتتان وخمسة دنانير وثلثان وحبتان، وغلة الف وسبعمائة اردب:

قمح، ثمانمائة واربعون اردبا.

شعير، ثمانمائة[483] واثنا عشر اردبا.

كمون، اربعة وثلاثون اردبا.

سلجم، اربعة عشر اردبا.

تفصيله:

خراج الراتب بما فيه من الموقوف عن الخراب الداثر في جهة من تسحب وسقط بالوفاة، وعدا الفار[484] على راتبه، مما ورد اصلا وموقوفًا حفظا لذكره على العادة، ماتتان وخمسة دنانير وثلثان وحبتان. تفصيل:

الاصل، عن ثلاثة وخمسين فدانا وثلث وربع وحبتين، مائة واثنان وثمانون دينارا ونصف وثلث ودانق. تفصيله:

كرم، قطيعة خمسة دنانير وثلث الفدان، عن اثنين وعشرين فدانا وثلثين[485] وثمن، مائة واحد وعشرون دينارا ونصف قيراط وحبة.

شجر راتب، قطيعة دينارين، عن اثنين وعشرين فدانا وثلث وحبة، اربعة واربعون دينارا وثلثان وحبتان.

قطن، بالقطيعة، عن ستة فدادين ونصف وثلث وثمن وحبة، ثلاثة عشر دينارا[486] وثلثان وربع[487] وحبتان.

نيلة بالقطيعة، عن ربع وثمن وحبة، نصف وربع وحبتان.

حنا، عن فدان واحد[488] وسدس وحبتين، ديناران وربع وثمن وحبة.

الاضافة، اثنان وعشرون دينارا ونصف وثلث ونصف قيراط.

خراج زراعة المزارعين، اصلا واضافة، الف وسبعمائة واحد وخمسون اردبا، على ما فصل.

وعليها لمقطعي العشر المعروف بابن المهراني، اثنان وثلاثون اردبا. تفصيله:

قمح، خمسة عشر اردبا.

شعير، خمسة عشر اردبا.

كمون، اردبان.

وعليها من الرسوم والكيالة والمراعي، عن اربعمائة وتسعة وعشرين درهما ونصف وثمن، عشرة دنانير وثلثان ونصف ثمن وحبة؛ وغلة، ثمانية وثمانون اردبا وثلثان وثمن. تفصيله:

قمح، اربعون اردبا وثلثان وثمن.

شعير، خمسة واربعون اردبا.

كمون، ثلاثة ارادب.

تفصيله:

الرسوم، ماتتان وتسعة وتسعون درهما ونصف، وغلة ثلاثة واربعون اردبا وثلثان وربع. تفصيله:

قمح، عشرون اردبا وثلثان وثمن.

شعير، عشرون اردبا وثلثان وثمن.

كمون، اردبان وثلث.

Land tax in cash, 205 2/3 2/72 dinars; and in grains, 1,700 ardabbs:

wheat, 840 ardabbs;

barley, 812 ardabbs;

cumin, 34 ardabbs;

rape, 14 ardabbs.

[The land tax in cash]:

Land tax on perennial plants — including the withheld payments for what has been destroyed and fallen into disuse, because of withdrawal or death, and for the perennial plants consumed by mice,[148] as basic assessment and as withheld payments which are recorded as is customary — 205 2/3 2/72 dinars:

the basic assessment, for 53 1/3 1/4 2/72 feddans, 182 1/2 1/3 1/144 dinars:

vineyards, at the rate of 5 1/3 dinars per feddan, for 22 2/3 1/8 feddans, 121 1/48 1/72 dinars;

fully grown trees, at the rate of 2 dinars [per feddan], for 22 1/3 1/72 feddans, 44 2/3 2/72 dinars;

cotton, at the same rate [of 2 dinars per feddan], for 6 1/2 1/3 1/8 1/72 feddans, 13 2/3 1/4 2/72 dinars;

indigo at the same rate [of 2 dinars per feddan], for 1/4 1/8 1/72 [feddan], 1/2 1/4 2/72 [dinar];

henna, for 1 1/6 2/72 feddan, 2 1/4 1/8 1/72 dinars.

The addition, 22 1/4 1/3 1/48 dinars;

Land tax on cultivation of the tenants, the basic assessment and the addition, 1,751 ardabbs, as specified.

For the *iqṭāʿ*-holders of the tithe known as Ibn al-Mihrānī, 32 ardabbs:

wheat, 15 ardabbs;

barley, 15 ardabbs;

cumin, 2 ardabbs.

The fees, the measurement fee and the pasture tax are 429 1/2 1/8 dirhams, which are 10 2/3 1/16 1/72 dinars; and in grains, 88 2/3 1/8 ardabbs:

wheat, 40 2/3 1/8 ardabbs;

barley, 45 ardabbs;

cumin, 3 ardabbs.

[The fees, the measurement fee and the pasture tax] in detail:

the fees are 299 1/2 dirhams; and in grains, 43 ardabbs 2/3 1/4:

wheat, 20 2/3 1/8 ardabbs;

barley, 20 2/3 1/8 ardabbs;

cumin, 2 1/3 ardabbs.

---

483 أ. س. يضيف: أردب.

484 ط. م.: النار.

485 أ. س.: وثلث.

486 أ. س.: فدانا.

487 أ. س. يضيف: وثمن.

488 أ. س. يضيف ويشطب: ونصف.

148 TM: *al-nār* (fire).

تفصيله:
شد الاحباس، اربعة دراهم.
رسم الجراريف، تسعون درهما.
رسم الحصاد، ثلاثة وخمسون درهما.
رسم الخفارة، خمسة عشر درهما.
رسم الكمون، مائة درهم.
رسم الاجران، سبعة وثلاثون درهما ونصف، وغلة، ثلاثة واربعون اردبا وثلثان وربع، على ما فصل.
الكيالة، اربعة واربعون اردبا ونصف وربع وثمن:
قمح، عشرون اردبا.
شعير، اربعة وعشرون اردبا وخمسة قراريط.
كمون، ثلثا اردب.[489]
المراعي، عن مائة وثلاثة وستين[490] راسا، مائة وثلاثون درهما وثمن. تفصيله:
راتب، قطيعة درهمين وربع الراس، عن ستة عشر راسا، ستة وثلاثون درهما.
طارئ، عن مائة وسبعة واربعين راسا، اربعة وثمانون درهما. تفصيله:
قطيعة درهم واحد الراس، عن سبعة وخمسين راسا، سبعة وخمسون درهما.
قطيعة ثلاثين درهما المائة، عن تسعين راسا، سبعة وعشرون درهما.
رسم المستخدمين، عشرة دراهم وثمن.
وعليها من الزكاة، تسعة وثلاثون دينارا ونصف وثمن وحبتان. تفصيله:
الخرص، احد وعشرون دينارا ونصف:
خرص العنب، عشرون دينارا.
خرص النخل، دينار واحد ونصف.
ثمن الاغنام، عن ثمانية وثلاثين راسا، ثمانية عشر دينارا وثمن وحبتان:
بياض، عن اثنى عشر راسا، اثنا عشر دينارا وربع.
شعارى، عن ستة وعشرين راسا، خمسة دنانير ونصف وربع وثمن وحبتان.
عن الاغنام، عن خمسة ارؤس، ديناران ونصف وربع.
عن الابل، عن احد وعشرين راسا، ثلاثة دنانير وثمن وحبتان.
وعليها من الاتبان، الفان وثمانمائة وسبعة وعشرون شنيفا.
رسم خولي البحر، قمح، اردب.
وعليها لديوان الاحباس، عينا، ديناران.
اهلها يزرعون من الاقصاب برسم معصرة الناحية، عشرة فدادين.
المربى بها من الفروج، ثمانمائة وخمسون طائرا. تفصيله:
للديوان المعمور بما فيه من اجرة التربية وهو الثلث، اربعمائة وخمسون.
للمقطع، اربعمائة.

وبها من التقاوي الديوانية برسم عمارتها الى اخر سنة احدى واربعين وستمائة، سبعمائة وثمانية وسبعون اردبا وثلث وربع ونصف ثمن:
قمح، اربعمائة وثمانية وثلاثون اردبا وربع وسدس.
شعير، ثلاثمائة وثلاثة وعشرون اردبا وثلث.
كمون، ثمانية ارادب ونصف وربع وثمن.
سلجم، ثلث وربع اردب.
سمسم، سبعة ارادب وقيراط ونصف.
زريعة بطيخ اخضر، ربع وثمن اردب.

[The fees] include:
supervision of endowments, 4 dirhams;
dredging fee, 90 dirhams;
harvest fee, 53 dirhams;
protection fee, 15 dirhams;
cumin fee, 100 dirhams;
threshing-floor fee, 37 ½ dirhams; and in grains, 43 ⅔ ¼ ardabbs, as specified.
The measurement fee, 44 ½ ¼ ⅛ ardabbs:
wheat, 20 ardabbs;
barley, 24 5/24 ardabbs;
cumin, ⅔ ardabb.
The pasture tax, for 163 heads, 130 ⅛ dirhams:
permanent pasture lands, at the rate of 2¼ dirhams per head, for 16 heads, 36 dirhams;
seasonal pasture lands, for 147 heads, 84 dirhams:
at the rate of one dirham per head, for 57 heads, 57 dirhams;
at the rate of 30 dirhams per 100 [heads], for 90 heads, 27 dirhams;
the government agents' fee, 10 ⅛ dirhams.

The alms-tax, 39 ½ ⅛ 2/72 dinars. In detail:
the estimate, 21 ½ dinars:
estimate of grapes, 20 dinars;
estimate of date palms, 1 ½ dinar;
monetary value of small cattle, for 38 heads, 18 ⅛ 2/72 dinars:
sheep, for 12 heads, 12 ¼ dinars;
goats, for 26 heads, 5 ½ ¼ ⅛ 2/72 dinars:
[levied on] goats, for five heads, 2 ½ ¼ dinars;
[levied on] camels, for 21 heads, 3 ⅛ 2/72 dinars.

Hay, 2,827 bales.

The fee of the overseer of the canal, wheat, 1 ardabb.

For the Ministry of Endowments, in specie, 2 dinars.

Its people sow 10 feddans of sugarcane, assigned to the press of the village.

The chickens reared in it, 850 birds:
for the prosperous Dīwān, including the rearing wage of a third, 450;
for the *iqṭāʿ*-holder, 400.

The seed advances from the Dīwān, assigned for its cultivation until the end of the year 641, 778 ⅓ ¼ 1/16 ardabbs:
wheat, 438 ¼ ⅙ ardabbs;
barley, 323 ⅓ ardabbs;
cumin, 8 ½ ¼ ⅛ ardabbs;
rape, ⅓ ¼ ardabb;
sesame, 7 1/24 1/48 ardabbs;
seeds of green watermelon, ¼ ⅛ ardabb.

489 أ. س.: ثلاثة أرادب.
490 أ. س.: عن ثلاثمائة وستين.

والذي انساق بها من الحاصل والموقوف والباقي في الايام السلطانية الكاملية قبل انتقالها للاقطاع الى اخر سنة اربع وثلاثين، عند ما كانت جارية في اقطاع الامير عز الدين بن درباس لسنة خمس وثلاثين وستمائة، عينا، مائتان واحد وثلاثون دينارا وربع وثمن وحبة؛ غلة، ستة الاف واربعمائة وستة وخمسون اردبا وربع وسدس:

قمح، ثلاثة الاف وملتان وستة وثملون اردبا ونصف وربع وثمن.

شعير، الفان وثمانمائة وخمسة ارادب وسدس وثمن.

فول، مائة اردب ونصف.

سمسم، اربعة ارادب وربع ونصف قيراط.

كمون، مائة وخمسة وثلاثون اردبا وثلث وربع.

سلجم، ملة وثلاثة وعشرون اردبا ونصف وثلث ونصف ثمن.

حلاوة، ستة عشر ظرفا. تفصيله:[491]

قند، تسع ابليج.

عسل دفن، سبعة امطار.

تفصيله:

ما انساق في معاملة الديوان السلطاني لاستقبال سنة ثلاثين والى اخر سنة اربع وثلاثين وستمائة، مائتان واحد وثلاثون دينارا وربع وثمن وحبة، وغلة اربعة الاف وتسعمائة وثلاثة وستون اردبا وربع ونصف قيراط. تفصيله:

قمح، الفان وخمسمائة وثلاثة وستون اردبا ونصف ونصف ثمن.

شعير، الفان وخمسة وثمانون اردبا وثلث ونصف قيراط.

فول، مائة اردب ونصف.

سمسم، اربعة ارادب وربع ونصف قيراط.

كمون، مائة وستة ارادب وسدس وثمن.

سلجم، مائة وثلاثة ارادب وسدس وثمن.

والحلاوة.

الحاصل خاصة، كمون، اردبان.

الموقوف عن الخراب الداثر، وما هو في جهة الجمالين،[492] مائتان وتسعة وعشرون دينارا وثلثان وربع ونصف ثمن والحلاوة.

الباقي، دينار واحد وثلث ونصف ثمن وحبة، وغلة، اربعة الاف وتسعمائة واحد وستون اردبا وربع ونصف قيراط على ما فصل.

ما انساق باقيا في معاملة الامير عز الدين بن درباس لسنة خمس وثلاثين وستمائة، الف واربعمائة وثلاثة وتسعون اردبا وثمن ونصف قيراط على ما فصل.

ومن حرف الباء، بور سينرو. هذه اللفظة عبارة عن ارض براح لا جدران بها[493] وكانت قديمة فخربت من ثلاث سنين وليس بها شجر ولا بساتين بل محاطب وطرفاء يزرعها اهل سينرو. وهي جارية في اقطاع جماعة من الاجناد. عبرتها جيشية ثلاثة الاف دينار، والمطلق لها من الماء من خليج سينرو مما يقسم من اسفله بخشبة تخص البر المنكور، عشر قبض صغار. مزارعوها اهل سينرو.

وارتفاعها مما جميعه متحصلا، خمسمائة اردب. تفصيله:

قمح، مائتان وخمسون اردبا.

وشعير، مائتان وخمسون اردبا.

وعليها من الرسوم والكيالة، عن احد عشر درهما وربع، ربع دينار ونصف قيراط وحبة؛ غلة، ثلاثون اردبا وثلث وربع. تفصيله:

491 ساقط من ط. م.: تفصيله.

492 أ. س.: الحمالين.

493 أ. س.: فيها.

The surplus, withheld and outstanding payments carried forward in its account since the days of Sultan al-Kāmil until the end of year [6]34, and when it was assigned as an *iqṭāʿ* to the amir ʿIzz al-Dīn ibn Dirbās in the year 635, are, in specie, 231 ¼ ⅛ 1/72 dinars; and in grains, 6,456 ¼ ⅙ ardabbs:

wheat, 3,286 ½ ¼ ⅛ ardabbs;

barley, 2,805 ⅙ ⅛ ardabbs;

broad beans, 100 ½ ardabbs;

sesame, 4 ¼ 1/48 ardabbs;

cumin, 135 ⅓ ¼ irddabs;

rape, 123 ½ ⅓ 1/16 ardabbs;

sweets (*ḥalāwa*), 16 containers (*ẓarfan*):

raw sugar, earthenware moulds (*abālīj*),[149] nine;

covered (*dafn*) molasses, 7 maṭars.[150]

[The surplus, withheld and outstanding payments] in detail:

The [surplus, withheld and outstanding payments] carried forward in the account of the royal Dīwān from the beginning of [6]30 to the end of 634 are 231 ¼ ⅛ 1/72 dinars; and in grains, 4,963 ¼ 1/48 ardabbs:

wheat, 2,563 ½ 1/16 ardabbs;

barley, 2,085 ⅓ 1/48 ardabbs;

broad beans, 100 ½ ardabbs;

sesame, 4 ¼ 1/48 ardabbs;

cumin, 106 ⅙ ⅛ ardabbs;

rape, 103 ⅙ ⅛ ardabbs;

the sweets.

[The payments registered in the accounts of the royal Dīwān in detail]:

The surplus, cumin, 2 ardabbs.

the withheld payments relating to derelict property that has fallen into disuse, and to the camel-drivers (?, *jammālīn*),[151] are 229 ⅔ ¼ 1/16 dinars and the sweets.

The outstanding payments, 1 ⅓ 1/16 1/72 dinar; and in grains, 4,961 ⅛ 1/48 ardabbs, as specified.

The arrears carried forward in the account of the amir ʿIzz al-Dīn ibn Dirbās for the year 635 [AD 1237–8] are 1,493 ⅛ 1/48 ardabbs, as specified.

Also beginning with the letter 'bā'': Būr Sīnarū.[152] This name refers to an open tract of land without any fences, as this village was deserted three years ago. There are no trees and orchards in it, but only firewood and tamarisks. The people of Sīnarū cultivate it, and it is assigned as an *iqṭāʿ* to a group of soldiers. Its fiscal value is 3,000 army dinars. The water allocated for this village from the lower section of Sīnarū Canal, allocated by a wooden [divisor], 10 small *qabḍas* (*qubaḍ ṣighār*). Its tenants are the people of Sīnarū.

149 The *ublūj* (pl. *abālīj*) was a cone-shaped earthenware mould, wide at the top and narrow at the bottom, used to separate the raw sugar (*qand*) from the black molasses (*ʿasal*). Definitions of its size vary, but Sato argues it held around 10 kg. See Sato, *Sugar*, pp. 43–46, including images of preserved vessels.

150 In al-Nuwayrī's account of sugar production, he explains that the *abālīj*, full of boiled juice, are brought to *bayt al-dafn*. Sato takes this to mean that they were covered with earth. When water was sprinkled on the surface, the molasses (*ʿasal*) flowed down, leaving behind the raw sugar; Sato, *Sugar*, pp. 43–45.

151 AS: *ḥammālīn* or *ḥimālayn*.

152 Modern location (uncertain): Sīnarū al-Baḥriyya (سينرو البحرية). Salmon, 'Répertoire', p. 56: Bawr Sīnarū. We identified it as Modern Sīnarū al-Baḥriyya — a location which is also in line with Shafei Bey's map.

قمح، ثلاثة عشر اردبا ونصف وربع ونصف قيراط.
شعير، ستة عشر اردبا ونصف وربع ونصف ثمن.

تفصيله:
رسم الاجران، احد عشر درهما وربع، وغلة ثلاثة عشر اردبا وخمسة قراريط:
قمح، ستة ارادب وثلث وربع ونصف قيراط.
شعير، ستة ارادب وربع ونصف قيراط.
الكيالة، عشرة ارادب:
قمح، ثلاثة ارادب.
شعير، سبعة ارادب.
نصف العشر، سبعة ارادب وربع وسدس:
قمح، اربعة ارادب وسدس.
شعير، ثلاثة ارادب وخمسة قراريط.

وعليها من الاتبان، خمسمائة شنيف.

والمربى بها من الفروج بما فيه من اجرة التربية وهو الثلث، ثلاثمائة فروج.

والمرتب بها من الرزق، ثلاثة عشر فدانا. تفصيله:
النجارون، فدانان.
المشايخ، سبعة فدادين.
الكلابون،[494] ثلاثة فدادين.
حارس المقسم، فدان.

والمخلد بها من التقاوي الديوانية، احد وعشرون اردبا وثلث وربع وثمن. تفصيله:
قمح، اربعة عشر اردبا وقيراط ونصف.
شعير، ستة ارادب وثلث وربع ونصف قيراط.
سلجم، اردب واحد وقيراط.

والذي جرت العادة باطلاقه للناحية من التقاوي عند ما كانت جارية في الخاص، مائة وثمانية عشر اردبا. تفصيله:
قمح، خمسة وتسعون[495] اردبا وربع وسدس وثمن.
شعير، اثنان وعشرون اردبا.
سلجم، ثلث وربع وثمن اردب.

ومن حرف الباء، ببيج انقاش. هذه البلدة عبارة عن بلدة متوسطة بين الكبر والصغر بينها وبين مدينة الفيوم مسافة ساعتين للراكب غربي الفيوم. تشمل على نخل مثمر وغير مثمر وكروم عنب يسير. وهي جارية[496] في اقطاع الامير عماد الدين بن طي واصحاب الامير شهاب الدين خضر امير شكار، واصحاب الامير حسام الدين بن ابي[497] علي، واصحاب الامير ركن الدين[498] خاص الترك، واصحاب الامير علم الدين سنجر الشريفي، واصحاب الامير فارس الدين اقطاي، واصحاب الامير سيف الدين الحميدي، واصحاب الامير جمال الدين اقوش المشرف. عبرتها جيشية، اربعة الاف وثلاثون دينارا. تشرب من شركة منية اقنى من المقسم المعروف بالعرين بما عدته اربع قبض ونصف. وبها جامع تقام فيه الجمعة.[499] اهلها بنو غصين فخذ من بني كلاب.

494 أ. س.: الكيالون.
495 أ. س.: وسبعون.
496 ساقط من أ. س.: جارية.
497 ساقط من أ. س.: أبي.
498 ساقط من أ. س.: الدين.
499 أ. س.: الخطبة.

Its revenues, in kind, 500 ardabbs:
wheat, 250 ardabbs;
barley 250 ardabbs.

The fees and the measurement fee are 11 ¼ dirhams, which are ¼ 1/48 1/72 dinar; and in grains, 30 ⅓ ¼ ardabbs:
wheat, 13 ½ ¼ 1/48 ardabbs;
barley, 16 ½ ¼ 1/16 ardabbs.

[The fees and the measurement fee] include:
Threshing-floor fee, 11 ¼ dirhams; and in grains, 13 5/24 ardabbs:
wheat, 6 ⅓ ¼ 1/48 ardabbs;
barley, 6 ¼ 1/48 ardabbs.
The measurement fee, 10 ardabbs:
wheat, 3 ardabbs;
barley, 7 ardabbs.

Half of the tithe [on the allowances], 7 ¼ ⅙ ardabbs:
wheat, 4 ⅙ ardabbs;
barley, 3 5/24 ardabbs.

Hay, 500 bales.

The chicken reared in it, including the rearing wage of a third, 300 chickens.

The established (*al-murattab*) allowances, 13 feddans:
the carpenters, 2 feddans;
the headmen, 7 feddans;
the dog handlers (*kallābūn*), 3 feddans;
the watchman of the divisor, 1 feddan.

The recorded seed advances in the Dīwān, 21 ⅓ ¼ ⅛ ardabbs:
wheat, 14 1/24 1/48 ardabbs;
barley, 6 ⅓ ¼ 1/48 ardabbs;
rape, 1 1/24 ardabb.

The seed advances which were customarily assigned to the village when it belonged to the private domain of the sultan, 118 ardabbs:
wheat, 95 ¼ ⅙ ⅛ ardabbs;
barley, 22 ardabbs;
rape, ⅓ ¼ ⅛ ardabb.

Also beginning with the letter 'bā'': Babīj Anqāsh.[153] This is a medium-sized village, two hours' ride from Madīnat al-Fayyūm, in the west of the province. It has date palms, both fruit-bearing and not, and a few grape vineyards. It is assigned as an *iqṭā*ʿ to the amir ʿImād al-Dīn ibn Ṭayy; and to the followers (*aṣḥāb*) of the amir Shihāb al-Dīn Khiḍr, *amīr shikār*;[154] and to the followers of the amir Ḥusām al-Dīn ibn Abī ʿAlī;[155] and to the followers of the amir Rukn al-Dīn Khāṣṣ

153 Modern location: Abū Dinqāsh/ ʿIzbat Dinqāsh (ابو دنقاش). Halm, *Ägypten*, p. 247; Salmon, 'Répertoire', p. 59; Savigny, *Description de l'Égypte*, p. 126: Abū Dinjāsh; de Sacy, *État des provinces*, p. 681; Ibn Mammātī, *Kitāb qawānīn al-dawāwīn*, p. 119: Babīj Inqāsh; Yāqūt, *Muʿjam al-Buldān*, I, 334; Ibn al-Jīʿān, *Kitāb al-tuḥfa*, p. 153; Ramzī, *Al-Qāmūs*, II/III, 71: Abū Dinqāsh/ ʿIzbat Dinqāsh.

154 Possibly to be identified with Shihāb al-Dīn Khiḍr, nephew of al-Asad al-Hakkārī, mentioned below.

155 Ḥusām al-Dīn ibn Abī ʿAlī, a free-born Kurdish amir from Hama. He became *ustādār* (Majordomo) for al-Ṣāliḥ, then vice-regent in Egypt, in the 1230s. In

ارتفاعها مما جميعه مستخرجا ومتحصلا، عينا، ثلاثة عشر دينارا؛ غلة، الف وثلاثمائة وسبعة وستون اردبا ونصف. تفصيله:

قمح، ستمائة وثلاثة وسبعون اردبا ونصف وربع.

شعير، ستمائة وثلاثة وسبعون اردبا ونصف وربع.

كمون، عشرون اردبا.

تفصيله:

الهلالي، عن اجرة الحانوت ستة دنانير.

المراعي، ديناران.

خراج الدويرات، خمسة دنانير.

خراج الغلة، مناجزة، الف وثلاثمائة وسبعة وستون اردبا ونصف، على ما تقدم تفصيله.

وعليها لمقطعي العشر المعروف بابن[500] المهراني ثلاثون اردبا، قمح وشعير نصفان.

وعليها من الرسوم والكيالة والمراعي، عن ماتتين واثنين وعشرين درهما، خمسة دنانير وربع وسدس وثمن وحبة؛ وغلة، تسعة وثمانون اردبا ونصف وربع وثمن. تفصيله:

قمح، ثلاثة واربعون اردبا وخمسة قراريط.

شعير، تسعة وثلاثون اردبا ونصف ونصف ثمن.

فول، ستة ارادب وقيراطان ونصف.

سمسم، اردب واحد.

تفصيله:

الرسوم، ماتتان ودرهمان وربع، وغلة، خمسة وستون اردبا ونصف ونصف ثمن. تفصيله:

قمح، تسعة وعشرون اردبا وثلث وربع وثمن.

شعير، ثلاثة وثلاثون اردبا ونصف ونصف ثمن.

فول، اردب واحد وربع وسدس وثمن.

سمسم، نصف وربع اردب.

تفصيله:

شد العين، اربعة دراهم.

شد الاحباس، اربعة دراهم.

رسم الحصاد، ثلاثة وخمسون درهما.

500 ساقط من أ. س.: ابن.

al-Turk;[156] and to the followers of the amir ʿAlam al-Dīn Sanjar al-Sharīfī; and to the followers of the amir Fāris al-Dīn Aqṭāy;[157] and to the followers of the amir Sayf al-Dīn al-Ḥumaydī;[158] and to the followers of the amir Jamāl al-Dīn Aqqūsh al-Mushrif.[159] Its fiscal value is 4,030 army dinars. It gets its water from [a canal] shared with Minyat Aqnā, from the divisor known as al-ʿArīn. Its quota is 4½ *qabḍas*. It has a congregational mosque, in which the Friday prayers are held. Its people are the Banū Ghuṣayn, a branch of the Banū Kilāb.

Its revenues in kind and in cash are in specie, 13 dinars; and in grains, 1,367 ½ ardabbs:

wheat, 673 ½ ¼ ardabbs;

barley, 673 ½ ¼ ardabbs;

cumin, 20 ardabbs.

[The revenues in specie] include:

lunar-calendar tax, for the rent of the shop, 6 dinars;

pasture tax, 2 dinars;

land tax on tree enclosures (*al-duwayrāt*), 5 dinars;

Munājaza land tax, in grains, 1,376 ½ ardabbs, as specified.

For the *iqṭāʿ*-holders of the tithe known as Ibn al-Mihrānī, 30 ardabbs of wheat and barley, half in each.

The fees, the measurement fee and the pasture tax, 222 dirhams, which are 5 ¼ 1/6 1/8 1/72 dinars; and in grains, 89 ½ ¼ 1/8 ardabbs:

wheat, 43 5/24 ardabbs;

barley 39 ½ 1/16 ardabbs;

broad beans, 6 2/24 1/48 ardabbs;

sesame, 1 ardabb.

[The fees, the measurement fee and the pasture tax] in detail:

the fees are 202 ¼ dirhams; and in grains, 65 ½ 1/16 ardabbs:

wheat, 29 ⅓ ¼ 1/8 ardabbs;

barley, 33 ½ 1/16 ardabbs;

broad beans, 1 ¼ 1/6 1/8 ardabb;

sesame, ½ ¼ ardabb.

[The fees] include:

supervision of the land survey, 4 dirhams;

supervision of endowments, 4 dirhams;

harvest fee, 53 dirhams;

642/1244, he was employed by al-Ṣāliḥ in his siege of Damascus; Humphreys, *From Saladin to the Mongols*, pp. 251, 276; Levanoni, 'The Mamluks' Ascent', pp. 128, 138.

156 Rukn al-Dīn Baybars Khāṣṣ al-Turk was a senior Ṣāliḥi amir and military commander. In 642/1244 he was employed by al-Ṣāliḥ in his siege of Damascus. Died 674/1275. Humphreys, *From Saladin to the Mongols*, pp. 276, 315–16, 321; Amitai, 'The Mamlūk officer class', p. 293.

157 Fāris al-Dīn Aqṭāy, a high ranking officer in the Mamluk army, and the commander of the Baḥriyya regiment in the late 1240s. Died in 1254. See Makīn b. al-ʿAmīd, *Taʾrīkh*, ed. by Claude Cahen, 'La Chronique des Ayyoubides d'al-Makin b. al-'Amīd', *Bulletin d'Études Orientales*, 15 (1955–57), 109–84 (pp. 159 [51], 164 [56]); Humphreys, *From Saladin to the Mongols*, pp. 326, 465n30.

158 The Ḥumaydiyya were one of the main Kurdish tribes represented in Saladin's army; Humphreys, *From Saladin to the Mongols*, pp. 30–31.

159 There were several Ṣāliḥī amirs by the name of Jamāl al-Dīn Aqqūsh, including Jamāl al-Dīn Aqqūsh al-Najībī, future governor of Syria; Amitai-Preiss, 'The Mamlūk Officer Class', p. 294 nos 13, 15, p. 299 no. 57.

رسم الخفارة، خمسة عشر درهما.
مصالحة السلجم، سبعون درهما.
رسم الاجران، ستة وخمسون درهما وربع وغلة، خمسة وستون اردبا ونصف ونصف ثمن، على ما فصل.
الكيالة، اربعة وعشرون اردبا وربع ونصف ثمن. تفصيله:
قمح، ثلاثة عشر اردبا ونصف.
شعير، ستة ارادب.
فول، اربعة ارادب ونصف ونصف ثمن.
سمسم، ربع اردب.
المراعي، عن ستين راسا، تسعة عشر درهما ونصف وربع. تفصيله:
قطيعة ثلاثين درهما المائة، عن عشرين راسا، ستة دراهم.[501]
قطيعة خمسة وعشرين المائة، عن اربعين راسا، عشرة دراهم.
رسم المستخدمين، ثلاثة دراهم ونصف وربع.

وعليها من الزكاة، عن ثمن ماشية، عن تسعة ارؤس، خمسة دنانير ونصف وثلث. تفصيله:
بقر احمر تبيع واحد، دينار.
اغنام، عن ثمانية ارؤس، اربعة دنانير ونصف وثلث. تفصيله:
بياض، عن راس واحد، دينار واحد وقيراطان.
شعارى، عن سبعة ارؤس، ثلاثة دنانير ونصف وربع.

عليها[502] لديوان الاحباس ديناران.

عليها من الاتبان، الف وثلاثمائة شنيف.

رسم خولي البحر بها، اردب واحد، قمحًا.

والمقرر على مزارعيها من الكشك والفريك، اردبان وثلث. تفصيله:
كشك، اردب وثلث.
فريك، اردب.

والمربى بها من الدجاج، خمسمائة وعشرون طائرا:
للديوان المعمور، بما فيه من اجرة التربية وهو الثلث، ثلاثمائة وعشرون.
للمقطعين، مائتا طائر.

والذي جرت به العادة باطلاقه للناحية من التقاوي، مائتا اردب:
قمح، مائة اردب.
شعير، مائة اردب.

والذي يسلف عليه بها من الشعير برسم الاصطبلات السلطانية، مائة خمسة[503] وعشرون اردبا.

protection fee, 15 dirhams;
settlement for rape, 70 dirhams;
threshing-floor fee, 56 ¼ dirhams; and in grains, 65 ½ 1/16 ardabbs, as specified.

The measurement fee, 24 ¼ 1/16 ardabbs:
wheat, 13 ½ ardabbs;
barley, 6 ardabbs;
broad beans, 4 ½ 1/16 ardabbs;
sesame ¼ ardabb.

The pasture fee, for 60 heads, 19 ½ ¼ dirhams:
at the rate of 30 dirhams per 100 [heads], for 20 heads, 6 dirhams;
at the rate of 25 per 100 [heads], for 40 heads, 10 dirhams;
the government agents' fee, 3 ½ ¼ dirhams.

The alms-tax, for the monetary value of livestock, nine heads, 5 ½ ⅓ dinars:
cows, for a yearling calf, 1 dinar;
small cattle, for eight heads, 4 ½ ⅓ dinars:
sheep, for one head, 1 2/24 dinar;
goats, for seven heads, 3 ½ ¼ dinars.

For the Ministry of Endowments, 2 dinars.

Hay, 1,300 bales.

The fee for the overseer of its canal, 1 ardabb of wheat.

The established levy of *kishk* and *farīk* dishes on the tenants, 2 ⅓ ardabbs:
kishk, 1 ⅓ ardabb;
farīk, 1 ardabb.

The chickens reared in it, 520 birds:
for the prosperous Dīwān, including the rearing wage of a third, 320;
for the *iqṭāʿ*-holders, 200 birds.

The seed advances customarily distributed in the village, 200 ardabbs:
wheat, 100 ardabbs;
barley, 100 ardabbs.

The barley assigned for the royal stables, which was paid for in advance, 125 ardabbs.

501 أ. س.: عن أربعين رأسا عشرة دراهم رسم المستخدمين.
502 أ. س. يضيف ويشطب: من الأتبان.
503 ساقط من ط. م.: خمسة.

ومن حرف الباء، ببيج انديركفورها خمسة[504] مناشئ. هذه البلدة بلدة كبيرة ولها مناشئ تنكر في باب الميم. بينها وبين مدينة الفيوم مسافة ساعتين للراكب من غربي الفيوم. تشتمل على اراضي الزرع خاصة ليس بها نخيل ولا بساتين ولا كروم. واما نكر مناشئها: منشاة شرف، منشاة ابي حاتم، منشاة ابريشة، منشاة الغصيني،[505] منشاة خامسة.

عبرتها جيشية، ستة الاف وثمانمائة وستة عشر دينارا. تشرب من بحر دلية من المقسم المعروف بالتبرون بما عدته اربعة وعشرون قبضة ماء. اهلها بنو غصين، فخذ من بني كلاب.

ارتفاعها، عينا، اربعة دنانير وسدس، وشعير الف وثلاثمائة وعشرون اردبا. تفصيله:

الهلالي، ديناران ونصف.
المراعي، دينار وثلثان.

مناجزة الغلات، الف وثلاثمائة وعشرون اردبا شعيرًا.

وعليها من خراج محاريث الرزق، شعير، مائة وعشرون اردبا.

عليها من الرسوم والكيالة والمراعي، عن مائتين واثنين وستين درهما ونصف، ستة دنانير وربع وسدس وثمن وحبتان، وغلة، سبعون اردبا. تفصيله:

قمح، خمسة ارادب وسدس ونصف ثمن.
شعير، احد وستون اردبا ونصف[506] وربع ونصف قيراط.
كمون، ثلاثة ارادب.

تفصيله:

الرسوم، مائتان وخمسة وثلاثون درهما ونصف; غلة، خمسة وخمسون اردبا ونصف ونصف ثمن. تفصيله:
قمح، خمسة ارادب وسدس ونصف ثمن.
شعير، ثمانية واربعون اردبا.
كمون، اردبان وثلث.
تفصيله:
رسم الجراريف، تسعون درهما.
رسم الحصاد، ثلاثة وخمسون درهما.
رسم الخفارة، خمسة عشر درهما.
مصالحة الكمون، ثلاثون درهما.
رسم الاجران، سبعة واربعون درهما ونصف، وغلة، خمسة وخمسون اردبا ونصف[507] ونصف ثمن، على ما فصل.
الكيالة، اربعة عشر اردبا وربع وسدس ونصف قيراط:
شعير، ثلاثة عشر اردبا ونصف وربع ونصف قيراط.
كمون، ثلثا اردب.
المراعي، عن احد وسبعين راسا، سبعة وعشرون درهما. تفصيله:
قطيعة ثلاثين درهما المائة، عن ثلاثين راسا، تسعة دراهم.
قطيعة درهم واحد، عن خمسة اروس، خمسة دراهم.
قطيعة خمسة وعشرين درهما المائة، ستة وثلاثون راسا، تسعة دراهم.
رسم المستخدمين، اربعة دراهم.

504 أ. س.: خمس.
505 أ. س.: العصيني.
506 ساقط من أ. س.: ونصف.
507 ساقط من أ. س.: ونصف.

Also beginning with the letter 'bā'': Babīj Andīr and its five hamlets.[160] This is a large village, and it has hamlets which will be mentioned under the letter 'mim'. It is two hours' ride from Madīnat al-Fayyūm, in the west of the province. Its lands are only cultivated with field crops, and there are no date palms, orchards or vineyards. As for its hamlets, these are: Munsha'at Sharaf, Munsha'at Abī Ḥātim, Munsha'at Ibrīsha, Munsha'at al-Ghuṣaynī and a fifth Munsha'a.

Its fiscal value is 6,816 Army Dinars. It gets its water from Dilya Canal, from the divisor known as al-Tabrūn. Its water quota is 24 *qabḍas*. Its people are the Banū Ghuṣayn, a branch of the Banū Kilāb.

Its revenues in specie are 4 ⅙ dinars; and in barley, 1,320 ardabbs.

[Its revenues in specie] include:
lunar-calendar tax, 2 ½ dinars;
pasture tax, 1 ⅔ dinar.

Munājaza land tax on grains, 1,320 ardabbs of barley.

The fees, the measurement fee and the pasture tax are 262 ½ dirhams, which are 6 dinars ¼ ⅙ ⅛ 2/72; and in grains, 70 ardabbs:
wheat, 5 ⅙ 1/16 ardabbs;
barley, 61 ½ ¼ 1/48 ardabbs;
cumin, 3 ardabbs.

[The fees, the measurement fee and the pasture tax] in detail:
The fees, 235 ½ dirhams, and in grains, 55 ½ 1/16 ardabbs:
wheat, 5 ⅙ 1/16 ardabbs;
barley, 48 ardabbs;
cumin, 2 ⅓ ardabbs.
[The fees] include:
dredging fee, 90 dirhams;
harvest fee, 53 dirhams;
protection fee, 15 dirhams;
settlement for cumin, 30 dirhams;
threshing-floor fee, 47 ½ dirhams; and in grains, 55 ardabbs ½ 1/16, as specified.
The measurement fee, 14 ¼ ⅙ 1/48 ardabbs:
barley, 13 ½ ¼ 1/48 ardabbs;
cumin, ⅔ ardabb.
The pasture fee, for 71 heads, 27 dirhams:
at the rate of 30 dirhams per 100 [heads], for 30 heads, 9 dirhams;
at the rate of one dirham [per head], for five heads, 5 dirhams;
at the rate of 25 dirhams per 100 [heads], [for] 36 heads, 9 dirhams;
the government agents' fee, 4 dirhams.

The land tax on the plough-shares of the allowances (*maḥārīth al-rizaq*), barley, 120 ardabbs.[161]

160 Modern location: Abū Jandīr (ابو جندير). Halm, *Ägypten*, p. 247; Salmon, 'Répertoire', pp. 68–69; Yāqūt, *Muʿjam al-Buldān*, I, 334; Ibn al-Jīʿān, *Kitāb al-tuḥfa*, p. 152; de Sacy, *État des provinces*, p. 681; Savigny, *Description de l'Égypte*, p. 126: Abūkandir; Ramzī, *Al-Qāmūs*, II/III, 81: Abū Jandīr.

161 As noted above, the plough-shares were shares in a village's arable lands, probably equal to a dozen feddans. They are mentioned in the survey only in connection with the *rizaq*, the tax-free land allocated to local officials. As these privileged lands were not subject to the lease contracts governing all other arable

وعليها من الزكاة، عن ثمن اغنام، عن سبعة اروس، خمسة دنانير وثلثان وثمن. تفصيله:

بياض، عن اربعة اروس اربعة دنانير وسدس.

شعارى، عن ثلاثة اروس، دينار ونصف وثمن.

وعليها من الاتبان، الف وثلاثمائة شنيف.

والذي يسلف عليه بها من الشعير برسم الاصطبلات السلطانية، تسعون اردبا.

والذي جرت العادة باطلاقه لها من التقاوي، شعير، مائتا[508] اردب.

والذي يربى بها من الفروج، الف طائر:

للديوان المعمور بما فيه من اجرة التربية وهو الثلث، ستمائة طائر.

للمقطعين، اربعمائة.

ومن حرف الباء، بياض. هذه البلدة عبارة عن بلدة متوسطة بينها وبين مدينة الفيوم مسافة اربع ساعات للراكب وهي تحت ذيل الجبل وهي[509] اخر عمل الفيوم من قبل[510] الشرق. عبرتها جيشية، عشرة الاف دينار وتسعة دنانير. تشرب من بحر الشرقية من مقسم جص مبنى بما عبرته اثنتا عشرة قبضة. اهلها بنو زرعة، فخذ من بني عجلان.

ارتفاعها، عينا، سبعة عشر دينارا، وغلة، الف وثمانمائة[511] وثمانون اردبا:

قمح، ثمانون اردبا.

شعير، الف وثمانمائة اردب.

تفصيله:

مال الهلالي، اثنا عشر دينارا.

المراعي، خمسة دنانير.

خراج الغلة، الف وثمانمائة وثمانون اردبا:

قمح، ثمانون اردبا.

شعير، الف وثمانمائة[512] اردبا.

وعليها من الرسوم والكيالة والمراعي، عن ثلاثمائة وسبعة وستين درهما، تسعة دنانير وسدس ودانق; غلة، تسعة وتسعون اردبا وثلث وربع وثمن. تفصيله:

قمح، عشرون اردبا وثلثان وربع ونصف قيراط.

شعير، ثمانية وستون اردبا ونصف وربع.[513]

فول، عشرة ارادب ونصف قيراط.

تفصيله:

الرسوم، مائتان وتسعة دراهم وربع، وغلة، تسعة وخمسون اردبا وثلث وربع وثمن:

قمح، اثنا عشر اردبا وثلثان وربع ونصف قيراط.[514]

شعير، ستة وثلاثون اردبا ونصف وربع.

فول، عشرة ارادب ونصف قيراط.[515]

The alms-tax, for the monetary value of seven heads of small cattle, 5 $\frac{2}{3}$ $\frac{1}{8}$ dinars:

sheep, for four heads, 4 $\frac{1}{6}$ dinars;

goats, for three heads, a dinar $\frac{1}{2}$ $\frac{1}{8}$.

Hay, 1,300 bales.

The barley assigned for the royal stables, which is paid for in advance, 90 ardabbs.

The seed advances which are customarily distributed in it, barley, 200 ardabbs.

The chickens reared in it, 1,000 birds:

for the prosperous Dīwān, including the rearing wage of a third, 600 birds;

for the *iqṭāʿ*-holders, 400.

Also beginning with the letter 'bāʾ': Bayāḍ.[162] This is a medium-sized village, four hours' ride from Madīnat al-Fayyūm. It is located at the foot of the mountain, at the easternmost edge of the province. Its fiscal value is 10,009 army dinars. It gets its water from al-Sharqiyya Canal,[163] from a plastered divisor with a weir. Its [water] quota is 12 *qabḍas*. Its people are the Banū Zarʿa, a branch of the Banū ʿAjlān.

Its revenues in specie, 17 dinars; and in grains, 1,880 ardabbs:

Wheat, 80 ardabbs;

Barley, 1,800 ardabbs.

[The revenues] in detail:

lunar calendar tax, 12 dinars;

pasture tax, 5 dinars;

Land tax on grains, 1,880 ardabbs.

Wheat, 80 ardabbs;

Barley, 1,800 ardabbs.

The fees, the measurement fee and the pasture tax are 367 dirhams, which are 9 dinars $\frac{1}{6}$ $\frac{1}{144}$; and in grains, 99 $\frac{1}{3}$ $\frac{1}{4}$ $\frac{1}{8}$ ardabbs:

wheat, 20 $\frac{2}{3}$ $\frac{1}{4}$ $\frac{1}{48}$ ardabbs;

barley, 68 $\frac{1}{2}$ $\frac{1}{4}$ ardabbs;

broad beans, 10 $\frac{1}{48}$ ardabbs.

[The fees, the measurement fee and the pasture tax] in detail:

The fees, 209 $\frac{1}{4}$ dirhams; in grains, 59 $\frac{1}{3}$ $\frac{1}{4}$ $\frac{1}{8}$ ardabbs:

wheat, 12 $\frac{2}{3}$ $\frac{1}{4}$ $\frac{1}{48}$ ardabbs;

barley, 36 $\frac{1}{2}$ $\frac{1}{4}$ ardabbs;

broad beans, 10 $\frac{1}{48}$ ardabbs.

508 أ. س.: مائة.

509 أ. س.: في.

510 أ. س.: قبلي.

511 أ. س.: ثلاثمائة.

512 أ. س.، ط. م. يضيفا ثمانون.

513 ساقط من أ. س.: شعير ثمانية وستون أردبا ونصف وربع.

514 ساقط من أ. س.: ونصف قيراط.

515 أ. س.: فول عشرة أرادب ونصف قيراط شعير ستة وثلاثون أردبا ونصف وربع.

land, they were subject to a different kind of land tax, identified here as *kharāj*. In other village entries this tax on the allowances is called *ʿushr*, the canonical tithe levied on privately-owned arable land.

162 Modern location: ʿIzbat al-Sharika al-Inglīziyya (عزبة الشركة). Halm, *Ägypten*, p. 250; Salmon, 'Répertoire', p. 44; Ibn al-Jīʿān, *Kitāb al-tuḥfa*, p. 153; de Sacy, *État des provinces*, p. 681; Ramzī, *Al-Qāmūs*, I, 182: ʿIzbat al-Sharika al-Inglīziyya, north of the Sīla train station.

163 Halm, *Ägypten*, p. 242, identifies it with Khalīj al-Awāṣī mentioned by al-Maqrīzī, *Kitāb al-mawāʿiẓ*, ed. by Wiet, I, 248/21; Salmon, 'Répertoire', p. 32, identifies it with Baḥr Sīla.

تفصيل ذلك:

رسم الجراريف، تسعون درهما.

رسم الخفارة، خمسة عشر درهما.

رسم الحصاد، ثلاثة وخمسون درهما.

رسم الاجران، احد وخمسون درهما وربع، وغلة، تسعة وخمسون اردبا وثلث وربع وثمن، على ما فصل.

الكيالة، اربعون اردبا. تفصيله:

قمح، ثمانية ارادب.

شعير، اثنان وثلاثون اردبا.

المراعي، عن اربعمائة وثلاثة وثلاثين راسا، مائة وسبعة وخمسون درهما ونصف وربع:

قطيعة مائة درهم المائة، عن ثلاثة عشر راسا، ثلاثة عشر درهما.

قطيعة ثلاثين درهما المائة، عن مائتين واربعة وخمسين راسا، ستة وسبعون درهما وثمن.

قطيعة خمسة وعشرين درهما المائة، عن مائة وستة وستين راسا، احد واربعون درهما ونصف.

رسم المستخدمين، سبعة وعشرين درهما وثمن.

وعليها من الزكاة، عن ثمن اغنام، عن ثمانية وعشرين راسا، احد وعشرين دينارا وقيراط وحبتان. تفصيله:

بياض، عن سبعة عشر راسا، ثمانية عشر دينارا وربع.

شعارى، عن احد عشر راسا، ديناران وثلثان وثمن وحبتان:

عن الاغنام، عن ثلاثة ارؤس، دينار واحد ونصف وثمن.

عن الابل، عن ثمانية ارؤس، دينار واحد وسدس وحبتان.

وعليها من الاتبان، الفا شنيف.

رسم خولي البحر بها، شعير، نصف وربع اردب.

وعليها لديوان الاحباس، ديناران.

والذي جرت العادة باطلاقه لها من التقاوي، ثلاثمائة وخمسة وعشرون اردبا:

قمح، ثمانون اردبا.

شعير، مائة وخمسون اردبا.

فول، خمسة وتسعون اردبا.

والذي بها من التقاوي السلطانية، مائة وخمسة وعشرون اردبا ونصف وثلث. تفصيله:

قمح، اربعة ارادب وثلث وربع ونصف ثمن.

شعير، اثنان وثلاثون اردبا وثلث وثمن.

فول، ثمانية وثمانون[516] اردبا وثلثان ونصف ثمن.

والمربى بها من الدجاج، ثمانمائة وخمسون طائرا. تفصيله:

للديوان المعمور، بما فيه من اجرة التربية وهو الثلث، اربعمائة وخمسون طائرا.

للمقطعين، اربعمائة طائر.

والذي يسلف عليه بها من الشعير برسم الاصطبلات السلطانية، ثلاثمائة وثمانون اردبا.

[The fees] include:

dredging fee, 90 dirhams;

protection fee, 15 dirhams;

harvest fee, 53 dirhams;

threshing-floor fee, 51 ¼ dirhams; and in grains, 59 ardabbs, ⅓ ¼ ⅛, as specified.

The measurement fee, 40 ardabbs:

wheat, 8 ardabbs;

barley, 32 ardabbs;

The pasture tax, for 433 heads, 157 ½ ¼ dirhams:

at the rate of 100 dirhams per 100 [heads], for 13 heads, 13 dirhams;

at the rate of 30 dirhams per 100 [heads], for 254 heads, 76 ⅛ dirhams;

at the rate of 25 dirhams per 100 [heads], for 166 heads, 41 ½ dirhams.

the government agents' fee, 27 ⅛ dirhams.

The alms-tax, which consists of the monetary value of 28 heads of small cattle, 21 1/24 2/72 dinars:

sheep, for 17 heads, 18 ¼ dinars;

goats, for 11 heads, 2 ⅔ ⅛ 2/72 dinars:

[levied on] goats, for three heads, 1 ½ ⅛ dinar;

[levied on] camels, for eight heads, 1 ⅙ 2/72 dinar.

Hay, 1,000 bales.

The fee of the overseer of the canal, barley ½ ¼ ardabb.

For the Ministry of Endowments, 2 dinars.

The seed advances customarily distributed in it, 325 ardabbs:

wheat, 80 ardabbs;

barley, 150 ardabbs;

broad beans, 95 ardabbs.

The royal seed advances are 125 ½ ⅓ ardabbs:

wheat, 4 ⅓ ¼ 1/16 ardabbs;

barley, 32 ⅓ ⅛ ardabbs;

broad beans, 88 ⅔ 1/16 ardabbs.

The chickens reared in it, 850 birds:

for the prosperous Dīwān, including the rearing wage of a third, 450 birds;

for the *iqṭāʿ*-holders, 400 birds.

The barley assigned for the royal stables, which is paid for in advance, 380 ardabbs.

---

516 أ. س.: ثلاثون.

ومن حرف الباء، بنديق. هذه البلدة عبارة عن مرج[517] فيه اخصاص تروى ايام النيل كما تروى الريف غير الفيوم وينصل عنها الماء للمصايد من[518] شرقي الفيوم. بينها وبين مدينة الفيوم مسافة ثلاثة ساعات للراكب. ليس بها[519] شجر ولا نخيل ولا بساتين ولا كروم وليس بها الا الزرع خاصة. وهي جارية في اقطاع الامير عز الدين خضر بن محمد الكيكاني واخوته. تروى من البحر بوردان بغير عبرة.

Also beginning with the letter ʻbāʼʼ: Bandīq.[164] This village consists of shacks over a meadow, watered during the period of the Nile's flooding like Lower Egypt, not like the Fayyum. The water escapes from it to the fisheries. It is at the east of the province, three hours' ride from Madīnat al-Fayyūm. There are no trees, date palms, orchards or vineyards in it, and its land is only used for field cultivation. It is assigned as an *iqṭāʻ* to the amir ʻIzz al-Dīn Khiḍr ibn Muḥammad al-Kīkānī and his brothers.[165] It gets its water from Waradān Canal, without [a water] quota.

ارتفاعها، مشاطرة، مما جميعه مستخرجا ومتحصلا، عينا، اربعون دينارا; وغلة، مائة وخمسة وخمسون اردبا:
قمح، خمسة عشر اردبا.
شعير، مائة واربعون اردبا.

Its revenue, in cash and in kind, is in specie, 40 dinars; and in grains, by *mushāṭara* land tax, 155 ardabbs:
wheat, 15 ardabbs;
barley, 140 ardabbs.

اهلها بنو زرعة، فخذ من بني عجلان.

Its people are the Banū Zarʻa, a branch of the Banū ʻAjlān.

عليها من الرسوم والكيالة والمراعي، عن مائتين واربعة وتسعين[520] درهما وثمن، سبعة دنانير وثلث ونصف قيراط وغلة، ستة ارادب وسدس:
قمح، اردبان ونصف وثلث.
شعير، ثلاثة ارادب وثلث.

The fees, the measurement fee and the pasture tax are 294 dirhams, which are 7 ⅓ 1/48 dinars; and in grains, 6 ⅙ ardabbs:
wheat, 2 ½ ⅓ ardabbs;
barley, 3 ⅓ ardabbs.

تفصيله:
الرسوم،
عن رسم الاجران، اربعة دراهم وربع وثمن، وغلة، اربعة ارادب وثلثان وربع:
قمح، اردبان وثلث.
شعير، اردبان وثلث وربع.
الكيالة، اردب وربع:
قمح، نصف اردب.
شعير، نصف وربع اردب.
المراعي، عن مائتين واحد وسبعين راسا، مائتان وتسعة وثمانون درهما ونصف وربع. تفصيله:
قطيعة مائة درهم المائة راس، عن احد وخمسين راسا، احد وخمسون درهما.
قطيعة سبعين درهما المائة، عن مائة وتسعين[521] راسا، مائة وثلاثة وثلاثين درهما.
قطيعة ثلاثين درهما المائة، عن ثلاثين راسا، تسعة دراهم.
رسم المستخدمين،[522] ستة عشر درهما ونصف وربع وثمن.

[The fees, the measurement fee and the pasture tax] in detail:
The fees:
threshing-floor fee, 4 ½ ⅛ dirhams; and in grains, 4 ⅔ ¼ ardabbs:
wheat, 2 ⅓ ardabbs;
barley, 2 ⅓ ¼ ardabbs.
The measurement fee: 1 ¼ ardabb:
wheat, ½ ardabb;
barley, ¾ ardabb.
The pasture tax, for 271 heads, 289 [= 209][166] ½ ¼ dirhams:
at the rate of 100 dirhams per 100 [heads], for 51 heads, 51 dirhams;
at the rate of 70 dirhams per 100 [heads], for 190 heads, 133 dirhams;
at the rate of 30 dirhams per 100 [heads], for 30 heads, 9 dirhams.
the government agents' fee,[167] 16 ½ ¼ ⅛ dirhams.

عليها من الزكاة، عن ثمن اغنام، عن ثلاثة ارؤس، ديناران وثمن. تفصيله:
بياض، عن راس واحد، دينار واحد.
شعارى، عن راسين، دينار وثمن.

The alms-tax, which consists of the monetary value of three heads of small cattle, 2 ⅛ dinars:
sheep, for one head, 1 dinar;
goats, for two heads, 1 ⅛ dinar.

وعليها من الاتبان، مائتا[523] شنيف.

517 ط. م.: برج.
518 أ. س.: فيها.
519 أ. س.: في.
520 أ. س.: عشرين.
521 أ. س.: سبعين.
522 أ. س.، ط. م.: الأجران.
523 أ. س.: مائة.

164 Modern location (uncertain): between Dimūh al-Dāthir and Sīla. Halm, *Ägypten*, p. 250; Salmon, 'Répertoire', p. 44; Ibn al-Jīʻān, *Kitāb al-tuḥfa*, p. 153: Baydīf; de Sacy, *État des provinces*, p. 681; Ramzī, *Al-Qāmūs*, I, 170: ʻIzbat Buṭrān Ismāʻīl in the lands of al-Rūbiyyāt, on canal al-Ahālī. We could not locate this ʻIzba. It is unlikely that Bandīq lay in the lands of al-Rūbiyyāt, as, according to al-Nābulusī, Bandīq was located three hours' ride east of the city, whereas al-Rūbiyyāt was located five hours' ride to the north-east. In addition, the two villages got their water from different canals and different divisors. We therefore decided to follow Shafei Bey's map, and to locate Bandīq between Dimūh al-Dāthir and Sīla.

165 Kīkān was the name of a Kurdish tribe, mentioned in earlier Islamic geographical texts. See Thomas Bois, Vladimir Minorsky, and David N. MacKenzie, 'Kurds, Kurdistān', *The Encyclopedia of Islam*, 2nd edn, V, 438–86; ʻAlī b. al-Ḥusayn b. ʻAlī al-Masʻūdī, *Al-Tanbīh wa'l-ishrāf*, ed. by M. J. de Goeje (Leiden: Brill, 1893; repr. Beirut: Dār Ṣādir, n.d.), pp. 88–91. The amir ʻIzz al-Dīn Khiḍr ibn Muḥammad al-Kīkānī and his companions or brothers had several *iqṭāʻ*-holdings in the Fayyum.

166 Correction in order to allow the sums below to add up.

167 MP and AS: *rasm al-ajrān* (threshing-floor fee) instead of *rasm al-mustakhdamīn*.

والذي بها من التقاوي الديوانية، سبعة وعشرون اردبا وسدس:
قمح، خمسة[524] عشر اردبا وثلث.
شعير، احد عشر اردبا.
سمسم، نصف وثلث اردب.

ومن حرف الباء، ببيج غيلان وكوم الرمل. هاتان[525] البلدتان عبارة عن بلدتين صغيرتين شرقي الفيوم الى القبلة، مجاورتين للبحر المنهى اليوسفي. تزرع الكتاتين والحبوب الشتوية زرع ريف. مسافتها اربع ساعات للراكب من مدينة الفيوم. مجموعتان في الاقطاع، عبرتهما ستة الاف دينار جيشية. اهلها بنو هانئ، فخذ من لواتة.

ارتفاعهما مما جميعه مستخرجا ومتحصلا، عينا، مائتان وعشرون دينارا وربع وحبتان؛ وغلة اربعمائة واثنا عشر اردبا وثلث وربع ونصف ثمن:
قمح، مائتان واثنان وستون اردبا وثلث وربع ونصف ثمن.
شعير، مائة وخمسون اردبا.

تفصيله:
المعدية، تسعة دنانير.
المراعي، خمسة عشر دينارا.
الخراجي مائة وستة وتسعون[526] دينارا وربع وحبتان؛ وغلة، اربعمائة واثنا عشر اردبا وثلث وربع ونصف ثمن، على ما فصل. تفصيله:
خراج السواقي، ستون دينارا.
خراج الكتان، مائة دينار وثمانية دنانير وخمسة قراريط وحبة.
خراج قرط اثنان وعشرون دينارا وثلثان وربع.
خراج الجلبان، خمسة دنانير وثمن وحبة.

المشاطرة، غلة، اربعمائة واثنا عشر اردبا وثلث وربع ونصف ثمن، على ما تقدم تفصيله.

وعليهما[527] من الرسوم والكيالة والمراعي، عن مائة وثلاثة وعشرين درهما، ثلاثة دنانير وقيراط[528] ونصف[529] وحبة، وغلة، سبعة عشر اردبا وربع وسدس وثمن. تفصيله:
قمح، اربعة ارادب وثلثان ونصف قيراط.
شعير، اثنا عشر اردبا ونصف وثلث ونصف قيراط.

تفصيله:
الرسوم، ثمانية وسبعون درهما، وغلة، اثنا عشر اردبا وقيراط. تفصيله:
قمح، اردبان وسدس ونصف قيراط.
شعير تسعة ارادب ونصف وثلث ونصف قيراط.
تفصيله:
رسم الحصاد، ثلاثة وخمسون درهما.
رسم الخفارة، خمسة عشر درهما.
رسم الاجران، عشرة دراهم، وغلة، اثنا عشر اردبا وقيراط. تفصيله:
قمح، اردبان وسدس ونصف قيراط.
شعير، تسعة ارادب ونصف وثلث ونصف قيراط.

524 ساقط من أ. س.: خمسة.
525 أ. س.: هذه.
526 أ. س.: سبعون.
527 أ. س.: عليها.
528 ساقط من أ. س.: وقيراط.
529 أ. س. يضيف: وثمن.

Hay, 200 bales.

Seed advances from the Dīwān, 27 1/6 ardabbs:
- wheat, 15 1/3 ardabbs;
- barley, 11 ardabbs;
- sesame 1/2 1/3 ardabb.

Also beginning with the letter 'bā'': Babīj Ghaylān[168] and Kawm al-Raml.[169] These two are small villages in the south-east of the Fayyum, near al-Manhā Canal, four hours' ride from Madīnat al-Fayyūm. Flax and winter cereals are sown here in the manner of Lower Egypt. They are grouped jointly as an *iqṭāʿ*, and their joint fiscal value is 6,000 army dinars. Their people are the Banū Hāniʾ, a branch of the Lawāta.

Their revenues in cash and kind are, in specie, 220 1/4 2/72 dinars; and in grains, 412 1/3 1/4 1/16 ardabbs:
- wheat, 262 1/3 1/4 1/16 ardabbs;
- barley, 150 ardabbs.

[The revenue] in detail:
- ferryboat, 9 dinars;
- permanent pasture tax, 15 dinars;
- land tax, 196 1/4 2/72 dinars; and in grains, 412 1/3 1/4 1/16 ardabbs, as specified.
- [The land tax in detail]:
  - land tax on [lands irrigated by] waterwheels, 60 dinars;
  - tax on flax, 108 5/24 1/72 dinars;
  - land tax on alfalfa, 22 2/3 1/4 dinars;
  - land tax on chickling vetch, 5 1/8 1/72 dinars;

Mushāṭara land tax, in grains, 412 1/3 1/4 1/16 ardabbs, as specified above.

The fees, the measurement fee and the pasture tax are 123 dirhams, which are 3 1/24 1/48 1/72 dinars; and in grains, 17 1/4 1/6 1/8 ardabbs:
- wheat, 4 2/3 1/48 ardabbs;
- barley, 12 1/2 1/3 1/48 ardabbs.

[The fees, the measurement fee and the pasture tax] in detail:
- the fees, 78 dirhams; and in grains, 12 1/24 ardabbs:
  - wheat, 2 1/6 1/48 ardabbs;
  - barley, 9 1/2 1/3 1/48 ardabbs.
- [The fees] include:
  - harvest fee, 53 dirhams;
  - protection fee, 15 dirhams;
  - threshing-floor fee, 10 dirhams; and in grains, 12 1/24 ardabbs:
    - wheat, 2 1/6 1/48 ardabbs;
    - barley, 9 1/2 1/3 1/48 ardabbs.

[168] Modern location: Manyal Hānī (عزبة المنيل). Halm, *Ägypten*, p. 248: Babīj Ghailān; Salmon, 'Répertoire', p. 40: Babīdj Ghaïlān et Kōm al-Raml; Ibn Mammātī, *Kitāb qawānīn al-dawāwīn*, p. 119: of al-Fayyūm; Yāqūt, *Muʿjam al-Buldān*, I, 334; Ibn Duqmāq, *Kitāb al-intiṣār*, V, 6: of al-Bahnasā; Ibn al-Jīʿān, *Kitāb al-tuḥfa*, p. 163: of al-Bahnasā; Ramzī, *Al-Qāmūs*, II/III, 164: Manyal Hānī.

[169] Modern location: Kawm al-Raml al-Baḥrī (كوم الرمل البحري). Ibn Mammātī, *Kitāb qawānīn al-dawāwīn*; Ramzī, *Al-Qāmūs*, II/III, 163: Kawm al-Raml al-Baḥrī.

الكيالة، خمسة ارادب ونصف:

قمح، اردبان ونصف.

شعير، ثلاثة ارادب.

المراعي طارئ، عن اربعة وثمانين راسا، خمسة واربعون درهما. تفصيله:

قطيعة مائة درهم المائة راس، عن تسعة عشر راسا، تسعة عشر درهما.

قطيعة ستين درهما المائة، عن اثنا عشر راسا، سبعة دراهم ونصف.

قطيعة خمسة وعشرين درهما المائة، عن ثلاثة وخمسين راسا، ثلاثة عشر درهما وربع.

رسم المستخدمين خمسة دراهم وربع.

وعليها من الزكاة، عن ثمن اغنام، عن اربع وثلاثين راسا، اربع عشر دينارا وربع وحبتان. تفصيله:

بياض، عن تسعة ارؤس، تسعة دنانير ونصف وربع.

شعارى، عن خمسة وعشرين راسا، اربعة دنانير ونصف وحبتان. تفصيله:

عن[530] الاغنام، عن راسين، دينار وقيراطان.

عن الابل، عن ثلاثة وعشرين راسا، ثلاثة دنانير وربع وسدس وحبتان.

وعليهما من الاتبان اربعمائة شنيف.

ومن حرف الباء، بُلْجُسُوق، من كفور خليج تنبطويه. هذه البلدة عبارة عن بلدة جيدة كبيرة قبلي الفيوم. بينها وبين مدينة الفيوم اربع ساعات للراكب. تشتمل على نخل يسير وجميزة واحدة وهي في عبرة اقطاع الخليج المذكور يخصها من جملة ستة وعشرين الفا مائتان وخمسون دينارا جيشية على حكم مقاسمة الاقطاع. شربها من بحر تنبطويه من الجهة القبلية بما عدته احدى عشرة قبضة وربع ماء. وبها جامع تقام فيه الجمعة وبها[531] كنيسة متهدمة. اهلها بنو حاتم فخذ من بني كلاب.

ارتفاعها، عن سبعمائة وعشرة دراهم، سبعة عشر دينارا ونصف وربع؛ وغلة، خمسمائة وثلاثون اردبا ونصف. تفصيله:

قمح، ثلاثمائة وثلاثة وخمسون اردبا وثلثان.

شعير وفول، مائة وستة وسبعون اردبا ونصف وثلث.

تفصيله:

مناجزة خراج القطن، عن سبعمائة وعشرة دراهم، سبعة عشر دينارا ونصف وربع.

خراج الغلة، خمسمائة وثلاثون اردبا ونصف على ما فصل.

وعليها من الرسوم والكيالة والمراعي، عن مائتين وسبعة وسبعين درهما ونصف، ستة دنانير وثلثان وربع ونصف ثمن، وغلة، اثنان وثلاثون اردبا وثلثان وثمن. تفصيله:

قمح، ثلاث عشر اردبا وثلث وربع ونصف ثمن.

شعير، خمسة عشر اردبا.

فول، اربعة ارادب وثمن ونصف قيراط.

تفصيله:

الرسوم، مائة وسبعة وتسعون درهما وثمن، وغلة، اربعة عشر اردبا وثلثان وربع. تفصيله:

قمح، ستة ارادب ونصف وربع ونصف قيراط.

شعير، ستة ارادب.

فول، اردبان وثمن ونصف قيراط.

530 أ. س.: على.

531 ساقط من ط. م.: بها.

The measurement fee, 5 ½ ardabbs:

wheat, 2 ½ ardabbs;

barley, 3 ardabbs.

The pasture tax on seasonal pasture, for 84 heads, 45 dirhams:

at the rate of 100 dirhams per 100 heads, for 19 heads, 19 dirhams;

at the rate of 60 dirhams per 100 [heads], for 12 heads, 7½ dirhams;

at the rate of 25 dirhams per 100 [heads], for 53 heads, 13¼ dirhams;

the government agents' fee, 5 ¼ dirhams.

The alms-tax, the monetary value of 34 heads of small cattle, 14 ¼ ²⁄₇₂ dinars:

sheep, for nine heads, 9 ½ ¼ dinars;

goats, for 25 heads, 4 ½ ²⁄₇₂ dinars:

[levied on] goats, for two heads, 1 ²⁄₂₄ dinar;

[levied on] camels, for 23 heads, 3 ¼ ⅙ ²⁄₇₂ dinars.

Hay, 400 bales.

Also beginning with the letter 'bā'': Buljusūq,[170] one of the hamlets (*kufūr*) of Tanabṭawayh Canal. This is a pleasant and large village in southern Fayyum, four hours' ride from Madīnat al-Fayyūm. It has a few date palms and one sycamore tree. It is included in the fiscal value of the *iqṭā*ᶜ of the aforementioned canal, and its share, out of the total of 26,250 army dinars, is subject to the rules of dividing the revenues (*muqāsama*) of the *iqṭā*ᶜ. It gets its water from Tanabṭawayh Canal, from the southern bank. Its [water] quota is 11¼ *qabḍas*. It has a congregational mosque, in which the Friday prayers are held, and a deserted church. Its people are the Banū Ḥātim, a branch of the Banū Kilāb.

Its revenue is 710 dirhams, which are 17 ½ ¼ dinars; and in grains, 530 ½ ardabbs:

wheat, 353 ⅔ ardabbs:

barley and broad beans, 176 ½ ⅓ ardabbs.

[The revenue] in detail:

munājaza land tax on cotton, 710 dirhams, which are 17 ½ ¼ dinars;

land tax on grains, 530 ½ ardabbs, as specified.

The fees, the measurement fee and the pasture tax are 277 ½ dirhams, which are 6 ⅔ ¼ ¹⁄₁₆ dinars; and in grains, 32 ⅔ ⅛ ardabbs:

wheat, 13 ⅓ ¼ ¹⁄₁₆ ardabbs;

barley, 15 ardabbs;

broad beans, 4 ⅛ ¹⁄₄₈ ardabbs.

[The fees, the measurement fee and the pasture tax] in detail:

The fees, 197 ⅛ dirhams; and in grains, 14 ⅔ ¼ ardabbs:

wheat, 6 ½ ¼ ¹⁄₄₈ ardabbs;

barley, 6 ardabbs;

broad beans, 2 ⅛ ¹⁄₄₈ ardabbs.

170 Possible modern location: Qaṣr al-Bāsil/ᶜIzbat al-Bāsil (عزبة الباسل/ قصر الباسل). Halm, *Ägypten*, p. 252; Salmon, 'Répertoire', pp. 70–71; Ibn al-Jīᶜān, *Kitāb al-tuḥfa*, p. 153: Buljūq; de Sacy, *État des provinces*, p. 682: Baljūq; Nabia Abbott, 'The Monasteries of the Fayyum', *The American Journal of Semitic Languages and Literatures*, 53. 1 (1936), 13–33 (p. 28): Buljsūk/Abū al-Jusūk/ Barsh; Ramzī, *Al-Qāmūs*, I, 167–68: Qaṣr al-Bāsil. We located it in ᶜIzbat al-Bāsil, five hundred metres north of the mountain — a location which is in line with al-Nābulusī's description.

تفصيله:
رسم الجراريف، خمسة واربعون درهما.
رسم الحصاد، ثلاثة وخمسون درهما ونصف.
رسم الخفارة، خمسة عشر درهما.
شد العين، ثمانية وخمسون درهما ونصف.
شد الاحباس، عشرة دراهم.
رسم الاجران، خمسة عشر درهما وثمن، وغلة، اربعة عشر اردبا وثلثان وربع، على ما فصل.
الكيالة، سبعة عشر اردبا ونصف وربع وثمن. تفصيله:
قمح، ستة ارادب ونصف وربع وثمن.
شعير، تسعة ارادب.
فول اردبان.
المراعي، عن مائة[532] وثلاثة وعشرين راسا، طارئ، ثمانون درهما وربع وثمن. تفصيله:
قطيعة مائة درهم المائة، عن احد وخمسين راسا، احد وخمسون درهما.
قطيعة ثلاثين درهما المائة، عن[533] اثنين وسبعين راسا، احد وعشرون درهما ونصف وثمن.
رسم المستخدمين، سبعة دراهم ونصف وربع.

وعليها من الزكاة،[534] عن ثمن اغنام، عن اربعة عشر راسا، ثمانية دنانير وثمن[535] وحبتان. تفصيله:
بياض، عن ستة اروس، ستة دنانير وسدس.
شعارى، عن ثمانية اروس، دينار واحد ونصف وثلث[536] وثمن وحبتان:
عن الاغنام، عن[537] راسين، دينار وقيراطان.
عن الابل، عن[538] ستة اروس، نصف وربع وثمن وحبتان.

وعليها من الجوالي، عن تسعة[539] نفر، ثمانية عشر دينارا. تفصيله:
مقيم بها نفر واحد، ديناران.
ناؤن عنها بالوجه القبلي، ثمانية نفر، ستة عشر دينارا.

عليها من الاتبان، الف وستمائة شنيف.

وعليها لديوان الاحباس، عينا، اثنا عشر دينارا.

المربى بها من الفروج، ستمائة طائر. تفصيله:
للديوان المعمور، بما فيه من اجرة التربية وهو الثلث، مائتان.
للمقطعين، اربعمائة طائر.

بها من التقاوي السلطانية فيما يخص الاجناد الكيكانية، ثمانون اردبا وثلثان. تفصيله:
قمح، ثلاثة وستون اردبا وثلث وربع وثمن.
شعير، ستة ارادب ونصف وثلث.
فول، تسعة ارادب ونصف وربع.[540]
بزق بصل، سدس اردب.
سمسم، خمسة قراريط.

[532] ساقط من أ. س.: مائة.
[533] ساقط من أ. س.: احد وخمسين رأسا احد وخمسون درهما. قطيعة ثلاثين درهما المائة عن.
[534] ساقط من ط. م.: من الزكاة.
[535] أ. س.: ثلث.
[536] أ. س.: ربع.
[537] ساقط من أ. س.: عن.
[538] ساقط من أ. س.: عن.
[539] أ. س.: ستة.
[540] أ. س.: ثلث.

[the fees] include:
dredging fee, 45 dirhams;
harvest fee, 53 ½ dirhams;
protection fee, 15 dirhams;
supervision of the land survey, 58 ½ dirhams;
supervision of endowments, 10 dirhams;
threshing-floor fee, 15 ⅛ dirhams; and in grains, 14 ⅔ ¼ ardabbs, as specified.

The measurement fee, 17 ½ ¼ ⅛ ardabbs:
wheat, 6 ½ ¼ ⅛ ardabbs;
barley, 9 ardabbs;
broad beans, 2 ardabbs.

The pasture tax on seasonal pasture lands, for 123 heads, 80 ¼ ⅛ dirhams:
at the rate of 100 dirhams per 100 [heads], for 51 heads, 51 dirhams;
at the rate of 30 dirhams per 100 [heads], for 72 heads, 21 ½ ⅛ dirhams;
the government agents' fee, 7 ½ ¼ dirhams.

The alms-tax, which is the monetary value of small cattle, for 14 heads, 8 ⅛ 2/72 dinars:
sheep, for six heads, 6 ⅙ dinars;
goats, for eight heads, a dinar ½ ⅓ ⅛ 2/72:
[levied on] goats, for two heads, 1 2/24 dinar;
[levied on] camels, for six heads, ½ ¼ ⅛ 2/72 [dinar].

The poll-tax, for nine individuals, 18 dinars:
those residing in it, for one individual, 2 dinars;
those absent from it, [residing] in the southern provinces, for eight individuals, 16 dinars.

Hay, 1,600 bales.

For the Ministry of Endowments, in specie, 12 dinars.

The chickens reared in it, 600 birds:
for the prosperous Dīwān, including the rearing wage of a third, 200;
for the *iqṭāʿ*-holders, 400 birds.

The royal seed advances, for the soldiers of the Kīkāniyya regiment,[171] 80 ⅔ ardabbs:
wheat, 63 ⅓ ¼ ⅛ ardabbs;
barley, 6 ½ ⅓ ardabbs;
broad beans, 9 ½ ¼ ardabbs;
onion seeds, ⅙ ardabb;
sesame, 5/24 [ardabb].

[171] These are the troops of the amir ʿIzz al-Dīn Khiḍr ibn Muḥammad al-Kīkānī, who had several *iqṭāʿ*-holdings in the Fayyum.

وبها من الرزق، ثمانية فدادين. تفصيله:
الخطابة، اربعة فدادين.
المشايخ، اربعة فدادين.

The allowances, 8 feddans:
the preachers, 4 feddans;
the headmen, 4 feddans.

والذي يسلف عليه بها من الشعير برسم الاصطبلات السلطانية، تسعة وعشرون اردبا.

The barley assigned for the royal stables, paid for in advance, 29 ardabbs.

اهلها يزرعون من الاقصاب السكر بدموشية، فدانين ونصفًا.

Its people sow sugarcane at Dumūshiyya, 2 ½ feddans.

باقيها في الايام الكاملية عند ما كانت جارية في الخاص لسنة اربع وثلاثين وستمائة وما قبلها مجموع في باقى قمبشا بحكم انها من كفورها.

Its arrears due from the days of al-Kāmil, when it belonged to the private domain of the sultan, for the year 634 and before that, are subsumed under the arrears of Qambashā, since it [Buljusūq] was [then] one of its hamlets.

ومن حرف التاء، ترسا. هذه البلدة عبارة عن بلدة متوسطة بين الكبيرة والصغيرة. بينها وبين مدينة الفيوم اكثر من مسافة ساعتين للراكب. وليس بها نخل ولا بساتين ولا شجر ولا كرم. بها مساجد غير مدونة، وذكر ان بها مدافن الصالحين. وهي جارية في اقطاع جماعة من المقطعين. عبرتها سبعة الاف وتسعمائة دينار جيشية. تشرب من خليج البر البحري اخر الجهة الشرقية من المدينة شركة الطارمة، ينقسم[541] من اسفل في خليجين تخص ترسا بخليج عشر قبض ونصف. بها جامع تقام فيه الجمعة. اهلها بنو سمالوس، فخذ من بني عجلان.

Beginning with the letter 'tā'': Tirsā.[172] This is a medium-sized village, more than two hours' ride from Madīnat al-Fayyūm. There are no date palms, orchards, trees or vineyards in it. It has unregistered mosques, and it has been said that some pious men are buried there. It is assigned as an *iqṭāʿ* to a group of *iqṭāʿ*-holders, and its fiscal value is 7,900 army dinars. It gets its water from a canal [that flows] from the northern bank [of the Main Canal] at the eastern edge of the city. [The canal] is shared with al-Ṭārima, and as it descends it splits into two canals. Tirsā is allocated 10½ *qabḍas* to its own canal. It has a congregational mosque, in which the Friday prayers are held. Its people are the Banū Samālūs, a branch of the Banū ʿAjlān.

ارتفاعها تسعة عشر دينارا، وغلة، الف وخمسمائة اردب:
قمح، اربعمائة اردب.
شعير، الف ومائة اردب.

Its revenue is 19 dinars; and in grains, 1,500 ardabbs:
wheat, 400 ardabbs;
barley, 1,100 ardabbs.

تفصيله:
الهلالي، ستة عشر دينارا.
المراعي، ثلاثة دنانير.

[The revenue] in detail:
lunar-calendar tax, 16 dinars;
pasture tax, 3 dinars;

خراج المناجزة، الف وخمسمائة اردب على ما فصل.

Munājaza land tax, 1,500 ardabbs, as specified.

وعليها من الرسوم والكيالة والمراعي، عن اربعمائة وستين درهما ونصف، احد عشر دينارا ونصف وحبة; وغلة، تسعة وتسعون اردبا وسدس ونصف قيراط. تفصيله:
قمح، تسعة وثلاثون اردبا وربع.
شعير، خمسون اردبا وسدس وثمن.
فول، تسعة ارادب وثلث وربع ونصف ثمن.

The fees, the measurement fee and the pasture tax are 460 ½ dirhams, which are 11 ½ 1/72 dinars; and in grains, 99 ⅙ 1/48 ardabbs:
wheat, 39 ¼ ardabbs;
barley, 50 ⅙ ⅛ ardabbs;
broad beans, 9 ⅓ ¼ 1/16 ardabbs.

تفصيله:
الرسوم، مائتان وستة وعشرون درهما وربع، وغلة، ثلاثة وستون اردبا وثمن ونصف قيراط. تفصيله:
قمح، تسعة وعشرون اردبا وخمسة قراريط.
شعير، ستة وعشرون اردبا وسدس وثمن.
فول، سبعة ارادب وثلث وربع وثمن.
تفصيله:
شد الاحباس، اثنا عشر درهما.
رسم الجراريف، تسعون درهما.
رسم الحصاد، ثلاثة وخمسون درهما.
رسم الخفارة، خمسة عشر درهما.
رسم الاجران، ستة وخمسون درهما وربع، وغلة، ثلاثة وستون اردبا وثمن ونصف قيراط، على ما فصل.

[The fees, the measurement fee and the pasture tax] in detail:
the fees, 226 ¼ dirhams; and in grains, 63 ⅛ 1/48 ardabbs:
wheat, 29 5/24 ardabbs;
barley, 26 ⅙ ⅛ ardabbs;
broad beans, 7 ⅓ ¼ ⅛ ardabbs.
[The fees] include:
supervision of endowments, 12 dirhams;
dredging fee, 90 dirhams;
harvest fee, 53 dirhams;
protection fee, 15 dirhams;
threshing-floor fee, 56 ¼ dirhams; and in grains, 63 ⅛ 1/48 ardabbs, as specified.

541 ط. م.: تنقسم.

172 Modern location: Tirsā (ترسا). Halm, *Ägypten*, p. 275; Salmon, 'Répertoire', p. 53; de Sacy, *État des provinces*, p. 182; Savigny, *Description de l'Égypte*, p. 130; Ibn Mammātī, *Kitāb qawānīn al-dawāwīn*, p. 123; Ibn al-Jīʿān, *Kitāb al-tuḥfa*, p. 154; Ramzī, *Al-Qāmūs*, II/III, 112: Tirsā.

الكيالة، ستة وثلاثون اردبا وقيراط. تفصيله:
قمح، عشرة ارادب وقيراط.
شعير، اربعة وعشرون اردبا.
فول، اردبان.
المراعي، عن خمسمائة وتسعة واربعين راسا طارئ، مائتان واربعة وثلاثون درهما وربع. تفصيله:
قطيعة درهم واحد الراس، عن اربعة ارؤس، اربعة دراهم.
قطيعة خمسين درهما المائة راس، عن مائتين واثنين وثلاثين راسا، مائة وستة عشر درهما.
قطيعة ثلاثين درهما المائة راس، عن ثلاثة وثلاثين راسا، عشرة دراهم.
قطيعة خمسة وعشرين درهما المائة، عن مائتين وثمانين راسا، سبعون درهما.
رسم المستخدمين، حسابا عن كل مائة راس ستة دراهم وربع، اربعة وثلاثون درهما وربع.

وعليها من الزكاة، عن ثمن تسعة ارؤس تسعة دنانير. تفصيله:
بقر احمر، تبيع واحد، دينار واحد.
اغنام، عن ثمانية ارؤس، ثمانية دنانير. تفصيله:
بياض، عن ستة ارؤس، ستة دنانير ونصف وربع.
شعارى، عن راسين دينار وربع.

عليها لديوان الاحباس، عينا، ستة دنانير.

وعليها من الجوالي، عن نفر واحد مقيم بها،[542] ديناران.

عليها من الاتبان، الف واربعمائة شنيف.

رسم خولي البحر بها، قمح، اردب واحد.

والذي يسلف عليه بها من الشعير برسم الاصطبلات السلطانية، ثلاثمائة اردب.

والذي جرت العادة به من الاصناف على مزارعيها، اردبان ونصف. تفصيله:
كشك، اردب واحد.
فريك، اردب واحد.
سويق، نصف اردب.

اهلها يزرعون من القصب الراس بعد برشه بابقارهم ورجالهم، سبعة فدادين، ويسقون من الخلفة اربعة فدادين.

والمربى بها من الفروج، سبعمائة وخمسون:
للديوان، اربعمائة وخمسون.
للمقطعين، ثلاثمائة طائر.

ومن حرف التاء، تطون. هذه البلدة عبارة عن بلدة صغيرة. كان قبليها بلدة تعرف بتطون دثرت وهي كبيرة وعمرت هذه وسميت باسمها. مزارعها شتوية وبها يسير من الاقطان. بينها وبين مدينة الفيوم مسافة ثلاث ساعات للراكب. وهي من نواحي خليج تنبطويه، جارية في اقطاع المقطعين مجموعة في الاقطاع في[543] جملة الخليج المذكور. شربها من بحر تنبطويه بما عبرته احدى عشرة قبضة وربع، وبرسم شرب اطفيح شلا[544] من حقوقها للشتوي والصيفي خمس قبض. اهلها بنو حاتم، فخذ من بني كلاب.[545]

542 ساقط من ط. م.: بها.
543 أ. س.: من.
544 ساقط من أ. س.: شلا.
545 ط. م.: أهلها بنو حاتم فخذ من بني كلاب. وبرسم شرب اطفيح شلا من حقوقها للشتوي والصيفي خمس قبض.

The measurement fee, 36 1/24 ardabbs:
- wheat, 10 1/24 ardabbs;
- barley, 24 ardabbs;
- broad beans, 2 ardabbs.

The pasture tax, for 549 heads of seasonal pasture lands, 234 ¼ dirhams:
- at the rate of one dirham per head, for four heads, 4 dirhams;
- at the rate of 50 dirhams per 100 heads, for 232 heads, 116 dirhams;
- at the rate of 30 dirhams per 100 heads, for 33 heads, 10 dirhams;
- at the rate of 25 dirhams per 100 [heads], for 280 heads, 70 dirhams;
- the government agents' fee, calculated at the rate of 6¼ dirhams for every 100 heads, 34 ¼ dirhams.

The alms-tax, which is the monetary value of nine heads, 9 dinars:
- cows, one yearling calf, 1 dinar;
- small cattle, for eight heads, 8 dinars:
  - sheep, for six heads, 6 ½ ¼ dinars;
  - goats, for two heads, 1¼ dinar.

For the Ministry of Endowments, in specie, 6 dinars.

The poll-tax, for one individual residing in it, 2 dinars.

Hay, 1,400 bales.

The fee of the overseer of the canal, wheat, 1 ardabb.

The barley assigned for the royal stables, which is paid for in advance, 300 ardabbs.

The foodstuffs customarily levied on its tenants, 2 ½ ardabbs:
- *kishk*, 1 ardabb;
- *farīq*, 1 ardabbs;
- *sawīq*, ½ ardabb.

Its people sow first-harvest sugarcane after tilling it by means of their cattle and men, 7 feddans. They irrigate 4 feddans of second harvest [sugarcane].

The chickens reared in it, 750:
- for the Dīwān, 450;
- for the *iqṭāʿ*-holders, 300 birds.

Also beginning with the letter 'tā'': Tuṭūn.[173] This is a small village. South of it there used to be a large village called Tuṭūn, but it has been deserted, and then this one was built and took over its name. It has winter cultivation, and some cotton cultivation. It is one of the villages of Tanabṭawayh Canal, three hours' ride from Madīnat al-Fayyūm. It is assigned as an *iqṭāʿ* to *iqṭāʿ*-holders, and grouped together under the *iqṭāʿ* of Tanabṭawayh Canal. It gets its water from that canal, with a quota of 11 ¼ *qabḍas*. Five *qabḍas* are assigned for the irrigation of Iṭfīḥ Shallā,[174] which is entitled to the water of this village for winter and summer cultivation. Its people are the Banū Ḥātim, a branch of the Banū Kilāb.

173 Modern location: Tuṭūn (تطون). Timm, *Das Christlich-Koptische Ägypten*, pp. 2887–92: Tebtynis (Tuṭun, Umm al-Barajāt, in Arabic); Trismegistos GEO ID 2287; Salmon, 'Répertoire', p. 70; Halm, *Ägypten*, p. 274: Taṭūn/Ṭalīt; Ibn al-Jīʿān, *Kitāb al-tuḥfa*, p. 154: Taṭūb Wa-Ṭalīb; de Sacy, *État des provinces*, p. 682: Taṭūb; Ramzī, *Al-Qāmūs*, II/III, 84: Tuṭūn. Tuṭūn is very well represented in the documentary evidence from the Abbasid and Fatimid periods, and, uniquely for the Fayyum, its Islamic site has been excavated. See Marie-Odile Rousset and Sylvie Marchand, 'Tebtynis 1998, travaux dans le secteur nord', *Annales Islamologiques*, 33 (1999), 185–262; Rousset and Marchand, 'Secteur nord de Tebtynis: Mission de 1999', *Annales Islamologiques*, 34 (2000), 387–436.

174 Modern location (uncertain): near ʿIzbat Salām (عزبة سلام). Halm, *Ägypten*, p. 247: Aṭfīḥ Shallā; Ramzī, *Al-Qāmūs*, I, 21: Kōm Iṭfīḥ, near ʿIzbat Qalamshāh.

ارتفاعها عينا، عن مناجزة القطن، عن سبعمائة وثمانية وثلاثين درهما، ثمانية عشر دينارا وربع وسدس ونصف قيراط وحبة; وغلة، عن المناجزة، ثمانمائة واثنان وستون اردبا ونصف. تفصيله:

قمح، خمسمائة وخمسة وسبعون اردبا.

شعير وفول، مائتان وسبعة وثمانون اردبا ونصف.

عليها من الرسوم والكيالة والمراعي، ما هو مختص بتطون، عن مائتين وستة وثمانين درهما وربع وثمن، سبعة دنانير وسدس; وغلة، خمسون اردبا وسدس ونصف قيراط. تفصيله:

قمح، اثنان وثلاثون اردبا وربع وسدس وثمن.

شعير، ستة ارادب ونصف وثلث ونصف قيراط.

فول، عشرة ارادب وثلثان وثمن.

تفصيله:

الرسوم، مائتان وتسعة عشر درهما ونصف، وغلة، اربعة واربعون اردبا وسدس ونصف قيراط. تفصيله:

قمح، تسعة وعشرون اردبا وربع وسدس وثمن.

شعير، ثلاثة ارادب ونصف وثلث ونصف قيراط.

فول، عشرة ارادب وثلثان وثمن.

تفصيله:

شد العين، ثمانية وخمسون درهما ونصف.

شد الاحباس، عشرة دراهم ونصف.

رسم الجراريف، خمسة واربعون درهما.

رسم الحصاد، ثلاثة وخمسون درهما.[546]

رسم الخفارة، خمسة عشر درهما.

رسم الاجران، سبعة وثلاثون درهما ونصف، وغلة، اربعة واربعون اردبا وسدس ونصف قيراط على ما فصل.

الكيالة، ستة ارادب، قمح وشعير نصفان.

المراعي[547]، ستة وستون درهما ونصف وربع وثمن. تفصيله:

قطيعة ثلاثين درهما المائة، عن احد وثمانين راسا، اربعة وعشرون درهما وربع.

قطيعة خمسة وعشرين درهما المائة، عن مائة وعشرين راسا، ثلاثون درهما.

رسم المستخدمين، اثنا عشر درهما ونصف وثمن.

اطفيح شلا من حقوق الناحية، رسم اجران وكيالة ومراعي، عن ثلاثة وخمسين درهما وربع وثمن، دينار واحد وثلث; وغلة، ثلاثة عشر اردبا ونصف وثلث ونصف قيراط:

قمح، عشرة ارادب.

فول، ثلاثة ارادب ونصف وثلث ونصف قيراط.

وعليها من الزكاة ما يخص تطون، عن ثمن اغنام، عن ثلاثة عشر راسا، تسعة دنانير ونصف وثلث وثمن. تفصيله:

بياض، عن ثمانية ارؤس، ثمانية دنانير ونصف.

شعارى، عن خمسة ارؤس، دينار واحد وثلث وثمن:

عن الاغنام، عن راسين، دينار واحد.

عن الابل، عن ثلاثة ارؤس، ثلث وثمن دينار.

ما يخص اطفيح شلا عن ثمن اغنام، عن اربعة ارؤس، ثلاثة دنانير وخمسة قراريط. تفصيله:

بياض، عن راسين، ديناران وثمن.

شعارى، عن راسين، دينار وقيراطان.

Its revenues in specie from *munājaza* land tax on cotton: 738 dirhams, which are 18 ¼ ⅙ ⅟₄₈ ⅟₇₂ dinars; and *munājaza* land tax in grains, 862 ½ ardabbs:

wheat, 575 ardabbs;

barley and broad beans, 287 ½ ardabbs.

The fees, the measurement fee and the pasture tax for Tuṭūn proper are 286 ¼ ⅛ dirhams, which are 7 ⅙ dinars; and in grains, 50 ⅙ ⅟₄₈ ardabbs:

wheat, 32 ¼ ⅙ ⅛ ardabbs;

barley, 6 ½ ⅓ ⅟₄₈ ardabbs;

broad beans, 10 ⅔ ⅛ ardabbs.

[The fees, the measurement fee and the pasture tax] include:

the fees, 219 ½ dirhams; and in grains, 44 ⅙ ⅟₄₈ ardabbs:

wheat, 29 ¼ ⅙ ⅛ ardabbs;

barley, 3 ½ ⅓ ⅟₄₈ ardabbs;

broad beans, 10 ⅔ ⅛ ardabbs.

[the fees] in detail:

supervision of the land survey, 58 ½ dirhams;

supervision of endowments, 10 ½ dirhams;

dredging fee, 45 dirhams;

harvest fee, 53 dirhams;

protection fee, 15 dirhams;

threshing-floor fees, 37 ½ dirhams; and in grains, 44 ⅙ ⅟₄₈ ardabbs, as specified.

The measurement fee, 6 ardabbs of wheat and barley, half in each.

The pasture tax, for 201 heads, 66 ½ ¼ ⅛ dirhams:

at the rate of 30 dirhams per 100 [heads], for 81 heads, 24 ¼ dirhams;

at the rate of 25 dirhams per 100 [heads], for 120 heads, 30 dirhams;

the government agents' fee, 12 ½ ⅛ dirhams.

The threshing-floor fee, the measurement fee and the pasture tax for Iṭfīḥ Shallā, which is included in the accounts of this village, are 53 ¼ ⅛ dirhams, which are 1 ⅓ dinar; and in grains, 13 ½ ⅓ ⅟₄₈ ardabbs:

wheat, 10 ardabbs;

broad beans, 3 ½ ⅓ ⅟₄₈ ardabbs.

The alms-tax on Tuṭūn proper, for the monetary value of 13 heads of small cattle, 9 ½ ⅓ ⅛ dinars:

sheep, for eight heads, 8 ½ dinars;

goats, for five heads, 1 ⅓ ⅛ dinar:

[levied on] small cattle, for two heads, 1 dinar;

[levied on] camels, for three heads, ⅓ ⅛ dinar.

[The alms-tax that pertains to] Iṭfīḥ Shallā, for the monetary value of four heads of small cattle, 3 ⁵⁄₂₄ dinars:

sheep, for two heads, 2 ⅛ dinars;

goats, for two heads, 1 ²⁄₂₄ dinar.

546 ساقط من أ. س.: رسم الحصاد ثلاثة وخمسون درهما.

547 ساقط من ط. م.: ستة أرادب قمح وشعير نصفان. المراعي.

We could not locate this ʿIzba. Al-Nābulusī does not provide any geographical information about this hamlet. We placed it near the modern village of ʿIzbat Salām.

وعلى اطفيح شلا لديوان الاحباس، ديناران.

وعليها من الاتبان، الف وستمائة شنيف.

والمربى بها من الفروج، ثمانمائة فروج. تفصيله:
للديوان المعمور، بما فيه من اجرة التربية وهو الثلث، اربعمائة طائر.
للمقطعين، اربعمائة طائر.

والمسلف عليه بها من الشعير برسم الاصطبلات السلطانية، ثلاثة واربعون اردبا ونصف.

والذي بها من التقاوي الديوانية، ثمانية ارادب وثلث ونصف ثمن. تفصيله:
قمح، ستة ارادب وقيراط.
فول، اردبان.
سمسم، ثلث ونصف قيراط.

اهلها يزرعون قصب السكر بدموشية، راس، ثلاثة فدادين.

ومن حرف الثاء، ثلاث.[548] هذه البلدة عبارة عن بلدة متوسطة بين الكبر والصغر. بينها وبين مدينة الفيوم ساعتان للراكب. بها نخل وشجر وبساتين وكرم. بها مساجد غير مدونة وذكر ان بها مدافن الصالحين. وهي جارية في اقطاع جماعة من المقطعين. عبرتها جيشية ثلاثة الاف وستمائة دينار. شربها من خليج من البر القبلي بعد خليج الاستنباط بغير بنيان، ليس له عبرة قبض. اهلها بنو جواب، فخذ من بني كلاب.

ارتفاعها مما جميعه مستخرجا ومتحصلا، ثمانية وخمسون دينارا وسدس ونصف قيراط؛ وغلة، خمسمائة وستة وسبعون اردبا. تفصيله:
قمح، مائتان وثمانية وثمانون اردبا.
شعير، مائتان وثمانية وثمانون[549] اردبا.

تفصيله:
مراعي، سبعة دنانير وسدس ونصف قيراط.
خراج الاحكار، احد وخمسون دينارا. تفصيله:
الاصل، قطيعة ديناران الفدان، عن اربعة وعشرين فدانا، ثمانية واربعون دينارا.
الاضافة، عن كل فدان ثمن دينار، ثلاثة دنانير.

خراج المناجزة، غلة، خمسمائة وستة وسبعون اردبا. تفصيله:
قمح، مائتان وثمانية وثمانون اردبا.
شعير، مائتان وثمانية وثمانون.

وعليها من الرسوم والكيالة والمراعي، عن مائتان وثمانية دراهم، خمسة دنانير وسدس ونصف قيراط وحبة؛ وغلة، سبعة وثلاثون اردبا وثلثان وربع. تفصيله:
قمح، سبعة عشر اردبا ونصف وثلث وثمن.
شعير، اربعة عشر اردبا وثلث وربع وثمن.
فول، خمسة ارادب وربع.

تفصيله:
الرسوم، مائة وثلاثة وسبعون درهما وربع وثمن، وغلة، عشرون اردبا وثلث وربع:
قمح، تسعة ارادب ونصف وثلث وثمن.
شعير، ستة ارادب وربع وسدس وثمن.
فول، ثلاثة ارادب وقيراطان.

[548] ط م.: ثلات ويورد البلدة من حرف التاء.
[549] أ س.: ثلاثون.

For the Ministry of Endowments, on Iṭfīḥ Shallā, 2 dinars.

Hay, 1,600 bales.

The chickens reared in it, 800 chickens:
for the prosperous Dīwān, including the rearing wage of a third, 400 birds;
for the *iqṭāʿ*-holders, 400 birds.

The barley assigned for the royal stables and paid for in advance, 43 ½ ardabbs.

The seed advances from the Dīwān, 8 1/3 1/16 ardabbs:
wheat, 6 1/24 ardabbs;
broad beans, 2 ardabbs;
sesame, 1/3 1/48 [ardabb].

Its people sow first harvest sugarcane at Dumūshiyya, 3 feddans.

Beginning with the letter 'thā'': Thalāth.[175] This is a medium-sized village, two hours' ride from Madīnat al-Fayyūm. It has date palms, trees, orchards and a vineyard. It has unregistered mosques, and it has been said that some pious men are buried there. It is assigned as an *iqṭāʿ* to a group of *iqṭāʿ*-holders. Its fiscal value is 3,600 army dinars. It gets its water from a canal without a weir, which issues from the southern bank [of the Main Canal], after al-Istinbāṭ Canal. It has no water quota. Its people are the Banū Jawwāb, a branch of the Banū Kilāb.

Its revenues in cash and kind are 58 1/6 1/48 dinars; and in grains, 576 ardabbs:
wheat, 288 ardabbs;
barley, 288 ardabbs.

[The revenue] in detail:
pasture tax, 7 1/6 1/48 dinars;
land tax on lands subject to long-term lease, 51 dinars:
basic assessment, at the rate of 2 dinars per feddan, for 24 feddans, 48 dinars;
the addition, [at a rate of] 1/8 dinar per feddan, 3 dinars.

Munājaza land tax in grains, 576 ardabbs:
wheat, 288 ardabbs;
barley, 288 [ardabbs].

The fees, the measurement fee and the pasture tax are 208 dirhams, which are 5 1/6 1/48 1/72 dinars; and in grains, 37 2/3 1/4 ardabbs:
wheat, 17 ½ 1/3 1/8 ardabbs;
barley, 14 1/3 1/4 1/8 ardabbs;
broad beans, 5 1/4 ardabbs.

[The fees, the measurement fee and the pasture tax] include:
The fees, 173 1/4 1/8 dirhams, and in grains, 20 1/3 1/4 ardabbs:
wheat, 9 ½ 1/3 1/8 ardabbs;
barley, 7 1/4 1/6 1/8 ardabbs;
broad beans, 3 2/24 ardabbs.

[175] Modern location: Talāt (تلات). Halm, *Ägypten*, p. 274: Talāt al-ʿUlyā; Salmon, 'Répertoire', p. 60; de Sacy, *État des provinces*, p. 682; Savigny, *Description de l'Égypte*, p. 128; Boinet Bey, *Dictionnaire géographique*: Talāt al-Maẓālīm; Ramzī, *Al-Qāmūs*, II/III, 98: Talāt.

تفصيله:

شد العين، احد وسبعون درهما.

رسم الحصاد، ثلاثة وخمسون درهما.

رسم الخفارة، خمسة عشر درهما.

رسم الجراريف، خمسة عشر درهما.

شد الاحباس، درهم واحد ونصف وربع وثمن.

رسم الاجران، سبعة عشر درهما ونصف، وغلة، عشرون اردبا وثلث وربع على ما تقدم.

الكيالة، سبعة عشر اردبا وثلث. تفصيله:

قمح، ثمانية ارادب.

شعير، سبعة ارادب وسدس.

فول، اردبان وسدس.

مراعي الاغنام الطارئ، عن مائة وتسعة ارؤس، اربعة وثلاثون درهما ونصف وثمن. تفصيله:

قطيعة خمسة وعشرين درهما المائة، عن العدة المذكورة، سبعة وعشرون درهما وربع.

رسم المستخدمين، سبعة دراهم وربع وثمن.

وعليها من الزكاة، ستة وعشرين دينارا وربع. تفصيله:

خرص العنب، احد وعشرون دينارا.

ثمن الماشية، عن ستة ارؤس، خمسة دنانير وربع. تفصيله:

بقر احمر، تبيع واحد، دينار واحد ونصف.

ثمن الاغنام، عن خمسة ارؤس، ثلاثة دنانير ونصف وربع. تفصيله:

بياض، عن راسين، ديناران وربع.

شعارى، عن ثلاثة ارؤس، دينار ونصف.

وعليها من الاتبان، تسعمائة وخمسون شنيفا.

اهلها يزرعون قصب السكر برسم معصرة سينرو باراضي الناحية، تسعة فدادين وربع وسدس. تفصيله:

راس، ستة فدادين وثلث.

خلفة، ثلاثة فدادين وقيراطان.

والذي يربى بها من الدجاج،[550] مائتان وثلاثون طائرا:

للديوان المعمور، بما فيه من اجرة التربية وهو الثلث، مائة وثلاثون طائرا.

وللمقطعين، مائة طائر.

وبها من التقاوي للمقطعين برسم عمارة الناحية، اثنان وتسعون اردبا، قمح وشعير نصفان.

والذي يسلف عليه بها من الشعير برسم الاصطبلات السلطانية، اربعون اردبا.

ومن حرف الجيم، جرفس. هذه البلدة عبارة عن بلدة صغيرة من كفور سنورس. وقد دثرت من تقادم الزمان[551] وهي الان ارض تزرع بغير جدار وهي من بحري الفيوم. مسافتها من مدينة الفيوم ساعتان للراكب. ومن حقوقها نخل وبساتين يستادى[552] الخراج عن ذلك للبلدة المذكورة. وهي من حقوق سنورس، جارية في اقطاع الامير شمس الدين محمد بن قيصر. لها من الماء من[553] بحر سنورس من المقسم المعروف بالشاذروان للشتوي والصيفي

550 أ. س.: الفروج.

551 أ. س.: السنين.

552 ط. م.: تساوي.

553 ساقط من ط. م.: الماء من.

[The fees] in detail:

supervision of the land survey, 71 dirhams;

harvest fee, 53 dirhams;

protection fee, 15 dirhams;

dredging fee, 15 dirhams;

supervision of endowments, 1 ½ ¼ ⅛ dirham;

threshing-floor fee, 17½ dirhams; and in grains, 20 ⅓ ¼ ardabbs, as specified.

the measurement fee, 17 ⅓ ardabbs:

wheat, 8 ardabbs;

barley, 7 ⅙ ardabbs;

broad beans, 2 ⅙ ardabbs.

the pasture tax on small cattle in seasonal pasture, for 109 heads, 34 ½ ⅛ dirhams:

at the rate of 25 dirhams per 100 [heads], for that number [of heads], 27 ¼ dirhams;

the government agents' fee, 7 ¼ ⅛ dirhams.

The alms-tax, 26 ¼ dinars:

the estimate of grapes, 21 dinars;

monetary value of livestock, for six heads, 5 ¼ dinars:

cows, one yearling calf, 1 ½ dinar;

monetary value of small cattle, for five heads, 3 ½ ¼ dinars:

sheep, for two heads, 2 ¼ dinars;

goats, for three heads, 1 ½ dinar.

Hay, 950 bales.

Its people sow 9 ¼ ⅙ feddans of sugarcane, assigned for the press at Sīnarū, in the lands of the village:

first harvest, 6 ⅓ feddans;

second harvest, 3 2/24 feddans.

The chickens reared in it, 230 birds:

for the prosperous Dīwān, including the rearing wage of a third, 130 birds;

for the *iqṭā*ᶜ-holders, 100 birds.

The seed advances for the *iqṭā*ᶜ-holders, towards the village's cultivation, 92 ardabbs of wheat and barley, half in each.

The barley assigned for the royal stables and paid for in advance, 40 ardabbs.

Beginning with the letter 'jīm': Jarfis.[176] This is a small village, one of the hamlets of Sinnūris. It was deserted a long time ago, but now the land is sown, with no fences. It lies in the north of the province, two hours' ride from Madīnat al-Fayyūm. Its rights for water are used for the cultivation of date palms and orchards, from which the land tax of the village is paid. It is included in the accounts of Sinnūris, [but separately] assigned as an *iqṭā*ᶜ to the amir Shams al-Dīn Muḥammad ibn Qayṣar. It has two *qabḍas* of water for winter and summer cultivation, drawn from Sinnūris Canal, from the divisor known as

[176] Modern location: Jarfis (جرفس). Halm, *Ägypten*, p. 257; Salmon, 'Répertoire', p. 51: Jarfas; Zéki, 'Une description', p. 38; Ibn al-Jīᶜān, *Kitāb al-tuḥfa*, p. 153: Jarīs; Ibn Mammātī, *Kitāb qawānīn al-dawāwīn*, p. 127: Kharfis; Ramzī, *Al-Qāmūs*, II/III, 112: Jarfis.

قبضتان. اهلها جابريون من القياصرة، فخذ من بني كلاب [= عجلان].[554] عبرتها جيشية الف دينار.

ارتفاعها، عينا، اربعة وستون دينارا وربع، وغلة، مائتان وستون اردبا ونصف وربع. تفصيله:

قمح، مائة واحد وثمانون اردبا وسدس.
شعير، خمسة وعشرون اردبا وثلث وربع.
فول، سبعة واربعون اردبا.
سمسم، سبعة ارادب.

تفصيله:

خراج العين بما فيه[555] مما هو موقوف عن[556] الداثر، وهو ستة عشر دينارا، اربعة وستون دينارا وربع.

مشاطرة الغلة، مائة واربعة وثمانون اردبا. تفصيله:

قمح، مائة وثلاثون اردبا.
شعير، سبعة واربعون اردبا.
سمسم، سبعة ارادب.

خراج قصب السكر، غلة، ستة وسبعون اردبا ونصف وربع. تفصيله:

قمح، احد وخمسون اردبا وسدس.
شعير، خمسة وعشرون اردبا وثلث وربع.

وعليها من الرسوم والكيالة عن اربعة وستين درهما ونصف، دينار واحد وثلث وربع وحبة؛ وغلة، ستة ارادب ونصف. تفصيله:

قمح، ثلاثة ارادب ونصف وربع.
شعير، اردبان ونصف وربع.
تفصيله:
رسم قلقاس، تسعة وخمسون درهما ونصف.
رسم الاجران، خمسة دراهم، وغلة، خمسة ارادب ونصف:
قمح، اردبان ونصف وربع.[557]
فول، اردبان ونصف وربع.
الكيالة، اردب واحد قمحًا.

وعليها من الزكاة، عن ثمن اغنام، عن خمسة ارؤس، دينار واحد وثلث وربع وحبة. تفصيله:

القراريه،[558] بياض، عن راس واحد، دينار واحد.
المنتجعون، شعارى، عن اربعة ارؤس، عن ابل، ثلث وربع وحبة.

وعليها من الاتبان، مائتان وستون شنيفا.

والذي جرت العادة باطلاقه للناحية من التقاوي، سبعة وخمسون اردبا وثلث:

قمح، اربعون اردبا.
فول، سبعة عشر[559] اردبا وثلث.

al-Shādhrawān. Its people are the Banū Jābir of the Qayāṣira, a branch of the Banū ʿAjlān.[177] Its fiscal value is 1,000 army dinars.

Its revenues, in specie, 64 ¼ dinars; and in grains, 260 ½ ¼ ardabbs:

wheat, 181 ⅙ ardabbs;
barley, 25 ⅓ ¼ ardabbs;
broad beans, 47 ardabbs;
sesame, 7 ardabbs.

The land tax in specie, 64 ¼ dinars, including 16 dinars as withheld payments on what had fallen into disuse.

Mushāṭara land tax on grains, 184 ardabbs:

wheat, 130 ardabbs;
barley, 47 ardabbs;
sesame, 7 ardabbs.

Land tax on sugarcane, in grains, 76 ½ ¼ ardabbs:[178]

wheat, 51 ⅙ ardabbs;
barley, 25 ⅓ ¼ ardabbs.

The fees and the measurement fee, 64 ½ dirhams, which are 1 ⅓ ¼ 1/72 dinar; and in grains, 6 ½ ardabbs:

wheat, 3 ½ ¼ ardabbs;
barley, 2 ½ ¼ ardabbs.
[The fees] include:
fee on colocasia, 59 ½ dirhams;
threshing-floor fee, 5 dirhams; and in grains, 5 ½ ardabbs:
wheat, 2 ½ ¼ ardabbs;
broad beans, 2 ½ ¼ ardabbs.
The measurement fee, 1 ardabb of wheat.

The alms-tax, for the monetary value of five heads of small cattle, 1 ⅓ ¼ 1/72 dinar:

local sheep, for one head, 1 dinar;
for four heads of goats levied on camels seeking pasture, ⅓ ¼ 1/72 [dinar].

Hay, 260 bales.

The seed advances customarily distributed in the village, 57 ⅓ ardabbs:

wheat, 40 ardabbs;
broad beans, 17 ⅓ ardabbs.

554 أ. س.; ط. م.: كلاب.
555 ساقط من أ. س.: بما فيه.
556 أ. س.: على.
557 ساقط من أ. س.: قمح أردبان ونصف وربع.
558 ط. م.: القزازيه، أ. س.: القراريه.
559 ساقط من أ. س.: عشر.

177 AS and MP: Banū Kilāb. Elsewhere the Qayāṣira are identified as a branch, or a sub-section, of the Banū ʿAjlān.

178 In this village, as well as in Shisfa, land tax on the cultivation of sugarcane was unusually paid in grains. In most villages sugarcane was cultivated on crown estates and was not subject to taxation at all. In a couple of other villages (Minyat Karbīs, Bāja) the sugarcane plantations were subject to a land tax in cash, with a low rate of one or two dinars per feddan.

ومن حرف الجيم، جردو. هذه البلدة عبارة عن بلدة كبيرة. بها نخل وكروم وعنب وسنط وجميز. وهي من غربي الفيوم. تزرع الحبوب الشتوية. بينها وبين مدينة الفيوم مسافة ساعة ونصف للراكب. جارية في اقطاع جماعة من المقطعين. عبرتها جيشية، اربعة الاف وخمسمائة وتسعة وثلاثون دينارا. شربها من مقسم بخشبة اخر البحر اليوسفي من البر البحري، شركة ابي كسا وببيج انشو وابشاية الرمان وطبهار، بما عبرته عما يخص الناحية ثمان قبض.

ارتفاعها مما جميعه مستخرجا ومتحصلا، عينا، تسعة وثمانون دينارا ونصف، وغلة، الف واربعمائة وعشرون اردبا. تفصيله:

قمح، سبعمائة وعشرة ارادب.
شعير، ستمائة وخمسة وستون اردبا.
سلجم، ثمانية ارادب.
كمون، سبعة ارادب.

تفصيله:

مال الهلالي، عن ضمان الحانوت، اثنا عشر دينارا.
مال المراعي، ثلاثة دنانير وربع وثمن.
الخراجي، اربعة وسبعون دينارا[560] وثمن، والغلة، على ما تقدم شرحه. تفصيله: خراج الراتب والاحكار، اصلا واضافة، اربعة وسبعون دينارا وثمن.

خراج مناجزة الغلة، الف واربعمائة وعشرون اردبا على ما فصل.

وعليها من الرسوم والمراعي والكيالة، عن ثلاثمائة وستة وتسعين درهما ونصف وربع وثمن، تسعة دنانير وثلثان وربع وحبة؛ وغلة، ستة وثمانون اردبا وثلث وربع. تفصيله:

قمح، اربعة واربعون اردبا وربع وسدس ونصف قيراط.
شعير، ستة وثلاثون اردبا.
فول، ستة ارادب وثمن ونصف قيراط.

تفصيله:

الرسوم، ثلاثمائة وستة واربعون درهما ونصف، وغلة، ستون اردبا وثلثان ونصف قيراط. تفصيله:
قمح، اربعة وثلاثون اردبا وربع وسدس ونصف قيراط.
شعير، ثلاثة وعشرون اردبا وثلثان وربع.
فول، اردبان وثلث.
تفصيله:
شد العين، سبعة وخمسون درهما.
شد الاحباس، ثمانية دراهم.
رسم الجراريف، تسعون درهما.
رسم الحصاد، ثلاثة وخمسون درهما.
رسم الخفارة، خمسة عشر درهما.
مصالحة السلجم، احد وسبعون درهما.
رسم الاجران، اثنان وخمسون درهما ونصف، وغلة، ستون اردبا وثلثان ونصف قيراط، على ما فصل.
الكيالة، خمسة وعشرون اردبا ونصف وثلث ونصف ثمن:
قمح، عشرة ارادب.
شعير، اثنا عشر اردبا وقيراطان.
فول، ثلاثة ارادب ونصف وربع ونصف ثمن.

560 أ. س.: أردبا.

Also beginning with the letter 'jīm': Jardū.[179] This is a large village, with date palms, vineyards of grapes, acacias and sycamores, as well as winter cereals. It is to the west of the Fayyum, an hour and a half's ride from Madīnat al-Fayyūm. It is assigned as *iqṭāʿ* to a group of *iqṭāʿ*-holders. Its fiscal value is 4,539 army dinars. It gets its water from a wooden [divisor], at the end of the Main Canal, on the northern bank. [This divisor] is shared with Abū Ksā, Babīj Unshū, Ibshāyat al-Rummān and Ṭubhār. The water quota assigned for the village is eight *qabḍas*.

Its revenues in cash and kind are, in specie, 39 ½ dinars; and in grains, 1,420 ardabbs:

wheat, 710 ardabbs;
barley, 665 ardabbs;
rape, 8 ardabbs;
cumin, 7 ardabbs.[180]

[the revenues] include:

lunar-calendar tax, for the concession of the shop, 12 dinars;
pasture tax, 3 ¼ ⅛ dinars;
land tax, 74 ⅛ dinars; and in grains, as previously specified. [The land tax in cash] consists of the land tax on perennial plants and on lands subject to long-term lease, the basic assessment and the addition.

Munājaza land tax of grains, 1,420 ardabbs, as specified.

The fees, the pasture tax and the measurement fee, 396 ½ ¼ ⅛ dirhams, which are 9 ⅔ ¼ 1/72 dinars; and in grains, 86 ⅓ ¼ ardabbs:

wheat, 44 ¼ ⅙ 1/48 ardabbs;
barley, 36 ardabbs;
broad beans, 6 ⅛ 1/48 ardabbs.

[The fees, the pasture tax and the measurement fee] include:

The fees, 346 ½ dirhams; and in grains, 60 ardabbs ⅔ 1/48:
wheat, 34 ¼ ⅙ 1/48 ardabbs;
barley, 23 ⅔ ¼ ardabbs;
broad beans, 2 ⅓ ardabbs.
[The fees] in detail:
supervision of the land survey, 57 dirhams;
supervision of endowments, 8 dirhams;
dredging fee, 90 dirhams;
harvest fee, 53 dirhams;
protection fee, 15 dirhams;
settlement for rape, 71 dirhams;
threshing-floor fee, 52 ½ dirhams; and in grains, 60 ⅔ 1/48 ardabbs, as specified.

[179] Modern location: Jardū (جردو). Timm, *Das Christlich-Koptische Ägypten*, pp. 1233–34: Kieratou (Jardū, in Arabic); Trismegistos GEO ID: 1100; Halm, *Ägypten*, p. 257; Ibn Mammātī, *Kitāb qawānīn al-dawāwīn*, p. 127; Ibn al-Jīʿān, *Kitāb al-tuḥfa*, p. 154: Jirdū; Salmon, 'Répertoire', p. 58: Jirdū; de Sacy, *État des provinces*, p. 682; Savigny, *Description de l'Égypte*, p. 127; Ramzī, *Al-Qāmūs*, II/III, 84: Jardū.

[180] The total adds up to only 1,390 ardabbs.

المراعي، عن مائة واثنين وسبعين راسا، اثنان وخمسون درهما وربع وثمن. تفصيله:
قطيعة ثلاثين درهما المائة، عن ثلاثة وتسعين راسا، ثمانية وعشرون درهما وثمن.
قطيعة خمسة وعشرين درهما المائة، عن سبعة وسبعين راسا، تسعة عشر درهما ونصف وربع.
رسم المستخدمين، اربعة دراهم ونصف.

وعليها من الزكاة، احد وخمسون دينارا وقيراط وحبتان. تفصيله:
جردو خلصة، تسعة واربعون دينارا وربع وسدس وحبتان. تفصيله:
خرص العنب، ثلاثة واربعون دينارا.
ثمن الماشية، عن تسعة ارؤس، ستة[561] دنانير وربع وسدس وحبتان. تفصيله:
بقر احمر، عن مسنة واحدة، ديناران ونصف وثلث وحبة.
ثمن الاغنام، عن ثمانية ارؤس، ثلاثة دنانير وثلث وربع وحبة. تفصيله:
بياض، عن راسين، ديناران.
شعارى، عن ستة ارؤس، دينار واحد وثلث وربع وحبة. تفصيله:
عن الاغنام، عن راسين،[562] دينار واحد.
عن الابل، اربعة ارؤس، ثلث وربع وحبة.
منشاة ابي سباع، عن ثمن راسين غنم، دينار واحد ونصف وثمن. تفصيله:
بياض، عن راس واحد، دينار واحد وثمن.
شعرية واحدة، نصف دينار.

وعليها من الاتبان، الفان وثلاثمائة وستة وعشرون شنيفا.

رسم خولي البحر بها، قمح، اردب واحد.

عليها لديوان الاحباس عينا، اربعة دنانير.

المربى بها من الفروج ستمائة طائر. تفصيله:
للديوان المعمور، بما فيه من اجرة التربية وهو الثلث، ثلاثمائة طائر.
وللمقطعين، ثلاثمائة طائر.

اهلها يزرعون الاقصاب برسم معصرة ببيج انشو، راس ثلاثون فدانا.

والذي يسلف عليه بها من الشعير برسم الاصطبلات السلطانية، مائة اردب.

والمقرر عليها من الفريك والكشك، اردبان نصفان.

والذي جرت العادة باطلاقه للناحية من التقاوي من حاصل المقطعين، غلة، مائتان وخمسة وخمسون اردبا. تفصيله:
قمح، مائة وخمسة وثلاثون اردبا.
شعير، مائة وعشرون اردبا.

ومن حرف الحاء، حدادة. هذه البلدة عبارة عن بلدة متوسطة بين الكبر والصغر. بها اصول اثل في كيمان الرمل بها منثورة لا ينتفع بها. وكان من غربيها بلدة كبيرة من قديم الزمان تسمى حدادة خربت وعمرت هذه على اسمها وهي من غربي الفيوم، بينها وبين مدينة الفيوم مسافة ثلاث ساعات للراكب. جارية في اقطاع جماعة من

561 أ. س.: تسعة.
562 ساقط من أ. س.: عن راسين.

The measurement fee, 25 ½ ⅓ 1/16 ardabbs:
wheat, 10 ardabbs;
barley, 12 2/24 ardabbs;
broad beans, 3 ½ ¼ 1/16 ardabbs.
The pasture tax, for 172[181] heads, 52 ¼ ⅛ dirhams:
at the rate of 30 dirhams per 100 [heads], for 93 heads, 28 ⅛ dirhams;
at the rate of 25 dirhams per 100 [heads], for 77 heads, 19 ½ ¼ dirhams;
the government agents' fee, 4 ½ dirhams.

The alms-tax, 51 1/24 2/72 dinars:
for Jardū proper, 49 ¼ ⅙ 2/72 dinars:
estimate of grapes, 43 dinars;
monetary value of livestock, for nine heads, 6 ¼ ⅙ 2/72 dinars:
cows, for a two-year old cow, 2 ½ ⅓ 1/72 dinars;
monetary value of small cattle, for eight heads, 3 ⅓ ¼ 1/72 dinars:
sheep, for two heads, 2 dinars;
goats, for six heads, 1 ⅓ ¼ 1/72 dinar:
[levied on] small cattle for two heads, 1 dinar;
[levied on] camels, four heads, ⅓ ¼ 1/72 [dinar].
[Alms-tax for] Munshaʾat Abī Sibāʿ,[182] for the monetary value of two heads of small cattle, 1 ½ ⅛ dinar:
sheep, for one head, 1 ⅛ dinar;
one goat, ½ dinar.

Hay, 2,326 bales.

Fee of the overseer of the canal, wheat, 1 ardabb.

For the Ministry of Endowments, in specie, 4 dinars.

The chickens reared in it, 600 birds:
for the prosperous Dīwān, including the rearing wage of a third, 300 birds;
for the *iqṭāʿ*-holders, 300 birds.

Its people sow sugarcane assigned for the press at Babīj Unshū, first harvest, 30 feddans.

The barley assigned for the royal stables and paid for in advance, 100 ardabbs.

The established levy of *kishk* and *farīk* dishes, 2 ardabbs, half in each.

The seed advances, customarily distributed in the village from the surplus (*ḥāṣil*) of the *iqṭāʿ*-holders, in grains, 255 ardabbs:
wheat, 135 ardabbs;
barley, 120 ardabbs.

Also beginning with the letter 'ḥāʾ': Ḥaddāda.[183] This is a medium-sized village, with trunks of tamarisks scattered among the sandy hillocks, which are of no benefit. The ruins of a large ancient village called Ḥaddāda are found to its west, and then this one was built up, taking its name. It is in the west of the province, three hours' ride from Madīnat al-Fayyūm. It is assigned as an *iqṭāʿ* to a group of

181 The total adds up to only 170 heads.

182 This hamlet is not mentioned in Chapter 5 or Chapter 7.

183 Modern location (uncertain): ʿIzbat al-Bāshawāt (عزبة الباشوات). Halm, *Ägypten*, p. 257; Salmon, 'Répertoire', p. 68; de Sacy, *État des provinces*, p. 681: Ḥaddādih; Ibn al-Jīʿān, *Kitāb al-tuḥfa*, p. 154. In line with al-Nābulusī's description and with Shafei Bey's map, we placed it near the modern ʿIzbat al-Bāshawāt.

المقطعين. عبرتها جيشية اربعة الاف وخمسمائة وثلاثة دنانير ونصف. لها من الماء برسم سقي الزراعة بها من بحر دلية من المقسم المعروف بالقلنبو اربعة وعشرون قبضة وثلثان صغار. اهلها بنو غصين فخذ من بني كلاب.

ارتفاعها، شعير، سبعمائة وثمانية وستون اردبا.

وعليها عن خراج محاريث الرزق ثلاثون اردبا، قمح وشعير نصفان.

وعليها من الرسوم والكيالة، عن احد وستين درهما ونصف وربع، دينار واحد وربع وسدس وثمن، وشعير عشرون اردبا وثلث. تفصيله:

رسم الحصاد، ثلاثة وخمسون درهما.
رسم الاجران، ثمانية دراهم ونصف وربع وتسعة ارادب ونصف وثمن.
الكيالة، عشرة ارادب وثلث وربع وثمن.

وعليها من الزكاة، عن ثمن اغنام، عن تسعة اروس، ثلاثة دنانير ونصف وربع:

بياض، عن راسين، ديناران.
شعارى، سبعة اروس، دينار واحد ونصف وربع. تفصيله:
عن الاغنام، عن راسين، دينار واحد.
عن الابل، عن خمسة اروس، نصف وربع دينار.

وعليها من الاتبان، ثمانمائة شنيف.

المربى بها من الفروج، ثلاثمائة وثمانون طائرا:

للديوان المعمور، مائة وثمانون طائرا، بما فيه من اجرة التربية وهو الثلث.
للمقطعين، مائتا طائر.

والذي يسلف عليه بها من الشعير برسم الاصطبلات السلطانية، ثمانون اردبا.

ومن[563] حرف الخاء، خور الرماد. هذه البلدة عبارة عن بلدة متوسطة بين الكبر والصغر. بها اصول سنط ودويرات وسواقي. تزرع الاقصاب والخضراوات وبها نخل ويزرع بها الحبوب الشتوية. بينها وبين مدينة الفيوم مسافة[564] نصف ساعة للراكب، من بحري الفيوم. المنتقلة عن المقطعين للخاص لمغل سنة اثنين واربعين. عبرتها جيشية ثلاثة الاف دينار. تشرب من خليج بغير بنيان للشتوي والصيفي من البر البحري بغير عبرة. اهلها بنو زرعة، فخذ من بني عجلان.[565]

ارتفاعها لسنة احدى واربعين وستمائة، عينا، عن خراج السواقي وغير ذلك، مائة وثلاثة وستون دينارا وثلثان وربع ودانق؛ وغلة، عن خراج المناجزة، تسعمائة واثنان وخمسون اردبا وثلثان. تفصيله:

قمح، ستمائة وثمانية وعشرون اردبا وثلثان.
شعير، مائة واثنان وستون اردبا.
فول، مائة واثنان وستون اردبا.

عليها من الكيالة، ستة وعشرون اردبا. تفصيله:

قمح، ثمانية عشر اردبا.
فول، ثمانية ارادب.

iqṭāʿ-holders. Its fiscal value is 4,503 ½ army dinars. Its water, assigned for the irrigation of the field crops, comes through the divisor of al-Qalanbū on Dilya Canal. [Its water quota] is 24 ⅔ small *qabḍas*. Its people are the Banū Ghuṣayn, a branch of the Banū Kilāb.

Its revenues in barley, 768 ardabbs.

The land tax on the ploughshares of the allowances, 30 ardabbs, wheat and barley, half in each.

The fees and the measurement fee are 61 ½ ¼ dirhams, which are 1 ¼ ⅙ ⅛ dinar; and in barley, 20 ⅓ ardabbs:

harvest fee, 53 dirhams;
threshing-floor fee, 8 ½ ¼ dirhams; and 9 ½ ⅛ ardabbs [of barley];
the measurement fee, 10 ⅓ ¼ ⅛ ardabbs.

The alms-tax, for the monetary value of nine heads of small cattle, 3 ½ ¼ dinars:

sheep, for two heads, 2 dinars;
goats, for seven heads, 1 ½ ¼ dinar:
[levied on] small cattle, for two heads, 1 dinar;
[levied on] camels, for five heads, ½ ¼ [dinar].

Hay, 800 bales.

The chickens reared in it, 380 birds:

for the prosperous Dīwān, 180 birds, including the rearing wage of a third;
for the *iqṭāʿ*-holders, 200 birds.

The barley assigned for the royal stables and paid for in advance, 80 ardabbs.

Beginning with the letter 'khā'': Khawr al-Rammād.[184] This is a medium-sized village, with trunks of acacias, enclosures and waterwheels. Sugarcane, green vegetables and winter cereals are also sown in it, as well as date palms. It is half an hour's ride from Madīnat al-Fayyūm, towards the north. It was transferred from the *iqṭāʿ*-holders to the private domain of the sultan for the yield of [6]42 [AD 1244–5]. Its fiscal value is 3,000 army dinars. It gets its water for winter and summer cultivation from a canal without a weir, issuing from the northern bank [of the Main Canal], without a [water] quota. Its people are the Banū Zarʿa, a branch of the Banū ʿAjlān.

Its revenues in specie for the year 641 [AD 1243–4], from land tax on [lands irrigated by] waterwheels and other things, 163 ⅔ ¼ 1/144 dinars; and in grains, from *munājaza* land tax, 952 ⅔ ardabbs:

wheat, 628 ⅔ ardabbs;
barley, 162 ardabbs;
broad beans, 162 ardabbs.

The measurement fee, 26 ardabbs:

wheat, 18 ardabbs;
broad beans, 8 ardabbs.

563 ساقط من أ. س.: ومن.
564 ساقط من أ. س.: مسافة.
565 أ. س.: كلاب.

184 Modern location: a quarter in the eastern part of the city. Halm, *Ägypten*, p. 259; Salmon, 'Répertoire', pp. 46–47; Zéki, 'Une description', p. 38; Ibn Mammātī, *Kitāb qawānīn al-dawāwīn*, p. 132; Ibn al-Jīʿān, *Kitāb al-tuḥfa*, p. 154; de Sacy, *État des provinces*, p. 682; Ramzī, *Al-Qāmūs*, II/III, 98–99: Dār al-Rammād.

وعليها من الزكاة، عن ثمن الماشية، عن ثمانية ارؤس، سبعة دنانير وربع وسدس وثمن. تفصيله:

بقر احمر، عن تبيع[566] واحد، دينار واحد.

ثمن الاغنام، عن سبعة ارؤس، ستة دنانير وربع وسدس وثمن. تفصيله:

بياض، عن خمسة ارؤس، خمسة دنانير وربع وسدس.

شعارى، عن راسين، دينار واحد وثمن.

وعليها من الاتبان، الف شنيف.

اهلها يزرعون قصب السكر برسم معصرة المدينة، وهو خمسة فدادين ونصف:

راس، ثلاثة ونصف.

خلفة، فدانان.

والمربى بها من الفروج، خمسمائة وعشرون طائرا. تفصيله:

للديوان المعمور، بما فيه من اجرة التربية وهو الثلث، ثلاثمائة وعشرون طائرا.

للمقطعين، مائتا طاير.

ومن حرف الخاء، خراب جندي والمصلوب. هذه البلدة عبارة عن بلدة متوسطة بين الكبر والصغر، بها دويرات تين ونخل ودي غير مثمر. تزرع الشتوي والصيفي وصيفيها ارز. وهي من شرقي الفيوم، مسافتها من مدينة الفيوم ساعة للراكب. جارية في اقطاع الامير بدر الدين المرندزي[567] ومن معه من الاجناد. لها خليج لسقي الناحية مبنى من البحر اليوسفي، عبرته خمس قبض، يسقى[568] الشتوي والارز بالناحية. عبرتها جيشية الف وسبعمائة وخمسون دينارا. اهلها بنو زرعة، فخذ من بني عجلان.

ارتفاعها مما جميعه مستخرجا ومتحصلا، عينا، ثلاثة دنانير ونصف؛ وغلة، ثمانمائة وثلاثة عشر اردبا ونصف وربع. تفصيله:

قمح، اربعمائة واثنان وثلاثون اردبا ونصف وثمن.

شعير، مائة وستون اردبا وثلثان ونصف قيراط.

فول، خمسة وستون اردبا وثلثان وربع ونصف قيراط.

ارز بقشره، مائة واربعة وخمسون اردبا ونصف.

تفصيله:

الهلالي، دينار واحد.

المراعي، دينار واحد.

خراج الراتب، دينار واحد ونصف.

مناجزة الغلات[569] الشتوي، ستمائة وتسعة وخمسون اردبا وربع على ما فصل.

مشاطرة الارز، مائة واربعة وخمسون اردبا ونصف.

عليها من الرسوم والكيالة والمراعي، عن مائة وتسعة واربعين درهما ونصف، ثلاثة دنانير وثلثان وثمن وحبتان؛ وغلة، ستة وثلاثون اردبا وثلثان وربع. تفصيله:

قمح، تسعة عشر اردبا وسدس وثمن.

شعير، عشرة[570] ارادب ونصف وثمن.

فول، سبعة ارادب.

566 أ. س.: تبيعين.

567 أ. س.: المزندزي.

568 أ. س.: تسقى.

569 أ. س.: الغلال.

570 ساقط من أ. س.: عشرة.

The alms-tax, consisting of the monetary value of eight heads of livestock, 7 ¼ ⅙ ⅛ dinars:

cows, a yearling calf, 1 dinar;

monetary value of small cattle, for seven heads, 6 ¼ ⅙ ⅛ dinars:

sheep, for five heads, 5 ¼ ⅙ dinars;

goats, for two heads, 1 ⅛ dinar.

Hay, 1,000 bales.

Its people sow 5½ feddans of sugarcane, assigned to the press of the city:

first harvest, 3½ [feddans];

second harvest, 2 feddans.

The chickens reared in it, 520 birds:

for the prosperous Dīwān, including the rearing wage of a third, 320 birds;

for the *iqṭāʿ*-holders, 200 birds.

Also beginning with the letter 'khāʾ': Kharāb Jundī and al-Maṣlūb.[185] This is a medium-sized village, with enclosures of figs and date-palm shoots that do not bear fruit. It has winter and summer crops; its summer crop is rice. It is in the east of the province, one hour's ride from Madīnat al-Fayyūm. [It is] assigned as an *iqṭāʿ* to the amir Badr al-Dīn al-Marandizī and his soldiers. It has an irrigation canal with a weir, [issuing] from the Main Canal. Its [water] quota is five *qabḍas*, used for the irrigation of winter crops and rice. Its fiscal value is 1,750 army dinars. Its people are the Banū Zarʿa, a branch of the Banū ʿAjlān.

Its revenues in cash and kind are, in specie, 3 ½ dinars; and in grains, 813 ½ ¼ ardabbs:

wheat, 432 ½ ⅛ ardabbs;

barley, 160 ⅔ 1/48 ardabbs;

broad beans, 65 ⅔ ¼ 1/48 ardabbs;

rice in hull, 154 ¼ ardabbs.

[Its revenues] include:

lunar-calendar tax, 1 dinar;

pasture tax, 1 dinar;

land tax on perennial plants, 1 ½ dinar;

Munājaza land tax on winter grains, 659 ½ ardabbs, as specified;

Mushāṭara land tax on rice, 154 ½ ardabbs.

The fees, the measurement fee and the pasture tax are 149 ½ dirhams, which are 3 ⅔ ⅛ 2/72 dinars; and in grains, 36 ⅔ ¼ ardabbs:

wheat, 19 ⅙ ⅛ ardabbs;

barley, 10 ½ ⅛ ardabbs;

broad beans, 7 ardabbs.

185 Modern location (uncertain): al-ʿĀmiriyya (العامرية). Halm, *Ägypten*, p. 264; Salmon, 'Répertoire', p. 46; Ibn al-Jīʿān, *Kitāb al-tuḥfa*, p. 152; de Sacy, *État des provinces*, p. 681; Savigny, *Description de l'Égypte*, p. 129; Ramzī, *Al-Qāmūs*, II/III, 97: Maṣlūb. We could not positively identify this village, although al-Maṣlūb Canal still exists. In line with al-Nābulusī's description, we estimate that it was near the modern village of al-ʿĀmiriyya. This identification is also in line with Shafei Bey's map.

الرسوم، مائة وثلاثة وثلاثون درهما وربع، وتسعة عشر اردبا:
قمح، ثمانية ارادب وربع.
شعير، خمسة ارادب وقيراطان.
فول، خمسة ارادب وثلثان.
تفصيله:
شد العين، اربعة دراهم.
رسم الجراريف، خمسة واربعون درهما.
رسم الحصاد، ثلاثة وخمسون درهما.
رسم الخفارة، خمسة عشر درهما.
رسم الاجران، ستة عشر درهما وربع، وغلة، تسعة عشر اردبا على ما فصل.
الكيالة، سبعة عشر اردبا وثلثان وربع:
قمح، احد عشر اردبا[571] وقيراط.
شعير، خمسة ارادب وربع وسدس وثمن.
فول، اردب واحد وثلث.
المراعي، عن اثنين وخمسين راسا طارئ، ستة عشر درهما وربع. تفصيله:
قطيعة خمسة وعشرين درهما المائة، عن العدة، ثلاثة عشر درهما وربع.
رسم المستخدمين، ثلاثة دراهم وربع.

وعليها من الزكاة، عن ثمن ماشية، عن اربعة اروس، اربعة دنانير[572] ونصف وثمن. تفصيله:
بقر احمر، تبيع واحد، ديناران.
اغنام، ثلاثة اروس، ديناران وثمن. تفصيله:
بياض، عن راسين، ديناران وقيراطان.
شعارى، عن راس واحد، ربع وسدس وثمن دينار.

وعليها من الاتبان، سبعمائة وتسعون شنيفا.

رسم خولي البحر بها، قمح، اردب واحد.

والمربى بها من الفروج، اربعمائة واربعون طائرا. تفصيله:
للديوان المعمور، بما فيه من اجرة التربية وهو الثلث، مائتان واربعون طائرا.
للمقطعين، مائتان.

ومن حرف الدال، دسيا. هذه البلدة عبارة عن بلدة متوسطة بين الكبر والصغر، بها نخل وسدر واصول سنط.[573] تزرع الشتوي لا غير. وهي من غربي الفيوم للقبلة، بينها وبين مدينة الفيوم ساعة ونصف للراكب. جارية في اقطاع جماعة من المقطعين. عبرتها جيشية اربعة الاف ومائتان وتسعة وثلاثون دينارا. لها خليج يسقى مزدرعاتها من بر البحر اليوسفي القبلي، مبنى مجصص، عبرته اربع قبض ماء. اهلها بنو غصين، فخذ من بني كلاب. من بحريها دير.

ارتفاعها مما جميعه مستخرجا ومتحصلا، عينا، عن المراعي، اربعة دنانير وسدس ونصف قيراط وحبة؛ وغلة، عن خراج المناجزة، الف ومائة اردب. تفصيله:
قمح، خمسمائة وخمسون اردبا.
شعير، خمسمائة وخمسون اردبا.[574]

The fees, 133 ¼ dirhams; [and in grains], 19 ardabbs:
- wheat, 8 ¼ ardabbs;
- barley, 5 2/24 ardabbs;
- broad beans, 5 ⅔ ardabbs.
- [The fees] in detail:
  - supervision of the land survey, 4 dirhams;
  - dredging fee, 45 dirhams;
  - harvest fee, 53 dirhams;
  - protection fee, 15 dirhams;
  - threshing-floor fee, 16 ¼ dirhams; and in grains, 19 ardabbs, as specified.
- The measurement fee, 17 ⅔ ¼ ardabbs:
  - wheat, 11 1/24 ardabbs;
  - barley, 5 ¼ ⅙ ⅛ ardabbs;
  - broad beans, 1 ⅓ ardabb.
- The pasture tax, for 52 heads of seasonal pasture lands, 16 ¼ dirhams:
  - at the rate of 25 dirhams per 100 [heads], for the tally above, 13 ¼ dirhams;
  - the government agents' fee, 3 ¼ dirhams.

The alms-tax, for the monetary value of four heads of livestock, 4 ½ ⅛ dinars:
- cows, for one yearling calf, 2 dinars;
- small cattle, for three heads, 2 ½ ⅛ dinars:
  - sheep, for two heads, 2 2/24 dinars;
  - goats, for one head, ¼ ⅙ ⅛ dinar.

Hay, 790 bales.

The fee of the overseer of the canal, wheat, 1 ardabb.

The chickens reared in it, 440 birds:
- for the prosperous Dīwān, including the rearing wage of a third, 240 birds;
- for the *iqṭā*ᶜ-holders, 200.

Beginning with the letter 'dāl': Disyā.[186] This is a medium-sized village, with date palms, sidr trees and acacia trunks, but only winter crops. It is in the south-west of the province, an hour and a half's ride from Madīnat al-Fayyūm. It is assigned as an *iqṭā*ᶜ to a group of *iqṭā*ᶜ-holders. Its fiscal value is 4,239 army dinars. It has a plastered canal with a weir, issuing from the south bank of the Main Canal. Its quota is four *qabḍa*s of water. Its people are the Banū Ghuṣayn, a branch of the Banū Kilāb. To its north there is a monastery.

Its revenue in cash and kind is in specie, from the pasture tax, 4 ⅙ 1/48 1/72 dinars; and in grains, from *munājaza* land tax, 1,100 ardabbs:
- wheat, 550 ardabbs;
- barley, 550 ardabbs.

571 ساقط من ط. م.: أردبا.
572 أ. س.: دينار ونصف.
573 ط. م.: صنط.
574 ساقط من ط. م.: شعير خمسمائة وخمسون أردبا.

186 Modern location: Disyā (دسيا). Halm, *Ägypten*, p. 254; Salmon, 'Répertoire', p. 62; Savigny, *Description de l'Égypte*, p. 127: Disya; Ibn Mammātī, *Kitāb qawānīn al-dawāwīn*, p. 139; Ramzī, *Al-Qāmūs*, II/III, 99: Disyā.

عليها من الرسوم والكيالة والمراعي، عن مائتين وسبعة وسبعين درهما ونصف، ستة دنانير وثلثان ونصف قيراط وحبة؛ وغلة، ستة وستون اردبا وثلث وثمن. تفصيله:

قمح، خمسة وثلاثون اردبا وثمن.

شعير، سبعة وعشون اردبا وخمسة قراريط.

فول، اربعة ارادب وثمن.

تفصيله:

الرسوم، مائة وخمسة وتسعون درهما ونصف وربع، وغلة، ستة وعشرون اردبا وثلث وثمن. تفصيله:

قمح، خمسة عشر اردبا وثمن.

شعير، سبعة ارادب وخمسة قراريط.

فول، اربعة ارادب وثمن.

تفصيله:

شد العين، عشرة دراهم.

شد الاحباس، اربعة دراهم.

رسم الحصاد، ثلاثة وخمسون درهما.

رسم الخفارة، خمسة عشر درهما.

رسم الجراريف، تسعون درهما.

رسم الاجران، ثلاثة وعشرون درهما ونصف وربع، وغلة، ستة وعشرون اردبا وثلث وثمن، على ما فصل.

الكيالة، اربعون اردبا:

قمح، عشرون اردبا.

شعير، عشرون اردبا.

المراعي، مائة وثمانية واربعون راسا، اثنان وسبعون درهما. تفصيله:

قطيعة درهم واحد الراس، عن احد عشر راسا، احد عشر درهما.

قطيعة خمسين درهما المائة، عن سبعين راسا، خمسة وثلاثون درهما.

قطيعة خمسة وعشرين درهما المائة، عن سبعة وستين راسا، ستة عشر درهما ونصف وربع.

رسم المستخدمين، تسعة دراهم وربع.

وعليها من الزكاة، عن ثمن اغنام، عن ستة اروس، خمسة دنانير وثمن.[575] تفصيله:

بياض، عن اربعة اروس، اربعة دنانير.

شعارى، عن راسين، دينار واحد وثمن.

وعليها من الاتبان، الف وثمانمائة شنيف.

وعليها لديوان الاحباس، ديناران.

رسم خولي البحر، قمح، اردب واحد.

المربى بها من الدجاج،[576] خمسمائة وثلاثون طائرا. تفصيله:

للديوان المعمور، بما فيه من اجرة التربية وهو الثلث، ثلاثمائة طائر.

للمقطعين، مائتان وثلاثون طائرا.[577]

The fees, the measurement fee and the pasture tax are 277 ½ dirhams, which are 6 ⅔ ¹⁄₄₈ ¹⁄₇₂ dinars; and in grains, 66 ⅓ ⅛ ardabbs:

wheat, 35 ⅛ ardabbs;

barley, 27 ⁵⁄₂₄ ardabbs;

broad beans, 4 ⅛ ardabbs.

[The fees, the measurement fee and the pasture tax] include:

The fees, 195 ½ ¼ dirhams; and in grains, 26 ⅓ ⅛ ardabbs:

wheat, 15 ⅛ ardabbs;

barley, 7 ⁵⁄₂₄ ardabbs;

broad beans, 4 ⅛ ardabbs.

[the fees] in detail:

supervision of the land survey, 10 dirhams;

supervision of endowments, 4 dirhams;

harvest fee, 53 dirhams;

protection fee, 15 dirhams;

dredging fee, 90 dirhams;

threshing-floor fee, 23 ½ ¼ dirhams; and in grains, 26 ⅓ ⅛ ardabbs, as specified.

The measurement fee, 40 ardabbs:

wheat, 20 ardabbs;

barley, 20 ardabbs.

The pasture tax, for 148 heads, 72 dirhams:

at the rate of one dirham per head, for 11 heads, 11 dirhams;

at the rate of 50 dirhams per 100 [heads], for 70 heads, 35 dirhams;

at the rate of 25 dirhams per 100 [heads], for 67 heads, 16 ½ ¼ dirhams;

the government agents' fee, 9 ¼ dirhams.

The alms-tax, for the monetary value of six heads of small cattle, 5 ⅛ dinars:

sheep, for four heads, 4 dinars;

goats, for two heads, 1 ⅛ dinar.

Hay, 1,800 bales.

For the Ministry of Endowments, 2 dinars.

The fee of the overseer of the canal, wheat, 1 ardabb.

The chickens reared in it, 530 birds:

for the prosperous Dīwān, including the rearing wage of a third, 300 birds;

for the *iqṭāʿ*-holders, 230 birds.

575 أ. س.: وثلث.

576 أ. س.: الفروج.

577 ساقط من أ. س.: تفصيله للديوان المعمور ما فيه من أجرة التربية وهو الثلث ثلاثمائة طائر للمقطعين مائتان وثلاثون طائرا.

والذي جرت العادة باطلاقه للناحية[578] من التقاوي، مائتان واثنان وعشرون اردبا:

قمح، مائة وتسعة عشر اردبا.

شعير، مائة وثلاثة ارادب.

وبها من التقاوي لمعاملة المحلول، قمح اثنا عشر اردبا ونصف وثلث.

والذي يسلف عليها بها من الشعير برسم الاصطبلات السلطانية، مائة اردب.

اهلها يزرعون من الاقصاب السكر برسم المعاصر بفانو ونقليفة، اربعة عشر فدانا ونصف وثلث. تفصيله:

راس، ثمانية فدادين ونصف وثلث.

خلفة، ستة فدادين.

ومن حرف الدال، دموشية. هذه البلدة عبارة عن بلدة كبيرة[579] فيها النخل والجميز. تزرع الصيفي والشتوي. وعليها حجر معصرة قصب وبها مرج تزرع الكتان والمقات والقمح والشعير بماء النيل، كما تزرع[580] الريف. وينصل[581] الماء الذي بالمرج المذكور بمصيدة. وكان بها ملاحة ينقل لها الماء بساقية من بئر نبع، فلما كان الذي يتحصل[582] منها لا يفي بالنفقة التي[583] عليها لرخص الملح، عطلت. وهي قبلي مدينة الفيوم، مسافة ساعة للراكب. مرتجعة للديوان المعمور لمغل سنة اثنتين واربعين وستمائة.

والمطلق لها من الماء ثلاث عشرة قبضة ونصف وثمن قبضة ونصف قيراط قبضة. تفصيله:

من خليج شركة لبوصير دفدنو،[584] قبضة وسدس وثمن وثلث قيراط.

من خليجين مبنيين مجصصين عبرتها ست قبض وثلث.

القلهانة الصغرى من حقوقها ارض بغير جدار.

من خليج تنبطويه، اربع قبض.

جزائر شداد من حقوقها. من خليج تنبطويه قبضتان.

بها جامع تقام فيه الجمعة. من قبليها دير يعرف بدير دموشية. اهلها بنو ربيعة، فخذ من بني كلاب. وبها معصرة ذات حجر واحد دائر بالابقار.

ارتفاعها، عينا، الف وثمانمائة وثمانية دنانير وربع وحبتان; وغلة، الف وثمانمائة واردبان ونصف. تفصيله:

قمح، تسعمائة واردب واحد وربع.

شعير، خمسمائة وخمسة عشر[585] اردبا وربع.

فول، ثلاثمائة وستة وثمانون اردبا وربع.

فدن، ثمانية وثلاثون فدانا ونصف. تفصيله:

قصب سكر، راس، اربعة وثلاثون فدانا.

فول اخضر، اربعة فدادين ونصف.

تفصيله:

مال الهلالي، عن اجرة الحانوت، سبعة دنانير ونصف.

مال المصايد، خمسة وعشرون دينارا.

مال الخراجي، الف وسبعمائة ستة وخمسون دينارا ونصف وربع وحبة; وغلة، الف وثمانمائة واردبان ونصف، على ما فصل.

578 أ. س.: لها.

579 ساقط من أ. س.: كبيرة.

580 أ. س.: يزرع.

581 أ. س.: يتصل.

582 أ. س.: يحصل.

583 ساقط من ط. م.: التي.

584 ط. م.: لأبى صير فدنو.

585 أ. س.: عشرون.

The seed advances customarily distributed in the locality, 222 ardabbs:

wheat, 119 ardabbs;

barley, 103 ardabbs.

The seed advances in the account of vacant *iqṭāʿ*-holding, wheat, 12 ½ ⅓ ardabbs.

The barley assigned for the royal stables and paid for in advance, 100 ardabbs.

Its people sow 14 ½ ⅓ feddans of sugarcane, assigned for the press at Fānū and Naqalīfa:

first harvest, 8 ½ ⅓ feddans;

second harvest, 6 feddans.

Also beginning with the letter 'dāl': Dumūshiyya.[187] This is a large village, with date palms and sycamores. It cultivates winter and summer crops. It has a stone for the press of sugarcane. It has a meadow sown with flax, cucurbitaceous fruits, wheat and barley, which are watered by the water of the Nile as in Lower Egypt. The water in this meadow escapes to a fishery, which used to be a salt mine. Water was brought to it from a spring-well by a waterwheel, but when the income from it did not cover the expenses, due to the low price of salt, it went out of use. It is one hour's ride south of Madīnat al-Fayyūm. It was returned to the prosperous Dīwān [for re-distribution to *iqṭāʿ*-holders] for the yield of 642 [AD 1244–5].

The water allocated to it, 13 ½ ⅛ 1/48 *qabḍas*:

1 ⅙ ⅛ 1/72 *qabḍa* from a canal shared with Būṣīr Difidnū and Difidnū;

6 ⅓ *qabḍas* from two plastered canals with weirs;

4 *qabḍas* from Tanabṭawayh Canal for al-Qalhāna al-ṣughrā (Little Qalhāna), which is an unfenced plot of land attached to it;

2 *qabḍas* from Tanabṭawayh Canal for Jazāʾir Shaddād, [also] attached to it.

It has a congregational mosque, in which the Friday prayers are held, and south of it there is a monastery known as the Monastery of Dumūshiyya. Its people are the Banū Rabīʿa, a branch of the Banū Kilāb. It has a press with one stone, turned by cattle.

Its revenues in specie are 1,808 ¼ 2/72 dinars; and in grains, 1,802 ½ ardabbs:

wheat, 901 ¼ ardabbs;

barley, 515 ¼ ardabbs;

broad beans, 386 ¼ ardabbs.

[Crown estate] feddans, 38 ½ feddans:

sugarcane, first harvest, 34 feddans;

green broad beans, 4 ½ feddans.

[The revenues] include:

lunar-calendar tax, for the rent of the shop, 7 ½ dinars;

tax on fisheries, 25 dinars;

land tax, 1,756 ½ ¼ 1/72 dinars; and in grains, 1,802 ½ ardabbs, as specified.

187 Modern location (uncertain): Dīr Al-ʿAzab (دير العزب). Timm, *Das Christlich-Koptische Ägypten*, p. 889: Mouch(e)is (Dumūshiyya in Arabic); Trismegostis GEO ID 5824: Mouchis; Halm, *Ägypten*, p. 255: Dumūshiya al-Mallāḥa; Salmon, 'Répertoire', p. 64; de Sacy, *État des provinces*, p. 682: Dubūshiyyat al-Malāḥa; Ramzī, *Al-Qāmūs*, I, 253: Tall Abū Khaṣa near al-Ḥādiqa by Baḥr al-Nazla, north of Qalahāna. Al-Nābulusī does not provide much geographical information about its location, but he mentions that there used to be a salt mine in its lands. Shafei Bey, 'Fayoum Irrigation', writes that he found out its location from the local peasants, and that the salt still oozes on the surface (p. 308). We located it near the present village of Dīr Al-ʿAzab.

تفصيله:
خراج الراتب، اصلا واضافة، ثلاثة دنانير وثلث.
خراج فدن العين، عن خراج الكتان والمقات، الف وسبعمائة وثمانية واربعون دينارا وقيراط وحبة.
المناجزة، خمسة دنانير وربع وثمن، والغلة على ما تقدم.
اجرة المبل،[586] اربعة عشر دينارا.
اين المساحة، خمسة دنانير وثلثان.

الوفر، اثنان وخمسون اردبا ونصف:
قمح، ستة وعشرون اردبا وربع.
شعير، خمسة عشر اردبا.
فول، احد عشر اردبا وربع.

وعليها من الرسوم والكيالة والمراعي، عن الف وثمانمائة واحد واربعين درهما وثمن، ستة واربعون دينارا ونصف قيراط؛ وغلة، سبعة وسبعون اردبا ونصف قيراط. تفصيله:
قمح، اثنان وثلاثون اردبا ونصف.
شعير، اربعة عشر اردبا وربع وسدس.
فول، ثلاثون اردبا وقيراطان.

تفصيله:
الرسوم، الف ومائتان وستة واربعون درهما ونصف؛ وغلة، ثمانية وثلاثون اردبا ونصف وثلث. تفصيله:
قمح، اثنان وعشرون اردبا.
شعير، ثلاثة ارادب وقيراطان.
فول، ثلاثة عشر اردبا ونصف وربع.
تفصيله:
شد الاحباس، ثلاثة عشر درهما ونصف.
رسم جراريف، تسعون درهما.
رسم حصاد، ثلاثة وخمسون درهما.
رسم خفارة، خمسة عشر درهما.
شد عين، الف واربعون درهما.
رسم اجران، خمسة وثلاثون درهما، وغلة، ثمانية وثلاثون اردبا ونصف وثلث، على ما فصل.
الكيالة، ثمانية وثلاثون اردبا وسدس ونصف قيراط:
قمح، عشرة ارادب ونصف.
شعير، احد عشر اردبا[587] وثلث ونصف قيراط.
فول، ستة عشر اردبا وثلث.
المراعي، عن ثمانمائة واحد عشر راسا، خمسمائة واربعة وتسعون درهما ونصف وثمن. تفصيله:
راتب، عن اربعة وعشرين راسا، اربعة وخمسون درهما.
طارئ، عن سبعمائة وسبعة وثمانين راسا، اربعمائة وتسعون درهما. تفصيله:
قطيعة درهم واحد الراس، عن مائتين وخمسة اروس، مائتان وخمسة دراهم.
قطيعة خمسين درهما المائة، عن خمسمائة واثنين وخمسين راسا، مائتان وستة وسبعون درهما.
قطيعة ثلاثين درهما المائة، عن ثلاثين راسا، تسعة دراهم.
رسم المستخدمين، خمسون درهما ونصف وثمن.

[The land tax] in detail:
land tax on perennial plants, the basic assessment and the addition, 3 ⅓ dinars;
land tax on cash crops assessed by feddans, from land tax on flax and cucurbitaceous fruits, 1,748 1/24 1/72 dinars;
munājaza land tax, 5 ¼ ⅛ dinars; and in grains, as previously specified.
rent for the flax rettery (*maball*), 14 dinars;
āʾīn (regulation?)[188] of the land survey (*al-misāḥa*), 5 ⅔ dinars;

The surcharge, 52 ½ ardabbs:
wheat, 26 ¼ ardabbs;
barley, 15 ardabbs;
broad beans, 11 ¼ ardabbs.

The fees, the measurement fee and the pasture fee, 1,841 ⅛ dirhams, which are 46 1/48 dinars; and in grains, 77 1/48 ardabbs:
wheat, 32 ½ ardabbs;
barley, 14 ¼ ⅙ ardabbs;
broad beans, 30 2/24 ardabbs.

[The fees, the measurement fee and the pasture fee] include:
The fees, 1,246 ½ dirhams; and in grains, 38 ½ ⅓ ardabbs:
wheat, 22 ardabbs;
barley, 3 2/24 ardabbs;
broad beans, 13 ½ ¼ ardabbs.
[The fees] in detail:
supervision of endowments, 13 ½ dirhams;
dredging fee, 90 dirhams;
harvest fee, 53 dirhams;
protection fee, 15 dirhams;
supervision of the land survey, 1,040 dirhams;
threshing-floor fee, 35 dirhams; and in grains, 38 ½ ⅓ ardabbs, as specified.
The measurement fee, 38 ⅙ 1/48 ardabbs:
wheat, 10 ½ ardabbs;
barley, 11 ⅓ 1/48 ardabbs;
broad beans, 16 ⅓ ardabbs.
The pasture tax, for 811 heads, 594 ½ ⅛ dirhams:
permanent pasture lands, for 24 heads, 54 dirhams;
seasonal pasture lands, for 787 heads, 490 dirhams:
at the rate of one dirham per head, for 205 heads, 205 dirhams;
at the rate of 50 dirhams per 100 [heads], for 552 heads, 276 dirhams;
at the rate of 30 dirhams per 100 [heads], for 30 heads, nine dirhams;
the government agents' fee, 50 ½ ⅛ dirhams.

586 أ. س.: المثل.
587 ساقط من أ. س.: أردبا.

188 See F. Gabrieli, 'āʾīn', *The Encyclopedia of Islam*, 2nd edn, I, 306–07.

وعليها من الزكاة، عن ثمن الماشية، عن احد عشر راسا، عشرة دنانير وثلثان وثمن:

بقر احمر، تبيع واحد، دينار واحد.

اغنام، عشرة ارؤس، تسعة دنانير وثلثان وثمن. تفصيله:

بياض، عن ثمانية ارؤس، ثمانية دنانير وثلثان.

شعارى، عن راسين، دينار واحد وثمن.

وعليها من الجوالي، عن ثمانية نفر بما فيه مما يحسب عن نفر واحد طراد الوحش، وهو نصف دينار، ستة عشر دينارا. تفصيله:

المقيمون بها، عن سبعة[588] نفر، اربعة عشر دينارا.

الناءون عنها بالوجه القبلي، نفر واحد، ديناران.

عليها من الاتبان، بما فيه من كفورها،[589] ثلاثة الاف[590] شنيف.

عليها لديوان الاحباس، عينا، اربعة دنانير.

رسم خولي البحر عليها، قمح، اردب واحد.

المربى بها من الدجاج،[591] اربعمائة وعشرون طائرا:

المستقر تربيته بالناحية، مائتا طائر.

المستجد تجديد تربيته برسم المطابخ السلطانية بما فيه من اجرة التربية وهو الثلث، مائتان وعشرون طائرا.[592]

والذي بها من التقاوي الديوانية برسم عمارة الناحية، الف وخمسة وعشرون اردبا وقيراطان. تفصيله:

قمح، مائتان وستة واربعون اردبا ونصف.

شعير، خمسة وستون اردبا ونصف وثلث.

فول، ستة وتسعون اردبا.

بزر كتان، ستمائة وستة عشر اردبا ونصف وربع.

والذي انساق بالناحية وكفورها حاصلا وموقوفا وباقيا في معاملة الديوان السلطاني الكاملي السعيد، عشرة الاف وسبعمائة وثلاثون دينارا وحبة; وغلة، الف وخمسمائة واربعة وثمانون اردبا وخمسة قراريط. تفصيله:

قمح، ثمانمائة وتسعة وتسعون اردبا وربع ونصف قيراط.

شعير، خمسمائة وعشرون اردبا وربع وثمن.

فول، مائة وعشرة ارادب ونصف وثمن.

جلبان، ثلاثة عشر اردبا وثلثان وربع ونصف قيراط.

كتان خشب، ثمانية الاف وثمانمائة وستة وثلاثون حبلا.

تفصيله:

الحاصل، خاصة كتان، ثمانية الاف وثمانمائة وستة وثلاثون حبلا.

الموقوف عن زائد قطيعة الكتان الموجوبة[593] لاستقبال سنة ثمان وعشرين وستمائة، وخراج الغرق لسنة ثلاثين، وما اوقف عن خراج المقات العاطبة المشهور حالها لسنة ثلاثين، وما اوقف عن تتمة السجلات والموقوف في جهة المعاملين عن القرض[594] برسم كلف كتانهم، ثلاثة الاف وستمائة وثمانية عشر دينارا وربع وسدس ونصف قيراط، وقمح ثلثا اردب.

الباقي بما فيه من الكتان المنفوض المحمول الى دار الوكالة السعيدة من موجود المعاملين بغير تقويم، وهو خمسمائة

588 ط. م.: تسعة.

589 ط. م.: كفرها.

590 ط. م.: ألف.

591 أ. س.: الفروج.

592 أ. س. يضيف المستقر تربيته لكنه مشطب.

593 أ. س.: الموجبه.

594 ط. م.: القرص.

The alms-tax, for the monetary value of 11 heads of livestock, 10 ⅔ ⅛ dinars:

cows, one yearling calf, 1 dinar;

small cattle, 10 heads, 9 ⅔ ⅛ dinars:

sheep, for eight heads, 8 ⅔ dinars;

goats, for two heads, 1 ⅛ dinar.

The poll-tax on eight individuals, 16 dinars. This includes ½ dinar for one 'beast-chaser' (*ṭarrād al-waḥsh*). [The poll-tax] in detail:

those residing in it, for seven individuals, 14 dinars;

those absent from it, [residing] in the southern region, one individual, two dinars.

Hay, including its hamlets, 1,000 / 3,000[189] bales.

For the Ministry of Endowments, in specie, 4 dinars.

The fee of the overseer of the canal, wheat, 1 ardabb.

The chickens reared in it, 420 birds:

the established rearing in the village, 200 birds;[190]

the addition of recently introduced rearing, assigned for the royal kitchens, including the rearing wage of a third, 220 birds.

The seed advances from the Dīwān, assigned for the village's cultivation, 1,025 2/24 ardabbs:

wheat, 246 ½ ardabbs;

barley, 65 ½ ⅓ ardabbs;

broad beans, 96 ardabbs.

grains of flax, 616 ½ ¼ ardabbs.

The surplus, withheld and outstanding payments carried forward in the account of the village and its hamlets in the Dīwān of the blessed Sultan al-Kāmil, 10,730 1/72 dinars; and in grains, 1,584 5/24 ardabbs:

wheat, 899 ¼ 1/48 ardabbs;

barley, 520 ¼ ⅛ ardabbs;

broad beans, 110 ½ ⅛ ardabbs;

chickling vetch, 13 [= 53][191] ⅔ ¼ 1/48 ardabbs;

flax fibers (*kattān khashab*), 8,836 bundles (*ḥabl*).[192]

In detail:

The surplus: 8,836 bundles.

The withheld payments:

the added tax rate on flax, which came into effect at the beginning of 628 [AD 1230–1];

withheld land tax on al-Gharq for [6]30;[193]

189 AS: 3,000. MP: 1,000.

190 As this village belongs to the royal domain, the 'established' rearing of chicken is the rearing for the direct benefit of the Sultan, parallel to the rearing allocated for the benefit of *iqṭāʿ*-holders in other villages.

191 Correction required to make up the totals; see also the list below.

192 Ibn Mammātī states that flax yield per feddan was up to 30 *ḥabl*, a measure of length, probably indicating the size of a bundle; *Qawānīn al-Dawāwīn*, ed. by ʿAṭiya, pp. 261–62. See references to 'ropes' in Moshe Gil, 'The Flax Trade in the Mediterranean in the Eleventh Century AD as Seen in Merchants' Letters from the Cairo Geniza', *Journal of Near Eastern Studies*, 63. 2 (2004), 81–96 (p. 84).

193 Al-Gharq was a water reservoir in the south of the Fayyum, mentioned as a source of water for several villages in the south-west. Alternatively, the phrase could be taken literally to mean 'land submerged by water'.

وخمسة اعدال ونصف وثمن، سبعة الاف ومائة واحد عشر دينارا ونصف[595] ونصف ثمن وحبة; وغلة، الف وخمسمائة وثلاثة وثمانون اردبا وربع وسدس وثمن:

قمح، ثمانمائة وثمانية وتسعون اردبا وثلث وربع ونصف قيراط.
شعير، خمسمائة وعشرون اردبا وربع وثمن.
فول، مائة وعشرة ارادب ونصف وثمن.
جلبان، ثلاثة وخمسون اردبا وثلثان وربع ونصف قيراط.

والمقرر تسليفه عليه من الفول برسم العوامل الديوانية سبعون اردبا.

ومن حرف الدال، دفدنُو. هذه البلدة عبارة عن بلدة كبيرة بها نخل وجميز. تزرع الشتوي والصيفي. بينها وبين مدينة الفيوم مسافة ساعتين للراكب وهي قبلي الفيوم. جارية في اقطاع المقطعين مجموعة العبرة في الاقطاع مع ابي صير بما جملته عشرة الاف دينار جيشية. والمطلق لها من الماء شركة ابي صير عما خصها بحق[596] الثلثين من الخليج المشترك مع دموشية ومن شركة اطسا، ما جملته اربع عشرة قبضة ونصف وربع قبضة[597] وسدس قيراط قبضة. وبها جامع تقام فيه الجمعة وبها كنيسة مختلة العمارة متهدمة.[598] اهلها بنو عامر فخذ من بني كلاب.

ارتفاعها عينا، عن الف ومائتين واثنين وسبعين درهما ونصف وربع، احد وثلاثون دينارا وثلثان وثمن وحبتان. تفصيله:

الحانوت، مائة وثمانون درهما وربع وثمن.
المصيدة، اربعة وثمانون درهما.[599]
خراج الرواتب والاحكار، سبعمائة وسبعة وعشرون درهما.
خراج القطن، مائة واربعة دراهم وربع وثمن.
رسم الاجران، ستة وخمسون درهما ونصف.
مراعي، الاغنام، مائة وعشرون درهما ونصف.

غلة، خارجا عما استثنى عن خراج اراضي المتسحبين وما تسلمه[600] مستخدمو الرسوم منسوبا الى انه متميز زائد عما ورد المحسوب على جاري العادة، وهو اربعمائة وستة واربعون اردبا وخمسة قراريط. تفصيله:

قمح، مائتان[601] واحد وسبعون اردبا وثلث وربع.
شعير وفول، مائة واربعة وسبعون اردبا ونصف وثمن.[602]

غلة، الفان ومائتان وسبعة وثلاثون اردبا وثلث وثمن. تفصيله:

قمح، الف واربعمائة وثمانية وتسعون اردبا وثلث وثمن.
شعير وفول، سبعمائة واثنا عشر اردبا وثلثان وربع.
سمسم، ستة وعشرون اردبا وقيراطان.

وعليها من الرسوم والكيالة والمراعي، اربعة عشر دينارا وثلثان وربع وحبة; وغلة، مائة وستون اردبا وقيراط ونصف. تفصيله:

قمح، مائة واربعة ارادب ونصف.
شعير، ثلاثة وثلاثون اردبا ونصف وربع ونصف قيراط.
سمسم، اردب واحد وثلثان وربع.

595 ساقط من أ. س.: ونصف.
596 ط. م.: نحو.
597 ط. م. يضيف: ربع.
598 أ. س.: منهدمة.
599 ساقط من أ. س.: درهما.
600 أ. س.: تسلموه.
601 ساقط من أ. س.: أربعمائة وستة وأربعون أردبا وخمسة قراريط. تفصيله قمح مائتان.
602 ساقط من أ. س.: وثمن.

withheld land-tax payment for the year [6]30 on rotted cucurbitaceous fruits, whose condition is well known;

the withheld adjustment to the registers (*tatimmat al-sijillāt*);

the withheld payments, for loans (*qarḍ*) to the cultivators that cover the expenditure on their flax;

[The total of the withheld payments is]: 3,618 ¼ ⅙ 1/48 dinars; and wheat, ⅔ ardabb.

The outstanding payments [in cash] are 7,111 ½ 1/16 1/72 dinars — this includes 505 ½ ⅛ bales (*aʿdāl*) of scutched flax, delivered to the blessed merchandise warehouse from the stocks of the cultivators without monetary evaluation; and in grains, 1,583 ¼ ⅙ ⅛ ardabbs:

wheat, 898 ⅓ ¼ 1/48 ardabbs;
barley, 520 ¼ ⅛ ardabbs;
broad beans, 110 ½ ⅛ ardabbs;
chickling vetch, 53 ⅔ ¼ 1/48 ardabbs.

The established amount of broad beans assigned for the Dīwān's cattle and paid for in advance, 70 ardabbs.

Also beginning with the letter 'dāl': Difidnū.[194] This is a large village, with date palms and sycamores, winter and summer crops. It is in the south of the province, two hours' ride from Madīnat al-Fayyūm. It is assigned as an *iqṭāʿ* to *iqṭāʿ*-holders. Its fiscal value, combined with that of Abū Ṣīr [Būṣīr Difidnū], is a total of 10,000 army dinars. It has the right to two-thirds of the water allocated to it in partnership with Abū Ṣīr, from the canal shared with Dumūshiyya, and from a [canal] shared with Iṭsā. All in all, its [water quota] is 14 ¾ 1/144 *qabḍa*. It has a congregational mosque, in which the Friday prayers are held, and a church, in poor condition and demolished. Its people are the Banū ʿĀmir, a branch of the Banū Kilāb.

Its revenues in specie are 1,272 ½ ¼ dirhams, which are 31 ⅔ ⅛ 2/72 dinars:

the shop, 180 ¼ ⅛ dirhams;
the fishery, 84 dirhams;
land tax on perennial plants and on lands subject to long-term lease, 727 dirhams;
land tax on cotton, 104 ¼ ⅛ dirhams;
threshing-floor fee, 56 ½ dirhams;
seasonal pasture [fee], 120 ½ dirhams.

[Its revenues] in grains, 2,237 ⅓ ⅛ ardabbs:

wheat, 1,498 ⅓ ⅛ ardabbs;
barley and broad beans, 712 ⅔ ¼ ardabbs;
sesame, 26 2/24 ardabbs.

The revenue in grains does not include the land tax on the lands of those who have fled, which was excluded; and what the government agents received, taking into account that this was distinctly in excess of the normal calculation. This amounts to 446 5/24 ardabbs: wheat, 271 ⅓ ¼ ardabbs; barley and broad beans, 174 ½ ⅛ ardabbs.

The fees, the measurement fee and the pasture fee, 14 ⅔ ¼ 1/72 dinars; and in

194 Modern location: Difinnū (دفنو). Timm, *Das Christlich-Koptische Ägypten*, p. 491: Tenenou (Difidnū/Difidnnū, in Arabic); Halm, *Ägypten*, p. 252; Salmon, 'Répertoire', p. 64; Zéki, 'Une description', p. 44; de Sacy, *État des provinces*, p. 682: Dafdnū; Savigny, *Description de l'Égypte*, p. 126: Difinnū; Ibn Mammātī, *Kitāb qawānīn al-dawāwīn*, p. 139; Ibn al-Jīʿān, *Kitāb al-tuḥfa*, p. 154; Ramzī, *Al-Qāmūs*, II/III, 84–85: Difinnū.

تفصيله:

الرسوم، مائتان وسبعون درهما ونصف، وغلة، احد وتسعون اردبا وقيراط ونصف. تفصيله:

قمح، ثمانية وخمسون اردبا وثلثان وربع.

شعير، عشرون اردبا ونصف وربع ونصف ثمن.

فول، تسعة ارادب ونصف وربع وثمن.

سمسم، اردب واحد وثلثان وثمن.

تفصيله:

شد العين، خمسة وعشرون درهما.

شد الاحباس، ثمانية دراهم.

رسم الجراريف، تسعون درهما.

رسم الحصاد، ثلاثة وخمسون درهما.

رسم الخفارة، خمسة عشر درهما.

رسم المدقات، درهمان.

رسم الاجران، سبعة وسبعون درهما ونصف، وغلة، احد وتسعون اردبا ونصف وثمن على ما فصل.

الكيالة، تسعة وستون اردبا. تفصيله:

قمح، خمسة واربعون اردبا وثلث وربع.

شعير، اثنا عشر اردبا ونصف وثلث وثمن.

فول، عشرة ارادب.

سمسم، ثلث وثمن اردب.

المراعي عن دفدنو وابي صير عن المحسوب على جاري العادة عن اغنام الفلاحين خاصة، ثمانية دنانير وسدس.

عليها من الزكاة، تسعة دنانير:

دولبة، دينار واحد ونصف.

خرص النخل، دينار واحد.

ثمن الماشية، عن سبعة اروس، ستة دنانير ونصف. تفصيله:

بقر احمر تبيع واحد، دينار واحد وربع.

ثمن اغنام، ستة اروس، خمسة دنانير وربع:

بياض، اربعة اروس، اربعة دنانير وثمن.

شعارى، راسين، دينار واحد وثمن.

عليها لديوان الاحباس، اربعة دنانير.

وعليها من الاتبان، الفان وستمائة شنيف.

رسم خولي البحر بها، اردبان، قمحًا.

والمربى بها من الفروج، سبعمائة وخمسون طائرا. تفصيله:

للديوان المعمور بما فيه من اجرة التربية وهو الثلث، اربعمائة وخمسون طائرا.

للمقطعين، ثلاثمائة طائر.

والذي يسلف بها من الشعير برسم الاصطبلات السلطانية، مائتان واربعة وثمانون اردبا.

اهلها يزرعون من القصب السكر بدموشية ما عدة فدنه ستة فدادين ونصف وثمن.

والمقرر على المعاملين من الفريك، اردب واحد.

grains, 160 1/24 1/48 ardabbs:

- wheat, 104 ½ ardabbs;
- barley, 33 ½ ¼ 1/48 ardabbs;
- sesame, 1 ⅔ ¼ ardabb.

[The fees, the measurement fee and the pasture fee] include:

- the fees, 270 ½ dirhams; and in grains, 91 1/24 1/48 ardabbs:
  - wheat, 58 ardabbs ⅔ ¼;
  - barley, 20 ardabbs ½ ¼ 1/16;
  - broad beans, 9 ½ ¼ ⅛ ardabbs;
  - sesame, 1 ⅔ ⅛ ardabb.
- [the fees] in detail:
  - supervision of the land survey, 25 dirhams;
  - supervision of endowments, 8 dirhams;
  - dredging fee, 90 dirhams;
  - harvest fee, 53 dirhams;
  - protection fee, 15 dirhams;
  - grinding fee (*al-midaqqāt*), 2 dirhams;
  - threshing-floor fee, 77 ½ dirhams; and in grains, 91 ½ ⅛ ardabbs, as specified.
- the measurement fee, 69 ardabbs:
  - wheat, 45 ⅓ ¼ arddabs;
  - barley, 12 ½ ⅓ ⅛ ardabbs;
  - broad beans, 10 ardabbs;
  - sesame, ⅓ ⅛ ardabb.
- the pasture fee for Difidnū and Abū Ṣīr, calculated on the basis of the normal number of the small cattle held by the peasants (*fallāḥūn*), 8 ⅙ dinars.

The alms-tax, 9 dinars:

- merchandise, 1 ½ dinar;
- estimate of date palms, 1 dinar;
- monetary value of livestock, for seven heads, 6 ½ dinars:
  - cows, one yearling calf, 1 ¼ dinar;
  - monetary value of small cattle, for six heads, 5 ¼ dinars:
    - sheep, for four heads, 4 ⅛ dinars;
    - goats, for two heads, 1 ⅛ dinar.

For the Ministry of Endowments, 4 dinars.

Hay, 2,600 bales.

Fee of the overseer of the canal, 2 ardabbs of wheat.

The chickens reared in it, 750 birds:

- for the prosperous Dīwān, including the rearing wage of a third, 450 birds;
- for the *iqṭā*ᶜ-holders, 300 birds.

The barley assigned for the royal stables and paid for in advance, 284 ardabbs.

Its people sow 6 ½ ⅛ feddans of sugarcane at Dumūshiyya.

The established levy of *farīk* dishes on the cultivators, 1 ardabb.

ومن حرف الدال، دنفارتي جردو واهريت. هاتان[603] البلدتان عبارة عن ست حلل فيها ودي وسنط وسدر وكروم عنب. تزرع الشتوي والصيفي. بينهما وبين مدينة الفيوم مسافة ساعة ونصف للراكب. وهما[604] من قبلي الفيوم للغرب. مجموعتان[605] في اقطاع الاميرين الاجلين سيف الدين ابن الامير سابق الدين، وعلاء الدين اخيه. عبرتهما جيشية، الفان وثلاثمائة دينار. والمطلق لهما[606] من الماء من مقسم ينقسم من قبلي مطول بجص، من ماء بحر منية اقنى، ما عدته اربع قبض مفردة. اهلهما بنو غصين فخذ من بني كلاب.

ارتفاعهما مما جميعه مستخرجا ومتحصلا، عينا، سبعة وعشرون دينارا; وغلة، الف واربعمائة واربعون اردبا. تفصيله:

قمح، سبعمائة وعشرون اردبا.

شعير، سبعمائة وعشرون اردب.

تفصيله:

مال الهلالي، عن الحانوت، عشرون دينارا.

المراعي، ثلاث دنانير.

خراج الدويرات، اربعة دنانير.

مناجزة الغلات، الف واربعمائة واربعون اردبا.

وعليها من الرسوم والكيالة، عن احد واربعين درهما وربع، دينار واحد ونصف قيراط وحبة; وغلة، ستون اردبا ونصف وربع ونصف ثمن. تفصيله:

قمح، ثلاثون اردبا وقيراط.

شعير، ثلاثون اردبا.

فول، نصف وربع اردب ونصف قيراط.

تفصيله:

رسم الاجران، احد واربعون درهما وربع، وغلة، تسعة واربعون اردبا وربع وثمن:

قمح، عشرون اردبا وقيراط.

شعير، ثمانية وعشرون اردبا ونصف ونصف ثمن.

فول، نصف وربع اردب ونصف قيراط.

الكيالة، احد عشر اردبا وربع وسدس ونصف قيراط:

قمح، عشرة ارادب.

شعير، اردب واحد وربع وسدس ونصف قيراط.

وعليها من الزكاة عن الاغنام، عن اثنى عشر راسا، ثمانية دنانير. تفصيله:

بياض، عن سبعة ارؤس، سبعة دنانير وربع.

شعارى، عن خمسة ارؤس، نصف وربع دينار.

والمربى بها من الفروج للمقطعين، اربعمائة واربعون طائرا.

وعليها من الاتبان، الف واربعمائة شنيف.

603 أ. س.: هذه.

604 أ. س.: وهي.

605 أ. س.: مجموعة.

606 أ. س.: لها.

Also beginning with the letter 'dāl': The Dinfāras of Jardū[195] and Ihrīt.[196] These two villages consist of six encampments (*ḥilal*). They have palm shoots, acacias, sidr trees and grape vineyards, winter and summer crops. They are an hour and a half's ride from Madīnat al-Fayyūm, towards the south-west of the province. They are jointly included in the *iqṭāʿ* of the two honourable amirs, Sayf al-Dīn, son of the amir Sābiq al-Dīn, and ʿAlāʾ al-Dīn, his brother.[197] Their fiscal value is 2,300 army dinars. They are allotted four *qabḍas* of water from a plastered divisor south of Muṭūl, from the water of Minyat Aqnā Canal. Their people are the Banū Ghuṣayn, a branch of the Banū Kilāb.

Their revenues in cash and kind are, in specie, 27 dinars; and in grains, 1,440 ardabbs:

wheat, 720 ardabbs;

barley, 720 ardabbs.

[This revenue] in detail:

lunar-calendar tax, for the shop, 20 dinars;

fixed pasture tax, 3 dinars;

land tax on enclosures, 4 dinars;

Munājaza land tax on grains, 1,440 ardabbs.

The fees and the measurement fee, 41 ¼ dirhams, which are 1 1/48 1/72 dinar; and in grains, 60 ½ ¼ 1/16 ardabbs:

wheat, 30 1/24 ardabbs;

barley, 30 ardabbs;

broad beans, ½ ¼ 1/48 ardabb.

[The fees and the measurement fee] in detail:

Threshing-floor fee, 41 ¼ dirhams; and in grains, 49 ¼ ⅛ ardabbs:

wheat, 20 1/24 ardabbs;

barley, 28 ½ 1/16 ardabbs;

broad beans, ½ ¼ 1/48 ardabb.

The measurement fee, 11 ¼ ⅙ 1/48 ardabbs:

wheat, 10 ardabbs;

barley, 1 ¼ ⅙ 1/48 ardabb.

The alms-tax, [the monetary value of] 12 heads of small cattle, 8 dinars:

sheep, for seven heads, 7 ¼ dinars;

goats, for five heads, ½ ¼ dinar.

The chickens reared in it for the *iqṭāʿ*-holders, 440 birds.

Hay, 1,400 bales.

195 Modern location (uncertain): ʿIzbat Muḥammad Fahmī (عزبة محمد فهمي). Halm, *Ägypten*, pp. 253–54; Salmon, 'Répertoire', p. 63; de Sacy, *État des provinces*, p. 682: Dinqāra; Ibn al-Jīʿān, *Kitāb al-tuḥfa*, p. 155: Dinqārat Jaradū; Ramzī, *Al-Qāmūs*, I, 256: near Jardū. We have no positive identification of this village, but in line with al-Nābulusī's description and with Shafei Bey's map, we located it near modern ʿIzbat Muḥammad Fahmī.

196 Modern location (uncertain): ʿIzbat ʿAbdallāh Bek al-Baḥrī (عزبة عبدالله بك البحري). Halm, *Ägypten*, p. 254; Salmon, 'Répertoire', p. 63; Ibn al-Jīʿān, *Kitāb al-tuḥfa*, p. 155: Dinqārat Ihrīt; Ramzī, *Al-Qāmūs*, I, 256: near Ihrīt. We have no positive identification of this village. In line with al-Nābulusī's description and with Shafei Bey's map, we located it near modern ʿIzbat ʿAbdallāh Bek al-Baḥrī.

197 Possibly a reference to Sābiq al-Dīn ʿUthmān, of the Banū al-Dāya, a prominent family in Aleppo under Nūr al-Din; Humphreys, *From Saladin to the Mongols*, pp. 32–33. One of his sons, ʿIzz al-Dīn Masʿūd, was the lord of Shayzar until his death in 1224; Jean-Michel Mouton, 'Shayzar', *The Encyclopedia of Islam*, 2nd edn, IX, 410–11.

ومن حرف الدال، دمشقين البصل. هذه البلدة عبارة عن بلدة كبيرة، شرقي الفيوم، من غربي المنهى. قريبة من طرف البحر الذي يخرج من المنهى الى الفيوم. تشتمل على نخل وجميز. يزرع بها البصل والقمح والسمسم والنيلة. وفي ايام الصيف ينقل لها الماء على اعناق الابقار. ويزرع في اراضيها التي تروى بالنيل القمح والشعير والكتان. بينها وبين مدينة الفيوم مسافة ثلاث ساعات للراكب. عبرتها جيشية، الف ومائتا دينار. وبها مسجد غير[607] مدون وكنيستان للنصارى. اهلها هوارة فخذ من بني لواتة.

ارتفاعها مما جميعه مستخرجا ومتحصلا، ثلاثمائة وستة دنانير ونصف؛ قمح، تسعة وستون اردبا. تفصيله:

مال المراعي،[608] اثنا عشر دينارا.

خراج[609] السواقي، مائتان وخمسة وخمسون دينارا.

خراج الكتان، احد وثلاثون دينارا.

خراج القرط ديناران.

خراج الجلبان، ستة دنانير ونصف.

المشاطرة، قمح تسعة وستون اردبا.

وعليها لمقطعي عشر المعروف بابن المهراني، اثنا عشر دينارا.

وعليها من الرسوم والكيالة والمراعي، عن ستمائة وتسعة وسبعين درهما ونصف وربع، سبعة عشر دينارا؛ وغلة، عشرة ارادب وقيراطان:

قمح، ستة[610] ارادب وقيراطان.

جلبان، اربعة ارادب.

تفصيله:

الرسوم، اربعمائة واربعة واربعون درهما ونصف، قمح، ثلاثة ارادب وقيراطان:

شد العين،[611] ثلاثمائة وتسعة وستون درهما.

شد احباس، خمسة دراهم.

رسم الحصاد، ثلاثة وخمسون درهما.

رسم الخفارة، خمسة عشر درهما.

رسم الاجران، درهمان ونصف، وقمح، ثلاثة ارادب وقيراطان.

كيالة، سبعة ارادب:

قمح، ثلاثة ارادب

جلبان، اربعة ارادب.

المراعي، طارئ، عن ستمائة وثلاثة وثلاثين راسا، مائتان وخمسة وثلاثون درهما وربع. تفصيله:

قطيعة درهم واحد الراس، عن خمسين راسا، خمسون درهما.

قطيعة خمسة وعشرين المائة، عن خمسمائة وثلاث وثمانين راسا، مائة وخمسة واربعون درهما ونصف وربع.

رسم المستخدمين حسابا عن كل مائة راس ستة دراهم وربع، تسعة وثلاثون درهما ونصف.

عليها من الزكاة عن ثمن اغنام، عن ثمانية ارؤس، سبعة دنانير وثمن. تفصيله:

بياض، عن ستة ارؤس، ستة دنانير وسدس.

شعارى، عن راسين، دينار واحد وثمن.

607 ساقط من أ. س.: غير.

608 أ. س.: الهلالي.

609 ساقط من أ. س.: خراج.

610 أ. س. يضيف قراريط لكنه مشطب.

611 ط. م.: شد عين.

Also beginning with the letter 'dāl': Dimashqīn al-Baṣal.[198] This is a large village in the east of the Fayyum, west of al-Manhā [Canal], near the edge of the canal which issues from al-Manhā toward the Fayyum. It has date palms and sycamores, and onions, wheat, sesame and indigo are sown in it. In the summer water is carried to it on cattle's necks, and in the lands that are watered by the Nile they sow wheat, barley and flax. It is three hours' ride from Madīnat al-Fayyūm. Its fiscal value is 1,200 army dinars. It has one unregistered neighbourhood mosque, and two Christian churches. Its people are the Hawwāra, a branch of the Banū Lawāta.

Its revenue in cash and in kind is 306 ½ dinars; [and in] wheat, 69 ardabbs. [The revenue] in detail:

permanent pasture tax / lunar-calendar taxes[199], 12 dinars;

land tax on [land watered by] waterwheels, 255 dinars;

land tax on flax, 31 dinars;

land tax on alfalfa, 2 dinars;

land tax on chickling vetch, 6 ½ dinars;

Mushāṭara land tax, wheat, 69 ardabbs.

For the *iqṭāᶜ*-holders of the tithe known as Ibn al-Mihrānī, 12 dinars.

The fees, measurement fee and the pasture fee, 679 ½ ¼ dirhams, which are 17 dinars; and in grains, 10 ²⁄₂₄ ardabbs:

wheat, 6 ²⁄₂₄ ardabbs;

chickling vetch, 4 ardabbs.

[The fees, measurement fee and the pasture fee] include:

The fees, 444 ½ dirhams; and in wheat, 3 ²⁄₂₄ ardabbs. In detail:

supervision of the land survey, 369 dirhams;

supervision of endowments, 5 dirhams;

harvest fee, 53 dirhams;

protection fee, 15 dirhams;

threshing-floor fee, 2 ½ dirhams; and in wheat, 3 ²⁄₂₄ ardabbs;

The measurement fee, 7 ardabbs:

wheat, 3 ardabbs;

chickling vetch, 4 ardabbs.

The pasture fee, for 633 heads of seasonal pasture lands, 235 ¼ dirhams:

at the rate of one dirham per head, for 50 heads, 50 dirhams;

at the rate of 25 [dirhams] per 100 [heads], for 583 heads, 145 ½ ¼ dirhams;

the government agents' fee, calculated at the rate of 6 ¼ dirhams per 100 heads, 39 ½ dirhams.

The alms-tax, for the monetary value of eight heads of small cattle, 7 dinars ⅙ ⅛:

sheep, for six heads, 6 ⅙ dinars;

goats, for two heads, 1 ⅛ dinar.

198 Modern location: Dimishqīn/ᶜIzbat Kamāl (عزبة كمال). Timm, *Das Christlich-Koptische Ägypten*, p. 865; Halm, *Ägypten*, p. 253; Salmon, 'Répertoire', p. 39; Ibn Mammātī, *Kitāb qawānīn al-dawāwīn*, p. 139; Yāqūt, *Muᶜjam al-Buldān*, II, 470: Dimashqīn; Ibn al-Jīᶜān, *Kitāb al-tuḥfa*, p. 154: Damashqīn; de Sacy, *État des provinces*, p. 682: Damashqīn; Savigny, *Description de l'Égypte*, p. 126; Ramzī, *Al-Qāmūs*, II/III, 99: Dimishqīn/ᶜIzbat Kamāl.

199 MP: permanent pasture tax; AS: lunar calendar taxes.

وعليها من الجوالي، عن اربعة وستين نفرا، مائة وثمانية وعشرون دينارا. تفصيله:

المقيمون بها،[612] عن اربعة وعشرين نفرا، ثمانية واربعون دينارا.

الناعون عنها، عن اربعين نفرا، ثمانون دينارا. تفصيله:

بالوجه البحري، عن[613] احد عشر نفرا، اثنان وعشرون دينارا.

بالوجه القبلي، عن تسعة وعشرين نفرا، ثمانية وخمسون دينارا.

عليها من الاتبان، ثمانون شنيفا.

عليها لديوان الاحباس، ديناران.

اهلها يعمرون الحيطان الدائرة على الاقصاب بما عدته اربعون نفرا.

اهلها يربون من الدجاج برسم المطابخ السلطانية، بما فيه مما يعتد به لهم عن اجرة التربية بحق الثلث وهو مائة فروج، ثلاثمائة فروج.

يبتاع من اهلها من زراعة سواقيهم من البصل الخشبي برسم زراعة الاواسي السلطانية بمدينة الفيوم، سعر ستة دراهم الاردب، مائتا اردب.

ومن حرف الدال، دموه الداثر. هذه البلدة عبارة عن بلدة صغيرة مستجدة بعد ان دثرت. بعض اراضيها تزرع بماء النيل كالريف وبعضها بالسقي كاراضي الفيوم. ليس بها شجر ولا نخل ولا كرم ولا بساتين ولا غروس بل ارض براح. بينها وبين مدينة الفيوم مسافة ساعتين للراكب. وهي من علو البلاد. عبرتها الف ومائتا دينار جيشية. لها خليج بغير عبرة لسقي[614] الشتوي[615] خاصة. اهلها بنو زرعة، فخذ من بني عجلان.

ارتفاعها مما جميعه مستخرجا ومتحصلا، عينا، ديناران ونصف؛ غلة، ثمانون اردبا. تفصيله:

قمح، ستون اردبا.

فول، عشرون اردبا.

تفصيله:

مراعي، ديناران ونصف.

خراج الغلة، ثمانون اردبا، على ما فصل.

عليها من الرسوم والكيالة والمراعي، عن احد وثلاثين درهما وربع، نصف وربع ونصف قيراط وحبة؛ وغلة، احد عشر اردبا وثلثان وربع ونصف ثمن. تفصيله:

قمح، اردبان وثلثان[616] وثمن.

شعير، ستة ارادب ونصف وثلث ونصف قيراط.

فول، اردبان وثلث.

تفصيله:

رسم الحصاد، خمسة وعشرون درهما.

رسم الاجران، ستة دراهم وربع، وغلة، سبعة ارادب وثلثان ونصف ثمن. تفصيله:

قمح، اردب واحد وربع وسدس وثمن.

شعير، ثلاثة ارادب ونصف وثلث ونصف قيراط.

فول، اردبان وثلث.

612 ساقط من ط. م.: بها.

613 ساقط من أ. س.: عن.

614 أ. س.: يسقي.

615 أ. س. يضيف: الشتوي.

616 أ. س.: وثلث.

The poll-tax, for 64 individuals, 128 dinars:

those residing in it, for 24 individuals, 48 dinars;

those absent from it, for 40 individuals, 80 dinars:

the northern region, for 11 individuals, 22 dinars;

the southern region, for 29 individuals, 58 dinars.

Hay, 800 bales.

For the Ministry of Endowments, 2 dinars.

Forty individuals from this village construct walls that encircle the sugarcane plantations.

Its people rear 300 chickens, assigned for the royal kitchens. This includes the rearing wage, calculated as one third, 100 chickens.

Its people sell 200 ardabbs of onion bulbs (?, *baṣal khashabī*)[200] from the produce of [lands irrigated by] their waterwheels, assigned for sowing in the crown estate in Madīnat al-Fayyūm, at a price of 6 dirhams per ardabb.

Also beginning with the letter 'dāl': Dimūh al-Dāthir.[201] This is a small village, which has been recently re-occupied after it had been deserted. Some of its land is cultivated with the water of the Nile like Lower Egypt, and some of it irrigated like the villages of the Fayyum. It has no trees, date palms, vineyards, gardens or orchards, but is only an open tract of land that lies on higher ground. The distance between it and Madīnat al-Fayyūm is two hours' ride. Its fiscal value is 1,200 army dinars. It has a canal without water quota, solely for the irrigation of winter crops. Its people are the Banū Zarʿa, a branch of the Banū ʿAjlān.

Its revenue in cash and in kind is, in specie, 2 ½ dinars; and in grains, 80 ardabbs:

wheat, 60 ardabbs;

broad beans, 20 ardabbs.

[The revenue] in detail:

fixed pasture tax, 2 ½ dinars;

land tax on grains, 80 ardabbs, as specified.

The fees, the measurement fee and the pasture fee are 31 ¼ dirhams, which are ½ ¼ 1/48 1/72 [of a dinar]; and in grains, 11 ⅔ ¼ 1/16 ardabbs:

wheat, 2 ⅔ ⅛ ardabbs;

barley, 6 ½ ⅓ 1/48 ardabbs;

broad beans, 2 ⅓ ardabbs.

[The fees, the measurement fee and the pasture fee] include:

harvest fee, 25 dirhams;

threshing-floor fee, 6 ¼ dirhams; and in grains, 7 ⅔ 1/16 ardabbs:

wheat, 1 ¼ ⅙ ⅛ ardabb;

barley, 3 ½ ⅓ 1/48 ardabbs;

broad beans, 2 ⅓ ardabbs.

200 We have not found other references to the term *baṣal khashabī* — 'woody' onions. Since these onions were to be re-sown in the crown estate in the city, it is likely the term refers to small bulbs. On the planting of onions and on varieties of onions, see also Abū al-Khayr al-Ishbīlī, *Kitāb al-filāḥa = Tratado De Agricultura*, ed. and trans. by Julia Maria Carabaza (Madrid: Agencia Espanõla de Cooperacion Internacional, 1991), pp. 209–15.

201 Modern location: Dimū (دمو). Ibn al-Jīʿān, *Kitāb al-tuḥfa*, p. 155; Halm, *Ägypten*, p. 254; Ibn Mammātī, *Kitāb qawānīn al-dawāwīn*, p. 124: Dumūh al-Bayḍāʾ; de Sacy, *État des provinces*, p. 682: Dumūh al-Dātir; Savigny, *Description de l'Égypte*, p. 128; Ramzī, *Al-Qāmūs*, II/III, 99: Dimū.

الكيالة، اربعة ارادب وربع. تفصيله:
قمح، اردب واحد وربع.
شعير، ثلاثة ارادب.

وعليها من الزكاة عن ثمن اغنام، عن اربعة اروس، ثلاثة دنانير وثمن. تفصيله:
بياض، عن راسين، ديناران.
شعارى، عن راسين، دينار واحد وثمن.

وعليها من الاتبان، ثمانون شنيفا.

اهلها يربون من الدجاج برسم المطابخ السلطانية، بما فيه من اجرة التربية وهو الثلث، مائة وخمسة فراريج.

والذي جرت العادة باطلاقه لها من التقاوي، خمسة وعشرون اردبا.

ومن حرف الدال، دموه اللاهون المعروف بكوم درى. هذه البلدة عبارة عن بلدة صغيرة، بها نخل وجميز وسواق ينقل الماء لها على اعناق الابقار. تزرع البصل والصيفي كالسمسم وغيره. ويزرع في اراضيها القمح والشعير ويسير كتان. بينها وبين مدينة الفيوم ثلاث ساعات للراكب. عبرتها الفان ومائتا دينار. اهلها هواريون.

ارتفاعها مما جميعه مستخرجا ومتحصلا، عينا، مائة واربعة وثلاثون دينارا؛ وغلة، خمسة وثلاثون اردبا. تفصيله:
شعير، سبعة عشر اردبا ونصف.
جلبان، سبعة عشر اردبا ونصف.

تفصيله:
ضمان المعدية، ستة دنانير.
المراعي، ديناران.
الخراج، عينا، مائة وستة وعشرون دينارا، والغلة على ما تقدم.

وعليها من الرسوم والمراعي، عن ثلاثمائة وثلاثة واربعين درهما، ثمانية دنانير وربع وسدس وثمن وحبتان. تفصيله:
الرسوم، مائة واثنان وخمسون درهما. تفصيله:[617]
شد العين، اربعة وثمانون درهما.
رسم الحصاد، ثلاثة وخمسون درهما.
خفارة، خمسة عشر درهما.
المراعي، عن اربعمائة وتسعة وثلاثين راسا، مائة واحد وتسعون درهما. تفصيله:
قطيعة درهم واحد الراس، عن اربعة وعشرون راسا، اربعة وعشرون درهما.[618]
قطيعة سبعين درهما المائة، عن ثمانية واربعين راسا، اثنان وثلاثون درهما ونصف وربع.
قطيعة ثلاثين درهما المائة، عن مائتين وتسعة وتسعين راسا، تسعة وثمانون درهما ونصف وربع.
قطيعة خمسة وعشرين درهما المائة، عن ثمانية وستين راسا، سبعة عشر درهما.
رسم المستخدمين، سبعة وعشرون درهما ونصف.

The measurement fee, 4 ¼ ardabbs:
wheat, 1 ¼ ardabb;
barley, 3 ardabbs.

The alms-tax, for the monetary value of four heads of small cattle, 3 ⅛ dinars:
sheep, for two heads, 2 dinars;
goats, for two heads, 1 ⅛ dinar.

Hay, 80 bales.

Its people rear 150 chickens assigned for the royal kitchens, including the rearing wage of a third.

The seed advances customarily distributed in it, 25 ardabbs.

Also beginning with the letter 'dāl': Dimūh al-Lāhūn, known as Kawm Durrī.[202] This is a small village, with date palms and sycamores, as well as waterwheels. Water is carried to it on cattle's necks. Onions are sown in it, as well as summer crops such as sesame and the like. Wheat, barley and a bit of flax are also sown. It is three hours' ride from Madīnat al-Fayyūm. Its fiscal value is 2,200 army dinars. Its people are the Hawwāra.

Its revenue in cash and kind is, in specie, 134 dinars; and in grains, 35 ardabbs:
barley, 17 ½ ardabbs;
chickling vetch, 17 ½ ardabbs.

[The revenue] in detail:
concession of the ferryboat, 6 dinars;
permanent pasture tax, 2 dinars;
land tax in specie, 126 dinars;
the grains, as above.

The fees and the pasture fee are 343 dirhams, which are 8 ¼ ⅙ ⅛ 2/72 dinars:
The fees, 152 dirhams:
supervision of the land survey, 84 dirhams;
harvest fee, 53 dirhams;
protection fee, 15 dirhams.
The pasture fee, for 439 heads, 191 dirhams:
at the rate of one dirham per head, for 24 heads, 24 dirhams;
at the rate of 70 dirhams per 100 [heads], for 58 heads, 32 ½ ¼ dirhams;
at the rate of 30 dirhams per 100 [heads], for 299 heads, 89 ½ ¼ dirhams;
at the rate of 25 dirhams per 100 [heads], for 68 heads, 17 dirhams;
the government agents' fee, 27 ½ dirhams.

617 ساقط من أ. س.: تفصيله.
618 ساقط من ط. م.: قطيعة درهم واحد الراس عن أربعة وعشرون رأسا أربعة وعشرون درهما.

202 Modern location: Hawwārat ʿAdlān (هوّارة عدلان). Ibn Mammātī, *Kitāb qawānīn al-dawāwīn*, p. 139; Ibn al-Jīʿān, *Kitāb al-tuḥfa*, p. 166 — belongs to al-Bahnasā; Halm, *Ägypten*, p. 255; Salmon, 'Répertoire', p. 39; Ramzī, *Al-Qāmūs*, II/III, 103: Hawwārat ʿAdlān. This village is well documented in the Banū Bifām archive of the eleventh century; see Gaubert and Mouton, *Hommes et villages*, pp. 12–13.

وعليها من الزكاة عن ثمن اغنام، عن اربعة اروس، ثلاثة دنانير ونصف وثمن. تفصيله:

بياض، عن ثلاثة اروس، ثلاثة دنانير وثمن.

شعارى، عن راس واحد، نصف دينار.

والذي يربى بها من الدجاج للديوان السلطاني المعمور[619] بما فيه من اجرة التربية وهو الثلث، مائتان وعشرة اطيار.

ومن حرف الدال، دهما. هذه البلدة عبارة عن بلدة كبيرة محدثة من قبلي مدينة الفيوم الى الغرب. بها اصول سنط وليس بها نخل ولا كروم ولا جميز ولا غروس. كانت تزرع الاقطان قبل ان تصرف المياه الى الاقصاب. فلما كثرت الاقصاب استوعبت جميع المياه فتعطلت الناحية عن زراعة القطن. ويزرع بها القمح والشعير والفول من جنس اراضي الفيوم. بينها وبين مدينة الفيوم ثلاث ساعات للراكب. داخلة في عبرة الاقطاع بالخليج المذكور. المطلق[620] لها من الماء من بحر دلية من المقسم المعروف بالتبرون، تسع قبض وثمن. اهلها بنو حاتم فخذ من بني كلاب.

ارتفاعها عينا، ثلاثة دنانير هلالي، وشعير خمسمائة وعشرون اردبا.

عليها من المراعي والرسوم والكيالة، عن مائة وسبعة وخمسين درهما ونصف، ثلاثة دنانير وثلثان وربع ونصف قيراط؛ وغلة، خمسة وعشرون اردبا ونصف وربع وثمن. تفصيله:

قمح، اردبان وثلث.

شعير، اثنان وعشرون اردبا ونصف وربع ونصف قيراط.

فول، نصف وربع ونصف قيراط.

تفصيله:

شد الاحباس، احد عشر درهما ونصف.[621]

رسم الجراريف، خمسة واربعون درهما.

رسم الخفارة، خمسة عشر درهما.[622]

رسم الحصاد، ثلاثة وخمسون درهما.

رسم الكمون، عشرون درهما.

رسم الاجران، ثلاثة عشر درهما، وغلة، اربعة عشر اردبا ونصف وربع وثمن. تفصيله:

قمح، اردبان وثلث.

شعير، احد عشر اردبا ونصف وربع ونصف قيراط.

الكيالة، احد عشر اردبا شعيرا.

وعليها من الزكاة عن ثمن الاغنام، عن اربعة اروس، ثلاثة دنانير وربع. تفصيله:

بياض، عن راسين، ديناران وثمن.

شعارى، عن راسين، دينار واحد وثمن.

وعليها لديوان الاحباس، ثلاثة دنانير.

وعليها من الاتبان، ستمائة شنيف.

والمسلف عليه بها من الشعير برسم الاصطبلات السلطانية، اربعون اردبا.

اهلها يزرعون القصب السكر بدموشية، راس، فدان واحد وسدس.

والمربى بها من الفروج، خمسمائة وستون فروج. تفصيله:

للديوان المعمور برسم المطابخ السلطانية، ثلاثمائة وستون فروجا، بما فيه من اجرة التربية وهو الثلث.

للمقطعين، مائتا طائر.

619 ساقط من أ. س.: المعمور.

620 أ. س.: المطلق المذكور لها.

621 ساقط من أ. س.: ونصف.

622 أ. س. يضيف: ونصف.

The alms-tax, for the monetary value of four heads of small cattle, 3 ½ ⅛ dinars:

sheep, for three heads, 3 ⅛ dinars;

goats, for one head, ½ dinar.

The chickens reared in it for the prosperous royal Dīwān, including the rearing wage of a third, 210 birds.

Also beginning with the letter 'dāl': Dahmā.[203] This is a large, recently occupied village, south-west of Madīnat al-Fayyūm. It has trunks of acacias, but no date palms, vineyards, sycamores or plantations. Cotton was sown in it before the water was diverted to the sugarcane. When the [cultivation of] sugarcane increased, it absorbed the entire amount of water, and the sowing of cotton in the village was discontinued. Wheat, barley and broad beans are cultivated in the manner of the villages of the Fayyum. It is three hours' ride from Madīnat al-Fayyūm. It is included in the fiscal value of the *iqṭāʿ* of Dilya Canal. The water allotted to it from Dilya Canal, through the divisor known as al-Tabrūn, is 9 ⅛ *qabḍas*. Its people are the Banū Ḥātim, a branch of the Banū Kilāb.

Its revenues in specie, 3 dinars from lunar calendar taxes; and in barley, 520 ardabbs.

The pasture fee, the fees and the measurement fee, 157 ½ dirhams, which are 3 ⅔ ¼ 1/48 dinars; and in grains, 25 ½ ¼ ⅛ ardabbs:

wheat, 2 ⅓ ardabbs;

barley, 22 ½ ¼ 1/48 ardabbs;

broad beans ½ ¼ 1/48 [ardabb].

[the fees] in detail:

supervision of endowments, 11 ½ dirhams;

dredging fee, 45 dirhams;

protection fee, 15 dirhams;

harvest fee, 53 dirhams;

cumin fee, 20 dirhams;

threshing-floor fee, 13 dirhams; and in grains, 14 ½ ¼ ⅛ ardabbs:

wheat, 2 ⅓ ardabbs;

barley, 11 ½ ¼ 1/48 ardabbs.

The measurement fee, 11 ardabbs of barley.

The alms-tax, for the monetary value of four heads of small cattle, 3 ¼ dinars:

sheep, for two heads, 2 ⅛ dinars;

goats, for two heads, 1 ⅛ dinar.

For the Ministry of Endowments, 3 dinars.

Hay, 600 bales.

The barley assigned for the royal stables and paid for in advance, 40 ardabbs.

Its people sow sugarcane in Dumūshiyya, first harvest, 1 ⅙ feddan.

The chickens reared in it, 560 chickens:

for the prosperous Dīwān and assigned for the royal kitchens, 360 chickens, including the rearing wage of a third;

for the *iqṭāʿ*-holders, 200 birds.

203 Modern location: Nawwāra (نوارة). Halm, *Ägypten*, p. 252: Dahmā = Dahmashā; Ibn al-Jīʿān, *Kitāb al-tuḥfa*, p. 166: Dahmashā; Salmon, 'Répertoire', p. 69; de Sacy, *État des provinces*, p. 682: Dahmashā; Ramzī, *Al-Qāmūs*, II/III, 87: Nawwāra.

ومن حرف الذال، ذات الصفاء وما عرف[623] بها وهو اخصاص النجار. هذه البلدة عبارة عن بلدة كبيرة مقسومة حارتين بينهما مشوار فرس. انقسم[624] سكانها لخلف[625] كان بينهم فتباعدوا في المساكن. تشتمل على البساتين الكثيرة والكروم الغزيرة والثمار المتكاثرة والفواكه الباهرة والنخيل المثمرة والحدائق المستكثرة والانهار الجارية وطاحون الماء الدائرة. تزرع جميع الحبوب كما تزرع بلاد الفيوم. وكان يزرع بها قديما السمسم ثم رقت الاراضي عنه فعوض عنه بالارز ثم ترك الارز بها من سنين لتوفير الماء على الاقصاب المحدثة في هذه السنين.

بينها وبين مدينة الفيوم مسافة اربع ساعات للراكب. وهي جارية في اقطاع جماعة من المقطعين. بها معصرة بظاهر اخصاص الحلاق ذات حجر واحد دائر بالماء. والمطلق لها من الماء لسقى الشتوي والصيفي من بحر يعرف بذات الصفاء، يخرج منه لسقي مطر طارس معروف بتلمنده، وتتساق بقية المياه الى الفسقية[626] اليوسفية تحت القبرا، تتقسم[627] على اخصاص الحلاق ومنية البطس وسرسنا وفرقس وابريزيا والزربي.

والذي يخص الناحية المنكورة مما هو مطلق في خليج مجصص مبنى له ثلاثة ابواب، احد وثلاثون قبضة. تفصيله:

باب شرقي، ثمانية عشر قبضة.

باب وسطاني مستجد للقصب لسنة تسعة وثلاثين وستمائة للديوان السلطاني، خمس قبض.

باب غربي البابين، يعرف بمقعد المراة، ثمان قبض.

وبها جامع تقام فيه الجمعة. ذكر ان فيه اسماء اناس من الصحابة مدفونين به. اهلها بنو جابر، فخذ من بني عجلان. عبرتها جيشية ثلاثة وخمسون الفا وثلاثمائة وثلاث[628] وثلاثون دينارا وثلث.

ارتفاعها، عينا، سبعمائة وستة واربعون دينارا وربع وسدس؛ وغلات، اربعة الاف وثلاثة عشر اردبا وسدس. تفصيله:

قمح، الفان وستمائة وستة وستون اردبا وثلثان.

شعير، الف وثلاثمائة وثلاثة وثلاثون اردبا وثلث.

سمسم، ثلاثة عشر اردبا وسدس.

ومن الفدن القصب، ثلاثة وخمسون فدانا وثلث.

تفصيله:

مل الهلالي، مائة واربعة وثمانون دينارا وربع وحبتان. تفصيله:

الحانوت، سبعة وستون دينارا وثلثان وربع وحبتان.

الطاحون، مائة وستة عشر دينارا وثلث.

مل الخراجي بما فيه من الداثر، وهو خمسة واربعون دينارا، خمسمائة واثنان وستون دينارا وثمن وحبة. والغلة والفدن على ما تقدم.

623 أ. س.: يعرف.
624 ساقط من أ. س.: انقسم.
625 أ. س. ط. م.: لخلف
626 أ. س.: لالفسقية.
627 أ. س.: ينقسم.
628 ساقط من أ. س.: وثلاث.

Beginning with the letter 'dhāl': Dhāt al-Ṣafā'[204] and its hamlet Akhṣāṣ al-Najjār. This is a large village divided into two quarters, with a short journey (*mishwār faras*) between them. [This is because] its inhabitants have become divided owing to a disagreement between them, and have drawn away from each other. The village has many gardens and abundant vineyards, plenty of splendid fruits, fruit-bearing date palms, numerous enclosed gardens, running streams and a turning watermill. All the varieties of cereals are cultivated, in the manner of the villages of the Fayyum. Sesame was sown in it in the past, but then its lands became unfit for it (*raqqat al-arāḍī ʿanhu*), and it was replaced by rice. Then, several years ago, rice was abandoned to provide water for the sugarcane, which was introduced during these years.

The distance between it and Madīnat al-Fayyūm is four hours' ride. It is included in the *iqṭāʿ* of a group of *iqṭāʿ*-holders. It has a press, in the outskirts of Akhṣāṣ al-Ḥallāq, with one stone turned by water. Water is allocated to it from Dhāt al-Ṣafā' Canal, for the irrigation of winter and summer crops. Water from this canal is [also] used for the irrigation of Miṭr Ṭāris, [through a canal] known as Tlmndh. The remainder of the water is directed toward the [the divisor known as] al-Fasqiyya al-Yūsufiyya, below al-Qubarā', [where] it is divided between Akhṣāṣ al-Ḥallāq, Minyat al-Baṭs, Sirisnā, Furqus, Ibrīziyā and al-Zarbī.

The [water] quota assigned for this village, through a plastered canal with a weir and three sluice gates, is 31 *qabḍas*:

an eastern sluice gate, 18 *qabḍas*;

a central sluice gate, newly built for the sugarcane in 639 [AD 1241–2], for the use of the royal Dīwān, 5 *qabḍas*;

a sluice gate to the west of these two, known as 'The Woman's Seat', 8 *qabḍas*.

It has a congregational mosque, in which the Friday prayers are held, and it is said that the names of several Companions of the Prophet who are buried in it are inscribed there. Its people are the Banū Jābir, a branch of the Banū ʿAjlān. Its fiscal value is 53,333 ⅓ army dinars.

Its revenue in specie is 746 ¼ ⅙ dinars; and in grains, 4,013 ⅙:

wheat, 2,666 ⅔ ardabbs;

barley, 1,333 ⅓ ardabbs;

sesame, 13 ⅙ ardabbs.

The feddans of sugarcane sowed, 53 ⅓ feddans.

[The revenue] in detail:

Lunar calendar taxes, 184 ¼ 2/72 dinars:

the shop, 67 ⅔ ¼ 2/72 dinars;

the mill, 116 ⅓ dinars;

Land tax — including that which has fallen into disuse, which is 45 dinars — 562 ⅛ 1/72 dinars; the grains and the feddans [of sugarcane], as specified above.

204 Modern location: Maʿṣarat Ṣāwī (معصرة صاوي). Halm, *Ägypten*, p. 253; Salmon, 'Répertoire', p. 49: Dhāt al-Ṣafā' = Akhṣāṣ al-Najjār; de Sacy, *État des provinces*, p. 682; Ibn Mammātī, *Kitāb qawānīn al-dawāwīn*, p. 142; Ibn al-Jīʿān, *Kitāb al-tuḥfa*, p. 154; Ramzī, *Al-Qāmūs*, II/III, 115: Maʿṣarat Ṣāwī.

تفصيله:

خراج الراتب والاحكار، اربعمائة وثمانية وستون دينارا وربع وثمن وحبة. تفصيله:

كرم كامل، قطيعة خمسة دنانير ونصف وثلث الفدان، عن ثمانية فدادين وثلث وربع ونصف ثمن، خمسون دينارا ونصف وحبة.

راتب، قطيعة دينارين وربع بالاضافة، عن ثلاثة وخمسين فدانا وربع وثمن وحبتين، مائة وثلاثة وعشرون دينارا وربع وحبتان.

قطن، قطيعة دينار واحد وربع الفدان بالاضافة، عن تسعة واربعين فدانا وثمن، احد وستون دينارا وربع وسدس.

حكر، قطيعة دينارين وثمن بالاضافة، عن مائة وتسعة فدادين وثلثين ونصف ثمن،[629] مائتان[630] وثلاثة وثلاثون دينارا وسدس وحبة.

خراج المناجزة والقرط ومؤنة النواب، احد وثمانون دينارا وربع. تفصيله:

المناجزة، المقرر على المزارعين خاصة عن زراعة القطاني، خمسون دينارا.

قرط، ثلاثة وعشرون دينارا وربع.

مؤنة النواب، ثمانية دنانير.

خراج فدن العين، عن القلقاس والثوم والخضر، اثنا عشر دينارا ونصف:

القلقاس، ستة دنانير وربع.

ثوم وخضر، ستة دنانير وربع.

خراج مناجزة الغلات والمتحصل من المشاطرة في السمسم خاصة، اربعة الاف وثلاثة عشر اردبا وسدس على ما فصّل.

زراعة الاوسية المباركة، قصب سكر مما جميعه راس، ثلاثة وخمسون فدانا وثلث.

وعليها من الرسوم والكيالة والمراعي، عن الف وتسعمائة[631] وثلاثة وثلاثين درهما وربع وثمن، ثمانية واربعون دينارا وثلث؛ وغلة، مائتان وثلاثة وستون اردبا ونصف وثمن. تفصيله:

قمح، مائة وثلاثة وعشرون اردبا وقيراطان ونصف.

وشعير، سبعة وسبعون اردبا وربع وسدس ونصف قيراط.

وفول، ستة وخمسون اردبا وثلث وربع ونصف ثمن.

جلبان، ستة ارادب وربع وسدس ونصف قيراط.

تفصيله:

الرسوم، اربعمائة واثنان وستون درهما ونصف، ومائة وستة عشر اردبا وسدس وثمن:

قمح، احد واربعون اردبا[632] وثلث وربع.

شعير، خمسة وثلاثون اردبا وخمسة قراريط.

فول، خمسة وثلاثون اردبا[633] وقيراط.

جلبان، اربعة ارادب وثلث وثمن.

تفصيله:

شد احباس، اثنان وثلاثون درهما.

رسم الجراريف، مائة واثنان وثمانون درهما ونصف.

رسم الحصاد، ثلاثة وخمسون[634] درهما.

رسم الخفارة، خمسة عشر درهما.

[land tax] in detail:

land tax on perennial plants and on lands subject to long-term lease, 468 ¼ ⅛ 1/72 dinars:

fully grown vineyard, at the rate of 5 ½ ⅓[205] dinars per feddan, for 8 ⅓ ¼ 1/16 feddans, 50 ½ 1/72 dinars;

perennial plants, at the rate of 2 dinars ¼ [per feddan], which incorporates the additional rate, for 53 ¼ ⅛ 2/72 feddans, 123 ¼ 2/72 dinars;

cotton, at the rate of 1 ¼ dinar per feddan, which incorporates the additional rate, for 49 ⅛ feddans, 61 ¼ ⅙ dinars;

land subject to long-term lease, at the rate of 2 ⅛ dinars, which incorporates the additional rate, for 109 ⅔ 1/16 feddans, 233 ⅙ 1/72 dinars.

munājaza land tax, alfalfa, and the provisions for the agents, 81 ¼ dinars:

the established *munājaza* land tax on the tenants, specifically for the cultivation of lentils (*qaṭānī*), 50 dinars;

alfalfa, 23 ¼ dinars;

provisions for the agents, 8 dinars.

land tax on cash crops, assessed by feddans, for colocasia, garlic and green vegetables, 12 ½ dinars:

colocasia, 6 ¼ dinars;

garlic and green vegetables, 6 ¼ dinar.

Munājaza land tax on grains, and the tax in kind from *mushāṭara* land tax on sesame, 4,013 ⅙ ardabbs, as specified.

The cultivation of sugarcane in the blessed crown estate, all of which is first harvest, 53 ⅓ feddans.

The fees, the measurement fee and the pasture fee are 1,933 ¼ ⅛ dirhams, which are 48 ⅓ dinars; and in grains, 263 ½ ⅛ ardabbs:

wheat, 123 5/48 ardabbs;

barley, 77 ¼ ⅙ 1/48 ardabbs;

broad beans, 56 ⅓ ¼ 1/16 ardabbs;

chickling vetch, 6 ¼ ⅙ 1/48 ardabbs.

[The fees, the measurement fee and the pasture fee] include:

the fees, 462 ½ dirhams; [and in grains] 116 ⅙ ⅛ ardabbs:

wheat, 41 ⅓ ¼ ardabbs;

barley, 35 5/24 ardabbs;

broad beans, 35 1/24 ardabbs;

chickling vetch, 4 ⅓ ⅛ ardabbs.

[The fees] in detail:

supervision of endowments, 32 dirhams;

dredging fee, 182 ½ dirhams;

harvest fee, 53 dirhams;

protection fee, 15 dirhams;

629 أ. س.: قيراط.

630 أ. س.: ثمانمائة.

631 أ. س.: وستمائة.

632 ساقط من أ. س.: أردبا.

633 ساقط من أ. س.: أردبا.

634 أ. س.: ثلاثون.

205 In both manuscripts, and according to the calculation, 5 ½ ⅓. Elsewhere in the treatise the rate for vineyards is uniformly 5 ⅓ dinar per feddan.

رسم القلقاس، ثمانون درهما.
رسم الاجران، مائة درهم، وغلة، مائة وستة عشر اردبا وسدس وثمن. تفصيله:
قمح، احد واربعون اردبا وثلث وربع.
شعير، خمسة وثلاثون اردبا وخمسة قراريط.
فول، خمسة وثلاثون اردبا وقيراط.
جلبان، اربعة ارادب وثلث وثمن.
الكيالة، مائة وسبعة واربعون اردبا وثلث. تفصيله:
قمح، احد وثمانون اردبا ونصف ونصف قيراط.
شعير، اثنان واربعون اردبا وسدس ونصف ثمن.
فول، احد وعشرون اردبا وثلث وربع ونصف قيراط.
جلبان، اردب واحد وثلثان وربع ونصف ثمن.
المراعي، عن ثمانمائة وستة وتسعين راسا، الف واربعمائة وتسعة وستون درهما ونصف وربع وثمن. تفصيله:
راتب، قطيعة درهمين وربع الراس، عن اربعمائة وثلاثة وثمانين راسا، الف وستة[635] وثمانون درهما ونصف وربع.
طارئ، عن اربعمائة وثلاثة عشر راسا، ثلاثمائة وسبعة وعشرون درهما. تفصيله:
قطيعة درهم واحد الراس، عن مائتين وثلاثة عشر راسا، مائتان وثلاثة عشر درهما.
قطيعة سبعين درهما المائة، عن مائة وعشرين راسا، اربعة وثمانون درهما.
قطيعة خمسين درهما المائة، عن ثلاثين[636] راسا، خمسة عشر درهما.
قطيعة ثلاثين درهما المائة، عن خمسين راسا، خمسة عشر درهما.[637]
رسم المستخدمين، ستة وخمسون درهما.[638]

وعليها من الزكاة، خمسة وعشرون دينارا وثمن. تفصيله:
دولبة، ثلاثة دنانير.
عن عقار، دينار واحد.
الخرص، احد عشر دينارا وربع. تفصيله:
خرص العنب، تسعة دنانير وربع.
خرص النخل،[639] ديناران.
ثمن الاغنام، عن اثنى عشر راسا، تسعة دنانير ونصف وربع وثمن:
بياض، عن سبعة ارؤس، سبعة دنانير وربع.
شعارى، عن خمسة ارؤس، ديناران ونصف وثمن.

وعلى الاحكار المعروفة بالنفيس[640] المطلق سقيها من بحر الناحية، زكاة عن خرص عنب، ثلاثة دنانير وربع.

وعليها من الجوالي، عن تسعين نفرا، مائة وثمانون دينارا. تفصيله:
المقيمون بها، ستة وخمسون نفرا، مائة واثنا عشر دينارا.
الناعون عنها بالوجه البحري والقبلي،[641] عن اربعة وثلاثين نفرا، ثمانية وستون دينارا. تفصيله:
الوجه البحري، ستة عشر نفرا، اثنان وثلاثون دينارا.
الوجه القبلي، ثمانية عشر نفرا، ستة وثلاثون دينارا.

colocasia fee, 80 dirhams;
threshing-floor fee, 100 dirhams; and in grains 116 1/6 1/8 ardabbs:
wheat, 41 1/3 1/4 ardabbs;
barley, 35 5/24 ardabbs;
broad beans, 35 1/24 ardabbs;
chickling vetch, 4 1/3 1/8 ardabbs.
The measurement fee, 147 1/3 ardabbs:
wheat, 81 1/2 1/48 ardabbs;
barley, 42 1/6 1/16 ardabbs;
broad beans, 21 1/3 1/4 1/48 ardabbs;
chickling vetch, 1 2/3 1/4 1/16 ardabb.
The pasture fee, for 896 heads, 1,469 1/2 1/4 1/8 dirhams:
permanent pasture lands at the rate of 2 1/4 dirhams per head, for 483 heads, 1,086 1/2 1/4 dirhams;
seasonal pasture lands, for 413 heads, 327 dirhams:
at the rate of one dirham per head, for 213 heads: 213 dirhams;
at the rate of 70 dirhams per 100 [heads], for 120 heads: 84 dirhams;
at the rate of 50 dirhams per 100 [heads], for 30 heads: 15 dirhams;
at the rate of 30 dirhams per 100 [heads], for 50 heads: 15 dirhams;
the government agents' fee, 56 dirhams.

The alms-tax, 25 1/8 dinars:
merchandise, 3 dinars;
real estate, 1 dinar;
the estimate, 11 1/4 dinars:
estimate of grapes, 9 1/4 dinars;
estimate of dates, 2 dinars;
monetary value of small cattle, for 12 heads, 9 1/2 1/4 1/8 dinars:
sheep, for seven heads, 7 1/4 dinars;
goats, for five heads, 2 1/2 1/8 dinars.

The alms-tax imposed on al-Nafīs (?), lands subject to long-term lease that draw water from the canal of the village, for the estimate of grapes, 3 1/4 dinar.

The poll-tax, for 90 individuals, 180 dinars:
those residing in it, for 56 individuals, 112 dinars;
those absent from it in the northern and southern regions, for 34 individuals, 68 dinars:
the northern region, for 16 individuals, 32 dinars;
the southern region, for 18 individuals, 36 dinars.

635 أ. س.: ستمائة.
636 أ. س.: خمسين.
637 ساقط من أ. س.: قطيعة ثلاثين درهما المائة، عن خمسين رأسا خمسة عشر درهما.
638 أ. س. يضيف: وثمن.
639 ساقط من أ. س.: تسعة دنانير وربع. خرص النخل.
640 أ. س.: بالبقيس.
641 ساقط من ط. م.: والقبلي.

وعليها من الاتبان سبعة الاف شنيف.

عليها لديوان احباس الجوامع والمساجد، عينا، ستة عشر دينارا.

رسم خولي البحر عليها اردبان، قمحًا.

اهلها يزرعون الاقصاب برسم معصرتها كفاية ما تحتاج اليه المعصرة.

والمربى بها من الفروج، الف وعشرة فراريج. تفصيله:
للديوان المعمور، بما فيه من اجرة التربية وهو الثلث، ثلاثمائة وستون طائرا.
للمقطعين، ستمائة وخمسون طائرا.

والذي يسلف عليها بها من الشعير برسم الاصطبلات السلطانية، مائة أردب.

والذي بها من التقاوي الديوانية بعد المجرى للمقطعين في تعويض تقاوي الجيزية، وهو خمسمائة واحد وثمانون اردبا وثلثان وربع ونصف قيراط، والمجرى بالوصولات المسيبة من الديوان المعمور، خمسة وستون اردبا وخمسة قراريط، سبعمائة واربعة وستون اردبا وثمن. تفصيله:
قمح، ثلاثمائة وسبعة وعشرون اردبا وقيراطان.
شعير، مائة وثمانون اردبا وربع وسدس ونصف قيراط.
فول، مائة وثمانية وسبعون اردبا ونصف وثلث[642] وثمن.
جلبان، ثلاثة عشر اردبا وقيراطان ونصف.
ارز بقشره اربعون اردبا ونصف وربع ونصف قيراط.
سمسم، ثلاثة وعشرون اردبا ونصف وربع ونصف قيراط.

والذي انساق بها من الحاصل[643] والموقوف والباقي لاستقبال سنة ثلاثين والى اخر سنة تسع وثلاثين في معاملة من ياتي ذكره، مائة وسبعة وثلاثون دينارا وسدس وثمن؛ غلة، سبعة وثلاثون الفا وسبعمائة وستة اراداب ونصف قيراط. تفصيله:
قمح، عشرون الفا وستمائة وتسعة وثلاثون اردبا وثمن ونصف قيراط.
شعير، ثمانية الاف وثلاثمائة وثمانية وثمانون اردبا ونصف ثمن.
فول، ثلاثة الاف وثمانمائة وثمانية وسبعون اردبا وثلثان[644] ونصف ثمن.
جلبان، ثمانية اراداب وربع وثمن.
سمسم، الفان وتسعمائة وثمانية اراداب ونصف وربع ونصف قيراط.
سلجم، اردبان وقيراطان ونصف.
ارز بقشره، الف وثمانمائة وثمانون اردبا ونصف وثلث.
عسل دفن، مطر واحد.

تفصيله:
ما انساق في معاملة الديوان السلطاني، مائة وستة دنانير وسدس وتسعة عشر الفا وسبعمائة وثمانية عشر اردبا ونصف قيراط. تفصيله:
قمح، عشرة الاف وثلاثمائة اردب[645] واردب واحد وقيراط.
شعير، ثلاثة الاف وثلاثمائة وثلاثة[646] وتسعون اردبا ونصف وربع ونصف ثمن.[647]
وفول، الف وتسعمائة وتسعة وسبعون اردبا وثلث ونصف ثمن.

642 ساقط من أ. س.: وثلث.
643 أ. س.: الحواصل.
644 ساقط من أ. س.: وثلثان.
645 ساقط من ط. م.: أردب.
646 ساقط من أ. س.: وثلاثة.
647 ط. م. يضيف: جلبان.

Hay, 7,000 bales.

For the Ministry of Endowments of Congregational and Neighbourhood Mosques, in specie, 16 dinars.

The fee of the overseer of the canal, 2 ardabbs of wheat.

Its people sow sugarcane assigned for its press, in a quantity sufficient for what the press requires.

The chickens reared in it, 1,010 chicks:
for the prosperous Dīwān, including the rearing wage of one-third, 360 birds;
for the *iqṭāʿ*-holders, 650 birds.

The barley assigned for the royal stables and paid for in advance, 100 ardabbs.

The seed advances from the Dīwān are 764 1/8 ardabbs. This is after transferring (*al-mujrā*) to the *iqṭāʿ*-holders compensation for the seed advances of the Giza district, amounting to 581 2/3 1/4 1/48 ardabbs; and after transferring 65 5/24 ardabbs according to the receipts issued (?, *al-mujrā bi'l-wuṣūlāt al-masība*) from the prosperous Dīwān.[206] [The seed advances] include:
wheat, 327 2/24 ardabbs;
barley, 180 1/4 1/6 1/48 ardabbs;
broad beans, 178 1/2 1/3 1/8 ardabbs;
chickling vetch, 13 5/48 ardabbs;
rice in hull, 40 1/2 1/4 1/48 ardabbs;
sesame, 23 1/2 1/4 1/48 ardabbs.

The surplus, withheld and outstanding payments carried forward with regard to it, from the outset of year [6]30 to the end of year [6]39, in the account of those who will be mentioned below, are 137 1/6 1/8 dinars; and in grains, 37,706 1/48 ardabbs:
wheat, 20,639 1/8 1/48 ardabbs;
barley, 8,388 1/16 ardabbs;
broad beans, 3,878 2/3 1/16 ardabbs;
chickling vetch, 8 1/4 1/8 ardabbs;
sesame, 2,908 1/2 1/4 1/48 ardabbs;
rape, 2 5/48 ardabbs;
rice in hull, 1,880 1/2 1/3 ardabbs;
covered molasses, 1 maṭar.

[The surplus, withheld and outstanding payments] in detail:
In the account of the royal Dīwān, 106 1/6 dinars; and 19,718 1/48 ardabbs:
wheat, 10,301 1/24 ardabbs;
barley, 3,393 1/2 1/4 1/16 ardabbs;
broad beans, 1,979 1/3 1/16 ardabbs;

206 On *wuṣūl* as a form of receipt issued by the Dīwān, see al-Nuwayrī, *Nihāyat al-arab*, VIII, 242–43, 253.

جلبان،[648] ثمانية ارادب وربع وثمن.
ارز بقشره، الف وثمانمائة وثمانون اردبا ونصف وثلث.
سمسم، الفان ومائة واثنان وخمسون اردبا وثلث وثمن.
سلجم، اردبان وقيراطان ونصف.
والعسل.
تفصيله:
الحاصل، سبعة دنانير وحبتان، وثلاثة وثلاثون اردبا وربع وسدس وثمن. تفصيله:
قمح، ثلاثة ارادب ونصف وثلث وثمن.
شعير، اردبان وثلثان[649] وربع ونصف قيراط.
فول،[650] تسعة ارادب وثلثان وربع ونصف قيراط.
جلبان، ثمانية ارادب وربع وثمن.
ارز بقشره، ثمانية ارادب وثلث.
عسل دفن، مطر واحد.
الموقوف عن الخراب الداثر لمدة خمس سنين اولها سنة ثلاثين واخرها سنة اربع وثلاثين وستمائة، ثلاثة عشر دينارا ونصف ونصف ثمن وحبة.
الباقي، خمسة وثمانون دينارا ونصف ونصف ثمن، وتسعة عشر الفا وستمائة واربعة وثمانون[651] اردبا وربع وسدس ونصف ثمن.[652] تفصيله:
قمح، عشرة الاف ومائتان وسبعة وتسعون اردبا وقيراطان.
شعير، ثلاثة الاف وثلاثمائة وتسعون اردبا ونصف وربع وثمن.
فول، الف وتسعمائة وتسعة وستون اردبا وثلث وثمن.
سمسم، الفان ومائة واثنان وخمسون اردبا وثلث وثمن.
ارز بقشره، الف وثمانمائة واثنان وسبعون اردبا ونصف.
سلجم، اردبان وقيراطان ونصف.
ما انساق في معاملة المرتجع عن الامراء لاستقبال سنة خمس وثلاثين وستمائة والى اخرسنة ثمان وثلاثين وستمائة، احد وثلاثون دينارا وثمن; وغلة، سبعة عشر الفا وتسعمائة وثمانية وثمانون[653] اردبا:
قمح، عشرة الاف وثلاثمائة وثمانية وثلاثون اردبا وقيراطان ونصف.
شعير، اربعة الاف وتسعمائة واربعة وتسعون اردبا وربع.
فول، الف وثمانمائة وتسعة وتسعون اردبا وثلث.
سمسم، سبعمائة وستة وخمسون اردبا وربع ونصف ثمن.

حرف الراء والزاى، خال.

ومن حرف السين، سنورس. هذه البلدة عبارة عن بلدة كبيرة، عروس[654] من عرائس الفيوم المشهورة وبلادها المذكورة. وهي بحري مدينة الفيوم، وبها المياه الكثيرة والبساتين الغزيرة وحدائق النخيل[655] والاعناب وشجر التين الكثير الجزيل. تزرع الحبوب كلها الشتوي والصيفي. بينها وبين مدينة الفيوم ثلاث ساعات للراكب. جارية في الخاص الشريف.

648 ساقط من ط. م. جلبان.
649 أ. س.: وثلث.
650 ساقط من ط. م. فول.
651 أ. س.: وأربعون.
652 ط. م. يضيف: أردب.
653 أ. س.: ثلاثون.
654 ساقط من ط. م. عروس.
655 أ. س.: والحدائق النخل.

chickling vetch, 8 ¼ ⅛ ardabbs;
rice in hull, 1,880 ½ ⅓ ardabbs;
sesame, 2,152 ardabbs ⅓ ⅛;
rape, 2 5/48 ardabbs;
the molasses.

Surplus payments, 7 2/72 dinars; and 33 ¼ ⅙ ⅛ ardabbs:
wheat, 3 ½ ⅓ ⅛ ardabbs;
barley, 2 ⅔ ¼ 1/48 ardabbs;
broad beans, 9 ⅔ ¼ 1/48 ardabbs;
chickling vetch, 8 ¼ ⅛ ardabbs;
rice in hull, 8 ⅓ ardabbs;
covered molasses, 1 maṭar.

Withheld payments on derelict property that had fallen into disuse for a period of five years, from [6]30 to 634, 13 ½ 1/16 1/72 dinars.

The outstanding payments, 85 ½ 1/16 dinars; and 19,684 ¼ ⅙ 1/16 ardabbs:
wheat, 10,297 2/24 ardabbs;
barley 3,390 ½ ¼ ⅛ ardabbs;
broad beans, 1,969 ⅓ ⅛ ardabbs;
sesame, 2,152 ⅓ ⅛ ardabbs;
rice in hull, 1,872 ½ ardabbs;
rape, 2 5/48 ardabbs.

Carried forward in the account of what is reclaimed from the amirs, from 635 to 638, 31 ⅛ dinars; and in grains, 17,988 ardabbs:
wheat, 10,338 5/48 ardabbs;
barley, 4,994 ¼ ardabbs;
broad beans, 1,899 ⅓ ardabbs;
sesame, 756 ¼ 1/16 ardabbs.

The letters rāʾ and zāʾ — blank [no village entries for these letters].

Beginning with the letter ʿsīnʾ: Sinnūris.[207] This is a large village, one of the famous brides and celebrated villages of the Fayyum. It lies north of Madīnat al-Fayyūm, and has much water, plentiful orchards, and gardens of date palms, grapes and abundant fig trees. All the varieties of cereals are cultivated, both winter and summer crops. It is three hours' ride from Madīnat al-Fayyūm. It is assigned to the illustrious private domain of the sultan.

207 Modern location: Sinnūris (سنورس). Timm, *Das Christlich-Koptische Ägypten*, pp. 2355–56: Psenhyris (Sinnauris in Arabic); Trismegistos GEO ID: 5120; Halm, *Ägypten*, p. 272: Sinnūris and Jarīs; Salmon, 'Répertoire', pp. 50–51; de Sacy, *État des provinces*, p. 683: Sinnūris and Ḥarīs; Savigny, *Description de l'Égypte*, p. 130; Ramzī, *Al-Qāmūs*, II/III, 113: Sinnūris.

لها من الماء لسقي الشتوي والاقصاب والصيفي والاملاك، من جملة بحر معروف بالناحية مما يتفرع من المقسم المعروف بالشاذروان، تسع عشرة[656] قبضة، ويرسم ارباب الرزق المرتبة من تقادم السنين اربع قبض. تفصيله:

القصاص، قبضة.

الخطابة، نصف قبضة.

الخفارة، قبضة.

المشيخة، نصف قبضة.

الخولة،[657] نصف وربع قبضة.

دير سنورس، ربع قبضة.

وبها من الاحجار لاعتصار الاقصاب، اربعة احجار دائرة. تفصيله:

بالابقار، بمعصرة الناحية ثلاثة احجار.

بالماء، بمعصرة بظاهر الناحية من غربيها، حجر واحد.

وبها جامع تقام فيه الجمعة وكنيستان، احداهما عامرة والاخرى غامرة في حدود الشونة الديوانية. ومن غربيها دير يعرف بدير سنورس. اهلها بنو قيصر فخذ من بني عجلان.

ارتفاعها عينا،[658] ستمائة وثمانية واربعون دينارا وثمن وحبتان؛ وغلة، اربعة الاف وخمسمائة وثمانية وستون اردبا ونصف وثمن. تفصيله:

قمح، الفان وتسعمائة واربعة واربعون اردبا وربع وسدس.

شعير، تسعمائة وستة وتسعون اردبا وسدس وثمن.

فول، خمسمائة واثنان وستون اردبا ونصف وربع وثمن.

سمسم، خمسة وثمانون اردبا وقيراط.

فدن، ثلاثمائة واربعة وخمسون فدانا ونصف ونصف قيراط وحبة. تفصيله:

قصب سكر، خارجا عن الزائد لسنة اثنتين، ثلاثمائة[659] وثمانية عشر فدانا وثمن ونصف قيراط وحبة.

تفصيله:

راس، مائتان واربعة واربعون فدانا وثلثان وربع.

خلفة، ثلاثة وسبعون فدانا وسدس ونصف ثمن وحبة.

تفصيل ذلك:

زراعة المزارعين بالنواحي، مائتان واثنان وعشرون فدانا وربع ونصف قيراط:

راس، مائة وتسعة واربعون فدانا وحبتان.

خلفة، ثلاثة وسبعون فدانا وسدس ونصف ثمن وحبة.

زراعة المرابعين:

خمسة وتسعون فدانا ونصف وربع وثمن وحبة، راس.

قلقاس، فدانان وربع وثمن.

قرط وفول، اربعة وثلاثون فدانا.

تفصيل ذلك:

مال الهلالي، ثلاثمائة واحد واربعون دينارا وثلث وربع وحبة. تفصيله:

الحوانيت، احد وثلاثون دينارا وثلث وربع ودانق.

الكتاني، تسعة دنانير.

القزازون، دينار واحد وثلثان[660] وربع ونصف قيراط وحبة.

الطاحون، مائة وتسعة وخمسون دينارا وقيراط وحبة.

معمل الفروج، مائة واربعون دينارا.

It gets 19 *qabḍa*s of water for the irrigation of winter crops, sugarcane, summer crops and for private estates (*al-amlāk*), out of the total of a canal named after the village [i.e., Sinnūris Canal], which branches off from the divisor known as al-Shādhrawān. Four *qabḍa*s of water are assigned to those entitled to long-established allowances:

the 'fable-tellers' (*al-quṣṣāṣ*), 1 *qabḍa*;

the Friday preachers, ½ *qabḍa*;

the guardsmen, 1 *qabḍa*;

the headmen, ½ *qabḍa*;

the overseers, ¾ *qabḍa*;

the monastery of Sinnūris ¼ *qabḍa*.

It has four turning stones for the pressing of sugarcane:

three stones turned by oxen, at the cane press of the village;

one stone turned by water, at a press located in the outskirts of the village, towards the west.

It has a congregational mosque, in which the Friday [prayers] are held, and two churches, one of them in use. The other, which lies at the boundaries of the granary of the Dīwān, is not. To the west there is a monastery known as the Monastery of Sinnūris. Its people are the Banū Qayṣar, a branch of the Banū ʿAjlān.

Its revenue in specie is 648 ⅛ 2/72 dinars; and in grains, 4,568 ½ ⅛ ardabbs:

wheat, 2,944 ¼ ⅙ ardabbs;

barley, 996 ⅙ ⅛ ardabbs;

broad beans, 562 ½ ¼ ⅛ ardabbs;

sesame, 85 1/24 ardabbs.

[Crown estate] feddans: 354 ½ 1/48 1/72 feddans. [This includes]:

sugarcane, not including the increment for the year [64]2, 318 ⅛ 1/48 1/72 feddans:

first harvest, 244 ⅔ ¼ feddans;

second harvest, 73 ⅙ 1/16 1/72 feddans.

[Sugarcane feddans] in detail:

cultivation by tenants in the villages, 222 ¼ 1/48 feddans:

first harvest, 149 2/72 feddans;

second harvest, 73 ⅙ 1/16 1/72 feddans;

cultivation by quarter-share labourers:

95 ½ ¼ ⅛ 1/72 feddans; [all of it] first harvest.

colocasia, 2 ¼ ⅛ feddans.

alfalfa and broad beans, 34 feddans.

[The revenue] in detail:

lunar-calendar taxes, 341 ⅓ ¼ 1/72 dinars:

the shops, 31 ⅓ ¼ 1/144 dinars;

the flax merchant, 9 dinars;

the weavers, 1 ⅔ ¼ 1/48 1/72 dinar;

the mill, 159 1/24 1/72 dinars;

the chicken hatchery, 140 dinars;

656 ساقط من أ. س.: عشرة.

657 أ. س.: الخولي.

658 ساقط من أ. س.: عينا.

659 أ. س. ط. م. يكررا: وثلاثمائة.

660 أ. س.: ديناران.

مال الخراجي، ثلاثمائة وستة دنانير وربع وسدس وثمن وحبة، والغلة والفدن. تفصيله:

زراعة المزارعين، مائتان وستة وتسعون دينارا وربع وسدس وثمن وحبة; والغلة على ما تقدم.

خراج الراتب والاحكار، مائتان وستة وثلاثون دينارا وثلث وربع وثمن ودانق. تفصيله:

المستقر، مائتان واربعة وعشرون دينارا وربع وثمن:

الاصل، عن سبعة وتسعين فدانا وربع وثمن وحبة، مائة وستة وسبعون دينارا ونصف وربع. تفصيله:

كرم، قطيعة خمسة دنانير وثلث الفدان، عن فدانين وربع، اثنا عشر دينارا.

راتب، عن تسعة وستين فدانا وثلث وربع وحبتين، مائة وتسعة وثلاثون دينارا وخمسة قراريط وحبة.

حكر، عن خمسة وعشرين فدانا ونصف وحبتين، خمسة وعشرون دينارا ونصف[661] وحبتان.

الاضافة، اثنان وعشرون دينارا وقيراطان وحبة.

زائد القطيعة، خمسة وعشرون دينارا ونصف وحبتان.

المستجد، اثنا عشر دينارا وثلث ودانق. تفصيله:

الاصل، عشرة دنانير ونصف وثلث وثمن ودانق. تفصيله:

كامل، عن اربعة فدادين وثلث وربع ونصف ثمن، تسعة دنانير وسدس وثمن.

غرس عامين، عن فدان وثلثين[662] ودانق، دينار وثلثان ودانق.

الاضافة، دينار واحد وربع وثمن.

خراج الزراعة، تسعة وثلاثون دينارا ونصف وثلث ودانق. تفصيله:

الاصل، عن خمسة وعشرين فدانا وسدس وثمن، خمسة وثلاثون دينارا وربع وسدس:

قطيعة ثلاثة دنانير الفدان، عن اربعة فدادين ونصف وثلث، اربعة عشر دينارا ونصف.

خضر وبادنجان، عن ثلث وثمن فدان، ثلثان وربع دينار.

قرط، عشرون فدانا، عشرون دينارا.

الاضافة، اربعة دنانير وربع وسدس ودانق.

المناجزة، اربعة الاف ومائة واربعة وثمانون اردبا وثلث وربع على ما فصل.

ثمن الراتبة الديوانية، ثلاثون دينارا.

زراعة الاوسية، فدن قصب سكر وقلقاس وقرط وفول اخضر، ثلاثمائة واربعة وخمسون فدانا ونصف ونصف قيراط وحبة، على ما فصل.

وفر الخراج المقرر، عن كل مائة اردب ثلاثة ارادب، مائة وخمسة وعشرون اردبا وربع وسدس وثمن. تفصيله:

قمح، احد وثمانون اردبا وثلثان وثمن.

شعير، ستة وعشرون اردبا وثلثان وثمن.

فول، اربعة عشر اردبا وربع وسدس وثمن.

سمسم، اردبان وربع وسدس.

The land tax, 306 ¼ ⅙ ⅛ 1/72 dinars; the grains and the [crown estate] feddans [as specified].

Cultivation by tenants, 296 [= 276][208] ¼ ⅙ ⅛ 1/72 dinars; and the grains as above. In detail:

Land tax on perennial plants and on lands subject to long-term lease, 236 ⅓ ¼ ⅛ 1/144 dinars:

The established tax (*al-mustaqarr*): 224 ¼ ⅛ dinars:

the basic assessment, for 97 ¼ ⅛ 1/72 feddans, 176 ½ ¼ dinars:

vineyards, at the rate of 5 ⅓ dinars per feddan, for 2 ¼ feddans, 12 dinars;

fully grown [plants], for 69 ⅓ ¼ 2/72 feddans, 139 5/24 1/72 dinars;

lands subject to long-term lease, for 25 ½ 2/72 feddans, 25 ½ 2/72 dinars.

the addition, 22 2/24 1/72 dinars;

the added tax-rate [on the lands subject to long-term lease], 25 ½ 2/72 dinars;

The recently planted area, 12 ⅓ 1/144 dinars:

the basic assessment, 10 ½ ⅓ ⅛ 1/144 dinars:

fully grown (*kāmil*), for 4 ⅓ ¼ 1/16 feddans, 9 ⅙ ⅛ dinars;

two-year old plants, for ⅔ 1/144 feddan, 1 ⅔ 1/144 dinar.

The addition, 1 ¼ ⅛ dinar.

land tax on field crops, 39 ½ ⅓ 1/144 dinars:

basic assessment, for 25 ⅙ ⅛ feddans, 35 ¼ ⅙ dinars:

at the rate of 3 dinars per feddan, for 4 ½ ⅓ feddans, 14 ½ dinars;

vegetables and eggplant, for ⅓ ⅛ feddan, ⅔ ¼ dinar;

alfalfa, for 20 feddans, 20 dinars.

the addition, 4 ¼ ⅙ 1/144 dinars.

Munājaza cultivation, 4,184 ⅓ ¼ ardabbs, as specified.

Monetary value of the perennials (?, *al-rātiba*) that belong to the Dīwān, 30 dinars.

Feddans of sugarcane, colocasia, alfalfa and green broad beans cultivated in the crown estate, 354 ½ 1/48 1/72 feddans, as specified.

The surcharge to the established land tax, at the rate of 3 ardabbs per 100 ardabbs, 125 ¼ ⅙ ⅛ ardabbs:

wheat, 81 ⅔ ⅛ ardabbs;

barley, 26 ⅔ ⅛ ardabbs;

broad beans, 14 ¼ ⅙ ⅛ ardabbs;

sesame, 2 ¼ ⅙ ardabbs.

661 ساقط من أ. س.: ونصف.

662 أ. س.: وثلث.

208 Correction to allow sums below to add up.

رسم الاجران، سبعة وستون اردبا وثمن:
قمح، ثمانية وعشرون اردبا وربع.
شعير، عشرون اردبا وربع.
فول، ثمانية عشر اردبا[663] ونصف وثمن.

الكيالة، مائة وثلاثة وعشرون اردبا وسدس ونصف قيراط. تفصيله:
قمح، اربعة وثمانون اردبا وثلثان وثمن.
شعير، ثمانية عشر اردبا وقيراط ونصف.
فول، سبعة عشر اردبا وثلث وربع وثمن.
سمسم، اردبان ونصف وثمن.

المتوفر من الحمولة، تسعة وخمسون اردبا وسدس ونصف قيراط:
قمح، اربعة عشر اردبا وثلث وثمن.
شعير، ثمانية عشر اردبا وربع وسدس ونصف قيراط.
فول، ستة وعشرون اردبا وسدس وثمن.

عشر الرزق، قمح، تسعة ارادب.

وعليها من الرسوم والمراعي، خارجا عن رسم الاجران والكيالة الوارد حملها في الارتفاع، عن تسعمائة وخمسة وستين درهما، اربعة وعشرون دينارا وثمن. تفصيله:
الرسوم، اربعمائة واثنان وثلاثون درهما. تفصيله:
شد الاحباس، اربعة وعشرون درهما.
رسم الجراريف، مائة وسبعون درهما.
رسم الحصاد، ثلاثة وخمسون درهما.
رسم الخفارة، خمسة عشر درهما.
رسم القلقاس، مائة وعشرة دراهم.
رسم الاجران، ستون درهما.
المراعي، عن مائتين وسبعة وسبعين راسا، خمسمائة وثلاثة وثلاثون درهما. تفصيله:
راتب، عن مائة واحد وتسعين راسا، اربعمائة وتسعة وعشرون درهما ونصف وربع.
طارئ، عن ستة وثمانين راسا ستة وثمانون درهما.
رسم المستخدمين، سبعة عشر درهما وربع.

وعليها من الزكاة، سبعة دنانير وثمن وحبة. تفصيله:
دولبة، نصف دينار.
خرص النخل، دينار واحد وثلث وحبة.
خرص العنب، ثلث وربع وثمن وحبة.
خرص الزيتون، نصف وثمن دينار.
ثمن اغنام، عن سبعة اروس، خمسة دنانير وسدس وثمن. تفصيله:
بياض، عن ثلاثة اروس ثلاثة دنانير وثمن.
شعارى، عن اربعة، ديناران وسدس.

وعليها من الجوالي، عن مائة واحد وعشرين نفرا، مائتان واثنان واربعون دينارا. من ذلك ما هو محسوب عن طرادين الوحش، عن اربعة وثلاثين نفرا، سبعة عشر دينارا. تفصيل ذلك:
عن المقيمين، عن مائة واثنى عشر نفرا، مائتان واربعة وعشرون دينارا.
الناءون عنها، عن تسعة انفار، ثمانية عشر دينارا. تفصيله:
الوجه البحري، عن اربعة انفار، ثمانية دنانير.
الوجه القبلي، عن خمسة انفار، عشرة دنانير.

[663] ساقط من أ. س.: وربع. شعير عشرون أردبا وربع. فول ثمانية عشر أردبا.

Threshing-floor fee, 67 1/8 ardabbs:
- wheat, 28 1/4 ardabbs;
- barley, 20 1/4 ardabbs;
- broad beans, 18 1/2 1/8 ardabbs.

The measurement fee, 123 1/6 1/48 ardabbs:
- wheat, 84 2/3 1/8 ardabbs;
- barley, 18 1/24 1/48 ardabbs;
- broad beans, 17 1/3 1/4 1/8 ardabbs;
- sesame, 2 1/2 1/8 ardabbs.

The supplementary (*al-mutawaffir*) transportation [fee], 59 1/6 1/48 ardabbs:
- wheat, 14 1/3 1/8 ardabbs;
- barley, 18 1/4 1/6 1/48 ardabbs;
- broad beans, 26 1/6 1/8 ardabbs.

The tithe on allowances, wheat, 9 ardabbs.

The fees and the pasture fee, excluding the threshing-floor fee in kind mentioned in the revenue section, are 965 dirhams, which are 24 1/8 dinars:
- the fees, 432 dirhams:
  - supervision of endowments, 24 dirhams;
  - dredging fee, 170 dirhams;
  - harvest fee, 53 dirhams;
  - protection fee, 15 dirhams;
  - colocasia fee, 110 dirhams;
  - threshing-floor fee, 60 dirhams.
- The pasture fee, for 277 heads, 533 dirhams:
  - permanent pasture lands, for 191 heads, 429 1/2 1/4 dirhams;
  - seasonal pasture lands, for 86 heads, 86 dirhams;
  - the government agents' fee, 17 1/4 dirhams.

The alms-tax, 7 1/8 1/72 dinars:
- merchandise, 1/2 dinar;
- estimate of dates, 1 1/3 1/72 dinar;
- estimate of grapes 1/3 1/4 1/8 1/72 [dinar];
- estimate of olives 1/2 1/8 dinar;
- monetary value of small cattle, for seven heads, 5 1/6 1/8 dinars:
  - sheep, for three heads, 3 1/8 dinars;
  - goats, for four [heads], 2 1/6 dinars.

The poll-tax, for 121 individuals, 242 dinars. Of this, 17 dinars are allotted for 'beast-chasers' (*ṭarrādūn al-waḥsh*), for 34 individuals. [The poll-tax] in detail:
- residing [in the village], for 112 individuals, 224 dinars;
- absent from the village, for nine individuals, 18 dinars:
  - the northern region, for four individuals, 8 dinars;
  - the southern region, for five individuals, 10 dinars.

وعليها من الاتبان، اربعة الاف ومائتا شنيف.

وعليها لديوان الاحباس، احد عشر دينارا وربع وثمن.

والمربى بها من الفروج، ستمائة وخمسون فروج:
المستقر، مائتان وتسعون فروجا.
المرتب تربيته لاستقبال سنة تسع وثلاثين وستمائة، بما فيه من اجرة التربية وهو الثلث، ثلاثمائة وستون فروجا.

والمقرر اطلاقه بها من الرزق لمن ياتي ذكره:
الخولة، ثمانية عشر فدانا عن ثلاثة انفار، لكل واحد[664] ستة فدادين.
المشايخ، نصف محراث ماء.
الخفراء، محراث ماء.
الخطابة، نصف محراث ماء.
القصاص، نصف محراث ماء ونصف فدان كرم وتين.
طرادون الوحش، ثمانية فدادين.
النجارون، محراث ماء.
رهبان دير سنورس، ثمن محراث ماء، وخراج ديناران ونصف وربع.

اهلها يزرعون من القصب ويسقون من الخلف، خارجا عن الزائد لسنة اثنتين، ما عدة فدنه ستة وسبعون فدانا ونصف وثلث وثمن. تفصيله:
راس، خمسون فدانا وخمسة قراريط.
خلفة، ستة وعشرون فدانا ونصف وربع.

والذي بها من التقاوي للمعاملين والمرابعين في الاقصاب الديوانية، عينا، مائة وثمانية وثلاثون دينارا ونصف وربع وحبة؛ وغلة، تسعمائة وسبعة ارادب وثلث وربع وثمن. تفصيله:
قمح، ستمائة واحد عشر اردبا وثلث وربع.
شعير، مائة وتسعة وثلاثون اردبا.
فول، مائة وسبعة وخمسون اردبا وثمن.

تفصيله:
تقاوي المعاملين، خاصة لعمارة سنة اثنتين، سبعمائة[665] تسعة وتسعون اردبا وثلث وربع وثمن:
قمح، خمسمائة وثلاثة ارادب وثلث وربع.
شعير، مائة وتسعة وثلاثون اردبا.
فول، مائة وسبعة وخمسون اردبا وثمن.
تقاوي المرابعين في الاقصاب المستجدة، اثنان واربعون دينارا.[666]
تقاوي المرابعين لسنة احدى وما قبلها، ستة وثمانون دينارا ونصف وربع وحبة، وقمح،[667] مائة وثمانية ارادب وثلثان.

والذي انساق موقوفا ومتاخرا وباقيا، ستمائة وخمسة وثمانون دينارا وثلث وربع وثمن وحبتان؛ وغلة، عشرة الاف وتسعمائة واربعة وثلاثون اردبا وثمن. تفصيله:
قمح، ثمانية الاف ومائة وخمسة وتسعون اردبا وربع.
شعير، الف وستمائة وثلاثة ارادب وثلثان ونصف ثمن.
فول، ستمائة وثلاثة وسبعون اردبا وسدس.
سمسم، تسعون اردبا وثلث وربع ونصف قيراط.
ارز بقشره، ثلاثمائة وسبعون اردبا وثلث.
سلجم، اردب واحد[668] وقيراط.

[664] أ. س.: نفر.
[665] أ. س.: وأربعمائة
[666] ساقط من أ. س.: تقاوى المرابعين في الأقصاب المستجدة اثنان وأربعون دينارا.
[667] أ. س.: قمح.
[668] ساقط من أ. س.: واحد.

Hay, 4,200 bales.

For the Ministry of Endowments, 11 ¼ ⅛ dinars.

The chickens reared in it, 650 chickens:
The established rearing, 290 chickens.
The set rearing since the beginning of 639, including the rearing wage of a third, 360 chickens.

The established allowances distributed in it, for those mentioned below:
the overseers, 18 feddans for three individuals; 6 feddans each.
the headmen, ½ ploughshare, water;[209]
the guardsmen, 1 ploughshare, water;
the Friday preachers, ½ ploughshare, water;
the 'fable-tellers' (*quṣṣāṣ*), ½ ploughshare, water and ½ feddan of grapes and figs;
the 'beast-chasers', 8 feddans;
the carpenters, 1 ploughshare, water;
the monks of Sinnūris Monastery, ⅛ ploughshare, water and land tax of 2 ½ ¼ dinars.

Its people sow sugarcane and irrigate second harvest [sugarcane] at a total of 76 ½ ⅓ ⅛ feddans, excluding the increment for the year [64]2:
first harvest 50 5/24 feddans;
second harvest, 26 ½ ¼ feddans.

The seed advances distributed in it for the cultivators and the quarter-share labourers in the sugarcane of the Dīwān are, in specie, 138 ½ ¼ 1/72 dinars; and in grains, 907 ⅓ ¼ ⅛ ardabbs:
wheat, 611 ⅓ ¼ ardabbs;
barley, 139 ardabbs;
broad beans, 157 ⅛ ardabbs;

[The seed advances] in detail:
seed advances for the cultivators, specifically for cultivation in [64]2, 799 ⅓ ¼ ⅛ ardabbs:
wheat, 503 ⅓ ¼ ardabbs;
barley, 139 ardabbs;
broad beans, 157 ⅛ ardabbs;
seed advances for the quarter-share labourers of the recently introduced sugarcane, 42 dinars;
seed advances for quarter-share labourers for the year [64]1 and previous years, 86 ½ ¼ 1/72 dinars; and in wheat, 108 ⅔ ardabbs.

[209] The text reads *miḥrāth mā'*. Nicolas Michel rightly suggests that this term refers to area that can be cultivated by one plough, combined with the turn of water rights that is needed to cultivate it. See Michel, 'Les rizaq iḥbāsiyya, terres agricoles en mainmorte dans l'Égypte mamelouke et ottomane: étude sur les dafātir al-aḥbās ottomans', *Annales Islamologiques*, 30 (1996), 105–98 (p. 110). Since on this list the *miḥrāth mā'* appears to be interchangeable with feddans of arable land, it likely refers to a unit of area — the plough-share, perhaps a dozen feddans, with the water rights probably attached to the land. Note that at the beginning of the entry there is a separate list of entitlements to water-rights by (mostly) the same officials.

تفصيله:

الموقوف عن الرواتب الديوانية التي نكر مقطعو بيهمو انها في[669] اراضيهم;

وفي جهة من بعد وتسحب وسقط بالوفاة بسنورس لاستقبال سنة ثلاثين والى اخر سنة احدى واربعين، والكفور لاستقبال سنة ثلاثين والى اخر سنة اربع وثلاثين;

وعن المزارعين بشلالة عما تاخر لهم من اجرة عزاق الاقصاب لسنة اربع وثلاثين وستمائة;

وعن المزارعين بمنشاة الطواحين عن خراج الجروي المنتقل الى معاملة مدينة الفيوم;

وزراعة الاقصاب برسم المدينة لسنة اربع وثلاثين وستمائة وما قبلها;

وما اوقف عن المزارعين المتسحبين عن خراج الجروي لسنة احدى وثلاثين وستمائة، والموقوف عن خراج الاستنباط لسنة احدى وثلاثين وستمائة وما قبلها;

والموقوف عن المزارعين ببيهمو عن خراج الارز لسنة اربع وثلاثين وستمائة[670] وغير ذلك:

ستمائة وسبعة وسبعون دينارا وسدس ودانق، وغلة ثمانمائة واربعة وستون اردبا وثلث وربع وثمن:

قمح، ثلاثمائة وتسعة وخمسون اردبا ونصف وثلث.

شعير، مائة وخمسة وخمسون[671] اردبا وربع وسدس ونصف قيراط.

فول، اربعة عشر اردبا وربع[672] وثمن.

سمسم، احد عشر اردبا ونصف وربع وثمن.

ارز بقشره، ثلاثمائة ثلاثة[673] وعشرون اردبا وسدس ونصف قيراط.

المتاخر لسنة اربعين وسنة احدى واربعين وستمائة، دينار وربع وثمن وحبة، وغلة، ثلاثمائة واربعة وعشرون اردبا وثلث ونصف ثمن. تفصيله:

قمح، ثلاثمائة واثنا عشر اردبا وثلثان وربع.

شعير، احد عشر اردبا وربع وسدس[674] ونصف ثمن.

والباقي الى اخر الايام السلطانية الكاملية[675] بسنورس وجميع كفورها لاستقبال سنة ثلاثين وستمائة الى اخر سنة اربع وثلاثين وستمائة، سبعة دنانير وسدس ودانق، وتسعة الاف وسبعمائة وخمسة واربعون اردبا ونصف قيراط. تفصيله:

قمح، سبعة الاف وخمسمائة واثنان وعشرون اردبا ونصف.

شعير، الف واربعمائة[676] وستة وثلاثون اردبا ونصف وربع ونصف ثمن.

فول، ستمائة وثمانية وخمسون اردبا وثلثان وثمن.

سمسم، ثمانية وسبعون اردبا وثلثان ونصف ثمن.

ارز بقشره، سبعة واربعون اردبا وثمن ونصف قيراط.

سلجم، اردب واحد وقيراط.[677]

669 أ. س.: من.

670 ساقط من أ. س.: عن خراج الارز لسنة أربع وثلاثين وستمائة.

671 أ. س.: عشرون.

672 ساقط من أ. س.: وربع.

673 ساقط من ط. م.: ثلاثة.

674 ساقط من ط. م.: وسدس.

675 أ. س.: الكاملية السلطانية.

676 أ. س.: ثلاثمائة.

677 ساقط من ط. م.: وقيراط.

The withheld, delayed (*muta'akhkhar*[an]) and outstanding payments carried over are 685 ⅓ ¼ ⅛ ²⁄₇₂ dinars; and in grains, 10,934 ⅛ ardabbs:

wheat, 8,195 ¼ ardabbs;

barley, 1,603 ⅔ ¹⁄₁₆ ardabbs;

broad beans, 673 ⅙ ardabbs;

sesame, 90 ⅓ ¼ ¹⁄₄₈ ardabbs;

rice in hull, 370 ⅓ ardabbs;

rape, 1 ¹⁄₂₄ ardabb.

[The withheld payments] in detail:

The withheld payments for the perennials (*rawātib*) that belong to the Dīwān, which the *iqṭā*ʿ-holders of Biyahmū claim to lie in their lands;

the withheld payments for those who drew away, fled, or died in Sinnūris from [6]30 to [6]41, and in the hamlets [of Sinnūris] from [6]30 to [6]34;

the withheld payments of the tenants of Shallāla, on account of the wages due to them for hoeing the sugarcane, dating to 634;

the withheld *jarwī*[210] land tax of the tenants in Munsha'at al-Ṭawāḥīn, which has been transferred to the account of Madīnat al-Fayyūm;

and the cultivation of sugarcane that was assigned for (the press in) Madīnat al-Fayyūm in 634 and earlier;

the withheld *jarwī* land tax of tenants who fled, for the year 631;

the withheld payments of the land tax of al-Istinbāṭ, for the year 631 and before that;

the withheld payments of land tax on rice by the tenants of Biyahmū for the year 634;

and other categories.

[The withheld payments amount to] 677 dinars ⅙ ¹⁄₁₄₄; and in grains, 864 ⅓ ¼ ⅛ ardabbs:

wheat, 359 ½ ⅓ ardabbs;

barley, 155 ¼ ⅙ ¹⁄₄₈ ardabbs;

broad beans, 14 ¼ ⅛ ardabbs;

sesame, 11 ½ ¼ ⅛ ardabbs;

rice in hull, 323 ⅙ ¹⁄₄₈ ardabbs.

The delayed payments for [6]40 and 641 [AD 1242–4] are 1 ¼ ⅛ ¹⁄₇₂ dinar; and in grains, 324 ⅓ ¹⁄₁₆ ardabbs:

wheat, 312 ⅔ ¼ ardabbs;

barley, 11 ¼ ⅙ ¹⁄₁₆ ardabbs.

The outstanding payments for Sinnūris and all of the hamlets included in its *iqṭā*ʿ at the end of the reign of the Sultan al-Kāmil, since the beginning of 630 up to the end of 634, are 7 ⅙ ¹⁄₁₄₄ dinars; and [in grains], 9,745 ¹⁄₄₈ ardabbs:

wheat, 7,522 ½ ardabbs;

barley, 1,436 ½ ¼ ¹⁄₁₆ ardabbs;

broad beans, 658 ⅔ ⅛ ardabbs;

sesame, 78 ⅔ ¹⁄₁₆ ardabbs;

rice in hull, 47 ⅛ ¹⁄₄₈ ardabbs;

rape, 1 ¹⁄₂₄ ardabb.

210 Certain products were weighed by *jarwī* raṭls, equalling 967 g (twice its standard value). According to Ibn Mammātī, products weighed in *jarwī* units included most fruits, cheese, and sugar — which is probably the intention here; Ibn Mammātī, *Kitāb qawānīn al-dawāwīn*, p. 361; Cooper, 'Ibn Mammati's Rules', pp. 341, 348.

ومن حرف السين، سرسنا. هذه البلدة عبارة عن بلدة كبيرة تزرع الصيفي والشتوي وبها نخل يسير مستجد. ليس بها شجر ولا كروم. بينها وبين مدينة الفيوم اربع ساعات للراكب وهي جارية في اقطاع الامير الاجل الكبير فارس الدين اقطاي المستعرب.[678] والمطلق لها من الماء لسقي الشتوي والصيفي الارز من الماء المتصل من بحر ذات الصفاء المساق الى المقسم المعروف بالفسقية اليوسفية تحت القبرا بخليج واحد مجصص ينقسم بين الناحية[679] وفرقس، عبرته اثنتان وعشرون قبضة، يخص سرسنا من اسفل في خليج مفرد عبرته ستة عشر قبضة ونصف ماء. وبها جامع تقام فيه الجمعة. خفرها لبني زرعة، فخذ من بني عجلان.

ارتفاعها ثلاثمائة واثنان وسبعون دينارا ونصف وثمن، وغلة، اربعة الاف وتسعمائة واردب واحد وقيراطان. تفصيله:

قمح، الفان وستمائة واحد وخمسون اردبا ونصف وربع.
شعير، ثمانمائة واردب واحد وقيراطان.
فول وجلبان، الف وتسعة وثمانون اردبا ونصف وربع.
ارز بقشره، من جملة الفي اردب، ثلاثمائة وتسعة واربعون اردبا وثلث.
كزبرة، ثلاثة ارادب وسدس.
زريعة ملوخية، ستة ارادب.

تفصيله:

الهلالي، عن اجرة الحانوت مائة وثمانية عشر دينارا.
مال الخراجي، مائتان واثنان واربعون دينارا ونصف وثمن، والغلة، على ما تقدم ذكره.
خراج الراتب والاحكار، مائتان واثنان واربعون دينارا ونصف وثمن. تفصيله:
المستقر، مائتان واربعة وثلاثون دينارا وثلث. تفصيله:
الاصل،[680] عن مائة وثمانية فدادين وسدس وثمن، مائتان وثمانية دنانير وسدس وثمن. تفصيله:
راتب وقلقاس، قطيعة دينارين الفدان، عن مائة فدان، مائتان دينار. تفصيله:
راتب، خمسة وتسعون فدانا.
وقلقاس، خمسة فدادين.
حكر، عن ثمانية فدادين وسدس وثمن، ثمانية دنانير وسدس وثمن.
الاضافة، ستة وعشرون دينارا وقيراط.
زائد القطيعة عن الحكر، ثمانية دنانير وسدس وثمن.
مؤنة النواب، اثنا عشر دينارا.

Also beginning with the letter 'sīn': Sirisnā.[211] This is a large village, with summer and winter crops and a few recently introduced date palms. There are no trees or vineyards in it.[212] It is four hours' ride from Madīnat al-Fayyūm. It is assigned as an *iqṭā*ʿ to the illustrious Grand Amir (*al-amīr al-ajall al-kabīr*)[213] Fāris al-Dīn Aqṭāy al-Mustaʿrab.[214] The water allocated to it for the purpose of irrigating the winter and the summer crops, that is rice, is drawn from Dhāt al-Ṣafāʾ Canal and carried to the divisor known as al-Fasqiyya al-Yūsufiyya below al-Qubarāʾ by means of a plastered canal, which is split between this village and Furqus. The canal's quota is 22 *qabḍas*. Sirisnā is served by a separate canal lower down, which has a water quota of 16 ½ *qabḍas*. It has a congregational mosque, in which the Friday prayers are held, and its protection is in the hands the Banū Zarʿa, a branch of the Banū ʿAjlān.

Its revenue is 372 ½ ⅛ dinars; and in grains, 4,901 2/24 ardabbs:

- wheat, 2,651 ½ ¼ ardabbs;
- barley, 801 2/24 ardabbs;
- broad beans and chickling vetch, 1,089 ½ ¼ ardabbs;
- rice in hull — out of a total of 2,000 ardabbs — 349 ⅓ ardabbs;
- coriander, 3 ⅙ ardabbs;
- seeds of Jew's mallow, 6 ardabbs.

[The revenue] in detail:

- lunar-calendar taxes, for the rent of the shop, 118 dinars;
- land tax, 242 ½ ⅛ dinars; and in grains, as above. [In detail]:
- land tax on perennial plants and on lands subject to long term lease, 242 ½ ⅛ dinars:
  - the established tax, 234 ⅓ dinars:
    - basic assessment, for 108 feddans ⅙ ⅛, 208 dinars ⅙ ⅛:
      - perennial plants and colocasia, at the rate of 2 dinars per feddan, for 100 feddans, 200 dinars:
        - perennial plants, 95 feddans;
        - colocasia, 5 feddans;
  - land subject to long-term lease, for 8 ⅙ ⅛ feddans, 8 ⅙ ⅛ dinars;
    - the addition, 26 1/24 dinars;
    - the additional tax-rate on lands subject to long-term lease, 8 ⅙ ⅛ dinars.
  - the provisions for the agents, 12 dinars.

211 Modern location: Sirisnā (سرسنا). Halm, *Ägypten*, p. 273; Salmon, 'Répertoire', pp. 47–48; de Sacy, *État des provinces*, p. 682: Sirsnī; Savigny, *Description de l'Égypte*, p. 130: Sirsnī; Ibn Mammātī, *Kitāb qawānīn al-dawāwīn*, p. 150; Yāqūt, *Muʿjam al-Buldān*, III, 211: Sarsanā; Ibn al-Jīʿān, *Kitāb al-tuḥfa*, p. 154; Ramzī, *Al-Qāmūs*, II/III, 112: Sirisnā.

212 This statement is found in both MP and AS, but is contradicted by the tax list of the village.

213 The title of senior commanders in the Ayyubid army; Humphreys, 'The Emergence of the Mamluk Army', p. 86.

214 A high-ranking Ṣāliḥī amir, who would be appointed Atabek (commander of the army) in 1257. He would eventually cast the deciding vote in favour of Baybars after the murder of Quṭuz; Amitai, 'The Mamlūk Officer Class', p. 292; Humphreys, *From Saladin to the Mongols*, pp. 330, 333, 345. Not the same as Fāris al-Dīn Aqṭāy, future commander of the Baḥriyya regiment.

678 أ. س.: المستغرب.
679 أ. س.: الناحيتين.
680 ساقط من ط. م.: الأصل.

عليها عن خراج الاستنباط لسنورس، مائة وثلاثة وخمسون اردبا ونصف:[681]

قمح، خمسة وثمانون اردبا ونصف وثمن.

شعير، خمسة وثلاثون اردبا ونصف[682] وثمن.

فول، اربعة وعشرون اردبا ونصف[683] وثمن.

سمسم، ثمانية ارادب ونصف[684] وثمن.

وعليها من الرسوم والمراعي والكيالة،[685] عن ثمانمائة وثمانين درهما وربع وثمن، اثنان وعشرون دينارا ونصف قيراط، وغلة، مائتان وخمسة وستون اردبا ونصف وربع ونصف ثمن. تفصيله:

قمح، مائة واثنا عشر اردبا وثلثان ونصف ثمن.

شعير، عشرون اردبا.

فول، اثنان وخمسون اردبا وثلث وربع.

جلبان، ثلاثون اردبا.

ارز بقشره، خمسون اردبا ونصف.

تفصيله:

الرسوم، مائتان واربعون درهما وربع، وغلة، سبعة وسبعون اردبا وثلثان ونصف ثمن:

قمح، تسعة واربعون اردبا وثلثان ونصف ثمن.

شعير، خمسة ارادب ونصف.

فول، خمسة عشر اردبا ونصف وثمن.[686]

جلبان، ستة ارادب ونصف وربع وثمن.

تفصيله:

شد الاحباس، ثلاثة عشر درهما ونصف.

رسم الجراريف، تسعون درهما.

رسم الحصاد، ثلاثة وخمسون درهما.

رسم الخفارة، خمسة عشر درهما.

رسم الاجران، ثمانية وستون درهما ونصف وربع، والغلة على ما تقدم.

الكيالة، مائة وثمانية وثمانون اردبا وقيراطان:

ارز بقشره، خمسون اردبا ونصف.

قمح، ثلاثة وستون اردبا.

شعير، اربعة عشر اردبا ونصف.

فول، ستة وثلاثون اردبا ونصف وثلث وثمن.

جلبان، ثلاثة وعشرون اردبا وثمن.

المراعي، عن ثلاثمائة وثلاثة وثلاثين راسا، ستمائة واربعون درهما ونصف وثمن. تفصيله:

راتب، عن مائتين وستة وخمسين راسا، خمسمائة وستة وسبعون درهما.

طارئ، عن سبعة وسبعين راسا، ثلاثة واربعون درهما ونصف وربع وثمن. تفصيله:

قطيعة مائة درهم المائة راس، عن ثلاثين راسا، ثلاثون درهما.[687]

قطيعة ثلاثين درهما المائة، عن سبعة واربعين راسا، ثلاثة عشر درهما ونصف وربع وثمن.

رسم المستخدمين، عشرون درهما ونصف وربع.

681 أ. س.: وربع.

682 أ. س.: عشرون أردبا وربع.

683 أ. س.: وربع.

684 أ. س.: وربع.

685 أ. س.: والكيالة والمراعي.

686 أ. س.: ونصف ثمن.

687 ساقط من أ. س.: ونصف وربع وثمن تفصيله قطيعة مائة درهم المائة رأس عن ثلاثين رأسا ثلاثون درهما.

The land tax on al-Istinbāṭ, [part of the land tax revenues] of Sinnūris, 153 ½ ardabbs:

- wheat, 85 ½ ⅛ ardabbs;
- barley, 35 ½ ⅛ ardabbs;
- broad beans, 24 ½ ⅛ ardabbs;
- sesame, 8 ½ ⅛ ardabbs.

The fees, the measurement fee, and the pasture fee are 880 ¼ ⅛ dirhams, which are 22 1/48 dinars; and in grains, 265 ½ ¼ 1/16 ardabbs:

- wheat, 112 ⅔ 1/16 ardabbs;
- barley, 20 ardabbs;
- broad beans, 52 ⅓ ¼ ardabbs;
- chickling vetch, 30 ardabbs;
- rice in hull, 50 ½ ardabbs.

[The fees, the measurement fee, and the pasture fee] include:

- the fees, 240 ¼ dirhams; and in grains, 77 ⅔ 1/16 ardabbs:
  - wheat, 49 ⅔ 1/16 ardabbs;
  - barley, 5 ½ ardabbs;
  - broad beans, 15 ½ ⅛ ardabbs,
  - chickling vetch, 6 ½ ¼ ⅛ ardabbs.
- [The fees] in detail:
  - supervision of endowments, 13 ½ dirhams;
  - dredging fee, 90 dirhams;
  - harvest fee, 53 dirhams;
  - protection fee, 15 dirhams;
  - threshing-floor fee, 68 ½ ¼ dirhams; and in grains, as specified above.
- The measurement fee, 188 2/24 ardabbs:
  - rice in hull, 50 ½ ardabbs;
  - wheat, 63 ardabbs;
  - barley, 14 ½ ardabbs;
  - broad beans, 36 ½ ⅓ ⅛ ardabbs;
  - chickling vetch, 23 ⅛ ardabbs.
- The pasture fee, for 333 heads, 640 ½ ⅛ dirhams:
  - permanent pasture lands, for 256 heads, 576 dirhams;
  - seasonal pasture tax, for 77 heads, 43 ½ ¼ ⅛ dirhams:
    - at the rate of 100 dirhams per 100 heads, for 30 heads, 30 dirhams;
    - at the rate of 30 dirhams per 100 [heads], for 47 heads, 13 ½ ¼ ⅛ dirhams;
  - the government agents' fee, 20 ½ ¼ dirhams.

وعليها من الزكاة، اربعة عشر دينارا وحبتان. تفصيله:
دولبة، نصف دينار.
خرص النخل، دينار واحد.
ثمن الماشية، عن احد عشر راسا، اثنا عشر دينارا ونصف وحبتان:
بقر احمر، عن مسنة واحدة، ثلاثة دنانير وربع وحبتان.
ثمن الاغنام، عن عشرة ارؤس، تسعة دنانير وربع. تفصيله:
بياض، عن ثمانية ارؤس، ثمانية دنانير وربع.
شعارى، راس واحد، دينار واحد.[688]

وعليها من الاتبان، اربعة الاف شنيف.

رسم خولي البحر، قمح، اردبان.

وعليها لديوان الاحباس اثنا عشر دينارا.

والمقرر بها من فدن الرزق، سبعة وثلاثون فدانا. تفصيله:
الخطابة، اثنا عشر فدانا.
النجارون، ثمانية فدادين.
الخفراء، خمسة عشر فدانا.
قيم الجامع، فدان واحد.
المؤذن، فدان واحد.

والمربى بها من الفروج للمقطع خاصة، خارجا عن تربية الديوان المعمور المرفوعة عن اهل الناحية لسنة احدى واربعين وستمائة على من تسحب منهم، ثمانمائة طائر.

والذي بها من التقاوي الديوانية، الفان وسبعمائة وثمانية وثلاثون اردبا وسدس. تفصيله:
قمح، الف واربعمائة وسبعون اردبا وثلث وربع وثمن.
شعير، مائتان وعشرون اردبا وربع وثمن.
فول، اربعمائة واحد وثمانون اردبا وثلث وثمن.
جلبان، خمسة عشر اردبا ونصف وثمن.
ارز بقشره، خمسمائة وخمسون اردبا.

والذي انساق في المعاملة من الحاصل الموقوف والباقي، مائتان وديناران وثلث. وغلة، ثمانمائة وثمانية واربعون اردبا وثلثان وثمن. تفصيله:
قمح، مائتان وثمانية وعشرون اردبا وربع وسدس ونصف ثمن.
شعير، مائة وتسعة وثلاثون اردبا.
فول، ثلاثمائة وثلاثة وعشرون اردبا وثلث ونصف قيراط.
سمسم، قيراط ونصف.
ارز بقشره، مائة وستة ارادب وربع وثمن.
جلبان، ثلاثة وعشرون اردبا وربع وسدس ونصف ثمن.
سلجم، ربع اردب.
كزبرة، ثمانية ارادب وثلث وثمن.
فريك، ثلاثة ارادب وثلثان.
ملوخية، خمسة عشر اردبا وثلثان.

[688] ساقط من أ. س.: دينار واحد.

The alms-tax, 14 2/72 dinars:
merchandise, ½ dinar;
estimate of dates, 1 dinar;
monetary value of livestock, for 11 heads, 12 ½ 2/72 dinars:
cows, for a two-year old cow, 3 ¼ 2/72 dinars;
monetary value of small cattle, for 10 heads, 9 ¼ dinars:
sheep, for eight heads, 8 ¼ dinars;
goats, for one head, 1 dinar.

Hay, 4,000 bales.

The fee of the overseer of the canal, wheat, 2 ardabbs.

For the Ministry of Endowments, 12 dinars.

The confirmed allowances of feddans, 37 feddans:
the preachers, 12 feddans;
the carpenters, 8 feddans;
the watchmen, 15 feddans;
the caretaker of the mosque, 1 feddan;
the muezzin, 1 feddan.

The chicken reared in it, solely for the *iqṭāʿ*-holder, 800 birds. This excludes the rearing for the prosperous Dīwān, from which the people of the village were exempted for the year 641, due to the flight of some of the inhabitants.

The seed advances from the Dīwān are 2,738 ⅙ ardabbs:
wheat, 1,470 ⅓ ¼ ⅛ ardabbs;
barley, 220 ¼ ⅛ ardabbs;
broad beans, 481 ⅓ ⅛ ardabbs;
chickling vetch, 15 ½ ⅛ ardabbs;
rice in hull, 550 ardabbs.

The surplus, withheld and outstanding payments carried forward in the account, 202 ⅓ dinars; and in grains, 848 ⅔ ⅛ ardabbs:
wheat, 228 ¼ ⅙ 1/16 ardabbs;
barley, 139 ardabbs;
broad beans, 323 ⅓ 1/48 ardabbs;
sesame 1/24 ½ ardabb;
rice in hull, 106 ¼ ⅛ ardabbs;
chickling vetch, 23 ¼ ⅙ 1/16 ardabbs;
rape, ¼ ardabb;
coriander, 8 ⅓ ⅛ ardabbs;
green wheat, 3 ⅔ ardabbs;
Jew's mallow, 15 ⅔ ardabbs.

تفصيله:

ما انساق في معاملة الديوان السلطاني، خمسة عشر دينارا وثلث وربع وثمن، وغلة، مائة واحد وعشرون اردبا وثلثان وربع ونصف قيراط:

قمح، ثلاثة ارادب وثلث.

فول، اردب واحد وسدس ونصف قيراط.

سمسم، قيراط ونصف.

ارز بقشره، تسعة وثمانون اردبا وربع.

جلبان، ثلاثة عشر وعشرون اردبا وربع وسدس ونصف ثمن.

سلجم، ربع اردب.

كزبرة، ثلث وربع وثمن اردب.

فريك، ثلاثة ارادب وثلثان.

الحاصل خاصة، مائة واربعة عشر اردبا وسدس ونصف ثمن:

فول، اردب واحد وسدس ونصف قيراط.

سمسم، قيراط ونصف.

ارز بقشره، تسعة وثمانون اردبا وربع.

جلبان، ثلاثة وعشرون اردبا وربع وسدس ونصف ثمن.

سلجم، ربع اردب.

الموقوف عن القرض باسم المعامليين، قمح، ثلاث ارادب وثلث.

الباقي، خمسة عشر دينارا وثلث وربع وثمن، وغلة، اربعة ارادب وربع وثمن. تفصيله:

كزبرة، ثلث اردب وربع وثمن.

فريك، ثلاثة ارادب وثلثان.

ما انساق في معاملة الامراء صارم الدين قايماز المسعودي وزين الدين موسى بن ابي[689] زكري، مائة وستة وثمانون دينارا ونصف وثمن، وغلة، سبعمائة وستة وعشرون اردبا ونصف وثلث ونصف قيراط. تفصيله:

قمح، مائتان وخمسة وعشرون اردبا وثمن ونصف قيراط.

شعير، مائة وتسعة وثلاثون اردبا.

فول، ثلاثمائة واثنان وعشرون اردبا وسدس.

ارز بقشره، سبعة عشر اردبا وثمن.

كزبرة سبعة ارادب ونصف وربع.

ملوخية، خمسة عشر اردبا وثلثان.

والمسلف عليه بها من الشعير برسم الاصطبلات السلطانية، مائة وخمسون اردبا.

ومن حرف السين، سيلة.[690] هذه البلدة عبارة عن بلدة متوسطة وتعرف ببلد يعقوب عليه السلام. وهي كانت من المدائن الكبار التي[691] كانت العدوة تعرف بها، وكذلك البلاد الشرقية كلها تعرف بها حتى قيل انه كان بها اربعون كنيسة دثرت الان الى ان صارت بين البلد الكبير والصغير.[692] تزرع القمح والشعير والفول، تشمل على نخيل واصيلات جميز. بينها وبين مدينة الفيوم مسافة ثلاث ساعات للراكب، وهي شرقي مدينة الفيوم. وقيل ان في اراضي هذه البلدة فدانا واحدا يعرف بفدان النبي يعقوب عليه السلام، وانه مائة اردب، وهو مجهول وكل غيط وقع هذا الفدان فيه بالقسمة يزيد ذلك الغيط مائة اردب ونظيره.

689 ساقط من أ. س.: أبي.

690 أ. س.: سيلا.

691 أ. س.: الدي.

692 أ. س.: الكبيرة والصغيرة.

[The surplus, withheld and outstanding payments] include:

That which was carried forward in the account of the royal Dīwān, 15 ⅓ ¼ ⅛ dinars; and in grains, 121 ⅔ ¼ 1/48 ardabbs:

wheat, 3 ⅓ ardabbs;

broad beans, 1 ⅙ 1/48 ardabb;

sesame 1/24 ½;

rice in hull, 89 ¼ ardabbs;

chickling vetch, 23 ¼ ⅙ 1/16 ardabbs;

rape, ¼ ardabb;

coriander ⅓ ¼ ⅛ ardabb;

green wheat, 3 ⅔ ardabbs.

[In detail]:

The surplus, 114 ⅙ 1/16 ardabbs:

broad beans, 1 ⅙ 1/48 ardabb;

sesame 1/24 1/48 [ardabb];

rice in hull, 89 ¼ ardabbs;

chickling vetch, 23 ¼ ⅙ 1/16 ardabbs;

rape ¼ ardabb;

The withheld payments, for loans to the cultivators, wheat, 3 ⅓ ardabbs.

The outstanding payments are 15 ⅓ ¼ ⅛ dinars; and in grains, 4 ardabbs ¼ ⅛:

coriander ⅓ ¼ ⅛ [ardabb];

green wheat, 3 ⅔ ardabbs.

What was registered in the accounts of the amirs Ṣārim al-Dīn Qāymāz al-Masʿūdī and Zayn al-Dīn Mūsā ibn Abī Zikrī is 186 ½ ⅛ dinars; and in grains, 726 ½ ⅓ 1/48 ardabbs:

wheat, 225 ⅛ 1/48 ardabbs;

barley, 139 ardabbs;

broad beans, 322 ⅙ ardabbs;

rice in hull, 17 ⅛ ardabbs;

coriander, 7 ½ ¼ ardabbs;

Jew's mallow, 15 ⅔ ardabbs.

The barley assigned for the royal stables and paid for in advance, 150 ardabbs.

Also beginning with the letter 'sīn': Sīla.[215] This is a medium-sized village, known as the village of Jacob, peace be upon him. It used to be a large city, and al-ʿIdwa, as well as all the villages in eastern Fayyum, were its hamlets (*tuʿraf bi-hā*). It is even said that there were forty churches in it, which are now all deserted. But then it became a medium-sized village. Wheat, barley and broad beans are sown in it, and it has date palms and trunks of acacia. It is three hours' ride from Madīnat al-Fayyūm, towards the east. It is said that in the lands of this village there is a feddan known as 'the feddan of the Prophet Jacob', may peace be upon him, and this feddan yields 100 ardabbs. This feddan is unknown, but when it falls in a field (*ghayṭ*) through the division [of the village lands] (*waqaʿa bi'l-qisma*), the field yields more than 100 ardabbs, or something like it.

215 Modern location: Sīla (سيلة). Halm, *Ägypten*, p. 269: Saila; Salmon, 'Répertoire', p. 45: Saïla; Ibn Mammātī, *Kitāb qawānīn al-dawāwīn*, p. 150; Yāqūt, *Muʿjam al-Buldān*, III, 300: Sayla; Ibn al-Jīʿān, *Kitāb al-tuḥfa*, p. 155: Sayala; Savigny, *Description de l'Égypte*, p. 129: Syleh; Quatremère, *Mémoires géographiques*, I, 413; Abū Ṣāliḥ, *Churches and Monasteries*, p. 209; Ramzī, *Al-Qāmūs*, II/III, 101: Sīla.

وهي جارية في اقطاع جماعة من المقطعين. لها من الماء للشتوي خاصة من بحر الشرقية مما ينقسم بمقاسم جص شركة شانة[693] وبياض ومقطول والربيات، اثنا عشر قبضة. عبرتها جيشية[694] ستة الاف ومائتا دينار. وبها جامع تقام فيه الجمعة، يذكر انه جامع يعقوب عليه السلام. وبها مسجد ابيض على كوم عال.[695] وبها كنيسة واحدة، ومن قبليها دير يعرف بدير سيلة. اهلها بنو زرعة، فخذ من بني كلاب.

ارتفاعها عينا مما جميعه مستخرجا ومتحصلا، خمسة عشر دينارا ونصف; وغلة، الفان وخمسمائة اردب. تفصيله:

قمح، ثمانمائة وثلاثة وثلاثون اردبا وثلث.

شعير، الف وستمائة وستة وستون اردبا وثلثان.

تفصيله:

الهلالي، ثمانية دنانير.

المراعي، سبعة دنانير ونصف.

المناجزة، غلة، الفان وخمسمائة اردب على ما فصل.

وعليها من الرسوم والكيالة والمراعي، عن خمسمائة وسبعين درهما ونصف وربع وثمن، ثلاثة عشر دينارا ونصف وربع ونصف قيراط; وغلة، مائة واثنان وعشرون اردبا ونصف وثلث ونصف ثمن. تفصيله:

قمح، تسعة وثلاثون اردبا.

شعير، ثلاثة وسبعون اردبا.

فول، عشرة ارادب ونصف وثلث ونصف ثمن.

تفصيله:

الرسوم، مائتان واثنان وخمسون درهما ونصف وثمن، وغلة، ثمانية وستون اردبا وربع ونصف قيراط. تفصيله:

قمح، ثلاثة وعشرون اردبا ونصف وربع وثمن.

شعير، ثلاثة وثلاثون اردبا ونصف.

فول، عشرة ارادب ونصف وثلث ونصف ثمن.

تفصيله:

شد الاحباس، اربعة وثلاثون درهما.

رسم الجراريف، تسعون درهما.

رسم الحصاد، ثلاثة وخمسون درهما.

رسم الخفارة، خمسة عشر درهما.

رسم الاجران، ستون درهما ونصف وثمن، والغلة.

الكيالة، اربعة وخمسون اردبا ونصف وثمن. تفصيله:

قمح، خمسة عشر اردبا وثمن.

شعير، تسعة وثلاثون اردبا ونصف.

المراعي، طارئ، عن خمسمائة وسبعة وتسعين راسا، ثلاثمائة وثمانية عشر درهما وربع. تفصيله:

قطيعة مائة درهم المائة، عن ستة وثلاثين راسا، ستة وثلاثون درهما.

قطيعة سبعين درهما المائة، عن مائة وثلاثة وثمانين راسا، مائة وخمسة وعشرون درهما ونصف وربع وثمن.

قطيعة خمسين درهما المائة، عن مائة وثلاثة واربعين راسا، احد وسبعون درهما ونصف.

693 أ. س.: شافه.

694 ساقط من أ. س.: جيشية.

695 أ. س.: عالي.

It is included in the *iqṭāʿ* of a group of *iqṭāʿ*-holders. It gets 12 *qabḍas* of water, allocated solely for winter crops, from al-Sharqiyya Canal, by plastered divisors shared with Shāna, Bayāḍ, Maqṭūl and al-Rubiyyāt. Its fiscal value is 6,200 army dinars. It has a congregational mosque, in which the Friday prayers are held, and it is said that this is the Mosque of Jacob, peace be upon him. It also has a white neighbourhood mosque, standing on a tall mound. There is one church, and south of it there is a monastery known as the Monastery of Sīla. Its people are the Banū Zarʿa, a branch of the Banū Kilāb.

Its revenue collected in cash and kind is, in specie, 15 ½ dinars; and in grains, 2,500 ardabbs:

wheat, 833 ⅓ ardabbs;

barley, 1,666 ⅔ ardabbs.

[The revenue] in detail:

lunar-calendar revenues, 8 dinars;

[permanent] pasture tax, 7 ½ dinars;

Munājaza land tax of grains, 2,500 ardabbs, as specified.

The fees, the measurement fee and the pasture fee are 570 ½ ¼ ⅛ dirhams, which are 13 ½ ¼ 1/48 dinars; and in grains, 122 ½ ⅓ 1/16 ardabbs:

wheat, 39 ardabbs;

barley, 73 ardabbs;

broad beans, 10 ½ ⅓ 1/16 ardabbs.

[The fees, the measurement fee and the pasture fee] in detail:

the fees, 252 ½ ⅛ dirhams; and in grains, 68 ¼ 1/48 ardabbs:

wheat, 23 ½ ¼ ⅛ ardabbs;

barley, 33 ½ ardabbs;

broad beans, 10 ½ ⅓ 1/16 ardabbs.

[the fees] in detail:

supervision of endowments, 34 dirhams;

dredging fee, 90 dirhams;

harvest fee, 53 dirhams;

protection fee, 15 dirhams;

threshing-floor fee, 60 ½ ⅛ dirhams; and the grains.

the measurement fee, 54 ½ ⅛ ardabbs:

wheat, 15 ⅛ ardabbs;

barley, 39 ½ ardabbs.

The pasture fee on seasonal pasture lands, for 597 heads, 318 ¼ dirhams:

at the rate of 100 dirhams per 100 [heads], for 36 heads, 36 dirhams;

at the rate of 70 dirhams per 100 [heads], for 183 heads, 125 dirhams ½ ¼ ⅛;

at the rate of 50 dirhams per 100 [heads], for 143 heads, 71 ½ dirhams;

قطيعة ثلاثين درهما المائة، عن خمسة عشر راسا، اربعة دراهم ونصف.[696]
قطيعة خمسة وعشرين درهما المائة، عن مائتين وعشرين راسا، خمسة وخمسون درهما.
رسم المستخدمين، خمسة وعشرين درهما وربع وثمن.

وعليها من الزكاة عن ثمن الماشية، عن ثمانية اروس، ثمانية دنانير. تفصيله:
بقر احمر، عن تبيع واحد، دينار وثمن.
ثمن الاغنام، عن سبعة اروس، ستة دنانير ونصف وربع وثمن. تفصيله:
بياض، عن ستة اروس، ستة دنانير وربع وثمن.
شعارى، عن راس واحد، نصف دينار.

عليها من الجوالي، عن عشرة انفار، عشرون دينارا. تفصيله:
المقيمون بها، سبعة انفار، اربعة عشر دينارا.
الناءون عنها، بالوجه القبلي، ثلاثة انفار، ستة دنانير.

وعليها من الاتبان، الفان وخمسمائة شنيف.

رسم خولي البحر بها، شعير، نصف اردب.

عليها لديوان الاحباس، عينا، سبعة عشر دينارا.

والذي جرت العادة باطلاقه للناحية من التقاوي، ثلاثمائة وثمانية عشر اردبا:
قمح، مائة وثلاثون اردبا.
شعير، مائة وخمسون اردبا.
فول، ثمانية وثلاثون اردبا.

والمقرر على المعاملين من الكشك والفريك، ثلاثة ارادب، نصفان.

والمطلق بها من الرزق، اربعة فدادين.

والمربى بها من الفروج، سبعمائة وخمسون فروجا. تفصيله:
للديوان المعمور، بما فيه من اجرة التربية وهو الثلث، اربعمائة وخمسون طائرا.
للمقطعين، ثلاثمائة.

والمسلف عليه بها من الشعير برسم الاصطبلات السلطانية، ثلاثمائة وعشرون اردبا.

ومن حرف السين، سينرو. هذه البلدة عبارة عن بلدة متوسطة بين الكبر والصغر. بها بساتين يسيرة، بها نخل واصول خروب وجميز. وكان بها كروم عنب دثرت لقلة الماء. تزرع الشتوي وصيفها اقصاب للديوان. وهي من غربي مدينة الفيوم، بينها وبين مدينة الفيوم مسافة ساعتين للراكب. جارية في اقطاع المقطعين. عبرتها ثمانية الاف دينار ومائة وخمسون دينارا جيشية. والمطلق لها من الماء من خليج شركة سينرو وبورها من البر البحري، يخص سينرو المذكورة اربعة عشر قبضة ماء. بها جامع تقام فيه الجمعة وبها كنيسة واحدة. اهلها، النصف منهم من بني جواب، والنصف الاخر اضابطة، فخذ من بني كلاب.

696 ساقط من أ. س.: قطيعة ثلاثين درهما المائة، عن خمسة عشر رأسا أربعة دراهم ونصف.

at the rate of 30 dirhams per 100 [heads], for 15 heads, 4 ½ dirhams;
at the rate of 25 dirhams per 100 [heads], for 220 heads, 55 dirhams;
the government agents' fee, 25 ¼ ⅛ dirhams.

The alms-tax, for the monetary value of eight heads of livestock, 8 dinars:
cows, for a yearling calf, 1 ⅛ dinar;
monetary value of small cattle, for seven heads, 6 ½ ¼ ⅛ dinars:
sheep, for six heads, 6 ¼ ⅛ dinars;
goats, for one head, ½ dinar.

The poll-tax, for ten individuals, 20 dinars:
those residing in it, for seven individuals, 14 dinars;
those absent from it, in the southern region, for three individuals, 6 dinars.

Hay, 2,500 bales.

The fee of the overseer of the canal, barley, ½ ardabb.

For the Ministry of Endowments, in specie, 17 dinars.

The seed advances customarily distributed in the locality, 318 ardabbs:
wheat, 130 ardabbs;
barley, 150 ardabbs;
broad beans, 38 ardabbs.

The established levy on the cultivators in *kishk* and *farīk* dishes, 3 ardabbs, half in each.

The allowances distributed in it, 4 feddans.

The chicken reared in it, 750 chickens:
for the prosperous Dīwān, including the rearing wage of a third, 450 birds;
for the *iqṭā*ʿ-holders, 300.

The barley assigned for the royal stables and paid for in advance, 320 ardabbs.

Also beginning with the letter 'sīn': Sīnarū.[216] This is a medium-sized village, with a few orchards, date palms and trunks of carob trees and sycamores. It used to have grape vineyards, but they fell into ruin due to lack of water. Winter crops are cultivated in it, and sugarcane that belongs to the Dīwān is grown in the summer. It lies two hours' ride west of Madīnat al-Fayyūm. It is assigned as an *iqṭā*ʿ to *iqṭā*ʿ-holders. Its fiscal value is 8,150 army dinars. The water distributed to it comes from a canal that branches off from the northern bank [of the Main Canal], shared by Sīnarū and its hamlet, Būr [Sīnarū]. The share of Sīnarū is 14 *qabḍas* of water. It has a congregational mosque, in which the Friday prayers are held, and one church. Half of its people belong to the Banū Jawwāb and the other half to the Aḍābiṭa, branches of the Banū Kilāb.

216 Modern location: Sīnarū (سينرو). Timm, *Das Christlich-Koptische Ägypten*, p. 2034: Psineuris; Trismegistos, GEO ID Psineuris. Halm, *Ägypten*, p. 272; Salmon, 'Répertoire', p. 56; Zéki, 'Une description', p. 43; de Sacy, *État des provinces*, p. 683; Savigny, *Description de l'Égypte*, p. 129; Amélineau, *La géographie*, p. 29: Senaoueh; Ibn Mammātī, *Kitāb qawānīn al-dawāwīn*, p. 150; Ibn al-Jīʿān, *Kitāb al-tuḥfa*, p. 155; Ramzī, *Al-Qāmūs*, II/III, 73: Sīnarū.

بها معصرة قصب سكر ذات حجر بالابقار. تزرع[697] باراضي الناحية برسم المعصرة المنكورة وعواملها، فدن، سبعة وتسعون فدانا وثلثان ونصف ثمن وحبة.[698] تفصيله:

قصب سكر، اربعة وثمانون فدانا وسدس ونصف ثمن وحبة:[699]

راس، اثنان وستون فدانا ونصف.

خلفة، احد وعشرون فدانا وثلثان ونصف ثمن وحبة.[700]

قرط وفول، ثلاثة عشر فدانا ونصف.

ارتفاعها عينا، مما جميعه مستخرجا، مائة وعشرة دنانير; غلة، مما جميعه متحصلا، الف واربعمائة وخمسون اردبا. تفصيله:

قمح، سبعمائة وخمسون اردبا.

شعير، سبعمائة اردب.

تفصيله:

الهلالي، ديناران.

المراعي، سبعة دنانير.

الخراجي، مائة ودينار واحد.

والغلة، تفصيله:

المناجزة، سبعمائة اردب، قمح وشعير نصفان.

المشاطرة، سبعمائة وخمسون اردبا. تفصيله:

قمح، اربعمائة اردب.

شعير، ثلاثمائة[701] وخمسون اردبا.

خراج الراتب، ثمانية عشر دينارا.

خراج القصب السكر، ثلاثة وثمانون[702] دينارا.

وعليها من الرسوم والمراعي والكيالة، عن ستمائة وسبعة[703] عشر درهما وربع وثمن، خمسة عشر دينارا وربع وسدس ونصف قيراط; وغلة، ثمانية وثمانون اردبا وثلث ونصف قيراط:

قمح، اثنان واربعون اردبا وثلث.

شعير، اربعون اردبا وثلث ونصف ثمن.

فول، اردبان ونصف وربع.

كمون، اردبان ونصف وربع وثمن.

تفصيله:

الرسوم، اربعمائة وتسعة وستون درهما وربع، وغلة، ستة واربعون اردبا ونصف وثلث وثمن. تفصيله:

قمح، اثنان وعشرون اردبا وثلث.

شعير، تسعة عشر اردبا وربع وسدس وثمن.

فول، اردبان ونصف وربع.

كمون، اردبان وثلث.

تفصيله:

شد الاحباس، ستة عشر درهما.

رسم الجراريف، تسعون درهما.

رسم الحصاد، ثلاثة وخمسون درهما.

رسم الخفارة، خمسة عشر درهما.

شد العين، تسعة واربعون درهما ونصف.

رسم قطع الثوم، مائتان وسبعة دراهم.

رسم الاجران، ثمانية وثلاثون درهما ونصف وربع، والغلة على ما فصل.

697 أ. س.: يزرع.

698 ط. م.: حبة.

699 ط. م.: حبة.

700 ط. م.: حبة.

701 أ. س. يضيف: أردب.

702 أ. س.: ثلاثون.

703 أ.س.: وستة.

It has a sugarcane press with one stone, [turned] by oxen. The [crown estate] feddans sown in the lands of the village, assigned for the press and its cattle, 97 ⅔ 1/16 1/72 feddans:

sugarcane, 84 ⅙ 1/16 1/72 feddans:

first harvest, 62 ½ feddans;

second harvest, 21 ⅔ 1/16 1/72 feddans.

Alfalfa and broad beans, 13 ½ feddans.

Its cash revenues, in specie, 110 dinars; and its revenues in kind, in grains, 1,450 ardabbs:

wheat, 750 ardabbs;

barley, 700 ardabbs.

[The revenue] in detail:

lunar-calendar revenues, 2 dinars;

[permanent] pasture tax, 7 dinars;

land tax, 101 dinars;

And in grains:

munājaza land tax, 700 ardabbs, wheat and barley, half in each;

mushāṭara land tax, 750 ardabbs:

wheat, 400 ardabbs;

barley, 350 ardabbs.

[the land tax in cash]:

land tax on perennial plants, 18 dinars;

land tax on sugarcane, 83 dinars.

The fees, the pasture fees and the measurement fee are 617 ¼ ⅛ dirhams, which are 15 ¼ ⅙ 1/48 dinars; and in grains, 88 ⅓ 1/48 ardabbs:

wheat, 42 ⅓ ardabbs;

barley, 40 ⅓ 1/16 ardabbs;

broad beans, 2 ½ ¼ ardabbs;

cumin, 2 ½ ¼ ⅛ ardabbs.

[The fees, the measurement fee and the pasture fee] in detail:

the fees, 469 ¼ dirhams; and in grains, 46 ½ ⅓ ⅛ ardabbs:

wheat, 22 ⅓ ardabbs;

barley, 19 ¼ ⅙ ⅛ ardabbs;

broad beans, 2 ½ ¼ ardabbs;

cumin, 2 ⅓ ardabbs.

[the fees] in detail:

supervision of endowments, 16 dirhams;

dredging fee, 90 dirhams;

harvest fee, 53 dirhams;

protection fee, 15 dirhams;

supervision of the land survey, 49 ½ dirhams;

[settlement] fee for the tax-rate on garlic (*rasm qaṭīʿat al-thūm*), 207 dirhams;

threshing-floor fee, 38 ½ ¼ dirhams; and in grains, as specified.

الكيالة، احد واربعون اردبا وثلث ونصف ثمن:

قمح، عشرون اردبا.

شعير، عشرون اردبا ونصف وثلث وثمن.

كمون، ربع وسدس ونصف قيراط.

المراعي، طارئ، عن اربعمائة وستة وثلاثين راسا، مائة وثمانية واربعون درهما وثمن. تفصيله:

قطيعة مائة درهم المائة، عن عشرة اروس، عشرة دراهم.

قطيعة ثلاثين درهما المائة، عن مائة واربعة وثمانين راسا، احد وخمسون درهما وربع وثمن.

قطيعة خمسة وعشرين درهما المائة، عن مائتين واثنين واربعين راسا، ستون درهما ونصف.

رسم المستخدمين، حسابا عن كل مائة راس ستة دراهم وربع، ستة وعشرون درهما وربع.

وعليها من الزكاة، ثمانية دنانير[704] ونصف وثلث:

خرص النخل، دينار واحد.

ثمن ماشية، عن ثمانية اروس، سبعة دنانير ونصف وثلث. تفصيله:

بقر احمر، تبيع واحد، دينار واحد ونصف.

ثمن الاغنام، عن سبعة اروس، ستة دنانير وثلث:

بياض، عن خمسة اروس، خمسة دنانير وثلث.

شعارى، عن راسين، دينار.

وعليها من الجوالي، عن تسعة انفار، ثمانية عشر دينارا. تفصيله:

المقيمون بها، عن ستة انفار، اثنا عشر دينارا.

الناءون عنها، عن ثلاثة انفار، ستة دنانير. تفصيله:

الوجه البحري، عن نفرين، اربعة دنانير.

الوجه القبلي، عن[705] نفر واحد، ديناران.

وعليها لديوان الاحباس، عينا، سبعة دنانير.

وعليها من الاتبان، ثلاثة الاف شنيف.

رسم خولي البحر بها، قمح، اردب واحد.

والمطلق بها من الرزق، ثمانية فدادين ونصف:

الخفراء، اربعة فدادين ونصف.

النجارون، اربعة فدادين.

اهلها يزرعون من القصب الراس ويسقون من الخلف برسم معصرة سينرو، خارجا عن الزائد في سنة اثنتين، سبعة وخمسون فدانا وقيراط. تفصيله:

راس، اثنان واربعون فدانا وربع وسدس وثمن ودانق.

خلفة، اربعة عشر فدانا وربع وسدس ونصف ثمن وحبة.[706]

والمسلف عليه بها من الشعير للاصطبلات السلطانية، مائة وخمسون اردبا.

والمربى بها من الفروج، ستمائة وخمسة وثمانون طائرا. تفصيله:

للديوان المعمور، بما فيه من اجرة التربية وهو الثلث، ثلاثمائة وستون طائرا.

للمقطعين، ثلاثمائة وخمسة وعشرون طائرا.

704 أ. س.: دراهم.

705 ساقط من ط. م.: عن.

706 ط. م.: حبة.

The measurement fee, 41 1/3 1/16 ardabbs:

wheat, 20 ardabbs;

barley, 20 1/2 1/3 1/8 ardabbs;

cumin, 1/4 1/6 1/48 [ardabb].

Pasture fee on seasonal pasture lands, for 436 heads, 148 1/8 dirhams:

at the rate of 100 dirhams per 100 [heads], for 10 heads, 10 dirhams;

at the rate of 30 dirhams per 100 [heads], for 184 heads, 51 1/4 1/8 dirhams;

at the rate of 25 dirhams per 100 [heads], for 242 heads, 60 1/2 dirhams;

the government agents' fee, calculated as 6 1/4 dirhams for every 100 heads, 26 1/4 dirhams.

The alms-tax, 8 1/2 1/3 dinars:

estimate of dates, 1 dinar;

monetary value of livestock, for eight heads, 7 1/2 1/3 dinars:

cows, for a yearling calf, 1 1/2 dinar;

monetary value of small cattle, for seven heads, 6 1/3 dinars:

sheep, for five heads, 5 1/3 dinars;

goats, for two heads, 1 dinar.

The poll-tax, for nine individuals, 18 dinars:

those residing in it, for six individuals, 12 dinars;

those absent from it, for three individuals, 6 dinars:

the northern region, for two individuals, 4 dinars;

the southern region, one individual, 2 dinars.

For the Ministry of Endowments, in specie, 7 dinars.

Hay, 3,000 bales.

The fee of the overseer of the canal, wheat, 1 ardabb.

The allowances allocated in it, 8 1/2 feddans:

for the watchmen, 4 1/2 feddans;

for the carpenters, 4 feddans.

Its people sow first-harvest sugarcane, and they irrigate second-harvest sugarcane, assigned for the press of Sīnarū. Excluding the increment for year [64]2, that amounts to 57 1/24 feddans:

first harvest, 42 1/4 1/6 1/8 1/144 feddans;

second harvest, 14 1/4 1/6 1/16 1/72 feddans.

The barley assigned for the royal stables and paid for in advance, 150 ardabbs.

The chickens reared in it, 685 birds:

for the prosperous Dīwān, including the rearing wage of a third, 360 birds;

for the *iqṭāʿ*-holders, 325 birds.

والمقرر على المعاملين من الكشك والفريك والسويق، ثلاثة ارادب:
كشك، اردب.
وفريك، اردب.
وسويق، اردب.

والذي جرت العادة باطلاقه من التقاوي لعمارة الناحية، مائة واحد وخمسون اردبا وقيراطان:
قمح، ثمانية وسبعون اردبا ونصف وربع.
شعير، اثنان وستون اردبا ونصف وثلث.
فول، تسعة ارادب ونصف.

ومن حرف السين، سدمنت. هذه البلدة عبارة عن بلدة متوسطة، بين الكبر والصغر. بها نخيل وشجر مقل وجميز. تروى من النيل وتزرع كما يزرع الريف. وهي مجاورة المنهى، قريبة من حافته. وبها الشونة التي يحزن بها مغل خليج تنبطويه. والشونة مجاورة لدير هناك. بينها وبين مدينة الفيوم نصف نهار للراكب. وهي جارية في اقطاع الامير الاجل فخر الدين امير شكار[707] والامير شجاع الدين التاجي.[708] عبرتها الف وتسعة دنانير[709] جيشية. بها مسجد غير مدون، ومن بحريها باراضي قمبشا،[710] في الجبل على بحر الفيوم دير يعرف بدير سدمنت. اهلها بنو هانئ، فخذ من بني كلاب.

ارتفاعها عينا، سبعة وعشرون دينار، مائة وتسعة وعشرون اردبا وثلث:
قمح، سبعة وسبعون اردبا وثلث.
شعير، اثنان وخمسون اردبا.

تفصيله:
مال الهلالي، عن ضمان المعدية، تسعة دنانير.
مال المصايد، ثمانية عشر دينارا.

مشاطرة الغلة، مائة وتسعة وعشرون اردبا وثلث، على ما فصل.

وعليه من الرسوم والكيالة والمراعي، عن مائة وتسعة وخمسين درهما وثمن، ثلاثة دنانير وثلثان وربع ونصف ثمن؛ وغلة، ثمانية ارادب ونصف وربع وثمن:
قمح، ستة ارادب وثمن.
فول، اردبان ونصف وربع.

تفصيله:
الرسوم، مائة وثلاثة عشر درهما وربع، وغلة، ستة ارادب ونصف وربع وثمن:
قمح، اربعة ارادب وثمن.
شعير، اردبان ونصف وربع.
تفصيله:
شد العين، تسعة وثلاثون درهما.
رسم الحصاد، ثلاثة وخمسون درهما.
رسم الخفارة، خمسة عشر درهما.
رسم الاجران، ستة دراهم وربع، والغلة.
الكيالة، قمح اردبان وثمن.
المراعي، طارئ، خمسة واربعون درهما ونصف وربع وثمن:
قطيعة خمسة وعشرين درهما المائة، عن مائة وستة واربعين راسا، ستة وثلاثون درهما ونصف.
رسم المستخدمين، تسعة دراهم وربع وثمن.

707 أ. س.: نكار.
708 أ. س.: الناجي.
709 ساقط من أ. س.: ألف وتسعة دنانير.
710 أ. س.: قنبشا.

The established levy on the cultivators in *kishk*, *farīk* and *sawīq* dishes, 3 ardabbs:
kishk, 1 ardabb;
farīk, 1 ardabb;
sawīq, 1 ardabb.

The seed advances customarily distributed for the village's cultivation, 151 2/24 ardabbs:
wheat, 78 ½ ¼ ardabbs;
barley, 62 ½ ⅓ ardabbs;
broad beans, 9 ½ ardabbs.

Also beginning with the letter 'sīn': Sidmant.[217] This is a medium-sized village, with date palms, bdellium trees (*muql*) and sycamores. It is watered by the Nile, and cultivated in the manner of Lower Egypt. It is adjacent to al-Manhā [Canal], near its bank. It has a granary, adjacent to a monastery there, in which the annual yield of Tanabṭawayh Canal is stored. It is half a day's ride from Madīnat al-Fayyūm. It is assigned as an *iqṭāʿ* to the illustrious (*al-ajall*)[218] amir Fakhr al-Dīn, *amīr shikār*, and to the amir Shujāʿ al-Dīn at-Tājī. Its fiscal value is 1,009 army dinars. It has a small, unregistered mosque. North of it, in the lands of Qambashā, in the mountain above the Main Canal, there is a monastery called Dayr Sidmant. Its people are the Banū Hāniʾ, a branch of the Banū Kilāb [=al-Lawāta].

Its revenues in specie are 27 dinars; and in grains, 129 ⅓ ardabbs:
wheat, 77 ⅓ ardabbs;
barley, 52 ardabbs.

[The revenue] in detail:
lunar-calendar taxes, for the concession of the ferryboat, 9 dinars;
fishery tax, 18 dinars;

Mushāṭara land tax, 129 ⅓ ardabbs, as specified.

The fees, the measurement fee and the pasture fee are 159 ⅛ dirhams, which are 3 ⅔ ¼ 1/16 dinars; and in grains, 8 ½ ¼ ⅛ ardabbs:
wheat, 6 ⅛ ardabbs;
broad beans, 2 ½ ¼ ardabbs.

[The fees, the measurement fee and the pasture fee] include:
the fees, 113 ¼ dirhams; and in grains, 6 ½ ¼ ⅛ ardabbs:
wheat, 4 ⅛ ardabbs;
barley, 2 ½ ¼ ardabbs.
[The fees] in detail:
supervision of the land survey, 39 dirhams;
harvest fee, 53 dirhams;
protection fee, 15 dirhams;
threshing-floor fee, 6 ¼ dirhams; and the grains.
The measurement fee, wheat, 2 ⅛ ardabbs.
The pasture fee on seasonal pasture lands, 45 ½ ¼ ⅛ dirhams:
at the rate of 25 dirhams per 100 [heads], for 146 heads, 36 ½ dirhams;
the government agents' fee, 9 ¼ ⅛ dirhams.

217 Modern location: Sidmant al-Jabal (سدمنت الجبل). Halm, *Ägypten*, p. 269; Ibn Duqmāq, *Kitāb al-intiṣār*, p. 5, p. 8 of al-Bahnasā; Ibn al-Jīʿān, *Kitāb al-tuḥfa*, p. 167: Sadamant of al-Bahnasā; Ramzī, *Al-Qāmūs*, II/III, 161: Sidmant al-Jabal, Coptic Posotoment (following Amélineau, *La géographie*).

218 The rank of *al-amīr al-ajall* designated military commanders of the second order, below the senior amirs. See Humphreys, 'The Emergence of the Mamluk Army', pp. 86ff (based on surviving inscriptions).

وعليها من الزكاة عن ثمن الماشية، عن سبعة ارؤس، ستة دنانير وثلث وحبتان. تفصيله:

بقر احمر، تبيع واحد، دينار واحد وخمسة قراريط وحبتان.

اغنام، عن ستة ارؤس، خمسة دنانير وثمن. تفصيله:

بياض، عن اربعة ارؤس، اربعة دنانير وثمن.

شعارى، عن راسين، دينار واحد.

وعليها من الاتبان، مائة وثلاثون شنيفا.

والمربي بها من الفروج للديوان السلطاني، بما فيه من اجرة التربية وهو الثلث، مائة وعشرون فروجا.

ومن حرف الشين، شسفة، من حقوق سنورس.[711] هذه البلدة عبارة عن بلدة صغيرة، فيها نخل ويسير من احكار كروم ودويرات تين وغيرها. وهي بحري الفيوم، بينها وبين مدينة الفيوم مسافة ساعتين ونصف للراكب. جارية في اقطاع الامير عز الدين خضر بن محمد الكيكاني واخوته بغير عبرة. لها من الماء المطلق في بحر سنورس المساق الى المقسم المعروف بالشاذروان لسقي الشتوي والصيفي بما عدته ثلاث قبض ونصف[712] ماء. وبرسم بستان زين الدين بن ابي سليمان، من اراضي الناحية، قبضة واحدة مرتبة. بها مسجد غير مدون. اهلها بنو قيصر فخذ من بني كلاب [= عجلان].[713]

ارتفاعها، عينا، عن المراعي والخراجي، خمسة وتسعون دينارا وسدس. تفصيله:

المراعي،[714] اربعة دنانير وثلث[715] ونصف ثمن.

الخراجي، على ما كان مقررا في الديوان السلطاني، تسعون دينارا ونصف وربع ونصف قيراط:

خراج الراتب، خمسة وثمانون دينارا وثلثان وثمن ودانق.

المستقر، ثمانية وستون دينارا وسدس ونصف ثمن وحبة.

الاصل، عن ثمانية وثلاثين فدانا وثلث وثمن وحبة، ستون دينارا وثلث وربع ونصف ثمن وحبة.[716] تفصيله:

كرم، عن ربع وثمن ودانق، ديناران ونصف قيراط وحبة.

شجر[717] راتب، عن عشرين فدانا ونصف ونصف قيراط وحبة، احد واربعون دينارا وقيراطان وحبتان.

حكر، عن سبعة عشر فدانا وربع وسدس وثمن وحبة، سبعة عشر دينارا وربع وسدس وثمن وحبة.

الاضافة، سبعة دنانير وثلث وربع.

القطيعة، سبعة عشر دينارا وربع وسدس وثمن وحبة.

خراج فدن العين، اربعة دنانير ونصف وثلث وثمن وحبة. تفصيله:

الاصل، عن ثلاثة فدادين ونصف وثلث ونصف قيراط، اربعة دنانير وربع وسدس ودانق.

قلقاس، عن خمسة قراريط ودانق، ثلث وربع ونصف ثمن دينار.

خضر، عن ثمن وحبة، ربع وحبتان.

قرط، عن ثلاثة فدادين ونصف، ثلاثة دنانير ونصف.

الاضافة، ربع وسدس وثمن ودانق.

711 ساقط من أ. س.: من حقوق سنورس.

712 ساقط من أ. س.: ونصف.

713 أ. س.، ط. م.: كلاب.

714 ساقط من أ. س.: والخراجي، خمسة وتسعون دينارا وسدس. تفصيله المراعي.

715 أ. س.: ونصف.

716 ط. م.: حبة.

717 ساقط من أ. س.: شجر.

The alms-tax, for the monetary value of seven heads of livestock, 6 1/3 2/72 dinars:

cows, for a yearling calf, 1 5/24 2/72 dinar;

small cattle, for six heads, 5 1/8 dinars:

sheep, for four heads, 4 1/8 dinars;

goats, for two heads, 1 dinar.

Hay, 130 bales.

The chickens reared in it for the royal Dīwān, including the rearing wage of a third, 120 chickens.

Beginning with the letter ‘shīn’: Shisfa,[219] included in the accounts of Sinnūris. This is a small village, with date palms, a few vineyards subject to long-term lease, enclosures of figs and other fruits. It lies in the north of the province, two and a half hours’ ride from Madīnat al-Fayyūm. It is assigned as an *iqṭāʿ* to the amir ʿIzz al-Dīn Khiḍr ibn Muḥammad al-Kīkānī and his brothers, without a fiscal value. The water allocated to it, in the amount of 3 1/2 *qabḍas*, is directed from Sinnūris Canal to the divisor known as al-Shādhrawān, for the irrigation of winter and summer crops. The orchard of Zayn al-Dīn ibn Abī Sulaymān which lies in the lands of the village is assigned one fixed (*murattaba*) *qabḍa*. It has a small, unregistered mosque. Its people are Banū Qayṣar, a branch of the Banū Kilāb [= ʿAjlān].[220]

Its revenues in specie, from fixed pasture tax and from land tax, are 95 1/6 dinars:

pasture [tax], 4 1/3 1/16 dinars;

the land tax, according to what is established in the royal Dīwān, 90 1/2 1/4 1/48 dinars:

land tax on perennial plants, 85 2/3 1/8 1/144 dinars:

the established: 68 1/6 1/16 1/72 dinars:

the basic assessment, for 38 1/3 1/8 1/72 feddans, 60 1/3 1/4 1/16 1/72 dinars:

vineyards, for 1/4 1/8 1/144 [feddan], 2 1/48 1/72 dinars;

perennial plants, for 20 1/2 1/48 1/72 feddans, 41 2/24 2/72 dinars;

land subject to long-term lease, for 17 1/4 1/6 1/8 1/72 feddans, 17 1/4 1/6 1/8 1/72 dinars.

the addition, 7 1/3 1/4 dinars.

[the added tax] rate, 17 1/4 1/6 1/8 1/72 dinars.

Land tax on cash-crops, assessed by feddans, 4 1/2 1/3 1/8 1/72 dinars:

the basic assessment, for 3 1/2 1/3 1/48 feddans, 4 1/4 1/6 1/144 dinars:

colocasia, for 5/24 1/144 [feddan], 1/3 1/4 1/16 dinar;

green vegetables, for 1/8 1/72 [feddan], 1/4 2/72 [dinar].

alfalfa, for 3 1/2 feddans, 3 1/2 dinars.

the addition 1/4 1/6 1/8 1/144 [dinar].

219 Modern location: Al-Zāwiya al-Khaḍrāʾ (الزاوية الخضراء). Halm, *Ägypten*, p. 271: Shasfa; Salmon, ‘Répertoire’, p. 51; Ibn al-Jīʿān, *Kitāb al-tuḥfa*, p. 156: Shashʿa; de Sacy, *État des provinces*, p. 683: Shashʿa; Ibn Mammātī, *Kitāb qawānīn al-dawāwīn*, 127: Shishfa; Ramzī, *Al-Qāmūs*, II/III, 109: Al-Zāwiya al-Khaḍrāʾ.

220 AS and MP: Banū Kilāb.

غلات، عن خراج المناجزة والاقصاب السكر، اربعمائة وستون اردبا:
قمح، ثلاثمائة اردب.
شعير، مائة وخمسون اردبا.
سمسم، عشرة ارادب.

عليها من الرسوم والكيالة والمراعي، عن ثلاثمائة خمسة وتسعين درهما وربع، تسعة دنانير ونصف وربع وثمن ودانق، وغلة، تسعة عشر اردبا وثلث:
قمح، اثنا عشر اردبا وقيراط.
فول، سبعة ارادب.
سمسم، سدس وثمن اردب.

تفصيله:
الرسوم، مائة وخمسة وعشرون درهما وربع، وغلة، احد عشر اردبا وثلثان وربع ونصف قيراط.
تفصيله:
قمح، سبعة ارادب وقيراط.
فول، اربعة ارادب ونصف وثلث ونصف ثمن.
تفصيله:
شد الاحباس، اربعة دراهم.
رسم جراريف، اثنان وعشرون درهما.
رسم الحصاد، ثلاثة وخمسون درهما.
رسم الخفارة، خمسة عشر درهما.
رسم القلقاس، عشرون درهما.
رسم الاجران، احد عشر درهما وربع، والغلة على ما تقدم.
الكيالة، سبعة ارادب وثلث ونصف ثمن:
قمح،[718] خمسة ارادب.
فول، اردبان وقيراطان ونصف.
سمسم، سدس وثمن اردب.
المراعي، عن مائتين واربعة وثلاثين راسا، مائتان وسبعون درهما. تفصيله:
راتب، عن ثلاثة وستين راسا، مائة واحد واربعون درهما ونصف وربع.
طارئ، عن مائة واحد وسبعين راسا، مائة[719] وثلاثة عشر درهما ونصف وثمن. تفصيله:
قطيعة درهم واحد الراس، عن تسعة واربعين راسا، تسعة واربعون درهما.
قطيعة سبعين درهما المائة، عن سبعين راسا، تسعة واربعون درهما.
قطيعة ثلاثين درهما المائة، عن اثنين وخمسين راسا، خمسة عشر درهما ونصف وثمن.
رسم المستخدمين، اربعة عشر درهما ونصف وثمن.

وعليها من الزكاة، عينا، سبعة دنانير ونصف. تفصيله:
خرص العنب، اربعة دنانير ونصف.
ثمن الاغنام، عن اربعة ارؤس، ثلاثة دنانير:
بياض، عن راسين ديناران.
شعارى، عن راسين دينار واحد.

وعليها من الاتبان، خمسمائة وخمسون شنيفا.

وعليها لديوان الاحباس ديناران.

718 أ. س.: قمح، أردب.
719 ساقط من ط. م.: مائة.

In grains, *munājaza* land tax and the sugarcane,[221] 460 ardabbs:
wheat, 300 ardabbs;
barley, 150 ardabbs;
sesame, 10 ardabbs.

The fees, the measurement fee and the pasture fee, 395 ¼ dirhams, which are 9 ½ ¼ ⅛ 1/144 dinars; and in grains, 19 ⅓ ardabbs:
wheat, 12 1/24 ardabbs;
broad beans, 7 ardabbs;
sesame ⅙ ⅛ ardabb,

[The fees, the measurement fee and the pasture fee] in detail:
the fees, 125 ¼ dirhams; and in grains, 11 ⅔ ¼ 1/48 ardabbs:
wheat, 7 1/24 ardabbs;
broad beans, 4 ½ ⅓ 1/16 ardabbs.
[the fees] in detail:
supervision of endowments, 4 dirhams;
dredging fee, 22 dirhams;
harvest fee, 53 dirhams;
protection fee, 15 dirhams;
colocasia fee, 20 dirhams;
threshing-floor fee, 11 ¼ dirhams, and the grains, as above.
The measurement fee, 7 ⅓ 1/16 ardabbs:
wheat, 5 ardabbs;
broad beans, 2 2/24 1/48 ardabbs;
sesame ⅙ ⅛ ardabb.
The pasture fee, for 234 heads, 270 dirhams:
permanent pasture lands, for 63 heads, 141 ½ ¼ dirhams;
seasonal pasture lands, for 171 heads, 113 ½ ⅛ dirhams:
at the rate of one dirham per head, for 49 heads, 49 dirhams;
at the rate of 70 dirhams per 100 [heads], for 70 heads, 49 dirhams;
at the rate of 30 dirhams per 100 [heads], for 52 head, 15 ½ ⅛ dirhams;
the government agents' fee, 14 ½ ⅛ dirhams.

The alms-tax, in specie, 7 ½ dinars:
estimate of grapes, 4 ½ dinars;
monetary value of four heads of small cattle, 3 dinars:
sheep, for two heads, 2 dinars;
goats, for two heads, 1 dinar.

Hay, 550 bales.

For the Ministry of Endowments, 2 dinars.

221 In both manuscripts.

اهلها يزرعون من الاقصاب السكر الراس ويسقون من الخلف برسم المعاصر بسنورس، ستة فدادين وسدس وثمن وحبتان. تفصيله:

راس، خمسة فدادين وسدس.

خلفة، فدانان وسدس وثمن وحبتان.

المربى بها من الفروج، ثلاثمائة فروج. تفصيله:

للديوان المعمور بما فيه من اجرة التربية وهو الثلث، مائتا طائر.

للمقطعين، مائة طائر.

والذي بها من التقاوي الديوانية، ثلاثة وسبعون اردبا. تفصيله:

قمح، ستون اردبا.

شعير، اربعة ارادب.

فول، ثمانية ارادب وثلث.

سمسم، ثلثا اردب.

ومن حرف الشين، شلالة، من حقوق سنورس. هذه البلدة عبارة عن بلدة صغيرة بها نخل ودويرات تين وغيره. تزرع الشتوي، القمح والشعير والفول. بينه وبين مدينة الفيوم مسافة ساعتين للراكب. جارية في اقطاع الامير الكبير علم الدين سنجر الحلبي بغير عبرة. لها من الماء المطلق ببحر سنورس في خليج بغير بنيان مفرد عبرته ست قبض. اهلها بنو قيصر فخذ من بني عجلان.

ارتفاعها عينا مما جميعه خراج ومراعي، ستة واربعون دينارا وثلث وحبة. تفصيله:

المراعي، ستة دنانير ونصف وربع.

خراج الراتب، تسعة وثلاثون دينارا وثلث وربع وحبة:

الاصل، عن عشرين فدانا ونصف ونصف قيراط وحبة، خمسة وثلاثون دينارا وسدس ونصف قيراط وحبة. تفصيله:

كرم، عن نصف ودانق، ديناران وثلث ونصف قيراط وحبة.[720]

راتب، عن اربعة فدادين وثلثين[721] وربع، تسعة دنانير ونصف وثلث.

قطن، قطيعة دينار واحد ونصف الفدان، عن خمسة عشر فدانا وقيراطان وحبتين، اثنان وعشرون دينارا وثلثان.

الاضافة، اربعة دنانير وثلث ونصف ثمن.

خراج القرط، ستة دنانير ونصف وربع.

الاصل، عن ستة فدادين، ستة دنانير.

الاضافة، نصف وربع دينار.

غلة، عن خراج المناجزة، خمسمائة وخمسة واربعون اردبا ونصف وثلث:

قمح، ثلاثمائة وسبعة وعشرون اردبا ونصف.

شعير، مائة وتسعة ارادب وسدس.

فول، مائة وتسعة ارادب وسدس.

عليها من الرسوم والكيالة، عن مائة وسبعين درهما وثمن، اربعة دنانير وربع، وغلة، اثنان اربعون اردبا وقيراطان:

قمح، ثمانية عشر اردبا ونصف وثمن.

شعير، عشرة ارادب.

فول، ثلاثة عشر اردبا وثلث وثمن.

720 ساقط من ط. م.: تفصيله كرم عن نصف ودانق ديناران وثلث ونصف قيراط وحبة.

721 أ. س.: وثلث.

Its people sow first-harvest sugarcane, and irrigate second-harvest sugarcane, assigned for the press at Sinnūris, 6 1/6 1/8 2/72 feddans:

first harvest, 5 1/6 feddans;

second harvest, 2[222] 1/8 2/72 feddans.

The chickens reared in it, 300 chickens:

for the prosperous Dīwān, including the rearing wage of a third, 200 birds;

for the *iqṭāʿ*-holders, 100 birds.

The seed advances of the Dīwān, 73 ardabbs:

wheat, 60 ardabbs;

barley, 4 ardabbs;

broad beans, 8 1/3 ardabbs;

sesame 2/3 ardabb.

Beginning with the letter 'shīn': Shallāla,[223] included in the accounts of Sinnūris. This is a small village, with date palms and enclosures of fig trees and other [trees]. Wheat, barley and broad beans are sown in the winter. It is two hours' ride from Madīnat al-Fayyūm. It is assigned as an *iqṭāʿ* to the Grand Amir (*al-amīr al-kabīr*)[224] ʿAlam al-Dīn Sanjar al-Ḥalabī,[225] without a fiscal value. It gets water from Sinnūris Canal, by means of a separate canal without a weir, which has a water quota of six *qabḍas*. Its people are the Banū Qayṣar, a branch of the Banū ʿAjlān.

Its revenues in specie, all of which come from land tax and pasture tax, are 46 1/3 1/72 dinars:

pasture tax, 6 1/2 1/4 dinars;

land tax on perennial plants, 39 1/3 1/4 1/72 dinars:

the basic assessment, for 20 1/2 1/48 1/72 feddans, 35 1/6 1/48 1/72 dinars:

vineyards, for 1/2 1/144 [feddan], 2 1/3 1/48 1/72 dinars;

fully grown trees, for 4 2/3 1/4 feddans, 9 1/2 1/3 dinars;

cotton, at the rate of 1 1/2 dinars per feddan, for 15 2/24 2/72 feddans, 22 2/3 dinars.

the addition, 4 1/3 1/16 dinars;

land tax on alfalfa, 6 1/2 1/4 dinars:

the basic assessment, for 6 feddans, 6 dinars;

the addition, 1/2 1/4 dinar;

Munājaza land tax on grains, 545 1/2 1/3 ardabbs:

wheat, 327 1/2 ardabbs;

barley, 109 1/6 ardabbs;

broad beans, 109 1/6 [ardabbs].

The fees and the measurement fee, 170 1/8 dirhams, which are 4 1/4 dinars; and in grains, 42 2/24 ardabbs:

wheat, 18 1/2 1/8 ardabbs;

barley, 10 ardabbs;

broad beans, 13 1/3 1/8 ardabbs.

222 Should be 'one feddan', or the total should be 'seven feddans'.

223 Modern location: al-Kaʿābī al-Jadīda (الكعابي الجديدة). Halm, *Ägypten*, p. 270: Shallāla/Malāliya; Salmon, 'Répertoire', p. 50; Ibn al-Jīʿān, *Kitāb al-tuḥfa*, p. 156: Shalāliyya al-Mudaddaliyya; de Sacy, *État des provinces*, p. 683; Ramzī, *Al-Qāmūs*, I, 299: al-Kaʿābī al-Jadīda.

224 The title of senior commanders in the Ayyubid army; Humphreys, 'The Emergence of the Mamluk Army', p. 86.

225 A high ranking Ṣāliḥī amir, who would later be appointed by Sultan Quṭuz as governor of Damascus; Amitai, 'The Mamlūk officer class', p. 294.

تفصيله:
الرسوم، مائة وسبعون درهما وثمن وثلاثة عشر اردبا وربع وسدس ونصف ثمن. تفصيله:
قمح، خمسة ارادب ونصف.
شعير، اربعة ارادب وثمن.
فول، ثلاثة ارادب ونصف وثلث ونصف قيراط.
وتفصيله:
شد الاحباس، اربعة دراهم.
رسم الجراريف، احد واربعون درهما.
شد العين، خمسة واربعون درهما.
رسم الحصاد، ثلاثة وخمسون درهما.
رسم الخفارة، خمسة عشر درهما.
رسم الاجران، اثنا عشر درهما وثمن، والغلة على ما تقدم.
الكيالة، ثمانية وعشرون اردبا وثلث وربع ونصف قيراط:
قمح، ثلاثة عشر اردبا وثمن.
شعير، خمسة ارادب ونصف وربع وثمن.
فول، تسعة ارادب وثلث وربع ونصف قيراط.

وعليه من الزكاة، ثمانية دنانير وقيراطان. تفصيله:
خرص العنب، ثلث وربع وثمن دينار.
ثمن الاغنام، عن عشرة ارؤس، سبعة دنانير وربع وثمن.
بياض، عن اربعة ارؤس، اربعة دنانير وربع.
شعارى، ستة ارؤس، ثلاثة دنانير وثمن.

وعليها لديوان الاحباس، عينا، ديناران.

وعليها من الاتبان، ستمائة وثلاثون شنيفا.

اهلها يزرعون من القصب السكر برسم المعاصر بسنورس، مما جميعه راس، عشرة فدادين ونصف وربع وثمن.

المربى بها من الفروج، ثلاثمائة وعشرون طائرا:
للديوان المعمور، بما فيه من اجرة التربية وهو الثلث، مائتا طائر.
للمقطعين، مائة وعشرون طائرا.

والمستقر عليها من الفريك، اردب.

والمستقر اطلاقه بها من الرزق، ستة فدادين:
المشايخ، فدان واحد.
النجارون، ثلاثة فدادين.
طرادون الوحش، فدانان.

والذي بها من التقاوي الديوانية، ثلاثة وتسعون اردبا ونصف. تفصيله:
قمح، ثمانية وستون اردبا.
شعير، خمسة عشر اردبا.
فول، عشرة ارادب ونصف.

[The fees, the measurement fee] in detail:
the fees, 170 ⅛ dirhams; and [in grains] 13 ¼ ⅙ 1/16 ardabbs:
wheat, 5 ½ ardabbs;
barley, 4 ⅛ ardabbs;
broad beans, 3 ½ ⅓ 1/48 ardabbs.
[the fees] in detail:
supervision of endowments, 4 dirhams;
dredging fee, 41 dirhams;
supervision of the land survey, 45 dirhams;
harvest fee, 53 dirhams;
protection fee, 15 dirhams;
threshing-floor fee, 12 ⅛ dirhams; and in grains, as specified.
The measurement fee, 28 ⅓ ¼ 1/48 ardabbs:
wheat, 13 ⅛ ardabbs;
barley, 5 ½ ¼ ⅛ ardabbs;
broad beans, 9 ⅓ ¼ 1/48 ardabbs.

The alms-tax, 8 2/24 dinars:
estimate of grapes ⅓ ¼ ⅛ dinar;
monetary value of small cattle, for 10 heads, 7 ¼ ⅛ dinars:
sheep, for four heads, 4 ¼ dinars;
goats, for six heads, 3 ⅛ dinars.

For the Ministry of Endowments, in specie, 2 dinars.

Hay, 630 bales.

Its people sow 10 ½ ¼ ⅛ feddans of sugarcane, all of it first harvest, which is assigned for the presses at Sinnūris.

The chickens reared in it, 320 birds:
for the prosperous Dīwān, including the rearing wage of a third, 200 birds;
for the *iqṭā*ʿ-holders, 120 birds.

The confirmed levy of *farīk* dishes, 1 ardabb.

The established allowances allocated in it, 6 feddans:
the headmen, 1 feddan;
the carpenters, 3 feddans;
'beast-chasers', 2 feddans.

The seed advances of the Dīwān distributed in it, 93 ½ ardabbs:
wheat, 68 ardabbs;
barley, 15 ardabbs;
broad beans, 10 ½ ardabbs.

ومن حرف الشين، شانة. من نواحي شرقية الفيوم، هذه البلدة عبارة عن بلدة كبيرة. وهذه اللفظة تطلق على بلدين احدهما عتيقة في ذيل الجبل في الوطاة، انتقل اهلها عنها الى الوطاة بحري البلد العتيق. وبنوا بلدة تعرف بشانة كاسم البلد العتيق وهي بلدة كبيرة. تشتمل هذه البلدة على خلق كثير. اكثر زرعها الشعير. واهل هذه البلدة اول من يزرع في الفيوم واول من يحصد فانهم يزرعون من النوروز اول توت من اشهر القبط.

ويقال ان هذه شانة العتيقة، الذي ارتحل اهلها عنها الى شانة المستجدة، هي اول قرية وضعت في الفيوم. وسبب انتقالهم عنها الى الثانية، ان مجاورتهم في لحف الجبل بلدة تعرف باللواسي[722] دثرت من سنين عديدة وبقيت اراضيها مهملة. ولما كثر اهل شانة، زرعوا في اراضي اللواسي.[723] فبعدت عليهم من شانة العتيقة انتقلوا الى قريب من اراضي اللواسي.[724] وقيل ان من جملة سبب انتقالهم قلة الماء لما كثرت الاقصاب بالفيوم.

وهي تزرع الحبوب الشتوية، وليس لها صيفي. وهي شرقي مدينة الفيوم، بينها وبين مدينة الفيوم[725] مسافة نصف نهار للراكب. جارية في اقطاع جماعة من المقطعين. عبرتها جيشية عشرة الاف وتسعة دنانير. والمطلق لها من الماء، من بحر الشرقية، اربعة وعشرون قبضة. بها جامع تقام فيه الجمعة. اهلها بنو زرعة، فخذ من بني عجلان.

ارتفاعها عينا، مما جميعه مستخرجا عن مل الهلالي، اربعون دينارا.

شعير عن مناجزة الغلات، اربعة الاف اردب.

وعليها من الرسوم والكيالة والمراعي، عن اربعمائة وسبعة دراهم ونصف وربع وثمن، عشرة دنانير وسدس ونصف قيراط وحبة؛ وغلة، مائة واثنان وتسعون اردبا:

شعير، مائة واثنان وثمانون اردبا.

فول، عشرة ارادب.

تفصيله:

الرسوم، مائتان وستة وثمانون درهما ونصف، وغلة، مائة وسبعة ارادب وربع، شعير. تفصيله:

شد الاحباس، اربعة دراهم ونصف.

رسم الجراريف، مائة وستة عشر درهما ونصف.

رسم الحصاد، ثلاثة وخمسون درهما.

رسم الخفارة، خمسة عشر درهما.

رسم الاجران، سبعة وتسعون درهما، والغلة على ما تقدم.

كيالة، اربعة وثمانون اردبا ونصف وربع. تفصيله:

شعير، اربعة وسبعون اردبا ونصف وربع.

فول، عشرة ارادب.

وعليها من المراعي الطارئ، عن ثلاثمائة وثمانية واربعين راسا، مائة واحد وعشرون درهما وربع وثمن. تفصيله:

قطيعة ثلاثين درهما المائة، عن مائتين واحد وخمسين راسا، خمسة وسبعون درهما وربع وثمن.

قطيعة خمسة وعشرين درهما المائة، عن سبعة وتسعين راسا، اربعة وعشرون درهما وربع.

رسم المستخدمين، احد وعشرون درهما ونصف وربع.

وعليها من الزكاة عن ثمن اغنام، عن ثمانية وعشرين راسا، تسعة عشر دينارا وثمن. تفصيله:

بياض، عن خمسة عشر راسا، ستة عشر دينارا.

شعارى، عن ثلاثة عشر راسا، ثلاثة دنانير وثمن.

722 أ. س.: بالكواسي.

723 أ. س.: بالكواسي.

724 أ. س.: بالكواسي.

725 ساقط من أ. س.: بينها وبين مدينة الفيوم.

Also beginning with the letter 'shīn': Shāna,[226] a large village in eastern Fayyum. The name applies to two villages. The old one is in a plain at the foot of the mountain. From there the inhabitants moved to the plain to the north, where they built a village known as Shāna, named after the old village. It is a large village, densely populated. Most of its crops consist of barley. The people of this village are the first to sow and the first to harvest in the Fayyum. They sow in Nawrūz, on the first day of Coptic month of Tūt [10 of September].

It is said that this ancient Shāna, from which its people moved to the new Shāna, was the first village occupied in the Fayyum. The reason for their relocation to the new village was that neighbouring them, at the foot of the mountain, was a village known as al-Lawāsī, which had been deserted many years ago. Its lands were neglected, and when the number of Shāna's inhabitants increased, they began sowing in the lands of al-Lawāsī. These lands were distant from the site of the old Shāna, so they moved nearer to the lands of al-Lawāsī. It is also said that among the reasons for their move was a dearth of water, due to the increase in [cultivation of] sugarcane at the Fayyum.

Winter cereals are sown in it, but no summer crops. It lies half a day's ride east of Madīnat al-Fayyūm. It is included in the *iqṭāʿ* of a group of *iqṭāʿ*-holders, with a fiscal value of 10,009 army dinars. The water allocated to it from al-Sharqiyya Canal is 24 *qabḍas*. It has a congregational mosque, in which the Friday prayers are held. Its people are the Banū Zarʿa, a branch of the Banū ʿAjlān.

Its revenues in specie, all of it from lunar-calendar taxes, 40 dinars; [and in grains], barley from *munājaza* land tax on grains, 4,000 ardabbs.

The fees, the measurement fee and the pasture fee are 407 ½ ¼ ⅛ dirhams, which are 10 dinars ⅙ 1/48 1/72; and in grains, 192 ardabbs:

barley, 182 ardabbs;

broad beans, 10 ardabbs.

[The fees, the measurement fee and the pasture fee] in detail:

the fees, 286 ½ dirhams; and in grains, 107 ¼ ardabbs, in barley:

supervision of endowments, 4 ½ dirhams;

dredging fee, 116 ½ dirhams;

harvest fee, 53 dirhams;

protection fee, 15 dirhams;

threshing-floor fee, 97 dirhams; and in grains, as specified.

The measurement fee, 84 ½ ¼ ardabbs:

barley, 74 ½ ¼ ardabbs;

broad beans, 10 ardabbs.

The pasture fee on seasonal pasture lands, for 348 heads, 121 ¼ ⅛ dirhams:

at the rate of 30 dirhams per 100 [heads], for 251 heads, 75 ¼ ⅛ dirhams;

at the rate of 25 dirhams per 100 [heads], for 97 heads, 24 ¼ dirhams;

the government agents' fee, 21 ½ ¼ dirhams.

The alms-tax, on the monetary value of small cattle, for 28 heads, 19 ⅛ dinars:

sheep, for 15 heads, 16 dinars;

goats, for 13 heads, 3 ⅛ dinars.

226 Modern location: ʿIzbat Qaṣr Shāna (عزبة قصر شانة). Halm, *Ägypten*, p. 270; Salmon, 'Répertoire', pp. 40–41; Yāqūt, *Muʿjam al-Buldān*, II, 287: Shanāna or Shāna — the first village built by the Qur'anic Yūsuf in the Fayyum; Ibn al-Jīʿān, *Kitāb al-tuḥfa*, p. 155: Shāba; de Sacy, *État des provinces*, p. 683: Shāba; [Abū Ṣāliḥ], *Churches*, p. 203: Shāna; al-Maqrīzī, *Kitāb al-mawāʿiẓ*, ed. by Wiet, I, 246: Sāna; Ramzī, *Al-Qāmūs*, I, 291: ʿIzbat Qaṣr Shāna.

وعليها من الاتبان، ستة الاف شنيف.

عليها لديوان الاحباس، ديناران.

رسم خولي البحر، شعير، ثلاثة ارادب.

والمقرر على المعاملين بها من الكشك والفريك، سبعة ارادب، نصفان.

والمربى بها من الفروج، الف ومائة طائر:
للديوان المعمور، بما فيه من اجرة التربية وهو الثلث، ستمائة طائر.
للمقطعين، خمسمائة طائر.

والذي جرت العادة باطلاقه لها من التقاوي على ما ثبت علمه[726] في الديوان متقدما، خمسمائة وستون اردبا:
قمح، مائة وستة وسبعون اردبا.
شعير، مائتا اردب.
فول، مائة واربعة وثمانون اردبا.

والذي يسلف عليه بها من الشعير برسم الاصطبلات السلطانية، اربعمائة وستة وخمسون اردبا.

ومن حرف الشين، ششها، من حقوق خليج دلية. هذه البلدة عبارة عن بلدة متوسطة عتيقة من البلاد العتق. بها نخل يسير وليس بها شجر ولا كروم. تزرع الحبوب الشتوية. وهي قبلي الفيوم، الى الغرب. بينها وبين مدينة الفيوم ثلاث ساعات للراكب. وهي من نواحي خليج دلية، مجموعة في جملة اقطاع الخليج المذكور. والمطلق لها من الماء من خليج دلية، من الماء المساق الى المقسم المعروف بالتبرون، خمس قبض وثلثان. بها جامع تقام فيه الجمعة. اهلها بنو غصين، فخذ من بني كلاب.

ارتفاعها، عينا، اربعة دنانير وثلثان ونصف قيراط. تفصيله:
الهلالي، ديناران.
المراعي، دينار واحد وربع.
ما يخص جمال الدين بن الهمام، دينار واحد وربع وسدس ونصف قيراط.

غلة، اربعمائة وخمسة وخمسون اردبا. تفصيله:
قمح، مائتان وثلاثة وستون اردبا وثلث.
شعير، مائة واحد وتسعون اردبا وثلثان.

وعليها من الرسوم والكيالة والمراعي، عن مائة وخمسة واربعين درهما ونصف وربع، ثلاثة دنانير وربع ونصف ثمن؛ وغلة، اثنان وثلاثون اردبا وربع ونصف ثمن. تفصيله:
قمح، عشرون اردبا وثلث.
شعير، احد عشر اردبا وثلثان وربع ونصف ثمن.

تفصيله:
الرسوم، مائة واحد وعشرون درهما وربع وثمن، وتسعة عشر اردبا وربع ونصف ثمن:
قمح، احد عشر اردبا وثلث.
شعير، سبعة ارادب وثلثان وربع ونصف ثمن.
تفصيله:
شد العين، اربعة دراهم ونصف.
شد الاحباس، ثمانية دراهم.
رسم الجراريف، اربعة وعشرون درهما.

726 أ. س.: عمله.

Hay, 6,000 bales.

For the Ministry of Endowments, 2 dinars.

The fee of the overseer of the canal, barley, 3 ardabbs.

The established levy of *kishk* and *farīk* dishes on the cultivators, 7 ardabbs, half in each.

The chickens reared in it, 1,100 birds:
for the prosperous Dīwān, including the rearing wage of a third, 600 birds;
for the *iqṭāʿ*-holders, 500 birds.

The seed advances customarily distributed in it, according to what had been confirmed (*thabata ʿilmu-hu*)[227] in the Dīwān for some years, 560 ardabbs:
wheat, 176 ardabbs;
barley, 200 ardabbs;
broad beans, 184 ardabbs.

The barley assigned for the royal stables and paid for in advance, 456 ardabbs.

Also beginning with the letter 'shīn': Shushhā,[228] included in the accounts of Dilya Canal. This is a medium-sized, ancient village. It has a few date palms, but no trees or vineyards. Winter cereals are sown in it. It lies in the south-west of the province, three hours' ride from Madīnat al-Fayyūm. It is one of the villages of Dilya Canal, and is included in the *iqṭāʿ* of that canal. The water quota allocated to it from Dilya Canal, from the water channelled to the divisor known as al-Tabrūn, is 5 ⅔ *qabḍas*. It has a congregational mosque, in which the Friday prayers are held. Its people are the Banū Ghuṣayn, a branch of the Banū Kilāb.

Its revenue in specie is 4 ⅔ 1/48 dinars:
lunar-calendar tax, 2 dinars;
pasture tax, 1 ¼ dinar;
[taxes that] go to (*yakhuṣṣu*) [the amir] Jamāl al-Dīn ibn al-Humām, 1 ¼ ⅙ 1/48 dinar.

[Its revenue] in grains, 455 ardabbs:
wheat, 263 ⅓ ardabbs;
barley, 191 ⅔ ardabbs.

The fees, the measurement fee and the pasture fee are 135 ½ ¼ dirhams, which are 3 ⅓ ¼ 1/16 dinars; and in grains, 32 ¼ 1/16 ardabbs:
wheat, 20 ⅓ ardabbs;
barley, 11 ⅔ ¼ 1/16 ardabbs.

[The fees, the measurement fee and the pasture fee] in detail:
the fees, 121 ¼ ⅛ dirhams; and [in grains] 19 ¼ 1/16 ardabbs:
wheat, 11 ⅓ ardabbs;
barley, 7 ⅔ ¼ 1/16 ardabbs.
[The fees] in detail:
supervision of the land survey, 4 ½ dirhams;
supervision of endowments, 8 dirhams;
dredging fee, 24 dirhams;

227 AS: *ʿamalu-hu*.

228 Modern location: ʿIzbat Maʿjūn Bek near al-Minyā/ Maʿjūn (معجون). Halm, *Ägypten*, p. 273; Salmon, 'Répertoire', p. 69; de Sacy, *État des provinces*, p. 683; Ibn al-Jīʿān, *Kitāb al-tuḥfa*, p. 156; Ramzī, *Al-Qāmūs*, I, 297: ʿIzbat Maʿjūn Bak near al-Minyā. We identified it with present day Maʿjūn.

رسم الحصاد، ثلاثة وخمسون درهما.
رسم الخفارة، خمسة عشر درهما.
رسم الاجران، ستة عشر درهما ونصف وربع وثمن، والغلة على ما فصل.
الكيالة، ثلاثة عشر اردبا. تفصيله:
قمح، تسعة ارادب.
شعير، اربعة ارادب.
المراعي، طارئ، اربعة وعشرون درهما وربع وثمن:
قطيعة خمسة وعشرين درهما المائة، عن ثمانية وسبعين راسا، تسعة عشر درهما ونصف.
رسم المستخدمين، اربعة دراهم ونصف وربع وثمن.

وعليها من الزكاة عن ثمن الماشية، عن اربعة اروس، اربعة دنانير ونصف. تفصيله:
بقر احمر، مسنة واحدة، ديناران.
ثمن الاغنام، عن ثلاثة اروس، ديناران ونصف. تفصيله:
بياض، عن راسين، ديناران.
شعارى، عن راس واحد، نصف دينار.

عليها من الاتبان تسعمائة وثلاثة وعشرون شنيف.

رسم خولي البحر به، اردب وثلثان: قمح نصف وثلث،[727] وشعير نصف وثلث.

عليها لديوان الاحباس، ثلاثة دنانير.

المربى بها من الفروج، خمسمائة وستون طائرا. تفصيله:
للديوان المعمور، بما فيه من اجرة التربية وهو الثلث، ثلاثمائة وستون طائرا.
للمقطعين، مائتا طائر.

والذي يسلف عليه بها من الشعير برسم الاصطبلات السلطانية، مائة اردب.

اهلها يزرعون من الاقصاب السكر برسم معصرة دموشية، فدانين وسدسا.

ومن حرف الشين، شدموه، من حقوق خليج دلية. هذه البلدة عبارة عن بلدة متوسطة، بين الكبر والصغر. فيه دويرات نخل وقليل كروم وغروس وجميز. تزرع الشتوي وكانت تزرع الصيفي الى ان كثرت الاقصاب. وهي من قبلي الفيوم، بينها وبين مدينة الفيوم مسافة ثلاث ساعات للراكب. مجموعة في جملة عبرة الاقطاع الجيشية بالخليج المذكور. لها من بحر دلية من الماء المساق الى المقسم المعروف بالقلنبو، ثمان قبض ونصف وربع ماء. اهلها بنو قريط وشاكر، فخذ من بني كلاب.

ارتفاعها، عينا،[728] سبعة دنانير وسدس وثمن ودانق:
هلالي، خمسة دنانير.
مراعي راتب، دينار واحد ونصف.
ما يخص اقطاع الامير جمال الدين بن الهمام من وجوه العين، ثلثان وثمن ودانق.

غلة، ثمانمائة اردب وسدس وثمن:
قمح، اربعمائة وستة وسبعون اردبا ونصف.
شعير، مائتان وستة وثلاثون اردبا ونصف وثلث.
فول، ثمانون اردبا ونصف وثلث.
سمسم، ستة ارادب وثمن.[729]

[727] ساقط من أ. س.: نصف وثلث.
[728] ساقط من أ. س.: عينا.
[729] ساقط من أ. س.: وثمن.

harvest fee, 53 dirhams;
protection fee, 15 dirhams;
threshing-floor fee, 16 ½ ¼ ⅛ dirhams; and in grains, as specified.
The measurement fee, 13 ardabbs:
wheat, 9 ardabbs;
barley, 4 ardabbs.
The pasture fee on seasonal pasture lands, 24 ¼ ⅛ dirhams:
at the rate of 25 dirhams per 100 [heads], for 78 heads, 19 ½ dirhams;
the government agents' fee, 4 ½ ¼ ⅛ dirhams.

The alms-tax, for the monetary value of four heads of livestock, 4 ½ dinars:
cows, one two-year old cow, 2 dinars;
monetary value of small cattle, for three heads, 2 ½ dinars:
sheep, for two heads, 2 dinars;
goats, for one head, ½ dinar.

Hay, 923 bales.

The fee of the overseer of the canal, 1 ⅔ ardabb:
wheat, ½ ⅓ [ardabb];
barley, ½ ⅓ [ardabb].

For the Ministry of Endowments, 3 dinars.

The chickens reared in it, 560 birds:
for the prosperous Dīwān, including the rearing wage of a third, 360 birds;
for the *iqṭāʿ*-holders, 200 birds.

The barley assigned for the royal stables and paid for in advance, 100 ardabbs.

Its people sow 2 ⅙ feddans of sugarcane, assigned for the press at Dumūshiyya.

Also beginning with the letter 'shīn': Shidmūh,[229] included in the accounts of Dilya Canal. This is a medium-sized village, with enclosures of date palms, a few vineyards, plantations and acacias. Winter crops are sown, and summer crops used to be sown until the [cultivation] of sugarcane increased. It lies in the south of the province, three hours' ride from Madīnat al-Fayyūm. It is included in the combined fiscal value, in army dinars, of the *iqṭāʿ* of the Dilya Canal. It is allocated water from that canal — 8 ½ ⅓ *qabḍas* — out of the water channelled to the divisor known as al-Qalanbū. Its people are the Banū Qurīṭ and Shākir, a branch of the Banū Kilāb.

Its revenue in specie is 7 ⅙ ⅛ 1/144 dinars:
lunar-calendar taxes, 5 dinars;
tax on permanent pasture lands, 1 ½ dinar;
revenues in cash that go to the *iqṭāʿ* of the amir Jamāl al-Dīn ibn al-Humām, ⅔ ⅛ 1/144 [of a dinar].

[Its revenues] in grains, 800 ⅙ ⅛ ardabbs:
wheat, 476 ½ ardabbs;
barley, 236 ½ ⅓ ardabbs;
broad beans, 80 ½ ⅓ ardabbs;
sesame, 6 ⅛ ardabbs.

[229] Modern location: Shidmūh (شدموه). Halm, *Ägypten*, p. 269: Shadamūh; Salmon, 'Répertoire', pp. 69–70; Ibn al-Jīʿān, *Kitāb al-tuḥfa*, p. 156: Sharamūh; de Sacy, *État des provinces*, p. 683: Sharmūh; Ramzī, *Al-Qāmūs*, II/III, 85: Shidmūh.

وعليها من الرسوم والكيالة والمراعي، عن مائة وسبعة وخمسين درهما ونصف وثمن، ثلاثة دنانير وثلثان وربع ونصف قيراط، وغلة احد وخمسون اردبا ونصف وربع ونصف قيراط:

قمح، اربعة وثلاثون اردبا ونصف ونصف قيراط.

شعير، احد عشر اردبا ونصف وثلث ونصف قيراط.

فول، خمسة ارادب وثلث ونصف ثمن.

تفصيله:

الرسوم، مائة وتسعة وثلاثون درهما ونصف وربع وثمن، وغلة، تسعة وعشرون اردبا ونصف وربع ونصف قيراط:

قمح، اربعة عشر اردبا ونصف ونصف قيراط.

شعير، تسعة ارادب ونصف وثلث ونصف قيراط.

فول، ثلاثة ارادب وثلث ونصف ثمن.

تفصيله:

شد العين، اربعة دراهم ونصف.

رسم الحصاد، ثلاثة وخمسون درهما.

رسم الخفارة، خمسة عشر درهما.

رسم الجراريف، ثلاثة وثلاثون درهما ونصف وربع.

شد الاحباس، ثمانية دراهم.

رسم الاجران، خمسة وعشرون درهما ونصف وثمن، وغلة، تسعة وعشرون اردبا[730] ونصف وربع ونصف قيراط:

قمح، اربعة عشر اردبا ونصف ونصف قيراط.

شعير، تسعة ارادب ونصف وثلث ونصف قيراط.

فول، ثلاثة ارادب وثلث ونصف ثمن.

الكيالة، اثنان وعشرون اردبا:

قمح، عشرون اردبا.

شعير، اردبان.

المراعي، طارئ، عن ثمانية وعشرين راسا، سبعة عشر درهما ونصف وربع:

قطيعة درهم واحد الراس، عن اثنى عشر راس[731] اثنا عشر درهما.

قطيعة خمسة وعشرين درهما المائة، عن ستة عشر راسا، اربعة دراهم.

رسم المستخدمين، درهم واحد ونصف وربع.

وعليها من الزكاة، عينا، خمسة دنانير وثمن. تفصيله:

خرص العنب، دينار واحد.

ثمن الاغنام، عن[732] خمسة ارؤس، اربعة دنانير وثمن:

بياض، عن ثلاثة ارؤس، ثلاثة دنانير وثمن.

شعارى، عن راسين دينار واحد.

وعليها من الاتبان، ستمائة وثمانون شنيفا.

رسم خولي البحر بها، اردب واحد وثلثان، قمح وشعير نصفان.

وعليها لديوان الاحباس، عينا، اربعة دنانير.

المربى بها من الفروج، ستمائة وخمسة وسبعون طائرا. تفصيله:

للديوان المعمور، بما فيه من اجرة التربية وهو الثلث، ثلاثمائة وستون طائرا.

للمقطعين، ثلاثمائة وخمسة عشر طائرا.

The fees, the measurement fee and the pasture fee are 157 ½ ⅛ dirhams, which are 3 ⅔ ¼ 1/48 dinars; and in grains, 51 ½ ¼ 1/48 ardabbs:

wheat, 34 ½ 1/48 ardabbs;

barley, 11 ½ ⅓ 1/48 ardabbs;

broad beans, 5 ⅓ 1/16 ardabbs.

[The fees, the measurement fee and the pasture fee] in detail:

the fees, 139 ½ ¼ ⅛ dirhams; and in grains, 29 ½ ¼ 1/48 ardabbs:

wheat, 14 ½ 1/48 ardabbs;

barley, 9 ½ ⅓ 1/48 ardabbs;

broad beans, 3 ⅓ 1/16 ardabbs.

[The fees] in detail:

supervision of the land survey, 4 ½ dirhams;

harvest fee, 53 dirhams;

protection fee, 15 dirhams;

dredging fee, 33 ½ ¼ dirhams;

supervision of endowments, 8 dirhams;

threshing-floor fee, 25 ½ ⅛ dirhams; and in grains, 29 ½ ¼ 1/48 ardabbs:

wheat, 14 ½ 1/48 ardabbs;

barley, 9 ½ ⅓ 1/48 ardabbs;

broad beans, 3 ⅓ 1/16 ardabbs.

The measurement fee, 22 ardabbs:

wheat, 20 ardabbs;

barley, 2 ardabbs.

The pasture fee on seasonal pasture lands, for 28 heads, 17 ½ ¼ dirhams:

at the rate of one dirham per head, for 12 heads, 12 dirhams;

at the rate of 25 dirhams per 100 [heads], for 17 heads, 4 dirhams;

the government agents' fee, 1 ½ ¼ dirhams.

The alms-tax, in specie, 5 ⅛ dinars:

estimate of grapes, 1 dinar;

monetary value of small cattle, for five heads, 4 ⅛ dinars:

sheep, for three heads, 3 ⅛ dinars;

goats, for two heads, 1 dinar.

Hay, 680 bales.

Fee of the overseer of the canal, 1 ⅔ ardabb, wheat and barley, half in each.

For the Ministry of Endowments, in specie, 4 dinars.

The chickens reared in it, 675 birds:

for the prosperous Dīwān, including the rearing wage of a third, 360 birds;

for the *iqṭāʿ*-holders, 315 birds.

730 ط. م.: ادربا.

731 ساقط من أ. س: سبعة عشر درهما ونصف وربع. قطيعة درهم واحد الرأس، عن اثنى عشر رأس .

732 ساقط من أ. س.: عن.

والمسلف عليه بها من الشعير برسم الاصطبلات السلطانية، اربعون اردبا.

اهلها يزرعون من القصب السكر الراس برسم معصرة دموشية، فدانا واحدا ونصفا.

ومن حرف الصاد، صنوفر. هذه البلدة عبارة عن بلدة صغيرة وهي من البلاد العتق قريبة من بحر الفيوم من شرقيه. تشتمل على نخل كثير واشجار وجميز وبساتين متعددة لملاكها قريبة من المدينة. بينها وبين مدينة الفيوم ساعة للراكب. وعبرتها جيشية الف وسبعمائة وخمسون دينارا. جارية في اقطاع اصحاب الطواشي شهاب الدين رشيد الصغير. شربها من خليج من البر[733] البحري برسم الناحية صورة مسقاة بغير عبرة بحكم علو الارض، للشتوي خاصة خارجا من السواقي. ولها خليجان صورة مساقي بغير بنيان ولا عبرة. عليها ساقيتان معروفتان لزراعة الخضر احداهما عامرة والاخرى معطلة.

ارتفاعها عينا مما جميعه مستخرجا ومتحصلا خمسة وخمسون دينارا:

مراعي، خمسة دنانير.

خراج الراتب عن البساتين، خمسون دينارا.

غلة، مشاطرة، احد وعشرون اردبا:

قمح، سبعة ارادب.

شعير، اربعة عشر اردبا.

عليها من الرسوم والكيالة والمراعي، عن مائة واربعة وتسعين درهما ونصف وربع، اربعة دنانير ونصف وثلث ونصف قيراط وحبة. وغلة، ثمانية ارادب وقيراط ونصف. تفصيله:

قمح، اربعة ارادب وخمسة قراريط.

شعير، ثلاثة ارادب وقيراطان.

فول، نصف وربع ونصف قيراط.

تفصيله:

الرسوم، مائة وستة وخمسون درهما وربع، وغلة، سبعة ارادب وسدس ونصف ثمن. تفصيله:

قمح، ثلاثة ارادب وثلث وربع وثمن.

شعير، اردبان ونصف وربع.

فول، نصف وربع ونصف قيراط.

تفصيله:

شد العين، اثنان وثلاثون درهما.

شد الاحباس، خمسة دراهم.

رسم الجراريف، خمسة واربعون درهما.

رسم الخفارة، خمسة عشر درهما.

رسم الحصاد، ثلاثة وخمسون درهما.

رسم الاجران، ستة دراهم وربع، والغلة.

كيالة، نصف وثلث اردب:

قمح، نصف اردب

شعير، ثلث اردب.

[733] أ. س.: البحر.

The barley assigned for the royal stables and paid for in advance, 40 ardabbs.

Its people sow 1 ½ feddans of first harvest sugarcane, assigned for the press at Dumūshiyya.

Beginning with the letter 'ṣād': Ṣunūfar.[230] This is a small village, one of the ancient villages, located near the Main Canal, on its eastern side, one hour's ride from Madīnat al-Fayyūm. It has many date palms, trees, sycamores and numerous orchards in private ownership near the city. Its fiscal value is 1,750 army dinars. It is assigned as an *iqṭāʿ* to the followers (*aṣḥāb*) of the *ṭawāshī* Shihāb al-Dīn Rashīd al-Ṣaghīr.[231] It gets its water from a canal assigned to the village, [which issues] from the northern bank [of the Main Canal]. This canal is in the form of an irrigation ditch without quota, due to the elevation of the land. [This canal is] solely for winter crops, not for the waterwheels. It has two other canals which resemble irrigation ditches, without weirs or water quota, over which there are two well-known waterwheels for the cultivation of green [vegetables]. One of the waterwheels is in use and the other is not.

Its revenues in cash and in kind are, in specie, 55 dinars:

pasture tax, 5 dinars;

land tax on perennial plants, on orchards, 50 dinars;

and in grains, *mushāṭara* land tax, 21 ardabbs:

wheat, 7 ardabbs;

barley, 14 ardabbs.

The fees, the measurement fee and the pasture fee are 194 ½ ¼ dirhams, which are 4 ½ ⅓ 1/48 1/72 dinars; and in grains, 8 1/24 1/48 ardabbs:

wheat, 4 5/24 ardabbs;

barley, 3 2/24 ardabbs;

broad beans, ½ ¼ 1/48 [ardabb].

[The fees, the measurement fee and the pasture fee] in detail:

the fees, 156 ¼ dirhams; and in grains, 7 ⅙ 1/16 ardabbs:

wheat, 3 ⅓ ¼ ⅛ ardabbs;

barley, 2 ½ ¼ ardabbs;

broad beans, ½ ¼ 1/48 [ardabb].

[the fees] in detail:

supervision of the land survey, 32 dirhams;

supervision of endowments, 5 dirhams;

dredging fee, 45 dirhams;

protection fee, 15 dirhams;

harvest fee, 53 dirhams;

threshing-floor fee, 6 ¼ dirhams; and in grains [as specified].

the measurement fee ½ ⅓ ardabb:

wheat, ½ ardabb;

barley, ⅓ ardabb.

[230] Moderm location: ʿIzbat Sunūfar (عزبة سنوفر). Timm, *Das Christlich-Koptische Ägypten*, p. 2035: Pseouenaphris (Ṣunūfar in Arabic); Halm, *Ägypten*, pp. 270–71; Salmon, 'Répertoire', p. 40: Ṣinūfar; Savigny, *Description de l'Égypte*, p. 127; Ibn Mammātī, *Kitāb qawānīn al-dawāwīn*, p. 150: Sanaufar; Ibn al-Jīʿān, *Kitāb al-tuḥfa*, p. 156; Ramzī, *Al-Qāmūs*, II/III, 101: ʿIzbat Sunūfar.

[231] Not identified in contemporary chronicles. Probably not the same as the senior *ṭawāshī* Shihāb al-Dīn Rashīd al-Kabīr, mentioned elsewhere in this treatise.

المراعي والرسوم طارئ، عن مائة واثنى عشر راسا، ثمانية وثلاثون درهما ونصف. تفصيله:

المراعي، قطيعة خمسة وعشرين درهما المائة، احد وثلاثون درهما ونصف.

رسم المستخدمين، سبعة دراهم.

عليها من الزكاة، ستة دنانير ونصف:

خرص النخل، ديناران ونصف.

ثمن الاغنام، عن خمسة ارؤس، اربعة دنانير. تفصيله:

بياض، عن ثلاثة ارؤس، ثلاثة دنانير.

شعارى، عن راسين، دينار واحد.

عليها من الاتبان، مائتان وستون شنيفا.

عليها لديوان الاحباس، ديناران.

المربى بها من الفروج، مائة واحد وستون طائرا. تفصيله:

للديوان المعمور، بما فيه من اجرة التربية وهو الثلث، ثمانون طائرا.

للمقطعين، احد وثمانون طائرا.

والذي جرت العادة باطلاقه لها من التقاوي برسم عمارة الناحية، ثلاثة وعشرون اردبا:

قمح، عشرة ارادب.

شعير وفول، ثلاثة عشر اردبا.

حرف الضاد، خل.

ومن[734] حرف الطاء، طما. هذه البلدة عبارة عن بيتين[735] في ارض براح، قبالة معصرة منشية[736] قاي. تزرع الحبوب الشتوية وتروى ري الريف من النيل لا من سقي كاراضي الفيوم. وهي شرقي الفيوم الى القبلة، بينها وبين مدينة الفيوم مسافة ثلاث ساعات للراكب. جارية في الخاص. اهلها بنو زرعة، فخذ من بني[737] لواتة [= عجلان].[738]

ارتفاعها، عينا، اربعة دنانير وثمن؛ وغلة، مناجزة تسجل باسم الفقيه تاج الدين ابن الشيخ ابي عبد الله محمد القرطبي.

عينا، عن اجرة المعدية، اربعة دنانير وثمن؛

وغلة، ثمانون اردبا، نصفان، قمح وشعير.

عليها من الرسوم والكيالة والمراعي، عن اربعة[739] واربعين درهما وثمن، دينار واحد وقيراطان ونصف، وجلبان خمسة ارادب. تفصيله:

رسم الاجران، ثلاثة دراهم ونصف وربع، وجلبان اربعة ارادب ونصف وثمن.

المراعي، اربعون درهما وربع وثمن.

734 ساقط من أ. س.: ومن.

735 أ. س.: بلدين.

736 أ. س.: منشاية.

737 ساقط من ط. م.: بني.

738 أ. س.; ط. م.: لواتة.

739 ساقط من أ. س.: أربعة.

the pasture fee and the fees [*sic*] on seasonal pasture lands, for 120 heads, 38 ½ dirhams:

the pasture fee at the rate of 25 dirhams per 100 [heads], 31 ½ dirhams;

the government agents' fee, 7 dirhams.

The alms-tax, 6 ½ dinars:

estimate of dates, 2 ½ dinars;

monetary value of small cattle, for five heads, 4 dinars:

sheep, for three heads, 3 dinars;

goats, for two heads, 1 dinar.

Hay, 260 bales.

For the Ministry of Endowments, 2 dinars.

The chickens reared in it, 161 birds:

for the prosperous Dīwān, including the rearing wage of a third, 80 birds;

for the *iqṭāʿ*-holders, 81 birds.

The seed advances customarily distributed in it for the village's cultivation, 23 ardabbs:

Wheat, 10 ardabbs;

barley and broad beans, 13 ardabbs.

The letter 'ḍād', blank [no village entry for this letter].

Beginning with the letter 'ṭāʾ': Ṭimā.[232] This village consists of two units (*baytayn*)[233] in an open tract of land, opposite the press of Munshaʾat Qāy. Winter cereals are sown in it. It is watered from the Nile in the manner of Lower Egypt, not irrigated in the manner of the Fayyum. It lies in the south-east, three hours' ride from Madīnat al-Fayyūm. It is assigned to the private domain of the Sultan. Its people are the Banū Zarʿa, a branch of the Banū Lawāta [= ʿAjlān].[234]

Its revenue in specie is 4 ⅛ dinars; and in grains, in *munājaza* land tax registered in the name (*tusajjal bi-ism*) of the jurist Tāj al-Dīn, son of the Shaykh Abū ʿAbdallāh Muḥammad al-Qurṭubī.[235]

[The revenues in detail]:

in specie, from the ferryboat rent, 4 ⅛ dinars;

in grains, 80 ardabbs, wheat and barley, half in each.

The fees, the measurement fee and the pasture fee are 44 ⅛ dirhams, which are 1 5/48 dinar; and in chickling vetch, 5 ardabbs:

threshing-floor fee, 3 ½ ¼ dirhams; and chickling vetch, 4 ½ ⅛ ardabbs;[236]

the pasture fee, 40 ¼ ⅛ dirhams.

232 Modern location: Ṭimā Fayyūm (طما فيوم). de Sacy, *État des provinces*, p. 683; Halm, *Ägypten*, p. 275; Salmon, 'Répertoire', p. 37; Ibn al-Jīʿān, *Kitāb al-tuḥfa*, p. 156; Ramzī, *Al-Qāmūs*, II/III, 162: Ṭimā Fayyūm.

233 AS: *baladayn* (two settlements).

234 AS and MP: Lawāta.

235 The celebrated Qurʾān commentator Abū ʿAbdallāh al-Qurṭubī, who died in Munyat Abī al-Khaṣīb, Upper Egypt, in 1272, and the most famous scholar associated with the Fayyum during the Ayyubid period. An anecdote reported by al-Ṣafadī has al-Qurṭubī visiting the Fayyum together with another famous Mālikī scholar, Shihāb al-Dīn al-Qarāfī. See Ṣalāḥ al-Dīn Khalīl ibn Aybak al-Ṣafadī, *Kitāb al-wāfī bi'l-wafayāt*, ed. by H. Ritter and S. Dedering (Istanbul/ Damascus/Wiesbaden: [n. pub.], 1949), II, 122 (no. 470). The jurist mentioned here is most likely his son.

236 Does not match the total ardabbs in the line above.

وعليها من الزكاة باسم المنتجعين اليها عن ثمن الاغنام، عن تسعة اروس، سبعة دنانير وربع:

بياض، عن خمسة اروس، خمسة دنانير وثمن.

شعارى، اربعة اروس، ديناران وثمن.

وعليها من الاتبان، ثمانون شنيفا.

والذي بها من التقاوي الديوانية، احد وخمسون اردبا:

قمح، ستة وعشرون اردبا.

فول، عشرة ارادب ونصف.

جلبان، اربعة عشر اردبا ونصف.

ومن حرف الطاء، طليت، من حقوق خليج تنبطويه، هذه البلدة عبارة عن بلدة مستجدة، قليلة السكان، تشتمل على نخيل محدث ما اطعم بعد وعلى دويرات تين محدثة اطعمت. وكانت هذه البلدة بلدة كبيرة عامرة دثرت على ما يقال من غلاء المستنصر. ثم استولى عليها السافي فردمها. واحدث في ذيل اراضيها هذه البيوت المستجدة. وهي قبلي الفيوم، بينها وبين مدينة الفيوم نصف نهار للراكب. وهي جارية في اقطاع جماعة من المقطعين بمعاملة[740] الرسوم والمراعي بغير عبرة. لها من الماء من خليج من[741] بحر تنبطويه مستجد في ايام الامير فخر الدين، عبرته عشرون قبضة. اهلها بنو حاتم فخذ من بني كلاب.

ارتفاعها، عينا، ثمانية دنانير وثلثان وربع ونصف قيراط وحبة؛ وغلة، سبعمائة وثلاثة وثمانون اردبا وسدس. تفصيله:

قمح، مائة وخمسة ارادب.

وشعير، ستمائة وسبعة عشر اردبا وثلث وثمن.

وسمسم، ستون اردبا وثلث وربع وثمن.

تفصيل ذلك:[742]

وجوه العين عن اجرة الحانوت المختص بالديوان وخراج الراتب والحكر، ثمانية دنانير وثلثان وربع ونصف قيراط وحبة.

زراعة الاواسي الديوانية، خمسمائة واربعة وسبعون اردبا وسدس. تفصيله:

شعير، خمسمائة وثلاثة عشر اردبا وثلث وثمن.

سمسم، ستون اردبا وثلث وربع وثمن.

المشاطرة عما هو جار في اقطاع المقطعين، مائتان وتسعة ارادب:

قمح، مائة وخمسة ارادب

شعير، مائة واربعة ارادب.

عليها من الرسوم والكيالة والمراعي، خمسة دنانير وقيراط وحبتان، وغلة، ستة وثلاثون اردبا وثلثان وثمن:

قمح، احد وعشرون اردبا ونصف وربع.

شعير، اثنا عشر اردبا وثلث وربع وثمن.

وسمسم، اردبان وثلث.

740 أ. س.: لمعاملة.

741 ساقط من أ. س.: من.

742 أ. س.: تفصيله.

The alms-tax, levied on those seeking pasture in it, for the monetary value of nine heads of small cattle, 7 ¼ dinars:

sheep, for five heads, 5 ⅛ dinars;

goats, four heads, 2 ⅛ dinars.

Hay, 80 bales.

The seed advances from the Dīwān, 51 ardabbs:

wheat, 26 ardabbs;

broad beans, 10 ½ ardabbs;

chickling vetch, 14 ½ ardabbs.

Also beginning with the letter 'ṭāʾ': Ṭalīt,[237] included in the accounts of Tanabṭawayh Canal. It is a new village, with few inhabitants. It has recent date-palm plantations, which have not yet borne fruit, and enclosures of recently planted fig trees, which have borne fruit. This village used to be large and populated, but it was deserted — so it is said — because of the shortages (*al-ghalāʾ*) during the days of al-Mustanṣir [Fatimid caliph, r. 428–87/AD 1036–94]. Then it was overtaken by dust and covered in it. Those new houses were then built on the edge of its lands. It is half a day's ride south of Madīnat al-Fayyūm. It is assigned as an *iqṭāʿ* to a group of *iqṭāʿ*-holders, including the revenue from fees and pasture fees, without a fiscal value. It gets water from a new canal [dug] in the days of the amir Fakhr al-Dīn, which issues from Tanabṭawayh Canal. Its [water] quota is 20 *qabḍas*. Its people are the Banū Ḥātim, a branch of the Banū Kilāb.

Its revenue in specie is 8 ⅔ ¼ 1/48 1/72 dinars; and in grains, 783 ⅙ ardabbs:

wheat, 105 ardabbs;

barley, 617 ⅓ ⅛ ardabbs;

sesame, 60 ⅓ ¼ ⅛ ardabbs.

[The revenue] in detail:

taxes in cash, including the rent of the shop that belongs to the Dīwān and the land tax on perennial plants and on lands subject to long-term lease, 8 ⅔ ¼ 1/48 1/72 dinars;

cultivation of the crown estates, 574 ⅙ ardabbs:

barley, 513 ⅓ ⅛ ardabbs;

sesame, 60 ⅓ ¼ ⅛ ardabbs.

Mushāṭara land tax on the lands that belong to the *iqṭāʿ* of the *iqṭāʿ*-holders, 209 ardabbs:

wheat, 105 ardabbs;

barley, 104 ardabbs.

The fees, the measurement fee and the pasture fee, 5 1/24 2/72 dinars; and in grains, 36 ⅔ ⅛ ardabbs:

wheat, 21 ½ ¼ ardabbs;

barley, 12 ⅓ ¼ ⅛ ardabbs;

sesame, 2 ⅓ ardabbs.

237 Modern location (uncertain): ʿIzbat ʿAbd al-Ghanī Abū Jalīl (عزبة عبد الغني ابو جليل). Timm, *Das Christlich-Koptische Ägypten*, pp. 2474–5: Talithis (Ṭalīt in Arabic); Trismegistos GEO ID 2236; Halm, *Ägypten*, p. 274; Salmon, 'Répertoire', p. 71; Ibn al-Jīʿān, *Kitāb al-tuḥfa*, p. 154: Ṭalīb; de Sacy, *État des provinces*, p. 682; Ramzī, *Al-Qāmūs*, I, 313: Kawm Ṭalīt, south of Dānīyāl in the lands of district of al-Gharq. We did not find Kawm Ṭalīt, so we located it in the modern village of ʿIzbat ʿAbd al-Ghanī Abū Jalīl, in line with Shafei Bey's map and with the Trismegistos project map. See 'Trismegistos Geo'<http://www.trismegistos.org/geo/detail.php?tm = 2236> [accessed 19 December 2017].

[تفصيله]:
رسم الاجران، ثمانية عشر درهما ونصف وربع، وغلة، اثنان وعشرون اردبا ونصف وثلث وثمن.
تفصيله:
قمح، ثلاثة عشر اردبا ونصف وربع.
شعير، سبعة ارادب وثلث وربع وثمن.
سمسم، اردب واحد ونصف.
الكيالة، ثلاثة عشر اردبا ونصف وثلث:
قمح، ثمانية ارادب.
شعير، خمسة ارادب.
سمسم، نصف وثلث اردب.
المراعي الطارئ، عن مائتين وخمسة وثلاثين راسا، مائة وثلاثة وثمانون درهما ونصف وربع وثمن. تفصيله:
قطيعة مائة درهم المائة، عن ستة[743] وتسعين راسا، ستة[744] وتسعون درهما.
قطيعة سبعين درهما المائة، عن اربعة وستين راسا، اربعة واربعون درهما ونصف وربع.
قطيعة خمسين درهما المائة، عن ثلاثين راسا، خمسة عشر درهما.
قطيعة ثلاثين درهما المائة، عن خمسة واربعين راسا، ثلاثة عشر درهما ونصف.
رسم المستخدمين، اربعة عشر درهما ونصف وثمن.

وعليها من الزكاة عن ثمن الاغنام، عن عشرة اروس، خمسة دنانير:
بياض، عن ثلاثة اروس، ثلاثة دنانير وثمن.
شعارى، عن سبعة اروس، دينار واحد ونصف وربع وثمن.

وعليها من الاتبان، اربعمائة شنيف.

رسم خولي البحر بها، قمح، اردب واحد.

والمربى بها من الفروج للديوان السلطاني السعيد، خارجا عن اجرة التربية وهو الثلث، ثلاثمائة طائر.

والمسلف عليه بها من الشعير برسم الاصطبلات السلطانية، خمسة وخمسون اردبا.

والذي بها من التقاوي الديوانية، بما فيه من بذار[745] اوسية الشعير الديوانية وهو خمسون اردبا، ثلاثمائة واردب واحد وثلث وربع ونصف ثمن وربع قيراط. تفصيله:
قمح، مائتان واردبان وثلث وربع وثمن.
شعير، ستة وسبعون اردبا ونصف.
فول، عشرون اردبا.
سمسم، اردبان وربع وسدس.
نيلة، نصف وربع قيراط.

ومن حرف الطاء، طبهار. هذه البلدة عبارة عن بلدة متوسطة تشتمل على بساتين وكروم ونخيل وتين. تزرع الشتوي لا غير. اراضيها عالية لا يصل اليها الماء الا بكلفة ويقل عنها عند احتراق الماء وربما عدمته بالكلية فيشرب اهلها من الابار.

743 أ. س.: سبعة.
744 أ. س.: سبعة.
745 أ. س.: بدار.

[The fees, the measurement fee and the pasture fee] in detail:
threshing-floor fee, 18 ½ ¼ dirhams; and in grains, 22 ½ ⅓ ⅛ ardabbs:
wheat, 13 ½ ¼ ardabbs;
barley, 7 ⅓ ¼ ⅛ ardabbs;
sesame, 1 ½ ardabbs.
The measurement fee, 13 ½ ⅓ ardabbs:
wheat, 8 ardabbs;
barley, 5 ardabbs;
sesame ½ ⅓ ardabb.
The pasture fee on seasonal pasture lands, for 235 heads, 183 ½ ¼ ⅛ dirhams:
at the rate of 100 dirhams per 100 [heads], for 96 heads, 96 dirhams;
at the rate of 70 dirhams per 100 [heads], for 64 heads, 44 ½ ¼ dirhams;
at the rate of 50 dirhams per 100 [heads], for 30 heads, 15 dirhams;
at the rate of 30 dirhams per 100 [heads], for 45 heads, 13 ½ dirhams;
the government agents' fee, 14 ½ ⅛ dirhams.

The alms-tax, for the monetary value of ten heads of small cattle, 5 dinars:
sheep, for three heads, 3 ⅛ dinars;
goats, for seven heads, 1 ½ ¼ ⅛ dinar.

Hay, 400 bales.

The fee for the overseer of the canal, wheat, 1 ardabb.

The chickens reared in it for the blessed royal Dīwān, excluding the rearing wage of a third, 300 birds.

The barley assigned for the royal stables and paid for in advance, 55 ardabbs.

The seed advances from the Dīwān, including 50 ardabbs of seeds to the barley crown estate, 301 ⅓ ¼ 1/16 1/96 ardabbs:
wheat, 202 ⅓ ¼ ⅛ ardabbs;
barley, 76 ½ ardabbs;
broad beans, 20 ardabbs;
sesame, 2 ¼ ⅙ ardabbs;
indigo, ½ 1/96 [ardabb].

Also beginning with the letter 'ṭāʾ': Ṭubhār.[238] This is a medium-sized village, with orchards, vineyards, date palms and figs. Winter crops are sown in it, but nothing else. Its lands are elevated and water does not reach them without additional effort. Water supply is scanty when the [Nile] water is at its lowest (*iḥtirāq al-māʾ*), and it may even cease altogether. During this period of seepage, its people drink from wells, and [additional] water is allocated to it when the vineyards are in need.

238 Modern location: Ṭubhār (طبهار). Halm, *Ägypten*, p. 275; Salmon, 'Répertoire', p. 58; Zéki, 'Une description', p. 44; de Sacy, *État des provinces*, p. 683; Savigny, *Description de l'Égypte*, p. 128; Ibn Mammātī, *Kitāb qawānīn al-dawāwīn*, p. 163; Ibn al-Jīʿān, *Kitāb al-tuḥfa*, p. 156: Ṭibhār; Ramzī, *Al-Qāmūs*, II/III, 73: Ṭubhār.

وتطلق[746] لها المياه عند حاجة الكروم اليها في زمن الاحتراق. وهي غربي الفيوم، بينها وبين مدينة الفيوم ثلاث ساعات للراكب. جارية في اقطاع جماعة من المقطعين بذات الصفاء. عبرتها في ديوان الجيوش المنصورة ثلاثة الاف ومائة وخمسون دينارا جيشية، تنقسم على عبرة مبلغها اربعون الف دينارا. والمطلق لها من الماء من خليج من المقسم الذي اخر[747] البحر الاعظم اليوسفي من الجهة البحرية شركة ابي كسا وبيبج انشو وابشاية[748] وجردو. والذي يخص الناحية ثمان قبض ماء. وبها جامع تقام فيه الجمعة. اهلها بنو غصين، فخذ من بني كلاب.

ارتفاعها، عينا، مما جميعه مستخرجا ومتحصلا، ستة وتسعون دينارا ونصف؛ غلة، الف وستمائة وسبعون اردبا وربع وثمن. تفصيله:

قمح، ثمانمائة ستة وثلاثون[749] اردبا وربع وثمن.

شعير، سبعمائة واحد وعشرون اردبا.

كمون، مائة وثلاثة ارادب.

سلجم، عشرة ارادب.

تفصيله:

مال الهلالي، عن اجرة الحانوت، اثنا عشر دينارا ونصف.

مال المراعي، اربعة دنانير.

خراج الراتب، ثمانون دينارا:

كرم كامل، عن ثمانية فدادين وقيراط ونصف وحبة، ثمانية واربعون دينارا وثلث وثمن.

شجر، عن سبعة فدادين وثلثين، ستة عشر دينارا ونصف.

قطن، عن ثلاثة فدادين وربع ونصف ثمن وحبة، خمسة دنانير ونصف وربع.

قصب فارسي، عن سدس ونصف ثمن وربع قيراط ربع وسدس وحبة.

نخل، عن مائتين[750] وثلاثة واربعين نخلة، سبعة دنانير وثلث وربع.

حكر، عن فدان واحد وثلث وثمن، دينار ونصف وثمن وحبتان.

مناجزة الغلات، الف وستمائة وسبعون اردبا وربع وثمن، على ما فصل.

عليها من الرسوم والكيالة والمراعي، عن خمسمائة وخمسة عشر درهما ونصف وثمن، اثنا عشر دينارا ونصف وثلث ونصف ثمن؛ وغلة، مائة وخمسة وعشرون اردبا وثلثان ونصف ثمن. تفصيله:

قمح، سبعة وستون اردبا[751] وثلث وربع ونصف قيراط.

وشعير، اثنان وخمسون اردبا وسدس وثمن.

وكمون، خمسة ارادب ونصف وثلث.

It lies in the west of the province, three hours' ride from Madīnat al-Fayyūm. It is assigned as an *iqṭāʿ* to some of the *iqṭāʿ*-holders of Dhāt al-Ṣafāʾ. Its fiscal value, according to the Dīwān of the army, is 3,150 army dinars, which is part of (*tanqasimu ʿalā*) a total fiscal value of 40,000 dinars.[239] Water is allocated to it from a canal, shared with Abū Ksā, Babīj Unshū, Ibshāyat [al-Rummān] and Jardū, which branches off from a divisor at the edge of the Main Canal, from the northern side. The village has rights to 8 *qabḍas* of water. It has a congregational mosque, in which the Friday prayers are held. Its people are the Banū Ghuṣayn, a branch of the Banū Kilāb.

Its revenues in cash and in kind are, in specie, 96 ½ dinars; and in grains, 1,670 ¼ ⅛ ardabbs:

wheat, 836 ¼ ⅛ ardabbs;

barley, 721 ardabbs;

cumin, 103 ardabbs;

rape, 10 ardabbs.

[The revenue] in detail:

lunar-calendar tax for the rent of the shop, 12 ½ dinars;

pasture tax, 4 dinars;

land tax on perennial plants, 80 dinars:

fully-grown vineyards, for 8 1/24 1/48 1/72 feddans, 48 ⅓ ⅛ dinars;

trees, for 7 ⅔ feddans, 16 ½ dinars;

cotton, for 3 ¼ 1/16 1/72 feddans, 5 ½ ¼ dinars;

Persian sugarcane (*qaṣab fārisī*), for ⅙ 1/16 1/96 [feddan], ¼ ⅙ 1/72 [dinar];

date palms, for 243[240] date palm trees, 7 ⅓ ¼ dinars;

[land tax on] lands subject to long-term lease, for 1 ⅓ ⅛ feddan, 1 ½ ⅛ 2/72 dinar.

Munājaza land tax, in grains, 1,670 ¼ ⅛ ardabbs, as specified.

The fees, the measurement fee and the pasture fee are 515 ½ ⅛ dirhams, which are 12 ½ ⅓ 1/16 dinars; and in grains, 125 ⅔ 1/16 ardabbs:

wheat, 67 ⅓ ¼ 1/48 ardabbs;

barley, 52 ⅙ ⅛ ardabbs;

cumin, 5 ½ ⅓ ardabbs.

746 أ. س.: ويطلق.

747 أ. س. يضيف: من.

748 أ. س.: وابشويه.

749 أ. س.: ثلاثمائة ستة وثمانون.

750 ساقط من أ. س.: مائتين.

751 ساقط من أ. س.: وثلثان ونصف ثمن تفصيله قمح سبعة وستون أردبا.

239 This a reference to the total fiscal value of a cluster of villages — most probably the other villages along the same canal that are listed in the following sentence.

240 AS: 43.

تفصيله:
الرسوم، ثلاثمائة واحد وعشرون درهما[752] وربع وثمن، وغلة، سبعة وسبعون[753] اردبا وثلثان ونصف ثمن:
قمح، خمسة واربعون اردبا وثلث وربع ونصف قيراط.
وشعير، ثمانية[754] وعشرون اردبا وسدس وثمن.
وكمون، ثلاثة ارادب ونصف وثلث.
تفصيله:
شد العين، خمسة وثمانون درهما.
شد الاحباس، اربعة عشر درهما.
رسم الجراريف،[755] تسعون درهما.
رسم الحصاد، ثلاثة وخمسون درهما.
رسم الخفارة، خمسة عشر درهما.
رسم الاجران، اربعة وستون درهما وربع وثمن، والغلة على ما فصل.
الكيالة، ثمانية واربعون اردبا:
قمح، اثنان وعشرون اردبا.
شعير، اربعة وعشرون اردبا.
كمون، اردبان.
المراعي، طارئ، عن خمسمائة وثلاثة وخمسين راسا، مائة واربعة وتسعون درهما وربع. تفصيله:
قطيعة ثلاثين درهما المائة، عن اربعمائة واحد[756] وثلاثين راسا، مائة واحد وعشرون درهما وربع.
قطيعة خمسة وعشرين درهما المائة، عن مائة واثنين وعشرين راسا، ثلاثون درهما ونصف.
رسم المستخدمين، اربعة وثلاثون درهما ونصف.

وعليها من الزكاة، اثنان وخمسون دينارا وربع وثمن. تفصيله:
الخرص، ستة واربعون دينارا ونصف. تفصيله:
خرص العنب، اربعة واربعون دينارا.
خرص النخل، ديناران ونصف.
ثمن الماشية، عن ستة ارؤس، خمسة دنانير ونصف وربع وثمن. تفصيله:
بقر احمر، تبيع واحد، ديناران وربع.
اغنام، عن خمسة ارؤس، ثلاثة دنانير ونصف وثمن. تفصيله:
بياض، عن راسين ديناران.
شعارى، ثلاثة ارؤس، دينارا واحد ونصف وثمن.

عليها لديوان الاحباس، عينا،[757] ثمانية دنانير.

عليها من الاتبان، الف وخمسمائة شنيف.

رسم خولي البحر بها، اردب واحد، قمحًا.

والمقرر على الفلاحين بها، سبعة ارادب:
كشك، ثلاثة ارادب.
وفريك، ثلاثة ارادب.
وسويق، اردب واحد.

اهلها يزرعون من الاقصاب السكر برسم معصرة ببيج انشو، ثلاثين فدانا.

[The fees, the measurement fee and the pasture fee] in detail:
the fees are 321 ¼ ⅛ dirhams; and in grains, 67[241] ⅔ 1/16 ardabbs:
wheat, 45 ⅓ ¼ 1/48 ardabbs;
barley, 28 ⅙ ⅛ ardabbs;
cumin, 3 ½ ⅓ ardabbs.
[The fees] in detail:
supervision of the land survey, 85 dirhams;
supervision of endowments, 14 dirhams;
dredging fee, 90 dirhams;
harvest fee, 53 dirhams;
protection fee, 15 dirhams;
threshing-floor fee, 64 ¼ ⅛ dirhams; and in grains, as specified.
The measurement fee, 48 ardabbs:
wheat, 22 ardabbs;
barley, 24 ardabbs;
cumin, 2 ardabbs.
The pasture fee on seasonal pasture lands, for 553 heads, 194 ¼ dirhams:
at the rate of 30 dirhams per 100 [heads], for 431 heads, 121 [= 131][242] ¼ dirhams;
at the rate of 25 dirhams per 100 [heads], for 122 heads, 30 ½ dirhams;
the government agents' fee, 34 ½ dirhams.

The alms-tax imposed, 52 ¼ ⅛ dinars:
the estimates, 46 ½ dinars:
estimate of grapes, 44 dinars;
estimate of dates, 2 ½ dinars;
monetary value of livestock, for six heads, 5 ½ ¼ ⅛ dinars:
cows, for a yearling calf, 2 ¼ dinars;
small cattle, for five heads, 3 ½ ⅛ dinars:
sheep, for two heads, 2 dinars;
goats, for three heads, 1 ½ ⅛ dinar.

For the Ministry of Endowments, in specie, 8 dinars.

Hay, 1,500 bales.

The fee of the overseer of the canal, 1 ardabb in wheat.

The established levy on the peasants (*fallaḥūn*), 7 ardabbs:
kishk, 3 ardabbs;
farīk, 3 ardabbs;
sawīq, 1 ardabb.

Its people sow 30 feddans of sugarcane, assigned for the press of Babīj Unshū.

752 أ. س.: دينارا.
753 ط. م.: وستون.
754 أ. س.: ثلاثة.
755 أ. س. يضيف: أربع وستون درهما وربع وثمن.
756 ط. م.: واحدى.
757 ساقط من ط. م.: عينا.

241 Should be 77.
242 Should be 131.

والمقرر تسليفه بالناحية من الشعير برسم الاصطبلات السلطانية، مائتا اردب.

والمربى بها من الفروج، خمسمائة طائر. تفصيله:
للديوان المعمور، بما فيه من اجرة التربية وهو الثلث، ثلاثمائة طائر.
للمقطعين، مائتا طائر.

والذي جرت العادة باطلاقه للناحية من التقاوي، مائتان واربعة وثمانون اردبا. تفصيله:
قمح، مائة وستون اردبا.
وشعير، مائة اردب.
كمون، اربعة وعشرون اردبا.

والذي بها من التقاوي الديوانية، ستة عشر اردبا وربع:
قمح، خمسة عشر اردبا.
شعير، واحد وربع.

حرف الظاء، خال.

ومن حرف العين، عنز. هذه البلدة عبارة عن بلدة صغيرة تشتمل على نخل صغير ودي. تزرع الشتوي لا غير. وهي غربي مدينة الفيوم، بينها وبين مدينة الفيوم مسافة ساعة ونصف للراكب. جارية في اقطاع المقطعين الشاهد بهم ديوان الجيوش المنصورة. عبرتها الفان وخمسمائة دينار جيشية. والمطلق لها من الماء لسقي الشتوي خاصة من خليج من البر القبلي، باب واحد، بغير عبرة. اهلها بنو جواب، فخذ من بني كلاب.

ارتفاعها، مما جميعه مستخرجا ومتحصلا، اربعة عشر دينارا. تفصيله:
مقات، ثمانية دنانير ونصف.
جزر، ثلاثة دنانير.
قرط ديناران[758] ونصف.

مشاطرة الغلة، خمسمائة وتسعة ارادب وثلثان. تفصيله:
قمح، مائة وخمسة وثمانون اردبا وثلث وربع وثمن.
شعير، مائتان واثنان وثلاثون اردبا وربع وسدس.
فول، احد وتسعون اردبا وربع وسدس وثمن.

وعليها من الرسوم والكيالة، عن مائة وعشرة دراهم ونصف وربع، ديناران ونصف وربع ونصف قيراط؛ وغلة، تسعة وعشرون اردبا ونصف وثمن. تفصيله:
قمح، تسعة ارادب ونصف وثمن.
شعير، اثنا عشر اردبا ونصف وربع وثمن.
فول، ستة ارادب ونصف وربع وثمن.

تفصيله:
الرسوم، مائة وعشرة دراهم ونصف وربع، وعشرون اردبا ونصف وثمن. تفصيله:
قمح، ستة ارادب ونصف وربع وثمن.
وشعير، ستة ارادب ونصف وربع وثمن.

758 أ. س.: دينار.

The established amount of barley in the village assigned for the royal stables and paid for in advance, 200 ardabbs.

The chickens reared in it, 500 birds:
for the prosperous Dīwān, including the rearing wage of one third, 300 birds;
for the *iqṭāʿ*-holders, 200 birds.

The seed advances customarily distributed in the locality, 284 ardabbs:
wheat, 160 ardabbs;
barley, 100 ardabbs;
cumin, 24 ardabbs.

The seed advances of the Dīwān [distributed] in it, 16 ¼ ardabbs:
wheat, 15 ardabbs;
barley, 1 ¼ ardabb.

The letter ẓāʾ, blank [no village entry for this letter].

Beginning with the letter 'ʿayn': ʿAnz.[243] This is a small village, with small shoots of date palms. Winter crops are sown in it, but nothing else. It lies an hour and a half's ride west of Madīnat al-Fayyūm. It is assigned as an *iqṭāʿ* to a group of *iqṭāʿ*-holders, whose names are attested by the Ministry of the Army. Its fiscal value is 2,500 army dinars. Water is allocated to it solely for the purpose for irrigating the winter crops, from a canal [that branches] off the southern bank [of the Main Canal], with one sluice-gate, without [water] quota. Its people are the Banū Jawwāb, a branch of the Banū Kilāb.

Its revenue in cash and in kind is, in specie, 14 dinars:
[land tax] on cucurbitaceous fruits, 8 ½ dinars;
[land tax on] carrot, 3 dinars;
[land tax on] alfalfa, 2 ½ dinars.

[and in kind], in *mushāṭara* land tax on grains, 509 ⅔ ardabbs:
wheat, 185 ⅓ ¼ ⅛ ardabbs;
barley, 232 ¼ ⅙ ardabbs;
broad beans, 91 ¼ ⅙ ⅛ ardabbs.

The fees and the measurement fee are 110 ½ ¼ dirhams, which are 2 ½ ¼ 1/48 dinars; and in grains, 29 ½ ⅛ ardabbs:
wheat, 9 ½ ⅛ ardabbs;
barley, 12 ½ ¼ ⅛ ardabbs;
broad beans, 6 ½ ¼ ⅛ ardabbs.

[The fees and the measurement fee] in detail:
the fees, 110 ½ ¼ dirhams; and [in grains], 20 ½ ⅛ ardabbs:
wheat, 6 ½ ¼ ⅛ ardabbs;
barley, 6 ½ ¼ ⅛ ardabbs;
[broad beans, 6 ½ ¼ ⅛ ardabbs].[244]

243 Modern location (uncertain): Al-Ḥamīdiyya al-Jadīda (الحميدية الجديدة). Halm, *Ägypten*, p. 246; Salmon, 'Répertoire', p. 59; de Sacy, *État des provinces*, p. 683; Ibn al-Jīʿān, *Kitāb al-tuḥfa*, p. 156; Ramzī, *Al-Qāmūs*, II/III, 102: Munshảat Fārūq (until 1929). We could not find the present day Munshảat Fārūq. In line with al-Nābulusī's description and with Shafei Bey's map, we located it near the modern village of al-Ḥamīdiyya al-Jadīda.

244 Omitted from both MP and AS but required by aggregates above.

تفصيله:
شد العين، اربعة دراهم.
رسم الحصاد، ثلاثة وخمسون درهما.
رسم الخفارة، خمسة عشر درهما.
رسم الجزر، عشرون درهما.
رسم الاجران، ثمانية عشر درهما ونصف وربع، والغلة.
الكيالة، تسعة ارادب:
قمح، ثلاثة ارادب.
شعير، ستة ارادب.

عليها من الزكاة عن ثمن شعرية، نصف دينار.

عليها من الاتبان، خمسمائة شنيف.

رسم خولي البحر بها، قمح، نصف اردب.

والمخلد بها من التقاوي للمقطعين، مائة واربعة وعشرون اردبا:
قمح، تسعة واربعون اردبا.
شعير، خمسون اردبا.
فول، خمسة وعشرون اردبا.

والمربى بها من الفروج، ثلاثمائة طائر:
للديوان المعمور، بما فيه من اجرة التربية وهو الثلث، مائة وخمسون طائرا.
وللمقطعين، مائة وخمسون طائرا.

حرف الغين، غابة باجة. هذه البلدة عبارة عن بلدة متوسطة بين الكبر والصغر، قبلي المدينة. بها نخل وسدر وسنط وصفصاف. وهي حارتين قبلية وبحرية وبحر دلية يشق وسطها. مسافتها من مدينة الفيوم مشوار فرس. داخلة في الاقطاع[759] مع باجة المقدم ذكرها للطواشي شهاب الدين رشيد الكبير بعبرة مبلغها ستة الاف دينار جيشية. اهلها بنو حاتم، فخذ من بني كلاب. والمطلق لها من الماء في خليجين ومسقاة من البر القبلي من البحر الاعظم اليوسفي، الخليج الاول عبرته خمس قبض، والخليج الثاني اربع قبض {بحكم علو اراضيها}. والمسقاة بغير بنيان ولا عبرة [بحكم علو اراضيها].[760]

ارتفاعها، عينا، ثمانية وستون دينارا وثلثان وربع ونصف ثمن وحبة، وغلة، الف وخمسمائة اردب:
قمح، ثمانمائة وسبعون اردبا.
شعير وفول، ستمائة وثلاثون اردبا.

تفصيل ذلك:
الهلالي، عن ضمان الحانوت، ستة دنانير.
المراعي، ثمانية دنانير.
الخراجي، اربعة وخمسون دينارا وثلثان وربع ونصف ثمن وحبة، والف وخمسمائة اردب على ما فصل.

[759] أ. س. يضيف: جارية.
[760] ط. م، أ. س.: بحكم علو أراضيها والمسقاة بغير بنيان ولا عبرة .

[The fees] in detail:
supervision of the land survey, 4 dirhams;
harvest fee, 53 dirhams;
protection fee, 15 dirhams;
carrot fee, 20 dirhams;
threshing-floor fee, 18 ½ ¼ dirhams; and in grains [as specified].
The measurement fee, 9 ardabbs:
wheat, 3 ardabbs;
barley, 6 ardabbs.

The alms-tax, for the monetary value of one goat, ½ dinar.

Hay, 500 bales.

The fee for the overseer of the canal, wheat, ½ ardabb.

The recorded seed advances for the *iqṭāʿ*-holders, 124 ardabbs:
wheat, 49 ardabbs;
barley, 50 ardabbs;
broad beans, 25 ardabbs.

The chickens reared in it, 300 birds:
for the prosperous Dīwān, including the rearing wage of one third, 150 birds;
for the *iqṭāʿ*-holders, 150 birds.

Beginning with the letter 'ghayn': Ghābat Bāja.[245] This is a medium-sized village, south of the city. It has date palms, sidr trees, acacias and willows. It consists of two quarters, southern and northern, and Dilya Canal cuts it in the middle. It is a short journey from Madīnat al-Fayyūm. It is included, together with the above mentioned village of Bāja, in an *iqṭāʿ* assigned to the *ṭawāshī* Shihāb al-Dīn Rashīd al-Kabīr,[246] for a fiscal value of 6,000 army dinars. Its people are the Banū Ḥātim, a branch of the Banū Kilāb.

Water is allocated to it from two canals and an irrigation ditch that issue from the southern bank of the Main Canal. The water quota in the first canal is 5 *qabḍas*; in the second canal it is 4 *qabḍas*. The irrigation ditch has no weir and no [water] quota due to the elevation of the land.

Its revenue is, in specie, 68 ⅔ ¼ 1/16 1/72 dinars; and in grains, 1,500 ardabbs:
wheat, 870 ardabbs;
barley and broad beans, 630 ardabbs.

[The revenue] in detail:
lunar-calendar tax, from the concession for the shop, 6 dinars;
pasture tax, 8 dinars;
land tax, 54 ⅔ ¼ 1/16 1/72 dinars; [and in grains] 1,500 ardabbs, as specified.

[245] Modern location (uncertain): ʿIzbat al-Sabala / Munshảat Rabīʿ / al-Ḥadiqa (الحادقة). Halm, *Ägypten*, p. 256: Ghābat Bāja = Munshảat al-Rabīʿīyīn; Salmon, 'Répertoire', pp. 65–66; Ibn al-Jīʿān, *Kitāb al-tuḥfa*, p. 156; de Sacy, *État des provinces*, p. 683; Savigny, *Description de l'Égypte*, p. 129: Manshyat Rabīʿ; Ramzī, *Al-Qāmūs*, I, 341: ʿIzbat al-Sabala, south of Madīnat al-Fayyūm. We have no positive identification of this village. We located it, in accordance with al-Nābulusī's description and with Shafei Bey's map, near the modern village of al-Ḥādiqa.

[246] One of the most prominent amirs under al-Ṣāliḥ, and a governor of Damascus in 1246. Later commander of the Egyptian army under Shajar al-Durr: Levanoni, 'The Mamluks' Ascent', 138; Humphreys, *From Saladin to the Mongols*, pp. 284, 290, 315.

المفادنات مما جميعه حكر، اربعة عشر دينارا وثلثان وربع ونصف ثمن وحبة. تفصيله:

الاصل، ثلاثة عشر دينارا وثلث وحبة.

الاضافة، دينار واحد وثلث وربع ونصف ثمن.

خراج المناجزة، اربعون دينارا، والغلة على ما تقدم.

وعليها من الرسوم والكيالة[761] والمراعي، عن اثنين وتسعين راسا ورسم المستخدمين، ستة دراهم وربع المائة راس، عن ثمانية وعشرين درهما ونصف وربع، ثلثان وحبتان; غلة، مما جميعه كيالة، اثنان وثلاثون اردبا ونصف وثلث:

قمح، اثنان وعشرون اردبا ونصف ثلث.

فول، عشرة ارادب.

عليها من الزكاة عن ثمن الماشية، عن احد عشر[762] راسا، احد عشر دينارا وثلثان وربع وحبتان. تفصيله:

بقر احمر تبيع واحد، دينار واحد ونصف وربع وثمن وحبتان.

عن الاغنام، عشرة ارؤس، عشرة دنانير وقيراط. تفصيله:

بياض عن تسعة ارؤس، تسعة دنانير ونصف.

شعارى، راس واحد، ربع وسدس وثمن دينار.

عليها من الاتبان في الضريبة، الف ومائتا شنيف.

رسم خولي البحر بها، قمح، ثلثا اردب.

والمربى بها من الفروج، خمسمائة وعشرون طائرا. تفصيله:

للديوان المعمور، بما فيه من اجرة التربية وهو الثلث، ثلاثمائة وعشرون طائرا.

للمقطعين، مائتا طائر.[763]

والذي بها من التقاوي المرتجعة للديوان المعمور، مائة وثمانية عشر اردبا. تفصيله:

قمح، اثنان وتسعون اردبا.

شعير، ثلاثة عشر اردبا.

فول، ثلاثة عشر اردبا.

والمسلف عليه بها من الشعير برسم الاصطبلات السلطانية، مائتان وخمسون اردبا.[764]

حرف الفاء، فانو. هذه البلدة عبارة عن بلدة متوسطة بين الكبر والصغر، بحري الفيوم. كانت عامرة فيما سلف فتسحب من اهلها جماعة من جور مقطعيهم. وكان بها كروم دثرت ولم يبق الا معالمها. ولها موضع يقال له الملائد. وبها حدائق نخل وتين وتفاح ومشمش وكمثرى واترج.

[Land tax assessed by] feddans, all of it from lands subject to long-term lease, 14 ⅔ ¼ 1/16 1/72 dinars:

the basic assessment, 13 ⅓ 1/72 dinars;

the addition, 1 ⅓ ¼ 1/16 dinar.

Munājaza land tax, 40 dinars; and in grains, as specified above.

The fees, the measurement fee and the pasture fee for 92 heads, 28 ½ ¼ dirhams, which are ⅔ 2/72 [dinars], including the government agents' fee at a rate of 6 ¼ dirhams per 100 heads; and in grains, all of it from the measurement fee, 32 ½ ⅓ ardabbs:

wheat, 22 ½ ⅓ ardabbs;

broad beans, 10 ardabbs.

The alms-tax, on the monetary value of eleven heads of livestock, 11 ⅔ ¼ 2/72 dinars:

cows, for a yearling calf, 1 ½ ¼ ⅛ 2/72 dinar;

small cattle, for ten heads, 10 1/24 dinars:

sheep, for nine heads, 9 ½ dinars;

goats, for one head, ¼ ⅙ ⅛ dinar.

Hay, according to the [Dīwān's] register (*fī al-ḍarība*), 1,200 bales.[247]

The fee of the overseer of the canal, wheat, ⅓ ardabb.

The chickens reared in it, 520 birds:

for the prosperous Dīwān, including the rearing wage of a third, 320 birds;

for the *iqṭāʿ*-holders, 200 birds.

The seed advances reclaimed [from *iqṭāʿ*-holders] for the prosperous Dīwān, 118 ardabbs:

wheat, 92 ardabbs;

barley, 13 ardabbs;

broad beans, 13 ardabbs.

The barley assigned for the royal stables and paid for in advance, 250 ardabbs.

The letter 'fāʾ': Fānū.[248] This is a medium-sized village, in the north of the Fayyum. It used to be cultivated, but a group of its inhabitants fled due to the tyranny of their *iqṭāʿ*-holders. It had vineyards that fell into ruin, and nothing remained except their traces. It has a hamlet (*mawḍiʿ*) called al-Malāʾid. It has gardens of date palms, figs, peaches, apricots, pears and citrons.

761 ساقط من ط. م.: والكيالة.

762 أ. س.: وعشرون.

763 ساقط من أ. س.: تفصيله للديوان المعمور، بما فيه من أجرة التربية وهو الثلث، ثلاثمائة وعشرون طائرا. للمقطعين مائتا طائر.

764 أ. س.: مائتا أردب وخمسون.

247 On *ḍarība* as a list made in the Dīwān, see al-Nuwayrī, *Nihāyat al-arab*, VIII, 242. The reference here is to the old register of the levy of hay, last updated in 633 AH, which al-Nābulusī reports to have found in the Dīwān (see above, Chapter 9).

248 Modern location (uncertain): the northern part of Naqalīfa (نقليفة). Timm, *Das Christlich-Koptische Ägypten*, pp. 921–23: Phanou; Trismegistos GEO ID: 1746; Halm, *Ägypten*, p. 255: Fānū/Naqalīfa; Salmon, 'Répertoire', pp. 54–55; de Sacy, *État des provinces*, p. 683; Abū Sāliḥ, *Churches and Monasteries*, p. 209; Savigny, *Description de l'Égypte*, p. 129; Ibn Mammātī, *Kitāb qawānīn al-dawāwīn*, pp. 167, 196; Ibn al-Jīʿān, *Kitāb al-tuḥfa*, p. 157; Ramzī, *Al-Qāmūs*, II/III, 110: Minshāt Fānū is nowadays al-Sīliyyīn (near Fidīmīn) but Ramzī notes that this is the location of one of the hamlets of Fānū, and not of Fānū itself. Ramzī's identification is not in line with al-Nābulusī's statement that [Naqalīfa] bordered Fānū. We therefore located Fānū, following Shafei Bey, 'Fayoum Irrigation', at the northern part of modern Naqalīfa.

وكان بها حجران يدور احدهما بالماء والاخر بالعوامل، فدثر الحجر الذي يدور بالعوامل من سنين متعددة وعوض عنه حجر الماء، ثم تعطل الذي يدور بالماء من سنين من هذا التاريخ وهو سنة اثنتين واربعين. تعتصر[765] اقصابه لسنة ثلاث واربعين وستمائة بمعصرة نقليفة. وسبب تعطيل هذا الحجر الداثر[766] ان ماءه اذا اداره وخرج منه، لا ينتفع به في الزرع ويضيع مجانا خلاف الاحجار الدائرة الان المستمرة الدوران في كل سنة.

وبهذه البلدة نفسها دويرة نخل يسير عن جانبها من بحريها.

وهذه البلدة مجاورة لنقليفة تذكر معها وربما انضمت معها في حقوقها، فلهذا وصفت معها وان لم تكن في حرف الفاء.[767] وهذه نقليفة عبارة عن بلدة كبيرة تشتمل على نخل كثير وتين وزيتون غزير، متاخمة لها. بينهما خطوات يتخاطب اهل البلدين وكل منهما في موضعه وجدار فانو في ارض نقليفة.

بينهما وبين مدينة الفيوم مسافة ساعتين للراكب. جاريتان في الخاص الشريف يشربان الان من خليج يعرف بنقليفة وخليج يعرف بمنية كربيس من البر البحري وهما مختلطان من اسفل صورة خليج واحد وهو صورة بابين متسعين ليس لهما عبرة فتذكر لسقي شتويهما وصيفهما واقصابهما وبساتينهما. وتسقى منها الاقصاب المزدرعة باراضي منية كربيس برسم معصرة مدينة الفيوم. وينقسم الماء المطلق في البابين المذكورين من اسفل بين فانو ونقليفة في الشتوي نصفين [و]زمن الصيف بين اقصاب نقليفة والمدينة بالنسبة.

والدائر بنقليفة بمعصرة قصب سكر ثلاثة احجار بالابقار. وبفانو اثار حجر دائر بالماء واقصابه تعتصر الان بمعصرة نقليفة. وذكر ان سبب تعطيله تلاف المياه التي يدور بها وكونها لم يكن تحتها اراض للزراعة.

بهما جامعان تقام فيهما الجمعة وبهما كنائس اربعة. تفصيله: نقليفة كنيسة، وفانو ثلاث كنائس خراب. ومن غربي فانو دير يعرف بدير فانو. اهل نقليفة قياصرة واهل فانو بنو جابر، الفخذان من بني عجلان.

ارتفاعهما عينا، ستمائة وسبعة وعشرون دينارا وقيراط ونصف، وغلة، اربعة الاف وسبعمائة وستة وتسعون اردبا وثلث وربع ونصف قيراط. تفصيله:

قمح ثلاثة الاف ومائة واحد وستون اردبا.
شعير، سبعمائة وثلاثة وتسعون اردبا وسدس ونصف ثمن.
وفول، ثمانمائة واثنان واربعون اردبا وربع وثمن.

وفدن، ثلاثمائة وثمانية فدادين ونصف وربع وثمن. تفصيله:

قصب سكر، مائتان وسبعة وستون فدانا ونصف وربع وثمن. تفصيله:
راس، مائة وسبعة وسبعون فدانا وثلث وربع وثمن.
وخلفة، تسعون فدانا وسدس.
قرط وفول، احد واربعون فدانا.

765 أ. س.: يعتصر.
766 ط. م.: الدائر.
767 من هنا بياض ناقص في أ. س. لحد نهاية بلدة فدمين.

It had two [press] stones — one turned by water, and the other by cattle. The stone turned by cattle fell into disuse many years ago. It was replaced by the stone turned by water. Then the one turned by water broke down some years before this date, which is [6]42 [AD 1244–5]. For the year 643 [AD 1245–6], its sugarcane is pressed at the press of Naqalīfa. The reason that this stone went out of use is that when water turns it and exits, it cannot be used for cultivation, and thus goes wasted. This is unlike the stones in use now, which turn continuously every year.

In the village itself, on its northern side, there is an enclosure of a few date palms.

This village is adjacent to Naqalīfa.[249] The two are mentioned here together, and sometimes the one is considered a subsidiary of the other. Therefore, Naqalīfa is described here, even though it does not begin with the letter 'fā''. The village of Naqalīfa is a large, populous village. It has many date palms, figs and abundant olive trees. It borders Fānū, and they are just a few steps away from each other. The people of both villages can talk to each other without leaving their own village. The fences of Fānū are in the land of Naqalīfa.

The two villages are two hours' ride from Madīnat al-Fayyūm. They are assigned to the lofty private domain of the sultan. They presently get their water from a canal known as Naqalīfa and a canal known as Minyat Karbīs, [issuing] from the northern bank [of the Main Canal]. The two canals merge lower down to form one canal, with two wide sluice gates and no [water] quota, for the irrigation of their winter and summer crops, their sugarcane and their orchards. These [canals] water the sugarcane sown in the land of Minyat Karbīs, which is assigned to the press at Madīnat al-Fayyūm. The water allocated by the two sluice gates lower down the canal is divided equally between the winter crops of Fānū and Naqalīfa; [and] during the summer, divided proportionally between the sugarcanes of Naqalīfa and the city.

In Naqalīfa there are three stones turned by oxen at the sugarcane press. In Fānū there are remains of a stone turned by water, but its sugarcane is now pressed at the press of Naqalīfa. As has been mentioned, it stopped working because the water by which it turns goes wasted, since there are no lands below it which are suitable for cultivation.

The two villages have two congregational mosques, in which the Friday prayers are held, and four churches: Naqalīfa, one church; Fānū, three churches, deserted. To the west of Fānū there is a monastery known as the monastery of Fānū.

The people of Naqalīfa are the Banū Qayṣar and the people of Fānū are the Banū Jābir — both are branches of the Banū ʿAjlān.

Their revenue in specie, 627 1/24 1/2 dinars; and in grains, 4,796 1/3 1/4 1/48 ardabbs:

- wheat, 3,161 ardabbs;
- barley, 793 1/6 1/16 ardabbs;
- broad beans, 842 1/4 1/8 ardabbs.

The [crown estate] feddans, 308 1/2 1/4 1/8 feddans:

- sugarcane, 267 1/2 1/4 1/8 feddans:
  - first harvest, 177 1/3 1/4 1/8 feddans;
  - second harvest, 90 1/6 feddans;
- alfalfa and broad beans, 41 feddans.

249 Modern location: Naqālīfa (نقاليفة). Timm, *Das Christlich-Koptische Ägypten*, p. 1727; Halm, *Ägypten*, p. 267; Salmon, 'Répertoire', p. 55; Ibn al-Jīʿān, *Kitāb al-tuḥfa*, p. 157; de Sacy, *État des provinces*, p. 683: Naqalīfa; Abū Sālīḥ, *Churches*, p. 209; Quatremère, *Mémoires*, I, 413; Savigny, *Description de l'Égypte*, p. 129: Naqālīfa; Ramzī, *Al-Qāmūs*, II/III, 116: Naqālīfa, notes that its ancient name was Nakourhabeg.

تفصيل ذلك:
مال الهلالي، تسعون دينارا وربع ونصف ثمن. تفصيله:
الطاحون الدائرة بالماء بارض فانو، خمسون دينارا.
الحانوت بالناحيتين، خمسة وعشرون دينارا.
الفروج بالناحيتين، اثنا عشر دينارا ونصف.
السدر، ديناران ونصف وربع ونصف ثمن.

مال الخراجي وبذل المستخدمين، خمسمائة وستة وعشرون دينارا ونصف، والغلة، وبما فيه من الرسوم والكيالة والمتوفر من اجرة الحمولة، اربعة الاف وسبعمائة وستة وتسعون اردبا وثلث وربع ونصف قيراط، على ما فصل باصنافه. تفصيله:
زراعة المزارعين، اربعمائة وسبعة وثلاثون دينارا ونصف وثمن ودانق. تفصيله:
خراج الراتب والاحكار بما فيه من الخراب الداثر عن من بعد وتسحب وسقط بالوفاة ولم يوجد له موجود مما اورد حفظا انكره، اربعمائة وخمسة عشر دينارا ونصف ودانق. تفصيله:
الاصل، عن مائة واثنين وثلاثين فدانا وربع ونصف قيراط وحبة، ثلاثمائة واربعة وخمسون دينارا وربع ونصف ثمن. تفصيله:
كرم كامل، قطيعة خمسة دنانير وثلث الفدان، عن ثمانية وعشرين فدانا وربع وسدس وثمن وحبة، مائة واثنان وخمسون دينارا وسدس وثمن.
راتب، قطيعة ديناران الفدان، عن اربعة وثمانين فدانا وثمن ودانق، مائة وثمانية وستون دينارا وربع وحبة:
عن حنا، تسعة فدادين وخمسة قراريط، ثمانية عشر دينارا وربع وسدس.
خضر، عن ثلثي فدان، دينار واحد وثلث.
ثوم، نصف وثلث ودانق، دينار وثلثان وحبة.
قطن، عن ستة فدادين ونصف وربع وثمن ودانق، عشرة دنانير وربع ونصف ثمن وحبة.
حكر، عن فدانين، ديناران.
الاضافة، اربعة واربعون دينارا وسدس وثمن.
زائد القطيعة، ديناران.
زائد المساحة، اربعة عشر دينارا ونصف وحبتان.

خراج فدن العين، اثنان وعشرون دينارا ونصف. تفصيل:
الاصل، عن عشرين فدانا، عشرون دينارا.
الاضافة، ديناران ونصف.

مناجزة الغلات، اربعة الاف واربعمائة اردب. تفصيله:
قمح، الفان وتسعمائة وثلاثة وثلاثون اردبا وثلث.
شعير، سبعمائة وثلاثة وثمانون اردبا وثلث.
فول، سبعمائة وثلاثة وثلاثون اردبا وثلث.

تفصيله:
فانو، الف وستمائة اردب:
قمح، الف وستة وستون اردبا وثلثان.
شعير، مائتان وستة وستون اردبا وثلثان.
فول، مائتان وستة وستون اردبا وثلثان.
نقليفة، الفان وثمانمائة اردب. تفصيله:
قمح، الف وثمانمائة وستة وستون اردبا وثلثان.
شعير، اربعمائة وستة وستون اردبا وثلثان.
فول، اربعمائة وستة وستون اردبا وثلثان.

[The revenue] in detail:
lunar-calendar taxes, 90 ¼ 1/16 dinars:
the mill turned by water in the lands of Fānū, 50 dinars;
the shops in the two villages, 25 dinars;
the [concession for sale of] chickens in the two villages, 12 ½ dinars;
sidr trees, 2 ½ ¼ 1/16 dinars.

Land tax in cash and the *badhl* of the government agents,[250] 526 ½ dinars; and in grains, including the fees, the measurement fee and the supplementary transportation fee, 4,796 ⅓ ¼ 1/48 ardabbs, as specified according to the various categories.

[The land tax] in detail:
cultivation by tenants, 437 ½ ⅛ 1/144 dinars:
land tax on perennial plants and on lands subject to long-term lease — including the deserted lands of those who kept away, fled, or died without leaving an heir, mentioned here for the record — 415 ½ 1/144 dinars:
the basic assessment, for 132 ¼ 1/48 1/72 feddans, 354 ¼ 1/16 dinars:
fully-grown vineyards, at a rate of 5 ⅓ dinars per feddan, for 28 ¼ ⅙ ⅛ 1/72 feddans, 152 ⅙ ⅛ dinars;
[land tax on] perennial plants, at a rate of 2 dinars per feddan, for 84 ⅛ 1/144 feddans, 168 ¼ 1/72 dinars;
henna, for 9 5/24 feddans, 18 ¼ ⅙ dinars;
green [vegetables], for ⅔ feddan, 1 ⅓ dinar;
garlic, for ½ ⅓ 1/144 [feddan], 1 ⅔ 1/72 dinar;
cotton, for 6 ½ ¼ ⅛ 1/144 feddans, 10 ¼ ⅙ 1/72 dinars;
lands subject to long-term lease, for 2 feddans, 2 dinars.
the addition, 44 ⅙ ⅛ dinars.
the added tax-rate [on long-term lease], 2 dinars;
the increment of the land-survey (*zāʾid al-misāḥa*), 14 ½ 2/72 dinars.

Land tax on cash-crops assessed by feddans, 22 ½ dinars:
the basic assessment, for 22 feddans, 20 dinars;
the addition, 2 ½ dinars.

Munājaza land tax, in grains, 4,400 ardabbs:
wheat, 2,933 ⅓ ardabbs;
barley, 783 ⅓ ardabbs;
broad beans, 733 ⅓ ardabbs.

[*Munājaza* land tax] in detail:
Fānū, 1,600 ardabbs:
wheat, 1,066 ⅔ ardabbs;
barley, 266 ⅔ ardabbs;
broad beans, 266 ⅔ ardabbs.
Naqalīfa, 2,800 ardabbs:
wheat, 1,866 ⅔ ardabbs;
barley, 466 ⅔ ardabbs;
broad beans, 466 ⅔ ardabbs.

---

250 Reading *badhl* is confirmed by both AS and MP. On this term, see above, and compare al-Nuwayrī, *Nihāyat al-arab*, VIII, 202.

البذل[768] من جملة مائة دينار، بعد المستقر متميزا في الهلالي وهو احد عشر دينارا وثمن ودانق، ثمانية وستون دينارا ونصف وثلث ونصف قيراط وحبة. تفصيله:

في خراج الراتب عن المستجد، عن ثمانية فدادين وربع وسدس وثمن ودانق، اصلا واضافة، عشرون دينارا.

ما يسجله جرار بن مجير عن بركة عقيل، عن عشرة فدادين، احد عشر دينارا وربع.

تتمة الجملة على زراعة القلقاس والخضر وغيره، سبعة وخمسون دينارا وثلث وربع ونصف قيراط وحبة.

وفر الخراج المقرر على المعاملين، حسابا عن كل مائة اردب ثلاثة ارادب، مائة واثنان وثلاثون اردبا. تفصيله:

قمح، ثمانية و ثمانون اردبا.

شعير، اثنان وعشرون اردبا.

فول، اثنان وعشرون اردبا.

مؤنة النواب، ثمانية دنانير.

رسم الكروم، ديناران وربع.

رسم الاجران، مائة وسبعة ارادب وثلث ونصف ثمن. تفصيله:

قمح، احد وخمسون اردبا وثلث.

وشعير، عشرون اردبا وثلث وربع.

فول، خمسة وثلاثون اردبا وثلث وربع ونصف ثمن.

كيالة، مائة وعشرة ارادب ونصف ونصف قيراط:

قمح، اثنان وسبعون اردبا وثلثان ونصف قيراط.

شعير، عشرة ارادب وثلثان.

فول، سبعة وعشرون اردبا وسدس.

الحمولة، ستة واربعون اردبا وثلثان ونصف قيراط. تفصيله:

قمح، خمسة عشر اردبا وثلث وربع ونصف ثمن.

شعير، ستة ارادب وثلثان وربع ونصف ثمن.

فول، اربعة وعشرون اردبا وقيراط ونصف.

زراعة الاواسي الديوانية، ثلاثمائة وثمانية فدادين ونصف وربع ونصف ثمن، على ما تقدم تفصيله.

وعليها من الرسوم والمراعي والكيالة، خارجا عن رسم الغلة والكيالة الواردة في ارتفاع الخاص مما تقدم ذكره فيه، عن تسعمائة واحد وسبعين درهما وربع وثمن، اربعة وعشرون دينارا وسدس وثمن. تفصيله:

الرسوم، اربعمائة وثمانية وثلاثون درهما وثمن. تفصيله:

شد الاحباس، اربعة وعشرون درهما:

فانو، خمسة عشر درهما.

نقليفة، تسعة دراهم.

رسم الجراريف، مائة وثمانون درهما:

فانو، تسعون درهما.

نقليفة، تسعون درهما.

رسم الخفارة، ثلاثون درهما:

فانو، خمسة عشر درهما.

نقليفة، خمسة عشر درهما.

768 ط. م.: البذل، بياض في أ. س.

The *badhl* of the government agents, out of a total of 100 dinars — after deducting the amount established as subsumed (?, *mutamayyiz*[an]) under the category of lunar-calendar taxes, which is 11 ⅛ 1⁄144 dinars — is 88[251] ½ ⅓ 1⁄48 1⁄72 dinars:

for land tax on newly-introduced perennial plants, including the basic assessment and the addition, for 8 ¼ ⅙ ⅛ 1⁄144 feddans, 20 dinars;

what is registered in the name of Jirār ibn Mujīr for Birkat ʿAqīl, for 10 feddans, 11 ¼ dinars;

the adjustment to the total, for the cultivation of colocasia, greens and other crops, 57 ⅓ ¼ 1⁄48 1⁄72 dinars.

The established surcharge added on to the land tax of the cultivators, calculated at a rate of 3 ardabbs per 100, 132 ardabbs:

wheat, 88 ardabbs;

barley, 22 ardabbs;

broad beans, 22 ardabbs.

The provisions for the agents, 8 dinars.

Vineyards fee, 2 ¼ dinars.

Threshing-floor fee, 107 ⅓ 1⁄16 ardabbs:

wheat, 51 ⅓ ardabbs;

barley, 20 ⅓ ¼ ardabbs;

broad beans, 35 ⅓ ¼ 1⁄16 ardabbs.

The measurement fee, 110 ½ 1⁄48 ardabbs:

wheat, 72 ⅔ 1⁄48 ardabbs;

barley, 10 ⅔ ardabbs:

broad beans, 27 ⅙ ardabbs.

Transportation [fee], 46 ⅔ 1⁄48 ardabbs:

wheat, 15 ⅓ ¼ 1⁄16 ardabbs;

barley, 6 ⅔ ¼ 1⁄16 ardabbs;

broad beans, 24 1⁄24 1⁄48 ardabbs.

The cultivation of the crown estates, 308 ½ ¼ 1⁄16 feddans, as specified above.

The fees, the pasture fee and the measurement fee [threshing-floor fee][252] — excluding the fees in grains and the measurement fee recorded in the revenues of the private domain of the sultan, as previously mentioned — 971 ½ ⅛ dirhams, which are 24 ⅙ ⅛ dinars:

The fees are 438 ⅛ dirhams:

supervision of endowments, 24 dirhams:

Fānū, 15 dirhams;

Naqalīfa, 9 dirhams;

dredging fee, 180 dirhams:

Fānū, 90 dirhams;

Naqalīfa, 90 dirhams;

protection fee, 30 dirhams:

Fānū, 15 dirhams;

Naqalīfa, 15 dirhams;

251 MP: 68. Missing in AS.

252 Both AS and MP have 'measurement fee', but this should be 'the threshing-floor fee', as is clear from the following sentence.

رسم الحصاد، مائة وستة دراهم:
فانو ثلاثة وخمسون درهما.
نقليفة، ثلاثة وخمسون درهما.
رسم الاجران، ثمانية وتسعون درهما وثمن:
فانو، احد وثلاثون درهما ونصف وربع وثمن.
نقليفة، ستة وستون درهما وربع.
المراعي، عن مائتين وخمسة وخمسين راسا، خمسمائة وثلاثة وثلاثون درهما وربع. تفصيله:
راتب، قطيعة درهمين وربع الراس، عن مائتين وعشرة ارؤس، اربعمائة واثنان وسبعون درهما ونصف.
طارئ، قطيعة درهم واحد الراس، عن خمسة واربعين راسا، خمسة واربعون درهما.
رسم المستخدمين، خمسة عشر درهما ونصف وربع.

وعليهما من الزكاة، ثمانية وثلاثون دينارا ونصف. تفصيله:
فانو، اربعة عشر دينارا ونصف وثمن. تفصيله:
الخرص، اربعة دنانير ونصف وربع. تفصيله:
خرص العنب، ديناران ونصف.
خرص الزيتون، ديناران وربع.
ثمن الاغنام، عن ثلاثة عشر راسا، تسعة دنانير ونصف وربع وثمن. تفصيله:
بياض، عن ستة ارؤس، ستة دنانير وربع.
شعارى، سبعة ارؤس، ثلاثة ونصف وثمن.
نقليفة، ثلاثة وعشرون دينارا ونصف وربع وثمن. تفصيله:
الخرص، ثمانية عشر دينارا وربع وثمن:
خرص النخل، تسعة دنانير.
خرص الزيتون، تسعة دنانير وربع وثمن.
ثمن الاغنام، عن سبعة ارؤس، خمسة دنانير ونصف. تفصيله:
بياض، عن ثلاثة ارؤس، ثلاثة دنانير وربع.
شعارى، عن اربعة ارؤس، ديناران وربع.

وعليها من الجوالي، ثمانية وتسعون دينارا:
فانو، عن ثمانية وعشرين نفرا، ستة وخمسون دينارا، بما في ذلك مما هو محسوب عن طرادين الوحش وهو عن نفرين، دينار واحد. تفصيله:
المقيمون بها، عن ثمانية عشر نفرا، ستة وثلاثون دينارا.
الناعون عنها، عن عشرة انفار، عشرون دينارا. تفصيله:
بالوجه البحري، عن سبعة انفار، اربعة عشر دينارا.
بالوجه القبلي، عن ثلاثة انفار، ستة دنانير.
نقليفة، عن احد وعشرين نفرا، اثنان واربعون دينارا. تفصيله:
المقيمون بها، عن تسعة انفار، ثمانية عشر دينارا.
الناعون عنها، عن اثنى عشر انفار، اربعة وعشرون دينارا. تفصيله:
الوجه البحري، عن ستة انفار، اثنا عشر دينارا.
الوجه القبلي، عن ستة انفار، اثنا عشر دينارا.

وعليهما من الاتبان، خمسة الاف شنيف.

رسم خولي البحر بهما، اردبان، قمحا. تفصيله:
فانو، اردب.
نقليفة، اردب.

وعليهما لديوان الاحباس، عينا، احد عشر دينارا.

harvest fee, 106 dirhams:
Fānū, 53 dirhams;
Naqalīfa, 53 dirhams;
threshing-floor fee, 98 ⅛ dirhams:
Fānū, 31 dirhams ½ ¼ ⅛;
Naqalīfa, 66 ¼ dirhams.
The pasture fee, for 255 heads, 533 ¼ dirhams:
permanent pasture lands at the rate of 2 ¼ dirhams per head, for 210 heads, 472 ½ dirhams;
seasonal pasture lands at the rate of one dirham per head, for 45 heads, 45 dirhams;
the government agents' fee, 15 ½ ¼ dirhams.

The alms-tax for both villages, 38 ½ dinars:
Fānū, 14 ½ ⅛ dinars:
the estimate, 4 ½ ¼ dinars:
estimate of grapes, 2 ½ dinars;
estimate of olives, 2 ¼ dinars;
monetary value of small cattle, for thirteen heads, 9 ½ ¼ ⅛ dinars:
sheep, for six heads, 6 ¼ dinars;
goats, for seven heads, 3 ½ ⅛ dinars;
Naqalīfa, 23 ½ ¼ ⅛ dinars:
the estimate, 18 ¼ ⅛ dinars:
estimate of dates, 9 dinars;
estimate of olives, 9 ¼ ⅛ dinars;
monetary value of small cattle, for seven heads, 5 ½ dinars:
sheep, for three heads, 3 ¼ dinars;
goats, for four heads, 2 ¼ dinar.

The poll-tax, 98 dinars:
Fānū, for twenty-eight individuals, 56 dinars. This sum includes what is allotted to the 'beast-chasers', 1 dinar for two individuals;
those residing in it, for eighteen individuals, 36 dinars;
those absent from it, for ten individuals, 20 dinars:
In the northern region, for seven individuals, 14 dinars;
In the southern region, for three individuals, 6 dinars;
Naqalīfa, for 21 individuals, 42 dinars:
those residing in it, for nine individuals, 18 dinars;
those absent from it, for 12 individuals, 24 dinars:
the northern region, for six individuals, 12 dinars;
the southern region, for six individuals, 12 dinars.

Hay from the two villages, 5,000 bales.

اهلها يزرعون من الاقصاب السكر ويسقون من الخلف ما عدته ثلاثة وتسعون فدانا وثلثان وثمن:

راس، خمسة وستون فدانا وثلثان وثمن.

خلفة، ثمانية وعشرون فدانا.

والمطلق بهما من الرزق، خمسة واربعون فدانا:

خولة الاقصاب، عن نفرين لكل واحد منهما خمسة فدادين، عشرة فدادين.

القصاص، فدانان.

طرادون الوحش، اربعة فدادين.

الخطباء بالناحيتين، ثلاثة عشر فدانا:

فانو، ثمانية فدادين.

نقليفة، خمسة فدادين.

النجارين، عشرة فدادين.

الدير بفانو، فدانان.

المشايخ بفانو، اربعة فدادين.

والمربى بهما من الفروج سبعمائة طائر. تفصيله:

المستقر تربيته، اربعمائة طائر.

المرتب تربيته برسم المطابخ السلطانية، بما فيه من اجرة التربية وهو الثلث، ثلاثمائة فروج، نصفان.

والمزدرع بهما من الاقصاب الراس والمسقى من الخلف لسنة احدى واربعين وستمائة، مائتان وسبعة وستون فدانا ونصف وربع وثمن. تفصيله:

راس، مائة وسبعة وسبعون فدانا وثلث وربع وثمن.

خلفة، تسعون فدانا وسدس.

والذي بهما من التقاوي المطلقة والمخلدة الى اخر سنة اثنتين، عينا، ثمانية وخمسون دينارا وقيراطان وحبتان؛ وغلة، الف ومائة وتسعة وثمانون اردبا وثلثان وربع. تفصيله:

قمح، سبعمائة وستون اردبا وربع وسدس وثمن.

شعير، مائتان وعشرة ارادب ونصف وربع.

فول، مائتان وسبعة عشر اردبا وقيراط.

بسلة، ثلثا اردب.

زريعة بطيخ اخضر، ثلثان وربع اردب.

من ذلك ما هو باسم مرابعي الاقصاب، عينا، اربعة وتسعون دينارا وثلث وربع وثمن وحبة، وقمح، اربعة وخمسون اردبا ونصف وربع وثمن.

والذي انساق بها من الموقوف والباقي الى اخر سنة احدى واربعين، ثمانمائة ودينار واحد وثلثان وربع؛ وغلة، سبعة الاف ومائتان واردب واحد وثلثان وربع ونصف قيراط. تفصيله:

قمح، خمسة الاف وستة وثمانون اردبا وقيراط.

شعير، الف وتسعمائة واربعة وثلاثون اردبا وثلث وربع ونصف ثمن.

فول، مائة وتسعة وتسعون اردبا ونصف قيراط.

The fee of the overseer of the canal in the two villages, 2 ardabbs of wheat:

Fānū, 1 ardabb;

Naqalīfa, 1 ardabb.

For the Ministry of Endowments, in specie, 11 dinars.

The people of the two villages sow sugarcane and irrigate second-harvest sugarcane, at the amount of 93 ⅔ ⅛ feddans:

first harvest, 65 ⅔ ⅛ feddans;

second harvest, 28 feddans.

The allowances distributed in it, 45 feddans:

The overseers of the sugarcane, two individuals with 5 feddans each, 10 feddans;

the 'fable-tellers', 2 feddans;

the 'beast-chasers', 4 feddans;

the Friday preachers in the two villages, 13 feddans:

Fānū, 8 feddans;

Naqalīfa, 5 feddans;

the carpenters, 10 feddans;

the monastery in Fānū, 2 feddans;

the headmen in Fānū, 4 feddans.

The chickens reared in them, 700 birds:

the established rearing, 400 birds;

the set rearing assigned for the royal kitchens, including the rearing wage of a third, 300 chickens — half for each [village].

The first-harvest sugarcane sown in it, and the second-harvest irrigated in it for the year 641, 267 ½ ¼ ⅛ feddans:

first harvest, 177 ⅓ ¼ ⅛ feddans;

second harvest, 90 ⅙ feddans.

The amount of seed advances distributed [in them] and recorded [in the Dīwān] up to the end of [64]2 is, in specie, 58 2/24 2/72 dinars; and in grains, 1,189 ⅔ ¼ ardabbs:

wheat, 760 ¼ ⅙ ⅛ ardabbs;

barley, 210 ½ ¼ ardabbs;

broad beans, 217 1/24 ardabbs;

peas (*bisilla*), ⅔ ardabb;

seeds of green watermelons, ⅔ ¼ ardabb.

[The seed advances above] include what is assigned to the quarter-share labourers of sugarcanes, which is, in specie, 94 ⅓ ¼ ⅛ 1/72 dinars;[253] and in wheat, 54 ½ ¼ ⅛ ardabbs.

The withheld and outstanding payments carried forward up to the end of [6]41, 801 dinars ⅔ ¼;[254] and in grains, 7,201 ⅔ ¼ 1/48 ardabbs:

wheat, 5,086 1/24 ardabbs;

barley, 1,934 ⅓ ¼ 1/16 ardabbs;

broad beans, 199 1/48 ardabbs;

253 There seems to be a mistake in the accounts here, as the amount of cash assigned to the quarter-share labourers, at 94 52/72 dinars, is larger than the total of advances in cash, 58 8/72 dinars, mentioned a few lines earlier in the text.

254 The total of the withheld and outstanding payments cited below adds up to only 765 11/12 dinars.

سمسم، سدس وربع قيراط اردب.

سلجم، اردب وقيراط.

بطيخ اخضر، اردب واحد وربع قيراط.

عسل دفن، مطران.

والموقوف خاصة:

عن عطلة الطاحون بفانو لسنة تسع وثلاثين وستمائة؛

وعن من بعد وتسحب وسقط بالوفاة في الايام السلطانية وايام المقطعين، وعن كرم العادي عليها النار؛

وعن جرار بن مجير عن المكرر عليه، وعن رسم الكروم الخراب الداثر؛

وعن ضمان الفروج؛

وعن ما انكسر على الجمال الجدية؛

مما جميعه لاستقبال سنة ثلاثين وستمائة والى اخر سنة احدى واربعين وستمائة، عينا، سبعمائة وثلاثة وسبعون دينارا ونصف وثلث ونصف ثمن، وعسل دفن، مطران.

الباقي: ثمانية وعشرون دينارا ونصف قيراط، وغلة، سبعة الاف ومائتان واردب واحد وثلثان وربع ونصف قيراط. تفصيله:

قمح، خمسة الاف وستة وثمانون اردبا وقيراط.

شعير، الف وتسعمائة واربعة وثلاثون اردبا وثلث وربع وثمن.[769]

فول، مائة وتسعة وسبعون اردبا ونصف قيراط.

زريعة بطيخ، اردب وربع قيراط.

سمسم، سدس اردب ونصف وربع قيراط.

سلجم، اردب وقيراط.

ومن حرف الفاء، فرقس. هذه البلدة عبارة عن بلدة متوسطة بين الكبر والصغر، وهي من شرقي الفيوم [ا]لبحري. وهي عامرة اهلة، وبها نخل وشجرات تين. بينها وبين مدينة الفيوم مسافة ثلاث ساعات للراكب. عبرة اقطاعها الفا دينار جيشية. جارية في اقطاع الامير جمال الدين عيسى والامير فتح الدين يحيى بن جمال الدين احمد، والي الفيوم كان. بها جامع شريف ترجى فيه اجابة الدعوات. لها من الماء من بحر ذات الصفاء، من الماء المساق الى الفسقية اليوسفية تحت القبرا بخليج للشتوي والارز، خمس قبض ونصف. اهلها بنو زرعة، فخذ من بني عجلان.

ارتفاعها مما جميعه مستخرجا ومتحصلا، عينا، سبعة عشر دينارا؛ غلة، ثمانمائة وثلاثون اردبا. تفصيله:

قمح، اربعمائة وخمسون اردبا.

شعير، مائة وعشرون اردبا.

فول، مائتا اردب.

ارز بقشره، ستون اردبا.

تفصيله:

الهلالي عن الحانوت، اثنا عشر دينارا.

المراعي، خمسة دنانير.

المشاطرة، غلة، ثمانمائة وثلاثون اردبا على ما فصل.

769 ط. م. يضيف: ثمن.

sesame, ⅙ 1/96 ardabb;

rape, 1 1/24 ardabb;

green watermelons, 1 1/96 ardabb;

covered molasses, 2 maṭars.

The withheld payments in detail:

on account of the suspension of the mill at Fānū in 639;

on account of those who kept away, fled or died, [either] when the village belonged to the private domain of the sultan or when it belonged to *iqṭāʿ*-holders;

on account of a vineyard consumed by fire;[255]

on account of Jirār ibn Mujīr, for the double charges (*al-mukarrar*) on him;

on account of the fee of the deserted vineyards;

on account of the concession for [the sale of] chickens;

and on account of what was broken over the *al-jadiyya* camels (?).

All of these [withheld payments] date to the period from the beginning of 630 until the end of 641. It is, in specie, 737 ½ ⅓ 1/16 dinars; and in covered molasses, two maṭars.

The outstanding payments are 28 1/48 dinars; and in grains, 7,201 ⅔ ¼ 1/48 ardabbs:

wheat, 5,086 1/24 ardabbs;

barley, 1,934 ⅓ ¼ ⅛ ardabbs;

broad beans, 179 1/48 ardabbs;

seeds of watermelons, 1 1/96 ardabb;

sesame, ⅙ 1/48 1/96 ardabb;

rape, 1 1/24 ardabb.

Also beginning with the letter 'fāʾ': Furqus.[256] This is a medium-sized village in the north-east of the province, three hours' ride from Madīnat al-Fayyūm. It is inhabited and populous, with date palms and fig trees. The fiscal value of its *iqṭāʿ* is 2,000 army dinars, and it is assigned to the amir Jamāl al-Dīn ʿĪsā and to the amir Fatḥ al-Dīn Yaḥyā ibn Jamāl al-Dīn Aḥmad, who was (?) governor of the Fayyum (*wālī al-Fayyūm kāna*). It has an illustrious congregational mosque, where supplications may be answered. It gets its water from Dhāt as-Ṣafāʾ Canal, out of the water channelled towards the [divisor known as] al-Fasqiyya al-Yūsufiyya below al-Qubarāʾ, by means of a canal for winter crops and rice. [The quota is] 5 ½ *qabḍas*. Its people are the Banū Zarʿa, a branch of the Banū ʿAjlān.

Its revenue in cash and in kind is, in specie, 17 dinars; and in grains, 830 ardabbs:

wheat, 450 ardabbs;

barley, 120 ardabbs;

broad beans, 200 ardabbs;

rice in hull, 60 ardabbs.

[The revenue] in detail:

lunar-calendar tax for the shop, 12 dinars;

pasture tax, 5 dinars;

Mushāṭara land tax, in grains, 830 ardabbs, as specified.

255 Arabic: *nār*, but could be a mistake for *faʾr* (mice), mentioned in other village entries as a hazard to cultivation.

256 Modern location: Furquṣ (فرقص). Halm, *Ägypten*, p. 256: Furquṣ; Salmon, 'Répertoire', p. 48; Ibn Mammātī, *Kitāb qawānīn al-dawāwīn*, p. 199: Bū Furqus; Ibn al-Jīʿān, *Kitāb al-tuḥfa*, p. 157; de Sacy, *État des provinces*, p. 683; Ramzī, *Al-Qāmūs*, II/III, 114: Furquṣ, Coptic Purgos, ancient Ouomte (following Amélineau, *La géographie*).

عليها عن خراج الاستنباط لسنورس، احد وخمسون اردبا وربع:
قمح، ثمانية وعشرون اردبا وثلث وثمن.
شعير، احد عشر اردبا وثلثان وثمن.
فول، ثمانية ارادب وسدس.
سمسم، اردبان ونصف وثلث.

Land tax on al-Istinbāṭ, part of [the land tax revenues of] Sinnūris, 51 ¼ ardabbs:
wheat, 28 ⅓ ⅛ ardabbs;
barley, 11 ⅔ ⅛ ardabbs;
broad beans, 8 ⅙ ardabbs;
sesame, 2 ½ ⅓ ardabbs.

عليها من الرسوم والكيالة، عن اربعين درهما، دينار واحد وغلة، اثنان وسبعون اردبا ونصف وثلث. تفصيله:
قمح، سبعة وثلاثون اردبا ونصف وثمن.
شعير، اثنان وعشرون اردبا ونصف.
فول، اثنا عشر اردبا وثلث وربع وثمن.

The fees and the measurement fee are 40 dirhams, which are 1 dinar; and in grains, 62 ½ ⅓ ardabbs:
wheat, 37 ½ ⅛ ardabbs;
barley, 22 ½ ardabbs;
broad beans, 12 ⅓ ¼ ⅛ ardabbs.

تفصيله:
رسم الاجران، اربعون درهما، وغلة، اربعة واربعون اردبا ونصف وثلث:
قمح، عشرون اردبا ونصف وثمن.
شعير، ستة عشر اردبا ونصف.
فول، سبعة ارادب وثلث وربع وثمن.
الكيالة، ثمانية وعشرون اردبا:
قمح، سبعة عشر اردبا.
شعير، ستة ارادب.
فول، خمسة ارادب.

[The fees and the measurement fee] in detail:
Threshing-floor fee, 40 dirhams; and in grains, 44 ½ ⅓ ardabbs:
wheat, 20 ½ ⅛ ardabbs;
barley, 16 ½ ardabbs;
broad beans, 7 ⅓ ¼ ⅛ ardabbs.
The measurement fee, 28 ardabbs:
wheat, 17 ardabbs;
barley, 6 ardabbs;
broad beans, 5 ardabbs.

وعليها من الزكاة عن ثمن اغنام، عن خمسة اروس، اربعة دنانير ونصف وربع. تفصيله:
بياض، عن اربعة اروس، اربعة دنانير وربع.
شعارى، عن راس واحد، نصف دينار.

The alms-tax, for the monetary value of five heads of small cattle, 4 ½ ¼ dinars:
sheep, for four heads, 4 ¼ dinars;
goats, for one head, ½ dinar.

وعليها من الاتبان، الف شنيف.

Hay, 1,000 bales.

وعليها لديوان الاحباس اربعة دنانير.

For the Ministry of Endowments, 4 dinars.

رسم خولي البحر بها، قمح، نصف اردب.

The fee of the overseer of the canal, wheat, ½ ardabb.

والذي بها من التقاوي المخلدة للمقطعين برسم عمارة الناحية، مائتان وخمسة وخمسون اردبا ونصف وربع. تفصيله:
قمح، مائة وخمسون اردبا.
شعير، ثلاثون اردبا.
فول، خمسة وسبعون اردبا ونصف وربع.

The recorded seed advances for the *iqṭāʿ*-holders, assigned for the village's cultivation, 255 ½ ¼ ardabbs:
wheat, 150 ardabbs;
barley, 30 ardabbs;
broad beans, 75 ½ ¼ ardabbs.

والذي بها من الفروج، ستمائة وثلاثون طائرا. تفصيله:
للديوان المعمور، بما فيه من اجرة التربية وهو الثلث، اربعمائة وثلاثون طائرا.
للمقطعين، مائتا طائر.

The chickens [reared] in it, 630 birds:
for the prosperous Dīwān, including the rearing wage of a third, 430 birds;
for the *iqṭāʿ*-holders, 200 birds.

والذي يسلف عليه بها من الشعير برسم الاصطبلات السلطانية، مائة اردب.

The barley assigned for the royal stables and paid for in advance, 100 ardabbs.

ومن حرف الفاء، فدمين. هذه البلدة عبارة عن بلدة متوسطة، بين الكبر والصغر، وهي بحري الفيوم مما يلي الغرب. تشتمل على نخل وتين وزيتون في واد قريب منها من شرقيها. بينها وبين مدينة الفيوم مسافة ساعتين للراكب. جارية في اقطاع الاجناد. عبرتها جيشية اربعة الاف وستمائة دينار. بها جامع تقام فيه الجمعة. اهلها بنو جواب، فخذ من بني كلاب. والمطلق لها من الماء لسقى الشتوي والاقصاب الديوانية المزدرعة بحجر سنهور، باب بغير جص، ليس لمزارعيه صيفي، ثمان قبض.

Also beginning with the letter 'fā'': Fidimīn.[257] This is a medium-sized village in the north-west of the provicne, two hours' ride from Madīnat al-Fayyūm. It has date palms, figs and olives in a nearby ravine, to the east. It is assigned as an *iqṭāʿ* to soldiers, with a fiscal value of 4,600 army dinars. It has a congregational mosque, in which the Friday prayers are held. Its people are the Banū Jawwāb, a branch of the Banū Kilāb. Water is distributed to it from an unplastered sluice gate, for the irrigation of winter crops and the sugarcane of the Dīwān [assigned] for the press in Sanhūr, but not for summer crops. The water quota is 8 *qabḍas*.

[257] Modern location: Fidīmīn (فديمين). Timm, *Das Christlich-Koptische Ägypten*, pp. 957–58: Phentemin (Fidmīn in Arabic); Trismegistos GEO ID: 1970; Halm, *Ägypten*, pp. 255–56; Salmon, 'Répertoire', p. 55; Zéki, 'Une description', p. 38; Ibn Mammātī, *Kitāb qawānīn al-dawāwīn*, p. 167; de Sacy, *État des provinces*, p. 683: Fadmaīn; Savigny, *Description de l'Égypte*, p. 129: Fidimyn; Ibn al-Jīʿān, *Kitāb al-tuḥfa*, p. 157: Fadamain; Ramzī, *Al-Qāmūs*, II/III, 114: Fidīmīn.

ارتفاعها مما جميعه مستخرجا ومتحصلا، مائة وسبعة وثلاثون دينارا وسدس وثمن ودانق؛ وغلة، سبعمائة وخمسون اردبا. تفصيله:

قمح، ثلاثمائة وخمسة وسبعون اردبا.

وشعير، ثلاثمائة وخمسة وسبعون اردبا.

تفصيله:

الهلالي، اثنا عشر دينارا.

المراعي، ديناران وسدس وثمن ودانق.

خراج الراتب، ثلاثة وعشرون دينارا.

خراج قصب السكر، مائة دينار.

مناجزة الغلات، سبعمائة وخمسون اردبا، قمح وشعير نصفان.

عليها من الرسوم والكيالة والمراعي، عن مائتين وثلاثة واربعين درهما ونصف وثمن، ستة دنانير؛ وغلة، اربعة وستون اردبا وثلث ونصف ثمن. تفصيله:

قمح، ثمانية وعشرون اردبا وثلثان ونصف ثمن.

شعير، ثمانية وعشرون اردبا وثلثان وربع.

فول، ستة ارادب وثلث وثمن.

كمون، سدس وثمن اردب.

تفصيله:

الرسوم، مائتان وثلاثة وثلاثون درهما ونصف، وغلة، ثلاثة واربعون اردبا وثلث ونصف ثمن. تفصيله:

قمح، ستة عشر اردبا وثلثان ونصف ثمن.

وشعير، تسعة عشر اردبا وثلثان وربع.

وفول، ستة ارادب وثلث وثمن.

وكمون، سدس وثمن اردب.

تفصيله:

شد العين، ثلاثون درهما.

شد الاحباس، ثمانية دراهم.

رسم الجراريف، تسعون درهما.

رسم الحصاد، ثلاثة وخمسون درهما.

رسم الخفارة، خمسة عشر درهما.

رسم الاجران، سبعة وثلاثون درهما ونصف، والغلة.

الكيالة، احد وعشرون اردبا:

قمح، اثنا عشر اردبا.

شعير، تسعة ارادب.

المراعي، طارئ، عشرة دراهم وثمن:

المراعي خاصة، عن ثمانية عشر راسا، تسعة دراهم.

رسم المستخدمين، درهم واحد وثمن.

عليها من الزكاة، تسعة دنانير وثلثان وربع وحبتان:

خرص الزيتون، اربعة دنانير.

ثمن الماشية، عن اثنى عشر راسا، خمسة دنانير وثلثان وربع وحبتان:

بقر احمر، تبيع واحد، دينار واحد وربع.

ثمن الاغنام، عن احد عشر راسا، اربعة دنانير وثلثان وحبتان. تفصيله:

بياض، عن راسين، ديناران وسدس.

وشعارى، عن تسعة ارؤس، ديناران ونصف وحبتان.

عليها من الاتبان، الف وستمائة شنيف.

Its revenue in cash and kind is in specie, 137 ⅙ ⅛ 1/144 dinars; and in grains, 750 ardabbs:

wheat, 375 ardabbs;

barley, 375 ardabbs.

[The revenue] in detail:

lunar-calendar tax, 12 dinars;

fixed pasture tax, 2 ⅙ ⅛ 1/144 dinars;

land tax on perennial plants, 23 dinars;

land tax on sugarcane, 100 dinars.

Munājaza land tax in grains, 750 ardabbs, wheat and barley, half in each.

The fees, the measurement fee and the pasture fee are 243 ½ ⅛ dirhams, which are 6 dinars; and in grains, 64 ⅓ 1/16 ardabbs:

wheat, 28 ⅔ 1/16 ardabbs;

barley, 28 ⅔ ¼ ardabbs;

broad beans, 6 ⅓ ⅛ ardabbs;

cumin ⅙ ⅛ ardabb.

[The fees, the measurement fee and the pasture fee] in detail:

the fees, 233 ½ dirhams; and in grains, 43 ⅓ 1/16 ardabbs:

wheat, 16 ⅔ 1/16 ardabbs;

barley, 19 ⅔ ¼ ardabbs;

broad beans, 6 ⅓ ⅛ ardabbs;

cumin ⅙ ⅛ ardabb.

[the fees] in detail:

supervision of the land survey, 30 dirhams;

supervision of endowments, 8 dirhams;

dredging fee, 90 dirhams;

harvest fee, 53 dirhams;

protection fee, 15 dirhams;

threshing-floor fee, 37 ½ dirhams; and in grains [as specified].

The measurement fee, 21 ardabbs:

wheat, 12 ardabbs;

barley, 9 ardabbs.

The pasture fee on seasonal pasture lands, 10 ⅛ dirhams:

pasture tax proper, for 18 heads, 9 dirhams;

the government agents' fee, 1 ⅛ dirham.

The alms-tax, 9 ⅔ ¼ 2/72 dinars:

estimate of olives, 4 dinars;

monetary value of livestock, for twelveheads, 5 ⅔ ¼ 2/72 dinars:

cows, for one yearling calf, 1 ¼ dinar;

monetary value of small cattle, for eleven heads, 4 ⅔ 2/72 dinars:

sheep, for two heads, 2 ⅙ dinars;

goats, for nine heads, 2 ½ 2/72 dinars.

Hay, 1,600 bales.

رسم خولي البحر بها، اردب واحد.

عليها لديوان الاحباس، عينا، اربعة دنانير.

وبها من الرزق، ثلاثة عشر فدانا:
المشايخ، تسعة فدادين.
الخفراء، اربعة فدادين.

والمخلد بها من التقاوي للمقطعين، مائة واثنان وستون اردبا، قمح وشعير نصفان.

اهلها يزرعون من القصب السكر برسم معصرة سنهور، خارجا عن الزيادة لسنة اثنتين، خمسة وثلاثون فدانا وسدس:
راس، اربعة وعشرون فدانا.
خلفة،[770] احد عشر فدانا وسدس.

والمربى بها من الفروج، اربعمائة وعشرة اطيار:
للديوان، بما فيه من اجرة التربية وهو الثلث، مائتان وعشرة اطيار.
للمقطعين، مائتا[771] طائر.

والذي يسلف عليها بها من الشعير برسم الاصطبلات السلطانية، مائة اردب.

ومن حرف القاف، قمبشا. هذه البلدة عبارة عن بلدة كبيرة،[772] قبلي الفيوم. وهي ام لخليج تنبطويه وتشتمل على نخل يسير وكروم عنب. بينها وبين مدينة الفيوم مسافة اربع ساعات للراكب. مجموعة في عبرة الاقطاع مع كفورها بما جملته ستة وعشرون الفا ومائتان وخمسون دينارا.

والمطلق لها من الماء من بحر تنبطويه من المقسم، الشتوي والصيفي، خمسة واربعون قبضة. تفصيله:
قمبشا خاصة، احد واربعون قبضة ونصف.[773]
الصيفي بطليت عوضا من الاقصاب، ثلاث قبض ونصف.

ولها من ماء الغرق رزقة لخفارة جسر الغرق، عرض قبضة ونصف في سمك اربع قبض.

جارية في اقطاع جماعة من المقطعين الكيكانية والحميدية والامير بدر الدين المرندزي واصحاب الامير شهاب الدين خضر وغيرهم. وبها جامع تقام فيه الجمعة. اهلها بنو ربيعة، فخذ من بني كلاب.

ارتفاعها، عينا، مائتان وخمسة وسبعون دينارا وسدس ونصف قيراط وحبة؛ وغلات، ثلاثة الاف وسبعمائة وسبعون اردبا. تفصيله:
قمح، الفان وخمسمائة وثلاثة عشر اردبا وثلث.
شعير وفول، الف ومائتان وستة وخمسون اردبا وثلثان.
قطن حب، اربعة واربعون قنطارا وسدس.

تفصيله:
مال الهلالي عن اجرة الحانوت، تسعون دينارا.
الخراجي، عن خراج الراتب والقطن المقرر على المعاملين، مائة وخمسة وثمانون دينارا وسدس ونصف قيراط وحبة.

770 من هنا يستأنف أ. س.
771 أ. س.: مائة.
772 أ. س. يضيف: وهي.
773 أ. س.: وحبتان.

Fee for the overseer of the canal, 1 ardabb.

For the Ministry of Endowments, in specie, 4 dinars.

The allowances, 13 feddans:
the headmen, 9 feddans;
the guardsmen, 4 feddans.

The registered seed advances for the *iqṭāᶜ*-holders, 162 ardabbs of wheat and barley, half in each.

Its people sow 35 ⅙ feddans of sugarcane, assigned for the press at Sanhūr, excluding the increment for [64]2:
first harvest, 24 feddans;
second harvest, 11 ⅙ feddans.

The chickens reared in it, 410 birds:
for the prosperous Dīwān, including the rearing wage of a third, 210 birds;
for the *iqṭāᶜ*-holders, 200 birds.

The barley assigned for the royal stables and paid for in advance, 100 ardabbs.

Beginning with the letter 'qāf': Qambashā.[258] This is a large village in the south of the Fayyum, and the main village on Tanabṭawayh Canal. It has a few date palms and grape vineyards. It is four hours' ride from Madīnat al-Fayyūm. It is included in the fiscal value of the *iqṭāᶜ* [of Tanabṭawayh Canal] together with the other villages in its accounts, at a total of 26,250 army dinars.

The water allocated to it from Tanabṭawayh Canal through a divisor, for winter and summer crops, is 45 *qabḍas*:
Qambashā proper, 41 ½ *qabḍas*;
for summer cultivation in Ṭalīt, in compensation for the sugarcane, 3 ½ *qabḍas*.

It also gets water from [the reservoir] of al-Gharq, as an allowance for protecting the dike (*jisr*) of al-Gharq, a width of ½ *qabḍa*, and a height of 4 *qabḍas*.

It is assigned as an *iqṭāᶜ* to a group of *iqṭāᶜ*-holders: al-Kīkāniyya, al-Ḥumaydiyya, the amir Badr al-Dīn al-Marandizī, the followers of the amir Shihāb al-Din Khiḍr and others. It has a congregational mosque, in which the Friday prayers are held. Its people are the Banū Rabīᶜa, a branch of the Banū Kilāb.

Its revenue is, in specie, 275 ⅙ 1/48 1/72 dinars; and in grains, 3,770 ardabbs:
wheat, 2,513 ⅓ ardabbs;
barley and broad beans, 1,256 ⅔ ardabbs:
cotton seed, 44 ⅙ qinṭārs.

[The revenue] in detail:
lunar-calendar tax for the rent of the shop, 90 dinars;
the established land tax on perennial plants and on cotton due from the cultivators, 185 ⅙ 1/48 1/72 dinars; and in grains, as specified above.

258 Modern location: Qalamshāh (قلمشاة). Halm, *Ägypten*, p. 267; Salmon, 'Répertoire', p. 71; Zéki, 'Une description', p. 43; de Sacy, *État des provinces*, p. 683: Qumbishā; Ibn al-Jīᶜān, *Kitāb al-tuḥfa*, p. 157: Qumbushā; Ramzī, *Al-Qāmūs*, II/III, 85–86: Qalamshāh.

والغلة على ما تقدم تفصيله.

وعليها من الرسوم والكيالة والمراعي، عن الف[774] ومائتين وعشرة دراهم ونصف وثمن،[775] ثلاثون دينارا وربع وحبة؛ وغلة، مائة وثمانية[776] ارادب وسدس وثمن. تفصيله:

قمح، احد وستون اردبا وربع.

شعير، احد عشر اردبا ونصف.

فول، خمسة وثلاثون اردبا وربع وسدس وثمن.

تفصيله:

الرسوم، خمسمائة وتسعة وستون درهما وربع، وغلة، خمسة وستون اردبا وثلثان وثمن. تفصيله:

قمح، احد واربعون اردبا وربع.

شعير، احد عشر اردبا ونصف.

فول، ثلاثة عشر اردبا وقيراط.

تفصيله:

شد العين، مائتان وستة وثلاثون درهما.

شد الاحباس، اربعة وعشرون درهما.

رسم الجراريف، مائة واثنان وثمانون درهما ونصف.

رسم الحصاد، ثلاثة وخمسون درهما.

رسم الخفارة، خمسة عشر درهما.[777]

رسم الاجران، ثمانية وخمسون درهما ونصف وربع، وغلة، خمسة وستون اردبا وثلثان وثمن:

قمح، احد واربعون اردبا وربع.

شعير، احد عشر اردبا ونصف.

فول، ثلاثة عشر اردبا وقيراط.

كيالة، اثنان واربعون اردبا ونصف:

قمح، عشرون اردبا.

فول، اثنان وعشرون اردبا ونصف.

المراعي، طارئ، عن ثمانمائة وستين راسا، ستمائة واحد واربعون درهما وربع وثمن:

قطيعة مائة درهم المائة راس، عن ثلاثمائة واثنين وستين راسا، ثلاثمائة واثنان وستون درهما.

قطيعة خمسين درهما المائة راس، عن اربعمائة وخمسة ارؤس، مائتان ودرهمان ونصف.

قطيعة خمسة وعشرون درهما المائة، عن ثلاثة وتسعين راسا، ثلاثة وعشرون درهما وربع.

رسم المستخدمين، ثلاثة وخمسون درهما ونصف وثمن.

وعليها من الزكاة، عينا، سبعة وعشرون دينارا وقيراط. تفصيله:

دولبة، نصف دينار.

خرص العنب، سبعة دنانير ونصف وربع.

ثمن الماشية، عن احد وثلاثين راسا، ثمانية عشر دينارا وثلثان وثمن. تفصيله:

بقر احمر، عن مسنة واحدة، ديناران ونصف وربع.

ثمن الاغنام، عن ثلاثين راسا، سبعة عشر دينارا وقيراط:

بياض، عن تسعة ارؤس، تسعة دنانير ونصف.

شعارى، عن احد وعشرين راسا، ستة دنانير وربع وسدس وثمن.

The fees, the measurement fee and the pasture tax are 1,210 ½ ⅛ dirhams, which are 30 ¼ 1/72 dinars; and in grains, 108 ⅙ ⅛ ardabbs:

wheat, 61 ¼ ardabbs;

barley, 11 ½ ardabbs;

broad beans, 35 ¼ ⅙ ⅛ ardabbs.

[The fees, the measurement fee and the pasture tax] in detail:

the fees, 569 ¼ dirhams; and in grains, 65 ⅔ ⅛ ardabbs:

wheat, 41 ¼ ardabbs;

barley, 11 ½ ardabbs;

broad beans, 13 1/24 ardabbs.

[The fees] in detail:

supervision of the land survey, 236 dirhams;

supervision of endowments, 24 dirhams;

dredging fee, 182 ½ dirhams;

harvest fee, 53 dirhams;

protection fee, 15 dirhams;

threshing-floor fee, 58 ½ ¼ dirhams; and in grains, 65 ⅔ ⅛ ardabbs:

wheat, 41 ¼ ardabbs;

barley, 11 ½ ardabbs;

broad beans, 13 1/24 ardabbs.

The measurement fee, 42 ½ ardabbs:

wheat, 20 ardabbs;

broad beans, 22 ½ ardabbs.

The pasture tax on seasonal pasture lands, for 860 heads, 641 ¼ ⅛ dirhams:

at the rate of 100 dirhams per 100 heads, for 362 heads, 362 dirhams;

at the rate of 50 dirhams per 100 heads, for 405 heads, 20 ½ dirhams;

at the rate of 25 dirhams per 100 [heads], for 93 heads, 23 ¼ dirhams;

the government agents' fee, 53 ½ ⅛ dirhams.

The alms-tax, in specie, 27 1/24 dinars:

merchandise, ½ dinar;

estimate of grapes, 7 ½ ¼ dinars;

monetary value of livestock, for 31 heads, 18 ⅔ ⅛ dinars:

cows, for a two-year old cow, 2 ½ ¼ dinars;

monetary value of small cattle, for 30 heads, 17 1/24 dinars:

sheep, for nine heads, 9 ½ dinars;

goats, for 21 heads, 6 ¼ ⅙ ⅛ dinars.

774 أ. س.: ألفين.

775 ساقط من أ. س.: وثمن.

776 أ. س.: وثلاثة.

777 أ. س يضيف: رسم الخفارة خمسة عشر درهما رسم الحصاد ثلاثة وخمسون درهما.

وعليها من الجوالي، عن ستة نفر، اثنا عشر دينارا. تفصيله:
المقيمون بها، عن خمسة نفر، عشرة دنانير.
الناعون عنها بالوجه القبلي، نفر واحد ديناران.

The poll-tax, for six individuals, 12 dinars:
those residing in it, for five individuals, 10 dinars;
those absent from it in the southern region, one individual, 2 dinars.

وعليها من الاتبان، ستة الاف وستمائة[778] شنيف.

Hay, 1,600 bales.

عليها لديوان الاحباس، عينا، اثنا عشر دينارا.

For the Ministry of Endowments, in specie, 12 dinars.

وبها من الرزق، ثلاثة وسبعون فدانا. تفصيله:
الخطابة، اثنا عشر فدانا.
النجارون، اثنا عشر فدانا.
الخفراء، اثنا عشر فدانا.
المشايخ، اثنا عشر فدانا.
حراس المقاسم، اربعة فدادين.
حراس الجبل والطريق، احد عشر فدانا.
الرهبان بالديرة مجاورون لها، عشرة فدادين:
دير سدمنت، خمسة فدادين.
دير النقلون، خمسة فدادين.

The allowances, 73 feddans:
the preachers, 12 feddans;
the carpenters, 12 feddans;
the guardsmen, 12 feddans;
the headmen, 12 feddans;
the watchmen of the divisors, 4 feddans;
the watchmen of the mountains and the roadways, 11 feddans;
the monks in the monasteries nearby, 10 feddans:
the monastery of Sidmant, 5 feddans;
the monastery of al-Naqlūn, 5 feddans.

اهلها يزرعون من الاقصاب السكر برسم معصرة دموشية ما فدنه احد عشر فدانا وثلث وربع وثمن راس.

Its people sow first harvest sugarcane assigned for the press at Dumūshiyya, 11 ⅓ ¼ ⅛ feddans.

اهلها يربون من الفروج الفين وثمانمائة طائر. تفصيله:
للديوان المعمور، بما فيه من اجرة التربية وهو الثلث، الف ومائتا طائر.
للمقطعين، الف وستمائة طائر.

Its people rear chickens, 2,800 birds:
for the prosperous Dīwān, including the rearing wage of a third, 1,200 birds;
for the *iqṭāʿ*-holders, 1,600 birds.

وبها من التقاوي الديوانية، ثلاثمائة وستة وتسعون اردبا وقيراطان ونصف. تفصيله:
قمح، مائتان وستة وستون اردبا وثلثان.
وشعير، سبعة واربعون اردبا.
فول، اثنان وثمانون اردبا وسدس وثمن.
سمسم، ثمن[779] ونصف قيراط.

The seed advances of the Dīwān are 396 2/24 1/48 ardabbs:
wheat, 266 ⅔ ardabbs:
barley, 47 ardabbs;
broad beans, 82 ⅙ ⅛ ardabbs;
sesame, ⅛ 1/48 [ardabb].

وبها من التقاوي للمقطعين، ثمانمائة وستة وسبعون اردبا. تفصيله:
قمح، خمسمائة واربعة وثمانون اردبا.
شعير وفول، مائتان واثنان وتسعون اردبا.

The seed advances for the *iqṭāʿ*-holders, 876 ardabbs:
wheat, 584 ardabbs;
barley and broad beans, 292 ardabbs.

والذي شهد به الديوان المعمور عما انساق بالناحية وكفورها من الباقي الى اخر الايام الكاملية عند ما كان الثلث منها جاريا في الخاص، لاستقبال سنة ثلاثين وستمائة والى اخر سنة اربع وثلاثين وستمائة، بما فيه مما شرح انه حاصل، ثلث ونصف ثمن اردب:
سمسم، سدس وثمن.
قرطم، قيراطان ونصف.[780]

The outstanding payments of the village and its hamlets up to the end of the reign of al-Kāmil [in 635/1238], when a third of it belonged to the private domain of the sultan, as recorded and attested by the prosperous Dīwān, relate to a period from the beginning of 630 up to the end of 634. That included what was marked as surplus payments, which are ⅓ 1/16 of an ardabb:
sesame ⅙ ⅛ [ardabb];
safflower (*qirṭim*), 2/24 1/48 [ardabb]

عينا، ربع وثمن ودانق. غلة، ستة الاف ومائة واربعة وسبعون اردبا ونصف اردب وثلث اردب ونصف قيراط[781] وربع قيراط. تفصيله:
قمح، ثلاثة الاف وسبعمائة واربعة وخمسون اردبا ونصف وربع ونصف قيراط.
شعير، الف وستمائة وخمسة عشر اردبا ونصف.
فول، سبعمائة وخمسة اراداب ونصف وثلث وثمن.[782]

[The total of surplus and outstanding payments,] in specie ¼ ⅛ 1/144 [dinar]; and in grains, 6,174 ½ ⅓ 1/48 1/96 ardabbs:
wheat, 3,754 ½ ¼ 1/48 ardabbs;
barley, 1,615 ½ ardabbs;
broad beans, 705 ½ ⅓ ⅛ ardabbs;

778 ساقط من أ. س.: وستمائة.
779 ساقط من أ. س.: ثمن.
780 أ. س. ط. م. يضيفان: ورق نيلة، اثنا عشر أردبا.
781 ط. م.: ألف ومائة وستون أردبا وسدس ونصف.
782 أ. س.: ونصف أردب وثلث أردب وثمن أردب.

كمون، ثلاثة وستون اردبا ونصف وثلث وثمن.[783]
سمسم، تسعة ارادب ونصف وربع[784] وثمن[785] وربع قيراط.
سلجم، ثلاثة ارادب.
فريك، اردبان.
كزبرة، ربع اردب[786] ونصف قيراط.
برسيم، ربع[787] وسدس اردب.
زريعة فجل، اربعة ارادب.
جلبان، ثلاثة ارادب.
قرطم، قيراطان ونصف.
ورق نيلة، اثنا عشر اردبا.
ثوم يابس، ثمانية قناطير وربع ونصف ثمن.

والذي يسلف عليه بها من الشعير برسم الاصطبلات السلطانية، مائتان وعشرون اردبا.

ومن حرف القاف، قشوش. هذه البلدة عبارة عن بلدة صغيرة على حافة بحر الفيوم من شرقيه. تشتمل على نخل وسدر ومن قبليها وبحريها نخل اوقاف على مدرسة المالكية على ما ذكر. وبحريها نخل املاك للناس عليه خراج لمقطعيها. بينها وبين مدينة الفيوم مشوار فرس. جارية في اقطاع الطواشي شمس الدين الدكز[788] والطواشي صارم الدين حطلبا الكبشي.[789] عبرتها، الفا دينار جيشية. وبها جامع تقام فيه الجمعة. اهلها بنو زرعة فخذ من بني عجلان. شربها من ثلاث مساقي لسقي الشتوي خاصة، بغير بنيان لعلو ارضها ليس لهم عبرة، من البر البحري.

ارتفاعها مما جميعه مستخرجا ومتحصلا، عينا، ستة[790] وثلاثون دينارا ونصف، وغلة، اربعمائة اردب، قمح وشعير نصفان. تفصيله:
المراعي، خمسة دنانير.
الخراجي، احد وثلاثون دينارا ونصف، والغلة.

وعليها من الرسوم والكيالة والمراعي، عن مائة وخمسة وثمانين درهما وربع وثمن، اربعة دنانير ونصف وثمن وحبة؛ وغلة، اثنان وعشرون اردبا وربع. تفصيله:
قمح، احد عشر اردبا وربع وثمن.
وشعير، تسعة ارادب ونصف.
وفول، اردب واحد وربع وثمن.

783 أ. س.: ونصف أردب وثلث أردب وثمن أردب.
784 أ. س.: ونصف أردب وربع أردب.
785 ساقط من أ. س.: وثمن.
786 ساقط من ط. م.: أردب.
787 أ. س. يضيف: أردب.
788 أ. س.: الدكر. ط. م الذكن.
789 أ. س.: الكيشى.
790 أ. س.، ط. م.: تسعة.

cumin, 63 ½ ⅓ ⅛ ardabbs;
sesame, 9 ½ ¼ ⅛ 1/96 ardabbs;
rape, 3 ardabbs;
farīk dish, 2 ardabbs;
coriander, ¼ 1/48 [ardabb];
clover, ¼ ⅙ ardabb;
seeds of radishes (*fujl*), 4 ardabbs;
chickling vetch, 3 ardabbs;
safflower, 5/48 [ardabb];
indigo leaves, 12 ardabbs;
dry garlic, 8 ¼ 1/16 qinṭārs.

The barley assigned for the royal stables and paid for in advance, 220 ardabbs.

Also beginning with the letter 'qāf': Qushūsh.[259] This is a small village, on the bank of the Main Canal, to its east. It has date palms and sidr trees. To its south and north there are date palms belonging to endowments of the Malikite Madrasa, as was mentioned.[260] North of it there are also date palms in private ownership, which pay land tax to the *iqṭā*ʿ-holders. It is a short journey from Madīnat al-Fayyūm. It is assigned as an *iqṭā*ʿ to the *ṭawāshī* Shams Al-Dīn Ildekiz[261] and to the *ṭawāshī* Ṣārim al-Dīn Ḥuṭlubā al-Kabshī[262] with a fiscal value of 2,000 army dinars. It has a congregational mosque, in which the Friday prayers are held. Its people are the Banū Zarʿa, a branch of the Banū ʿAjlān. It gets its water, solely for winter crops, from the northern bank [of the Main Canal] through three irrigation ditches without weirs or quota, due to the elevation of its land.

Its revenue in cash and in kind is, in specie, 36 ½ dinars; and in grains, 400 ardabbs, wheat and barley, half in each.

[the revenue] in detail:
permanent pasture tax, 5 dinars;
land tax, 31 ½ dinars; and in grains [as specified].

The fees, the measurement fee and the pasture tax are 185 ¼ ⅛ dirhams, which are 4 ½ ⅛ 1/72 dinars; and in grains, 22 ¼ ardabbs:
wheat, 11 ¼ ⅛ ardabbs;
barley, 9 ½ ardabbs;
broad beans, 1 ¼ ⅛ ardabb.

259 Modern location: Quḥāfa (قحافة). Halm, *Ägypten*, p. 268: Qushush; Salmon, 'Répertoire', p. 40: Kouchoūsh; Ibn Mammātī, *Kitāb qawānīn al-dawāwīn*, p. 170: Qushush; Ibn al-Jīʿān, *Kitāb al-tuḥfa*, p. 157; de Sacy, *État des provinces*, p. 683; Ramzī, *Al-Qāmūs*, II/III, 101–02: Quḥāfa, notes that in his day there was still a family in this village called al-Qushūsha.

260 The list of the properties of the Malikite Madrasa has not been mentioned yet; it actually comes towards the end of the treatise.

261 MP: al-Dhakn, AS: al-Dakr. This is likely to be a corruption of a Turkic name, possibly Shams al-Dīn Ildekiz al-Wazīrī, governor of Nablus in 637/1239 in the service of al-Nāṣir Dāʾūd; Makīn, *Taʾrīkh*, p. 151 (43).

262 Probably Ṣārim al-Dīn Khuṭlubā, a *mamlūk* of Fakhr al-Dīn Jaharkas, who was one of Saladin's most senior amirs. After Jaharkas' death, Ṣārim al-Dīn was appointed as guardian of his son, and had effective control over his *iqṭā*ʿ in South Lebanon until 1219, when he received new lands from al-Muʿaẓẓam; Humphreys, *From Saladin to the Mongols*, pp. 144, 164. This is possibly the same as Ṣārim al-Dīn Quṭlū or Khuṭlubā al-Tibnīnī, mentioned as governor of Jerusalem in 1200; Hans L. Gottschalk, *Al-Malik Al-Kāmil von Egypten und Seine Zeit: Eine Studie zur Geschichte Vorderasiens und Egyptens in der Ersten Hälfte des 7./13. Jahrhunderts* (Wiesbaden: Harrassowitz, 1958), p. 29. Another officer by the name of Khuṭlubā received the entire Fayyum as iqṭāʿ in 1181–82; Halm, *Ägypten*, p. 268; Rabie, *The Financial System*, p. 42. AS: al-Kīshā instead of al-Kabshī.

تفصيله:
الرسوم، مائة وثمانية واربعون درهما ونصف، وغلة، اربعة عشر اردبا ونصف وربع:
قمح، سبعة ارادب وربع وثمن.
شعير، ستة ارادب.
فول، اردب واحد وربع وثمن.
تفصيله:
شد العين، سبعة عشر درهما.
شد الاحباس، ستة دراهم.[791]
رسم الجراريف، خمسة واربعون درهما.
رسم الحصاد، ثلاثة وخمسون درهما.
رسم الخفارة، خمسة عشر درهما.
رسم الاجران، اثنا عشر درهما ونصف، والغلة على ما تقدم.
الكيالة، سبعة ارادب ونصف:
قمح، اربعة ارادب.
وشعير، ثلاثة ارادب ونصف.
المراعي والرسم،[792] ستة وثلاثون درهما ونصف وربع وثمن. تفصيله:
المراعي خاصة، خمسة وعشرون درهما المائة، عن مائة وثمانية عشر راسا، تسعة وعشرون درهما ونصف.
رسم المستخدمين، سبعة دراهم وربع وثمن.

وعليها من الزكاة، سبعة دنانير وثلثان وربع. تفصيله:
خرص النخل، دينار واحد ونصف.
ثمن الماشية، عن سبعة ارؤس، ستة دنانير وربع وسدس. تفصيله:
بقر احمر، تبيع واحد، ثلثا دينار.
ثمن اغنام، عن ستة ارؤس، خمسة دنانير ونصف وربع. تفصيله:
بياض، عن خمسة ارؤس، خمسة دنانير وربع.
شعارى، عن راس واحد، نصف دينار.

وعليها من الاتبان، ستمائة شنيف.

وعليها لديوان الاحباس ديناران ونصف.

وبها من فدن الرزق باسم الخطيب بها، اربعة فدادين.

والمقرر على فلاحيها من الكشك والفريك والسويق، اردب واحد وربع ونصف قيراط:
كشك، ثلث وربع اردب.
فريك، ثلث وثمن اردب.
سويق، سدس ونصف ثمن اردب.

والذي جرت العادة باطلاقه من التقاوي لعمارتها من جهة المقطعين، مائة واردبان:
قمح، ستة وسبعون اردبا.
وشعير، ستة وعشرون اردبا.

والمربى بها من الدجاج، اربعمائة طائر. تفصيله:
للديوان المعمور، بما فيه من اجرة التربية وهو الثلث، ثلاثمائة طائر.
للمقطعين، مائة طائر.

791 ساقط من أ. س.: شد الأحباس ستة دراهم.
792 ساقط من أ. س.: والرسم.

[The fees, the measurement fee and the pasture tax] in detail:
the fees, 148 ½ dirhams; and in grains, 14 ½ ¼ ardabbs:
wheat, 7 ¼ ⅛ ardabbs;
barley, 7 ardabbs;
broad beans, 1 ¼ ⅛ ardabb.
[the fees] in detail:
supervision of the land survey, 17 dirhams;
supervision of endowments, 6 dirhams;
dredging fee, 45 dirhams;
harvest fee, 53 dirhams;
protection fee, 15 dirhams;
threshing-floor fee, 12 ½ dirhams; and in grains, as specified.
The measurement fee, 7 ½ ardabbs:
wheat, 4 ardabbs;
barley, 3 ½ ardabbs.
The pasture fee and the [government agents'] fee, 36 ½ ¼ ⅛ dirhams:
the pasture fee proper, at a rate of 25 dirhams per 100 [heads], for 118 heads, 29 ½ dirhams;
the government agents' fee, 7 ¼ ⅛ dirhams.

The alms-tax, 7 ⅔ ¼ dinars:
estimate of date palms, 1 ½ dinar;
monetary value of livestock, for seven heads, 6 ¼ ⅙ dinars:
cows, for a yearling calf ⅔ dinar;
monetary value of small cattle, for six heads, 5 ½ ¼ dinars:
sheep, for five heads, 5 ¼ dinars;
goats, for one head, ½ dinar.

Hay, 600 bales.

For the Ministry of Endowments, 2 ½ dinars.

The feddan allowances, which are in the name of the preacher, 4 feddans.

The established levy on its peasants in *kishk*, *farīk* and *sawīq* dishes, 1 ¼ 1/48 ardabb:
kishk, ⅓ ¼ ardabb;
farīk, ⅓ ⅛ ardabb;
sawīq, ⅙ 1/16 ardabb.

The customary seed advances distributed in it by the *iqṭā*ᶜ-holders for the purpose of its cultivation, 102 ardabbs:
wheat, 76 ardabbs;
barley, 26 ardabbs.

The chickens reared in it, 400 birds:
for the prosperous Dīwān, including the rearing wage of a third, 300 birds;
for the *iqṭā*ᶜ-holders, 100 birds.

والمسلف عليها بها من الشعير برسم الاصطبلات السلطانية، مائة اردب.

اهلها يزرعون[793] القصب السكر برسم معصرة المدينة، وهو راس وخلفة، فدانان. تفصيله:

راس، فدان واحد.

خلفة، فدان واحد.

حرف الكاف، كنبوت. وليس في حرف الكاف غيرها. هذه البلدة عبارة عن بلدة صغيرة من جملة بلاد خليج دلية. ليس بها سكان. وتزرع اراضيها بالمرتب لها من الماء فلاحون البلاد الذي حولها. بينها وبين مدينة الفيوم ثلاث ساعات وهي قبلي الفيوم وليس بها شجر ولا نخل ولا حولها سوى المحاطب. وهي مجموعة في عبرة اقطاع الخليج المذكور. لها من الماء من بحر دلية من المقسم المعروف بالتبرون ما عدته ست قبض وربع ماء. اهلها بنو حاتم، فخذ من بني كلاب.

ارتفاعها، مائتان وستة وتسعون[794] اردبا ونصف. تفصيله:

قمح، خمسة وتسعون اردبا.

شعير، مائتان واردب واحد ونصف.

عليها من الرسوم والكيالة، عن مائة واربعة عشر[795] درهما ونصف، ديناران ونصف وثلث وحبتان؛ وغلة، تسعة عشر اردبا وثلثان وثمن:

قمح، تسعة عشر اردبا ونصف قيراط.

فول، نصف وربع ونصف قيراط.

تفصيله:

الرسوم، مائة واربعة عشر درهما[796] ونصف، وغلة، تسعة ارادب وثلثان وثمن:

قمح، تسعة ارادب ونصف قيراط.

فول، نصف وربع ونصف قيراط.

تفصيله:

شد العين، ثلاثة دراهم.

شد الاحباس، ستة دراهم.

رسم الخفارة، خمسة عشر درهما.

رسم الحصاد، ثلاثة وخمسون درهما.

رسم الجراريف، ثمانية وعشرون درهما ونصف وربع.

رسم الاجران، ثمانية دراهم ونصف وربع، وغلة، تسعة ارادب وثلثان وثمن، على ما فصل.

كيالة، شعير، عشرة ارادب.

وعليها من الزكاة عن ثمن راسين غنم، دينار ونصف:

بياض، راس واحد، دينار واحد.

شعرية، نصف دينار.

عليها من الاتبان، مائتا شنيف.

رسم خولي البحر بها، اردب واحد وثلثان. تفصيله:

قمح، نصف وثلث.

شعير، نصف وثلث.

793 أ. س. يضيف: من.

794 أ. س.: أربعون.

795 أ. س.: أربعين.

796 أ. س.: أردبا.

The barley assigned for the royal stables and paid for in advance, 100 ardabbs.

Its people sow 2 feddans of sugarcane assigned for the press in Madīnat al-Fayyūm, first and second harvest:

first harvest, 1 feddan;

second harvest, 1 feddan.

The letter 'kāf': Kanbūt.[263] There are no other villages beginning in the letter 'kāf'. This is a small village, included in the total [fiscal value] of the villages of Dilya Canal. There are no inhabitants in it. Its lands are sown by the peasants of the surrounding villages with the water allocated to it. It is at the south of the Fayyum, three hours' [ride] from Madīnat al-Fayyūm. There are no trees or date palms in it, and there is nothing around it except for firewood. It is included in the fiscal value of Dilya Canal. It gets its water from that canal, from the divisor known as al-Tabrūn, 6 ¼ *qabḍas*. Its people are the Banū Ḥātim, a branch of the Banū Kilāb.

Its revenue is 296 ½ ardabbs:

wheat, 95 ardabbs;

barley, 201 ½ ardabbs.

The fees and the measurement fee, 114 ½ dirhams, which are 2 ½ ⅓ 2/72 dinars; and in grains, 19 ⅔ ⅛ ardabbs:

wheat, 19 1/48 ardabbs;

broad beans ½ ¼ 1/48 [ardabb].

[The fees and the measurement fee] in detail:

the fees, 114 ½ dirhams; and in grains, 9 ⅔ ⅛ ardabbs:

wheat, 9 1/48 ardabbs;

broad beans ½ ¼ 1/48 [ardabb].

[The fees] in detail:

supervision of the land survey, 3 dirhams;

supervision of endowments, 6 dirhams;

protection fee, 15 dirhams;

harvest fee, 53 dirhams;

dredging fee, 28 ½ ¼ dirhams;

threshing-floor fee, 8 ½ ¼ dirhams; and in grains, 9 ⅔ ⅛ ardabbs, as specified.

The measurement fee, barley, 10 ardabbs.

The alms-tax, for the monetary value of two heads of small cattle, 1 ½ dinar:

one sheep, 1 dinar;

one goat, ½ dinar.

Hay, 200 bales.

Fee for the overseer of the canal, 1 ⅔ ardabb:

wheat ½ ⅓;

barley ½ ⅓.

263 Modern location (uncertain): ʿIzbat ʿAbd al-ʿĀl (عزبة عبد العال). Halm, *Ägypten*, pp. 260–61; Salmon, 'Répertoire', p. 70; Ibn al-Jīʿān, *Kitāb al-tuḥfa*, p. 157; de Sacy, *État des provinces*, p. 683; Ramzī, *Al-Qāmūs*, I, 390: al-Saʿda. We have no positive identification of this village. In line with al-Nābulusī's description (that it received its water from Dilya Canal, from the divisor known as al-Tabrūn), we placed it near the present village of ʿIzbat ʿAbd al-ʿĀl.

وعليها لديوان الاحباس، ديناران.

ومن[797] حرف الميم، منية الاسقف. هذه البلدة عبارة عن بلدة صغيرة على حافة بحر الفيوم من جهة الغرب. بيوتها[798] في البساتين. يحف بها النخل والاشجار وتشتمل على بساتين. فيها انواع الفواكه كالمشمش والعنب والكمثرى والخروب والمحمضات كالنارنج والليمون. وفيها السفرجل والرمان. بينها وبين مدينة الفيوم مشوار فرس. جارية في اقطاع الامير عز الدين خضر بن محمد الكيكاني واخوته، بعبرة مبلغها الف وخمسمائة دينار جيشية. شربها في ايام النيل من خليج يعرف باقنى لسقيها وسقي[799] باجة. خفارتها[800] لبني زرعة، فخذ من بني كلاب. وبها كنيسة.

ارتفاعها، عينا، مما جميعه مستخرجا، مائتان وتسعة وعشرون دينارا ونصف وثمن. تفصيله:

الهلالي، ثلاثة عشر دينارا. تفصيله:

المدبغة، سبعة دنانير.

القزازون، ستة دنانير.

خراج البساتين، مائتان وستة عشر دينارا ونصف وثمن.

وعليها رسم الخفارة، عن خمسة عشر درهما، ربع وثمن دينار.

وعليها من الزكاة عن خرص النخل، اربعة دنانير ونصف وربع.

وعليها من الجوالي، عن ستة وخمسين نفرا، مائة واثنا عشر دينارا. تفصيله:

المقيمون بها، عن سبعة[801] واربعين نفرا، اربعة وتسعون دينارا.

الناءون عنها بالوجه البحري، عن تسعة انفار، ثمانية عشر دينارا.

اهلها يربون من الفروج برسم المطابخ السلطانية، بما فيه من اجرة التربية وهو الثلث، ثلاثمائة فروج.

ومن حرف الميم، منية كربيس والاخصاص المعروفة بابي عصية. هذان الموضعان يذكران معا بحكم ان اخصاص ابي عصية تابع لمنية كربيس، داخل في ارتفاعها، وهي كفر من كفورها. وتشتمل منية كربيس على نخل وخروب وجميز ويحف بها دويرات تين وبساتين للملاك يقومون بخراجها لمقطعها.[802] وهي بحري الفيوم مما يلي الغرب. بينها وبين مدينة الفيوم مسافة نصف ساعة للراكب.

وابو عصية عبارة عن كفر[803] صغير يكون دون عشرة ابيات الى حافة واد[804] على حافة تندود. في هذا الوادي اعين جارية يستقى منها[805] ويشرب اذا انقطع ماء البحر. ياوى الى هذا الوادي وقت السحر من الاطيار المسموع ما لا يحصر عدده ولا يضبط نوعه.

797 ساقط من أ. س.: ومن.

798 أ. س.: يتلوها.

799 أ. س.: ويسقي.

800 أ. س.: خفرها.

801 أ. س.: ستة.

802 أ. س.: لمقطعيها.

803 ط. م.: كفير.

804 أ. س.: الوادي.

805 ساقط من أ. س.: منها.

For the Ministry of Endowments, 2 dinars.

Beginning with the letter 'mīm': Minyat al-Usquf.[264] This is a small village, on the bank of the Main Canal, to its west. Its houses are within orchards,[265] and it is surrounded by date palms and trees. Its orchards contain various fruits such as apricots, grapes, pears, carobs, citrus fruits like bitter orange and lemon, quinces and pomegranates. It is a short journey from Madīnat al-Fayyūm. It is assigned as an *iqṭāʿ* to the amir ʿIzz al-Dīn Khiḍr ibn Muḥammad al-Kīkānī and his brothers, with a fiscal value of 1,500 army dinars. It gets its water, during the period of the high Nile, from a canal known as Aqnā, designated for its irrigation and the irrigation of Bāja. Its protection is at the hands of the Banū Zarʿa, a branch of the Banū Kilāb [= Banū ʿAjlān]. It has a church.

Its revenue in cash, in specie, is 229 ½ ⅛ dinars:

lunar-calendar tax, 13 dinars:

the tannery, 7 dinars;

the weavers, 6 dinars;

land tax on orchards, 216 ½ ⅛ dinars.

The protection fee, 15 dirhams, which are ¼ ⅛ dinar.

The alms-tax, for the estimate of the date palms, 4 ½ ¼ dinars.

The poll-tax, for 56 individuals, 112 dinars:

those residing in it, for 47 individuals, 94 dinars;

those absent from it, in the northern region, for nine individuals, 18 dinars.

Its people rear chickens assigned for the royal kitchens, including the rearing wage of a third, 300 chickens.

Also beginning with the letter 'mīm': Minyat Karbīs,[266] and the Akhṣāṣ known as Abū ʿUṣayya.[267] These two places are mentioned together since Akhṣāṣ Abū ʿUṣayya is subordinate to Minyat Karbīs, is included in its revenues, and is one of its hamlets. Minyat Karbīs has date palms, carobs and sycamores, and is surrounded by enclosures of figs and orchards in private ownership, paying land tax to its *iqṭāʿ*-holder. It is at the north-west of the province, half an hour's ride from Madīnat al-Fayyūm.

Abū ʿUṣayya is a small hamlet, with no more than ten houses, on the bank of a ravine, next to [the press known as] Tandūd. In this ravine there are flowing springs, which are used for irrigation and drinking when the canal water is cut off. At daybreak, countless birds of song, of unlimited varieties, seek refuge in this ravine.

264 Modern location (uncertain): the eastern part of the city, near the central train station. Ibn al-Jīʿān, *Kitāb al-tuḥfa*, p. 155; Timm, *Das Christlich-Koptische Ägypten*, pp. 1666–7; Halm, *Ägypten*, p. 271: ʾUsquf/Sāqiyat al-Qummuṣ; Salmon, 'Répertoire', p. 41; de Sacy, *État des provinces*, p. 682: Sāqiyat al-Qummuṣ wa'l-ʾUskuf; Ramzī, *Al-Qāmūs*, I, 273; 428: ʿIzbat al-ʿAqrab. We could not find this ʿIzba — probably because, as noted by Ramzī, it has been overtaken by the expanding city. Timm notes, however (p. 1667), that it was close to the location of the central train station. We located it on the map accordingly, and this is also in line with Shafei Bey's identification.

265 AS: *yatlū-hā fī al-basātīn*.

266 Modern location: Zāwiyat al-Karādsa (زاوية الكرادسة). Salmon, 'Répertoire', p. 53; Ibn al-Jīʿān, *Kitāb al-tuḥfa*, p. 151; Ibn Mammātī, *Kitāb qawānīn al-dawāwīn*: Minyat Kabūs; Zéki, 'Une description', p. 41; Savigny, *Description de l'Égypte*, p. 129: al-Zāwiya al-Karāniyya; Ramzī, *Al-Qāmūs*, II/III, 100: Zāwiyat al-Karādsa.

267 Modern location: ʿIzbat Ḥarfūsh (عزبة حرفوش). Halm, *Ägypten*, p. 245; Salmon, 'Répertoire', p. 53; Ibn al-Jīʿān, *Kitāb al-tuḥfa*, p. 151; Ramzī, *Al-Qāmūs*, II/III, 100: ʿIzbat Ḥarfūsh.

جارية في اقطاع الطواشي الاخص علم الدين سنجر[806] العدلاني بعبرة مبلغها ثلاثة الاف وخمسمائة دينار جيشية. شربها الشتوي من خليج فانو، بحكم ان خليجها اضيف لنقليفة وفانو على ما تقدم شرحه فيهما، ومسقاه من البحر الاعظم يسقى احكار ورثة ابن الاشقر. وعليها ساقيتان احداهما على بستان القاضي الاسعد بن جلال الدين والاخرى لورثة ابن الاشقر بغير عبرة. ليس له عبرة تذكر لعلو ناحيته. اهلها بنو جابر، كرابسة، فخذ من بني عجلان.

ارتفاعها مما جميعه مستخرجا ومتحصلا، عينا، مائتان وخمسة وستون[807] دينارا وثلث ونصف قيراط، وغلة، ثلاثمائة وثلاثة وعشرون اردبا. تفصيله:

قمح، مائة وسبعة وسبعون[808] اردبا.
شعير، ستة وستون اردبا وثلث.
فول، خمسة وسبعون اردبا ونصف.
كراويا، اردبان ونصف.
سلجم، اردب وثلثان.

تفصيله:

مال الهلالي، عن حكر طاحون الماء، عن ستين درهما، دينار ونصف.
مال المراعي، عشرة دنانير ونصف وثمن.
مال الخراجي وثمن ثمرة النخل، مائتان وثلاثة وخمسون دينارا وسدس ونصف ثمن؛ غلة، ثلاثمائة وثلاثة وعشرون اردبا، على ما فصل.

الخراجي خاصة، مائتان وتسعة واربعون دينارا وسدس ونصف ثمن، والغلة:

خراج الراتب والاحكار، اصلا واضافة، خمسة وثمانون دينارا ونصف وربع ونصف ثمن.
خراج الاقصاب المزدرعة للديوان السلطاني برسم معصرة المدينة، عن مائة فدان مائة دينار.
خراج اللواز واراضي المروج والخروس العالية، تسعة وخمسون دينارا وثلثان وربع.
خراج القرط ثلاثة دنانير ونصف.

مشاطرة الغلة بما فيه من القداحة والعشر، ثلاثمائة وثلاثة وعشرون اردبا، على ما فصل.

ثمن ثمرة النخل اربعة دنانير.

806 أ. س.: سحر.
807 أ. س.: سبعون، لكنه يضبطها لستون.
808 أ. س.: ستون.

It is assigned as an *iqṭāᶜ* to the *ṭawāshī al-akhaṣṣ*[268] ᶜAlam al-Dīn Sanjar al-ᶜAdlānī, with a fiscal value of 3,500 army dinars. It is watered in the winter from the Fānū Canal, since its canal was joined up with Naqalīfa and Fānū as explained above in their entry. An irrigation ditch issuing from the Main Canal irrigates the lands subject to long-term lease belonging to the heirs of Ibn al-Ashqar. It has two waterwheels, one of them [provides water] for the orchard of the judge al-Asᶜad ibn Jalāl al-Dīn, and the other belongs to the heirs of Ibn al-Ashqar. It has no [water] quota, due to the elevation of the area. Its people are the Karābisa[269] of the Banū Jābir, a branch of the Banū ᶜAjlān.

Its revenue in cash and in kind is, in specie, 265 ⅓ 1⁄48 dinars; and in grains, 323 ardabbs:

wheat, 177 ardabbs;
barley, 66 ⅓ ardabbs;
broad beans, 75 ½ ardabbs;
caraway, 2 ½ ardabbs;
rape, 1 ⅔ ardabb.

[The revenue] in detail:

lunar-calendar tax, for the long-term lease of the watermill, 60 dirhams, which are 1 ½ dinar;
fixed pasture tax, 10 ½ ⅛ dinars;
land tax in cash and the monetary value of the yield of dates, 253 ⅙ 1⁄16 dinars; and in grains, 323 ardabbs, as specified.

The land tax proper, 249 ⅙ 1⁄16 dinars; and the grains:

land tax on perennial plants and on lands subject to long-term lease, the basic assessment and the addition, 85 ½ ¼ 1⁄16 dinars;
land tax on sugarcanes, cultivated for the royal Dīwān, assigned for the press at the city, for 100 feddans, 100 dinars;
land tax on *al-lawāz* (?),[270] and on pasturing meadows and elevated *khirs*[271] land, 59 ⅔ ¼ dinars;
land tax on alfalfa, 3 ½ dinars;

Mushāṭara land tax in grains, including the *qidāḥa* (?)[272] and the tithe (*al-ᶜushr*), 323 ardabbs, as specified.

Monetary value of the yield of dates, 4 dinars.

268 The rank of *al-amīr al-akhaṣṣ* is not attested in surviving Ayyubid inscriptions; Humphreys, 'The Emergence of the Mamluk Army', p. 86. The context here suggests that this is a military commander of the second rank, comparable to *al-amīr al-ajall*.

269 Earlier in the treatise, the Karābisa are mentioned twice as a sub-section of the Aḍābiṭa, a branch of the Banū Kilāb. The Banū Jābir are mentioned elsewhere as a branch of the Banū ᶜAjlān.

270 Context suggests this is a type of soil, like the *khirs* mentioned in the next sentence. Perhaps *al-lawāz* (اللواز) is a mistake for *al-sawād* (السواد), arable clay soil.

271 Poor quality grazing land in which obstacles to cultivation are deeply rooted, but which, with clearing and effort, can become very productive. See Ibn Mammātī, *Kitāb qawānīn al-dawāwīn*, p. 203; Cooper, 'Ibn Mammati's Rules', p. 36.

272 Context suggests this is a measurement fee, called elsewhere in the treatise *kiyāla*. Perhaps etymologically connected to *qadaḥ*, pl. *aqdāḥ*, a dry measure of 1⁄96 ardabb.

وعليها من الرسوم والكيالة والمراعي، عن اربعمائة وثلاثة[809] دراهم، عشرة دنانير وقيراطان؛ وغلة، ثمانية وعشرون اردبا ونصف وربع ونصف ثمن. تفصيله:

قمح، تسعة عشر اردبا ونصف وربع وثمن.

شعير، ثلاثة ارادب وقيراطان.

فول، خمسة ارادب ونصف وثلث ونصف قيراط.

تفصيله:

الرسوم، مائتان واربعة وستون درهما ونصف وربع وثمن، وغلة، تسعة عشر اردبا وثلث وربع ونصف ثمن. تفصيله:

قمح، اثنا عشر اردبا وثلث وربع وثمن.

شعير، ثلاثة ارادب وقيراطان.

فول، ثلاثة ارادب ونصف وثلث ونصف قيراط.

تفصيل ذلك:

شد العين، خمسة وثمانون درهما.

شد الاحباس، خمسة دراهم.

رسم الجراريف، تسعون درهما.[810]

رسم الحصاد، ثلاثة وخمسون درهما.

رسم الخفارة، خمسة عشر درهما.

رسم الاجران، ستة عشر درهما ونصف وربع وثمن، والغلة على ما تقدم.

كيالة، تسعة ارادب وسدس. تفصيله:

قمح، سبعة ارادب وسدس.

فول، اردبان.

المراعي الطارئ، عن مائتين وثلاثة وثمانين[811] راسا، مائة وثمانية[812] وثلاثون درهما وثمن. تفصيله:

قطيعة سبعين درهما[813] المائة، عن خمسة وعشرين راسا، سبعة عشر درهما ونصف.[814]

قطيعة خمسين درهما المائة، عن مائة واربعين راسا، سبعون درهما.

قطيعة ثلاثين درهما المائة، عن سبعين راسا، احد وعشرون درهما.

قطيعة خمسة وعشرين درهما المائة، عن ثمانية واربعين راسا، اثنا عشر درهما.

رسم المستخدمين، سبعة عشر درهما ونصف وثمن.

وعليها من الزكاة، اثنا عشر دينارا وثلثان وربع. تفصيله:

منية كربيس، اربعة دنانير:

خرص النخل، دينار.

المواشي، عن ثلاثة ارؤس، ثلاثة دنانير. تفصيله:

بقر احمر، عن تبيع واحد، دينار واحد ونصف.[815]

اغنام، عن راسين، دينار واحد ونصف:

بياض، راس واحد، دينار واحد.

شعارى، راس، نصف دينار.

The fees, the measurement fee and the pasture tax are 403 dirhams, which are 10 2/24 dinars; and in grains, 28 ½ ¼ 1/16 ardabbs:

- wheat, 19 ½ ¼ ⅛ ardabbs;
- barley, 3 2/24 ardabbs;
- broad beans, 5 ½ ⅓ 1/48 ardabbs.

[The fees, the measurement fee and the pasture tax] in detail:

- the fees, 264 ½ ¼ ⅛ dirhams; and in grains, 19 ⅓ ¼ 1/16 ardabbs:
  - wheat, 12 ⅓ ¼ ⅛ ardabbs;
  - barley, 3 2/24 ardabbs;
  - broad beans, 3 ½ ⅓ 1/48 ardabbs.
- [The fees] in detail:
  - supervision of the land survey, 85 dirhams;
  - supervision of endowments, 5 dirhams;
  - dredging fee, 90 dirhams;
  - harvest fee, 53 dirhams;
  - protection fee, 15 dirhams;
  - threshing-floor fee, 16 ½ ¼ ⅛ dirhams; and in grains, as specified.
- The measurement fee, 9 ⅙ ardabbs:
  - wheat, 7 ⅙ ardabbs;
  - broad beans, 2 ardabbs.
- The pasture tax on seasonal pasture lands, for 283 heads, 138 ⅛ dirhams:
  - at the rate of 70 dirhams per 100 [heads], for 25 heads, 17 ½ dirhams;
  - at the rate of 50 dirhams per 100 [heads], for 140 heads, 70 dirhams;
  - at the rate of 30 dirhams per 100 [heads], for 70 heads, 21 dirhams;
  - at the rate of 25 dirhams per 100 [heads], for 48 heads, 12 dirhams;
  - the government agents' fee, 17 ½ ⅛ dirhams.

The alms-tax, 12 ⅔ ¼ dinars:

- Minyat Karbīs, 4 dinars:
  - estimate of date palms, 1 dinar;
  - [monetary value of] livestock, for three heads, 3 dinars:
    - cows, for a yearling calf, 1 ½ dinar;
    - small cattle, for two heads, 1 ½ dinar:
      - sheep, one head, 1 dinar;
      - goats, for one head, ½ dinar.

809 أ. س.: وثلاثين.

810 أ. س.: تسع دراهم.

811 أ. س.: ثلاثين.

812 أ. س.: وثلاثة.

813 أ. س.: سبع دراهم.

814 ساقط من أ. س.: ونصف.

815 ساقط من أ. س.: واحد ونصف.

اخصاص ابي عصية، ثمانية دنانير وثلثان وربع. تفصيله:
خرص النخل، ديناران ونصف وربع وثمن.
ثمن الماشية، عن ستة ارؤس، ستة دنانير وقيراط.
تفصيله:
بقر احمر، تبيع واحد، دينار واحد وربع.
ثمن الاغنام، عن خمسة ارؤس، اربعة دنانير وثلثان وثمن. تفصيله:
بياض، عن اربعة ارؤس، اربعة دنانير وربع.
شعارى، عن راس، ربع وسدس وثمن دينار.

عليها لديوان الاحباس، ديناران.

عليها من الاتبان في الضريبة العتيقة، تسعمائة شنيف.

رسم خولي البحر بها، قمح، نصف اردب.

والمقرر على مزارعيها من الكشك والفريك، ثلاث ارادب، نصفان.

والذي رتبه المقطع بها من الرزق، تسعة فدادين طين سواد. تفصيله:
للمشايخ، ستة فدادين.
الخفراء، ثلاثة فدادين.

والمربى بها من الفروج، اربعمائة وثلاثون فروجا. تفصيله:
للديوان المعمور، بما فيه من اجرة التربية وهو الثلث، مائة وثمانون طائرا.
للمقطع،[816] مائتان وخمسون طائرا.

اهلها يزرعون من القصب السكر برسم معصرة المدينة ما عدة فدنه اربعة عشر فدانا وربع وسدس وثمن. تفصيله:
راس، اثنا عشر فدانا وسدس وثمن.
خلفة، فدانان وربع.

والذي يسلف عليه بها من الشعير برسم الاصطبلات السلطانية، اربعون اردبا.

والذي جرت العادة باطلاقه لها من التقاوي، ثمانية وستون اردبا ونصف:
قمح، خمسون اردبا.
شعير، ثمانية ارادب ونصف.
فول، عشرة ارادب.

ومن حرف الميم، منشاة ابن كردي من كفور سنورس. هذه البلدة[817] عبارة عن بلدة صغيرة تشتمل على قليل شجر سنط وودي نخل مستجد. وهي من بحري الفيوم. بينهما وبين مدينة الفيوم مسافة ثلاث ساعات للراكب. جارية في اقطاع جماعة من المقطعين بغير عبرة. شربها من الماء المطلق ببحر سنورس من المقسم المعروف بالشاذروان تسقى الشتوي والصيفي بما عبرته خمس قبض ونصف ماء. اهلها بنو جابر، فخذ من بني عجلان.

ارتفاعها، بما فيه مما هو متوفر للديوان المعمور خارجا عن اقطاع المقطعين وهو عينا ستة دنانير ونصف وثلث، سمسم ثلاثة عشر اردبا وربع، عينا، عن خراج الراتب، ستة دنانير[818] ونصف وثلث ودانق؛ غلة، مما جميعه متحصلا من خراج الغلات، ستمائة وتسعة عشر اردبا ونصف. تفصيله:

816 أ. س.: للمقطعين.
817 ساقط من ط. م.: البلدة.
818 ساقط من أ. س.: دنانير.

Akhṣāṣ Abū ʿUṣayya, 8 ⅔ ¼ dinars:
estimate of the date palms, 2 ½ ¼ ⅛ dinars;
monetary value of livestock, for six heads, 6 1/24 dinars:
cows, for a yearling calf, 1 ¼ dinar;
monetary value of small cattle, for five heads, 4 ⅔ ⅛ dinars:
sheep, for four heads, 4 ¼ dinars;
goats, for one head, ¼ ⅙ ⅛ dinar.

For the Ministry of Endowments, 2 dinars.

Hay in the [Dīwān's] old register (*al-ḍarība al-ʿatīqa*), 900 bales.

The fee of the overseer of the canal, wheat, ½ ardabb.

The confirmed levy of *kishk* and *farīk* on the tenants, 3 ardabbs, half in each.

The allowances allocated by the *iqṭāʿ*-holder, 9 feddans of arable land (*ṭīn sawād*):[273]
the headmen, 6 feddans;
the guardsmen, 3 feddans.

The chickens reared in it, 430 chickens:
for the prosperous Dīwān, including the rearing wage of a third, 180 birds;
for the *iqṭāʿ*-holder, 250 birds.

Its people cultivate sugarcane assigned for the press at the city, 14 ¼ ⅙ ⅛ feddans:
first harvest, 12 ⅙ ⅛ feddans;
second harvest, 2 ¼ feddans.

The barley assigned for the royal stables and paid for in advance, 40 ardabbs.

The seed advances customarily distributed, 68 ½ ardabbs:
wheat, 50 ardabbs;
barley, 8 ½ ardabbs;
broad beans, 10 ardabbs.

Also beginning with the letter 'mīm': Munshaʾat Ibn Kurdī,[274] a hamlet of Sinnūris. This is a small village, with few acacia trees and recently planted shoots of date palms. It is in the north of the province, three hours' ride from Madīnat al-Fayyūm. It is assigned as an *iqṭāʿ* to a group of *iqṭāʿ*-holders, without fiscal value. It is irrigated by the water of Sinnūris Canal, allocated by the divisor known as al-Shādhrawān. Its water quota, for the irrigation of winter and summer crops, is 5 ½ *qabḍas*. Its people are the Banū Jābir, a branch of the Banū ʿAjlān.

Its revenue, consisting of what is rendered (*mutawaffir*) to the prosperous Dīwān, in specie, from land tax on perennial plants, 6 ½ ⅓ 1/144 dinars; and in grains, entirely from land tax on grains, 619 ½ ardabbs:

273 The term *arḍ sawād* is the common term for arable clay soil in Fatimid documents from the Fayyum. See two examples, among many, in Gaubert and Mouton, *Hommes et villages*, nos. 5 and 6.

274 Modern location: Jabala (جبلة). Halm, *Ägypten*, pp. 262–63: Manshiyat Ibn Kurdī = Jabala; Salmon, 'Répertoire', p. 51; Ibn al-Jīʿān, *Kitāb al-tuḥfa*, p. 158: Manshiyat Ibn Kurdī known as Ḥīla; Ramzī, *Al-Qāmūs*, II/III, 112: Jabala.

قمح، اربعمائة اردب.
شعير، مائتا اردب.
سمسم، تسعة عشر اردبا ونصف.

عليها من الرسوم، عن مائة وستين درهما وثمن، اربعة دنانير؛ وغلة، ستة وخمسون اردبا وربع وسدس وثمن. تفصيله:

قمح، ثمانية وعشرون اردبا وثمن ونصف قيراط.
وشعير، ستة عشر اردبا.
وفول، عشرة ارادب وثلث ونصف ثمن.
سمسم، اردبان.

تفصيله:

الرسوم، عن الاجران، ستة وعشرون درهما وربع، وغلة، احد وثلاثون اردبا وقيراط. تفصيله:
قمح، ثلاثة عشر اردبا وثمن ونصف قيراط.
شعير، ستة ارادب.
فول، عشرة ارادب وثلث ونصف ثمن.
سمسم، اردب واحد ونصف.
الكيالة، خمسة وعشرون اردبا ونصف. تفصيله:
قمح، خمسة عشر اردبا.
شعير، عشرة ارادب.
سمسم، نصف اردب.
المراعي، عن مائة واربعة ارؤس، مائة وثلاثة وثلاثون درهما ونصف وربع وثمن. تفصيله:
راتب، عن اثنين وعشرين راسا، اربعون درهما ونصف.
طارئ، عن اثنين وثمانين راسا، سبعة وسبعون درهما ونصف وربع وثمن. تفصيله:
قطيعة درهم واحد الراس، عن ستة وسبعين راسا، ستة وسبعون درهما.
قطيعة ثلاثين درهما المائة، عن ستة وسبعين ارؤس، درهم[819] واحد ونصف وربع وثمن.
رسم المستخدمين، ستة دراهم ونصف.

وعليها من الزكاة عن ثمن اغنام، عن اربعة ارؤس، ثلاثة دنانير وربع وثمن. تفصيله:
بياض، عن راسين، ديناران وربع.[820]
شعارى، عن راسين، دينار واحد وثمن.

وعليها من الاتبان، الف وعشرون شنيفا.

والمربى بها من الفروج، ثلاثمائة وعشرة فراريج. تفصيله:
للديوان المعمور بما فيه من اجرة التربية وهو الثلث،[821] مائتا طائر.
للمقطعين، مائة وعشرة فراريج.

اهلها يزرعون من[822] الاقصاب برسم المعاصر لسنورس، ثمانية عشر فدانا ونصف وثلث وحبتان. تفصيله:
راس، ثلاثة عشر فدانا ونصف وثمن وحبتين.
خلفة، خمسة فدادين وخمسة قراريط.

wheat, 400 ardabbs;
barley, 200 ardabbs;
sesame, 19 ½ ardabbs.

That excludes [the revenue of] the *iqṭāʿ* of the *iqṭāʿ*-holders, which is, in specie, 6 ½ ⅓ dinars; [and in grains], sesame, 13 ¼ ardabbs.

The fees are 160 ⅛ dirhams, which are 4 dinars; and in grains, 56 ¼ ⅙ ⅛ ardabbs:
wheat, 28 ⅛ 1/48 ardabbs;
barley, 16 ardabbs;
broad beans, 10 ⅓ 1/16 ardabbs;
sesame, 2 ardabbs.

The fees in detail:
threshing-floor fee, 26 ¼ dirhams; and in grains, 31 1/24 ardabbs:
wheat, 13 ⅛ 1/48 ardabbs;
barley, 6 ardabbs;
broad beans, 10 ⅓ 1/16 ardabbs;
sesame, 1 ½ ardabb.
The measurement fee, 25 ½ ardabbs:
wheat, 15 ardabbs;
barley, 10 ardabbs;
sesame, ½ ardabb.
The pasture tax, for 104 heads, 133 ½ ¼ ⅛ dirhams:
permanent pasture lands, for 22 heads, 49 ½ dirhams;
seasonal pasture lands, for 82 heads, 77 ½ ¼ ⅛ dirhams:
at the rate of one dirham per head, for 76 heads, 76 dirhams;
at the rate of 30 dirhams per 100 [heads], for six heads, 1 ½ ¼ ⅛ dirham;
the government agents' fee, 6 ½ dirhams.

The alms-tax, for the value of small cattle, for four heads, 3 ¼ ⅛ dinars:
sheep, for two heads, 2 ¼ dinars;
goats, for two heads, 1 ⅛ dinar.

Hay, 1,020 bales.

The chickens reared in it, 310 chickens:
for the prosperous Dīwān, including the rearing wage of a third, 200 birds;
for the *iqṭāʿ*-holders, 110 chickens.

Its people cultivate sugarcane assigned for the presses at Sinnūris, 18 ½ ⅓ 2/72 feddans:
first harvest, 13 ½ ⅛ 2/72 feddans;
second harvest, 5 5/24 feddans.

819 أ. س.: دينار.
820 ساقط من أ. س.: وربع.
821 ساقط من أ. س.: وهو الثلث.
822 ساقط من ط. م.: من.

والذي بها من التقاوي السلطانية، مائة وستة وستون اردبا. تفصيله:

قمح، مائة وعشرون اردبا.

شعير، ستة وعشرون اردبا.

فول، عشرون اردبا.

ومن تقاوي السمسم، نصف اردب.

والمسلف عليها بها من الشعير برسم الاصطبلات السلطانية، اربعون اردبا.

والذي انساق بها من الباقي[823] في الايام السلطانية الكاملية قبل انتقالها للاقطاع من جملة ما ورد بسنورس بحكم انها مجتمعة في الخاص مع كفورها.

ومن حرف الميم، منشاة الطواحين من كفور سنورس. هذه البلدة عبارة عن بلدة صغيرة وهي من بحري الفيوم تشتمل على حدائق نخل ودويرات كرم عنب وتين ومشمش وخضراوات وسنط. بينها وبين مدينة الفيوم مسافة[824] نصف ساعة للراكب. جارية في اقطاع الامير عز الدين خضر بن محمد الكيكاني واخوته بغير عبرة. شربها من الماء المطلق ببحر سنورس من المقسم المعروف بالشاذروان، لسقي الشتوي والصيفي، ثلاثة قبضات ماء. اهلها بنو قيصر، فخذ من بني عجلان.

ارتفاعها، عينا، مائة وسبعة[825] وسبعون دينارا، وغلة، خمسمائة اردب. تفصيله:

قمح، ثلاثمائة واحد وثلاثون اردبا وثلث.

فول، مائة وخمسة وستون اردبا وثلثان.

سمسم، ثلاثة ارادب.

تفصيله:

خراج الراتب والجروي وفدن العين،[826] مائة وسبعة وستون دينارا. من ذلك موقوف عن[827] المتسحبين والمتوفين، خمسة وعشرون دينارا.

خراج الغلات، خمسمائة اردب، على ما فصل.

وعليها من الرسوم والكيالة والمراعي، عن مائة وسبعة وخمسين درهما ونصف، ثلاثة دنانير وثلثان وربع ونصف قيراط؛ وغلة، عشرون اردبا ونصف وثلث ونصف قيراط. تفصيله:

قمح، ثلاثة عشر اردبا ونصف وربع وثمن.

شعير، اردبان وثمن.

وفول، اربعة ارادب ونصف وثلث ونصف قيراط.

تفصيله:

الرسوم، مائة وثمانية دراهم وربع وثمن، وغلة، اثنا عشر اردبا وقيراطان[828] ونصف. تفصيله:

قمح، ستة ارادب ونصف وربع وثمن.

شعير، اردب واحد وربع وثمن.

فول، ثلاثة ارادب ونصف وثلث ونصف قيراط.

تفصيله:

شد العين، خمسة عشر درهما.

شد الاحباس، سبعة دراهم ونصف.

رسم الجراريف، سبعة دراهم وربع.

---

823 ط. م.: التقاوي.

824 ساقط من أ. س.: مسافة.

825 أ. س.: وتسعة.

826 أ. س.، ط. م.: خراج الراتب والجروي وفر العين.

827 أ. س.: على.

828 أ. س.: وقيراط.

The royal seed advances in it, 166 ardabbs:

wheat, 120 ardabbs;

barley, 26 ardabbs;

broad beans, 20 ardabbs.

The seed advances of sesame, ½ ardabb.

The barley assigned for the royal stables and paid for in advance, 40 ardabbs.

The outstanding payments carried over, dating from the reign of Sultan al-Kāmil and since before it was allocated as *iqṭāʿ*, are included in the total of Sinnūris, since [Sinnūris] was joined up with its hamlets when it formed part of the private domain of the sultan.

Also beginning with the letter 'mīm': Munshaʾat al-Ṭawāḥīn,[275] included in the accounts of Sinnūris. This is a small village in the north of the province, half an hour's ride from Madīnat al-Fayyūm. It has gardens of date palms and enclosures of vineyards, figs, apricots, green vegetables and acacias. It is assigned as an *iqṭāʿ* to the amir ʿIzz al-Dīn Khiḍr ibn Muḥammad al-Kīkānī and his brothers, without fiscal value. It is irrigated by water from Sinnūris Canal, from the divisor known as al-Shādhrawān. Its water quota, for the irrigation of winter and summer crops, is three *qabḍas* of water. Its people are the Banū Qayṣar, a branch of the Banū ʿAjlān.

Its revenue in specie is 177 dinars; and in grains, 500 ardabbs:

wheat, 331 ⅓ ardabbs;

broad beans, 165 ⅔ ardabbs:

sesame, 3 ardabbs.

[The revenue] in detail:

land tax on perennial plants, the *jarwī* land tax and cash crops assessed by feddans,[276] 167[277] dinars. Of that, 25 dinars are withheld for those who fled or died.

land tax on grains, 500 ardabbs as specified.

The fees, the measurement fee and the pasture tax are 157 ½ dirhams, which are 3 ⅔ ¼ 1/48 dinars; and in grains, 20 ½ ⅓ 1/48 ardabbs:

wheat, 13 ½ ¼ ⅛ ardabbs;

barley, 2 ⅛ ardabbs;

broad beans, 4 ½ ⅓ 1/48 ardabbs.

In detail:

the fees, 108 ¼ ⅛ dirhams; and in grains, 12 5/48 ardabbs:

wheat, 6 ½ ¼ ⅛ ardabbs;

barley, 1 ¼ ⅛ ardabb;

broad beans, 3 ½ ⅓ 1/48 ardabbs.

[the fees] in detail:

supervision of the land survey 15 dirhams;

supervision of endowments, 7 ½ dirhams;

dredging fee, 7 ¼ dirhams;

---

275 Modern location: Munshâat ʿAbdallāh (منشاة عبدالله). Halm, *Ägypten*, p. 263: Manshīyat al-Ṭawwāḥīn; Salmon, 'Répertoire', p. 52; Ibn al-Jīʿān, *Kitāb al-tuḥfa*, p. 158; Ramzī, *Al-Qāmūs*, II/III, 102: Munshâat ʿAbdallāh.

276 AS and MP: *al-rātib wa'l-jarwī wafr al-ʿayn*; amended to: *al-rātib wa'l-jarwī wa-fudun al-ʿayn*. '*al- jarwī*' (الجروي) may also be a copyist mistake for *al-sawāqī* (السواقي), 'waterwheels'.

277 Note the discrepancy with the total of 177 dinars mentioned in the preceding lines.

رسم الحصاد، ثلاثة وخمسون درهما.
رسم الخفارة، خمسة عشر درهما.
رسم الاجران، عشرة دراهم ونصف وثمن، وغلة، اثنا عشر اردبا وقيراطان ونصف، على ما فصل.
كيالة ثمانية ارادب ونصف وربع:
قمح، سبعة ارادب.
شعير، نصف وربع اردب.
فول، اردب واحد.
المراعي، عن تسعين راسا، تسعة واربعون درهما وثمن. تفصيله:
قطيعة درهم واحد الراس، عن ثمانية وعشرين راسا، ثمانية وعشرون درهما.
قطيعة خمسة وعشرين درهما المائة، عن اثنين وستين راسا، خمسة عش درهما.
رسم المستخدمين، خمسة دراهم ونصف وثمن.

وعليها من الزكاة عن ثمن اغنام:
بياض، عن راسين ديناران وربع.

عليها من الاتبان، اربعمائة شنيف.

عليها لديوان الاحباس، دينار واحد.

اهلها يزرعون من الاقصاب برسم المعاصر[829] بسنورس، ستة فدادين ونصف وربع. تفصيله:
راس، اربعة فدادين ونصف وربع.
خلفة، فدانان.

والمربى بها من الفروج، مائتا طائر. تفصيله:
للديوان المعمور، بما فيه من اجرة التربية وهو الثلث، مائة طائر.
للمقطعين، مائة طائر.

والذي بها من التقاوي السلطانية، خمسة وخمسون اردبا:
قمح، خمس وثلاثون اردبا.
شعير، ستة ارادب.
فول، اربعة عشر اردبا.

وباقي الناحية المذكورة في الايام الكاملية وموقوفها لسنة اربع وثلاثين وستمائة وما قبلها داخل في معاملة صفقة سنورس بحكم ان هذه الناحية من كفورها.

ومن حرف الميم، منية اقنى وكفورها. هذه البلدة عبارة عن بلدة كبيرة غربية الفيوم، اخر عمل[830] الفيوم.[831] تشتمل هذه البلدة على نخل وشجرات من الزيتون والتين وشجرات نارنج ومنظرة وبستان وحمام انشاها الملك المفضل رحمه الله تعالى لما كان مقطع الفيوم. فخربها اهل البلد جهلا[832] منهم وعدوان. ثم لما ولى للفيوم الامير بدر الدين المرندزي عمرها واصلحها، فلما صرف من الفيوم عاد الفلاحون واوغادهم الى العدوان عليها وخربوها دفعة ثانية.

829 أ. س.: المعصرة.
830 أ. س.: العمل.
831 ساقط من أ. س.: الفيوم.
832 ط. م.: جهل.

harvest fee, 53 dirhams;
protection fee, 15 dirhams;
threshing-floor fee, 10 ½ ⅛ dirhams; and in grains, 12 $\frac{2}{24}$ $\frac{1}{48}$ ardabbs, as specified.
The measurement fee, 8 ½ ¼ ardabbs:
wheat, 7 ardabbs;
barley, ½ ¼ ardabb;
broad beans, 1 ardabb.
The pasture tax, for 90 heads, 49 ⅛ dirhams:
at the rate of one dirham per head, for 28 heads, 28 dirhams;
at the rate of 25 dirhams per 100 [heads], for 62 heads, 15 dirhams;
the government agents' fee, 5 ½ ⅛ dirhams.

The alms-tax, for the monetary value of small cattle:
sheep, for two heads, 2 ¼ dinar.

Hay, 400 bales.

For the Ministry of Endowments, 1 dinar.

Its people sow sugarcane assigned for the presses at Sinnūris, 6 ½ ¼ feddans:
first harvest, 4 ½ ¼ feddans;
second harvest, 2 feddans.

The chickens reared in it, 200 birds:
for the prosperous Dīwān, including the rearing wage of a third, 100 birds;
for the *iqṭāʿ*-holders, 100 birds.

The royal seed advances, 55 ardabbs:
wheat, 35 ardabbs;
barley, 6 ardabbs;
broad beans, 14 ardabbs.

The outstanding payments of this village, dating from the reign of [Sultan] al-Kāmil, and its withheld payments for 634 [AD 1236–7] and earlier, are included in the joint account for Sinnūris, since this village is one of its hamlets.

Also beginning with the letter 'mīm': Minyat Aqnā and its hamlets.[278] This is a large village, in the west of the Fayyum, right at the edge of the province. It has date palms, olive, fig and orange trees; a belvedere, an orchard and a bathhouse. [The bathhouse] was built by al-Malik al-Mufaḍḍal,[279] may God have mercy upon him, when he was the *iqṭāʿ*-holder of the Fayyum.

278 Modern location (uncertain): ʿIzbat al-ʿAwnī (عزبة العوني). Halm, *Ägypten*, p. 265; Salmon, 'Répertoire', pp. 58–59; Zéki, 'Une description', p. 41; de Sacy, *État des provinces*, p. 684: Minyat Afnā; Ibn al-Jīʿān, *Kitāb al-tuḥfa*, p. 158: Minyat Afnā; Ramzī, *Al-Qāmūs*, I, 427–28: Minyat Aqnā, near the modern village of al-Misharrak. We have no positive identification of this village, but according to al-Nābulusī, it was located at the western edge of the province, near the lake, opposite to where Waradān Canal terminated. Shafei Bey, 'Fayoum Irrigation', p. 309, claims that he identified Minyat Aqnā by the remains of the public bathhouse (see above), which the peasants still remembered. He also notes that the nearby canal is called to this day Baḥr al-Ḥammām (canal of the bathhouse). However, the location he assigned to Minyat Aqnā appears too far to the west from the central areas of cultivation, and is not in line with our conclusion that Minyat Aqnā Canal followed the route of the modern Wadi Nazla. We therefore located Minyat Aqnā close to the mouth of the modern Nazla ravine, near the village of ʿIzbat al-ʿAwnī (عزبة العوني).

279 Mufaḍḍal Quṭb al-Dīn, brother of Sultan al-Kāmil, who held the entire province as *iqṭāʿ* in 619/1222. See Makīn, *Taʾrīkh*, pp. 133–34; Sato, *State and Rural Society*, p. 81.

فلما مررت عليها قررت مع اهل البلد ان يعمروها من اموالهم والتزموا بعمارتها.

تتخرق المياه في وسط هذه البلدة. تشتمل على ثلاث حارات متسعة الارض كثيرة الزرع. يركب الماء في الانيال العالية اذا نفس عن[833] بحر الفيوم المياه في البطس الى بركة الصيد المعروفة بها يغطى[834] شيئا من اراضيها يقل به ارتفاعها. وتنكشف[835] في السنين القليلة الانيال من اراضيها ما يزرعه اهلها ويكثر به ارتفاعها كما جرى في هذه السنة وهي سنة اثنتين واربعين.

وهذه البركة من عجائب الوجود وعجائب المصنوعات. وذلك انها مصب لفضلات مياه الفيوم جميعها. متى علا النيل وسامت حافتى[836] البحر وخيف على بلاد الفيوم واقصابها من جميع نواحيها، كسرت تراع من ناحية البطس وهو عبارة عن محتفر عظيم على بحر الفيوم. وله قنطرة ما بين صنوفر المقدم ذكرها وقشوش ذات بابين يغلقان ايام الانيال[837] القليلة ويفتحان ايام الانيال[838] الكثيرة. يخرج منها ماء عظيم ويرميان الى هذا المحتفر.

واذا[839] لم يغن فتح هذين البابين اللذين بهذه القناطر، كسرت[840] التراع من علو بحر الفيوم مما يقابل مرج دموشية الى هوارة. وعند هوارة البحرية منصل اخر كان محكم البناء فدثر، ولم يبق الا معالم هذا المنصل الذي دثر ودثرت معالمه، يخرج منه من الماء اضعاف ما يخرج من ماء[841] البطس قدر عشر مرات. ثم الماء الذي يخرج منه ومن التراع التي بينه وبين البطس ومن بابي البطس يرمى جميعه الى الموضع المحتفر الذي يسمى بالبطس. ويمر جميعه الى بركة الصيد المذكورة التي في ارض منية اقنى.

يكون الذي يخرج من هذه المياه من هذه الفوهات المذكورة والتراع المشهورة قدر المياه التي تخرج من بحر منجا بالاعمال الشرقية يوم كسره. يدوم جريان هذا الماء مع كثرته الى هذه البركة مدة شهرين خارجا عما يخرج من بحر الفيوم ونيله[842] وحافتيه الى البركة مدة النيل وبعده باشهر. فلا يؤثر فيها الا اثرا يسيرا من تغطية بعض المزارع بمنية اقنى وبمويه ومنية البطس.

وهذه البركة مسافتها مسافة يوم كامل للراكب طولا وعرضها مسافة ساعتين للراكب. احد حافتي هذه البركة الجبل والاخر مزارع منية اقنى ومنية البطس. كان بها قناطر يمر الناس عليها من احد جانبيها الى الجانب الاخر وعبارة للماء يمر الماء على هذه القناطر الى جانب البركة الى الاراضي التي تلي الجبل. تزرع تلك بالماء الذي يمر على القناطر اليها من بحر الفيوم من الفوهة التي يصل الماء فيها الى الناحية. اتلفها الماء من سنين عديدة وصارت بعض الاراضي التي تلي الجبل تزرع بالسواقي من البركة المذكورة وليس فيها الان سوى ساقية واحدة.

833 أ. س.: اذا.
834 ط. م.: يعطى.
835 أ. س.: وينكشف.
836 أ. س.: حافة.
837 أ. س.: الانيلة.
838 أ. س.: الانيلة.
839 أ. س.: وان.
840 أ. س.: كثرت.
841 ساقط من أ. س.: ماء.
842 أ. س.: ويدلية.

Then the villagers destroyed it out of ignorance and resentment. When the amir Badr al-Dīn al-Marandizī became the governor of the Fayyum, he rebuilt and restored it. Yet when he was discharged from the Fayyum, the peasants and their scoundrels attacked it again, and they destroyed it for the second time. When I visited it, I ordered the villagers to rebuild it at their expense, and they committed themselves to do so.

The water goes through the center of this village, which is divided into three quarters, each with spacious land and plentiful cultivation. In years of high Nile inundations, water from the Main Canal is released into [the drainage canal of] al-Baṭs, and then the water flows towards the fishery lake, which is known by its name [i.e., Minyat Aqnā]. As a result, some of the village lands are submerged, and its revenues are reduced. In years of lower inundations, however, these lands are exposed and are sown by the villagers. Its revenues then increase, as happened this year, which is [6]42 [AD 1244–5].

This lake is one of the marvels of creation, and one of the wonders of man-made structures, as it is the outlet for the entire surplus waters of the Fayyum. When the Nile rises and the water reaches the level of the banks of the [Main] Canal, and there is fear for the lands of the Fayyum and their sugarcane, drainage canals (*turaʿ*) are breached towards the direction of al-Baṭs. This drainage canal consists of a great trench branching off the Main Canal. It has an arch, located between Ṣunūfar and Qushūsh, with two sluice gates, which are closed in periods of low Nile levels. They are opened when the Nile waters are high, and then huge amount of water flows through them into the great trench.

When the opening of the two sluice gates of the arches is not sufficient, other drainage canals, located at the upper part of the Main Canal opposite the meadow of Dumūshiyya towards Hawwāra, are breached. There is also another outlet at Hawwāra al-Baḥriyya, which was solidly built, but had fallen into ruin and only its remains are visible. The water that escapes through this ruined outlet is ten times more than the water of [the drainage canal of] al-Baṭs. Then, all the water that escapes through this drainage canal, the drainage canals between it and al-Baṭs, and through the two sluice gates at al-Baṭs — all of it is cast into the trench called al-Baṭs and flows in its entirety into the aforementioned fishing lake, which is at the lands of Minyat Aqnā.

The water that escapes through these openings and the well-known drainage canals is equivalent to the amount of the water that escapes from [Abū al-] Munajjā Canal[280] at the district of al-Sharqiyya on the day it is breached. The abundant flow of the water to this lake continues for a period of two months. This excludes the water which escapes towards the lake from the Main Canal, from its lower end and from its banks during the period of the Nile's [inundation], and in the months after it. [Yet all] this has only minimal impact on the lake, causing some of the fields of Minyat Aqnā, Bamawayh and Minyat al-Baṭs to be submerged.

The length of this lake is a full day's ride, and its width is two hours' ride. One bank of this lake is at [the foot of] the mountain, and the other bank is at the cultivated fields of Minyat Aqnā and Minyat al-Baṭs. It used to have arches in it, which allowed people to pass from one side to the other, and served as aqueducts (*ʿabbāra li'l-māʾ*). The water passed across these arches to the other side of the lake, towards the lands at the foot of the mountain. These lands were cultivated by means of the water that passed over the arches, and which came from the opening in the Main Canal that served the village [i.e., Minyat Aqnā]. Over the course of many years, the water had damaged the arches. Some of the lands that lie at the foot of the mountain came to be cultivated with waterwheels, [which raise water] from the lake. Currently there is only one waterwheel on the lake.

280 Also known as the al-Afḍalī canal, it was dug by the Fatimids and inaugurated in the year 506/1112–13, following six years of arduous work. See Shelomoh D. Goitein, *A Mediterranean Society: The Jewish Communities of the Arab World as Portrayed in the Documents of the Cairo Geniza*, I: *Economic Foundations* (Berkeley: University of California Press, 1967), pp. 298–99.

وفي هذه البركة المنكورة من الصيد ما لا يحصى جنسه ولا نوعه. يكثر صيدها في شحة النيل ويقل اذا كان عاليا لاتساعها وطلب السمك الاعماق فيها.[843] ومن غرائب ما جرى فيها واستفاض بين اهل البلاد انه في سنة اثنتين واربعين وستمائة في فصل الشتاء عصف يوما ريح باردة موجها وبرد ماءها فمات فيها من السمك الفراخ الكبار ما لا يحكى انه رئي في بحر من البحار الكبار. وبقى هذا السمك الذي مات على اطرافها للرائي كالجسور العظيمة حتى اخبرني خولي البحر، وهو متحرز[844] في قوله لم احرز عليه كذبا من ساعة وصولي البلاد الى الان حين عمل هذا الكتاب، انه مشى على طرف هذه البركة من بكرة الى الليل فوجد الاسماك المنكورة اربعة صفوف: صف فراخ كبار بطول البركة كالجسر العظيم، شيئا فوق شيء كالبناء المرصوص، وبعده[845] اخر بلطى الذي يصاد من البركة ويجلب الى مصر وسائر البلاد، وصف اخر لبيس كنلك، وصف اخر سمك يسمى بالشال كنلك. وشاهد الادهان خارجة من هذه الاسماك كالماء الجاري وورد اليها الطير والوحش ياكلون منها.

يجتمع في هذه البركة للصيد ما ينيف عن ثلاثين مركبا. ورايت السمك المسمى باللبيس يخرج من هذه البركة اذا دخل ماء النيل اليها الى القناطر التي تحت مسجد ابن فحل قريب مدينة الفيوم. فيصيد الناس من الخليج المنكور ويكثر هذا الصيد الى ان يباع كل خمسة قناطير بتسعة[846] دراهم سواد. هذا واخبرني[847] جماعة ان قبل[848] هذه السنة بيع ثلاثة قناطير سمك بربع درهم سواد بصورة ان صيادا دفع له شخص ربع درهم على ان يطرح وما طلع فيها كان له. فطرح فطلع فيها ستون سمكة كل واحدة وزنها خمسة ارطال.

جارية في اقطاع جماعة من المقطعين بعبرة مبلغها اثنان وخمسون الفا واربعمائة وخمسة وعشرون دينارا. شربها من الماء من البحر المعروف بالناحية، المساق الى المقسم المعروف بالعرين بخشبة، خمسون قبضة. والمطلق لدقلوه من ماء الغرق عشرون قبضة. بها جامع تقام فيه الجمعة. اهلها اضابطة، فخذ من بني كلاب.

ارتفاعها مجموعة مع كفورها عينا، ستمائة دينار وربع وسدس؛ وغلة، ثلاثة عشر الفا ومائتان وستة وعشرون اردبا. تفصيله:
قمح، ثمانية الاف وثمانمائة وسبعة عشر اردبا وثلث.
شعير وفول، اربعة الاف واربعمائة وثمانية ارادب وثلثان.

تفصيله:
الهلالي عن اجرة الحانوت، مائة واربعون دينارا.
بركة الصيد، اربعمائة دينار.
خراج الراتب عن العامر خاصة، خارجا عن الخراب وهو احد وثلاثون دينارا وثلثان ونصف ثمن، عشرة دنانير وربع وسدس.
خراج العين المقرر على المعاملين، خارجا عما وضعه المقطعون عن المزارعين بدقلوه وهو خمسة دنانير، خمسون دينار.

In this lake, there are countless types and varieties of fishes. Fishing increases during the dry season of the Nile, and decreases when the Nile is high, because the lake then expands, and the fishes search for its depths. One of the strange things that happened there, well-known among the villagers, is that during the winter of 642 [AD 1244–5] a cold wind had blown one day, stirring up its waves and cooling down its water. Then large *firākh* fishes started dying in it, at a quantity which no one is said to have ever seen in any of the great seas. The fish that died remained on its shores, and appeared like great dikes, to the extent that the overseer of the canal informed me — and he is careful in what he says, I have never caught him lying from the time of my arrival at the province until now, when this book is being prepared — that he walked along the shores of this lake from early morning until night time, and found the fishes arranged in four layers along the length of the lake like a great dike. First, a layer of the large *firākh* fishes, and then — stacked on top of that layer, like a stratified building — a layer of *bulṭī* (Tilapia Nilotica, perch), which are being fished in the lake, and are brought to Cairo and to the rest of the country; then another similar layer of *labīs* (Nile carp); and another similar layer of a fish called *shāl* (cat-fish). He also saw fish-oil oozing from these fishes like flowing water. Birds and beasts then came to feed on them.

More than 30 fishing boats operate in this lake. I have seen that, as the water from the Nile reaches it, the fish called *labīs* come out of the lake towards the arches below the mosque of Ibn Fiḥl, near Madīnat al-Fayyūm. People fish from this canal, and the fishing is so plentiful that five *qinṭār*s are sold for nine[281] black dirhams. I was informed by a group of people that before this year[282] three *qinṭār*s of fish were even sold for one fourth of a black dirham. It happened so: someone paid a fisherman one fourth of a dirham for casting his net, on the condition that what was caught would be his. The fisherman then cast his net and he brought up 60 fishes, each weighing five *raṭl*s.

It is assigned as an *iqṭāʿ* to a group of *iqṭāʿ*-holders, with the fiscal value of 52,425 [army] dinars. It gets its water from the canal named after the locality [i.e., Minyat Aqnā Canal], directed towards the divisor known as al-ʿArīn. Its water quota, allocated by means of a wooden [divisor], is 50 *qabḍa*s. The water allocated to Diqlawa,[283] from the water of [the reservoir of] al-Gharq, is 20 *qabḍa*s. [Minyat Aqnā] has a congregational mosque, in which the Friday prayers are held. Its people are the Aḍābiṭa, a branch of the Banū Kilāb.

Its revenue, together with its hamlets, is in specie, 600 ¼ ⅙ dinars; and in grains, 13,226 ardabbs:

wheat, 8,817 ⅓ ardabbs;

barley and broad beans, 4,408 ⅔ ardabbs.

[The revenue] in detail:

lunar-calendar taxes, for the rent of the shop, 140 dinars;

the fishing lake, 400 dinars;

land tax on perennial plants, solely for cultivated land — excluding the uncultivated land (*al-kharāb*), which is 31 ⅔ 1/16 dinars — 10 ¼ ⅙ dinars;

the established land tax on cash-crops levied on the cultivators — excluding the tax remission for the tenants of Diqlawa by the *iqṭāʿ*-holders, which is 5 dinars — 50 dinars.

843 ط. م.: الاغماق منها.
844 أ. س.: محترز.
845 أ. س.: وبعد.
846 أ. س.: بسبعة.
847 أ. س. يضيف: ان.
848 ساقط من أ. س.: ان قبل.

281 AS: seven.

282 AS: in this year.

283 Modern location: Qaṣr al-Jibālī (قصر الجبالي). Halm, *Ägypten*, p. 254: Diqlauh; Salmon, 'Répertoire', p. 62; Ibn al-Jīʿān, *Kitāb al-tuḥfa*, p. 158; Ramzī, *Al-Qāmūs*, I, 247: Qaṣr al-Jibālī.

خراج الغلة، مناجزة، من جملة ثلاثة عشر الف اردب[849] بعد ما وضعه المقطعون عن المزارعين المتسحبين وهو تسعمائة اردب، اثنا عشر الفا ومائة اردب. تفصيله:

قمح، ثمانية الاف وستة وستون اردبا وثلثان.

شعير وفول، اربعة الاف وثلاثة وثلاثون اردبا وثلث.

الوفر المقرر على المعاملين، حسابا عن كل مائة اردب ثلاثة ارادب، ثلاثمائة وثلاثة وستون اردبا:

قمح، مائتان واثنان واربعون اردبا.

وشعير وفول، مائة واحد وعشرون اردبا.

الكيالة، ثلاثمائة وثلاثة وستون اردبا. تفصيله:

قمح، مائتان واثنان واربعون اردبا.

وشعير، مائة واحد وعشرون اردبا.

رسم الاجران ووفرها، اربعمائة اردب. تفصيله:

قمح، مائتان وستة وستون اردبا وثلثان.

شعير وفول، مائة وثلاثة وثلاثون اردبا وثلث.

وعليها من الرسوم والكيالة والمراعي، عن الف واربعمائة وستة وثمانين درهما وربع، سبعة وثلاثون دينارا وسدس، وذلك خارجا عن الغلة الواردة ارتفاع الناحية. تفصيله:

الرسوم، ثلاثمائة وثمانية وتسعون درهما. تفصيله:

رسم حصاد، ثلاثة وخمسون درهما.

رسم الاجران، ثلاثمائة وخمسة واربعون درهما.

المراعي، عن سبعمائة وثلاثة وعشرين راسا، الف وثمانية وثمانون درهما وربع. تفصيله:

راتب، قطيعة درهمين وربع الراس، عن مائتين واثنتين وثمانين راسا، ستمائة واربعة وثلاثون درهما ونصف.

طارئ، عن اربعمائة واحد واربعين راسا، اربعمائة وثمانية دراهم. تفصيله:

قطيعة درهم واحد الراس، عن ثلاثمائة وثلاثة وتسعين راسا، ثلاثمائة وثلاثة وتسعون درهما.

قطيعة ثلاثين درهما المائة، عن ثمانية واربعين راسا، خمسة عشر درهما.

رسم المستخدمين، خمسة واربعون درهما ونصف وربع.

عليها من الزكاة، تسعة وثمانون دينارا وثلث وربع ونصف قيراط وحبة:

منية اقنى، عن ثمن اغنام، عن اربعة وثمانين راسا، ستة وخمسون دينارا وربع وسدس ونصف ثمن وحبة. تفصيله:

بياض، عن اثنين وثلاثين راسا، سبعة وثلاثون دينارا ونصف ونصف ثمن وحبة.

شعارى، عن اثنين وخمسين راسا، ثمانية عشر دينارا وثلثان وربع.

منشاة الوسط من حقوقها، عن ثمن اغنام، عن احد وعشرين راسا، عشرة دنانير وخمسة قراريط وحبة. تفصيله:

بياض، عن خمسة ارؤس، خمسة دنانير وربع.

شعارى، عن ستة عشر راسا، اربعة دنانير ونصف وثلث وثمن وحبة.

منشاة غيلان من حقوقها، عن ثمن الاغنام، عن سبعة وعشرين راسًا، احد وعشرون دينارا وربع وثمن وحبتان. تفصيله:

بياض، عن ثلاثة عشر راسا، اربعة عشر دينارا ونصف.

شعارى، عن اربعة عشر راسا، ستة دنانير ونصف وربع وثمن وحبتان.

849 ساقط من أ. س.: أردب.

Munājaza land tax in grains, a total of 13,000 ardabbs, of which 900 ardabbs were remitted by the *iqṭāʿ*-holders on account of the tenants who fled. [It comes up to] 12,100 ardabbs:

wheat, 8,066 ⅔ ardabbs:

barley and broad beans, 4,033 ⅓ ardabbs.

The established surcharge on the cultivators, calculated at 3 ardabbs per 100 ardabbs, 363 ardabbs:

wheat, 242 ardabbs;

barley and broad beans, 121 ardabbs.

The measurement fee, 363 ardabbs:

wheat, 242 ardabbs;

barley and broad beans, 121 ardabbs.

Threshing-floor fee and its surcharge, 400 ardabbs:

wheat, 266 ⅔ ardabbs:

barley and broad beans, 133 ⅓ ardabbs.

The fees, the measurement fee and the pasture tax are 1,486 ¼ dirhams, which are 37 ⅙ dinars. This excludes the fees in kind mentioned above in the revenues of the village.

[The fees, the measurement fee and the pasture tax] in detail:

the fees, 398 dirhams:

harvest fee, 53 dirhams;

threshing-floor fee, 345 dirhams.

The pasture fee, for 723 heads, 1,088 ¼ dirhams:

permanent pasture lands at the rate of 2 ¼ dirhams per head, for 282 heads, 634 ½ dirhams;

seasonal pasture lands, for 441 heads, 408 dirhams:

at the rate of one dirham per head, for 393 heads, 393 dirhams;

at the rate of 30 dirhams per 100 [heads], for 48 heads, 15 dirhams;

the government agents' fee, 45 ½ ¼ dirhams.

The alms-tax, 39 ⅓ ¼ 1/48 1/72 dinars:

Minyat Aqnā, for the monetary value of small cattle, for 84 heads, 56 ¼ ⅙ 1/48 1/72 dinars:

sheep, for 32 heads, 37 ½ 1/16 1/72 dinars;

goats, for 52 heads, 18 ⅔ ¼ dinars.

Munsha'at al-Wasaṭ — included in its accounts — for the monetary value of small cattle, for 21 heads, 10 5/24 1/72 dinars:

sheep, for five heads, 5 ¼ dinars;

goats, for 16 heads, 4 ½ ⅓ ⅛ 1/72 dinars.

Munsha'at Ghaylān — included in its accounts — for the monetary value of small cattle, for 27 heads, 21 ¼ ⅛ 2/72 dinars:

sheep, for 13 heads, 14 ½ dinars;

goats, for 14 heads, 6 ½ ¼ ⅛ 2/72 dinars.

دقلوه، دينار واحد ونصف. تفصيله:
بياض، عن راس واحد، دينار واحد.
شعرية، نصف دينار.

Diqlawa, 1 ½ dinar:
sheep, for one head, 1 dinar;
one goat, ½ dinar.

وعليها من الاتبان، ثلاث عشر الفا وخمسمائة شنيف.

Hay, 13,500 bales.

رسم خولي البحر بها، ثلاثة ارادب. تفصيله:
قمح، اردبان؛
وشعير، اردب واحد.

The fee of the overseer of the canal, 3 ardabbs:
wheat, 2 ardabbs;
barley, 1 ardabb.

وعليها لديوان احباس الجوامع والمساجد عينا، تسعة دنانير:
عن منية اقنى، ستة دنانير.[850]
وعن برشتوت من حقوقها، ثلاثة دنانير.

For the Ministry of the Endowments of Congregational and Neighbourhood Mosques, in specie, 9 dinars:
for Minyat Aqnā, 6 dinars;
and for Burjtūt,[284] included in its accounts, 3 dinars.

والمطلق عليها من الرزق، محراث واحد وثلث وربع. ما تفصيله:
المشايخ، محراث واحد وربع وثمن.
الخفراء، خمسة قراريط محراث.

The allowances allocated in it, 1 ⅓ ¼ ploughshare:
the headmen, 1 ¼ ⅛ ploughshare;
the guardsmen, 5/24 of a ploughshare.

والمسلف به من الشعير على مشايخ دقلوة برسم الاصطبلات السلطانية، مائة اردب وذلك خارجا عما يبتاع من منية اقنى من الاجناد والمشايخ من الفول لعلوفة العوامل الديوانية، وهو مما يزيد على الف اردب.

The barley assigned for the royal stables, for which the headmen in Diqlawa are paid for in advance, 100 ardabbs. This excludes the broad beans sold by the headmen and the soldiers from Minyat Aqnā as fodder for the cattle of the Dīwān, which is more than 1,000 ardabbs.

والمربى بها من الفروج، الف وسبعمائة وسبعة اطيار. تفصيله:
للديوان المعمور، بما فيه من اجرة التربية وهو الثلث، ستمائة طائر.
للمقطعين، الف ومائة وسبعة اطيار.

The chickens reared in it, 1,707 birds:
for the prosperous Dīwān, including the rearing wage of a third, 600 birds;
for the *iqṭāʿ*-holders, 1,107 birds.

والمربى بدقلوه للديوان المعمور، ثلاثمائة طائر بما فيه من اجرة التربية.

The [chickens] reared in Diqlawa, for the prosperous Dīwān, including the rearing wage, 300 birds.

والذي جرت العادة باطلاقه للناحية[851] من التقاوي، عينا، سبعة دنانير ونصف، وغلة، الف وستمائة وخمسة واربعون اردبا وثلث. تفصيله:
قمح، تسعمائة واحد وثمانون اردبا وثلث وربع ونصف ثمن.
شعير، ثلاثمائة واحد وثلاثون اردبا ونصف ونصف ثمن.
فول، ثلاثمائة واثنان وعشرون اردبا ونصف وثلث ونصف ثمن.
سمسم، تسعة ارادب وسدس وثمن.[852]

The seed advances customarily distributed in the locality, in specie, 7 ½ dinars; and in grains, 1,645 ⅓ ardabbs:
wheat, 981 ⅓ ¼ 1/16 ardabbs;
barley, 331 ½ 1/16 ardabbs;
broad beans, 322 ½ ⅓ 1/16 ardabbs;
sesame, 9 ⅙ ⅛ ardabbs.

والمخلد بها من التقاوي السلطانية، خارجا عن المجرى للمقطعين بها عوضا عن تقاويهم المحتاط عليها بالاعمال الجيزية، وهو تسعمائة واثنان واربعون اردبا ونصف قيراط الف وخمسة وعشرون اردبا وسدس وثمن. تفصيله:
قمح، خمسمائة واربعة وسبعون اردبا وثلثان وربع.
وشعير، مائتان وثمانية وثمانون اردبا وقيراطان ونصف.
فول، مائة واربعة وخمسون اردبا وقيراط.
سمسم، ثمانية ارادب وسدس ونصف ثمن.

The registered royal seed advances in it — excluding what is transferred to the *iqṭāʿ*-holders, in compensation for their seed advances that are kept in reserve (*al-muḥtāṭ ʿalayhā*) in the district of Giza, which are 942 1/48 ardabbs — 1,025 ⅙ ⅛ ardabbs:
wheat, 574 ⅔ ¼ ardabbs;
barley, 288 2/24 1/48 ardabbs;
broad beans, 154 1/24 ardabbs;
sesame, 8 ⅙ 1/16 ardabbs.

والذي انساق بها من الحاصل والموقوف والباقي في معاملة الديوان السلطاني، عينا، مائة وثلاثة دنانير وثلث وربع وثمن، وغلة، خمسة الاف وخمسمائة واربعة وثمانون اردبا وثلث وربع. تفصيله:
قمح، ثلاثة الاف واثنان وسبعون اردبا وثلثان ونصف ثمن.
شعير، الف وسبعمائة وسبعة وثلاثون اردبا وقيراط ونصف.
فول، سبعمائة وثمانية وستون اردبا وسدس ونصف ثمن.

The surplus, withheld and outstanding payments carried forward in the account of the royal Dīwān, in specie, 103 ⅓ ¼ ⅛ dinars; and in grains, 5,584 ⅓ ¼ ardabbs:
wheat, 3,072 ⅔ 1/16 ardabbs;
barley, 1,737 1/24 1/48 ardabbs;
broad beans, 768 ⅙ 1/16 ardabbs;

850 ساقط من ط. م.: ستة دنانير.
851 أ. س.: لها.
852 ساقط من أ. س.: سمسم تسعة أرادب وسدس وثمن، لكنه يضيفه في الحاشية.

284 In MP and AS: Barshtūt instead of Burjtūt, the form that appears elsewhere in the treatise. Modern location: al-Ḥāmūlī (الحمولي). Timm, *Das Christlich-Koptische Ägypten*, pp. 1917–21: Phantoou (Burjtūt in Arabic); Ramzī, *Al-Qāmūs*, II/III, 84: al-Ḥāmūlī.

سمسم، ثلث اردب.
كمون، اربعة ارادب وثمن.
برسيم، اردب وثلثان.
بزر [=بزق ؟] [853] بصل، ربع وسدس ونصف قيراط اردب.

sesame, ⅓ ardabb;
cumin, 4 ⅛ ardabbs;
clover 1 ⅔ ardabb;
onion seeds ¼ ⅙ 1/48 [ardabb].

وذلك لسنة تسع وثلاثين وستمائة وما قبلها. تفصيله:

These [payments] are for 639 [AD 1241–2] and previous years.

الحاصل خاصة، المتردد في الحساب، دينار واحد وثلث وربع وثمن وحبتان، وغلة، ثلاثمائة وثلاثة وثلاثون اردبا وسدس ونصف ثمن. تفصيله:
قمح، اربعة وعشرون اردبا وثلث وربع ونصف ثمن.
شعير، مائتان وثمانية وتسعون اردبا وربع وسدس.
فول، خمسة ارادب وربع ونصف قيراط.
سمسم، ثلث اردب.
كمون، اربعة ارادب وثمن.
بزق بصل، ربع وسدس ونصف قيراط.
الموقوف عن الخراب الداثر وعن الزيادة في الخراج لسنة ست وثلاثين وستمائة وما قبلها، اثنان وتسعون دينارا وسدس وحبة، وغلة، الفان واربعمائة وخمسة وخمسون اردبا وثلث وربع وثمن. تفصيله:
قمح، الف واربعمائة اردب وثلثان وثمن.
شعير، خمسمائة وسبعة وعشرون اردبا وثلث وربع.
فول، خمسمائة وسبعة وعشرون اردبا وثلث.
الباقي، عينا، تسعة دنانير وثلثان وثمن، وغلة، الفان وتسعمائة وخمسة وتسعون اردبا وثلث وربع ونصف ثمن. تفصيله:
قمح، الف وستمائة وسبعة واربعون اردبا وسدس وثمن.
شعير، تسعمائة واحد عشر اردبا وقيراط ونصف.
فول، مائتان وخمسة وثلاثون اردبا ونصف وثمن.
برسيم، اردب واحد وثلثان.

[The surplus, withheld and outstanding payments] in detail:
The surplus, repeated in the account (?, *al-mutaraddid fī al-ḥisāb*), is 1 ⅓ ¼ ⅛ 2/72 dinar; and in grains, 333 ⅙ 1/16 ardabbs:
wheat, 24 ⅓ ¼ 1/16 ardabbs;
barley, 298 ¼ ⅙ ardabbs;
broad beans, 5 ¼ 1/48 ardabbs;
sesame, ⅓ ardabb;
cumin, 4 ⅛ ardabbs;
onion seeds ¼ ⅙ 1/48 [ardabb].
The withheld payments on derelict and deserted land, and regarding the increment of land tax for the year 636 and earlier, 92 ⅙ 1/72 dinars; and in grains, 2,455 ⅓ ¼ ⅛ ardabbs:
wheat, 1,400 ⅔ ⅛ ardabbs;
barley, 527 ⅓ ¼ ardabbs;
broad beans, 527 ⅓ ardabbs.
The outstanding payments, in specie, 9 ⅔ ⅛ dinars; and in grains, 2,995 ⅓ ¼ 1/16 ardabbs:
wheat, 1,647 ⅙ ⅛ ardabbs;
barley, 911 1/24 1/48 ardabbs;
broad beans, 235 ½ ⅛ ardabbs;
clover, 1 ⅔ ardabb.

وذلك لسنة تسع وسبع وست وخمس وثلاثين وستمائة.

This is for the years 635, 636, 637 and 639.

ومن حرف الميم، مقران. هذه البلدة[854] عبارة عن بلدة كبيرة من نواحي خليج دلية. مجموعة في عبرة ارتفاع الخليج المذكور. ليس بها نخل ولا شجر. مسافتها من مدينة الفيوم ثلاث ساعات للراكب. اهلها بنو قريط[855] وشاكر، فخذ من بني كلاب. المطلق لها من الماء ما ياتي بيانه من بحر خليج دلية من المقسم المعروف بالقلنبو، احدى عشرة قبضة وثلثان. ومن ماء الغرق من اعلى الماء مسقاة عرض قبضتين في سمك اربع قبض.

Also beginning with the letter 'mīm': Muqrān.[285] This is a large village, one of the villages of Dilya Canal, and is included in the fiscal value of that Canal. There are no date palms or trees in it. It is three hours' ride from Madīnat al-Fayyūm. Its people are the Banū Qurīṭ and [the Banū] Shākir, a branch of the Banū Kilāb. The water allocated to it from Dilya Canal, as will be explained, through the divisor known as al-Qalanbū, is 11 ⅔ *qabḍas*; and from the water of [the reservoir of] al-Gharq, from the high water level (*min aʿlā al-māʾ*), through an irrigation ditch, is at a width of 2 *qabḍas* and height of 4 *qabḍas*.

ارتفاعها عن الهلالي والخراجي والمراعي، عينا، سبعة دنانير وربع، وغلة، عن خراج الغلات، الف وسبعة وثمانون اردبا وسدس وثمن. تفصيله:
قمح، ستمائة وستة واربعون اردبا ونصف.
شعير، مائتان وثلاثة وتسعون اردبا[856] ونصف.[857]
فول، مائة وسبعة وثلاثون اردبا ونصف.
سمسم، تسعة ارادب وثلثان وثمن.

Its revenue from lunar-calendar taxes, land tax and pasture tax, in specie, 7 ¼ dinars; and in grains, from land tax on grains, 1,087 ⅙ ⅛ ardabbs:
wheat, 646 ½ ardabbs;
barley, 293 ½ ardabbs;
broad beans, 137 ½ ardabbs;
sesame, 9 ⅔ ⅛ ardabbs.

853 أ. س.; ط. م.: بزر.
854 ساقط من أ. س.: البلدة.
855 أ. س.: قريظ.
856 ساقط من أ. س.: أردبا.
857 أ. س. يضيف: وثلث.

285 Modern location (uncertain): Near ʿIzbat al-Wābūr (عزبة الوابور) just south of Shidmūh. Halm, *Ägypten*, pp. 266–67; Salmon, 'Répertoire', p. 68; Ibn al-Jīʿān, *Kitāb al-tuḥfa*, p. 157: Miqrāt; de Sacy, *État des provinces*, p. 684: Miqrāt; ʿAlī Mubārak, *Al-Khiṭaṭ al-Tawfīqiyya al-jadīda li-Miṣr al-Qāhira wa-muduniha wa-bilādihā al-qādima wa'l-shāhira*, 2nd edn (Cairo: Dār al-Kutub, 1969), XVI, 62: Umm Qrān; Ramzī, *Al-Qāmūs*, I, 413: Tel Abū al-Tūr, south of Shidmūh. We have no positive identification for this village.

عليها من الرسوم والكيالة، عن مائة وثلاثة واربعين درهما ونصف، ثلاثة دنانير وثلث وربع، وغلة، ستة وثلاثون اردبا ونصف قيراط. تفصيله:

قمح، ثمانية عشر اردبا ونصف.

شعير، خمسة عشر اردبا وثلثان وربع ونصف ثمن.

فول، اردب واحد وربع[858] وسدس وثمن.

الرسوم، مائة وثلاثة واربعون درهما ونصف، وغلة، تسعة وعشرون اردبا وثلثان. تفصيله:

قمح، اربعة عشر اردبا وثمن ونصف قيراط.

شعير، ثلاثة عشر اردبا وثلثان وربع[859] ونصف ثمن.

فول، اردب واحد وربع وسدس وثمن.

تفصيل ذلك:

شد احباس، تسعة دراهم ونصف.

رسم الجراريف، احد واربعون درهما.

رسم حصاد، ثلاثة وخمسون درهما.

رسم خفارة، خمسة عشر درهما.

رسم الاجران، خمسة وعشرون درهما، وغلة، تسعة وعشرون اردبا وثلثان، على ما فصل.

كيالة، ستة ارادب وثلث ونصف قيراط. تفصيله:

قمح، اربعة ارادب وثلث ونصف قيراط.

شعير، اردبان.

عليها من الزكاة عن خمسة عشر راسا، ستة دنانير وثلث وربع وثمن وحبتان. تفصيله:

بياض، عن اربعة ارؤس، اربعة دنانير وربع.

شعارى، عن احد عشر راسا، ديناران وثلث وثمن وحبتان.

عليها من الاتبان، الف شنيف.

رسم خولي البحر بها، غلة، اردبان وثلثان، قمح وشعير نصفان.

عليها لديوان الاحباس وعلى قمنا بجوش من حقوقها، اربعة دنانير وثلثان. تفصيله:

مقران، اربعة دنانير.

قمنا بجوش، ثلثا دينار.

والذي جرت العادة بتربيته من الفروج للمقطعين[860] بالناحية، اربعمائة واثنان وثلاثون طائرا.

ومن حرف الميم، مطر طارس. هذه البلدة عبارة عن بلدة كبيرة، عروس من عرائس الفيوم المذكورة بها. تشتمل هذه البلدة على البساتين الرائقة والانهار الدافقة والاشجار اليانعة والثمار المتتابعة. تشتمل بساتينها على البرك[861] الكبيرة والفواكه الغزيرة. وتعم بخيرها الصادر والوارد تتخرقها الانهار طول الليل والنهار. ومن فواكهها الكمثرى الكثير والنخل الغزير والمشمش والاعناب. تمير بفاكهتها البلاد فهي عروس، توشحت اشجارها من الثمار بقلائد وغروس اطلعت على تجارها الفوائد.

858 أ. س. يضيف: وربع.
859 ساقط من أ. س.: وربع.
860 أ. س.: من المقطعين.
861 أ. س.: البركة.

The fees and the measurement fee are 143 ½ dirhams, which are 3 ⅓ ¼ dinars; and in grains, 36 1/48 ardabbs:

wheat, 18 ½ ardabbs;

barley, 15 ⅔ ¼ 1/16 ardabbs;

broad beans, 1 ¼ ⅙ ⅛ ardabb.

[The fees and the measurement fee] in detail:

The fees, 143 ½ dirhams; and in grains, 29 ⅔ ardabbs:

wheat, 14 ardabbs, ⅛ 1/48;

barley, 13 ⅔ ¼ 1/16 ardabbs;

broad beans, 1 ¼ ⅙ ⅛ ardabb.

[the fees] in detail:

supervision of endowments, 9 ½ dirhams;

dredging fee, 41 dirhams;

harvest fee, 53 dirhams;

protection fee, 15 dirhams;

threshing-floor fee, 25 dirhams; and in grains, 29 ⅔ ardabbs, as specified.

The measurement fee, 6 ⅓ 1/48 ardabbs:

wheat, 4 ⅓ 1/48 ardabbs;

barley, 2 ardabbs.

The alms-tax, [for the monetary value of livestock], for 15 heads, 6 ⅓ ¼ ⅛ 2/72 dinars:

sheep, for four heads, 4 ¼ dinars;

goats, for 11 heads, 2 ⅓ ⅛ 2/72 dinars.

Hay, 1,000 bales.

The fee of the overseer of the canal, in grains, 2 ⅔ ardabbs of wheat and barley, half in each.

For the Ministry of Endowments, on this village and on Qumnā Bajūsh,[286] included in its accounts, 4 ⅔ dinars:

Muqrān, 4 dinars;

Qumnā Bajūsh ⅔ dinar.

The chickens customarily reared in the locality for the *iqṭā*ʿ-holders, 432 birds.

Also beginning with the letter 'mīm': Miṭr Ṭāris.[287] This is a large village, a bride among the brides of the Fayyum. It has delightful orchards, flowing streams, trees bearing ripe fruit and an abundance of produce. Its orchards contain large ponds and plentiful fruits, and their agreeable nature engulfs the passer-by. Streams pass through it by day and by night. It produces abundant pears, plentiful date palms, apricots and grapes, and it supplies the entire land with its fruits. It is a bride, whose trees are adorned by fruits like necklaces, and whose plantations show its merchants the path to profits.

286 We have no positive identification of this village. Ramzī, *Al-Qāmūs*, I, 353: Maṣraf Abū ʿAwḍ. Ramzī mentions that it appears in al-Waṭwāṭ's *Mabāhij al-Fikr wa manāhij al-ʿibar* as Qamqīnā.

287 Modern location: Miṭr Ṭāris (مطر طارس). Timm, *Das Christlich-Koptische Ägypten*, pp. 1641–2: Mētrodōrōn Kome; Trismegistos GEO ID 1366; Halm, *Ägypten*, pp. 264–65; Salmon, 'Répertoire', p. 47; Zéki, 'Une description', p. 40; de Sacy, *État des provinces*, p. 684: Miṭrṭārish; Savigny, *Description de l'Égypte*, p. 129; Ibn Mammātī, *Kitāb qawānīn al-dawāwīn*, p. 191; Ibn al-Jīʿān, *Kitāb al-tuḥfa*, p. 157: Maṭar Ṭārish; Ramzī, *Al-Qāmūs*, II/III, 115: Miṭr Ṭāris.

وهي بحري الفيوم الى الشرق. بينها وبين مدينة الفيوم مسافة ساعتين للراكب. جارية في الخاص الشريف. شربها من بحر ذات الصفاء بالخليج المعروف بتلمنده، بماء عبرته ثماني عشرة قبضة. بها جامع تقام فيه الجمعة. اهلها بنو زرعة فخذ من افخاذ بني عجلان.

ارتفاعها عينا، الف واحد وستون دينارا وربع وسدس وثمن وحبتان. وغلة، خمسة الاف وثلاثمائة وثلاثة وسبعون اردبا ونصف وربع. تفصيله:

قمح، الف وتسعمائة وستة وخمسون اردبا.

شعير، ستمائة وثمانية وستون اردبا وربع وسدس ونصف قيراط.

فول، الف وسبعة ارادب ونصف ونصف ثمن.

ارز بقشره، الف وسبعمائة واحد واربعون[862] اردبا ونصف وربع.

فدن قصب سكر، ستة وسبعون فدانا. تفصيله:

راس، احد وخمسون فدانا.

خلفة، خمسة وعشرون فدانا.

تفصيله:

مال الهلالي، ستة وسبعون دينارا وثمن وحبتان. تفصيله:

الحانوت، اثنان وستون دينارا وثمن وحبتان.

الفروج، خمسة عشر دينارا.

خراج الراتب، ثمانمائة وسبعة وخمسون دينارا ونصف وربع وثمن وحبتان. تفصيله:

المستقر، ثمانمائة واحد وخمسون دينارا وثلث وربع وثمن. تفصيله:

الاصل، عن ثلاثمائة واحد وسبعين فدانا وثمن ونصف قيراط، ستمائة وسبعة وتسعون دينارا. تفصيله:

كرم، عن ستة فدادين وثلثين ونصف قيراط، خمسة وثلاثون دينارا وثلثان.

شجر راتب، عن مائتي وستة وتسعين فدانا ونصف وربع وثمن وحبة، خمسمائة وثلاثة وتسعون دينارا ونصف وربع وحبتان.

حكر، عن سبعة وستين فدانا وربع وسدس وثمن وحبتين، سبعة وستون دينارا وربع وسدس وثمن وحبتان.

الاضافة، سبعة وثمانون دينارا وثمن.

زائد القطيعة، سبعة وستون دينارا وربع وسدس وثمن وحبتان.

المستظهر به، ستة دنانير وسدس وحبتان. تفصيله:

الاصل، عن فدانين وثلثين وربع ونصف ثمن وحبة، ثلاثة دنانير وثلث وربع ونصف قيراط وحبة. تفصيله:

راتب، عن ثلثي فدان وثمن، دينار واحد وثلث وثمن. تفصيله:

كامل، عن ثلثي فدان، دينار واحد وثلث.

غرس عامين، عن ثمن فدان، ثمن دينار.

حكر، عن فدانين وثمن ونصف قيراط[863] وحبة، ديناران وثمن ونصف قيراط وحبة.

الاضافة، ربع وسدس دينار.

زائد القطيعة، ديناران وثمن ونصف قيراط وحبة.

It is in the north-east of the Fayyum, two hours' ride from Madīnat al-Fayyūm. It is assigned to the honourable private domain of the sultan. It gets its water from Dhāt al-Ṣafāʾ Canal, through the channel known as Tlmndh. Its water quota is 18 *qabḍas*. It has a congregational mosque, in which the Friday prayers are held. Its people are the Banū Zarʿa, a branch of the Banū ʿAjlān.

Its revenue in specie is 1,061 ¼ ⅙ ⅛ ²⁄₇₂ dinars; and in grains, 5,373 ½ ¼ ardabbs:

wheat, 1,956 ardabbs;

barley, 668 ¼ ⅙ ¹⁄₄₈ ardabbs;

broad beans, 1,007 ½ ¹⁄₁₆ ardabbs;

rice in hull, 1,741 ½ ¼ ardabbs.

Sugarcane [on the crown estate], 76 feddans:

first harvest, 51 feddans;

second harvest, 25 feddans;

[The revenue] in detail:

lunar-calendar taxes, 76 ⅛ ²⁄₇₂ dinars:

the shop, 62 ⅛ ²⁄₇₂ dinars;

[concession for sale of] chickens, 15 dinars.

land tax on perennial plants, 857 ½ ¼ ⅛ ²⁄₇₂ dinars:

the established tax, 851 ⅓ ¼ ⅛ dinars:

the basic assessment, for 371 ⅛ ¹⁄₄₈ feddans, 697 dinars:

vineyards, for 6 ⅔ ¹⁄₄₈ feddans, 35 ⅔ dinars;

fully grown trees, for 296 ½ ¼ ⅛ ¹⁄₇₂ feddans, 593 ½ ¼ ²⁄₇₂ dinars;

land tax on lands subject to long-term lease, for 67 ¼ ⅙ ⅛ ²⁄₇₂ feddans, 67 ¼ ⅙ ⅛ ²⁄₇₂ dinars.

the addition, 87 ⅛ dinars.

the added tax-rate [on long-term lease], 67 ¼ ⅙ ⅛ ²⁄₇₂ dinars.

The newly introduced (*al-mustaẓhar*)[288] [perennial plants], 6 ⅙ ²⁄₇₂ dinars:

the basic assessment, for 2 ⅔ ¼ ¹⁄₁₆ ¹⁄₇₂ feddans, 3 ⅓ ¼ ¹⁄₄₈ ¹⁄₇₂ dinars:

land tax on perennial plants, for ⅔ ⅛ feddan, 1 ⅓ ⅛ dinar:

fully-grown, for ⅔ feddan, 1 ⅓ dinar;

two-year old plants, for ⅛ feddan, ⅛ dinar;

lands subject to long-term lease, for 2 ⅛ ¹⁄₄₈ ¹⁄₇₂ feddans, 2 ⅛ ¹⁄₄₈ ¹⁄₇₂ dinars;

the addition ¼ ⅙ dinar;

the added tax-rate [on long-term lease], 2 ⅛ ¹⁄₄₈ ¹⁄₇₂ dinars.

862 أ. س.: سبعون.

863 ط. م. يضيف: نصف.

288 On *al-mustaẓhar bi-hi* (or *bi-hā*) as 'recently introduced', similar to *al-mustajidd*, see al-Nuwayrī, *Nihāyat al-arab*, VIII, 201, 209. It seems that *al-mustaẓhar bi-hi* is a fiscal term that refers specifically to revenues added to the *iqṭāʿ* unit, while *mustajidd* refers to newly planted crops and trees.

خراج الزراعة، اثنان وسبعون دينارا ونصف وثلث ونصف ثمن. تفصيله:
الاصل، اربعة وستون دينارا وثلثان وثمن. تفصيله:
خضر وثوم، عن ثلاثة وعشرين فدانا وثلث ونصف ثمن، ستة واربعون دينارا وثلثان وثمن.[864]
قلقاس، ثمانية عشر دينارا. تفصيله:
قطيعة خمسة دنانير الفدان، عن ثلاثة فدادين، خمسة عشر دينارا.
قطيعة ثلاثة دنانير الفدان، عن فدان واحد، ثلاثة دنانير.
الاضافة، ثمانية دنانير وقيراطان ونصف.

المناجزة، غلة، خمسة الاف ومائة واحد وتسعون اردبا. تفصيله:
قمح، الف وثمانمائة وتسعة وتسعون اردبا.
شعير، ستمائة وثلاثة واربعون اردبا.
فول، تسعمائة وثمانية وخمسون اردبا.
ارز بقشره، الف وستمائة واحد وتسعون اردبا.

المشاطرة فيما ياتي ذكره،[865] ثلاثة عشر دينارا وثلثان ونصف قيراط وحبة:
المقات، اثنا عشر دينارا ونصف.
السمسم، دينار وسدس ونصف قيراط وحبة.

تتمة البذل،[866] تسعة وثلاثون دينارا وثلثان وربع.

زراعة الاوسية، ستة وسبعون فدانا. تفصيله:
راس، احد وخمسون فدانا.
خلفه، خمسة وعشرون فدانا.

الوفر، مائة وخمسة وخمسون اردبا[867] وثلثان وثمن. تفصيله:
قمح، سبعة وخمسون اردبا.
شعير، تسعة عشر اردبا وسدس وثمن.
فول، ثمانية وعشرون اردبا ونصف وربع.
ارز بقشره، خمسون اردبا ونصف وربع.

الحمولة، ستة وعشرون اردبا ونصف وثلث وثمن. تفصيله:
شعير، ستة ارادب وثمن ونصف قيراط.
فول، عشرون اردبا ونصف وربع ونصف ثمن.

وعليها من الرسوم والكيالة والمراعي، عن الف وستمائة وخمسة وتسعين درهما ونصف وربع وثمن، اثنان واربعون دينارا وثلث ونصف ثمن؛ وغلة، مائة وثمانية وثمانون اردبا وثلثان وربع. تفصيله:
قمح، ستون اردبا وربع وسدس.
شعير، سبعة وعشرون اردبا ونصف.
فول، ثمانية وثلاثون اردبا وثلثان.
ارز بقشره، اثنان وستون اردبا وثلث.

Land tax [assessed by feddans], 72 ½ ⅓ 1/16 dinars:
the basic assessment, 64 ⅔ ⅛ dinars:
green [vegetables] and garlic, for 23 ⅓ 1/16 feddans, 46 ⅔ ⅛ dinars;
colocasia, 18 dinars:
at the rate of 5 dinars per feddan, for 3 feddans, 15 dinars;
at the rate of 3 dinars per feddan, for 1 feddan, 3 dinars.
the addition, 8 2/24 1/48 dinars.

Munājaza land tax on grains, 5,191 ardabbs:
wheat, 1,899 ardabbs;
barley, 643 ardabbs;
broad beans, 958 ardabbs;
rice in hull, 1,691 ardabbs.

Mushāṭara land tax, as will be listed below, 13 ⅔ 1/48 1/72 dinars:
Cucurbitaceous fruits, 12 ½ dinars;
sesame, 1 ⅙ 1/48 1/72 dinar.

The adjustment of the *badhl*,[289] 39 ⅔ ¼ dinars.

Cultivation of the crown estate, 76 feddans:
first harvest, 51 feddans;
second harvest, 25 feddans;

The surcharge, 155 ⅔ ⅛ ardabbs:[290]
wheat, 57 ardabbs;
barley, 19 ⅙ ⅛ ardabbs;
broad beans, 28 ½ ¼ ardabbs;
rice in hull, 50 ½ ¼ ardabbs.

The transportation fee, 26 ½ ⅓ ⅛ ardabbs:
barley, 6 ⅛ 1/48 ardabbs;
broad beans, 20 ½ ¼ 1/16 ardabbs.

The fees, the measurement fee and the pasture tax are 1,695 ½ ¼ ⅛ dirhams, which are 42 ⅓ 1/16 dinars; and in grains, 188 ⅔ ¼ ardabbs:
wheat, 60 ¼ ⅙ ardabbs;
barley, 27 ½ ardabbs;
broad beans, 38 ⅔ ardabbs:
rice in hull, 62 ⅓ ardabbs.

864 ساقط من أ. س.: وثمن.
865 ساقط من أ. س.: فيما يأتي ذكره.
866 ط. م.: قيمة البذل.
867 أ. س.، ط. م.: فدانا.

289 MP: *qīmat al-badhl* (value of the *badhl*).
290 MP and AS: feddans.

تفصيله:
الرسوم، تسعمائة واربعة وعشرون درهما وربع، وغلة، ستة وثلاثون اردبا وقيراط:
قمح، احد عشر اردبا.
شعير، اثنا عشر اردبا ونصف.
فول، اثنا عشر اردبا وربع وسدس وثمن.
تفصيله:
شد الاحباس، ثلاثة عشر درهما ونصف.
رسم الجراريف، تسعون درهما.
رسم الحصاد، ثلاثة وخمسون درهما.
رسم الخفارة، خمسة عشر درهما.
رسم قطيعة ثوم، ستمائة درهم.
رسم الجزر، اربعون درهما.
رسم القلقاس، اربعة وثمانون درهما.
رسم الاجران، ثمانية وعشرون درهما ونصف وربع، وغلة، ستة وثلاثون اردبا وقيراط على ما فصل.
كيالة، مائة واثنان وخمسون اردبا ونصف وربع وثمن:
قمح، تسعة واربعون اردبا وربع وسدس.
شعير، خمسة عشر اردبا.
فول، ستة وعشرون اردبا وثمن.[868]
ارز بقشره، اثنان وستون اردبا وثلث.[869]
المراعي، عن ثلاثمائة وثمانية وثلاثين راسا، سبعمائة واحد وسبعون درهما ونصف وثمن. تفصيله:
راتب، قطيعة درهمين[870] وربع الراس، عن ثلاثمائة وثلاثين راسا، سبعمائة واثنان واربعون درهما ونصف.
طارئ، قطيعة درهم واحد الراس، عن ثمانية ارؤس، ثمانية دراهم.
رسم المستخدمين، حسابا عن كل مائة ستة دراهم وربع، احد وعشرون درهما وربع.

عليها من الزكاة، مائة وثمانية دنانير وقيراط وحبة. تفصيله:
الخرص، ستة وتسعون دينارا ونصف. تفصيله:
خرص العنب، احد وستون دينارا ونصف.
خرص النخل، خمسة وثلاثون دينارا.
ثمن الماشية، عن عشرة ارؤس، احد عشر دينارا وربع وسدس وثمن وحبة. تفصيله:
بقر احمر، عن مسنة واحدة، ثلاثة دنانير ونصف وثلث وثمن وحبة.
عن ثمن الاغنام، عن تسعة ارؤس، سبعة دنانير وثلث وربع. تفصيله:
بياض، عن خمسة ارؤس، خمسة دنانير وربع.
شعارى، عن اربعة ارؤس، ديناران وثلث.

وعليها من الجوالي، عن ثلاثين نفرا، ستون دينارا. تفصيله:
المقيمون بها، عن تسعة عشر نفرا، ثمانية وثلاثون دينارا.
الناءون عنها، عن احد عشر نفرا، اثنان وعشرون دينارا. تفصيله:
الوجه البحري، عن نفر واحد، ديناران.
الوجه القبلي، عن عشرة انفار، عشرون دينارا.

وعليها من الاتبان، ثلاثة الاف وخمسمائة شنيف.

[868] أ. س.: وثلث.
[869] ساقط من أ. س.: وثلث.
[870] أ. س.: درهم.

[The fees, the measurement fee and the pasture tax] in detail:
the fees, 924 ¼ dirhams; and in grains, 36 1/24 ardabbs:
wheat, 11 ardabbs;
barley, 12 ½ ardabbs;
broad beans, 12 ¼ ⅙ ⅛ ardabbs.
[The fees] in detail:
supervision of endowments, 13 ½ dirhams;
dredging fee, 90 dirhams;
harvest fee, 53 dirhams;
protection fee, 15 dirhams;
[settlement] fee for the tax-rate on garlic, 600 dirhams;
[settlement] fee on carrots, 40 dirhams;
[settlement] fee on colocasia, 84 dirhams;
threshing-floor fee, 28 ½ ¼ dirhams; and in grains, 36 1/24 ardabbs, as specified.
the measurement fee, 152 ½ ¼ ⅛ ardabbs:
wheat, 49 ¼ ⅙ ardabbs;
barley, 15 ardabbs;
broad beans, 26 ⅛ ardabbs;
rice in hull, 62 ⅓ ardabbs.
The pasture tax, for 338 heads, 771 ½ ⅛ dirhams:
permanent pasture lands at the rate of 2 ¼ dirhams per head, for 330 heads, 742 ½ dirhams;
seasonal pasture lands, at the rate of one dirham per head, for eight heads, 8 dirhams;
The government agents' fee, calculated at 6 ¼ dirhams for every 100 [heads], 21 ¼ dirhams.

The alms-tax, 108 1/24 1/72 dinars:
the estimate, 96 ½ dinars:
estimate of grapes, 61 ½ dinars;
estimate of date palms, 35 dinars;
monetary value of livestock, for 10 heads, 11 ¼ ⅙ ⅛ 1/72 dinars:
cows, for a two-year old cow, 3 ½ ⅓ ⅛ 1/72 dinars;
monetary value of small cattle, for nine heads, 7 ⅓ ¼ dinars:
sheep, for five heads, 5 ¼ dinars;
goats, for four heads, 2 ⅓ dinars.

The poll-tax, for 30 individuals, 60 dinars:
those residing in it, for 19 individuals, 38 dinars;
those absent from it, for 11 individuals, 22 dinars:
in the northern region, for one individual, 2 dinars;
in the southern region, for 10 individuals, 20 dinars.

Hay, 3,500 bales.

عليها لديوان الاحباس ستة دنانير.

رسم خولي[871] البحر بها، قمح، اردبان.

والمطلق بها لارباب الرزق خمسة عشر فدانا. تفصيله:
الخفراء، ستة فدادين.
النجارون، تسعة فدادين.

والمربى بها من الدجاج عن المستقر تربيته بغير اجرة، الف وخمسون طائرا.

اهلها يزرعون من القصب السكر ويسقون من الخلفة بحق نصف المزدرع بالناحية، برسم معصرة القبرا، ثمانية وثلاثون فدانا. تفصيله:
راس، خمسة وعشرون فدانا ونصف.
خلفة، اثنا عشر فدانا ونصف.

والذي بها من التقاوي الى اخر عمل[872] سنة اثنتين واربعين وستمائة للمزارعين والمرابعين في الاقصاب والخضر، عينا، اثنان واربعون دينارا وثلث وربع وثمن وحبتان؛ وغلة، الف وثلاثمائة وثمانية وعشرون اردبا ونصف وثلث. تفصيله:
قمح، اربعمائة وثلاثة وثلاثون اردبا.
شعير، مائة وخمسون اردبا.
فول، ثلاثمائة وخمسون اردبا.
ارز بقشره، ثلاثمائة وخمسة وتسعون اردبا.[873]
سلجم، نصف وثلث اردب.

والذي جرت العادة بايقافه من خراج الناحية عن الخراب الداثر، سبعة وخمسون دينارا وثلث وربع وثمن وحبة.

والذي انساق بها من الباقي في معاملة الامير جمال الدين اقوش المستعرب والامير عز الدين امير شكار، خارجا عما بها من البواقي الديوانية لسنة اربع وثلاثين وستمائة وما قبلها عند ما كانت جارية في الخاص قبل انتقالها للمقطعين، الشاهد بجملة الحاصل والموقوف والباقي بالعدوة وسرسنا ومطرطارس عند ما كانت صفقة واحدة في الايام الكاملية، سقى الله عهدها صوب الرحمة[874]، الحسبانات المخلدة بالدواوين المعمورة، جملته عينا، ثلاثمائة وديناران ونصف[875] قيراط؛ وغلة، خمسة الاف وثلاثة وثمانون اردبا وثلث وربع ونصف ثمن، لاستقبال سنة خمس وثلاثين وستمائة والى اخر سنة اربعين وستمائة، ثمانية وخمسون دينارا وقيراطان ودانق؛ وغلة، الفان وثلاثمائة[876] واحد وستون اردبا وثلثان ونصف ثمن. تفصيله:
قمح، تسعمائة وسبعون[877] اردبا وثلث ونصف ثمن.
شعير، اربعمائة واثنان وستون اردبا ونصف ونصف ثمن.
فول، خمسمائة وسبعة وثلاثون اردبا وثلث.
ارز بقشره، ثلاثمائة واحد وتسعون اردبا وربع وسدس ونصف قيراط.

For the Ministry of Endowments, 6 dinars.

The fee of the overseer of the canal, wheat, 2 ardabbs.

Allocated for those entitled to allowances, 15 feddans:
the guardsmen, 6 feddans;
the carpenters, 9 feddans.

The established rearing of chickens, without [rearing] wage, 1,050 birds.

Its people sow sugarcane and irrigate second harvest [sugarcane] assigned for the press at al-Qubarā᾽. They have a right to half of what is sown in the locality (*bi-ḥaqq niṣf al-muzdaraᶜ bi'l-nāḥiya*), [which is] 38 feddans:
first harvest, 25 ½ feddans;
second harvest, 12 ½ feddans.

The seed advances for the tenants and the quarter-share labourers of sugarcane and green [vegetables], up to the end of 642, in specie, 42 ⅓ ¼ ⅛ 2/72 dinars; and in grains, 1,328 ½ ⅓ ardabbs:
wheat, 433 ardabbs;
barley, 150 ardabbs;
broad beans, 350 ardabbs;
rice in hull, 395 ardabbs;
rape, ½ ⅓ ardabb.

The land tax customarily withheld, on account of derelict and deserted lands, 57 dinars ⅓ ¼ ⅛ 1/72.

The tax arrears carried over in the account of the amir Jamāl al-Dīn Aqqūsh al-Mustaᶜrab and the amir ᶜIzz al-Dīn, amīr *shikār*, since the beginning of 635 until the end of the year 640, 58 2/24 1/144 dinars; and in grains, 2,361 ⅔ 1/16 ardabbs:
wheat, 970 ⅓ 1/16 ardabbs;
barley, 462 ½ 1/16 ardabbs;
broad beans, 537 ⅓ ardabbs;
rice in hull, 391 ¼ ⅙ 1/48 ardabbs.

That excludes the outstanding payments to the Dīwān for 634 and previous years, when it was assigned to the private domain of the sultan, before it was transferred to the *iqṭāᶜ*-holders. These attest to the joint total of the surplus, withheld and outstanding payments for al-ᶜIdwa, Sirisnā and Miṭr Ṭāris, as they formed one fiscal unit during the days of al-Kāmil, may God show compassion and approval on his age. The account registered in the prosperous Dīwān's totals is, in specie, 302 1/48 dinars; and in grains, 5,083 ⅓ ¼ 1/16 ardabbs.

871 ساقط من أ. س.: خولى، لكنه يضيفه على الهامش.
872 ط. م.: عمارة.
873 ساقط من أ. س.: فول ثلاثمائة وخمسون أردبا. أرز بقشره ثلاثمائة وخمسة وتسعون أردبا.
874 أ. س. يضيف: والرضوان.
875 ساقط من أ. س.: ونصف.
876 أ. س.: ستمائة.
877 أ. س.: ستون.

ومن حرف الميم، مسجد عائشة، وتسمى[878] ارضها بالعاقولة. هذا المكان عبارة عن بيوت اخصاص بين محاطب كثيرة ليس بها شجر ولا غرس ولا خضر. قليلة الارض من غربية الفيوم مجاورة الحنبوشية ودقلوه. بينها وبين مدينة الفيوم اربع ساعات للراكب. جارية في اقطاع الطواشي شمس الدين الكوراني. شربها من ماء الغرق المعروف بقمبشا[879] مما ينصرف من باب القبو ويقسم على دقلوه وارض العاقولة المعروفة بمسجد عائشة، رضي الله عنها[880]، شركة دقلوه من جملة اربعة وعشرين قبضة، بعد ما يخص دقلوه عشرون قبضة وثلثان، ثلاث قبض وثلث. اهلها اضابطة، فخذ من بني كلاب.

ارتفاعها، مشاطرة غلة، خمسة وسبعون اردبا:

قمح، ثلاثون اردبا.

شعير، خمسة واربعون اردبا.

عليها من الرسوم والكيالة، عن خمسة دراهم، ثمن دينار، وغلة، تسعة ارادب. تفصيله:

قمح، اربعة ارادب ونصف وربع.

شعير، اربعة ارادب وربع.

تفصيله:

رسم الاجران خمسة دراهم، وغلة، خمسة ارادب ونصف. تفصيله:

قمح، اردبان ونصف وربع.

وشعير، اردبان ونصف وربع.

كيالة، ثلاثة ارادب ونصف:

قمح، اردبان.

شعير، اردب ونصف.[881]

وعليها من الزكاة عن ثمن اغنام، عن اربعة اروس، ثلاثة دنانير وربع. تفصيله:

بياض، عن راسين، ديناران وثمن.

شعارى، عن راسين، دينار واحد وثمن.

عليها من الاتبان، خمسمائة شنيف.

والذي بها من التقاوي الديوانية لسنة خمس وثلاثين وستمائة، قمح، عشرون اردبا.

ومن حرف الميم، منشاة اولاد عرفة، من حقوق خليج دلية. هذه البلدة بلدة صغيرة تشتمل على شجر ونخيل ودويرات تين وخوخ واصول خروب وسدر. من قبلي مدينة الفيوم، بينها وبين مدينة الفيوم مسافة ساعة للراكب. في عبرة الاقطاع من الخليج المذكور. شربها من بحر خليج دلية قبل[882] المقاسم، بما فيه من الخفارة، قبضتان ماء. من قبلي الناحية دير يعرف بابي شنودة. اهلها بنو عامر، فخذ من بني كلاب.

ارتفاعها، عينا، عشرة دنانير وربع. تفصيله:

مراعي، ديناران ونصف.

خراج، سبعة دنانير ونصف وربع.

878 أ. س.: ويسمى.

879 أ. س.: قنبشا.

880 ساقط من ط. م.: رضي الله عنها.

881 ساقط من أ. س.: ونصف.

882 أ. س.: قبلي.

Also beginning with the letter 'mīm': Masjid ʿĀʾisha.[291] Its land is called al-ʿĀqūla. This place consists of shacks amid abundant firewood. It has no trees, plantations or green [vegetables], and very little land. It is in the west of the province, in the vicinity of al-Ḥanbūshiyya and Diqlawa, four hours' ride from Madīnat al-Fayyūm. It is assigned as an *iqṭāʿ* to the *ṭawāshī* Shams al-Dīn al-Kūrānī. It gets its water from [the reservoir of] al-Gharq, [also] known as Qambashā, from water that drains through the sluice gate of the Arch (*bāb al-Qabw*), and is then divided between Diqlawa and the land of al-ʿĀqūla, also known as Masjid ʿĀʾisha, may God be pleased with her. It shares with Diqlawa a total of 24 *qabḍas*, of which 20 ⅔ *qabḍas* are assigned to Diqlawa, and 3 ⅓ *qabḍas* [are allocated to it]. Its people are the Aḍābiṭa, a branch of the Banū Kilāb.

Its revenue, from *mushāṭara* land tax on grains, is 75 ardabbs:

wheat, 30 ardabbs;

barley, 45 ardabbs.

The fees and the measurement fee are 5 dirhams, which are ⅛ dinar; and in grains, 9 ardabbs:

wheat, 4 ½ ¼ ardabbs;

barley, 4 ¼ ardabbs.

[The fees and the measurement fee] in detail:

threshing-floor fee, 5 dirhams; and in grains, 5 ½ ardabbs:

wheat, 2 ½ ¼ ardabbs;

barley, 2 ½ ¼ ardabbs.

The measurement fee, 3 ½ ardabbs:

wheat, 2 ardabbs;

barley, 1 ½ ardabb.

The alms-tax, for the monetary value of small cattle, for four heads, 3 ¼ dinars:

sheep, for two heads, 2 ⅛ dinars;

goats, for two heads, 1 ⅛ dinar.

Hay, 500 bales.

The seed advances from the Dīwān for the year 635, wheat, 20 ardabbs.

Also beginning with the letter 'mīm': Munshaʾat Awlād ʿArafa,[292] included in the accounts of Dilya Canal. This is a small village, with trees, date palms, enclosures of figs and peaches, trunks of carob and sidr trees. It is one hour's ride south of Madīnat al-Fayyūm. It is included in the fiscal value of the *iqṭāʿ* of the [Dilya] canal. It gets its water from Dilya Canal, before[293] the divisors, two *qabḍas* of water, including what is allocated as [allowance for those providing] protection. To the south of the village there is a monastery known as Abū Shinūda (Shenute). Its people are the Banū ʿĀmir, a branch of the Banū Kilāb.

Its revenue in specie is 10 ¼ dinars:

fixed pasture tax, 2 ½ dinars;

land tax, 7 ½ ¼ dinars;

291 Modern location (uncertain): ʿIzbat Aḥmad dhū al-Fiqār (عزبة احمد ذو الفقار). Halm, *Ägypten*, p. 264; Salmon, 'Répertoire', p. 61; de Sacy, *État des provinces*, p. 684; Ibn al-Jīʿān, *Kitāb al-tuḥfa*, p. 157. There is no positive identification of this village, but in line with al-Nābulusī's description, and following Shafei Bey's map, we identified it with ʿIzbat Aḥmad dhū al-Fiqār.

292 Modern location: Maʿṣarat ʿArafa (معصرة عرفة). Halm, *Ägypten*, p. 262: Manshīat Awlād ʿArafa; Salmon, 'Répertoire', p. 66; de Sacy, *État des provinces*, p. 684; Ibn al-Jīʿān, *Kitāb al-tuḥfa*, p. 158; Ramzī, *Al-Qāmūs*, II/III, 87: Maʿṣarat ʿArafa.

293 AS: south of (*qiblī*).

غلة، مناجزة، مائتان وخمسون اردبا:
قمح، مائة واربعة وستون اردبا.
وشعير، ستة وثمانون اردبا.

عليها من الرسوم والكيالة، عن سبعة وتسعين درهما ونصف وربع، ديناران وربع وسدس وحبتان؛ وغلة، ستة وعشرون اردبا وثلث وربع وثمن. تفصيله:
قمح، ثلاثة عشر اردبا وخمسة قراريط.
وشعير، ثلاثة عشر اردبا ونصف.

تفصيله:
الرسوم، سبعة وتسعون درهما ونصف وربع، وغلة، تسعة ارادب ونصف وثمن:
قمح، اربعة ارادب وثمن.
فول، خمسة ارادب ونصف.
تفصيله:
شد الاحباس، درهمان.
رسم الجراريف، احد وعشرون درهما.[883]
رسم الحصاد، ثلاثة وخمسون درهما.
رسم الخفارة، خمسة عشر درهما.
رسم الاجران، ثمانية دراهم ونصف وربع، والغلة على ما فصل.
كيالة، سبعة عشر اردبا وقيراطان:
قمح، تسعة ارادب وقيراطان.
فول، ثمانية ارادب.

وعليها من الزكاة، ستة دنانير وسدس وحبة. تفصيله:
خرص النخل، دينار واحد ونصف.
ثمن المواشي، عن خمسة اروس، اربعة دنانير وثلثان وحبة.
تفصيله:
بقر احمر، تبيع واحد، ثلثا دينار وربع وحبة.
اغنام، عن اربعة اروس، ثلاثة دنانير ونصف وربع:
بياض، عن ثلاثة اروس، ثلاثة دنانير وربع.
شعارى، عن راس واحد، نصف دينار.

عليها من الاتبان، مائتان وخمسون شنيفا.

وعليها لديوان الاحباس، عينا، نصف دينار.

اهلها يربون من الفروج، مائة وتسعين طائرا. تفصيله:
للديوان المعمور، بما فيه من اجرة التربية وهو الثلث، مائة وخمسون طائرا.
للمقطعين، اربعون طائرا.

اهلها يزرعون من القصب السكر فدانا واحدا وقيراطان، راس.

والمسلف عليه بها من الشعير برسم الاصطبلات السلطانية خمسة وعشرون اردبا.

And in *munājaza* land tax on grains, 250 ardabbs:
wheat, 164 ardabbs;
barley, 86 ardabbs.

The fees and the measurement fee are 97 ½ ¼ dirhams, which are 2 ¼ ⅙ 2⁄72 dinars; and in grains, 26 ⅓ ¼ ⅛ ardabbs:
wheat, 13 5⁄24 ardabbs;
barley, 13 ½ ardabbs.

[The fees and the measurement fee] in detail:
the fees, 97 ½ ¼ dirhams; and in grains, 9 ½ ⅛ ardabbs:
wheat, 4 ⅛ ardabbs;
broad beans, 5 ½ ardabbs.
[The fees] in detail:
supervision of endowments, 2 dirhams;
dredging fee, 21 dirhams;
harvest fee, 53 dirhams;
protection fee, 15 dirhams;
threshing-floor fee, 8 ½ ¼ dirhams; and in grains as specified.
The measurement fee, 17 2⁄24 ardabbs:
wheat, 9 2⁄24 ardabbs;
broad beans, 8 ardabbs.

The alms-tax is 6 ⅙ 1⁄72 dinars:
estimate of date palms, 1 ½ dinar;
monetary value of livestock, for five heads, 4 ⅔ 1⁄72 dinars:
cows, for a yearling calf ⅔ ¼ 1⁄72 dinar;
small cattle, for four heads, 3 ½ ¼ dinars:
sheep, for three heads, 3 ¼ dinars;
goats, for one head, ½ dinar.

Hay, 250 bales.

For the Ministry of Endowments, in specie, ½ dinar.

Its people rear chickens, 190 birds:
for the prosperous Dīwān, including the rearing wage of a third, 150 birds;
for the *iqṭā*ʿ-holders, 40 birds.

Its people sow 1 2⁄24 feddan of sugarcane, first harvest.

The barley assigned for the royal stables and paid for in advance, 25 ardabbs.

883 ساقط من ط. م.: درهما.

ومن حرف الميم، منيه ششها. هذه البلدة عبارة عن بلدة كبيرة[884] تشتمل على اشجار ونخيل[885] وكروم وتين وعنب ونارنج. من قبلي الفيوم، بينها وبين مدينة الفيوم مسافة ساعتين للراكب. من نواحي خليج دلية في عبرة اقطاع الخليج المذكور. شربها من بحر دلية بخليج قبل مقسم معروف بطرفا، بماء عدته قبضتان ونصف وثمن. والمطلق لرزقة عز الدين بن حصن من التبرون، نصف قبضة ماء. بها[886] جامع تقام فيه الجمعة. اهلها بنو غصين، فخذ من بني كلاب.

ارتفاعها، عينا، هلالي ومراعي وخراجى، ثمانية وستون دينارا وسدس وثمن وحبتان؛ وغلة، مناجزة، اصلا واضافة، اربعمائة واربعة عشر اردبا ونصف وربع. تفصيله:

قمح، مائتان وثمانية واربعون اردبا ونصف وثلث.

شعير، اثنان وثمانون اردبا ونصف وثلث وثمن.

عليها من الرسوم والكيالة والمراعي، عن مائة واثنين وسبعين درهما ونصف،[887] اربعة دنانير وربع ونصف ثمن؛ وغلة، ثمانية وثلاثون اردبا وربع وسدس ونصف ثمن. تفصيله:

قمح، اثنان وعشرون اردبا وثلثان وثمن.

شعير، اربعة عشر اردبا وثمن ونصف قيراط.

فول، اردب واحد وربع وسدس وثمن.

تفصيله:

الرسوم، مائة واربعة وثلاثون درهما وربع وثمن، وغلة، اربعة وعشرون اردبا وثلثان وربع ونصف ثمن. تفصيله:

قمح، خمسة عشر اردبا وسدس وثمن.

وشعير، ثمانية ارادب وثمن ونصف قيراط. وفول، اردب واحد وربع وسدس وثمن.

تفصيله:

شد الاحباس، درهمان ونصف.

شد العين، احد وثلاثون درهما.

رسم الجراريف، احد عشر درهما.

رسم الحصاد، ثلاثة وخمسون درهما.

رسم الخفارة، خمسة عشر درهما.

رسم الاجران، احد وعشرون درهما ونصف وربع وثمن، والغلة على ما تقدم تفصيله.

الكيالة، ثلاثة عشر اردبا ونصف:

قمح، سبعة ارادب.

شعير، ستة ارادب.

المراعي، عن مائة[888] واثنين وعشرين راسا، ثمانية وثلاثون درهما وثمن. تفصيله:

قطيعة خمسة وعشرين درهما المائة، عن العدة المذكورة، ثلاثون درهما ونصف.

رسم المستخدمين، سبعة دراهم ونصف وثمن.

وعليها من الزكاة، تسعة عشر دينارا وربع وثمن:

الخرص، اربعة عشر دينارا. تفصيله:

خرص العنب، ثلاثة عشر دينارا.

خرص النخل، دينار واحد.

884 ساقط من أ. س.: كبيرة.

885 ساقط من ط. م.: ونخيل.

886 أ. س.: فيها

887 أ. س.: وحبة.

888 ساقط من أ. س.: مائة.

Also beginning with the letter 'mīm': Minyat Shushhā.[294] This is a large village, with trees, date palms, vineyards, figs, grapes and oranges. It is at the south of the province, two hours' ride from Madīnat al-Fayyūm. It is one of the villages of Dilya Canal, and is included in the *iqṭāʿ* of that canal. It gets its water, at the amount of 2 ½ ⅛ *qabḍas*, from Dilya Canal, by means of a channel [that branches off] before a divisor known as Ṭarfā (?).[295] The water allocated to the allowance of ʿIzz al-Dīn ibn Ḥiṣn[296] from [the divisor known as] al-Tabrūn, ½ *qabḍa* of water. It has a congregational mosque, in which the Friday prayers are held. Its people are Banū Ghuṣayn, a branch of the Banū Kilāb.

Its revenue is, in specie, from lunar-calendar taxes, pasture tax and land tax, 68 ⅙ ⅛ 2/72 dinars; and in grains, from the basic assessment and the addition of *munājaza* land tax, 414 ½ ¼ ardabbs:

wheat, 248 ½ ⅓ ardabbs;

barley, 82 ½ ⅓ ⅛ ardabbs.

The fees, the measurement fee and the pasture tax are 172 ½ dirhams, which are 4 ¼ 1/16 dinars; and in grains, 38 ¼ ⅙ 1/16 ardabbs:

wheat, 22 ⅔ ⅛ ardabbs;

barley, 14 ⅛ 1/48 ardabbs;

broad beans, 1 ¼ ⅙ ⅛ ardabb.

[The fees, the measurement fee and the pasture tax] in detail:

the fees are 134 ¼ ⅛ dirhams; and in grains, 24 ⅔ ¼ 1/16 ardabbs:

wheat, 15 ⅙ ⅛ ardabbs;

barley, 8 ⅛ 1/48 ardabbs;

broad beans, 1 ¼ ⅙ ⅛ ardabb.

[The fees] in detail:

supervision of endowments, 2 ½ dirhams;

supervision of the land survey, 31 dirhams;

dredging fee, 11 dirhams;

harvest fee, 53 dirhams;

protection fee, 15 dirhams;

threshing-floor fee, 21 ½ ¼ ⅛ dirhams; and in grains, as above.

The measurement fee, 13 ½ ardabbs:

wheat, 7 [½] ardabbs;

barley, 6 ardabbs.

The pasture tax, for 122 heads, 38 ⅛ dirhams:

at the rate of 25 dirhams per 100 [heads], for that number [of heads], 30 ½ dirhams;

the government agents' fee, 7 ½ ⅛ dirhams.

The alms-tax, 19 ¼ ⅛ dinars:

the estimate, 14 dinars:

estimate of grapes, 13 dinars;

estimate of date palms, 1 dinar.

294 Modern location: Minyat al-Ḥayṭ (منية الحيط). Halm, *Ägypten*, p. 266; Salmon, 'Répertoire', p. 66: Minīa Chouchahā; de Sacy, *État des provinces*, p. 684: Miniat Shushihā; Ramzī, *Al-Qāmūs*, II/III, 83: al-Minyā; I, p. 297: Minyat Shushhā = Minyat al-Ḥayṭ.

295 This divisor is not mentioned elsewhere in the treatise. The two divisors on Dilya canal that are mentioned are al-Tabrūn and al-Qalanbū.

296 Possibly the same as Ḥiṣn [al-Din] ibn Mutrif (?), mentioned in the entry for al-Aḥkar.

ثمن المواشي، ستة ارؤس، خمسة دنانير وربع وثمن. تفصيله:
بقر احمر، تبيع واحد، دينار واحد ونصف وربع.
ثمن الاغنام، عن خمسة ارؤس، ثلاثة دنانير ونصف وثمن:
بياض، عن راسين، ديناران.
شعارى، عن ثلاثة ارؤس، دينار واحد ونصف وثمن.

وعليها من الاتبان، خمسمائة شنيف.

رسم خولي البحر بها، اردب واحد وثلثان:
قمح، نصف وثلث اردب.
وشعير، نصف وثلث اردب.

والمربى بها من الفروج، اربعمائة واثنان وثلاثون فروجا. تفصيله:
للديوان المعمور،[889] بما فيه من اجرة التربية وهو الثلث، ثلاثمائة واربعون طائرا.
للمقطعين، اثنان وتسعون طائرا.

والمسلف عليه بها[890] من الشعير برسم الاصطبلات السلطانية، ستون اردبا.

والذي بها من التقاوي للامير جمال الدين بن الهمام الحميدي، اربعة وخمسون اردبا وسدس:
قمح، ستة وثلاثون اردبا.
شعير، ثمانية عشر اردبا.

ومن حرف الميم، منتارة. هذه البلدة عبارة عن بلدة صغيرة ليس فيها سوى شجر تين وسنط وهي بين المحاطب. وهي غربي الفيوم الى القبلة، بينها وبين مدينة الفيوم اربع ساعات للراكب. من كفور خليج دلية، مجموعة في عبرة الاقطاع بالخليج المذكور. شربها من بحر يعرف بدلية من الماء المساق الى المقسم المعروف بالتبرون، بماء عدته سبع قبض وربع وسدس. اهلها بنو غصين، فخذ من بني كلاب.

ارتفاعها، عينا، عن المراعي، دينار واحد وربع؛ غلة، اربعمائة وثمانون اردبا. تفصيله:
قمح، مائتان وثلاثون اردبا.
شعير، مائتان وخمسون اردبا.

وعليها من الرسوم والكيالة، عن مائة واثنين وعشرين درهما، ثلاثة دنانير وقيراط وحبة؛ وغلة، ثلاثة وعشرون اردبا وسدس وثمن. تفصيله:
قمح، اردب واحد وربع وسدس وثمن.
شعير، احد وعشرون اردبا ونصف وربع.

تفصيله:
رسوم،[891] عن مائة واثنين وعشرين درهما، ثلاثة دنانير وقيراط وحبة، وغلة اثنا عشر اردبا وربع وسدس وثمن. تفصيله:
قمح، اردب واحد وربع وسدس وثمن.
شعير، احد عشر اردبا.
تفصيله:
شد الاحباس، ثمانية دراهم.
رسم الجراريف، اربعة وثلاثون درهما ونصف وربع.
رسم الحصاد، ثلاثة وخمسون درهما.

monetary value of livestock, for six heads, 5 ¼ ⅛ dinars:
cows, for a yearling calf, 1 ½ ¼ dinar;
monetary value of small cattle, for five heads, 3 ½ ⅛ dinars:
sheep, for two heads, 2 dinars;
goats, for three heads, 1 ½ ⅛ dinar.

Hay, 500 bales.

The fee of the overseer of the canal, 1 ⅔ ardabb:
wheat, ½ ⅓ ardabb;
barley, ½ ⅓ ardabb.

The chickens reared in it, 432 chickens:
for the prosperous Dīwān, including the rearing wage of a third, 340 birds;
for the *iqṭāʿ*-holders, 92 birds.

The barley assigned for the royal stables and paid for in advance, 60 ardabbs.

The seed advances for the amir Jamāl al-Dīn ibn al-Humām al-Ḥumaydī, 54 ⅙ ardabbs:
wheat, 36 ardabbs;
barley, 18 ardabbs.

Also beginning with the letter 'mīm': Mintāra.[297] This is a small village, with nothing except fig trees and acacias, and it lies amid brushwood. It is in the south-west of the province, four hours' ride from Madīnat al-Fayyūm. It is one of the hamlets of Dilya Canal, and included in the fiscal value of the *iqṭāʿ* of that canal. It gets its water, at the amount of 7 ¼ ⅙ *qabḍas*, from Dilya canal, from the water directed to the divisor known as al-Tabrūn. Its people are the Banū Ghuṣayn, a branch of the Banū Kilāb.

Its revenue, in specie, from pasture tax, 1 ¼ dinar; and in grains, 480 ardabbs:
wheat, 230 ardabbs;
barley, 250 ardabbs.

The fees and the measurement fee are 122 dirhams, which are 3 1/24 1/72 dinars; and in grains, 23 ⅙ ⅛ ardabbs:
wheat, 1 ¼ ⅙ ⅛ ardabb;
barley, 21 ½ ¼ ardabbs.

[The fees and the measurement fee] in detail:
The fees, 122 dirhams, which are 3 1/24 1/72 dinars; and in grains, 12 ¼ ⅙ ⅛ ardabbs:
wheat, 1 ¼ ⅙ ⅛ ardabb;
barley, 11 ardabbs.
[The fees] in detail:
supervision of endowments, 8 dirhams;
dredging fee, 34 ½ ¼ dirhams;
harvest fee, 53 dirhams;

889 ساقط من أ. س.: تفصيله للديوان المعمور، لكنه يضيفه على الهامش.
890 ساقط من ط. م.: بها.
891 أ. س.: رسم.

297 Modern location (uncertain): near the village of ʿIzbat al-Kāshif (عزبة الكاشف). Halm, *Ägypten*, p. 265; Salmon, 'Répertoire', p. 70; al-Maqrīzī, *Kitāb al-mawāʿiẓ*, ed. by Wiet, I, 249: Santariya; Ibn al-Jīʿān, *Kitāb al-tuḥfa*, p. 158; Boinet Bey, *Dictionnaire géographique*, s.v. al-Mandara. We have no positive identification of this village, but in line with al-Nābulusī's description (see above), we placed it near the modern village of ʿIzbat al-Kāshif.

رسم الخفارة، خمسة عشر درهما.[892]
رسم الاجران، احد عشر درهما وربع، وغلة، اثنا عشر اردبا وربع وسدس وثمن.
الكيالة، عشرة ارادب ونصف وربع، شعير.

وعليها من الزكاة عن ثمن اغنام، عن خمسة اروس، ثلاثة دنانير وربع وثمن. تفصيله:
بياض، عن راس واحد، دينار واحد وثمن.
شعارى، عن اربعة اروس، ديناران وربع.

وعليها من الاتبان، الف ومائتان وسبعون شنيفا.

عليها لديوان الاحباس، عينا، ثلاثة دنانير.

والمربى بها من الفروج، ثلاثمائة وتسعون طائرا:
للديوان المعمور، بما فيه من اجرة التربية وهو الثلث، مائتان واربعون طائرا.
للمقطعين، مائة وخمسون طائرا.

والمسلف عليه بها من الشعير برسم الاصطبلات السلطانية، عشرون اردبا.

ومن حرف الميم، منية البطس. هذه البلدة عبارة عن بلدة كبيرة تشتمل على نخل ودي وسنط[893] ودمنة كبيرة. وهي بحري مدينة الفيوم، بينها وبين مدينة الفيوم مسافة اربع ساعات للراكب. جارية في اقطاع المقطعين وهم اصحاب الامير حسام الدين بن ابي علي، والامير ركن الدين بيبرس خاص الترك الكبير، والامير افتخار الدين ياقوت اليمني، واصحاب الامير شهاب الدين خضر ابن اخي الاسد الهكاري،[894] واصحاب الامير سعد الدين ابي بكر بن محمد الحميدي، واجناد الحلقة المنصورة. عبرتها جيشية، ثمانية الاف وسبعمائة وستون دينارا. شربها من بحر ذات الصفاء[895] المطلق من تحت المسجد المعروف بابن فحل، من المقسم المعروف بالفسقية اليوسفية، تحت القبرا في خليج واحد مجصص لسقي الشتوي والصيفي بالناحية، بما عدته ثلاث عشرة قبضة وثلثان ماء. بها جامع تقام فيه الجمعة. اهلها بنو سمالوس، فخذ من بني عجلان.

ارتفاعها مما جميعه مستخرجا ومتحصلا، عينا، مائة وديناران ونصف وربع؛ وغلة، الف وسبعمائة وستة وخمسون اردبا. تفصيله:
قمح، ثمانمائة وستة وسبعون اردبا.
شعير وفول، ثمانمائة وستة وسبعون اردبا.
كشك، اردبان.
فريك، اردبان.

تفصيله:
الهلالي، عن اجرة الحانوت، اربعة واربعون دينارا.
المراعي، ثمانية دنانير ونصف وربع.
خراج المقات، خمسون دينارا.

مناجزة الغلات، الف وسبعمائة وستة وخمسون اردبا، على ما فصل.

892 ساقط من أ. س.: رسم الخفارة خمسة عشر درهما.
893 أ. س.: صنط.
894 أ. س.: المكاري.
895 ط. م.: الصفا.

protection fee, 15 dirhams;
threshing-floor fee, 11 ¼ dirhams; and in grains, 11 ¼ ⅙ ⅛ ardabbs.
The measurement fee, barley, 10 ½ ¼ ardabbs.

The alms-tax, for the monetary value of small cattle, for five heads, 3 ¼ ⅛ dinars:
sheep, for one head, 1 ⅛ dinar;
goats, for four heads, 2 ¼ dinar.

Hay, 1,270 bales.

For the Ministry of Endowments, in specie, 3 dinars.

The chickens reared in it, 390 birds:
for the prosperous Dīwān, including the rearing wage of a third, 240 birds;
for the *iqṭāʿ*-holders, 150 birds.

The barley assigned for the royal stables and paid for in advance, 20 ardabbs.

Also beginning with the letter 'mīm': Minyat al-Baṭs.[298] This is a large village, with date palm shoots, acacia and a large heap of manure (*dimna*). It lies in the north of the province, four hours' ride from Madīnat al-Fayyūm. It is assigned as an *iqṭāʿ* to *iqṭāʿ*-holders: the followers of the amir Ḥusām al-Dīn ibn Abī ʿAlī; the amir Rukn al-Dīn Baybars Khāṣṣ al-Turk al-Kabīr; the amir Iftikhār al-Dīn Yāqūt al-Yamanī; the followers of the amir Shihāb al-Dīn Khiḍr ibn Akhī al-Asad al-Hakkārī;[299] the followers of the amir Saʿīd al-Dīn Abū Bakr ibn Muḥammad al-Ḥumaydī; and the soldiers of the victorious *ḥalqa* corps. Its fiscal value is 8,760 army dinars. It gets water for irrigating winter and summer crops, at the amount of 13 ⅔ *qabḍas*, from Dhāt al-Ṣafāʾ Canal, through a single plastered channel, which branches off beneath the neighbourhood mosque known as Ibn Fiḥl [in Madīnat al-Fayyūm], and then through the divisor known as al-Fasqiyya al-Yūsufiyya below al-Qubarāʾ. It has a congregational mosque, in which the Friday prayers are held. Its people are the Banū Samālūs, a branch of the Banū ʿAjlān.

Its revenue in cash and in kind, in specie, 102 ½ ¼ dinars; and in grains, 1,756 ardabbs:
wheat, 876 ardabbs;
barley and broad beans, 876 ardabbs;
kishk, 2 ardabbs;
farīk, 2 ardabbs.

[The revenue] in detail:
lunar-calendar tax, for the rent of the shop, 44 dinars;
pasture tax, 8 ½ ¼ dinars;
land tax on cucurbitaceous fruits, 50 dinars.

Munājaza land tax on grains, 1,756 ardabbs, as specified.

298 Modern location: Ṭāmiya (طامية). Halm, *Ägypten*, pp. 265–66; Salmon, 'Répertoire', p. 52; Ibn Mammātī, *Kitāb qawānīn al-dawāwīn*, p. 191: al-Baṭsh; Ibn al-Jīʿān, *Kitāb al-tuḥfa*, p. 158: Minyat al-Baṭṭ; Ramzī, *Al-Qāmūs*, II/III, 113–14: Ṭāmiya.

299 AS: al-Makkārī. Asad al-Dīn al-Hakkārī was a leading amir during the campaign against the Franks in 617/1220; Makīn, *Taʾrīkh*, p. 133 (25). A regiment of Hakkārī Kurdish troops was still present in al-Kāmil's army; Humphreys, *From Saladin to the Mongols*, p. 162.

عليها من خراج الاستنباط المعروف بسنورس، ثمانية وتسعون اردبا وثمن. تفصيله:

قمح، اثنان وخمسون اردبا ونصف.

شعير، اثنان وعشرون اردبا وثلث وربع.

فول، خمسة عشر اردبا ونصف وربع وثمن.

سمسم، ثمانية ارادب وسدس.

وعليها من الرسوم والكيالة، عن خمسمائة وثمانية وثمانين درهما وربع، اربعة عشر دينارا وثلثان[896] ونصف قيراط وحبة؛ وغلة، مائة وخمسة وثلاثون اردبا ونصف وربع وثمن. تفصيله:

قمح، ثمانية وسبعون اردبا ونصف وثلث ونصف قيراط.

شعير، ثلاثون اردبا.

فول، ستة وعشرون اردبا وثلثان ونصف قيراط.

سمسم، ثلاثة ارادب.

تفصيله:

الرسوم، ثلاثمائة وثمانية وثلاثون درهما وربع، وغلة، ثمانية وتسعون اردبا وثلث وربع وثمن. تفصيله:

قمح، تسعة وخمسون اردبا ونصف وثلث ونصف قيراط.

وشعير، اثنا عشر اردبا وسدس.

وفول، ستة وعشرون اردبا وثلثان ونصف قيراط.

تفصيله:

شد العين، اربعون درهما.

شد الاحباس، اربعة عشر درهما.

رسم الجراريف، تسعون درهما.

رسم الحصاد، ثلاثة وخمسون درهما.

رسم الخفارة، خمسة عشر درهما.

رسم الجزر،[897] اربعون درهما.

رسم الاجران، ستة وثمانون درهما وربع، وغلة، ثمانية وتسعون اردبا وثلث وربع وثمن على ما تقدم.[898]

كيالة، سبعة وثلاثون اردبا وسدس:

قمح، تسعة عشر اردبا.

شعير، سبعة عشر اردبا ونصف وثلث.

سمسم، ثلث اردب.[899]

المراعي الطارئ،[900] عن ستمائة وثلاثة وسبعين راسا، مائتان وخمسون درهما. تفصيله:

قطيعة درهم واحد الراس، عن خمسة ارؤس، خمسة دراهم.

قطيعة خمسين درهما المائة، عن تسعين راسا، خمسة واربعون درهما.

قطيعة ثلاثين درهما المائة، عن مائتين وسبعين راسا، احد وثمانون درهما.

قطيعة خمسة وعشرين درهما المائة، عن ثلاثمائة وثمانية ارؤس، سبعة وسبعون درهما.

رسم المستخدمين، اثنان واربعون درهما.

Land tax on al-Istinbāṭ, part of [the land-tax revenues of] Sinnūris, 98 ⅛ ardabbs:

wheat, 52 ½ ardabbs;

barley, 22 ⅓ ¼ ardabbs;

broad beans, 15 ½ ¼ ⅛ ardabbs;

sesame, 8 ⅙ ardabbs.

The fees, the measurement fee [and the pasture fee] are 588 ¼ dirhams, which are 14 ⅔ ¹⁄₄₈ ¹⁄₇₂ dinars; and in grains, 135 ½ ¼ ⅛ ardabbs:

wheat, 78 ½ ⅓ ¹⁄₄₈ ardabbs;

barley, 30 ardabbs;

broad beans, 26 ⅔ ¹⁄₄₈ ardabbs;

sesame, 3 ardabbs.

[The fees, the measurement fee and the pasture fee] in detail:

the fees, 338 ¼ dirhams; and in grains, 98 ⅓ ¼ ⅛ ardabbs:

wheat, 59 ½ ⅓ ¹⁄₄₈ ardabbs;

barley, 12 ⅙ ardabbs;

broad beans, 26 ⅔ ¹⁄₄₈ ardabbs.

[The fees] in detail:

supervision of the land survey, 40 dirhams;

supervision of endowments, 14 dirhams;

dredging fee, 90 dirhams;

harvest fee, 53 dirhams;

protection fee, 15 dirhams;

carrot fee, 40 dirhams;

threshing-floor fee 86 ¼ dirhams; and in grains, 98 ⅓ ¼ ⅛ ardabbs, as specified above.

The measurement fee, 37 ⅙ ardabbs:

wheat, 19 ardabbs;

barley, 17 ½ ⅓ ardabbs;

sesame, ⅓ ardabb.

The pasture tax on seasonal pasture lands, for 673 heads, 250 dirhams:

at the rate of one dirham per head, for five heads, 5 dirhams;

at the rate of 50 dirhams per 100 [heads], for 90 heads, 45 dirhams;

at the rate of 30 dirhams per 100 [heads], for 270 heads, 81 dirhams;

at the rate of 25 dirhams per 100 [heads], for 308 heads, 77 dirhams;

the government agents' fee, 42 dirhams.

---

896 أ. س. يضيف: وربع.

897 أ. س.: الجزار.

898 ط. م. يضيف تفصيله.

899 أ. س.: ثلاثة أرادب.

900 أ. س.: عن طارى.

وعليها من الزكاة عن ثمن اغنام، عن اثنى عشر راسا، عشرة دنانير وربع وسدس وثمن. تفصيله:

منية البطس العامرة، عن سبعة ارؤس، ستة دنانير ونصف. تفصيله:

بياض، عن خمسة ارؤس، خمسة دنانير وربع وثمن.

شعارى، عن راسين، دينار واحد وثمن.

منية البطس الخراب، عن خمسة ارؤس، اربعة دنانير وقيراط. تفصيله:

بياض، عن راسين، ديناران وسدس.

شعارى، عن ثلاثة ارؤس، دينار واحد ونصف وربع وثمن.

وعليها من الاتبان الف وسبعمائة شنيف.

رسم خولي البحر بها، اردبان، قمحًا.

عليها لديوان الاحباس، عينا، ستة دنانير.

والمربى بها من الفروج، الف ومائتا طائر:

للديوان المعمور، بما فيه من اجرة التربية وهو الثلث، ستمائة طائر.

للمقطعين، ستمائة طائر.

والذي يسلف عليه بها من الشعير برسم الاصطبلات السلطانية، مائة اردب.

ومن حرف الميم، منية الديك وبني مجنون وشلمص. هذه منية الديك والموضعان التابعان لها عبارة عن معبر واحد وهي ثلاث دمن متقاربات يجمعهم الارتفاع. فاما منية الديك فتشتمل على نخل كثير لا غير وجميزات. واما بنو مجنون فعبارة عن بلدة متوسطة، بين الكبر والصغر، تشتمل على نخل وسنط[901] وجميز وصفصاف ليس بالكثير.[902] واما شلمص، فعبارة عن بلد صغير، يشتمل[903] على جميزة واحدة ونخلة.[904] لها نخل في الاحكار متباعد عنها منشوب.[905] غربي المدينة بينهم وبين مدينة الفيوم مسافة نصف ساعة للراكب. جارية في اقطاع اصحاب الطواشي شهاب الدين رشيد. عبرتهم جيشية، الفان وخمسمائة دينار. شربهم على ما ياتي بيانه من البر البحري من البحر الاعظم اليوسفي:

خليج بني مجنون، للشتوي خاصة، باب واحد بغير بناء لعلو اراضيها، بغير عبرة.

يتلو خليج عنز شلمص ما هو للشتوي.

خليج صورة مسقاة عال، بغير عبرة، ما هو للصيفي.

مسقاة صغيرة بغير عبرة ما هو للبساتين بها.

مسقاة صغيرة يسقى منها عند الحاجة وتسد، تقدير قبضة واحدة.

اهلها بنو مجنون، فخذ من بني كلاب.

901 أ. س.: وصنط.
902 أ. س.: الكثر.
903 أ. س.: تشتمل.
904 ساقط من أ. س.: ونخلة.
905 ط. م.: منسوب.

The alms-tax, for the monetary value of small cattle, for 12 heads, 10 ¼ ⅙ ⅛ dinars:

Minyat al-Baṭs, the inhabited part, for seven heads, 6 ½ dinars:

sheep, for five heads, 5 ¼ ⅛ dinars;

goats, for two heads, 1 ⅛ dinar;

Minyat al-Baṭs, the deserted part (*al-kharāb*), for five heads, 4 1/24 dinars:

sheep, for two heads, 2 ⅙ dinars;

goats, for three heads, 1 ½ ¼ ⅛ dinar.

Hay, 1,700 bales.

The fee of the overseer of the canal, wheat, 2 ardabbs.

For the Ministry of Endowments, in specie, 6 dinars.

The chickens reared in it, 1,200 birds:

for the prosperous Dīwān, including the rearing wage of a third, 600 birds;

for the *iqṭā*ʿ-holders, 600 birds.

The barley assigned for the royal stables and paid for in advance, 100 ardabbs.

Also beginning with the letter 'mīm': Minyat al-Dīk,[300] Banū Majnūn,[301] and Shalmaṣ.[302] Minyat al-Dīk and the two settlements that are attached to it lie along the same path (*maʿbar*), and comprise of three adjacent heaps of manure (*diman*). The three form one fiscal unit. Minyat al-Dīk has many date palms and sycamores, but no other trees. Banū Majnūn is a medium-sized village, with date palms, acacias, sycamores and willows, but not in abundance. Shalmaṣ is a small village, with one sycamore and one date palm, although unripe (*manshūb*)[303] date palms are found in lands subject to long-term lease which lie further from it. They are half an hour's ride west of Madīnat al-Fayyūm. They are assigned as an *iqṭā*ʿ to the followers of the *ṭawāshī* Shihāb al-Dīn Rashīd[304] with a fiscal value of 2,500 army dinars. They get their water, as will be described, from the north bank of the Main Canal:

the canal of Banū Majnūn, a canal solely for winter crops, has one sluice gate, without a weir and without quota, due to the elevation of its land;

the canal of ʿAnz Shalmaṣ, for the irrigation of winter crops;

a canal in the form of an irrigation ditch, on high ground, without quota, for summer crops;

a small irrigation ditch, without quota, for the orchards;

a small irrigation ditch, used for irrigation when the need arises, and then blocked. The amount of water is approximately 1 *qabḍa*.

Their people are the Banū Majnūn, a branch of the Banū Kilāb.

300 Modern location: al-Mandara (المندرة). Halm, *Ägypten*, p. 266; Salmon, 'Répertoire', p. 54; de Sacy, *État des provinces*, p. 684; Savigny, *Description de l'Égypte*, p. 129; Ibn Mammātī, *Kitāb qawānīn al-dawāwīn*, p. 191; Ibn al-Jīʿān, *Kitāb al-tuḥfa*, p. 158; Ramzī, *Al-Qāmūs*, II/III, 98: al-Mandara. Later on in the treatise, a subsidiary hamlet of Minyat al-Dīk is named al-Manẓara.

301 Modern location: Banī Ṣāliḥ (بني صالح). Halm, *Ägypten*, pp. 249–50; Salmon, 'Répertoire', p. 54; de Sacy, *État des provinces*, p. 681; Ibn al-Jīʿān, *Kitāb al-tuḥfa*, p. 153; Ramzī, *Al-Qāmūs*, II/III, 98: Banī Ṣāliḥ.

302 Modern location (uncertain): ʿIzbat al-Jalābiyya (عزبة الجلابيّة). Salmon, 'Répertoire', p. 54. We have no positive identification of this village, but in line with al-Nābulusī's statement that Minyat al-Dīk, Banū Majnūn, and Shalmaṣ were adjacent, we placed Shalmaṣ near the modern village of ʿIzbat al-Jalābiyya.

303 MP: *mansūb*.

304 There are two officers of this name and honorific mentioned in the treatise as *iqṭā*ʿ-holders in the Fayyum. One was the *ṭawāshī* Shihāb al-Dīn Rashīd al-Kabīr ('the greater') and the other known as the *ṭawāshī* Shihāb al-Dīn Rashīd al-Ṣaghīr ('the lesser'). It is impossible to determine who is intended here.

ارتفاعها مما جميعه مستخرجا ومتحصلا، عينا، ثمانية وسبعون دينارا ونصف وثمن، وغلة، خمسمائة وخمسة وثلاثون اردبا ونصف. تفصيله:[906]

قمح، مائتان وخمسة واربعون اردبا ونصف.

شعير وفول، مائتان وتسعون اردبا.

تفصيله:

منية الديك وشلمص، ثمانية وخمسون دينارا ونصف وربع، وغلة، ثلاثمائة اردب. تفصيله:

قمح، مائة وخمسون اردبا.

شعير وفول، مائة وخمسون اردبا.

بنو مجنون، تسعة عشر دينارا وثمن، وغلة، مائتان وخمسة وثلاثون اردبا ونصف. تفصيله:

قمح، خمسة وتسعون اردبا ونصف.

شعير، مائة[907] وعشرة ارادب.

فول، ثلاثون اردبا.

وعليها لمقطعي العشر المعروف بابن المهراني، خمسون اردبا، قمح وشعير، نصفان.

وعليها من الرسوم والكيالة والمراعي، عن مائتين وثمانية وستين درهما ونصف، ستة دنانير وثلثان ونصف قيراط وحبة، وغلة، سبعة واربعون اردبا وثلث ونصف قيراط. تفصيله:

قمح، ثلاثة وعشرون اردبا وسدس.

شعير، سبعة عشر اردبا وثمن ونصف قيراط.

فول، سبعة ارادب وقيراط.

تفصيله:

الرسوم، مائتان وخمسة واربعون درهما ونصف، وغلة، احد وثلاثون اردبا وثلث ونصف قيراط.

تفصيله:

قمح، احد عشر اردبا وسدس.

شعير، ثلاثة عشر اردبا وثمن ونصف قيراط.

فول، سبعة ارادب وقيراط.

تفصيله:

شد العين، اثنان واربعون درهما.

رسم الجراريف، تسعون درهما.

رسم الحصاد، ثلاثة وخمسون درهما.

رسم الخفارة، خمسة عشر درهما.

رسم الجزر، ثمانية عشر درهما.

رسم الاجران، سبعة وعشرون درهما ونصف، وغلة، احد وثلاثون اردبا وثلث ونصف قيراط على ما فصل.

الكيالة، ستة عشر اردبا:

قمح، اثنا عشر اردبا.

شعير، اربعة ارادب.

المراعي، ثلاثة وعشرون درهما. تفصيله:

قطيعة خمسة وعشرين درهما المائة، عن اربعة وسبعين راسا، ثمانية عشر درهما ونصف.

رسم المستخدمين، اربعة دراهم ونصف.

Their revenue in cash and in kind is, in specie, 78 ½ ⅛ dinars; and in grains, 535 ½ ardabbs:

- wheat, 245 ½ ardabbs;
- barley and broad beans, 290 ardabbs.

[The revenue] in detail:

- Minyat al-Dīk and Shalmaṣ, 58 ½ ¼ dinars; and in grains, 300 ardabbs:
  - wheat, 150 ardabbs;
  - barley and broad beans, 150 ardabbs;
- Banū Majnūn, 19 ⅛ dinars, and in grains, 235 ½ ardabbs:
  - wheat, 95 ½ ardabbs;
  - barley, 110 ardabbs;
  - broad beans, 30 ardabbs.

For the *iqṭā*ᶜ-holders of the tithe known as Ibn al-Mihrānī, 50 ardabbs of wheat and barley, half in each.

The fees, the measurement fee and the pasture tax are 268 ½ dirhams, which are 6 ⅔ 1/48 1/72 dinars; and in grains, 47 ⅓ 1/48 ardabbs:

- wheat, 23 ⅙ ardabbs;
- barley, 17 ⅛ 1/48 ardabbs;
- broad beans, 7 1/24 ardabbs.

[The fees, the measurement fee the pasture tax] in detail:

- The fees, 245 ½ dirhams; and in grains, 31 ⅓ 1/48 ardabbs:
  - wheat, 11 ⅙ ardabbs;
  - barley, 13 ⅛ 1/48 ardabbs;
  - broad beans, 7 1/24 ardabbs.
- [The fees] in detail:
  - supervision of the land survey, 42 dirhams;
  - dredging fee, 90 dirhams;
  - harvest fee, 53 dirhams;
  - protection fee, 15 dirhams;
  - carrot fee, 18 dirhams;
  - threshing-floor fee, 27 ½ dirhams; and in grains, 31 ⅓ 1/48 ardabbs, as specified.
- The measurement fee, 16 ardabbs:
  - wheat, 12 ardabbs;
  - barley, 4 ardabbs.
- The pasture tax, 23 dirhams:
  - at the rate of 25 dirhams per 100 [heads], for 74 heads, 18 ½ dirhams;
  - the government agents' fee, 4 ½ dirhams.

906 ساقط من أ. س.: تفصيله.

907 أ. س. يضيف: أردب.

عليها من الزكاة، اثنا عشر دينارا ونصف وثمن. تفصيله:
بنو مجنون، خمسة دنانير وثمن. تفصيله:
خرص النخل، دينار واحد.
ثمن الماشية، عن اربعة اروس، اربعة دنانير وثمن. تفصيله:
بقر احمر، عن تبيع واحد، ديناران.
ثمن اغنام، عن ثلاثة اروس، ديناران وثمن. تفصيله:
بياض، عن راس، دينار واحد وقيراط.
شعارى، عن راسين، دينار واحد وقيراطان.
منية الديك، سبعة دنانير ونصف:
خرص النخل، سبعة دنانير.
ثمن الاغنام، عن شعرية واحدة، نصف دينار.
وعلى المنظرة من حقوقها، ثمن ماشية، عن راسين، دينار واحد وثلثين وثمن. تفصيله:
بقر احمر، تبيع واحد، دينار.
اغنام، عن شعرية، ربع وسدس وثمن.

The alms-tax, 12 ½ ⅛ dinars:
Banū Majnūn, 5 ⅛ dinars:
estimate of date palms, 1 dinar;
monetary value of livestock, for four heads, 4 ⅛ dinars:
cows, for a yearling calf, 2 dinars;
monetary value of small cattle, for three heads, 2 ⅛ dinars:
sheep, for one head, 1 1/24 dinar,
goats, for two heads, 1 2/24 dinar.
Minyat al-Dīk, 7 ½ dinars:
estimate of date palms, 7 dinars;
monetary value of small cattle, for goats, one head, ½ dinar.
Al-Manẓara, included in its accounts, for the monetary value of livestock, for two heads, 1 ⅔ ⅛ dinar:
cows, for a yearling calf, 1 dinar;
small cattle, for goats, one head, ¼ ⅙ ⅛ [dinar].[305]

عليها من الاتبان، الف وسبعمائة شنيف:
بنو مجنون، الف ومائتان.
شلمص، خمسمائة شنيف.

Hay, 1,700 bales:
Banū Majnūn, 1,200 [bales];
Shalmaṣ, 500 bales.

والذي بها من التقاوي للمقطعين، مائة وثلاثة وستون[908] اردبا. تفصيله:
منية الديك، احد وثمانون اردبا. تفصيله:
قمح، خمسة واربعون اردبا.
شعير، ثمانية عشر اردبا.
فول، ثمانية عشر اردبا.
بنو مجنون، اثنان وثمانون اردبا:
قمح، اربعة واربعون اردبا.
شعير، ثمانية وعشرون اردبا.
فول، عشرة ارادب.

The seed advances for the *iqṭāʿ*-holders, 163 ardabbs:
Minyat al-Dīk, 81 ardabbs:
wheat, 45 ardabbs;
barley, 18 ardabbs;
broad beans, 18 ardabbs;
Banū Majnūn, 82 ardabbs:
wheat, 44 ardabbs;
barley, 28 ardabbs;
broad beans, 10 ardabbs.

والمربى بها من الفروج ثمانمائة طائر. تفصيله:
للديوان المعمور، بما فيه من اجرة التربية وهو الثلث، مائة وخمسون طائرا.[909] تفصيله:
بنو مجنون، مائة طائر.
منية الديك، خمسون طائرا.
للمقطعين، ستمائة وخمسون طائرا.

The chickens reared in them, 800 birds:
for the prosperous Dīwān, including the rearing wage of a third, 150 birds:
Banū Majnūn, 100 birds;
Minyat al-Dīk, 50 birds.
for the *iqṭāʿ*-holders, 650 birds.

والمسلف عليه بها من الشعير برسم الاصطبلات السلطانية، مائة اردب.

Barley assigned for the royal stables and paid for in advance, 100 ardabbs.

اهلها يزرعون من الاقصاب ويسقون من الخلف برسم معصرة سينرو، خارجا[910] عن المستجد لسنة اثنتين واربعين وستمائة، اثنى عشر فدانا وقيراطين ونصف قيراط وحبة. تفصيله:
راس، سبعة فدادين وثلثان وربع ونصف قيراط وحبة.
وخلفة، اربعة فدادين وسدس.

Their people sow sugarcane and irrigate second harvest, assigned for the press at Sīnarū, excluding what was newly [planted] in the year 642, 12 2/24 1/48 1/72 feddans:
first harvest, 7 ⅔ ¼ 1/48 1/72 feddans;
second harvest, 4 ⅙ feddans.

[908] أ. س.: ثلاثون.
[909] أ. س. يضيف: للمقطعين.
[910] ساقط من أ. س.: خارجا.

[305] The sums for the alms-tax of al-Manẓara do not add up.

ومن حرف الميم، مطول وتبعها بحر قريط[911] مما جمعهما الارتفاع والاقطاع. فاما مطول فعبارة عن بلدة كبيرة تشتمل على نخل وزيتون وجميز ودويرات كثيرة، كرم عقل[912] وشجرة واحدة توت. وبها مقاسم منية اقنى وما معها من البلاد. وهي غربية الفيوم، بينها وبين مدينة الفيوم ساعتان للراكب. واما بحر بنى قريط[913] فعبارة عن اربع مناشئ تشتمل كل منها على نخل وسدر وسنط.[914] على خليج المنية ثلاث مناشئ وفي المزارع منشاة. بينها وبين مدينة الفيوم مسافة ثلاث ساعات للراكب. جارية في اقطاع جماعة من المقطعين. عبرتها جيشية، سبعة الاف وثلاثمائة وخمسون دينارا. شربها من خليج[915] من البر القبلي اليوسفي، باب واحد، مبنى مجصص، عبرته ست قبض. بها جامع تقام فيه الجمعة. اهلها بنو عامر، فخذ من بني كلاب.

ارتفاعها مما جميعه مستخرجا ومتحصلا، عينا، تسعة وعشرون دينارا، وغلة، الفان وتسعمائة واربعون اردبا. تفصيله:

قمح، الف واربعمائة وسبعون اردبا.

شعير، الف واربعمائة وسبعون اردبا.

تفصيله:

الهلالي، عن الحانوت، ثمانية عشر دينارا.

المراعي، احد عشر دينارا.

مناجزة الغلات، الفان وتسعمائة واربعون اردبا، على ما فصل.

عليها من الرسوم والكيالة والمراعي، عن اربعمائة وعشرة دراهم وثمن، عشرة دنانير وربع؛ وغلة، مائة وستة وتسعون اردبا وثمن. تفصيله:

قمح، مائة وثلاثة ارادب وثلث.

شعير، خمسة وسبعون اردبا وسدس.

فول، سبعة عشر[916] اردبا ونصف وثمن.

تفصيله:

الرسوم، ثلاثمائة واربعة دراهم ونصف، وغلة، مائة وخمسة وعشرون اردبا وثمن. تفصيله:

قمح، سبعة وستون اردبا وثلث.

شعير، اربعون اردبا وسدس.

فول، سبعة عشر اردبا ونصف وثمن.

تفصيله:

شد العين، ثلاثون درهما.

شد الاحباس، ستة دراهم ونصف.

رسم الجراريف، تسعون درهما.

رسم الحصاد، ثلاثة وخمسون درهما.

رسم الخفارة، خمسة عشر درهما.

رسم الاجران، مائة وعشرة دراهم، وغلة، مائة وخمسة وعشرون اردبا وثمن، على ما فصل.

كيالة، احد وسبعون اردبا. تفصيله:

قمح، ستة وثلاثون اردبا.

شعير، خمسة وثلاثون اردبا.

911 أ. س.: قريظ.

912 أ. س.: عقل كرم.

913 أ. س.: قريظ.

914 أ. س.: صنط.

915 أ. س.: الخليج.

916 ساقط من أ. س.: عشر.

Also beginning with the letter 'mīm': Muṭūl[306] and Baḥr Banī Qurīṭ,[307] which is attached to it. The two villages form one fiscal unit and one *iqṭāʿ* unit. Muṭūl is a large village, with date palms, olives and sycamores and many enclosures, recently planted vineyard (*karm ʿuqal*) and one mulberry tree. The divisors of Minyat Aqnā and of its hamlets are here. It is in the west of the province, two hours' ride from Madīnat al-Fayyūm. Baḥr Banī Qurīṭ consists of four hamlets. Each of them has date palms, sidr trees and acacias. Three of these hamlets are on Minyat [Aqnā] Canal, and one is in the fields. It is three hours' ride from Madīnat al-Fayyūm. The two villages are assigned as an *iqṭāʿ* to a group of *iqṭāʿ*-holders with a fiscal value of 7,350 army dinars. They get their water from a plastered canal with a weir, [issuing] from the south bank of the Main Canal, through one sluice gate. Its water quota is 6 *qabḍas*. It has a congregational mosque, in which the Friday prayers are held. Its people are the Banū ʿĀmir, a branch of the Banū Kilāb.

Their revenue in cash and kind is, in specie, 29 dinars; and in grains, 2,940 ardabbs:

wheat, 1,470 ardabbs;

barley, 1,470 ardabbs.

[Their revenue] in detail:

lunar-calendar tax, for the shop, 18 dinars;

pasture tax, 11 dinars;

Munājaza land tax on grains, 2,940 ardabbs, as specified.

The fees, the measurement fee and the pasture tax are 410 ⅛ dirhams, which are 10 ¼ dinars; and in grains, 196 ⅛ ardabbs:

wheat, 103 ⅓ ardabbs;

barley, 75 ⅙ ardabbs;

broad beans, 17 ½ ⅛ ardabbs.

[The fees, the measurement fee and the pasture tax] in detail:

the fees, 304 ½ dirhams; and in grains, 125 ⅛ ardabbs:

wheat, 67 ⅓ ardabbs;

barley, 40 ⅙ ardabbs;

broad beans, 17 ½ ⅛ ardabbs.

[The fees] in detail:

supervision of the land survey, 30 dirhams;

supervision of endowments, 6 ½ dirhams;

dredging fee, 90 dirhams;

harvest fee, 53 dirhams;

protection fee, 15 dirhams;

threshing-floor fee, 110 dirhams; and in grains, 125 ⅛ ardabbs, as specified.

The measurement fee, 71 ardabbs:

wheat, 36 ardabbs;

barley, 35 ardabbs.

306 Modern location: Muṭūl (مطول). Halm, *Ägypten*, p. 267: Muṭūl/Baḥr; Salmon, 'Répertoire', p. 63; de Sacy, *État des provinces*, p. 684; Savigny, *Description de l'Égypte*, p. 127: Turʿat Muṭūl; Ibn Mammātī, *Kitāb qawānīn al-dawāwīn*, p. 191; Ibn al-Jīʿān, *Kitāb al-tuḥfa*, p. 157; Ramzī, *al-Qāmūs*, II/III, 87: Muṭūl.

307 Modern location: ʿIzbat Baḥr Abū al-Mīr (عزبة بحر ابو المير). Halm, *Ägypten*, p. 249: Baḥr Banī Qarīṭ south of Muṭūl; Ramzī, *Al-Qāmūs*, II/III, 84: Baḥr Banī Qurīṭ was named during the Ottoman period Baḥr Abū Namīr. Later on, the name was changed to Baḥr Abū al-Mīr. We located it near the modern village of ʿIzbat Baḥr Abū al-Mīr.

المراعي، طارئ، عن مائتين واحد وثلاثين راسا، مائة وخمسة دراهم ونصف وثمن. تفصيله:
قطيعة درهم واحد الراس، عن خمسة واربعين راسا، خمسة واربعون درهما.[917]
قطيعة ثلاثين درهما المائة، عن اثنى عشر راسا، ثلاثة دراهم ونصف وثمن.
قطيعة خمسة وعشرين درهما المائة، عن [مائة][918] اربعة وسبعين راسا، ثلاثة واربعون درهما ونصف.
رسم المستخدمين، ثلاثة عشر درهما ونصف.

عليها من الزكاة، ستة وعشرون دينارا وثلث وربع وثمن. تفصيله:
مطول، ثلاثة عشر دينارا ونصف وثمن. تفصيله:
خرص النخل، دينار واحد وربع.
ثمن المواشي عن اثنى عشر راسا، اثنى عشر دينارا وربع وثمن. تفصيله:
بقر احمر، مسنة واحدة، ثلاثة دنانير.
ثمن الاغنام، عن احد عشر راسا، تسعة دنانير وربع وثمن:
بياض، عن ستة ارؤس، ستة دنانير ونصف وربع.
شعارى، عن خمسة ارؤس، ديناران ونصف وثمن.
بحر بني قريط، عن ثمن الماشية، عن اربعة عشر راسا، ثلاثة عشر دينارا وقيراطان. تفصيله:
بقر احمر، عن مسنة واحدة، ثلاثة دنانير.
اغنام، عن ثلاثة عشر راسا، عشرة دنانير وقيراطان. تفصيله:
بياض، عن ستة ارؤس، ستة دنانير وثلث.
شعارى، عن سبعة[919] ارؤس، ثلاثة دنانير ونصف وربع.

عليها من الجوالي، عن اربعة نفر مقيمين بها، ثمانية دنانير.

عليها لديوان الاحباس، اربعة دنانير.

عليها من الاتبان، الفان وثمانمائة وخمسة وتسعون شنيفا.

رسم خولي البحر بها، قمح، اردب واحد.

وبها من التقاوي المخلدة للمقطعين برسم عمارة الناحية، ثلاثمائة وثلاثة وخمسون اردبا:
قمح، مائة وستة وسبعون اردبا ونصف.
شعير، مائة وستة وسبعون اردبا ونصف.

اهلها يزرعون من الاقصاب ويسقون من الخلف برسم معصرة حجر الماء بسنهور، خارجا عن الزائد لسنة اثنتين واربعين وستمائة، اربعة واربعين فدانا ونصف وربع. تفصيله:
راس، احد وثلاثون فدانا وربع.
خلفة، ثلاثة عشر فدانا ونصف.

والمقرر على المعاملين من الكشك والفريك، ستة ارادب:
كشك، ثلاثة ارادب.
فريك، ثلاثة ارادب.

917 ساقط من أ. س.: درهم واحد الرأس، عن خمسة وأربعين رأسا، خمسة وأربعون درهما.
918 ساقط من أ. س.; ط. م.
919 أ. س.: ستة.

The pasture tax on seasonal pasture lands, for 231 heads, 105 ½ ⅛ dirhams:
at the rate of one dirham per head, for 45 heads, 45 dirhams;
at the rate of 30 dirhams per 100 [heads], for 12 heads, 3 ½ ⅛ dirhams;
at the rate of 25 dirhams per 100 [heads], for [1]74[308] heads, 43 ½ dirhams;
the government agents' fee, 13 ½ dirhams.

The alms-tax, 26 ⅓ ¼ ⅛ dinars:
Muṭūl, 13 ½ ⅛ dinars:
the estimate of date palms, 1 ¼ dinar;
monetary value of livestock, for 12 heads, 12 ¼ ⅛ dinars:
cows, for a two-year old cow, 3 dinars;
monetary value of small cattle, for 11 heads, 9 ¼ ⅛ dinars:
sheep, for six heads, 6 ½ ¼ dinars;
goats, for five heads, 2 ½ ⅛ dinars.
Baḥr Banī Qurīṭ, the monetary value of livestock, for 14 heads, 13 ²⁄₂₄ dinars:
cows, for a two-year old cow, 3 dinars;
small cattle, for 13 heads, 10 ²⁄₂₄ dinars:
sheep, for six heads, 6 ⅓ dinars;
goats, for seven heads, 3 ½ ¼ dinars.

The poll-tax, for four individuals residing in it, 8 dinars.

For the Ministry of Endowments, 4 dinars.

Hay, 2,895 bales.

The fee of the overseer of the canal, wheat, 1 ardabb.

The recorded seed advances for the *iqṭāʿ*-holders, assigned for the village's cultivation, 353 ardabbs:
wheat, 176 ½ ardabbs;
barley, 176 ½ ardabbs.

Its people sow sugarcanes and irrigate second-harvest sugarcane, assigned for a press in Sanhūr with a stone turned by water, excluding the increment for the year 642, 44 ½ ¼ feddans:
first harvest, 31 ¼ feddans;
second harvest, 13 ½ feddans.

The established levy on the cultivators in *kishk* and *farīk* dishes, 6 ardabbs:
kishk, 3 ardabbs;
farīk, 3 ardabbs.

308 MP and AS: 74.

والمربى بها من الفروج، الف وخمسون طائرا. تفصيله:
للديوان المعمور بما فيه من اجرة التربية وهو الثلث، ستمائة طائر.
للمقطعين، اربعمائة وخمسون طائرا.

والمسلف عليه بها من الشعير برسم الاصطبلات السلطانية، خمسمائة اردب.

ومن حرف الميم، مقطول والربيات وهي تبعها[920] في الاقطاع والارتفاع. فاما مقطول فعبارة عن بلدة صغيرة ليس بها نخل ولا شجر في وسط المزارع من نواحي شرقية الفيوم البحري. بينها وبين مدينة الفيوم مسافة[921] اربع ساعات للراكب. واما الربيات فعبارة عن بلدة كبيرة متاخمة للمحتفر المسمى بالبطس على جنبه الشرقي. ليس فيها شجر ولا نخل وبها منظرة صغيرة طين بناها مقطعها[922] والناحية بحري الفيوم للشرق. بينها وبين مدينة الفيوم مسافة خمس ساعات لراكب. جارية في اقطاع جماعة من المقطعين. عبرتها جيشية ستة الاف وستمائة دينار. شربها من بحر الشرقية بماء عبرته اثنتا عشرة قبضة. اهلها بنو زرعة، فخذ من بني عجلان.

ارتفاعها مما جميعه مستخرجا ومتحصلا عينا، ثلاثة وثلاثون دينارا ونصف وربع وثمن وحبتان، وغلة، الفان وثمانمائة وثمانون اردبا. تفصيله:
قمح، الف واربعمائة واربعون اردبا.
شعير، الف واربعمائة واربعون اردبا.

تفصيله:
الهلالي، عن الحانوت، اربعة وعشرون دينارا.
المراعي، تسعة دنانير ونصف وربع وثمن وحبتان.

المناجزة، غلة، الفان وثمانمائة وثمانون اردبا، على ما فصل.

عليها من الرسوم والمراعي والكيالة، عن ثلاثمائة وسبعين درهما وثمن، تسعة دنانير وربع؛ وغلة، مائة وعشرة ارادب وثلثان وربع ونصف قيراط. تفصيله:
قمح، اربعة واربعون اردبا وسدس.
شعير، تسعة وخمسون اردبا وقيراط ونصف.
فول، سبعة ارادب وثلث وربع وثمن.

تفصيله:
الرسوم، مائتان وثلاثة وثلاثون درهما ونصف وثمن، وغلة، خمسة وثمانون اردبا وربع وسدس ونصف قيراط. تفصيله:
قمح، تسعة وثلاثون اردبا وسدس.
شعير، ثمانية وثلاثون اردبا ونصف ونصف ثمن.
فول، سبعة ارادب وثلث وربع وثمن.
تفصيله:
رسم الحصاد، ثلاثة وخمسون درهما.
رسم الخفارة، خمسة عشر درهما.
رسم الجراريف، تسعون درهما.
رسم الاجران، خمسة وسبعون درهما ونصف وثمن، والغلة على ما تقدم.
الكيالة، خمسة وعشرون اردبا ونصف:
قمح، خمسة ارادب.
شعير، عشرون اردبا ونصف.

The chickens reared in it, 1,050 birds:
for the prosperous Dīwān, including the rearing wage of a third, 600 birds;
for the *iqṭāᶜ*-holders, 450 birds.

The barley assigned for the royal stables and paid for in advance, 500 ardabbs.

Also beginning with the letter 'mīm': Maqṭūl[309] together with al-Rubiyyāt,[310] which is joined to it in one fiscal and *iqṭāᶜ* unit. Maqṭūl is a small village, with no date palms or trees. It lies in the middle of fields in the north-east of the province, four hours' ride from Madīnat al-Fayyūm. Al-Rubiyyāt is a large village, adjacent to the trench of al-Baṭs, on its eastern side. It too has no trees or date palms, but it has a small belvedere (*manẓara)* made of clay, which was built by the *iqṭāᶜ*-holder. This village is in the north-east of the Fayyum, five hours' ride from Madīnat al-Fayyūm. It is assigned as an *iqṭāᶜ* to a group of *iqṭāᶜ*-holders, with a fiscal value of 6,600 army dinars. It gets its water from al-Sharqiyya Canal. Its water quota is 12 *qabḍas*. Its people are the Banū Zarᶜa, a branch of the Banū ᶜAjlān.

Its revenue in cash and in kind is, in specie, 33 ½ ¼ ⅛ 2/72 dinars; and in grains, 2,880 ardabbs:
wheat, 1,440 ardabbs;
barley, 1,440 ardabbs.

[The revenue] in detail:
lunar-calendar tax, for the shop, 24 dinars;
pasture tax, 9 ½ ¼ ⅛ 2/72 dinars.

Munājaza land tax in grains, 2,880 ardabbs, as specified.

The fees, the pasture tax and the measurement fee are 370 ⅛ dirhams, which are 9 ¼ dinars; and in grains, 110 ⅔ ¼ 1/48 ardabbs:
wheat, 44 ⅙ ardabbs;
barley, 59 1/24 1/48 ardabbs;
broad beans, 7 ⅓ ¼ ⅛ ardabbs.

[The fees, the pasture tax and the measurement fee] in detail:
the fees, 233 ½ ⅛ dirhams; and in grains, 85 ¼ ⅙ 1/48 ardabbs:
wheat, 39 ⅙ ardabbs;
barley, 38 ½ 1/16 ardabbs;
broad beans, 7 ⅓ ¼ ⅛ ardabbs.
[The fees] in detail:
harvest fee, 53 dirhams;
protection fee, 15 dirhams;
dredging fee, 90 dirhams;
threshing-floor fee, 75 ½ ⅛ dirhams; and in grains, as mentioned above.
The measurement fee, 25 ½ ardabbs:
wheat, 5 ardabbs;
barley, 20 ½ ardabbs.

920 أ. س.: معها.
921 ساقط من ط. م.: مسافة.
922 أ. س.: مقطعوها.

309 Modern location: al-Maqātla (المقاتلة). Halm, *Ägypten*, p. 264: Maqṭūl/Rubayyāt; Salmon, 'Répertoire', p. 45; Ibn al-Jīᶜān, *Kitāb al-tuḥfa*, p. 157; Ibn Mammātī, *Kitāb qawānīn al-dawāwīn*, p. 192: Maqṭal (with al-Rubiyyāt); Ramzī, *Al-Qāmūs*, II/III, 111: al-Maqātla.

310 Modern location: al-Rūbiyyāt (الروبيّات). Halm, *Ägypten*, p. 268; Ibn al-Jīᶜān, *Kitāb al-tuḥfa*, pp. 152, 157 (with Maqṭūl); de Sacy, *État des provinces*, p. 684; Ramzī, *Al-Qāmūs*, II/III, 108–09: al-Rūbiyyāt, Roman Touroubesti (following Amélineau, *La géographie*).

المراعي، عن اربعمائة وثمانية عشر راسا طارئ، مائة وستة وثلاثون درهما ونصف. تفصيله:

قطيعة ثلاثين درهما المائة، عن مائة وتسعة عشر راسا، خمسة وثلاثون درهما ونصف وثمن.

قطيعة خمسة وعشرين درهما المائة، عن مائتين وتسعة وتسعين راسا، اربعة وسبعون درهما ونصف وربع.

رسم المستخدمين، ستة وعشرون درهما وثمن.

وعليها من الزكاة عن ثمن اغنام، عن اربعة اروس ثلاثة دنانير وربع وسدس. تفصيله:

بياض، عن راسين، ديناران وسدس.

شعارى، عن راسين، دينار واحد وربع.

عليها من الاتبان، الفان وثمانمائة شنيف.

عليها لديوان الاحباس، عينا،[923] ديناران.

رسم خولي البحر بها، شعير، نصف وربع اردب.

والمربى بها من الفروج، الف وخمسون فروجا. تفصيله:

للديوان المعمور، بما فيه من اجرة التربية وهو الثلث، اربعمائة وخمسون طائرا.

للمقطعين، ستمائة طائر.

عليها من الفريك، اربعة ارادب.

والذي يسلف عليه بها من الشعير برسم الاصطبلات السلطانية، ثلاثمائة واربعة وخمسون اردبا.

حرف النون، نقليفة. هذه البلدة عبارة عن بلدة كبيرة ذات نخيل كثيرة[924] واشجار غزيرة وتين وزيتون. يجمعها وفانو الارتفاع على ما تقدم ذكره في حرف الفاء. وهي بحري الفيوم. بينه وبين مدينة الفيوم قرب[925] ثلاث ساعات للراكب وهي مشروحة في باب الفاء.

ومن حرف النون، ناموستين. هاتان البلدتان[926] عبارة عن بلدتين صغيرتين متقاربتين يجمعهما الارتفاع والاقطاع. وهما على شط البحر الذي يخرج ماؤه على حجر المنهى ويمر بهما ويؤتى[927] الى النيل. من شرقية الفيوم، بينهما وبين مدينة الفيوم مسافة اربع ساعات للراكب. جاريتان في اقطاع المقطعين. ترويان بالنيل ري الريف. عبرتهما جيشية الفان واربعمائة دينار. اهلهما[928] بنو منكنيت، فخذ من لواتة.

ارتفاعهما مما جميعه مستخرجا ومتحصلا، عينا، خراجا مقررا كتان وغيره، اصلا واضافة، مائة ودينار واحد؛ غلة، مناجزة ثلاثمائة اردب. تفصيله:

قمح، مائة وخمسون اردبا

فول، مائة وخمسون اردبا.

عليها من الرسوم والكيالة، عن مائة واربعة وعشرين درهما ونصف، ثلاثة دنانير وقيراطان ونصف؛ غلة، ستة وثلاثون اردبا ونصف وثلث:

قمح، ستة عشر اردبا وثلث.

فول، عشرون اردبا ونصف.

The pasture tax on seasonal pasture lands, for 418 heads, 136 ½ dirhams:

at the rate of 30 dirhams per 100 [heads], for 119 heads, 30 ½ ⅛ dirhams;

at the rate of 25 dirhams per 100 [heads], for 299 heads, 74 ½ ¼ dirhams;

the government agents' fee, 26 ⅛ dirhams.

The alms-tax, for the monetary value of small cattle, for four heads, 3 ¼ ⅙ dinars:

sheep, for two heads, 2 ⅙ dinars;

goats, for two heads, 1 ¼ dinar.

Hay, 2,800 bales.

For the Ministry of Endowments, in specie, 2 dinars.

The fee of the overseer of the canal, barley, ½ ¼ ardabb.

The chickens reared in it, 1,050 chickens:

for the prosperous Dīwān, including the rearing wage of a third, 450 birds;

for the *iqṭāʿ*-holders, 600 birds.

farīk, 4 ardabbs.

Barley assigned for the royal stables and paid for in advance, 354 ardabbs.

The letter 'nūn': Naqalīfa. This is a large village, with many date palms, abundant trees, figs and olives. Its revenue is combined with that of Fānū, as mentioned earlier under the letter 'fāʾ'. It is at the north of the province, nearly three hours' ride from Madīnat al-Fayyūm. It is presented in detail under the letter 'fāʾ'.

Beginning with the letter 'nūn': Nāmūsatayn.[311] These are two small adjacent villages, which are joined together as one fiscal and *iqṭāʿ* unit. They lie on the bank of the channel fed by the water escaping from above the stone dam on al-Manhā Canal. This channel then passes through these two villages, before reaching [back to] the Nile. They are to the east of the province, four hours' ride from Madīnat al-Fayyūm. They are assigned as an *iqṭāʿ* to a group of *iqṭāʿ*-holders. They are irrigated by the Nile, in the manner of Lower Egypt. Their fiscal value is 2,400 army dinars. Their people are the Banū Munkanīt, a branch of the Lawāta.

Their revenue in cash and in kind is, in specie, from the established land tax on flax and other crops, including the basic assessment and the additional rate, 101 dinars; and in grains, from *munājaza* land tax, 300 ardabbs:

wheat, 150 ardabbs;

broad beans, 150 ardabbs.

The fees and the measurement fee are 124 ½ dirhams, which are 3 ²⁄₂₄ ¹⁄₄₈ dinars; and in grains, 36 ½ ⅓ ardabbs:

wheat, 16 ⅓ ardabbs;

barley, 20 ½ ardabbs.

923 ساقط من أ. س.: عينا.

924 ساقط من أ. س.: كثيرة.

925 أ. س.: قريب.

926 ساقط من ط. م.: لبلدتان.

927 أ. س.: بها وبونا ؟ .

928 أ. س.: أهلها.

311 Modern location (uncertain): near Maʿṣarat Abū Ṣīr (معصرة ابو صير). Salmon, 'Répertoire', p. 41; Ibn al-Jīʿān, *Kitāb al-tuḥfa*, p. 159: Nāmūsa, at the province of Bahnasā; Ramzī, *Al-Qāmūs*, II/III, 128: Al-Nawāmīs. We have no positive identification of these two villages. In line with al-Nābulusī's description, we placed them near the modern village of Maʿṣarat Abū Ṣīr. This location is also in line with Shafei Bey's map.

تفصيله:
الرسوم، مائة واربعة وعشرون درهما ونصف، غلة، ثلاثون اردبا ونصف وثلث. تفصيله:
قمح، اثنا عشر اردبا وثلث.
شعير، ثمانية عشر اردبا ونصف.
تفصيله:
رسم الحصاد، ثلاثة وخمسون درهما.
رسم الخفارة، خمسة عشر درهما.
شد العين، احد وثلاثون درهما ونصف.
رسم الاجران، خمسة وعشرون درهما، وغلة، ثلاثون اردبا ونصف وثلث، على ما فصل.
كيالة، ستة ارادب:
قمح، اربعة ارادب.
شعير، اردبان.

عليها من الزكاة عن ثمن الماشية،[929] عن تسعة اروس، سبعة ونصف وثلث وثمن. تفصيله:
بقر احمر، تبيع واحد، دينار واحد وربع.
اغنام، عن ثمانية اروس، ستة دنانير وثلث وربع وثمن. تفصيله:
بياض، عن اربعة اروس، اربعة دنانير وثلث.
شعارى، عن اربعة اروس، ديناران وربع وثمن.

وعليها من الاتبان، ثلاثمائة شنيف.

والمربى بها من الفروج، اربعمائة وثمانون فروجا. تفصيله:
للديوان المعمور، بما فيه من اجرة التربية وهو الثلث، مائتان واربعون طائرا.
للمقطعين، مائتان واربعون طائرا.

والذي جرت العادة باطلاقه لها من التقاوي، ستة وستون اردبا:
قمح، اربعون اردبا.
شعير وفول، ستة وعشرون اردبا.

والذي بها من التقاوي[930] الديوانية، اردب وثلث وثمن:
قمح، اردب وسدس.
شعير، سدس وثمن.

والمسلف عليه بها من الفول برسم علوفة[931] العوامل الديوانية، خمسون اردبا.

حرف الهاء، هوارة دموشية. هذه البلدة[932] عبارة عن بلدة صغيرة تشتمل على نخل وجميز وسدر وهي على الشط القبلي من بحر الفيوم. وهي شرقي مدينة الفيوم بينها وبين مدينة الفيوم مسافة ساعة ونصف للراكب. جارية في اقطاع المقطعين، مرتجعة للديوان لسنة اثنتين واربعين وستمائة. أهلها هوارة، فخذ من لواتة. تروى بماء النيل.

[The fees and the measurement fee] in detail:
the fees, 124 ½ dirhams; and in grains, 30 ½ ⅓ ardabbs:
wheat, 12 ⅓ ardabbs;
barley, 18 ½ ardabbs.
[The fees] in detail:
harvest fee, 53 dirhams;
protection fee, 15 dirhams;
supervision of the land survey, 31 ½ dirhams;
threshing-floor fee, 25 dirhams; and in grains, 30 ½ ⅓ ardabbs, as specified.
The measurement fee, 6 ardabbs:
wheat, 4 ardabbs;
barley, 2 ardabbs.

The alms-tax, for the monetary value of nine heads of livestock, 7 ½ ⅓ ⅛ [dinars]:
cows, for a yearling calf, 1 ¼ dinar;
small cattle, for eight heads, 6 ⅓ ¼ ⅛ dinars:
sheep, for four heads, 4 ⅓ dinars;
goats, for four heads, 2 ¼ ⅛ dinars.

Hay, 300 bales.

The chickens reared in it, 480 chickens:
for the prosperous Dīwān, including the rearing wage of a third, 240 birds;
for the *iqṭāʿ*-holders, 240 birds.

The seed advances customarily distributed in it, 66 ardabbs:
wheat, 40 ardabbs;
barley and broad beans, 26 ardabbs.

The seed advances from the Dīwān, 1 ⅓ ⅛ ardabb:
wheat, 1 ⅙ ardabb;
barley, ⅙ ⅛ [ardabb].

The broad beans assigned for the fodder of the cattle of the Dīwān and paid for in advance, 50 ardabbs.

The letter 'hā'': Hawwārat Dumūshiyya.[312] This is a small village with date palms, sycamores and sidr trees. It is on the south bank of the Main Canal, an hour and a half's ride east of Madīnat al-Fayyūm. It is assigned as an *iqṭāʿ* to *iqṭāʿ*-holders, but was returned to the Dīwān in 642. Its people are the Hawwāra, a branch of the Lawāta. It is irrigated by the water of the Nile.

929 أ. س.: ماشية.
930 ساقط من أ. س.: ستة وستون أردبا: قمح أربعون أردبا شعير وفول ستة وعشرون أردبا. والذي بها من التقاوي.
931 ساقط من أ. س.: علوفة.
932 ساقط من أ. س.: البلدة.

312 Modern location: ʿIzbat ʿAlī Farāj (عزبة علي فراج). Ibn al-Jīʿān, *Kitāb al-tuḥfa*, p. 158: Hawwāra al-Qibliyya; de Sacy, *État des provinces*, p. 684; Savigny, *Description de l'Égypte*, p. 126: Hawwāra al-Kabīr; Boinet Bey, *Dictionnaire géographique*, s.v. *Hawwārat ʿAdlān*; Salmon, 'Répertoire', p. 37: Hawwārat Doumoūchya; Halm, *Ägypten*, p. 259: Hawwāra al-Qibliyya = Hawwārat Dumūshiya; Ramzī, *Al-Qāmūs*, I, 471: ʿIzbat ʿAlī Farāj.

ارتفاعها، عينا، ثمانية وستون دينارا ونصف وربع وحبتان. تفصيله:
خراج فدن العين، ثمانية وستون دينارا ونصف وربع وحبتان.
خراج فدن العين، خمسة وثلاثون دينارا وقيراط ونصف. تفصيله:
الاصل، عن ثلاثة عشر فدانا ونصف وثلث وثمن، اثنان وثلاثون دينارا ونصف وثمن. تفصيله:
كتان، عن ثلاثة فدادين وثمن ونصف قيراط، احد عشر دينارا.
مقات، قطيعة دينارين الفدان، عن عشرة فدادين ونصف وربع ونصف ثمن، احد وعشرون دينارا ونصف وثمن.
الاضافة، ديناران وربع وسدس ونصف قيراط.
خراج السواقي، اصلا واضافة، ثلاثة وثلاثون دينارا ونصف وربع.

ثمن العشب والقرط، فول ثلاثون اردبا.

عليها من الزكاة عن ثمن اغنام، عن ثلاثة اروس، ديناران ونصف وربع وثمن. تفصيله:
بياض، عن راسين، ديناران وربع وثمن.
شعرية واحدة، نصف دينار.

عليها من الاتبان من جملة المقرر على دموشية، مائة وخمسون شنيفا.

والذي بها من التقاوي الديوانية، غلة، ستة وخمسون اردبا وثلثان. تفصيله:
قمح، ثلاثة ارادب وسدس.
شعير، ثمانية واربعون اردبا ونصف.
فول، خمسة ارادب.

ومن حرف الهاء، هيشة دموشية. هذه البلدة عبارة عن غابة في ارض دموشية وخليج تنبطويه. استخرجها فخر الدين عثمان رحمه الله تعالى لما كان مقطعها وعمرها منشية وصارت الان بليدة.[933] تشتمل على ودي نخل صغير وقليل سنط صغير. وهي قبلي مدينة الفيوم بينها وبين مدينة الفيوم مسافة ساعتين للراكب. شربها من بحر تنبطويه في اربع مساق لزرع الشتوي والصيفي، اربع قبض ماء. اهلها بنو حاتم، فخذ من بني كلاب.

ارتفاعها، عينا، احد عشر دينارا، وغلة، ستمائة وستة وعشرون اردبا وربع. تفصيله:
قمح، اربعمائة واثنا عشر اردبا.
شعير، مائة وثلاثة ارادب.
فول، مائة وثلاثة ارادب.
سمسم، ثمانية ارادب وربع.
تفصيله:
خراج فدن العين، عشرة دنانير ونصف وربع.
الاصل، عن خمسة فدادين، عشرة دنانير.
الاضافة، نصف وربع دينار.
خراج القلقاس، دينار وربع.
مناجزة الغلات، ستمائة وثمانية ارادب. تفصيله:
قمح، اربعمائة اردب.
شعير، مائة اردب.
فول، مائة اردب.
سمسم، ثمانية ارادب.

933 أ. س.: البلدة.

Its revenue in specie is 68 ½ ¼ ²⁄₇₂ dinars:
land tax on cash-crops, 68 ½ ¼ ²⁄₇₂ dinars:
land tax on cash-crops [assessed by] feddans, 35 ¹⁄₂₄ ¹⁄₄₈ dinars:
the basic assessment, for 13 ½ ⅓ ⅛ feddans, 32 ½ ⅛ dinars:
flax, for 3 ⅛ ¹⁄₄₈ feddans, 11 dinars;
cucurbitaceous fruits, at the rate of 2 dinars per feddan, for 10 ½ ¼ ¹⁄₁₆ feddans, 21 ½ ⅛ dinars.
the addition, 2 ¼ ⅙ ¹⁄₄₈ dinars.
land tax on [lands irrigated by] waterwheels, including the basic assessment and the additional rate, 33 ½ ¼ dinars.

The value (*thaman*) of herbage and alfalfa, 30 ardabbs of broad beans.

The alms-tax imposed on it, for the monetary value of three heads of small cattle, 2 ½ ¼ ⅛ dinars:
sheep, for two heads, 2 ¼ ⅛ dinars;
goats, one head, ½ dinar.

Hay, out of the established levy on Dumūshiyya, 150 bales.

The seed advances from the Dīwān, in grains, 56 ⅔ ardabbs:
wheat, 3 ⅙ ardabbs;
barley, 48 ½ ardabbs;
broad beans, 5 ardabbs.

Also beginning with the letter 'hā'': Hayshat Dumūshiyya.[313] This village consists of a thicket in the land of Dumūshiyya and Tanabṭawayh Canal. [The amir] Fakhr al-Dīn ʿUthmān — may God the exalted have mercy on him — prepared it for cultivation (*istakhrajahā*) when he was its *iqṭā*ʿ-holder, and built it as a hamlet. It has now become a small village, which has small shoots of date palms and a few small acacias. It lies two hours' ride south of Madīnat al-Fayyūm. It gets 4 *qabḍas* of water from Tanabṭawayh Canal by four irrigation ditches, for winter and summer crops. Its people are the Banū Ḥātim, a branch of the Banū Kilāb.

Its revenue, in specie, is 11 dinars; and in grains, 626 ¼ ardabbs:
wheat, 412 ardabbs;
barley, 103 ardabbs;
broad beans, 103 ardabbs;
sesame, 8 ¼ ardabbs.

[The revenue] in detail:
land tax on cash-crops assessed by feddans, in specie, 10 ½ ¼ dinars:
the basic assessment, for 5 feddans, 10 dinars;
the addition, ½ ¼ dinar;
land tax on colocasia, 1 ¼ dinar;

Munājaza land tax in grains, 608 ardabbs:
wheat, 400 ardabbs;
barley, 100 ardabbs;
broad beans, 100 ardabbs;
sesame, 8 ardabbs.

313 Modern location: Munshảat Rabīʿ (منشاة ربيع). There are no references in other sources to this village, but Shafei Bey marks it on his map as Munshảat Rabīʿ, located near the modern village of Qalahāna.

الوفر، ثمانية عشر اردبا وربع. تفصيله:
قمح، اثنا عشر اردبا.
شعير، ثلاثة ارادب.
فول، ثلاثة ارادب.
سمسم، ربع اردب.

عليها من الرسوم والكيالة والمراعي، عن مائة وثلاثة دراهم ونصف وربع، ديناران وثلث وربع وحبة، وغلة، سبعة وثلاثون اردبا ونصف ونصف ثمن. تفصيله:
قمح،[934] اربعة وعشرون اردبا وربع وثمن.
شعير، ثمانية ارادب وثلث.[935]
فول، ثلاثة[936] ارادب ونصف وثلث ونصف قيراط.
سمسم، اردب واحد.

تفصيله:
رسم الاجران، ستة عشر درهما وربع، وغلة، تسعة عشر اردبا وربع ونصف ثمن. تفصيله:
قمح، اثنا عشر اردبا وربع وثمن.
شعير، اردبان وثلث.
فول، ثلاثة ارادب ونصف وثلث ونصف قيراط.
سمسم، نصف وربع اردب.
كيالة، ثمانية عشر اردبا وربع. تفصيله:
قمح، اثنا عشر اردبا.
شعير، ستة ارادب.
سمسم، ربع اردب.
المراعي، طارئ، عن مائة وسبعة وعشرين راسا، سبعة وثمانون درهما ونصف. تفصيله:
قطيعة درهم واحد الراس، عن اثنين وعشرين راسا، اثنان وعشرون درهما.
قطيعة سبعين درهما المائة، عن خمسة وعشرين راسا، سبعة عشر درهما ونصف.
قطيعة خمسين درهما المائة،[937] عن ثمانين راسا، اربعون درهما.
رسم المستخدمين، ثمانية دراهم.

عليها من الزكاة عن ثمن اغنام،[938] عن خمسة ارؤس، اربعة دنانير ونصف وربع وثمن:
بياض، عن اربعة ارؤس، اربعة دنانير وربع.
شعارى، عن راس واحد، نصف وثمن دينار.

عليها من الاتبان من جملة المقرر على دموشية، ستمائة شنيف.

والمربى بها من الفروج للديوان المعمور، بما فيه من اجرة التربية وهو الثلث، مائتان وخمسة وعشرون فروجا.

والذي بها من التقاوي الديوانية، مائة واحد وسبعون اردبا ونصف:
قمح، مائة وستة وعشرون اردبا ونصف.
شعير، ستة وعشرون اردبا.
فول، ثمانية عشر اردبا.
سمسم، اردب.

والذي يسلف عليه بها من الفول برسم العوامل الديوانية، ثلاثون اردبا.

934 أ. س. يضيف: تفصيله قمح.
935 أ. س. يضيف: ونصف قيراط.
936 ساقط من أ. س.: ثلاثة، لكنه يضيفه على الهامش.
937 ساقط من أ. س.: المائة.
938 ساقط من أ. س.: ثمن أغنام.

The surcharge, 18 ¼ ardabbs:
wheat, 12 ardabbs;
barley, 3 ardabbs;
broad beans, 3 ardabbs;
sesame, ¼ ardabb.

The fees, the measurement fee and the pasture tax are 103 ½ ⅓ dirhams, which are 2 ⅓ ¼ 1/72 dinars; and in grains, 37 ½ 1/16 ardabbs:
wheat, 24 ¼ ⅛ ardabbs;
barley, 8 ⅓ ardabbs;
broad beans, 3 ½ ⅓ 1/48 ardabbs;
sesame, 1 ardabb.

[The fees, the measurement fee and the pasture tax] in detail:
threshing-floor fee, 16 ¼ dirhams; and in grains, 19 ¼ 1/16 ardabbs:
wheat, 12 ¼ ⅛ ardabbs;
barley, 2 ⅓ ardabbs;
broad beans, 3 ½ ⅓ 1/48 ardabbs;
sesame, ½ ¼ ardabb.
The measurement fee, 18 ¼ ardabbs:
wheat, 12 ardabbs;
barley, 6 ardabbs;
sesame, ¼ ardabb.
The pasture tax on seasonal pasture lands, for 127 heads, 87 ½ dirhams:
at the rate of one dirham per head, for 22 heads, 22 dirhams;
at the rate of 70 dirhams per 100 [heads], for 25 heads, 17 ½ dirhams;
at the rate of 50 dirhams per 100 [heads], for 80 heads, 40 dirhams;
the government agents' fee, 8 dirhams.

The alms-tax, for the monetary value of small cattle, for five heads, 4 ½ ¼ ⅛ dinars:
sheep, for four heads, 4 ¼ dinars;
goats, for one head, ½ ⅛ dinar.

Hay, out of the established levy on Dumūshiyya, 600 bales.

The chickens reared for the prosperous Dīwān, including the rearing wage of a third, 225 chickens.

The seed advances from the Dīwān, 171 ½ ardabbs:
wheat, 126 ½ ardabbs;
barley, 26 ardabbs;
broad beans, 18 ardabbs;
sesame, 1 ardabb.

The broad beans assigned for the cattle of the Dīwān and paid for in advance, 30 ardabbs.

ومن حرف الهاء، هوارة البحرية. هذه البلدة عبارة عن بلدة صغيرة. تشتمل على نخل قليل ودي وسدر[939] وتين وجميز. وهي من شرقية الفيوم على شط بحر الفيوم البحري. بينها وبين مدينة الفيوم مسافة ساعة للراكب. جارية في اقطاع الامير الاجل عز الدين الكيكاني ومن معه. عبرتها جيشية ثمانمائة دينار. تروى بماء النيل. اهلها بنو زرعة، فخذ من بني عجلان.

ارتفاعها، عينا، ثمانون دينارا،[940] وغلة، ستون اردبا:
قمح، ثلاثون اردبا.
فول، ثلاثون اردبا.

تفصيله:
مال المراعي، عشرة دنانير.
خراج الكتان وغيره، سبعون دينارا.

المشاطرة، ستون اردبا، قمح وفول نصفان.

عليها من الرسوم والكيالة والمراعي، عن مائة وثمانية وسبعين درهما ونصف وربع، اربعة دنانير وربع وسدس وحبتان، وغلة، اربعة ارادب وقيراطان. تفصيله:
قمح، اردبان وقيراط.
فول، اردبان وقيراط.

تفصيله:
الرسوم، اربعة وسبعون درهما ونصف، وغلة، ثلاثة ارادب وقيراطان:
قمح، اردب واحد وربع وسدس وثمن.
فول، اردب واحد وربع وسدس وثمن.
تفصيله:
شد العين، اربعة دراهم.
رسم الحصاد، ثلاثة وخمسون درهما.
رسم الخفارة، خمسة عشر درهما.
رسم الاجران، درهمان ونصف وثلاثة ارادب وقيراطان، قمح وشعير نصفان.
كيالة، اردب واحد، قمح وفول نصفان.
المراعي، عن مائتين وخمسة وعشرين راسا طارى، مائة واربعة دراهم وربع. تفصيله:
قطيعة خمسين درهما المائة، عن مائة وستة وثلاثين راسا، ثمانية وستون درهما.
قطيعة خمسة وعشرين درهما المائة، عن تسعة وثمانين راسا، اثنان وعشرون درهما ونصف.
رسم المستخدمين، اربعة عشر درهما.

عليها من الزكاة عن ثمن اغنام، عن تسعة ارؤس، سبعة دنانير ونصف وثلث وحبتان. تفصيله:
بياض، عن خمسة ارؤس، خمسة دنانير ونصف وربع.
شعارى، عن اربعة ارؤس، ديناران وقيراطان وحبتان.

عليها من الاتبان، ستون شنيفا.

والمربى بها من الفروج للديوان المعمور، بما فيه من اجرة التربية وهو الثلث، تسعون فروجا.

939 ساقط من أ. س.: وسدر.

940 ط. م.: ثمانون دينارا عينا.

Also beginning with the letter 'hā'': Hawwāra al-Baḥriyya.[314] This is a small village, with a few date palm shoots, sidr trees, figs and sycamores. It is in the east of the province, on the northern bank of the Main Canal, one hour's ride from Madīnat al-Fayyūm. It is assigned as an *iqṭā*ᶜ to the illustrious amir ᶜIzz al-Dīn al-Kīkānī and his men, with fiscal value of 800 army dinars. It is irrigated by the water of the Nile. Its people are the Banū Zarᶜa, a branch of the Banū ᶜAjlān.

Its revenue is, in specie, 80 dinars; and in grains, 60 ardabbs:
wheat, 30 ardabbs;
broad beans, 30 ardabbs.

[The revenue] in detail:
fixed pasture tax, 10 dinars;
land tax on flax and other crops, 70 dinars.

Mushāṭara land tax, 60 ardabbs, wheat and broad beans, half in each.

The fees, the measurement fee and the pasture tax are 178 ½ ¼ dirhams, which are 4 ¼ ⅙ 2/72 dinars; and in grains, 4 2/24 ardabbs:
wheat, 2 1/24 ardabbs;
broad beans, 2 1/24 ardabbs.

[The fees, the measurement fee and the pasture tax] in detail:
the fees, 74 ½ dirhams; and in grains, 3 2/24 ardabbs:
wheat, 1 ¼ ⅙ ⅛ ardabb;
broad beans, 1 ¼ ⅙ ⅛ ardabb.
[The fees] in detail:
supervision of the land survey, 4 dirhams;
harvest fee, 53 dirhams;
protection fee 15 dirhams;
threshing-floor fee, 2 ½ dirhams; [and in grains] 3 2/24 ardabbs, wheat and barley, half in each.
The measurement fee, 1 ardabb, wheat and broad beans, half in each.
The pasture tax on seasonal pasture lands, for 225 heads, 104 ¼ dirhams:
at the rate of 50 dirhams per 100 [heads], for 136 heads, 68 dirhams;
at the rate of 25 dirhams per 100 [heads], for 89 heads, 22 ½ dirhams;
the government agents' fee, 14 dirhams.

The alms-tax, for the monetary value of small cattle, for nine heads, 7 ½ ⅓ 2/72 dinars:
sheep, for five heads, 5 ½ ¼ dinars;
goats, for four heads, 2 2/24 2/72 dinars.

Hay, 60 bales.

The chickens reared for the prosperous Dīwān, including the rearing wage of a third, 90 chickens.

314 Modern location: Hawwārat al-Maqṭaᶜ (هوارة المقطع). Timm, *Das Christlich-Koptische Ägypten*, p. 1099: Hawwārat al-Maqṭaᶜ; Halm, *Ägypten*, p. 259: Hawwāra al-Baḥriyya = Hawwārat al-Maqṭaᶜ; Savigny, *Description de l'Égypte*, p. 127: Hawwārat al-Ṣaghīr; Ibn al-Jīᶜān, *Kitāb al-tuḥfa*, p. 158; Ramzī, *Al-Qāmūs*, II/III, 103: Hawwārat al-Baḥriyya = Hawwārat al-Maqṭaᶜ.

[فصل]: مناشئ النواحي التي ياتي ذكرها

المقدم ذكر النواحي الداخل ارتفاع هذه المناشئ في البلاد المذكورة

مناشئ الاستنباط وعدتهم سبعة:

المخصوبة. هذه المنشاة عبارة عن[941] بيوت طين متوسطة. بها جميزة كبيرة ونخل وسنط.

منشاة شرف. هذه المنشاة عبارة عن بيوت قلائل ليس بها اشجار.

منشاة الصفصاف. هذه المنشاة عبارة عن بيوتات[942] قلائل بها برج حمام واشجار[943] نخل وسدر وصفصاف.

منشاة المقاسم. هذه المشاة عبارة عن بيوت قلائل ليس بها نخل ولا اشجار.

منشاة سراج. هذه المنشاة عبارة عن بيوت طين قلائل بها نخل كثير.

منشاة ابي سالم. هذه المنشاة عبارة عن بيوت كثيرة بها نخل وجميز وسنط.

منشاة تعرف ببرك البيض. هذه المنشاة عبارة عن بيوت قلائل بها جدران نخل وعقل كرم.

مناشئ اهريت، وعدتهم ثلاثة:

منشاة تعرف بببيج النيلة وتعرف بجروفة.[944] هذه المنشاة عبارة عن بيوت متوسطة بها صفصاف وسنط.

منشاة العثامنة. هذه المنشاة عبارة عن بيوت كثيرة بها نخل واصول تين.

منشاة بطاح. هذه المنشاة عبارة عن بيوت قلائل بها نخل كثير وودي وسنط.

منشاة اقلول. هذه المنشاة تعرف بابراهيم الجعفري. عبارة عن بيوت متوسطة بين الكبر والصغر، بها نخل وسدر.

منشاة اطسا. هذه المنشاة تعرف باولاد بكير، عبارة عن بيوت قلائل بها نخل مثمر وتين وسدر.

منشاة بارض الصفاونة. هذه المنشاة تعرف بالسواقي الهمامية المنصوبة على خليج منية اقنى.[945] عبارة عن بيوت متوسطة يسكنها مرابعو[946] القصب السكر المزردع برسم معصرة بلالة. بها سنط[947] وصفصاف.

مناشئ بلالة، وعدتهم اربعة:

منشاة المطوع، معروفة[948] بابي علاق. هذا المنشاة عبارة عن بيوت كثيرة بها نخل مثمر وشجرة خروب.

منشاة اولاد ابي زكري. هذه المنشاة عبارة عن بيوت متوسطة بها نخل واصول عنب.

منشاة عثمان. هذه المنشاة عبارة عن بيوتات[949] قلائل بها نخل واصول تين.

منشاة اولاد زيدان. هذه المنشاة معروفة بالاكراد، عبارة عن بيوت متوسطة بها مسجد وبرج حمام ودويرات تين[950] ونخل.

941 ساقط من أ. س.: عن.
942 أ. س.: بويتات.
943 ساقط من أ. س.: وأشجار.
944 ط. م.: بجرو.
945 ط. م.: دلية وأقنى.
946 ط. م.: مرابعون.
947 أ. س.: صنط.
948 أ. س.: تعرف.
949 أ. س.: بويتات.
950 ساقط من ط. م.: تين.

[Section]: The hamlets of villages.

The mother villages, under which the revenues of the hamlets are subsumed, are listed first.

Hamlets of al-Istinbāṭ, seven in number:

al-Makhṣūba. This hamlet consists of a medium number of mud houses. It has a large sycamore tree, date palms and acacias.

Munshaʾat Sharaf. This hamlet consists of a few houses. There are no trees in it.

Munshaʾat al-Ṣafṣāf. This hamlet consists of a few houses. It has a dovecote, date palms, sidr trees and willow trees.

Munshaʾat al-Maqāsim. This hamlet consists of a few houses. There are no date palms in it and no trees.

Munshaʾat Sirāj. This hamlet consists of a few mud houses. It has many date palms.

Munshaʾat Abū Sālim. This hamlet consists of many houses. It has date palms, sycamores and acacias.

Munshaʾa known as Birak al-Bayḍ. This hamlet consists of a few houses. It has walled gardens of date palms and recently planted vines.

Hamlets of Ihrīt, three in number:

Munshaʾa known as Babīj al-Nīla and as Jarūfa.[315] This hamlet consists of a medium number of houses. It has willows and acacia.

Munshaʾat al-ʿAthāmina. This hamlet consists of many houses. It has date palms and trunks of fig trees.

Munshaʾat Biṭāḥ. This hamlet consists of a few houses. It has many date palms, shoots and acacias.

Munshaʾat Uqlūl. This hamlet, which is known as Ibrāhīm al-Jaʿfarī, consists of a middling number of houses. It has date palms and sidr trees.

Munshaʾat Iṭsā. This hamlet, also known as Awlād Bakīr, consists of a small number of houses. It has fruit-bearing date palms, figs and sidr trees.

Munshaʾa in the land of al-Ṣafāwina. This hamlet is known by the Humāmī waterwheels, which are set up on Minyat Aqnā[316] Canal. It consists of a medium number of houses, occupied by quarter-share labourers who cultivate sugarcane, assigned for the press in Bilāla. It has acacias and willows.

Hamlets of Bilāla, four in number:

Munshaʾat al-Muṭawwiʿ, known as Abū ʿAllāq. This hamlet consists of many houses. It has fruit-bearing date palms and carob trees.

Munshaʾat Awlād Abū Zikrī. This hamlet consists of a medium number of houses. It has date palms and grape trunks.

Munshaʾat ʿUthmān. This hamlet consists of a few small houses. It has date palms and trunks of fig trees.

Munshaʾat Awlād Zaydān. This hamlet is known as al-Akrād [the Kurds]. It consists of a medium number of houses. It has a mosque, a dovecote, enclosures of figs and date palms.

315 MP: Jarū.

316 MP: *khalīj Dilya wa-Aqnā* instead of *khalīj Minyat Aqnā*. MS Dār al-Kutub 1594 leaves blank.

مناشئ بمويه، وعدتهم ستة:

منشاة نعيم. هذه المنشاة عبارة عن بيوتات قلائل بها سنط[951] وودي نخل.

منشاة ابن عسكر. غربي بمويه تعرف بالكوم الاحمر. هذه المنشاة عبارة عن اخصاص قصب ريحي بها سنطة[952] واحدة.

منشاة المقاسم. هذه المنشاة تعرف بالطاحون، عبارة عن بيوتات قلائل بها اصول زيتون ونخل.

منشاة تعرف بالقلاوة وتعرف بابي يوسف القطيطاي. هذه المنشاة عبارة عن اخصاص قصب قلائل ليس بها غروس.

منشاة غربي البلد تعرف بعنتر. هذه المنشاة عبارة عن اخصاص قصب ليس بها اشجار.

منشاة تعرف بسنهور. عبارة عن بيوت متوسطة، بها نخل وتين وزيتون وصفصاف. يسكنها بنو مطير.[953]

مناشئ ببيج اندير، وعدتهم خمسة:

منشاة تعرف بشرف بن عشم.[954] هذه المنشاة عبارة عن بيوت متوسطة ليس بها اشجار.

منشاة ابي حاتم. هذه المنشاة عبارة عن بيوت متوسطة بها سنط.[955]

منشاة تعرف باولاد ابراشه. هذه المنشاة عبارة عن بيوت متوسطة بين الكبر والصغر ليس به اشجار.

منشاة الغصيني. هذه المنشاة عبارة عن اخصاص قصب قلائل ليس بها اشجار.

منشاة مستجدة على خليج العاقولة. هذه المنشاة عبارة عن بيوت قلائل ليس بها اشجار.

منشاة بنديق. هذه المنشاة تعرف بالبور. عبارة عن اخصاص قصب ريحي وبيوت طين قلائل وبها سنط.

منشاة جردو. هذه المنشاة تعرف بالهلالي، عبارة عن بيوت قلائل بها جميزة واصول عنب.

منشاة دسيا. هذه المنشاة تعرف بالمرج والاكراد، عبارة عن بيوت متوسطة. بها جميز.

مناشئ دنفارة اهريت،[956] وعدتهم ثلاثة:

منشاة ابي خزعل. هذه المنشاة عبارة عن بيوت قلائل ليس بها اشجار.

منشاة ابي عزيز وتعرف بعلكان. هذه المنشاة عبارة عن بيوت متوسطة، فيها صفصاف وسدر.

منشاة خلاص. هذه المنشاة عبارة عن بيوت قلائل بها نخل مثمر.

951 أ. س.: صنط.
952 أ. س.: صنطة.
953 ط. م.: مطر.
954 أ. س.: غشم.
955 أ. س.: صنط.
956 ط. م.: تنفارة اهريت.

Hamlets of Bamawayh, six in number:

Munsha'at Naʿīm. This hamlet consists of a few small houses. It has acacias and shoots of date palms.

Munsha'at Ibn ʿAskar, which is known as al-Kawm al-Aḥmār. It lies west of Bamawayh. This hamlet consists of shacks made of *rīḥī*[317] reeds. It has one acacia tree.

Munsha'at al-Maqāsim. This hamlet is known as al-Ṭāḥūn ['the Mill']. It consists of a few houses (*buyūtāt*). It has trunks of olive trees and date palms.

Munshaʾa known as al-Qilāwa, and also as Abū Yūsuf al-Qaṭīṭāy (?). It consists of a few reed shacks. There are no trees in it.

Munshaʾa west of the village [Bamawayh], known as ʿAntar. It consists of reed shacks. There are no trees in it.

Munshaʾa known as Sanhūr.[318] It consists of a medium number of houses. It has date palms, figs, olives and willows. It is inhabited by the Banū Muṭayr.

Hamlets of Babīj Andīr, five in number:

Munshaʾa known as Sharaf ibn ʿIshm (?). It consists of a medium number of houses. There are no trees in it.

Munsha'at Abū Ḥātim. This hamlet consists of a medium number of houses. It has trunks of acacia.

Munshaʾa known as Awlād Ibrāsha.[319] It consists of a medium number of houses. There are no trees in it.

Munsha'at al-Ghuṣaynī. This hamlet consists of a small number of reed shacks. There are no trees in it.

A recently built Munshaʾa on the al-ʿĀqūla Canal. It consists of a few houses. There are no trees in it.

Munshaʾat Bandīq. This hamlet is known as al-Būr ['the fallow land']. It consists of shacks made of *rīḥī* reeds and a few mud houses. It has acacias.

Munshaʾat Jardū. This hamlet, also known as al-Hilālī, consists of a few houses. It has one sycamore and vine trunks.

Munshaʾat Disyā. This hamlet, also known as al-Marj ('the Meadow'), and as al-Akrād ('the Kurds'), consists of a medium number of houses. It has sycamores.

Hamlets of Dinfārat Ihrīt, three in number:

Munsha'at Abū Khazʿal. It consists of a small number of houses. There are no trees in it.

Munsha'at Abū ʿAzīz, also known as ʿAlikān. It consists of a medium number of houses. It has willows and sidr trees.

Munsha'at Khalāṣ. It consists of a few houses. It has fruit-bearing date palms.

317 Edward W. Lane and Stanley Lane-Poole, *An Arabic-English Lexicon*, repr. edn, 8 vols (New York: Ungar, 1956), I, 1181, has '*rayyiḥa*, plural *rīḥah*: a plant that appears at the roots, or lower parts, of trees remaining from the preceding year; or, a plant that has become green after its leaves and the upper parts of its branches have dried'.

318 Modern location: Sanhūr al-Baḥriyya (سنهور البحرية). Timm, *Das Christlich-Koptische Ägypten*, pp. 2291–2: Psenharyo; Trismegistos GEO ID 1956: Psenharyo; Halm, *Ägypten*, p. 249: Sanhūr = Bamawayh; Ibn Mammātī, *Kitāb qawānīn al-dawāwīn*, p. 118; Ibn al-Jīʿān, *Kitāb al-tuḥfa*, p. 153: Bamawayh and Sanhūr; Ramzī, *Al-Qāmūs*, II/III, 112–13: Sanhūr. Ramzī notes that the two villages of Bamawayh and Sanhūr were joined together and came to be known as Sanhūr, because the name Bamawayh was more difficult to pronounce. In contrast, Shafei Bey, 'Fayoum Irrigation', p. 39, argues that the two villages remained distinct up to modern times, and that al-Nābulusī's Bamawayh is indeed Sanhūr, but al-Nābulusī's Sanhūr is Sanhūr al-Baḥriyya.

319 Appears as Munshaʾat Ibrīsha in Chapter 7 sbove.

مناشئ دنفارة جردو،[957] اثنتان:

منشاة ابي سالم. عبارة عن بيوت متوسطة ليس بها اشجار.

منشاة موسى. عبارة عن بيوت متوسطة بين الكبر والصغر، ليس بها اشحار.

منشاة ذات الصفاء، تعرف باخصاص النجار. عبارة عن بويتات قلائل بها تين وكمثرى.

منشاة منية كربيس، تعرف باخصاص ابي عصية. عبارة عن بلدة متوسطة بها مسجد وجميزة ونخل كثير وطاحون ماء، وبحريها اهليلج اصفر شجرتان.

منشاة فدمين. عبارة عن بيوت قلائل بها جميزة ونخل.

منشاة فانو، تعرف بالمقاسم والملائد. عبارة عن بيوت متوسطة، بها دويرات نخل وتين وكمثرى وعنب ورمان وخوخ ومشمش.

مناشئ منية اقنى، وعدتهم سبعة:

منشاة غيلان. عبارة عن بيوت متوسطة بها سنط[958] وودي نخل.

منشاة الوسط. عبارة عن بيوت متوسطة بها سنطتان.[959]

منشاة الاثلة، تعرف بزيد بن كثير. عبارة عن اخصاص خطب طرفا، ليس بها اشجار.

منشاة حويت. عبارة عن بيوت قلائل ليس بها اشجار.

منشاتان يعرفان بالفحامتين، البرانية والجوانية. بينهما مسافة ساعتين. عبارة عن بيوت قلائل، دثر اكثرها بحكم رغبة المزارعين عن القيام بها.

منشاة تعرف بدقلوه. عبارة عن اخصاص قصب وبيوت طين بها نخل ودي.

منشاة منية البطس، تعرف بمنية البطس القديمة. عبارة عن بيوت كثيرة بها نخل.

منشاة مطول، تعرف بزعازع[960] بن الرحالة. عبارة عن بيوت قلائل ليس بها اشجار.

مناشئ مقران، اثنتان:

منشاة شرقية. عبارة عن بيوت متوسطة ليس بها ساكن[961] الان وليس بها اشجار.

منشاة تعرف بقمنا بجوش، وتعرف بالمنصورة. عبارة عن بيوت قلائل متفرقة. بها دويرات تين ونخل.

منشاة تعرف بالشيخ[962] ابي عبدالله القحافي. في ارض اطفيح شلا، من حقوق تطون من خليج تنبطويه. عبارة عن بيوت متوسطة يسكنها الفقراء. بها رباط زاوية ومسجد تقام فيه الجمعة. وبها بستان نخل وتين، وقف على الزاوية من الايام الكاملية، سقى الله عهدها صوب الرحمة.[963]

957 ط. م.: تنفارة وجردو.
958 أ. س.: صنط.
959 أ. س.: صنطان.
960 أ. س.: بزعارع.
961 أ. س.: سكن.
962 ساقط من أ. س.: بالشيخ.
963 أ. س. يضيف: والرضوان.

Hamlets of Dinfārat Jardū, two:

Munsha'at Abū Sālim. It consists of a medium number of houses. There are no trees in it.

Munsha'at Mūsā. It consists of a medium number of houses. There are no trees in it.

Munsha'at Dhāt al-Ṣafā', known as Ahkṣāṣ al-Najjār. It consists of a few houses. It has fig and pear trees.

Munsha'at Minyat Karbīs, known as Akhṣāṣ Abū ʿUṣayya. It is a medium-sized village. It has a mosque and a water mill, sycamores and many date palms. North of it there are two trees of yellow emblic myrobalan (*ihlīlaj aṣfar*).

Munsha'at Fidimīn. It consists of a few houses. It has sycamores and date palms.

Munsha'at Fānū, also known as al-Maqāsim and as al-Malā'id. It consists of a medium number of houses. It has enclosures of date palms, figs, pears, grapes, pomegranates, peaches and apricots.

Hamlets of Minyat Aqnā, seven in number:

Munsha'at Ghaylān. It consists of a medium number of houses. It has acacias and shoots of date palms.

Munsha'at al-Wasaṭ. It consists of a medium number of houses. It has two acacias.

Munsha'at al-Athila, also known as Zayd ibn Kathīr. It consists of huts made of tamarisk wood. There are no trees in it.

Munsha'at Ḥuwayt. It consists of a few houses. There are no trees in it.

Two hamlets known as al-Faḥḥāma al-Barrāniyya [the Outer Faḥḥāma], and al-Faḥḥāma al-Juwāniyya [the Inner Faḥḥāma]. The distance between the two of them is two hours' [walk?]. They consist of a few houses, which are mostly deserted, since the tenants do not want to live there.

Munsha'a known as Diqlawa. It consists of reed shacks and mud houses. It has shoots of date palms.

Munsha'at Minyat al-Baṭs, known as Minyat al-Baṭs al-Qadīma [the 'old']. It consists of a large number of houses. It has date palms.

Munsha'at Muṭūl, known as Zaʿāziʿ ibn al-Raḥḥāla ('the storms of the traveller'). It consists of a small number of houses. There are no trees in it.

Hamlets of Muqrān, two:

Munsha'at al-Sharqiyya. It consists of a medium number of houses. There are no inhabitants in it now, and there are no trees in it.

Munsha'a known as Qumnā Bajūsh, and as al-Manṣūra. It consists of a few scattered houses. It has enclosures of fig trees and date palms.

Munsha'a known as al-Shaykh Abū ʿAbdallāh al-Qaḥāfī, in the land of Iṭfīḥ Shallā, included in the accounts of Tuṭūn, [itself] part of Tanabṭawayh Canal. It consists of a medium number of houses, occupied by Sufis (*al-fuqarā'*).[320] It has a Sufi lodge (*ribāṭ zāwiya*) and a mosque, in which Friday prayers are being held. It has a garden of date palms and fig trees, which were endowed for the benefit of the lodge during the days of al-Kāmil — may God shower his age with compassion and approval.

320 The location of a Sufi institution in the lands of Iṭfīḥ Shallā points to remarkable continuity with the Coptic past, known to us through documentary evidence. In a deed published by Abbott and dated 336/947, a Coptic woman called Tūsāna grants real estate to a monastery known as Shallā. See Abbott, 'The Monasteries of the Fayyūm', p. 158.

فصل: مالم يعين بناحية عن مراعي الجاموس وعجز معاملة المراعي، مائة وسبعة وخمسون دينارا وثلث ونصف قيراط. تفصيله:

عجز ارتفاع المراعي، مائة وثلاثة دنانير.

مراعي الجاموس، اربعة وخمسون دينارا وثلث ونصف قيراط.

كيالة، مما لم يعين بناحية الاستنباط بسنورس، عشرة ارادب وربع وسدس:

قمح، خمسة ارادب وثلث.

شعير، اردبان وثلث.

فول، اردب ونصف وربع.

سمسم، اردب واحد.

فصل: ارتفاع الاراضي والسواقي الجارية في وقف المدارس والخانقاة بمدينة الفيوم، خارجا عن النواحي الواردة في اماكنها، ما بين:[964]

المدرسة المالكية المظفرية التقوية، مائة وثمانية وثمانون دينارا ونصف وثلث. تفصيله:

عينا، ستة وخمسون دينارا وسدس.

ورقا، عن خمسة الاف وثلاثمائة وستة دراهم ونصف وثمن، مائة واثنان وثلاثون دينارا وثلثان. تفصيله:

الارض التي بين خليجي[965] سنورس وذات الصفاء، ثمانية سواقي، عينا، احد وخمسون دينارا وثلثان، وورقا، ثلاثة الاف وثلاثمائة وستة وعشرون درهما ونصف.

بقشوش، ارض الساقيتين، ثلاثمائة وتسعون درهما.

بكوم الضبع يعرف بارض الحنا، مائة وعشرون درهما.

قبالة كوم يعرف بقصر فارس، ارض بها انشاب مساحتها خمسة فدادين ونصف وثلث ودانق، مائتان وثلاثة وعشرون درهما وربع وثمن.

بجوار قنطرة الجراحي، ارض تعرف بالفسقية، خراجها اربعة دنانير ونصف.

بالمنظرة، ارض البستان بها المشتمل على النخل والجميز والخيار الشُنبر، سبعمائة وستة واربعون درهما ونصف وربع.

المدرسة الشافعية الحسامية،

من البستان المشتمل على النخل والليمون والخيار الشنبر والجميز الذي بمنية الاسقف، وهو عشرة اسهم ونصف سهم، من اربعة وعشرين سهما شركة ورثة القاضي رشيد الدين ابي علي ومن يشركهم، عن خمسمائة وعشرين درهما، ثلاثة عشر دينارا. ومتولى الوقف يقوم بخراج الحصة للمقطعين في كل سنة مائة وسبعة وسبعين درهما.

الخانقاة الصلاحية، على مشايخ[966] الصوفية المقيمين بها والمترددين اليها، اربعون دينارا. تفصيله:

ارض البستان المعروف بالغزال من البر البحري والبحر الاعظم اليوسفي، اثنان وعشرون دينارا.

ارض البستان المعروف بكوم الرقيق من البر القبلي والبحر[967] الاعظم اليوسفي، اثنا عشر دينارا.

احكار[968] البساتين، ستة دنانير.

[964] ط. م.: مائتين.

[965] أ. س.: خليج.

[966] أ. س.: مصالح.

[967] ط. م.: والبحري.

[968] أ. س. يضيف: أرض.

Section: The revenues from the pasture of water buffalos, which were not allocated to any of the villages, and the shortfall in the pasture accounts, come to 157 ⅓ 1/48 dinars:

shortfall in pasture revenues, 103 dinars;

revenues from the pasture of water buffalos, 54 ⅓ 1/48 dinars.

The measurement fee for [land tax on] al-Istinbāṭ, part of [the land-tax revenues of] Sinnūris, which was not allocated to any of the villages, 10 ¼ ⅙ ardabbs:

wheat, 5 ⅓ ardabbs;

barley, 2 ⅓ ardabbs;

broad beans, 1 ½ ¼ ardabb;

sesame, 1 ardabb.

Section: The revenues from lands and waterwheels endowed for the madrasas and the Sufi lodge (*khānaqāh*) in Madīnat al-Fayyūm, excluding the villages which were mentioned in their appropriate places:

the Malikite al-Muẓaffariyya al-Taqawiyya Madrasa,[321] 188 ½ ⅓ dinars:

in gold coins, 56 ⅙ dinars;

in *waraq* dirhams, 5,306 ½ ⅛ dirhams, which are 132 ⅔ dinars:[322]

[The revenue of al-Muẓaffariyya al-Taqawiyya] in detail:

eight waterwheels in the land between Sinnūris and Dhāt al-Ṣafāʾ Canals, in specie, 51 ⅔ dinars; and in *waraq* dirhams, 3,326 ½ dirhams;

in Qushūsh, 'the land of the two water-wheels', 390 dirhams;

in Kawm al-Ḍabʿ, 'the Field of Henna', 120 dirhams;

land with plantations, opposite a mound known as Qaṣr Fāris, with an area of 5 ½ ⅓ 1/144 feddans, 223 ¼ ⅛ dirhams;

land known as al-Fasqiyya, near the arch of al-Jarāḥī, whose land tax is 4 ½ dinars;

in al-Manẓara, an orchard of date palms, sycamores and golden shower trees (*khiyār shanbar*, cassia fistula), 746 ½ ¼ dirhams.

The Shafiʿite al-Ḥusāmiyya Madrasa:

10 ½ shares (*sahm*) in an orchard in Minyat al-Usquf, with date palms, lemons, golden shower trees and sycamores, out of 24 shares, in partnership with the heirs of the Qāḍī Rashīd al-Dīn Abū ʿAlī and their partners, 520 dirhams, which are 13 dinars. The administrator of the endowment pays every year the land tax of this portion (*ḥiṣṣa*) to the *iqṭāʿ*-holders, 177 dirhams.

Al-Khānaqāh al-Ṣalāḥiyya, for the benefit of the Sufi shaykhs residing in it and those who visit it, 40 dinars.

The land of the orchard known as al-Ghazzāl, off the northern bank of the Main Canal, 22 dinars.

The land of the orchard known as Kawm al-Raqīq, off the southern bank of the Main Canal, 12 dinars.

Orchards in lands subject to long-term lease, 6 dinars.

[321] A madrasa established by the Ayyubid prince Taqī al-Dīn al-Muẓaffar ʿUmar, who held the Fayyum as *iqṭāʿ* between 579/1183 and 582/1186. It was called the Taqawiyya, or al-Muẓaffariya al-Taqawiyya, after his name. See al- Maqrīzī, *Kitāb al-mawāʿiẓ*, ed. by Sayyid, IV, 458; Ibn Khallikān, *Wafayāt al-aʿyān*, ed. by ʿAbbās, III, 456.

[322] This indicates an exchange rate of 1:40 between the dinar and the *waraq* dirham, the standard exchange rate between dinars and dirhams observed elsewhere in the treatise.

فصل: والذي مقرر على عربان البلاد بالفيوم اذا رسم بخروجهم في الخدمة لما يعرض من المهام، اربعمائة فارس.

النصف من ذلك باسم بني عجلان وبني سمالوس، مائتا فارس. تفصيله:

بنو عجلان خاصة، عن عشرة اسهم، مائة وستة وستون فارسا وثلثان.

بنو سمالوس عن سهمين، ثلاثة وثلاثون فارسا وثلث.

والنصف الثاني باسم بني كلاب، مائتا فارس. تفصيله:

بنو حاتم وبنو عامر، عن عشرة قراريط ثلاثة وثمانون فارسا وثلث. تفصيله:

بنو حاتم، ثلاثة اخماس، خمسون فارسا.

بنو عامر، الخمسان[969]، ثلاثة وثلاثون فارسا وثلث.

الانفار التي ياتي ذكرها، مما يقسم على اربعة عشر سهما، مائة وستة عشر فارسا وثلثان على خمسة انفار ونصف وربع. تفصيله:

الجوابون، عشرون فارسا وثلث.

الغصينيون، عشرون فارسا وثلث.

الاضابطة، عشرون فارسا وثلث.

الربعيون، عشرون فارسا وثلث.

الجعفري والقريطي والمجنوني،[970] عن نفر واحد ونصف وربع، خمسة وثلاثون فارسا.

فصل: ولما رسم بعمل جسر المحرقة بالاعمال الجيزية في اواخر سنة اثنتين واربعين وستمائة، ورد مرسوم كريم سلطاني الى الفيوم بان يخرج الى الجسر المشار اليه من بلاد الفيوم مائة جرافة. وزع ذلك على ما ياتي بيانه:

ابشاية الرمان، اربع قطع وربع وسدس.

اهريت ودنفارتها، قطعة واحدة ونصف.

اخصاص العجميين، قطعة وثلث.

الملالية، ثلث قطعة.

الطارمة، قطعة وثلثان.

اللاهون وام النخارير، قطعة وثلث.

ام السباع، نصف قطعة.

الهيشة المعروفة باللاهون، ثلث قطعة.

الحمام، قطعة واحدة.

الاستنباط قطعة ونصف.

ابريزيا والزربي، نصف وثلث قطعة.

اطسا، ربع قطعة.

اخصاص الحلاق، نصف قطعة.

ابو كسا، قطعتان ونصف وربع.

شانة، ثلاث قطع.

سيلة، قطعة ونصف.

بياض، قطعة ونصف وربع.

بمويه، اربع قطع ونصف وربع.

بيبج انشو، قطعة وثمن.

بور سينرو، ثلث قطعة.

بنديق، ثمن قطعة.

بيبج فرح، قطعة وسدس.

بيبج انقاش، ثلثا قطعة.

Section: The established levy on the Arab tribesmen (*al-ʿurbān*) of the lands of the Fayyum, when orders are issued for their departure for military service, for any duty that may arise, 400 riders (*fāris*):

One half from among the Banū ʿAjlān and the Banū Samālūs — 200 riders:

the Banū ʿAjlān proper, for 10 shares out of 24, 166 ⅔ riders;

the Banū Samālūs, for 2 shares out of 24, 33 ⅓ riders.

The second half is from among the Banū Kilāb, 200 riders:

the Banū Ḥātim and the Banū ʿĀmir, for 10 shares out of 24, 83 ⅓ riders:

the Banū Ḥātim, three fifths, 50 riders;

the Banū ʿĀmir, two fifths, 33 riders.

14 shares [out of 24], which are 116 ⅔ riders, divided into 5 ¾ units (*anfār*):

the Banū Jawwāb, 20 ⅓ riders;

the Banū Ghuṣayn, 20 ⅓ riders;

the al-Aḍābiṭa, 20 ⅓ riders;

the Banū Rabīʿa (*al-rabʿiyyūn*), 20 ⅓ riders;

the Banū Jaʿfar, the Banū Qurīṭ and the Banū Majnūn,[323] for 1¾ unit, 35 riders.

Section: When the construction of the Muḥraqa Dike (*jisr*) in the district of Giza was ordered at the end of 642 [AD 1244–5], a noble royal decree was sent to the Fayyum [ordering] that 100 dredging tools (*jurrāfa*) should be sent to the dike from the lands of the Fayyum. These were distributed as follows:

Ibshāyat al-Rummān, 4 ¼ ⅙ units (*qiṭaʿ*);

Ihrīt and its Dinfāra, 1 ½ unit;

Akhṣāṣ al-ʿAjamiyyīn, 1 ⅓ unit;

al-Malāliyya, ⅔ unit;

al-Ṭārima, 1 ⅔ unit;

al-Lāhūn and Umm al-Nakhārīr, 1 ⅓ unit;

Umm al-Sibāʿ, ½ unit;

al-Haysha, known as al-Lāhūn, ⅓ unit;

al-Ḥammām, 1 unit;

al-Istinbāṭ, 1 ½ unit;

Ibrīzyā and al-Zarbī, ½ ⅓ unit;

Iṭsā, ¼ unit;

Akhṣāṣ al-Ḥallāq, ½ unit;

Abū Ksā, 2 ½ ¼ units;

Shāna, 3 units;

Sīla, 1 ½ unit;

Bayāḍ, 1 ½ ¼ units;

Bamawayh, 4 ½ ¼ units;

Babīj Unshū, 1 ⅛ unit;

Būr Sīnarū, ⅓ unit;

Bandīq, ⅛ unit;

Babīj Faraḥ, 1 ⅙ unit;

Babīj Anqāsh, ⅔ unit;

Babīj Ghaylān and Kawm al-Raml, ½ unit;

---

969 أ. س.: الخمسين.

970 ط. م.: المجنوبي.

323 MP: *al-majnūbī*.

بيبج غيلان وكوم الرمل، نصف قطعة.
غابة باجة، نصف قطعة.
بيبج اندير، قطعة وثمن.
ترسا، قطعة.
ثلاث، نصف قطعة.[971]
جردو ودنفارتها، قطعة واحدة وربع وسدس وثمن.
حدادة، ثلثا قطعة.
خور الرماد، ثلثا قطعة.
خليج تنبطويه، خمس قطع وثلثان. تفصيله:
قمبشا،[972] ثلاث قطع وربع.
بلجسوق، ثلثا وثمن قطعة.
تطون، ثلثا وثمن قطعة.
المَهيمسِي، نصف قطعة.
القلهانة، ثلث قطعة.
خليج دلية،[973] خمس قطع وثلث وربع. تفصيله:
بلالة، نصف وربع قطعة.
منشاة اولاد عرفة، ثلث قطعة.
ششها، ثلث قطعة.
منية ششها، ثلث قطعة.
دهما، نصف قطعة.
بشطا، ربع قطعة.
منتارة، ربع قطعه.
اقلول، نصف قطعه.
كنبوت، ثلث قطعة.
الصفاونة، ثلث قطعة.
شدموه، ثلثا قطعة.
مقران، قطعة.

غير ذلك:
المصلوب، نصف وثمن قطعة.
ذات الصفا، اربع قطع وثلث.
دموشية، قطعة وربع.
منشاة ربيع، ربع وثمن قطعة.
هوارة، ثمن قطعة.
دسيا، نصف وثلث قطعة.
دمشقين، سدس قطعة.
دموه الداثر، سدس قطعة.
دفدنو وبوصير، قطعتان ونصف.
دموه اللاهون، قيراطان من قطعة.
سنورس، قطعتان ونصف وربع.
شسفة، سدس وثمن قطعة.
منشاة ابن كردي، ثلثا قطعة.
شلالة، ثلث قطعة.
جرفس، سدس قطعة.
بيهمو، ثلثا وثمن قطعة.
ابهيت، ثلثا قطعة.
منشاة الطواحين، ثلث قطعة.
سينرو، قطعة وثلث.

Ghābat Bāja, ½ unit;
Babīj Andīr, 1 ⅛ unit;
Tirsā, 1 unit;
Thalāth, ½ unit;
Jardū and its Dinfāra, 1 ¼ ⅙ ⅛ units;
Ḥaddāda, ⅔ unit;
Khawr al-Rammād ⅔ unit;
Tanabṭawayh Canal, 5 ⅔ units:
Qambashā, 3 ¼ units;
Buljusūq, ⅔ ⅛ unit;
Tuṭūn, ⅔ ⅛ unit;
al-Mahīmsī, ½ unit;
al-Qalhāna, ⅓ unit.
Dilya Canal, 5 ⅓ ¼ units:
Bilāla, ½ ¼ unit;
Munshaʾat Awlād ʿArafa, ⅓ unit;
Shishhā, ⅓ unit;
Minyat Shishhā, ⅓ unit;
Dahmā, ½ unit;
Bushṭā, ¼ unit;
Mintāra, ¼ unit;
Uqlūl, ½ unit;
Kanbūt, ⅓ unit;
al-Ṣafāwina, ⅓ unit;
Shidmūh, ⅔ unit;
Muqrān, 1 unit.

The remaining villages are:
al-Maṣlūb, ½ ⅛ unit;
Dhāt al-Ṣafāʾ, 4 ⅓ units;
Dumūshiyya, 1 ¼ unit;
Munshaʾat Rabīʿ, ¼ ⅛ unit;
Hawwāra, ⅛ unit;
Disya, ½ ⅓ unit;
Dimashqīn [al-Baṣal], ⅙ unit;
Dimūh al-Dāthir, ⅙ unit;
Difidnū and Būṣīr, 2 ½ units;
Dimūh al-Lāhūn, ²⁄₂₄ unit;
Sinnūris, 2 ½ ¼ units;
Shisfa, ⅙ ⅛ unit;
Munshaʾat ibn Kurdī, ⅔ unit;
Shallāla, ⅓ unit;
Jarfis, ⅙ unit;
Biyahmū, ⅔ ⅛ unit;
Ibhīt, ⅔ unit;
Munshaʾat al-Ṭawāḥīn, ⅓ unit;
Sīnarū, 1 ⅓ unit;
Sidmant, ¼ unit;
Ṣunūfar, ⅙ unit;

971 ساقط من أ. س.: (ثلاث) نصف قطعة.
972 أ. س.: قنبشا.
973 أ. س.، ط. م.: دلاية.

سدمنت، ربع قطعة.
صنوفر، سدس قطعة.
طبهار، قطعة.
طليت، ثلث قطعة.
العدوة، قطعة وربع وسدس.
سرسنا، ثلاث قطع.
عنز، ثلث قطعة.
فانو، قطعة وسدس.
نقليفة، قطعتان.
فدمين، نصف وربع قطعة.
فرقس،[974] قطعة ونصف.
قشوش، ثمن قطعة.
منية اقنى، تسع قطع.
مطر طارس، ثلاث قطع ونصف وربع.
منية البطس، قطعة ونصف.
منية الديك وبنو مجنون، نصف قطعة.
مطول، قطعتان.
مقطول والربيات، قطعتان ونصف.
منية كربيس، ثلث قطعة.
العاقولة، خمسة قراريط قطعة.
ناموسة، نصف قطعة.
هوارة البحرية، ثمن قطعة.
منية الاسقف، ثمن قطعة.
باجة، ربع قطعة.

وتفصيل التوزيع يزيد عن المائة جرافة بشيء[975] يسير، الا انه لم يخرج منها سوى خمسة وتسعين قطعة.

Ṭubhār, 1 unit;
Ṭalīt, ⅓ unit;
al-ʿIdwa, 1 ¼ ⅙ units;
Sirisnā, 3 units;
ʿAnz, ⅓ unit;
Fānū, 1 ⅙ unit;
Naqalīfa, 2 units;
Fidimīn, ½ ¼ unit;
Furqus, 1 ½ unit;
Qushūsh, ⅛ unit;
Minyat Aqnā, 9 units;
Miṭr Ṭāris, 3 ½ ¼ units;
Minyat al-Baṭs, 1 ½ unit;
Minyat al-Dīk and Banū Majnūn, ½ unit;
Muṭūl, 2 units;
Maqṭūl and al-Rubiyyāt, 2 ½ units;
Minyat Karbīs, ⅓ unit;
al-ʿĀqūla, 5/24 unit;
Nāmūsa, ½ unit;
Hawwāra al-Baḥriyya, ⅛ unit;
Minyat al-Usquf, ⅛ unit;
Bāja, ¼ unit.

The detailed allocation [of dredging tools per villages] slightly exceeds 100, but only 95 units have been delivered.

دعاء مبارك مستجاب نختم به هذا الكتاب.

اللهم اني اسئلك بحرمة من دعا بذمتك واستجار بعزك واعتصم بحبلك واستوطن في كنفك ولم يثق الا بك، صل على محمد وعلى ال محمد، واجعل لي من امري وهمي فرجا ومخرجا بفضلك ورحمتك يا ارحم الراحمين.

اللهم[976] خلد ملك مولانا السلطان وانصره وارزقني عاطفة من عواطفه اعود بها الى وطني واسكن الى سكني الاقي بها سرور النفس وافارق من قارنته من غير الجنس امين يا رب العالمين. تم[977] الكتاب والحمد لله[978] رب العالمين.[979] والحمد لله تعالى وعونه وحسن توفيقه وصلواته على خير خلقه محمد وعلى اله وصحابته وازواجه وذرياته وتابعيه صلاة وسلاما دائمين الى يوم الدين.[980] صنف سنة احدى واربعين وستمائة.

A blessed prayer, may it be granted, with which we conclude this book.

By God, I ask you by the sanctity of the one who has appealed for your protection, and who has sought refuge in your glory; the one who has held fast to your covenant, who has settled under your wing, and who has trusted you alone. Bless Muḥammad and the family of Muḥammad, and save me and relieve me from all my troubles and concerns, by Your Benevolence and Grace, O most Gracious One.

O God, preserve the reign of our lord the sultan, and make him victorious, and provide me with his [the Sultan's] affectionate benevolence, with which I may return to my homeland and to my dwelling, in which I will find happiness of soul, and be separated from those with whom I kept company but who were not of the same breed (*min ghayr al-jins*). Amen, oh Lord of the Universe.

This book has been completed,[324] praise be to the Glorious Lord, with His help and the good fortune that He bestows, and His prayers, for the best of his creation — Muḥammad, his family, his companions, his spouses, his descendants and his followers — constant prayer and peace be upon them, until the day of judgment. Composed in the year 641 [AD 1243–4].

974 أ. س.: فرقص.
975 أ. س.: شيء.
976 ساقط من أ. س.: اللهم.
977 أ. س.: نجز.
978 أ. س.: حمد الله.
979 ساقط من أ. س.: رب العالمين.
980 ساقط من ط. م.: والحمد لله تعالى وعونه وحسن توفيقه وصلواته على خير خلقة محمد وعلى آله وصحابته وأزواجه وذرياته وتابعيه صلاة وسلاما دائمين الى يوم الدين.

324 MP: *tamma al-kitāb* instead of *najaza al-kitāb*. MP omits the following sentence: حمد الله تعالى وعونه وحسن توفيقه وصلواته على خير خلقة محمد وعلى آله وصحابته وأزواجه وذرياته وتابعيه صلاة وسلاما دائمين الى يوم الدين (praise be to the Glorious Lord, with His help and the good fortune that He bestows, and His prayers, for the best of his creation — Muḥammad, his family, his companions, his spouses, his descendents and his followers — constant prayer and peace be upon them, until the day of judgement).

Bibliography

Abbott, Nabia, 'The Monasteries of the Fayyum', *The American Journal of Semitic Languages and Literatures*, 53. 1 (1936), 13–33

Abū Ṣāliḥ the Armenian, *Churches and Monasteries of Egypt*, ed. and trans. by Basil T. A. Evetts, Anecdota Oxoniensia, Semitic Series, 7 (Oxford: Clarendon Press, 1895)

Abū Shāma, Shihāb al-Dīn, *Tarājim rijāl al-qarnayn al-sādis wa'l-sābiʿ al-maʿrūf biʾl-dhayl ʿalā al-rawḍatayn*, ed. by Muḥammad al-Kawtharī (Cairo: Maktab Nashr al-Thaqāfa al-Islamiyya, 1947)

Alschech, Eli, 'Islamic Law, Practice and Legal Doctrine: Exempting the Poor from the Jizya under the Ayyubids (1171–1250)', *Islamic Law and Society*, 10. 3 (2003), 348–75

Amélineau, Émile, *La géographie de l'Egypte à l'époque copte* (Le Caire: Imprimerie nationale, 1893)

Amitai-Preiss, Reuven, 'The Mamluk Officer Class during the Reign of Sultan Baybars', in *War and Society in the Eastern Mediterranean, 7th–15th Centuries*, ed. by Yaacov Lev (Leiden: Brill, 1997), pp. 267–300

Ashtor, Eliyahu, 'Makāyīl and Mawāzīn', *The Encyclopedia of Islam*, 2nd edn, VI, 117–21

Baioumy, Hassan M., Hajime Kayanne, and Ryuji Tada, 'Reconstruction of Lake-Level and Climate Changes in Lake Qarun, Egypt, during the Last 7000 Years', *Journal of Great Lakes Research*, 36. 2 (2010), 318–27

Ball, John, *Contributions to the Geography of Egypt* (Cairo: The Government Press, 1939)

Becker, Carl, 'Miṣr, c. 2. The Historical Development of the Capital of Egypt', *The Encyclopedia of Islam*, 2nd edn, VII, 147–52

Boinet Bey, Amédée, *Dictionnaire géographique de l'Égypte* (Le Caire: Imprimerie nationale, 1899)

Bois, Thomas, Vladimir Minorsky, and David N. MacKenzie, 'Kurds, Kurdistān', *The Encyclopedia of Islam*, 2nd edn, V, 438–86

Borsch, Stuart J., *The Black Death in Egypt and England: A Comparative Study* (Austin: University of Texas Press, 2009)

Bosworth, Charles, E., 'Misāḥa, a.1. In the Central Islamic Lands', *The Encyclopedia of Islam*, 2nd edn, VII, 137–38

Bresc, Cécile, 'Quseir al-Qadim: A Hoard of Islamic Coins from the Ayyubid Period', *Revue numismatique*, 6. 164 (2008), 407–36

Butzer, Carl, *Early Hydraulic Civilization in Egypt: A Study in Cultural Ecology* (Chicago: University of Chicago Press, 1976)

Cahen, Claude, 'La Chronique des Ayyoubides d'al-Makin b. al-ʿAmīd', *Bulletin d'Études Orientales*, 15 (1955–57), 109–84

——, 'Contribution á l'étude des impots dans l'Égypt médiévale', *Journal of the Economic and Social History of the Orient*, 5 (1962), 244–78

——, 'Douanes et commerce dans les ports méditerranéens de l'Égypte médiévale d'après le Minhādj d'al-Makhzūmī', *Journal of the Economic and Social History of the Orient*, 7. 3 (1964), 217–314

——, *Makhzūmiyyāt: études sur l'histoire économique et financière de l'Égypte médiévale* (Leiden: Brill, 1977)

——, 'Quelques aspects de l'administration égyptienne médiévale vus par un de ses fonctionnaires', *Bulletin de la Faculté des Lettres de Strasbourg*, 26. 4 (1948), 97–118

——, 'Le régime des impôts dans le Fayyûm ayyûbide', *Arabica*, 3. 1 (1956), 8–30; repr. in *Makhzûmiyyât: Études sur l'histoire économique et financière de l'Égypte médievale* (Leiden: Brill, 1977), pp. 194–216

Caton-Thompson, Gertrude, and Elinor Wight Gardner, *The Desert Fayum: Vol. I* (London: Royal Anthropological Institute of Great Britain and Ireland, 1934)

Cooper, Richard S., 'The Assessment and Collection of Kharāj Tax in Medieval Egypt', *Journal of the American Oriental Society*, 96. 3 (1976), 365–82

——, 'Ibn Mammati's Rules for the Ministries: Translation with Commentary of the Qawānīn al-Dawāwīn' (unpublished doctoral dissertation, University of California, Berkeley, 1973)

——, 'Land Classification Terminology and the Assessment of the Kharāj Tax in Medieval Egypt', *Journal of the Economic and Social History of the Orient*, 17. 1 (1974), 91–102

Cuno, Kenneth M., *The Pasha's Peasants: Land, Society and Economy in Lower Egypt, 1740–1858* (Cambridge: Cambridge University Press, 1992)

Al-Dhahabī, Shams al-Dīn, *Taʾrīkh al-Islām wa-wafayāt al-mashāhīr wa'l-aʿlām*, ed. by ʿAbd al-Salām al-Tadmurī, 52 vols (Beirut: Dār al-Kitāb al-ʿArabī, 1987–99)

Al-Dimyāṭī, ʿAbd al-Muʾmin, *Le dictionnaire des autorités (Muʿǧam al-Šuyūḫ)*, ed. by Georges Vajda (Paris: CNRS, 1962)

Dols, Michael W., *Medieval Islamic Medicine: Ibn Riḍwān's Treatise 'On the prevention of bodily ills in Egypt'*, ed. by Adil S. Gamal, trans. by Michael W. Dols (Berkeley: University of California Press, 1984)

Dozy, Reinhart P. A., *Supplément aux dictionnaires arabes*, 2 vols (Leiden: Brill, 1881)

Eddé, Anne-Marie, 'Kurdes et Turcs dans l'armée ayyoubide de Syrie du Nord', in *War and Society in the Eastern Mediterranean, 7th–15th Centuries*, ed. by Yaacov Lev (Leiden: Brill, 1997), pp. 225–36

Eychenne, Mathieu, 'La production agricole de Damas et de la Ghūṭa au XIVᵉ siècle: diversité, taxation et prix des cultures maraîchères d'après al-Jazarī (m.739/1338)', *Journal of Economic and Social History of the Orient*, 56. 4–5 (2013), 569–630

Gabrieli, Francesco, 'Āʾīn', *The Encyclopedia of Islam*, 2nd edn, I, 306–07

Gaubert, Christian, and Jean-Michel Mouton, *Hommes et villages du Fayyoum dans la documentation papyrologique Arabe (Xᵉ–XIᵉ Siècles)* (Le Caire: Institut français d'archéologie orientale, 2014)

Gil, Moshe, 'The Flax Trade in the Mediterranean in the Eleventh Century AD as Seen in Merchants' Letters from the Cairo Geniza', *Journal of Near Eastern Studies*, 63. 2 (2004), 81–96

Goitein, Shelomoh D., 'The Exchange Rate of Gold and Silver Money in Fatimid and Ayyubid Times: A Preliminary Study of the Relevant Geniza Material', *Journal of the Economic and Social History of the Orient*, 8 (1965), 1–46

—, *A Mediterranean Society: The Jewish Communities of the Arab World as Portrayed in the Documents of the Cairo Geniza*, I: *Economic Foundations* (Berkeley: University of California Press, 1967)

Gottschalk, Hans L., *Al-Malik Al-Kāmil von Egypten und Seine Zeit: Eine Studie zur Geschichte Vorderasiens und Egyptens in der Ersten Hälfte des 7./13. Jahrhunderts* (Wiesbaden: Harrassowitz, 1958)

Halm, Heinz, *Ägypten nach den Mamlukischen Lehensregistern* (Wiesbaden: Reichert, 1982)

Hassan, Fekri A., 'Historical Nile Floods and Their Implications for Climatic Change', *Science*, 212 (1981), 1142–45

—, 'Holocene Lakes and Prehistoric Settlements of the Western Fayoum, Egypt', *Journal of Archeological Science*, 13 (1986), 483–501

Hassan, Fekri A., and others, 'Modelling Environmental and Settlement Change in the Fayum', *Egyptian Archaeology*, 29 (2006), 37–40

Haug, Brendan J., '360 Days of Summer: Experiencing the Fluvial in Egypt's Fayyūm', paper presented at the conference 'Shifting Fluvial Landscapes in the Roman World: New Directions in the Study of Ancient Rivers' (University of Oxford, 26–27 June, 2014)

—, 'Watering the Desert: Environment, Irrigation, and Society in the Premodern Fayyūm, Egypt' (unpublished doctoral dissertation, University of California, Berkeley, 2012)

Heck, Paul L., *The Construction of Knowledge in Islamic Civilization: Qudāma B. Jaʿfar and his Kitāb Al-Kharāj Wa-ṣināʿat Al-kitāba*, Islamic History and Civilizations: Studies and Texts, 42 (Leiden: Brill, 2002)

Hinz, Walther, 'dhirāʿ', *The Encyclopedia of Islam*, 2nd edn, II, 232

—, *Islamische Masse und Gewichte: Umgerechnet ins Metrische System*, Handbuch der Orientalistik, 1 (Leiden: Brill, 1970)

Humphreys, R. Stephen, 'The Emergence of the Mamluk Army', *Studia Islamica*, 45 (1977), 67–99

—, 'The Emergence of the Mamluk Army (Conclusion)', *Studia Islamica*, 46 (1977), 147–82

—, *From Saladin to the Mongols* (Albany: State University of NY Press, 1977)

—, *Islamic History: A Framework for Inquiry* (Princeton: Princeton University Press, 1991)

Ibn Duqmāq, Ibrāhīm ibn Muḥammad ibn Aydmar al-ʿAlāʾī, *Kitāb al-intiṣār li-wāsiṭat ʿiqd al-amṣār*, ed. by Karl Vollers (Le Caire: Imprimerie nationale, 1893)

Ibn al-Ḥājj, Muḥammad b. Muḥammad, *al-Madkhal*, 4 vols (Beirut: Dār al-Fikr, 1990)

Ibn al-Jīʿān, Yaḥyā ibn al-Maqarr, *Kitāb al-tuḥfa as-sanīya bi-asmāʾ al-bilād al-miṣrīya* (Le Caire: Bibliothèque Khédiviale, 1898)

Ibn Khallikān, Shams al-Dīn Abū al-ʿAbbas Aḥmad Ibn Muḥammad, *Wafayāt al-aʿyān wa-anbāʾ abnāʾ al-zamān*, ed. by Iḥsān ʿAbbās, 8 vols (Beirut: Dar Ṣāder, 1968)

Ibn Qudāma al-Maqdīsī, ʿAbd al-Raḥmān b. Muḥammad, *al-Mughnī wa'l-sharḥ al-kabīr*, 7 vols (Riyadh: Maktabat al-Riyaḍ al-Ḥadītha, 1981)

Ibn Mammātī, Asʿad, *Kitāb qawānīn al-dawāwīn*, ed. ʿAziz S. ʿAṭiya (Cairo: Al-Jamʿiyya al-zirāʿiyya al-malikiyya, 1943; repr. Cairo: Madbuli, 1996)

Ibn Shaddad, ʿIzz al-Dīn, *Al-Aʿlāq al-khaṭīra fī dhikr umarāʾ al-shām wa'l-jazīra (Taʾrīkh al-Jazīra)*, ed. by Yaḥyā ʿAbbāra, 2 vols (Damascus: Wizārat al-Thaqāfa waʾl-Irshād al-Qawmī, 1977–78)

—, *Description de la syrie du nord*, trans. by Anne-Marie Eddé-Terrasse (Damascus: Presses de l'Ifpo, 1984)

Ibn Taghrībirdī, Abū al-Maḥāsin Yūsuf, *Al-Nujūm al-zāhira fi mulūk Miṣr wa'l-Qāhira*, 16 vols (Cairo: al-Muʾasasah al-Miṣriyyah al-ʿĀmma li'l-Taʾlīf wa'l-Ṭibāʿa wa'l-Nashr, 1963–71)

Ibn Taymiyya, Taqī al-Dīn, *Majmūʿat al-fatāwā li-shaykh al-Islām Ibn Taymiiyya*, ed. by ʿAbd al-Rahmān ibn Muḥammad Ibn Qāsim and Muḥammad ibn ʿAbd al-Raḥmān Ibn Qāsim, 37 vols (Riyadh: Matābiʿ al-Riyāḍ, 1961)

Ibn Wāṣil, Muḥammad ibn Sālim, *Mufarrij al-kurūb fī akhbār banī ayyūb*, ed. Jamāl al-Dīn al-Shayyāl, Ḥasanayn al-Rabīʿ, and Saʿīd ʿĀshūr, 5 vols (Cairo: Maṭbūʿāt Idārat Iḥyāʾ al-Turāth al-Qadīm, Wizārat al-Maʿārif al-Miṣriyya, 1977)

Ibrahim, Mahmood, 'The 727/1327 Silk Weavers' Rebellion in Alexandria: Religious Xenophobia, Homophobia, or Economic Grievances', *Mamlūk Studies Review*, 16 (2012), 123–42

Igarashi, Daisuke, *Land Tenure, Fiscal Policy and Imperial Power in medieval Syro-Egypt* (Chicago: Middle Eastern Documentation Center, 2015)

Al-Ishbīlī, Abū al-Khayr, *Kitāb al-filāḥą = Tratado de Agricultura*, ed. and trans. by Julia Maria Carabaza (Madrid: Agencia Espanōla de Cooperacion Internacional, 1991)

Keatings, Kevin, and others, 'Ostracods and the Holocene Palaeolimnology of Lake Qarun, with Special Reference to Past Human–Environment Interactions in the Faiyum (Egypt)', *Hydrobiologia*, 654 (2010), 155–76

Keenan, James, G., 'Byzantine Egyptian Villages', in *Egypt in the Byzantine World, 300–700*, ed. by Roger S. Bagnall (Cambridge: Cambridge University Press, 2007), pp. 226–43

——, 'Deserted Villages: From the Ancient to the Medieval Fayyum', *Bulletin of the American Society of Papyrologists*, 40 (2003), 119–40

——, 'Fayyum Agriculture at the End of the Ayyubid Era: Nabulsi's Survey', in *Agriculture in Egypt from Pharaonic to Modern Times*, ed. by Alan K. Bowman and Eugene Rogan, Proceedings of the British Academy, 96 (Oxford: Oxford University Press, 1999), pp. 287–99

——, 'Landscape and Memory: al-Nabulsi's Taʾrikh al-Fayyum', *Bulletin of the American Society of Papyrologists*, 42 (2005), 203–12

Konig, Ingeborg, 'Die Oase Al-Fayyum nach ʿUtman an-Nabulsi: Ein Beitrage zur Wirschaftsgeschichte Agyptens um die Mitte des 13. Jahrhunderts n. Chr' (unpublished master's thesis, Albert-Ludwigs-Universitat zu Freiburg im Bresigau, 1966)

Kopf, L., 'al- Djawharī', *The Encyclopedia of Islam*, 2nd edn, II, 495–97

Krol, Alexei A., 'The "Disappearing" Copts of Fayyām', in *And the Earth is Joyous…: Studies in Honour of Galina A. Belova*, ed. by Sergei Ivanov and Marina Tolmacheva (Москва: ЦЕИ РАН, 2015), pp. 142–62

Kumakura, Wakako, 'Tax Survey Records of the First Year of the Ottoman Rule in Egypt, Contained in the Ayasofia Manuscript with Fakhr al-Dīn ʿUthmān al-Nābulsī's Taʾrīkh al-Fayyūm', *Journal of Asian and African Studies*, 89 (2015), 79–118 (in Japanese, with edited Arabic text)

Lane, Edward W., and Stanley Lane-Poole, *An Arabic-English Lexicon*, repr. edn, 8 vols (New York: Ungar, 1956)

Levanoni, Amalia, 'The Mamluks' Ascent to Power in Egypt', *Studia islamica*, 72 (1990), 121–44

Lévi-Provençal, Évariste, 'al-Maghrib', *The Encyclopedia of Islam*, 2nd edn, V, 1184–1209

Al-Makhzūmī, Abū al-Ḥasan Ibn ʿUthmān, *Al-Muntaqā min kitāb al-minhāj fī ʿilm kharāj misṛ*, ed. by Claude Cahen and Yūsuf Rāghib (al-Qāhirah: Institut français d'archéologie orientale, 1986)

Makīn b. al-ʿAmīd, *Taʾrīkh*, ed. by Claude Cahen as 'La Chronique des Ayyoubides d'al-Makin b. al-'Amīd', *Bulletin d'Études Orientales*, 15 (1955–57), 109–84

Al-Maqrīzī, Taqī al-Dīn Aḥmad ibn ʿAlī ibn ʿAbd al-Qādir, *Kitāb al-mawāʿiẓ wa'l-iʿtibār fī dhikr al-khiṭaṭ wa'l-āthār*, ed. by Ayman Fu'ad Sayyid, 4 vols (London: Mu'asasat al-Furqān li'l-Turāth al-Islāmī, 2002)

——, *Kitāb al-mawāʿiẓ wa'al-iʿtibār fī dhikr al-khiṭaṭ wa'l-āthār*, ed. by Gaston Wiet, 5 vols (Frankfurt am Main: Institute for the History of Arabic-Islamic Science at the Johann Wolfgang Goethe University, 1994)

Al-Masʿūdī, ʿAlī b. al-Ḥusayn b. ʿAlī, *Al-Tanbīh wa'l-ishrāf*, ed. by M. J. de Goeje (Leiden: Brill, 1893; repr. Beirut: Dār Ṣādir, n.d.)

Mehringer, Peter J., Kenneth L. Peterson, and Fekri A. Hassan, 'A Pollen Record from Birket Qarun and the Recent History of the Fayum', *Quaternary Research*, 11 (1979), 238–56

Michel, Nicolas, 'Devoirs fiscaux et droits fonciers: la condition des fellahs égyptiens (13ᵉ–16ᵉ siècles)', *Journal of the Economic and Social History of the Orient*, 43. 4 (2000), 521–78

——, 'Les rizaq iḥbāsiyya, terres agricoles en mainmorte dans l'Égypte mamelouke et ottomane: étude sur les dafātir al-aḥbās ottomans', *Annales Islamologiques*, 30 (1996), 105–98

——, 'Les services communaux dans les campagnes égyptiennes au début de l'époque ottomane', in *Sociétés rurales ottomanes / Ottoman Rural Societies*, ed. by Mohammad Afifi, Rachida Chih Brigitte Marino, and Nicolas Michel, Cahier des Annales islamologiques, 25 (Le Caire: Institut français d'archéologie orientale, 2005), pp. 19–46

——, 'Travaux aux digues dans la vallée du Nil aux époques papyrologique et ottomane: une comparaison', *Cahier de recherches de l'institut de papyrologie et d'égyptologie de Lille*, 25 (2005), 253–76

Mouton, Jean-Michel, 'Shayzar', *The Encyclopedia of Islam*, 2nd edn, IX, 410–11

Mubārak, 'Ali, *Al-Khiṭaṭ al-tawfīqiyya al-jadīda li-Miṣr al-Qāhirah wa-mudunihā wa-bilādihā al-qādima wa'l-shāhira*, 2nd edn, 20 vols (Cairo: Dār al-Kutub, 1969)

Al-Nābulusī, Abū ʿAmr ʿUthmān B. Ibrāhīm, *Kitāb lumaʿ al-qawānīn al-muḍiyya fī dawāwīn al-diyār al-miṣriyya*, ed. by Carl Becker and Claude Cahen, *Bulletin d'études Orientales*, 16 (1960), 1–78, 119–34

——, *The Sword of Ambition: Bureaucratic Rivalry in Medieval Egypt*, ed. and trans. by Luke Yarbrough (New York: New York University Press, 2016)

——, *Ta'rīkh al- Fayyūm wa-bilādihi*, ed. by Bernhard Moritz (Cairo: al-Maṭbaʿa al-Ahliyya, 1898; repr. in Fuat Sezgin, Mazen Amawi, Carl Ehrig-Eggert and Eckhard Neubauer, eds, *Studies of the Faiyūm Together with 'Taʾrīḫ al-Faiyūm wa-Bilādihī' by Abū ʿUthmān an-Nābulusī (d. 1261)*, Islamic Geography, 54 facs. edn (Frankfurt: Institute for the History of Arabic-Islamic Science at the Johann Wolfgang Goethe University, 1992)

Al-Nawawī, Yaḥyā bin Sharaf, *Kitāb al-majmūʿ: Sharḥ al-muhadhdhab*, ed. by Muḥammad Najīb al-Muṭīʿī, 12 vols (Beirut: Dār Iḥyāʾ al-Turāth al-ʿArabī, 2001)

Al-Nuwayrī, Shihāb al-Dīn Aḥmad b. ʿAbd al-Wahhāb, *Nihāyat al-arab fī funūn al-adab*, ed. by Aḥmad Zakī Pāsha and others, 33 vols (Cairo: al-Muʾasasa al-Miṣriyya al-ʿĀmma li'l-Taʾlīf wa'l-Tarjama wa'l-Ṭibāʿa wa'l-Nashr, 1923–97)

Owen, Charles A., and Charles C. Torrey, 'Scandal in the Egyptian Treasury: A Portion of the *Luma' al-Qawānīn* of 'Uthman ibn Ibrāhīm al-Nābulusī: Introductory Statement', *Journal of Near Eastern Studies*, 14. 2 (1955), 70–96

Pellat, Charles, 'Ibn Harma', *The Encyclopedia of Islam*, 2nd edn, III, 786

Phillipps, Rebecca, and others, 'Lake Level Changes, Lake Edge Basins and the Paleoenvironment of the Fayum North Shore, Egypt, during the Early to Mid-Holocene', *Open Quaternary*, 2. 2 (2016), 1–12

Pococke, Richard, *A Description of the East, and Some other Countries*, 2 vols (London: Bowyer, 1745)

Al-Qalqashandī, Shihāb al-Dīn Aḥmad b. ʿAlī, *Ṣubḥ al-aʿshā fī ṣināʿat al-inshāʾ*, ed. by Muḥammad ʿAbd al-Rasūl Ibrāhīm, 14 vols (Cairo: Dār al-Kutub al-Khidīwiyya, 1913–22; repr. 1964)

Quatremère, Étienne M., *Mémoires géographiques et historiques sur l'Égypte, et sur quelques contrées voisines: recueillis et extraits des manuscrits coptes, arabes, etc., de la Bibliothèque Impériale*, 2 vols (Paris: Schoell, 1811)

Rabbat, Nasser O., *The Citadel of Cairo: A New Interpretation of Royal Mamluk Architecture*, Islamic History and Civilizations: Studies and Texts, 14 (Leiden: Brill, 1995)

Rabie, Hassanein, *The Financial System of Egypt, A.D. 1169-1341* (London: Oxford University Press, 1972)

Rāgib Yūsuf, 'Les archives d'un gardien du monastère de Qalamūn', *Annales Islamologiques*, 29 (1995), 25–57

—, *Marchands d'étoffes du Fayyoum au IIIe/IXe siècle d'après leurs archives (actes et lettres)* (Le Caire: Institut français d'archéologie orientale, 1982)

—, *Transmission de biens, mariage et répudiation a Uqlul, village du Fayyoum, au Ve–XIe siècle* (Le Caire: Institut français d'archéologie orientale, 2016)

Ramzī, Muḥammad, *Al-Qāmūs al-jughrāfī liʾl-bilād al-miṣriyya min ʿahd qudamāʾ al-Miṣriyyīn ilā sana 1945*, 2 vols (Cairo: Dār al-Kutub al-Miṣriyya, 1953)

Rapoport, Yossef, 'Invisible Peasants, Marauding Nomads: Taxation, Tribalism and Revolt in Mamluk Egypt', *Mamlūk Studies Review*, 8. 2 (2004), 1–22

Rapoport, Yossef, and Ido Shahar, 'Irrigation in the Medieval Islamic Fayyum: Local Control in a Large-Scale Hydraulic System', *Journal of the Economic and Social History of the Orient*, 55 (2012), 1–31

Richards, D. S., 'The Qasāma in Mamlūk Society: Some Documents from the Ḥaram Collection in Jerusalem', *Annales Islamologues*, 25 (1990), 245–84

—, 'al-Ṣāliḥ Nadjm al-Dīn Ayyūb', *The Encyclopedia of Islam*, 2nd edn, VIII, 988–89

Richter, A., 'al-Ḳalyūb', *The Encyclopedia of Islam*, 2nd edn, IV, 514–15

Rousset, Marie-Odile, and Sylvie Marchand, 'Secteur nord de tebtynis: Mission de 1999', *Annales Islamologiques*, 34 (2000), 387–436

—, 'Tebtynis 1998, travaux dans le secteur nord', *Annales Islamologiques*, 33 (1999), 185–262

Rufus of Ephesus, *On Melancholy*, ed. by Peter E. Pormann (Tubingen: Mohr Siebeck, 2008)

De Sacy, Antoine Isaac Silvestre, *État des provinces et des villages de l'Égypte* (Strassburg: Treuttel et Würtz, 1810)

Al-Ṣafadī, Ṣalāḥ al-Dīn Khalīl ibn Aybak, *Kitāb al-wāfī bi'l-wafayāt*, ed. by H. Ritter and S. Dedering, 3 vols (Istanbul/Damascus/ Wiesbaden: [n. pub.], 1949)

Salmon, Georges, M., 'Répertoire géographique de la province du fayyoūm d'après le *Kitāb taʾrīkh al-fayyoūm d'an-nāboulsī*', *Bulletin de l'Institut Français d'Archéologie Orientale*, 1 (1901), 29–77

Sato, Tsugikata, *State and Rural Society in Medieval Islam* (Leiden: Brill, 1997)

—, 'Sugar in the Economic Life of Mamluk Egypt', *Mamlūk Studies Review*, 8. 2 (2004), 87–107

—, *Sugar in the Social Life of Medieval Islam* (Leiden: Brill, 2014).

Savigny, Marie Jules-César, *Description de l'Égypte, ou recueil des observations et des recherches qui ont été faites en Égypte pendant l'expédition de l'armée française, publié par les ordres de sa majesté l'empereur Napoléon le Grand: planches*, Histoire naturelle, 18 (Paris: Panckoucke, 1827)

Schultz, Warren, C., 'The Mechanisms of Commerce', in *The New Cambridge History of Islam: Volume 4, Islamic Cultures and Societies to the End of the Eighteenth Century*, ed. by Robert Irwin (Cambridge: Cambridge University Press, 2010), pp. 332–54

—, 'The Monetary History of Egypt, 642–1517', in *The Cambridge History of Egypt*, I: *Islamic Egypt, 640–1517*, ed. by Carl F. Petry (Cambridge: Cambridge University Press, 1998), pp. 318–38

Sezgin, Fuat, and others, eds, *Studies of the Faiyūm Together with 'Taʾrīḫ al-Faiyūm wa-Bilādihī' by Abū ʿUthmān an-Nābulusī (d. 1261)*, Islamic Geography, 54 (Frankfurt: Institute for the History of Arabic-Islamic Science at the Johann Wolfgang Goethe University, 1992)

Shafei Bey, Ali, 'Fayoum Irrigation as Described by Nabulsi in 1245 A.D.', *Bulletin de la Société de géographie d'Égypte*, 20. 3 (1940), 283–327

Sijpesteijn, Petra, *Shaping a Muslim State: The World of a Mid-Eighth-Century Egyptian Official* (Oxford: Oxford University Press, 2013)

Silverstein, Adam J., *Postal Systems in the Pre-Modern Islamic World* (Cambridge: Cambridge University Press, 2007)

Sourdel, Dominique, 'ʿIzz al-Dīn Ibn Shaddād', *The Encyclopedia of Islam*, 2nd edn, III, 933

Steenbergen, Jo Van, 'Taqwim al-Buldan al-Misriya (CUL Qq 65): Identifying a Late Medieval Cadastral Survey of Egypt', in *Egypt and Syria in the Fatimid, Ayyubid and Mamluk Eras*, IV: *Proceedings of the 9th and 10th International Colloquium Organized at the Katholieke Universiteit Leuven in May 2000 and May 2001*, ed. by U. Vermeulen and J. Van Steenbergen, Orientalia Lovaniensia Analecta, 140 (Leuven: Peeters, 2005), pp. 477–91

Tassie, Geoff, 'Modelling Environmental and Settlement Change in the Fayum', *Egyptian Archaeology*, 29 (2006), 37–40

Al-Thaʿālibī, Abū Manṣūr, *Thimār al-qulūb fī al-muḍāf wa'l-mansūb* (Cairo: Dār al-Maʿārif, 1982)

Timm, Stefan, *Das Christlich-Koptische Ägypten in Arabischer Zeit: Eine Sammlung Christlicher Stätten in Ägypten in Arabischer Zeit, unter Ausschluss von Alexandria, Kairo, des Apa-Mena-Klosters (dēr Abū Mina), eer Skētis (Wādi N-Naṭrūn) und der Sinai-Region* (Wiesbaden: Reichert, 1984)

Toussoun, Omar, *Mémoire sur l'histoire du Nil* (Caire: Imprimerie de l'Institut français d'archéologie orientale, 1925)

Vallet, Eric, *L'Arabie marchande: état et commerce sous les sultans rasūlides du Yémen, 626-858/1229-1454* (Paris: Publications de la Sorbonne, 2010)

Udovitch, Avram, L., 'Fals', *The Encyclopedia of Islam*, 2nd edn, II, 768–69

Yāqūt, ibn 'Abd Allāh al-Ḥamawī, *Muʿjam al-buldān*, 5 vols (Beirut: Dār Ṣawār li'l-Ṭibāʿa wa'l-Nashr, 1956)

—, *Muʿjam al-buldān*, ed. by Muḥammad Amīn al-Khānḥabī, X vols (Cairo: Maṭbaʿat al-Saʿāda, 1906)

Yarbrough, Luke, 'Introduction', in al-Nābulusī, *The Sword of Ambition: Bureaucratic Rivalry in Medieval Egypt*, ed. and trans. by Luke Yarbrough (New York: New York University Press, 2016), pp. xix–xxiii

Zéki, Aḥmad Bey, 'Une description arabe du fayyoūm au VIIᵉ siècle de l'hégire', *Bulletin de la société Khédiviale de Géographie*, 5 (1899), 253–95

Zysow, Aron, 'Zakāt', *The Encyclopedia of Islam*, 2nd edn, XI, 406–22

Index of Common Fiscal and Agricultural Terms

The following common fiscal terms and crops appear in most village entries in the tax register and are repeated throughout most pages of the edition and translation. We therefore excluded them from the general index.

The fiscal terms are explained in chapter 2, 'Decoding the *Villages of the Fayyum*', pp. 13–22. The list below indicates the sections in chapter 2 that are relevant for each term.

The data of the tax register is best approached via a digital format. The lists of taxes, including the key terms below, have been keyed into Excel spread sheets, together with their numerical value per village. These are available through a dedicated webpage hosted by the School of History at Queen Mary University of London (<https://projects.history.qmul.ac.uk/ruralsocietyislam>).

Index of Villages and Hamlets Described in the 'Villages of the Fayyum'

Bold numbers indicate a village's main entry.

General Index

The Medieval Countryside

All volumes in this series are evaluated by an Editorial Board, strictly on academic grounds, based on reports prepared by referees who have been commissioned by virtue of their specialism in the appropriate field. The Board ensures that the screening is done independently and without conflicts of interest. The definitive texts supplied by authors are also subject to review by the Board before being approved for publication. Further, the volumes are copyedited to conform to the publisher's stylebook and to the best international academic standards in the field.

Titles in Series

The Rural History of Medieval European Societies: Trends and Perspectives, ed. by Isabel Alfonso (2007)

Eva Svensson, *The Medieval Household: Daily Life in Castles and Farmsteads, Scandinavian Examples in their European Context* (2008)

Land, Power, and Society in Medieval Castile: A Study of Behetría Lordship, ed. by Cristina Jular Pérez-Alfaro and Carlos Estepa Díez (2009)

Survival and Discord in Medieval Society: Essays in Honour of Christopher Dyer, ed. by Richard Goddard, John Langdon, and Miriam Müller (2010)

Feudalism: New Landscapes of Debate, ed. by Sverre Bagge, Michael H. Gelting, and Thomas Lindkvist (2011)

Scale and Scale Change in the Early Middle Ages: Exploring Landscape, Local Society, and the World Beyond, ed. by Julio Escalona and Andrew Reynolds (2011)

José Ramón Díaz de Durana, *Anonymous Noblemen: The Generalization of Hidalgo Status in the Basque Country (1250–1525)* (2011)

Settlement and Lordship in Viking and Early Medieval Scandinavia, ed. by Bjørn Poulsen and Søren Michael Sindbæk (2011)

Britons, Saxons, and Scandinavians: The Historical Geography of Glanville R. J. Jones, ed. by P. S. Barnwell and Brian K. Roberts (2012)

Ferran Garcia-Oliver, *The Valley of the Six Mosques: Work and Life in Medieval Valldigna* (2012)

Town and Countryside in the Age of the Black Death: Essays in Honour of John Hatcher, ed. by Mark Bailey and Stephen Rigby (2012)

Town and Country in Medieval North Western Europe: Dynamic Interactions, edited by Alexis Wilkin, John Naylor, Derek Keene, and Arnoud-Jan Bijsterveld (2015)

Crisis in the Later Middle Ages: Beyond the Postan–Duby Paradigm, ed. by John Drendel (2015)

Alasdair Ross, *Land Assessment and Lordship in Medieval Northern Scotland* (2015)

Power and Rural Communities in Al-Andalus: Ideological and Material Representations, ed. by Adela Fábregas and Flocel Sabaté (2015)

Peasants and Lords in the Medieval English Economy: Essays in Honour of Bruce M. S. Campbell, ed. by Maryanne Kowaleski, John Langdon, and Phillipp R. Schofield (2015)

Eline Van Onacker, *Village Elites and Social Structures in the Late Medieval Campine Region* (2017)

Yossef Rapoport, *Rural Economy and Tribal Society in Islamic Egypt: A Study of al-Nābulusī's 'Villages of the Fayyum'* (2018)

Peter Hoppenbrouwers, *Village Community and Conflict in Late Medieval Drenthe* (2018)